INTRODUCING THE ✦ NEW TESTAMENT

COMPLETELY REVISED AND UPDATED

JOHN DRANE

A LION BOOK

Copyright © 1986, 1999 John Drane

Published by
Lion Publishing plc
Sandy Lane West, Oxford, England
www.lion-publishing.co.uk
ISBN 0 7459 3984 8 (hb)
ISBN 0 7459 4410 8 (pb)

First edition 1986
Revised edition 1999
10 9 8 7 6 5 4 3 2 1 0

A catalogue record for this book is available
from the British Library

Typeset in 9.5/12 Poppl Pontifex
and 9.5/11 Humanist 777 Light Condensed
Printed and bound in Spain

Picture acknowledgments

AKG London/Erich Lessing: 129, 145, 431
British Library: 471
British Museum: 39, 47, 62, 189, 236, 262, 443
Dover Publications: 67, 71, 85, 99, 126, 140, 154
E.T. Archive: 394
Israel Museum, Jerusalem: 42
Jon Arnold: 21, 52, 105, 437
Julie Baines: 15, 17, 22, 26 (all), 31, 143, 150, 200,
201, 247, 264, 309, 311, 328, 360, 390
Landesmuseum, Trier/H. Thornig: 258
Lion Publishing: 18, 55, 164, 232, 283, 286, 290,
292, 296, 301, 305, 306, 308, 315, 319, 324, 338,
349, 350, 352, 447, 469/Collection British
Museum 363/David Reddick 44, 153/David
Townsend 56, 91, 101, 245, 253/John Rylands
Museum 470/Mark Astle 80, 357/Pauline O'Boyle
354/Phil Manning 93/Simon Bull 48, 123, 277,
433, 446/Stanley Willcocks 148
Maritime Museum, Haifa: 391
Mary Evans Picture Library: 30, 112, 211 (all),
223, 224, 396, 398, 427, 462, 463, 465
Middle East Archive/Alisdair Duncan: 418
Museum of London: 24
Popperfoto: 116, 118
Scala: 273
SCM Press: 229
Sonia Halliday Photographs: 13, 25, 33, 41,
246/Andre Held 384/Barry Searle 374, 267/Jane
Taylor 16, 153, 429, 435
The Stock Market: 278/W. Braun 36
V&A Picture Library, by courtesy of the Trustees
of the V&A: 198
Werner Forman Archive/British Museum: 299
Zev Radovan: 27, 214, 342, 343, 347, 448

All maps and charts: Joshua Smith

Contents

Special Articles

1 The Beginning of the Story

The New Testament documents the rise of one of the most remarkable religious and social movements the world has ever seen. In their own day, the first Christians were accused of turning the world upside down with their message (Acts 17:6), and they have influenced every subsequent generation in history. The twenty-seven books of the New Testament contain stories of their deeds, accounts of their activities, together with letters and other occasional writings produced by this innovative group of people in the process of taking their message to the furthest reaches of the world as they knew it. It provides its readers with a unique archive of social history, for this is no domesticated, disinfected collection of writings: it bears testimony to the debates and disputes among the first followers of Jesus as they wrestled with the significance of his unique life and ministry, and even the stories of Jesus' own life are presented not in one agreed version, but through the perspectives of four different writers, each of whom displays their own characteristic insights into the meaning of the events they describe.

It is no exaggeration to claim that no other book from the ancient world has made such a lasting impact on world civilization. New Testament passages like Jesus' Sermon on the Mount (Matthew 5 – 7) or Paul's great hymn in praise of love (1 Corinthians 13) are acclaimed as outstanding literary compositions, even by those who have little time for their essential message. This is all the more surprising in light of the relative unsophistication of the New Testament writers. Not more than one or two of them can have had any sort of formal Greek education, and some of their books (Mark's Gospel, for example) would not be highly rated among scholars of ancient literature. Yet that has not dismayed the millions of people all over the world who still read the New Testament regularly and discover in its pages a personal inspiration for their daily living. It has the capacity to speak to people of different cultures, and at all periods of history, in a way that is highly distinctive, maybe unique. Though written in generally remote places of the ancient Roman empire, by people who were an oppressed and persecuted minority, its message still speaks with great power to spiritual searchers in all times and places.

Its contents can seem disparate and unconnected, and indeed it is

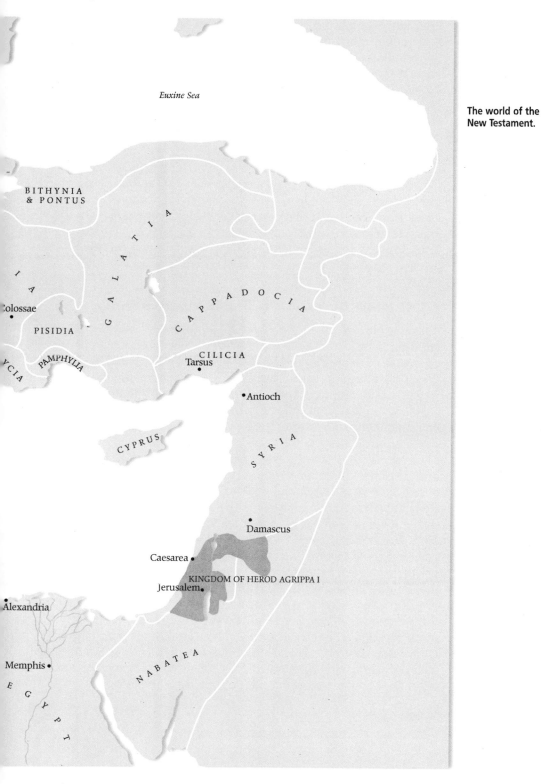

Euxine Sea

The world of the New Testament.

BITHYNIA & PONTUS

GALATIA

CAPPADOCIA

olossae

PISIDIA

PAMPHYLIA

CILICIA
Tarsus

Antioch

CYPRUS

SYRIA

Damascus

Caesarea

KINGDOM OF HEROD AGRIPPA I

Jerusalem

Alexandria

Memphis

NABATEA

EGYPT

like a small library, containing diverse types of literature, compiled by many different authors, at different points during the first century AD. But, for all its diversity, the New Testament has one central focus. These books are all part of the same story. They reflect the fervour and devotion of the first followers of Jesus Christ, but more than that: they claim that the story of Jesus is the grand metanarrative of all history – the one big story that gives meaning and significance to all the small stories of everyday human experience and insight. Through their faith in this one person, the New Testament writers found the fragments of their own experience transformed into something more glorious than they could possibly have imagined. Regardless of the cost – and it often included suffering and death – they were determined to share this life-giving story with others. The shared conviction that this was the way to find true fulfilment and meaning lies at the back of all their writings. But behind their accounts of their own faith experiences stands the life of just one remarkable person, Jesus of Nazareth.

From Jesus of Nazareth to early Christianity

Jesus was born about 4BC into an ordinary working-class Jewish family, but (unusually for someone with no formal religious training) he went on to make a name for himself as a religious teacher (Matthew 2:1; Luke 2:1–7). He was in the public gaze for little more than three years before his life was tragically cut short by his execution on a Roman cross (Luke 23:33), yet in that short time he delivered a message that was to exert a crucial influence not only on his own people, but on the subsequent course of world history.

In one sense, Jesus' lifestyle was not particularly remarkable in the context of the Palestinian countryside where he lived and worked. There were hundreds of wandering teachers ('rabbis'), all of them men (never women) of exceptional gifts and insight who would gather round them small groups of disciples to perpetuate their teachings after they were gone. The stories about Jesus in the New Testament gospels describe how he himself followed this pattern, with twelve special followers to whom he entrusted the essentials of his teachings (Matthew 10:1–4), though they also report that on more than one occasion thousands of people flocked to listen to him (Mark 6:30–44; 8:1–9). However, what really distinguished Jesus from other rabbis of his day, was the fact that it was not among simple peasants on the shores of the inland Sea of Galilee that his teaching made its greatest impact. In a very short time after his death, his personality and his beliefs were having a profound effect in places far removed from the shores of Palestine.

A new faith

Within twenty years of Jesus' crucifixion, every major centre of Roman civilization could boast at least one group of his followers. The list of nationalities present in Jerusalem to hear Peter's first public sermon reads like a roll-call of most of the cities in the ancient world: 'We are from Parthia, Media, and Elam; from Mesopotamia, Judea, and Cappadocia; from Pontus and Asia, from Phrygia and Pamphylia, from Egypt and the regions of Libya near Cyrene. Some of us are from Rome, both Jews and Gentiles converted to Judaism, and some of us are from Crete and Arabia...' (Acts 2:9–11) – and their inclusion at this point in the Christian story was obviously not just wishful thinking, for in a very short time we have hard evidence of thriving Christian communities in Rome, Corinth, Ephesus, Philippi, Antioch in Syria and many other Mediterranean cities, not to mention far-flung places such as Ethiopia, Byzantium, and Alexandria in Egypt (Acts 8:26–39).

It was not long before these new followers of Jesus began to exert an increasingly powerful influence on life even in Rome itself. Writing of events in AD49, less than twenty years after the death of Jesus, the Roman historian Suetonius described a series of riots that led the emperor Claudius to expel the Jewish population from the city. According to him, the cause of all the trouble was a person whom he calls 'Chrestus' (Suetonius, *Life of Claudius* 25.4). There has been much debate as to who Suetonius believed this 'Chrestus' actually was, but there seems little doubt that the events he was describing were brought about by arguments over the teaching of those Roman Jews who had

Fishing on Lake Galilee: most of Jesus' followers were ordinary people from rural Galilee.

become followers of Jesus, and were hailing him as the expected 'Messiah' (a Hebrew term, whose equivalence in Latin was *Christus*, *Christos* in Greek, and hence the eventual common reference to 'Jesus Christ').

Opposition

It was not long before the popular media of the Roman world turned their attention to these followers of Jesus, describing their activities in lurid terms and portraying them not only as people with weird religious ideas, but people who were a threat to the safety and security of the Roman state:

> *The Christians form among themselves secret societies that exist outside the system of laws... an obscure and mysterious community founded on revolt and on the advantage that accrues from it... They form a rabble of profane conspiracy. Their alliance consists in meetings at night with solemn rituals and inhuman revelries... They despise temples as if they were tombs. They disparage the gods and ridicule our sacred rites... Just like a rank growth of weeds, the abominable haunts where this impious confederacy meet are multiplying all over the world... To venerate an executed criminal and... the wooden cross on which he was executed is to erect altars which befit lost and depraved wretches (Origen,* Against Celsus *8.17; 3.14; Minucius Felix,* Octavius *8.4; 9.1–6).*

The Christians themselves naturally saw things differently. Far from worshipping 'an executed criminal', these men and women who were causing such social upheaval firmly believed that their Jesus was not dead, but was really and truly alive, and was with them wherever they went (Acts 2:32). This was perhaps the one crucial factor which ensured the lasting success of the whole Christian movement. Because they believed that Jesus was not dead, but alive, his first followers were prepared to take the most incredible risks in spreading their message. Beatings, imprisonments, shipwrecks, and persecutions of all kinds – even death – were commonplace in the life of the early churches (Acts 12:1–5; 2 Corinthians 11:23–27). But the spectacular results that accompanied their endeavours made even the suffering infinitely worthwhile.

Changing the world

Of course, we look back on all this with the wisdom of hindsight. We know that the church did in fact survive and spread. But if we put ourselves in the position of those first followers of Jesus, it is very obvious that their success was by no means a foregone conclusion. Indeed, quite the opposite, for by normal standards everything was against them. Jesus himself was a Jew, as were all his original disciples, and though in some circles in the Roman empire the Jewish faith was respected, anti-Semitism was common. There was particular disdain for those Jews who lived in Palestine, who were often regarded by the Roman establishment as an incomprehensible, fanatical and unbalanced race. In addition, neither Jesus nor his followers were of high social standing, coming as they did from rural Galilee. It was hard enough for such people to gain a hearing even in their own religious capital, Jerusalem, let alone to communicate effectively with educated Greeks and Romans in the wider world beyond their own limited experience. Yet this is precisely what they did, as a movement that began spontaneously in a country on the edge of Roman civilization suddenly became an important social and political, as well as religious, force at the very centre of life in the empire. So what was their secret? What did Jesus and his teaching really mean – and why did his followers feel compelled to take it to the furthest corners of the world they knew? Why did they not stay at home instead, to be a reforming movement in their own Jewish religion? And just how did these hill-billies from the backwoods of Palestine manage to communicate the message of Jesus so successfully to the cultured inhabitants of ancient cities in Italy and Greece?

To find the answers to these questions, we need first to understand the world where they lived.

The Greek heritage

There is no such thing as a culture that comes from nowhere. We are all heirs to the past. In the world of the first Christians, the outward forms of administration and government were those of the Roman empire, but its cultural roots were embedded in a different world altogether. The way people spoke and thought, their aspirations and achievements, and their hopes and fears all went back to pre-Roman times. For though the Romans had shown themselves to be skilled in technology, building impressive roads and water-supply systems wherever they went, the underlying ideology of their empire had its real origins some 300 years before the time of Jesus, in the vision of Alexander the Great (356–323BC).

Alexander rose to fame almost overnight. He began as the son of a little-known local ruler in Macedonia, but he was such a brilliant general that, within a very short time, he was able to defeat armies much more prestigious than his own, and establish himself as undisputed emperor of the whole of the world that was then known to people living in the Mediterranean lands. The great Persian empire fell to his troops, followed by Egypt, and ultimately by other lands even further to the east. Just ten years after his first major success against the Persians, Alexander died at the early age of only thirty-three. But by then his empire stretched from Greece in the west to the Indian sub-continent in the east.

Alexander the Great (356–323BC), whose policy of Hellenization created a world in which it was easy for Christianity to spread.

Politically, it did not survive his death intact. After much squabbling among Alexander's generals, his territories were divided, and it was nearly 300 years later that they were finally reunited, when the Roman Octavian (63BC–AD14) eventually secured the eastern end of the Mediterranean Sea for his own empire.

Hellenism

Octavian was himself a brilliant strategist. But he owed much of his lasting success to the fact that there was already a far-reaching cultural unity among almost all the nations he had conquered. In spite of their diverse national traditions, people throughout the Mediterranean world were deeply conscious of being part of a wider world. In both east and west, people had common hopes, similar educational opportunities, and much the same way of understanding life. They even spoke the same language: Greek.

All this sprang directly from the genius of Alexander the Great. Unlike many other dictators, Alexander was not addicted to the exercise of power just for its own sake. He was not a brutish, uncultured person. In his youth he had been a student of the great Greek philosopher Aristotle, and he never forgot what he had learned from him. Alexander was a fanatic for

The triumphal arch at Palmyra in Syria. It was in Hellenistic cities that Christianity spread most rapidly.

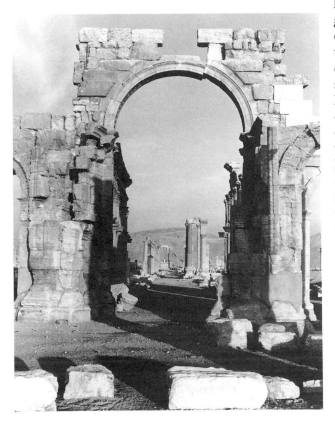

his own native culture, and was genuinely convinced that civilization had reached its ultimate goal with the Greek way of life. He was determined to share it with the whole world, and he took steps to ensure that Greek customs, religion and philosophy – even the Greek language – would all be adopted throughout his domains. Cities were built everywhere in the Greek style, incorporating Greek temples, theatres and sports arenas. The way of life that resulted – 'Hellenism' – was to last for nearly 1,000 years after Alexander's death, and have a profound impact on the future course of the whole of Western civilization. Throughout its early centuries, the Christian church could not afford to ignore this massive cultural and ideological edifice. Church leaders eventually found themselves forced to articulate, even redefine, their faith in terms of the Hellenistic world-view, and the consequences of their doing so are still affecting the Christian church today.

The degree to which any particular nation accepted this Hellenistic culture naturally varied from place to place. Sometimes the changes were only superficial. The names of local gods and goddesses might be changed into Greek forms, but their worship often continued on in much the same way. In addition, ordinary working people had little time or opportunity for philosophical debates and sports activities, and it was generally the ruling classes who became most involved in such pursuits. They were also the ones who most often used the Greek language, for it meant they could make international contacts without the tedious necessity of learning several languages. But the Greek influence was everywhere, and in one way or another it penetrated to all sections of society.

It was in this Greek-dominated world that the earliest Christians proclaimed their message. For all its size and diversity, it was a world that was easy to reach with the good news about Jesus. There were few language problems; cultural barriers were minimal; and by the Roman age great roads were being built which would make it easy to travel from one part of the empire to another. But these were not the only factors that moulded the world of the first Christians. For by the first century AD many people also had other concerns.

Philosophy

Alexander had been inspired by a love for the great classical Greek philosophers. But by the time of the New Testament, their heyday was long past. Those who succeeded the original generation of creative thinkers were not of the same intellectual calibre, and much philosophy was concerned with detailed arguments about things that to ordinary people seemed trivial and irrelevant. But there were some whose ideas were more accessible than others, and who therefore attracted a following among many ordinary citizens.

Alexander the Great portrayed as a god on a coin minted by Lysimachus, king of Thrace from 306 to 281BC.

THE STOICS

These were quite an influential group in the New Testament period. This school of thought was founded by Zeno (335–263BC). He was a native of Cyprus, but went to Athens and eventually set up his own school in the *Stoa Poikile* ('the Porch'), from which the name 'Stoic' was derived.

Stoic philosophy was based on a belief that both the world and its people ultimately depend on just one principle: 'Reason'. Since the world itself operates by this standard, people who want to enjoy a good life must 'live in harmony with nature'. They could do this primarily through following their conscience, for that itself was also inspired by 'Reason'. This was something people could only do for themselves, and Stoics therefore laid great emphasis on living a life of 'self-sufficiency'. Many of them were widely respected for their high standards of personal

The Parthenon in Athens, home to many of the ancient Greek philosophers, and still a place of influence in New Testament times.

morality. It was not uncommon for them to be prepared to commit suicide sooner than lose their self-respect and dignity. Chrysippus (d.c. 206BC) ensured Stoicism's survival as an influential school of thought, and in the following centuries it went through several phases. In the early Christian period its most famous advocates were Seneca (4BC–AD65, Epictetus (AD55–135) and Marcus Aurelius (AD121–180).

Inevitably, this way of understanding life did not convince everyone – not least because it did not seem to tackle the social realities of the day. If 'Reason' filled and inspired everything, then why were all people not the same? Why were there so many slaves condemned to eke out a wretched existence? The Stoic could reply that, in their minds, slaves were equal to the emperor, a claim that provided very little consolation either for slaves or those who were concerned for their welfare.

THE EPICUREANS

These were another popular philosophical group in the Hellenistic age. They too had an ancient pedigree, tracing their origin back to the Greek Epicurus (341–270BC). Epicureans adopted a totally different view of life. Though many Greeks had debated what happens at death, they would have none of it. Death is the end, they said, and the only real way to make sense of life is to be as detached as possible from it. A good life consists in 'pleasure'. For Epicurus, this had meant things like friendship and peace of mind. But many of his followers interpreted it differently, and gained a reputation for reckless living.

These and other philosophical groups had many followers among the intellectual classes in New Testament times, but they never had much appeal for ordinary people. They were seldom able to stem the fears of the working classes, and in any case it was time-consuming and intellectually demanding to organize one's life this way. As a result,

Greek philosophy had few points of contact with the mass of the people, who were not highly intellectual and had little opportunity for the leisurely pursuit of personal morality.

Religion

Many people found it more natural to make sense of life in terms of religion, but for those who took Hellenism seriously, few certainties could remain. While the philosophers had produced systems of thought that were often incomprehensible, they had also questioned many traditional religious beliefs. There were those who still worshipped the old Greek and Roman gods, but they knew that many educated people had claimed to be able to prove that such deities did not really exist. International movements of trade and people had also made Europeans more conscious of the existence of other gods and goddesses in the eastern part of the Roman empire. Did they exist – and if so, how could they relate to life in the great urban centres of Greece and Italy?

Such ambiguities eventually led to what can appropriately be described as a failure of nerve in the Hellenistic world. While the philosophers had discredited traditional ways of making sense out of life, they had failed to establish a plausible alternative, and as a result huge numbers of people found themselves in a moral and spiritual vacuum. There was no shortage of religious ideas that could fill the gap, and people whose confidence in their inherited spiritualities had been eroded were ready to try anything that might give them new hope in an uncertain world.

Countries on the eastern fringe of the Hellenistic world had their own ancient religions, which were largely unknown to those living in the urban centres of the western empire. What little was known of them seemed to suggest they were more 'spiritual' than the rationalistic and materialist world-views of western thinkers. These factors, combined with a natural curiosity about the unknown, generated an increasing interest in non-western faiths. The fact that some of them at least looked as if they were compatible with the more accessible conclusions of Greek philosophy only served to heighten their appeal. Two aspects of western philosophy seemed especially congenial to these eastern faiths:

■ In order to explain the existence of evil in the world, philosophers had often argued that this world is neither the only world, nor is it the best. There is, they suggested, another world of goodness and light, and that is the most important sphere of existence. People belong to it because they have a 'soul', a spark of light that is related not to bodily existence in this world, but to spiritual existence in the other world. Our brief existence here is merely an unfortunate encumbrance, and to find true meaning and fulfilment it is necessary to escape the body (which had been castigated as 'the prison of the soul' by Pythagoras).

■ Alongside the moral philosophy of people like Plato, another major strand in Greek thinking had been concerned with natural philosophy –

what would now be referred to as science – working out how things work, and how the universe fits together. As Roman and Greek thinkers explored the mysteries of the universe, they found themselves fascinated by the movements of the planets and the stars, which seemed to operate with such precision and regularity that many believed the key to the whole of life was somehow locked up within them.

So the way was prepared for the penetration of many oriental religions into the Roman empire. For a long time astrology had been of great interest to eastern sages. So had the possibility of reincarnation. It was not long before these speculations were combined with the conclusions of Greek scientists to produce a new kind of religious movement in the Hellenistic world.

GNOSTICISM .
This is a term often used to describe this movement today. There is a good deal of uncertainty about its precise origins, and a lot of disagreement as to whether it existed in the early first century, or whether it developed only later as a result of the spread of the Christian message itself. There is positive evidence of its existence in the second

---

Traditional Greek religion

Greek and Roman religion were very similar, indeed the same gods feature in each under different names. By the fifth century BC twelve gods and goddesses were identified by name as the key deities in the pantheon. They each had their own quite narrow sphere of influence, and worshippers would not follow their own favourites, but would pay some homage to them all in order that every aspect of human experience might be blessed by divine attention.

The twelve major deities were generally thought of as living in an extended family at Zeus' palace on Mount Olympus (hence the term 'Olympians' by which they were often known). Other deities existed, and were known as the 'chthonians' (from the Greek word *chthon*, meaning 'earth'), though they were not imagined to be in opposition to the Olympians, either morally or spiritually. The chthonians were not entirely negative influences, though gods of the underworld and of death were

certainly prominent among their number. But there were also positive gods within their ranks: food, for instance, grows in the earth, and even Zeus could have an earthbound, chthonic aspect to his character. Indeed, most of the leading gods had an endless list of adjectives applied to them, which defy neat classification. Individual communities constantly sought to define the qualities and powers of their particular deities as being in some way distinctive and different from the wider spirituality that was shared with other people throughout the Hellenistic world. Thus, for example, the 'Zeus of mountain tops' had qualities not possessed by 'Zeus of the city', or (to give an example that features in the New Testament, 'Artemis of Ephesus' (Acts 19:28) would bestow blessings and favours that would not be available to devotees of Artemis as she was revered in other Hellenistic cities.

Though gods might be portrayed in human form and, like people, originated from Mother Earth, they were never born, nor did they eat regular food, or grow old,

and third centuries AD, from Gnostic documents as well as from the writings of church leaders who wrote to denounce it. At that time it was obviously a widespread religious movement. It is unlikely that Gnosticism existed in any organized form in the New Testament period, though these later groups did not construct their systems out of nothing but incorporated materials that had been in circulation for a long time. Several New Testament books appear to refer to notions that later became central to Gnostic thinking, and it is obvious that these ideas were floating around independently in the religious atmosphere of the earlier Hellenistic age.

Gnostic thinking was based on the belief that there are two worlds: the world of spirit, where God is, which is pure and holy; and the world of matter, where people are, and which is evil and corrupted. A God who is holy and pure, Gnostics argued, can by definition have no involvement in what goes on in the material world. Salvation (however it might be defined) cannot be related to life here, but can only be a quality to be found in the other, spiritual world. A person's best chance of finding ultimate meaning is therefore to escape from this material world into the spiritual one, and discover true fulfilment there. For most Gnostics, this chance to escape came at death, when the soul left the

---

or die. If there had been a golden age when gods and people mingled freely with one another, that time was long since past, and for now there was a great gulf between the two modes of existence. There was however a third group, namely the heroes, who might also be worshipped, though being lower than the gods. A hero was typically a mortal who had died, having achieved great things, and whose tomb might become a centre of devotion.

Hellenistic religion had no organized central structure that could impose a uniform belief system at all the many local shrines. Though individual deities had their own priests, there was no recognized professional priesthood, and being a priest was not a full-time job. Authority in religious matters generally rested with those who had secular power, which in the household meant the father, while in the city-states it would be the local magistrates, or even the assembly of all citizens. The most important religious functionaries were often seers, who would deliver oracles

interpreting the divine will to any who asked their opinion – which they did, on matters as diverse as personal guidance, healing, the development of national

Mount Olympus, traditional home of the gods in Greek mythology.

body behind. But not everyone would be automatically qualified to reach the world of spirit. To do so, a person must have a divine 'spark' embedded in their nature, otherwise they would simply return to this world to start another meaningless round of bodily existence. Even those who possess this spark of deity can never be absolutely certain of finding ultimate release, for the evil creator of this world (the *Demiurge*) and his accomplices (the *Archons*) jealously guard every entrance to the world of spirit. To get past them, the spark must be enlightened about its own nature and the nature of true salvation. For this, 'knowledge' (the Greek word was *gnosis*) was required. When Gnostics spoke of 'knowledge' they did not have in mind an intellectual knowing of religious dogmas, or indeed of science. They referred to a mystical experience, a direct 'knowing' of the supreme God.

In practical terms, this kind of belief could lead to two quite opposite extremes. Some argued that their aim of complete liberation from the grasp of the material world could best be achieved by a rigorous asceticism which would effectively deny the reality of their bodily human existence. But there were others who believed that, by virtue of their mystical 'knowledge', they had already been released from all material ties, and therefore what they did in their present life

---

Traditional Greek religion *continued*

The sanctuary of Apollo at Delphi. The oracle in residence here was consulted by all Greek and many foreign states before embarking on major undertakings.

policies, or military campaigns. The oracle at Delphi was one of the most highly respected sources of such spiritual insight.

This was a religion of observance, in which the need to ensure ongoing security and prosperity in the various spheres of everyday life was the dominant factor, rather than (as in Christianity) matters of belief about God or the nature of the world and its people. Devotion was expressed through acts of respect directed towards the deities, with different gods or goddesses being recognized for their

influence in different circumstances and at different stages of life. For this reason, to speak of Greek or Roman religion as if it was some special sort of ritual or belief system, is misleading. Religious observance, in which the intrinsic reality of the gods and goddesses was recognized, was simply an everyday part of life, intended to preserve social stability, whether it be in the context of rites of passage, or of legal transactions, or military expeditions, or any other concern that people might have. Hellenistic spirituality was therefore not at all individualistic, and the notion of having a personal relationship with one of the gods would not have been a regular part of it. From a sociological point of view it was all about maintaining the well-being of the community, by observing the correct social forms at the right times and in the right places. This could easily be done, for example, by the head of a household acting on behalf of all members of a family, or by local magistrates as representatives of an entire community.

was totally irrelevant to their ultimate spiritual destiny. They saw it as their duty to spoil everything connected with life in the material world, including especially its standards of morality and what were regarded as conventional forms of behaviour. They might therefore promote anarchic and undisciplined behaviour as part of their spiritual quest.

It is not difficult to trace connections between this outlook and various groups who are mentioned in the New Testament, though we must remember there is no evidence that it had all been worked into a comprehensive system at this period. Nevertheless, Paul's letters to the church in Corinth often seem to be criticizing views that would certainly be congenial to later Gnostics, while Colossians, 1 John and Revelation also seem to be concerned with debates about people who were seeking to expound the Christian faith in similar terms.

MYSTERY RELIGIONS

Direct emotional experience of God also played a key role in the various mystery religions which sprang up in the Roman empire. Mithraism was one of the best known of these, and was very popular especially among the officers in the Roman army. But there were many others, associated with the gods of Asia Minor and Egypt as well as traditional Greek

---

Appropriate sites for devotion did not need to be special shrines or temples, and many thousands of *herms* (stone pillars with the head of the god Hermes on top and a phallic symbol in front) have been discovered at roadsides, or on street corners, inviting passers-by to seek the god's protection, and in the process recognizing their solidarity with the community in which the *herm* was located.

Sacrifice was the usual way to win the favour of the gods – usually of animals, though corn or fruit could also be offered. Far from being a gloomy occasion, this was generally a time for festivity and celebration, for only the poorest parts of sacrificial victims were actually offered to the gods, with the best cuts of meat then being eaten in a communal banquet. There was of course a serious side to it all, and worshippers regularly made offerings in order to win some particular favour from the deity. This was understood not so much as an attempt to bribe the gods, but more as a way of affirming that the human–divine relationship was a two-sided

affair operating in a cause and effect way that was predictable, and therefore orderly.

With the increasing influence of the philosophical thinkers, questions were inevitably raised about this belief system. In the earliest period, it had been taken for granted that the stories about the gods and their doings were about real deities, and what was described in these stories had actually happened. Under philosophical influence, the gods and their stories had been explained as symbols of some first force or abstract principle that lay behind the world, and while that did not invariably lead to an intellectual atheism or a discontinuation of the traditional forms of devotion, by the New Testament period cultural change (which included a fresh awareness of alternative religious traditions) was combining with growing spiritual uncertainty to undermine the easy acceptance of traditional Hellenistic beliefs – though they never disappeared entirely until they were eventually supplanted by Christianity itself centuries later.

practices. Like Gnosticism, these groups were by definition secret societies, and our specific knowledge of them is therefore inevitably limited. It seems likely however that many of them arose as developments from the various fertility religions which had been popular for thousands of years throughout the ancient Middle East. Their mythologies certainly seem to reflect the cycle of the seasons, as the new life of spring follows the barrenness of winter, all of it symbolized by the death and rebirth of the gods of fertility.

Mithraism was the most powerful mystery religion in the Roman empire in Paul's time. Worshippers believed that the god Mithras would save the faithful and help them to reach heaven. Here Mithras, a Persian god, is killing the bull as a sacrifice (Roman temple of Mithras, Wallbrook, London, England).

The ancient religions of Egypt and Palestine had generally celebrated this cyclical world-view in annual festivals in which priests and priestesses would act out the role of the deities, often in rituals with strong sexual overtones, and, in the Hellenistic mysteries, such rituals became mystical experiences for the individual worshipper. Their original mythology was transferred from the ongoing life of nature into the experience of individual people, who themselves spoke of undergoing the death and rebirth that had been so important to the prosperity of the ancient farmer.

A person could gain access to this mystical experience by way of an initiation ceremony. One account of the consecration of a priest tells how the subject was placed in a pit in the ground, covered with a wicker framework (Prudentius, *Peristephanon* X.1011–50). On this a bull (symbol of life and virility) was slaughtered, and its blood ran down and soaked the initiate. When the priest emerged, those around would fall down and worship him, for he himself had now been made divine through being drenched in the life of the bull. No doubt the initiation of a priest differed in some details from that of an ordinary person, but it is a safe guess that a similar pattern would be followed, while there is plenty of evidence to show that sexual rites of various kinds would often play a central part.

The Mysteries gave a sense of hope and security to their initiates, in both personal and social terms. Individuals gained a sense of personal meaning and purpose in life. They also became part of a distinctive group which shared the same secret experiences, and often operated as a mutual aid society in times of difficulty or hardship.

JUDAISM

This was also very popular in the Hellenistic world. There were a number of reasons for this, not least the fact that large numbers of Jews lived in most of the major towns and cities of the Roman empire. Wherever they went, they took their distinctive beliefs and lifestyle with them. While the Jewish communities were always conscious of a deep difference between themselves and their Gentile neighbours, they were not generally exclusive groups, and were usually more than happy for others to join them. Many Greeks and Romans were attracted.

From the perspective of city dwellers in the western empire, Judaism was essentially an eastern religion, and held all the attractions of mystery and intrigue that such an origin implied. But unlike the esoteric mystery cults, Judaism was not difficult for outsiders to understand. They could see its practical outworking in the everyday life of their Jewish friends, for its relevance depended not on secret experiences, but found expression in the ordinary life of the home. More important, enquirers could read the Jewish scriptures for themselves in their own Greek language, and make up their minds about it before committing themselves to involvement in the life of the Jewish community of faith.

Jewish teachers were not slow to exploit this openness to Judaism among those people who were not ethnically Jewish. Even in the time of Jesus, the persistence and enthusiasm of Jewish rabbis in sharing their faith with others, crossing land and sea to do so, was legendary (Matthew 23:15). Moreover, the Jewish emphasis on rigorous standards of personal and social morality found a warm reception among many thinking Greeks and Romans, who were dissatisfied with the permissiveness of their own culture. Some of them became full members of the Jewish faith, accepting all the demands of the Old Testament law to become 'proselytes'. Others merely accepted the Old Testament's moral teaching, and were given a lesser status as 'God-fearers'. These groups played a significant role in the developing life of the early Christian church. One of the first non-Jewish Christians mentioned in the New Testament – Cornelius, the Roman centurion – was a 'God-fearer' (Acts 10:1–48), and as the first Christian missionaries took their message into the wider Roman empire, they often found an enthusiastic response among such people. Indeed, Paul felt it was so important to share the message with these people that he made it a specific policy always to go first to the Jewish community in every town he visited.

Menorah carved on a column of the synagogue at Capernaum, dating from the end of the 2nd century AD.

CHRISTIANITY

This, then, was the world into which the first Christians brought their message about Jesus. It was a world that had been cut adrift from its roots, a world that was in search of a new self-understanding, and a world full of competing faiths and ideologies, all of them claiming to have the answers to the big questions of the day.

There are many ways in which the phenomenal success of the Christian faith in this context can be explained. But one of the key facts is simply that the Christian message addressed the key concerns of people in that culture at that point in time, and it was shared by people who had a clear understanding of what they needed to do in order to demonstrate its relevance to the everyday concerns of ordinary people. As the original followers of Jesus moved from their homeland on the fringes of the empire into the large urban centres of the western Mediterranean, they met people at their point of need. Not only were they able to engage with the questions that people were asking on an intellectual level, but in addition – and, if anything, even more significantly – the groups of Christian believers which they established throughout the empire demonstrated in a practical way the sense of purpose and meaning in life for which so many were searching.

Jesus' claim to be the fulfilment of the Old Testament faith gave

Traditional deities of Greece and Rome

Jupiter

Apollo

Zeus
Chief god, father of other gods; Roman Jupiter (Jove)

Hera
Sister and consort of Zeus; Roman Juno

Athena
Goddess of war, wisdom and the arts; Roman Minerva

Apollo
God of sun, prophecy, music, medicine, poetry; Roman Apollo

Athena

Artemis
Virgin goddess of chastity, the hunt and the moon; twin sister of Apollo; Roman Diana

Poseidon
God of sea, earthquakes, horses; brother of Zeus; Roman Neptune

Aphrodite
Goddess of love and beauty; Cytherea; Roman Venus

Hermes
God of commerce, invention, cunning, theft; messenger for other gods; patron of travellers and rogues; conductor of the dead to Hades; Roman Mercury

Hephaestus
Disabled god of fire and metalworking; Roman Vulcan

Ares
God of war; Roman Mars

Demeter
Goddess of agriculture, fertility, marriage; Roman Ceres

Dionysus
God of wine, ecstasy and orgasm; Roman Bacchus

Demeter

his followers a head start. Greeks and Romans – and expatriate Jews – naturally wanted to know what the Christians had to say, and because the Old Testament had already been translated into Greek, the earliest Christian missionaries had no difficulty at all in explaining their message in specific terms. In addition, Christianity had a certain curiosity value to the western city dwellers, as one of the many religions that were moving in from the east. Palestine itself was widely regarded as the very edge of the civilized land, and anything coming from that quarter would always be given a hearing by those who were disillusioned with their own religious heritage.

The early Christians could also appeal to those who were attracted to Gnosticism and the mystery religions. The whole thrust of Jesus' teaching was quite different from these world-denying systems of thought. But for that very reason it gave a more convincing explanation of life as it is in this world, rather than encouraging people to opt out and dream of the possibilities of life in some other world. The Christian message was firmly based on events that had taken place in the real

Jews and Judaism in the Roman empire

Most people assume that Palestine was the major homeland of the Jews in New Testament times. But in fact there were probably more Jews living in a city like Alexandria in Egypt than there were in Jerusalem itself, and overall there were significantly greater numbers living scattered throughout the major urban centres of the Roman empire than there were in Palestine. Josephus quotes the Latin author Strabo's comment that the Jewish nation 'has already made its way into every city, and it is not easy to find any place in the habitable world which has not received this nation, and in which it has not made its power felt' (Josephus, *Antiquities of the Jews* 14.7.2).

In Old Testament times, the land and people of Israel had been thought of as a self-contained geographical and national entity. Indeed, the Old Testament story is largely concerned with how Israel's ancestors had been gathered from various ethnic origins to be united in their common heritage, with its focus on their land, and the city of Jerusalem in particular. But by the time of Jesus the process was working

in reverse, and the Jewish people were living all over the world. This scattering, or *Diaspora* ('Dispersion'), had begun many centuries before in 586BC, when

River Euphrates near Babylon, home to a large Jewish population following Nebuchadnezzar's capture of Babylon in 586BC.

Nebuchadnezzar, king of Babylon, invaded the kingdom of Judah. As a way of imposing absolute control over the conquered nation, he took all the most gifted and influential inhabitants of Jerusalem off to a new life in Babylon. This was a disaster of immense proportions for the Jewish people. Politically, it was the final catastrophe, for never again were the Jewish people to enjoy an independent existence. Despite that, however, this Jewish exile in Babylon was to become one of the most creative forces in the whole history of Jewish religious history.

In the heyday of traditional Jewish

world of everyday experience – the life, death and resurrection of Jesus. It did not require believers to distance themselves from life as they experienced it, but to understand this material existence as the context in which God was active, and could be known in a personal way. Christians also affirmed that a good life could not be achieved by human ingenuity and, without denigrating the value of human rationality (as the mystery religions tended to do), they claimed that reason was not capable by itself of discerning the meaning of life. True satisfaction could only be found, they argued, through a close personal relationship with God, which through the work of God's Spirit shared some of the characteristics of the mystical experiences so popular at the time, but by virtue of being rooted in the life and teaching of Jesus of Nazareth was always grounded in the historical realities of life in this world. In addition, Christianity was not only concerned with individual self-fulfilment; through faith in Jesus believers found themselves part of a new social grouping – the church – that could offer a meaningful context for a corporate as well as an individual spirituality.

Jews and Judaism in the Roman empire *continued*

religion, the worship of the temple in Jerusalem had been of central importance. It was by regular visits to the temple and the offering of sacrifices there that people declared their loyalty to the God of Israel and their continued determination to obey the Law. But Nebuchadnezzar destroyed the temple, and though the remnants of the population who were left in Jerusalem still continued to worship in its ruins, even that consolation was not possible for those who had been removed to Babylon. Their feelings were expressed most poignantly in the words of Psalm 137:1–6:

> By the rivers of Babylon we sat down;
>   there we wept when we remembered
>   Zion.
> On the willows near by we hung up
>   our harps.
> Those who captured us told us
>   to sing;
> they told us to entertain them:
> 'Sing us a song about Zion.'
> How can we sing to the Lord in a
>   foreign land?
> May I never be able to play
>   the harp again
> if I forget you, Jerusalem!

In the event, Jerusalem was not forgotten, and it was not long before the exiles discovered that though at first it seemed inconceivable, they could indeed 'sing the Lord's songs in a foreign land'. It was in the synagogue that they did so. In a different social setting, some things just had to be different, and the local synagogue was not a replica of the temple back in Jerusalem. Worship in Jerusalem had been concerned with sacrifices, but this was no longer possible, and in the worship at the synagogue the central place of sacrifice had to be filled by something else. So a form of worship developed which allowed no place for sacrifice but instead placed a new emphasis on those traditional observances that could be carried out anywhere: prayer, the reading of the Torah, keeping the sabbath day, circumcision, and the observance of the ancient regulations concerning the preparation and consumption of food.

This adaptation of traditional Jewish worship was so successful that when Jews from Babylon were eventually able to return to their homeland, they took it with them. A bit later still, following the conquests of Alexander the Great, other enterprising Jews decided to emigrate

It is not difficult to see why and how the early Christians were able to fill the spiritual vacuum of the Hellenistic world so successfully. But the story of their faith is much more complex than just a haphazard coincidence of social factors in the ancient world. Indeed, it was not in this predominantly Greek world at all that the story had its beginnings and, to understand it fully, it is necessary to delve into the sometimes convoluted world of Jewish history and religion.

Palestine and its people

When Alexander conquered the ancient world, most nations went along with his policy of Hellenization. In many instances they accepted it only grudgingly, and quite often Hellenism made little impact on native customs. National institutions would be adjusted to conform with the Greek style, and the ruling classes in particular found it advantageous to adopt Greek habits, while the lives of ordinary people could remain virtually untouched by the Greek influence.

voluntarily to different parts of the Mediterranean world, and it was natural that they should adopt the synagogue as the central expression of their religious and national allegiance. By the time the first Christian missionaries were beginning to travel with their new message about Jesus, there was an extensive network of Jewish synagogues spread the length and breadth of the entire Roman empire.

Not all synagogues were exactly the same. In earlier times, the temple in Jerusalem had imposed a certain degree of central control over religious beliefs and practices, and it continued to do so in Palestine until its final destruction in AD70. But the synagogues were much freer to develop their own ways of thinking. The problems of being a Jew in Babylon were quite different from the challenges facing Jews in Rome, while the Egyptian city of Alexandria was different again. In each local centre, people had to work out for themselves how best to adapt their ancestral faith to the demands and opportunities of their new environments. Even within the same locality, different synagogues might reach different conclusions. In Rome, for example, some Jews were quite happy to go along with

many aspects of pagan society, even giving their children Latin or Greek names, and adopting the art-forms of Roman civilization, while others in the same city deplored what they saw as a dilution and betrayal of their ancestral faith, and stuck rigidly to a more traditional understanding of the laws of the Hebrew Bible.

We also know of Jews who became deeply interested in the study of Greek philosophy. The most famous of these was Philo, a Jew from the Egyptian city of Alexandria. We know few details of his life, but he must have been born some time before Jesus, and probably lived until the mid-forties of the first century AD. He was a member of an influential Jewish family, and some of his relatives became deeply involved in politics both in Egypt and elsewhere. But Philo was most interested in explaining the thinking of Greek writers, especially the Stoics. He found many of their ideas congenial, and set out to show how the Hebrew scriptures and Greek philosophy were really saying the same things in their own distinctive ways. In order to demonstrate this, he had to regard the traditional stories of his people as a kind of allegorical or symbolic presentation of the truths expounded by

Most nations around the Mediterranean world would have preferred to retain full control over their own lives, but they knew well enough that the realities of international politics obliged them to go along with the superpowers of the day. In any case, even if Alexander's policy of Hellenization was more thoroughgoing than anything imposed by most other ancient empires, it was not a new concept. For centuries, subject nations had demonstrated their subordination by accepting the culture of their conquerors. It was taken for granted that this would include at least a token allegiance to the religions of their overlords. Modern states change the image on their postage stamps or currency when a new ruler comes to power: in the ancient world, they changed the statues and altars in their temples. It can have come as no surprise to discover that under Greek rulers, subject nations would be expected to find a place for the Greek gods.

Most were willing to do so, but not the Jews of Palestine. For them, practical politics and deeply held religious convictions could not be reconciled quite so easily. For one thing, their ancestral faith had always insisted that there is just one God, and that this one God must be

---

Jews and Judaism in the Roman empire *continued*

Philo of Alexandria (c. 20BC –c. AD50), whose writings interpreted the Jewish scriptures using Greek categories of thought.

the philosophers. Orthodox Jews elsewhere in the empire would certainly have regarded Philo as a traitor to his religion, but he saw himself as a faithful interpreter who was proud of his ancestral traditions, and had no doubt that what he was doing was both worthwhile and necessary.

There was, however, one thing on which all the synagogues of the Roman world were united. This was in their use of the Greek language. As one generation succeeded another it was not long before the vast majority of Jews in the Mediterranean world could speak no other language, and so it became important that the ancient Jewish scriptures, originally written in Hebrew, should be translated into the language that most Jews now spoke and understood best.

The actual origins of the Greek Bible that was produced are shrouded in obscurity. According to one ancient legend, the Jews of Egypt managed to persuade the Egyptian king, Ptolemy II Philadelphus (285–247BC) to sponsor the project. The story tells how he sent to Jerusalem for seventy men who knew both Hebrew and Greek, and locked them up in seventy cells while each one produced his own translation. When their work was finished,

to everyone's amazement the seventy men not only expressed the same ideas, but also used the very same Greek words to do so – whereupon Ptolemy was so impressed, that he was immediately convinced of the divine origins of their work! Not everyone believed that sort of story even in the ancient world, and another ancient source, *The Letter of Aristeas*, implies that the translators set the precedent for almost all subsequent translations, and worked as a committee.

Probably neither of these stories by itself reflects the full account of what actually happened, and many scholars now believe that the Greek Septuagint version of the Jewish scriptures (the LXX) just evolved gradually over many generations. But wherever it came from, it had enormous influence and importance. It was widely used not only by Jews all over the Roman empire, but was also read by intelligent Romans who wanted to know more about the Jewish faith. It also became the Bible of the first Christian churches, and its easy accessibility greatly assisted the Christians in sharing their faith throughout the Hellenistic world.

worshipped without visual representations, and according to carefully prescribed regulations. Other nations could declare their allegiance to Zeus simply by placing his statue alongside their own gods and goddesses, and including him in the rituals that were already taking place. But Israel would never do this, and regarded it all as a complete denial of some of the most cherished aspects of the Old Testament faith.

Hellenism and Judaism

These religious misgivings among the Jewish people never amounted to much in the time of Alexander himself. Indeed, it was some considerable time after his death before they were to become a real issue, under the Greek ruler of Palestine, Antiochus IV Epiphanes (175–164BC). Antiochus was a member of the Seleucid dynasty, whose predecessors had always allowed the high priestly rulers in Jerusalem a good deal of local independence. Unfortunately, the high priesthood itself became the subject of an internal power struggle at exactly the same moment as Antiochus suffered a humiliating defeat in Egypt at the hands of the Romans (168BC). This hurt Antiochus' pride, and he was determined to reassert his authority by whatever means he could. The Jews were an easy target, and Antiochus marched on Jerusalem determined to show who was in charge. He knew enough to realize that the factional arguments about the priesthood were not purely political, but involved differences of opinion among the Jews themselves about their own religion. He neither understood nor cared for their faith, but if it was causing trouble, then Antiochus knew that its power would have to be diminished.

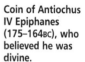

Coin of Antiochus IV Epiphanes (175–164BC), who believed he was divine.

He responded by inaugurating a thoroughgoing policy of enforced Hellenization. All the things that were most distinctive about Jewish life were banned, including circumcision, keeping the sabbath day, and reading the traditional scriptures. Even worse, Antiochus decreed that the temple in Jerusalem, the focal point of traditional Jewish worship, should be dedicated to the Greek god Zeus. To rub salt into the wounds, he opened the temple up to the whole population of the land, which included people who were not themselves Jewish believers. This kind of cultural integration had always been desirable to the Greek rulers of Palestine, but whereas his predecessors had taken a more pragmatic view, Antiochus believed it was now essential to stamp out Jewish distinctiveness in order to ensure his own political survival. Whether they liked it or not, and regardless of the consequences, everyone in the land would be united under the Greek religion in a thoroughly Greek way of life.

Antiochus had seriously underestimated the strength of Jewish religious feeling. It was one thing to erect altars to Greek gods – but it would be another thing altogether to persuade the Jews to worship at them. Antiochus' efforts to enforce his new regime only increased the determination of the Jewish people to fight back. It was not long before an armed resistance movement was established by Mattathias, a priest from the village of Modein, along with his five sons. They came to be known as the 'Maccabees', and their tactics of guerrilla warfare were so successful that it took only three years for Antiochus' troops to be defeated and for his policies to be reversed.

Jews and Romans

All this took place nearly 200 years before the time of Jesus. In the intervening period, the Greeks had been replaced by the Romans as the dominant superpower. But the Jews of Palestine never lost their firm determination to resist religious compromise and, if possible, to preserve their own rights to political self-determination.

This fiercely independent posture was largely the result of their belief that they had been specially chosen by God to rule the world under the leadership of God's promised deliverer, whom they called the 'Messiah'. At one time it had been possible for them to expect that this might happen in the normal course of history. Ancient stories from the days of David and Solomon, almost 1,000 years before the birth of Jesus, depicted them as one of the great world powers. Their more recent successes against Antiochus had shown that they were still a force to be reckoned with, but it was obvious to most Jews living in Palestine in Jesus' day that something of almost supernatural proportions would have to take place if they were ever to be released from the iron grip of Rome.

At the same time, not all Jews wanted to be freed from Roman rule. There were some sections of society in Palestine who found it was comfortable to be friendly with the Romans, and even among those who saw freedom as an ideal, there were not many who were prepared to take practical action to secure it.

The Romans had an unenviable task in Palestine. For them, its continuing security was essential, as it was the main eastern frontier of their entire empire. Even so, they were on occasion prepared to make allowances for Jewish scruples. When they appointed Herod the Great as ruler of Judea in 37BC, they hoped he would be acceptable to Jewish public opinion, for as well as being a person whom the Romans felt they could trust he was also half Jewish, a fact which they assumed would commend him to the Jewish people, and lessen some of their resistance to foreign rule.

Herod the Great

The story of Herod's rise to power, and indeed of the rest of his reign, is a classic tale of intrigue and ruthlessness. As a king he was a combination of diplomatic brilliance and personal insanity. Though there is no record of it outside the New Testament, the story of how he murdered the children of Bethlehem after Jesus was born (Matthew 2:16) is quite consistent with all that is known of his character and behaviour. Anyone who opposed his policies (or even just incurred his disfavour) could expect violent treatment. He never thought twice about killing even his own family: one of his wives, Mariamme, was executed on his orders, and he was involved in the murder of two of his own sons, Alexander and Aristobulus. Only five days before his death in 4BC he ordered the execution of yet another of his sons, Antipater, the one who had been expected to succeed him.

Yet Herod the Great was not called 'Great' for nothing, and in contrast to previous rulers Herod maintained peace and order throughout his territory. He was also responsible for a massive building programme: it was Herod the Great who started the building of a new temple at Jerusalem, which was still not finished during the lifetime of Jesus. He also built many other magnificent buildings in Jerusalem and Caesarea, and even in other Roman cities outside his own territory.

The three Herods

When Herod the Great died in 4BC the Romans divided his kingdom among his three remaining sons. With one possible exception, none of them was any better than his father.

Judea, the part of Palestine that included Jerusalem, was given to his

The Herodium is a fortress 7 m/12 km south of Jerusalem. Built by Herod the Great between 24 and 15BC, it stands on the spot where he achieved one of his most important victories over the Hasmoneans in 40BC.

son Archelaus. He was not allowed to call himself 'king' of Judea, as his father had been, but received the title 'ethnarch' instead. He ruled for only ten years: the Romans removed him from office. In AD6 Judea became a third-grade province of the Roman empire, under an officer of the upper-class equestrian rank, who was himself under the command of the Roman governor of Syria. These Roman rulers of Judea were later called 'procurators'. The best-known one, certainly in relation to the New Testament story, was Pontius Pilate, who governed Judea from AD26 to 36.

The northern part of Palestine was given to Antipas, another son of Herod. He was known as the 'tetrarch' of Galilee and Perea, and his territory included the village of Nazareth where Jesus grew up. Antipas was very much like his father, a crafty man who liked living in luxury. To make a name for himself he took great pride in the construction of massive public buildings. One of his major projects was the rebuilding of Sepphoris, a town only four miles from Nazareth. He also built the new town of Tiberias by Lake Galilee, and named it in honour of the Roman emperor Tiberius. It was Herod Antipas who had John the Baptist executed (Mark 6:17–29) and who was involved in the trials of Jesus (Luke 23:6–12).

A third brother, Philip, was given some territory to the north-east of Palestine when his father died. He founded the town of Caesarea Philippi at the foot of Mount Hermon. Of all the sons of Herod the Great, Philip was the only one who proved to be a balanced and humane ruler, and he survived as 'tetrarch of Iturea and Trachonitis' until the year AD34.

After Archelaus was replaced by a Roman governor, there were many revolts against the Romans in Judea. The Jews became more and more frustrated at not having control of their own affairs. The Romans for their part became less interested in trying to understand the special problems of the Jewish people. The oppression and corruption of many of the Roman rulers, encouraged by a rising tide of Jewish nationalism, continued to increase until eventually in the year AD66 a general revolt

Division of the kingdom on the death of Herod the Great.

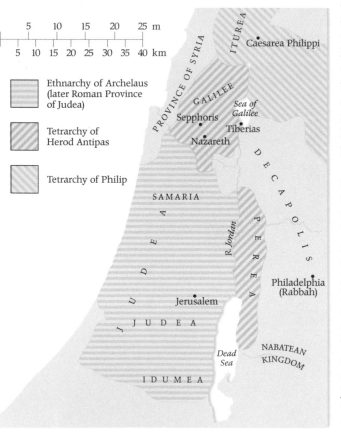

5   10   15   20   25 m
5 10 15 20 25 30 35 40 km

Ethnarchy of Archelaus (later Roman Province of Judea)

Tetrarchy of Herod Antipas

Tetrarchy of Philip

ITUREA
Caesarea Philippi
PROVINCE OF SYRIA
GALILEE
Sepphoris
Sea of Galilee
Tiberias
Nazareth
DECAPOLIS
SAMARIA
R. Jordan
PEREA
Jerusalem
Philadelphia (Rabbah)
JUDEA
Dead Sea
NABATEAN KINGDOM
IDUMEA

broke out. This revolt was finally crushed when Jerusalem was largely destroyed by the Roman general Titus in AD70.

Religious loyalties

The Jewish historian Josephus, who lived towards the end of the first century AD, and who was a friend of the Romans, reports that three main opinions were common among the Jews in Palestine: 'Jewish philosophy takes three forms. The followers of the first school are called Pharisees, of the second Sadducees, and the third sect, which has a reputation for being more disciplined, is the Essenes' (*Jewish Wars* 2.8.2). He also mentions a fourth group, called Zealots, but since he does not always include these among the philosophical sects, it seems likely that they formed a much looser kind of association (*Jewish Wars* 4.3.9). All these groups had their origins in the years following the Maccabean Revolt, and their actual membership was probably quite small, though most people would look to one of them for leadership, in much the same way as people nowadays might regularly vote for a particular political party, without joining it in a formal way as members. Three of these groups feature regularly in the New Testament: the Sadducees, the Pharisees and the Zealots.

Sadducees

The gospels of Matthew, Mark and Luke regularly mention the Sadducees along with the Pharisees, though in fact the two groups were not intrinsically related but were quite separate and actually held opposite opinions on almost everything. The Sadducees were only a small group, but were very influential because they consisted mainly of the more important priests in the temple at Jerusalem, and included only the most well-to-do classes of Jewish society. They were extreme conservatives in everything and disliked changes of any kind, especially changes which might affect the social status quo. Even if they believed theoretically in the coming of a Messiah, they generally had nothing to do with political protests, for that would only cause trouble with the Romans.

The name 'Sadducee' seems to mean 'son of Zadok', although the Sadducees were certainly not direct descendants of the priest Zadok mentioned in 2 Samuel 15:24–29. Other meanings for the name are also possible: either from the Hebrew word *sadiq*, meaning 'moral integrity' or 'righteousness'; or from the Greek word *syndicoi*, which could mean 'members of the council'. It is certainly true that the Jewish council of seventy (the Sanhedrin) had many Sadducees among its members, though since the remaining members were Pharisees, it is doubtful if this would be the origin of their distinctive name.

Sadducees were conservative not only in politics, but also in their understanding of Judaism. For them, the only religious teaching with any authority was the Law given by Moses in the first five books of the Hebrew Bible (the Pentateuch or Torah). They had no time either for

Facing page: Palestine in New Testament times.

the rest of the scriptures, or for anyone who tried to reinterpret or apply them in a more direct way to their own situation. This meant that they did not share with other Jews some of the beliefs of Judaism that were not explicitly contained in the Torah. For that reason, they did not generally believe that God had a purpose behind the events of history, while matters such as belief in a future life, resurrection, or a final judgment were regarded as unauthorized additions to the Jewish faith.

Pharisees

This was a much larger group, with maybe around 6,000 members at the time of Jesus. Many of them were professional students of the scriptures, but others had ordinary jobs. They were a national organization, with a large number of local groups found in most towns and villages throughout Palestine, each with their own officials and rules. They were probably the most influential religious group during Jesus' lifetime. The Sadducees disliked them because they believed and did things that went well beyond a literal understanding of the Law of Moses, but they were highly regarded by most ordinary people.

Modern Jews studying the Torah.

The Sadducees' chief complaint against the Pharisees was that they had collected many rules and regulations to explain what they saw as the real meaning of the Law. Though the Pharisees regarded the Hebrew scriptures as their supreme rule of life and belief, they also realized that

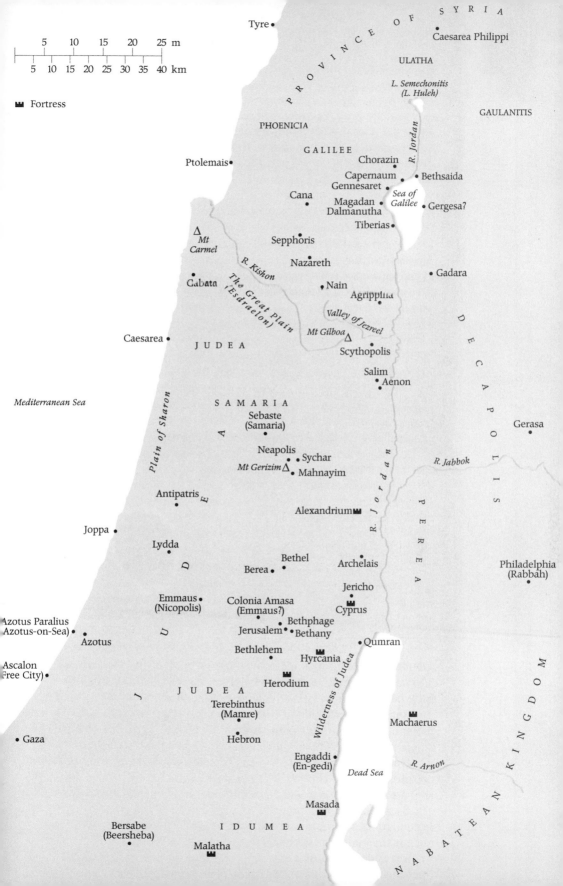

PROVINCE OF SYRIA

Tyre

Caesarea Philippi

ULATHA

L. Semechonitis
(L. Huleh)

GAULANITIS

PHOENICIA

GALILEE

Ptolemais

Chorazin

Capernaum
Gennesaret

Bethsaida

R. Jordan

Sea of
Galilee

Gergesa?

Cana

Magadan
Dalmanutha

Tiberias

Sepphoris

Nazareth

Gadara

Mt
Carmel

R. Kishon

Cabata

The Great Plain
('Esdraelon)

Nain

Agrippina

Valley of Jezreel

Mt Gilboa

D
E
C
A
P
O
L
I
S

Caesarea

JUDEA

Scythopolis

Salim
Aenon

Mediterranean Sea

SAMARIA

Sebaste
(Samaria)

Gerasa

Neapolis

Sychar

R. Jabbok

Mt Gerizim

Mahnayim

Plain of Sharon

Antipatris

Alexandrium

R. Jordan

P
E
R
E
A

Joppa

Lydda

Bethel

Archelais

Philadelphia
(Rabbah)

Berea

Jericho

Emmaus
(Nicopolis)

Colonia Amasa
(Emmaus?)

Cyprus

Azotus Paralius
(Azotus-on-Sea)

Bethphage

Jerusalem

Bethany

Azotus

Bethlehem

Qumran

Ascalon
(Free City)

Hyrcania

Wilderness of Judea

Herodium

JUDEA

Terebinthus
(Mamre)

Machaerus

Gaza

Hebron

Engaddi
(En-gedi)

R. Arnon

Dead Sea

N
A
B
A
T
E
A
N

K
I
N
G
D
O
M

Masada

Bersabe
(Beersheba)

IDUMEA

Malatha

5   10   15   20   25 m

5   10 15 20 25 30 35 40 km

▣ Fortress

it no longer had any direct application to the kind of society they lived in, and to remain relevant it would need to be explained in new ways. For example, the ten commandments instructed people to keep the sabbath day holy (Exodus 20:8). But what did that really mean in everyday terms? What should people do and not do on the sabbath day? To provide a practical answer to that kind of question, the Pharisees had developed a list of simple rules that could be applied by anybody.

One of the writings influenced by them, the *Pirke Aboth*, opened with the advice to 'make a fence for the Law', which meant, 'protect the Law from infringement by surrounding it with cautionary rules which can act as a warning notice to stop people before they get within breaking distance of the actual God-given commandments themselves'. This intention was praiseworthy enough, but there can be no doubt that eventually it led to the multiplication of petty rules to such an extent that keeping the Law easily became an onerous burden, rather than the joyful celebration of God's goodness which it was meant to be. A typical example would be the rules concerning the sabbath. Tailors were not allowed to go out carrying a needle late in the day before the sabbath, in case they were caught with it still in their pockets when the sabbath began. But like everyone else, they could go for a walk on the sabbath day – provided it was no further than 2,000 cubits, roughly two thirds of a mile, a distance determined by reference to the space between the people of Israel and the Ark of the Covenant when they first entered Canaan! This became known as the 'sabbath day's journey'.

In spite of the apparent absurdity of some of these notions, there can be no doubt that many Pharisees did actually keep these rules, and Josephus comments that 'the people of the cities hold them in the highest esteem, because they both preach and practise the very highest moral ideas' (*Antiquities* 18.1.3). Jesus denounced them for what he called 'hypocrisy', which in this context seems to have been a complaint that the keeping of their own sectarian rules and regulations had become more important than they deserved to be. In that respect, their mistake was one common to many religious groups, namely the claim that the only possible way to know God is to be a member of the group.

Jesus also differed from the Pharisees on more substantive grounds, for it seems that a person's ability to keep the Law had also become a form of social stratification, something that Jesus repeatedly questioned with his insistence that God had a special love for the outcasts and marginalized members of society, and a corresponding disdain for those who were conventionally religious. All that is known of the Pharisees makes it doubtful whether they could ever have said with Jesus: 'I came not to call the righteous, but sinners' (Mark 2:17).

The Pharisees had distinctive views on other subjects, of course. They accepted the authority of the whole of the Hebrew scriptures, and not just the Law of Moses. Unlike the Sadducees they had no difficulty in believing that there was a life after death. They might well have expected a Messiah to come and right the wrongs of their people, and though we have no record that they took part in open revolt against the Romans, they probably admired those people who did.

Zealots

These were the people who became most involved in direct action against the Romans. Conceptually, they probably shared many of the religious beliefs of the Pharisees, but their overriding conviction was that they could have no master but God, and for them that implied that driving out the Romans must be a top priority. Josephus identifies their founder as a man called Judas, a Galilean who led a revolt in AD6 at about the same time as Archelaus was removed from office by the Romans (*Jewish Wars* 2.8.1). He also reports that 'these men agree in everything with the opinions of the Pharisees, but they have an insatiable passion for liberty; and they are convinced that God alone is to be their only master and Lord... no fear can compel them to give this title to anyone else...' (*Antiquities* 18.1.6).

A Hebrew shekel, minted at the time of the first revolt against Roman rule, AD66–70.

 The Zealots continued as a guerrilla movement until the siege of Jerusalem in AD70, and perhaps even after that. At least one of Jesus' disciples, a man called Simon, was a Zealot, and it is often thought that Judas Iscariot was as well (Mark 3:18). But more typical Zealots seem to

The apocalyptists

A source of particular insight into the religious expectations that probably formed the background to the life and teaching of Jesus is those works known as the apocalyptic writings. This is a disparate collection of writings compiled over a considerable period of time, all of them containing speculative visions of the future. The term 'apocalypse' literally means 'a revealing of secrets', and it is unclear whether their authors (referred to as 'apocalyptists') formed a distinctive religious grouping, or whether they were individuals who belonged to some of the other groups mentioned by Josephus. Since these people are mostly known only through their writings, it is hard to be sure, though it is certainly unlikely, that any of the apocalyptists would have been Sadducees. The apocalyptists' central claim was that they had received new revelations from God, something that by definition the Sadducees would

not countenance, as they considered Moses to be the only one who had ever received divine revelation. It is easier to equate the apocalyptic writings with aspects of Pharisaic belief, for they placed great emphasis on God's predetermined plan for the history of the world.

 Whoever the apocalyptists might have been, their writings have a number of unusual characteristics which make them readily recognizable:
 ● They place strong emphasis on the life of heaven rather than the everyday world of human experience. Though events in this world are mentioned, they are important only insofar as they reveal something about events taking place in another, spiritual world. One apocalyptic writer states that 'the Most High has made not one world but two' (2 Esdras 7:50), and this viewpoint seems to have been widely shared by the apocalyptists. It was their job to reveal what was happening in God's world, and to assure their readers

have been people like Barabbas, whom the crowd chose to liberate in preference to Jesus (Mark 15:6–15), or the unnamed rabble-rouser with whom Paul was once confused (Acts 21:37–39).

Essenes

The Essenes are referred to by several ancient writers. Philo of Alexandria, the Latin author Pliny, and Josephus all mention them, though they are not explicitly named by any of the New Testament writers.

It is widely supposed that one section of the Essenes wrote the documents known as the Dead Sea Scrolls. This group had their headquarters at Qumran near the north-west corner of the Dead Sea. The people of Qumran probably had their origins among the religious supporters of the Maccabees, but became disenchanted with the corruption of their successors, the Hasmoneans. They chose to withdraw from mainstream society to live in an isolated community in the desert, where they could more easily preserve the traditions of religious and moral purity which they believed they could find in the Hebrew Bible.

Not all Essenes lived in this way, however, for Josephus says that they 'occupy no one city, but settle in large numbers in every town'. He also writes of others who, unlike the monastic groups, were married, though he does go to some pains to make it clear that they regarded

---

The apocalyptists
continued

that they had a central position in God's activities.

● The apocalyptic writings also emphasize dreams, visions and communications through angels. Since God is remote in a different world ('heaven'), intermediaries play a key role in dealings between people and God. A typical apocalypse is an extended report of how its writer received speculative visions and messages revealing what is happening in heaven.

● Corresponding with this is an unusual literary form. For the visions are not described in straightforward terms, but invariably use coded language. There are often references to esoteric passages in the books of the Hebrew prophets, and mythological beasts and symbolic numbers are used to represent nations or individuals.

● Apocalypses were normally written under the name of a great figure of the past. Enoch, Noah, Adam, Moses and Ezra are only a few of the ancient heroes who had apocalyptic works attributed to them.

This might have been necessary to protect the identities of their authors, because apocalypses were invariably written in circumstances of persecution. It could also have been the case that because the time of genuine prophecy was believed to have passed, prophets who wanted to get a hearing for their message had to attribute their work to somebody who had actually lived in the age when the Hebrew scriptures were in process of compilation. Revelation, the only New Testament book to use extensive apocalyptic imagery, is unique in this respect, and though there is a good deal of debate as to who its author actually was, he is named as a contemporary and friend of his readers, not someone from the distant past (Revelation 1:1–9).

Why did this kind of writing become so popular in the centuries immediately before the birth of Jesus? An attractive answer is that apocalyptic writing was a response to the difficult realities of life in

this not in relational terms, but only as a means of continuing the human race (*Jewish Wars* 2.8.2–13). There is also written evidence that another group lived in the desert near Damascus, whose organization was slightly different from the group at Qumran.

There is no clear account of the relationship between these various groups, nor any certain knowledge of how they might have been related to the Essenes apparently scattered throughout the towns and villages of Palestine. The community at Qumran is the best known, because of the

Qumran: view of the Essene settlement from the south west.

discovery of their writings, and at most points these documents are in harmony with the statements made by Josephus. The Dead Sea Scrolls reveal that the people of this community regarded themselves as the minority in Israel who were faithful to God's covenant. From their perspective, the rest of the nation, including especially the priests and religious leaders in Jerusalem, had wilfully jettisoned the true faith. Only their

---

Palestine at the time. The prophets had often suggested that the course of Israel's history was dependent on the nation's current spiritual attitudes. At times, it was almost as if they perceived a cause and effect relationship between religious faithfulness and political fortunes: when people were obedient to the Law of God they prospered and, if they weren't, they could expect hard times. These hard times had culminated most painfully in the capture of Jerusalem by Nebuchadnezzar in 586BC, and the exile of its population to Babylon. After only a short time in exile, the Jews had been allowed to return to their homeland, and those who returned were determined that they would not make the same mistakes as their ancestors.

A key part of the post-exilic reconstruction of the nation had been a rigorous reinterpretation of the Law, and an uncompromising application of its precepts to all aspects of national and personal life. As things turned out, however, these people did not prosper

either and, as time went on, the way to prosperity seemed to lie more in collaboration with outsiders such as the Romans than in remaining faithful to the ancient religious traditions. Those who tried to keep the faith alive found themselves more and more in a minority, while those who prospered often did so by sitting loosely to it, or even abandoning it altogether.

Apocalyptic writing might well have begun as an answer to this problem. Why did faithfulness not lead to prosperity? Why were good people suffering? Why did God not put an end to the power of evil forces? To these questions the apocalyptists answered that the present difficulties were only relative. Seen in the light of God's working throughout history, the good would eventually triumph and the oppressive domination of evil would soon be relaxed.

It is often asked whether Jesus had any connection with these apocalyptists and their visions of the heavenly world. Jesus

own leader, the 'Teacher of Righteousness', and his faithful followers had preserved knowledge of the true meaning of the ancient scriptures.

Like some of the other religious groupings, the Essenes looked forward to a day of crisis in history. At this time God's sovereignty over all things would be reaffirmed, and in the process all heretics would be banished, along with

The first three columns of the Great Isaiah Scroll from Qumran, one of the oldest known manuscripts of a part of the Hebrew Bible.

foreign enemies such as the Romans. The members of the group, rather than the whole Jewish nation, would be recognized as God's chosen people, and they would take over and purify the worship of God at the temple in Jerusalem. They expected three leaders to appear in connection with these events: the coming prophet who had been predicted by Moses (Deuteronomy 18:18–19); a royal Messiah who

---

The apocalyptists
continued

was certainly familiar with the ideas that the apocalyptists put forward, and used much of the same imagery and language in his own teachings (Mark 13; Matthew 24 – 25; Luke 21). But there are some important differences which should caution against a simplistic understanding which sees Jesus as just another apocalyptic visionary:

● Apocalyptic literature was always the report of visions and other insights into the heavenly world, given to humans through some special means. Jesus, however, did not base his teaching on visions and revelations of this kind, but spoke on his own authority. Moreover, his main concern was not with the affairs of some other, heavenly, world, but with life in this world. He did not reveal secrets; he made disciples and reminded them of their responsibilities to God, which always combined moral and social responsibilities as well as matters of belief.

● The apocalyptists were always concerned to encourage and comfort their readers by demonstrating that they were in the right, and their enemies would soon be overcome. But Jesus' teaching, even in what are called the 'apocalyptic discourses', was never designed to comfort his disciples. Nor did he suggest that they will automatically triumph over their enemies: on the contrary, Jesus made his teaching on the future an occasion to challenge his disciples' attitude to life, and regarded the time of God's intervention in human affairs as an occasion of judgment, for his disciples as much as for everyone else.

● There is no systematic view of the future in Jesus' teaching. This is quite different from the apocalyptic outlook, in which every detail of the future has already been mapped out in advance: there, it is all in God's predetermined plan, and those who hold the key to the coded language can know precisely what the future holds. Of course, there have been Christians who have produced systems of this kind on the basis of what they find in

would be a descendant of King David; and a priestly Messiah who would be the most important. In order to keep themselves in a constant state of readiness for these events, the Essenes of Qumran went through many ritual washings. Everything they did had some religious significance. Even their daily meals were an anticipation of the heavenly banquet which they believed would take place at the end of the age.

With the possible exception of the Sadducees, then, all the dominant religious groups in Palestine at the time of Jesus were hoping and praying that God would intervene to give new direction to the life of their people. They all had their own ideas about what God should do, and when and how it might all take place. Some, like the Zealots, were prepared to give God a helping hand when they thought it necessary. Others, such as the Pharisees and Essenes, believed that God's plan was fixed and predetermined and therefore could be neither changed nor enforced by human intervention. Over and above all this, no doubt many other people would be interested neither in political manoeuvring nor in theological disputes, but were still longing for a new direction in the fortunes of their nation. All these factors combined to produce a great sense of expectation, fuelled by much speculation about the meaning of the scriptures, and facilitated by the social and political ferment that ran like a metallic thread through the fabric that was life in Palestine at the time of the New Testament.

---

the New Testament, but the great variety of incompatible and contradictory understandings they have produced merely serves to emphasize the futile nature of such an undertaking. Jesus himself discounted the possibility that the divine plan might be uncovered so easily, and categorically asserted that he did not know it himself (Matthew 24:36; Mark 13:32). No apocalyptist would ever have said that.
● Apocalyptic writers were almost invariably pessimistic about the world and its history. Unlike the prophets of earlier generations, they despaired of God ever being able to work in the world. The forces of evil seemed too strong for that, and they saw the world running headlong to a final and tragic end. There was no point in trying to discover God at work in the midst of such evil, for God was not there. This is all in strong contrast to the outlook of Jesus, who made it abundantly plain that the 'kingdom of God' which he had come to inaugurate would affect the everyday life of ordinary people in this world (Luke

4:16–21). By both precept and example, he declared that God's will was not just something to be done 'in heaven', but was meant to impact the social and political realities of life here and now (Matthew 6:10).

There are then some fundamental differences between Jesus and the apocalyptists. He did not have an apocalyptic outlook on life. He occasionally gave his teaching in the language and imagery of the apocalyptic teachers, just as he referred to the 'golden rule' of the rabbis (Matthew 7:12). As a good teacher he realized that he needed to speak the language of his hearers, and it might well have been that many of the ordinary people of Palestine were most familiar with apocalyptic language. But, characteristically, Jesus took familiar concepts and gave them a new meaning.

Herod's Temple

Herod the Great began building the temple in Jerusalem in 19BC. The main building was complete by AD9 but work continued on it for many years after that. It was twice as high as Solomon's temple had been, and shone with gold decoration. This is an artist's impression of what it looked like.

The Holy of Holies, divided from the Holy Place by a curtain. The ark of the covenant stood here in Solomon's day, but no longer existed in Jesus' time.

The Holy Place, where the priests regularly burnt incense.

A bowl for ritual washings.

The temple area was a hill-top; Herod built a platform on it to make it level. It covered about 35 acres.

The altar where animals were sacrificed.

The court of the Gentiles. This was the only part in which non-Jews were allowed. The traders and money-changers worked here, and were turned out by Jesus.

Fort Antonia, where Roman soldiers were garrisoned.

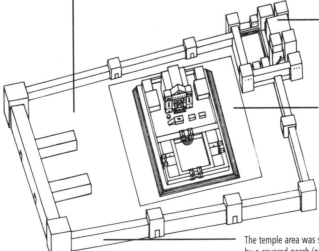

The central buidings were surrounded by steps and another wall.

The temple area was surrounded by a covered porch (or portico).

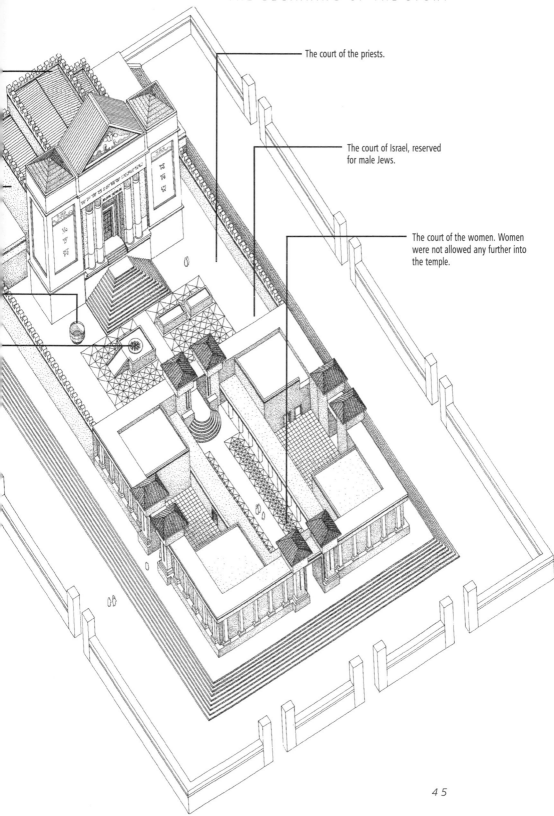

The court of the priests.

The court of Israel, reserved for male Jews.

The court of the women. Women were not allowed any further into the temple.

45

2 Jesus' Birth and Early Years

If there is one consistent theme that runs through all the stories of Jesus' birth, it is the repeated claim that ordinary people had more insight than religious experts when it came to understanding the significance of it all. The coming of the one who was later claimed to be the expected Messiah was recognized not predominantly by the great and the good but by those who, to a greater or lesser extent, were on the fringes of the cultured society of their day. The first chapter of Luke's Gospel paints a vivid picture of the little-known priest Zechariah and his wife Elizabeth praying expectantly for God to deliver their people, and being rewarded for their faithfulness by the announcement of the birth of their own son, later to be known as John the Baptist (Luke 1:5–28, 57–80).

Mary, the mother of Jesus, belonged to the same family. At the time of Jesus' conception and birth she was in the process of getting married to Joseph. This was an extended business, and it could take several months, with various betrothal ceremonies to get through before a couple were formally recognized as husband and wife. Joseph has traditionally been described as a carpenter, though the Greek word used to describe him (*tekton*) indicates that he was more likely a general builder, the kind of person who could turn his hand to just about anything in the construction industry. At the time, there was plenty of work in Palestine for such a person, so Joseph and Mary are unlikely to have been extremely poor. At the same time, they would not be rich. More importantly, from the religious perspective, as ordinary working people they would be regarded as quite unqualified when it came to understanding the Hebrew scriptures and applying them to the events of their own time in order to discern God's will for their people. They were part of the 'people of the land', whose endeavours were a necessary part of the national economy but whom the religious establishment would have considered incapable of spiritual insight.

The striking poetry of the hymn of praise sung by Mary, the Magnificat, emphasizes this theme (Luke 1:46–55), and all the leading characters in the nativity stories were lowly people. The first ones to hear the announcement of the fulfilment of the ancient promises with the birth of Jesus were some shepherds in the Judean hills (Luke

2:8–20), then Simeon and Anna in the temple (Luke 2:25–38). None of these people were of any significance to the world at large. The stories in the first chapters of Luke's Gospel emphasize that officialdom – whether political or religious – had no eyes with which to recognize Jesus. This lesson is repeated throughout the story of Jesus' life, as it becomes clear that to have a real understanding of God's actions in Christ even the most important people must become like little children (Luke 18:17).

When was Jesus born?

Deciding exactly when the birth of Jesus took place is not as simple a matter as it seems. The obvious thing to suppose is that Jesus was born between 1BC and AD1. But this has been known to be untrue for a long time, because of mistakes made as long ago as the sixth century in calculating the extent of the Christian era. In determining the likely date of Jesus' birth, there are four main pieces of evidence to be considered:

● According to Matthew 2:1, Jesus was born 'in Bethlehem of Judea in the reign of Herod the king', that is, before the death of Herod the Great in 4BC.

● Luke was much more interested in placing his story in the wider context of affairs in the Roman empire, and he says that Jesus was born during 'the first enrolment, when Quirinius was governor of Syria' (2:2). Josephus mentions an imperial representative called Quirinius being sent to Syria and Judea to take a census just after the beginning of the Christian era (*Jewish Antiquities* 18.1). This census, however, took place as part of the clearing-up operation after Herod the Great's son Archelaus had been deposed, which means it must have been in the year AD6 or 7 and could not therefore have been before the death of Herod the Great in 4BC. Because of this, it has been suggested that the person Luke calls 'Quirinius' might have been Saturninus, the imperial legate in Syria, who might have conducted a census in 6BC. However, there is no evidence that might explain how Luke could have confused the two, and in

the rest of his gospel, and also in his second volume, the book of Acts, he generally displays great care, and accuracy, in his use of the names and titles of Roman officials.

● At the same time, Luke's narrative does include other statements about the date of various important events in the life of Jesus. He records, for example, that Jesus was about thirty years old when he was baptized, and that this was 'in the fifteenth year of the reign of Tiberius Caesar' (3:1). Tiberius became ruler of the Roman empire in AD14, which would make the fifteenth year of his reign AD28. This calculation is complicated, however, by the fact that Tiberius had shared power with his predecessor Augustus from about AD11, which means that though he became emperor after Augustus died in AD14, for all practical purposes he had been the emperor for the previous three years as well. If, as is likely, Luke was reckoning the fifteenth year of Tiberius from AD11, that means Jesus would be thirty years old in AD25–26, which in turn would place his birth in either 5 or 4BC, and so before the death of Herod the Great.

● From time to time, some have tried to introduce a more scientific element into this debate, beginning with the bright star mentioned in Matthew 2:2 and calculating that there was a conjunction of certain planets about 6BC which might have been the same thing. Though such considerations cannot be entirely ruled out as admissible evidence, this kind of

A bronze head of Augustus (63BC – AD14) (Octavian), Roman emperor at the time of Jesus' birth.

Jesus grows up

Very little is known about Jesus' life as a child. His home was presumably the typical flat-roofed, one-roomed house of the time, built of clay. Joseph probably carried on his business from home, and various statements in the gospels imply that Jesus learned the same trade. Together they would make agricultural tools, furniture, and probably also worked on larger building projects. At the time when Jesus was

---

When was Jesus born? continued

approach would require a lot of imagination to be convincing.

There are then two pieces of evidence (one from Matthew, the other from Luke) indicating a date for Jesus' birth around 4BC, with a third piece of information also provided by Luke concerning the census under Quirinius which seems not to agree with this dating. Three possible explanations have been advanced in the effort to solve this problem:

Luke has been misunderstood
Several scholars propose that the apparent 'problem' as it has been outlined here simply does not exist . They point out that, from a grammatical point of view, it is perfectly possible to translate Luke 2:2 to read, 'This enrolment was before that made when Quirinius was governor of Syria', in place of the conventional translation, 'This was the first enrolment, when Quirinius

Jesus' birthplace: the town of Bethlehem, 9 km south of Jerusalem.

was governor of Syria'. Linguistically, this understanding is certainly plausible, though it would hardly be the most obvious meaning of the statement, and it does involve an implicit assumption that the text has somehow been corrupted in the process of transmission. Still, though this explanation of the matter is by no means universally held, some notable New Testament scholars have supported it, and continue to do so.

Luke made a mistake
Many more scholars take the simpler way out of the difficulty by concluding that Luke was mistaken in the information he provides regarding Quirinius. This is perhaps the most obvious explanation to adopt, though it also leaves some unanswered questions. Notable among these is the way that elsewhere in his writings where Luke refers to people and events in the Roman empire, he shows himself to have checked his sources very carefully. He needed to, for one of his purposes in writing was to commend the Christian faith to upper-class Hellenistic citizens, and in that context it would be especially important for his facts to be correct in relation to the life of the empire. We may therefore assume that Luke believed this information to be correct. Moreover, he presumably thought it was compatible with the other indication about dates that he gives

growing up, the ancient city of Sepphoris was being redesigned and rebuilt only a short distance from Nazareth, and this project must have created a huge demand for the skills of people involved in the construction industry. The city was completed shortly before Jesus began his public ministry of teaching, and it is tempting to imagine that both he and some of his band of disciples might have been thrown out of regular work at that time as the massive project was completed. It could also be that Joseph died about this time. He certainly seems to

---

when reporting the date of Jesus' baptism by John, which presupposes that Jesus was born in the reign of Herod the Great, and therefore something like ten years before the rule of the Quirinius whom Josephus mentions. These considerations do not of course prove that Luke got it right, only that he thought he had checked his sources carefully and did not believe he was giving out contradictory messages.

Luke does not tell the whole story
A different way of dealing with this matter begins not from the bare facts as reported in literary texts, but with a sociological understanding of how things could be made to happen in the furthest extremities of the Roman empire. Ruling Judea from Rome in AD7 was not the same thing as it would be today, with instant communication from one part of the world to another. In ancient Rome things were very different. Even in ideal conditions, it could take months for a decree signed by the emperor in Rome to be delivered to a distant province like Judea, and there was always a good chance that it might be delayed or even lost in the process. Messengers could be robbed or shipwrecked, or just disappear on the journey. At a later period, for example, the Emperor Caligula sent orders that his own statue should be erected in the temple at Jerusalem. The local governor was wiser than the emperor, and realized that this would create great resistance from the Jews, so he wrote and asked the emperor to think again. Caligula insisted on his plan going ahead, and wrote back to the governor to tell him so. The ship carrying

his message took three months to make the voyage from Rome to Judea. In the meantime, however, Caligula was assassinated and another ship that left Rome much later bearing the news of his death and the end of his policies, arrived twenty-seven days earlier than the first one!

When we take account of such simple practical problems of communication and government, it is obvious that conducting a census would not be a simple matter. In addition, Roman enrolments were carried out for tax purposes, and for that very reason were regularly resisted throughout the empire. One such census in Gaul, for example, was so unpopular among the people that it took forty years to complete! When all these considerations are taken into account, it is virtually certain that a census completed by Quirinius in AD6 or 7 must have taken a long time to carry through, and would be based on information collected much earlier than the date when it was finished.

The emperor Augustus was very keen on gathering statistics, and he might well have persuaded Herod the Great to carry out a census. Quirinius was sent in AD6 to clear up the mess left by Archelaus, and it is quite possible that he would use information gathered earlier rather than beginning the same tedious process all over again. If this was indeed the case, then there is no convincing reason to suppose that Luke's information about the census is contradictory to the rest of the evidence that he and other writers supply, all of which suggests that Jesus was born about 5BC.

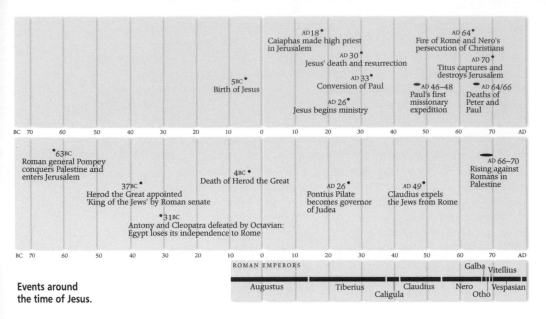

| BC 70 | 60 | 50 | 40 | 30 | 20 | 10 | 0 | 10 | 20 | 30 | 40 | 50 | 60 | 70 | AD |

AD 18•
Caiaphas made high priest
in Jerusalem

AD 64•
Fire of Rome and Nero's
persecution of Christians

AD 30•
Jesus' death and resurrection

AD 70•
Titus captures and
destroys Jerusalem

5BC•
Birth of Jesus

AD 33•
Conversion of Paul

AD 26•
Jesus begins ministry

AD 46–48
Paul's first
missionary
expedition

AD 64/66
Deaths of
Peter and
Paul

•63BC
Roman general Pompey
conquers Palestine and
enters Jerusalem

AD 66–70
Rising against
Romans in
Palestine

4BC•
Death of Herod the Great

37BC•
Herod the Great appointed
'King of the Jews' by Roman senate

AD 26•
Pontius Pilate
becomes governor
of Judea

AD 49•
Claudius expels
the Jews from Rome

•31BC
Antony and Cleopatra defeated by Octavian:
Egypt loses its independence to Rome

| BC 70 | 60 | 50 | 40 | 30 | 20 | 10 | 0 | 10 | 20 | 30 | 40 | 50 | 60 | 70 | AD |

ROMAN EMPERORS

**Events around
the time of Jesus.**

Augustus | Tiberius | Claudius | Galba Vitellius
Caligula | Nero | Vespasian
Otho

have disappeared from the scene during Jesus' early life, as he does not feature in the later stories of Jesus as an adult. Whenever Jesus' family are mentioned, it is only ever Mary and his brothers and sisters (Matthew 12:46; Mark 3:31; Luke 8:19). At his death, Jesus as the elder son of the family asked one of his senior disciples to take care of his mother Mary – another indication that Joseph was already dead (John 19:26–27).

Nazareth

Jesus obviously grew up in a simple home environment. But he also had the opportunity to gain some education. He was considered a suitable person to read the Old Testament in Hebrew in the synagogue at Nazareth, something that not everyone could do (Luke 4:16–20). There were organized schools in Palestine at this period, but most boys (never girls) would receive their education at the local synagogue. In addition, Nazareth itself must have been the kind of place where everyday life provided its own liberal education. It was not an important place, and is never mentioned in the rest of the Bible, or in any other contemporary literature. At one time, it was believed that Nazareth did not exist at the time of Jesus, but that is now known to be untrue, and various remains of water storage cisterns and other artifacts can be positively dated to this period. But it was never a large place, and even at its most expansive had a population of only about 200 people.

Its size alone would ensure that it was never mentioned in most official records, but in addition it was in Galilee – an area that was always despised by the strictest religious people, who felt that the inhabitants of Galilee were too relaxed in their dealings with explicitly non-Jewish culture. The reconstruction of Sepphoris as a Hellenistic city was not inconsistent in a place that was often called 'Galilee of the Gentiles', because it had more non-Jewish than Jewish residents. It was a great contrast to the southern province of Judea, whose people could more easily isolate their lifestyle from external influences – something that Jesus later criticized them for, claiming that they had too easily become introverted and self-centred, if not self-righteous and hypocritical. But Galilee was criss-crossed by major trading routes between east and west that ensured it would never be isolated from the wider life of the empire. Here Jesus would meet and mix with many people who were not Jewish, and he no doubt spent much of his time thinking and talking about the ideas of the Greeks and Romans as well as the religious heritage of his own people.

One of the special advantages of growing up in Galilee was that Jesus would probably be fluent in three languages. By now Hebrew was no longer the normal language of the Jewish people, and only continued in use because it was the language of the ancient scriptures. For several centuries, Aramaic had been the everyday language, and Jesus would use this at home and among his friends. This had originally been promoted by the Persian empire in the fifth and sixth centuries BC as its own international language, and had many similarities to Hebrew, which ensured its ready adoption throughout Palestine. However, since there were so many non-Jewish people in Galilee, Jesus must have spoken Greek as well, for this was the international language of commerce and government used everywhere throughout the whole of the Roman empire.

Jesus and his family

Apart from what we can infer from our knowledge of the kind of society in which Jesus was brought up, the New Testament tells us very little about his life before he was thirty years old. He was not the only child in his family. Mark 6:3 records how he returned to Nazareth as an adult teacher, and people found it hard to accept his message because they knew him only as 'the carpenter, the son of Mary, and the brother of James, Joseph, Judas, and Simon' – all of whom were still living in the village, along with some unnamed sisters. We know little about these brothers and sisters, though they were apparently believers in the very earliest days of the church (Acts 1:14), and James eventually became leader of the church in Jerusalem, though he was not a disciple during Jesus' lifetime. Mary herself is portrayed as constantly torn between discipleship and doubt, as she struggled to balance the needs of the various members of her family circle. But she was very firmly on Jesus' side, and features in the book of Acts as one of the leaders of the infant church (Acts 1:14).

Religiously, Jesus' family were obviously very committed to their ancestral faith. The one story about Jesus' childhood that the gospels do contain relates how on a pilgrimage to Jerusalem Jesus became separated from his parents, and when they eventually found him he was in the temple, discussing points of belief with the religious experts there (Luke 2:41–52). It is not easy to be more precise about the religious affiliations of Jesus' family, but some of them might have been Pharisees. James was certainly a conservative person later in life, even as a Christian, and according to one of his biographers he spent so much time in traditional Jewish prayers that his knees were like camel's knees! As a leader of the Jerusalem church he was able to stay in the city long after other Christians – including moderate Jewish believers like Peter – had been forced to leave. All these facts imply that he must have been quite traditional. Certainly, if some of Jesus' own relatives were Pharisees that could explain why he so often singled them out for special criticism, no doubt based on his first-hand experience of the way their theology had been applied in his own family circle.

Modern Nazareth: nothing now remains of the village that was Jesus' home.

The fact that the New Testament contains so little about Jesus' early life prompted later Christian writers to produce their own accounts of his childhood. From the second century and later, several such stories survive, with exotic titles like *The Gospel of the Nativity of Mary*, *The History of Joseph the Carpenter*, and *The Childhood Gospel of Thomas* (not to be confused with *The Gospel of Thomas*, which is a different kind of document altogether). Most of the stories contained in these 'gospels' are concerned with proving that Jesus had miraculous powers even as a child – powers, they claim, that he used to bring embarrassment both to his family and to the religious establishment. There is no reason to suppose that any of these accounts were based on authentic traditions about Jesus as a child: they were compiled in later generations by committed Christian believers who wanted on the one hand to satisfy natural curiosity about Jesus' origins, and also to enhance his reputation as a wonder-worker (something that, ironically, the New Testament gospels explicitly warn against).

John the Baptist

The next we hear of Jesus is when he was about thirty years old. His cousin, John the Baptist, had started a religious movement and had attracted quite a following. John lived a simple kind of life in the Judean desert, wearing clothes made of camel's hair and eating only the food of the desert, 'locusts and wild honey' (Mark 1:6).

John was by no means the only wandering prophet at that time. Many people were talking about the expected Messiah who would come to inaugurate some kind of new society. Further south in the same desert the people of Qumran were talking about similar things, and even later many rabble-rousers and prophets were able to attract people into the Judean desert in the hope of making a name for themselves and perhaps beginning a resistance movement that would banish the Romans from their land. One of John's most distinctive traits was that he quite specifically did not want to make a name for himself. He did not see himself as a messianic deliverer appointed by God to get rid of the political and social injustices of the time, but as 'a messenger', 'a voice' sent to bring the good news that the Messiah was about to come, and the nature of God's kingdom would soon be made plain (Mark 1:2–3).

Those who were familiar with the Hebrew scriptures knew that such a messenger would be like the Old Testament prophet Elijah (Malachi 4:5), and the gospel writers leave us in no doubt that they saw John the Baptist as this very person. Their descriptions of his way of life and of his message are closely modelled on the stories of Elijah in 1 Kings 17 – 19.

The New Testament and the Jewish historian Josephus both describe John's work as a call to the people to put their lives in order so that they would be morally fit to meet the person who was to establish God's new way of being (Josephus, *Antiquities of the Jews* 18.5.2). Earlier prophets had often condemned the people for their disobedience to the moral and spiritual standards God required of them, and declared that though they were still God's people, they could expect only judgment for their failure to live up to these expectations. Indeed, their judgment would be all the more severe because of the spiritual privilege they had enjoyed. John's message was exactly the same. He called on the people to be prepared to change their way of life, so they would be ready to meet God. Those who were willing to face up to the challenge showed their desire to change by being baptized. The Greek word from which this term is derived means 'to dip', and it was often used, for example, of the dyeing of clothes as they were immersed in a bath or tub. Baptism in the religious sense was just the same, except that it was people who were immersed, and they were dipped not in dye but in water. John's baptisms took place in the River Jordan.

Most Jews would have been familiar with baptism. It might have been used as a means of admitting Gentiles as proselytes or God-fearers into Judaism. It was certainly used in this way later. There is also ample evidence from the Dead Sea Scrolls that the Essenes used regularly repeated baptisms as a way of preserving their moral and religious purity. One of the most conspicuous features of the ruins of the monastery at Qumran is the incredibly complicated system of aqueducts and water tanks that was needed to provide sufficiently large quantities of water in the desert for the members of the community to undergo their baptismal rites. There were some differences, of course, and the rituals of people like the Essenes were not quite the same as the baptism of converts to Judaism. Unlike the ceremonial baptisms and washings that could be repeated over and over again at Qumran, proselyte baptism could only happen once, as it was not a rite of purification but of initiation, signalling the point at which a convert became a part of the faith community.

It is difficult to decide whether the background of John's ritual is to be found in repeated washings like those of the Essenes, or in the once-only baptism of Gentile converts. But the radical nature of John's message and the opposition he provoked would certainly be easier to understand if he was calling people who were already members of the covenant community to take part in something they would have regarded as appropriate only for those who were previously unbelievers. In John's view, however, some far-reaching changes of heart would be needed before his people could have any part in the new society that was about to dawn. They too would need to begin all over again, just as if they were Gentile people getting to know God for the first time.

Yet John did not see the full implications of what he was announcing. He saw the coming of the Messiah in conventional terms of judgment and condemnation, and described God's promised deliverer as a person who would chop down fruit trees that gave no fruit and burn the chaff away from the wheat (Luke 3:7–17). Admittedly, he appears to have seen with more clarity of spiritual vision than other religious people of his day, who took it for granted that the objects of God's anger would be the Romans. But he did not fully appreciate the true character of the 'kingdom of God', which in the teaching of Jesus turned out to be based less on damnation and judgment than on more generous qualities such as love, forgiveness and an unprejudiced concern for all kinds of people. This had always been the one thing that the ancient nation of Israel had found most difficult to understand, and it continued to cause problems even for Jesus' disciples, who could never quite grasp what it might mean for God's will to be done through self-denying service to others and suffering on their behalf (Mark 8:31–33). Though John announced the coming of the kingdom of God, the precise nature of what that might involve only became clear after the death and resurrection of Jesus.

Jesus is baptized

When Jesus came to John and asked to be baptized, John at first did not want to allow him to share in this symbol of repentance. After all, if Jesus really did have the special relationship with God which John believed he did, what could he possibly have to repent of? But Jesus assured John that he must take part in it, telling him: 'in this way we shall do all that God requires' (Matthew 3:15).

What did Jesus mean by saying this? The simple explanation is that Jesus felt he must identify himself with those who were ready to make sweeping changes in their lifestyles, and who would become his own first disciples. Far from separating him from other people, the gospels suggest that Jesus' special relationship with God was a powerful reason for becoming completely involved in the lives of the most ordinary folk. There are undoubtedly other undertones in these words, however, for in the context of the entire story of Jesus' life they link together the beginning and end of the story, implying that Jesus' baptism was in a sense the first step on the road to the cross, which was the climax and goal of his whole life. This is a theme that becomes more explicit when his death is later referred to as a 'baptism' in which God's will was more truly carried out than it had been in the days of John (Mark 10:38).

The gospels show Jesus' baptism by John as the start of an unfolding revelation of the exact nature of Jesus' relationship to God. According to Mark, on this occasion Jesus heard the words: 'You are my own dear Son. I am pleased with you' (Mark 1:11). This is a combination of statements found in two passages in the Hebrew Bible. First is an echo of Psalm 2:7: 'You are my son, today I have become your father.' In its original context, this statement referred to the kings of ancient Judah, who were regarded as reigning as the personal representatives of God, but by the time of Jesus it was widely understood as a prediction of the coming Messiah. In addition, however, there is a clear allusion to the poem of the suffering servant in Isaiah 42:1, where the servant is described as 'the one I have chosen, with whom I am pleased'. This concept of 'the servant of God' seems not to have been connected with the expectation of a Messiah before the time of Jesus.

The River Jordan. It was in this region that John the Baptist carried out his ministry.

The baptism stories, therefore, lay out two key themes that inform the rest of the story of Jesus. In them, Jesus is reassured of his own special relationship with God as the person who would inaugurate God's kingdom; and he was also reminded that to be this promised deliverer meant something very different from what most people expected. It was to include the acceptance of suffering and service as an essential part of his life, which would be a hard thing to work out in practical terms. But as he faced the challenge, the gospel writers remind their readers that Jesus was supported by God's personal presence, depicted at the baptism as the Holy Spirit symbolically coming to him in the form of a descending dove.

Jesus decides his priorities

The first three gospels tell how, immediately after he was baptized, Jesus was challenged to get his priorities right as God's promised deliverer, the Messiah. Mark mentions the temptations of Jesus only briefly, but Matthew and Luke both give more detailed accounts. They all place this period of self-appraisal at the very start of Jesus' public work, as a programmatic statement of his basic aims and objectives. But the issues raised in this story were continually cropping up in his ministry, for each of the temptations was an invitation to minister in a way that would bypass the suffering and humble service that Jesus ultimately knew to be God's way of doing things.

The first temptation was to bring about the messianic age by economic means, making stones into bread (Luke 4:1–4). There were certainly plenty of hungry people in the world who would have welcomed bread from any source. Indeed, Jesus himself was in the desert, and must have been hungry enough at the time. In addition, the ancient scriptures had often pictured the coming new age as a time of great material prosperity when the hungry would be fed and everyone's needs would be satisfied (Isaiah 25:6–8; 40:9–10; Ezekiel 39:17–20). Moreover, later stories show Jesus feeding the hungry on different occasions, so he was certainly not indifferent to the needs of starving people. There were therefore plenty of good reasons why Jesus should think it appropriate to be concerned with such matters. But he knew that the fame and popularity of an economic miracle-worker were not the same as suffering and service, and to establish a reputation on this basis alone would have been to deny the very essence of what God was calling him to do and be.

The Judean desert: traditional location for Jesus' temptations.

A word of God to the people of Israel at a crucial moment in their past history helped him to overcome the temptation: 'People cannot live by bread alone, but by every word that comes from the mouth of God' (Deuteronomy 8:3).

A similar temptation presented itself with the suggestion that he should throw himself down from one of the towers of the temple into the crowded courtyard below. Had he survived, that would certainly have been a dramatic demonstration to the whole nation that he was indeed endued with special powers. The miraculous and unusual had a special kind of appeal to the people whom Jesus knew best. Paul, who knew Judaism better than most, said it was characteristic of his people to 'demand signs' (1 Corinthians 1:22), though the same has been true of people in most cultures for most of history – including our own.

For Jesus, though, there was a more subtle underlying message here as well, for there was at least one ancient prophecy which seemed to suggest that the Messiah would suddenly appear in the temple in this kind of dramatic way (Malachi 3:1). This, together with a further promise that God would protect those who were ready to put their faith to the test (Psalm 91:9–16), presented a powerful argument for trying such a stunt. If Jesus was really God's Messiah, then should he not confirm his calling by trying out these promises to see if God really was on his side? Jesus was not afraid of the miraculous and the supernatural: there are many examples of that in the rest of his life. But he rejected the temptation to base his message purely on such sensationalism, again quoting the ancient scriptures to back up his judgment: 'You shall not put the Lord your God to the test' (Deuteronomy 6:16). The context of

Psalm 91 had made it clear that such promises of safety and security would be valid only for those who were prepared to live in obedient service to God's will – and for Jesus that was to mean service and suffering, not the arbitrary use of God's promises for his own ends.

The third temptation was to be a political Messiah. Luke places this one second, but Matthew puts it last, perhaps to emphasize its importance (Matthew 4:8–10). There is no doubt that this must have been the strongest of all temptations, for it was precisely what most people at the time were hoping that the Messiah would be. They also commonly believed that they would rule all the other nations in the new age that was coming, which no doubt explains the terms in which this temptation is presented to Jesus, to accept the authority of Satan in order to gain power over the world. The idea was made even more vivid by a vision of the splendour of the world's kingdoms. But Jesus realized again that this was far different from the kind of new society that he was to inaugurate. It was not that Jesus was unsympathetic to the deeply felt desire of his people for freedom: he had himself lived under the tyranny of Rome and had worked with his own hands to produce enough to pay Roman taxes. He was not unaware of the miserable condition of his people.

But he rejected political messiahship for two reasons. Firstly, he rejected the terms on which the devil offered it to him. According to the gospel narratives the devil offered to share sovereignty with Jesus. If Jesus accepted that the devil had authority over the universe as a whole, then he would be given limited political authority in exchange. That was something Jesus could not accept. His own commitment, and the commitment that he later demanded of his followers, was exclusively to God. To acknowledge the devil's power in any area of life would have been to deny God's ultimate authority. In addition, Jesus was offered the possibility of ruling by the 'authority' and 'glory' of an empire like that of the Romans. He knew that the nature of God's kingdom was to be quite different from the kind of authority to be found in an empire like that of the Romans. God's values and standards could never be imposed from outside, but would be nourished most effectively as people were set free to make their own choices not only about their relationship to God but also about how they could best create the new kind of social structures that would most closely reflect God's way of doing things.

It was not too difficult to reject this third temptation, and Jesus did so decisively. He would not try to impose a new authoritarianism on the world to replace the authoritarianism of Rome and the other empires that had preceded it. The 'kingdom of God' would not be the rule of tyranny and cruelty that some religious fanatics were hoping for, but something that would spring from the new, inner nature of those who were a part of it, as they discovered God in new ways and found themselves empowered to be the kind of people who would carry forward this new vision of a world transformed through the power of love and caring service.

The stories of Jesus' birth

The stories of how Jesus was born are certainly not the easiest parts of the gospels to understand. We have already seen that even the date of Jesus' birth presents a number of problems. But that difficulty is overshadowed by much larger questions about the whole nature of the stories, raised in a particularly pointed way by the repeated assertion in both Matthew and Luke that Mary was a virgin when Jesus was conceived (Matthew 1:18; Luke 1:26–27).

To be a virgin and pregnant is a contradiction in terms – so how are these stories to be understood? We can be sure that the gospel writers knew this well enough, which means that a key question surrounding the interpretation of their narratives relates to their genre or literary form. What kind of stories did the gospel writers think they were presenting here? The kind of literature a writer is creating has significant consequences for the way it is presented. In historical narrative, events are generally presented in a way that readers can imagine having happened, for while the details might be unique and distinctive, history writing depicts things that are similar to those we might expect to experience for ourselves. In poetry, however, things might be said that, as they are stated, are clearly untrue to historical fact. For example, when the English poet William Blake wrote his famous work *Jerusalem*, he described in graphic and realistic detail the miseries of the Industrial Revolution, and then imagined Jesus of Nazareth walking among it all. His readers got the point of his message, and appreciated it so much that his poem later became a classic definition of the self-understanding of the English – even though no one imagines for a moment that, in Blake's words, 'the Son of God' really did place his feet on 'England's green and pleasant land'. Similar examples could be found in the mythologies with which other nations around the world celebrate their distinctive identity.

So where would the gospel writers have placed their stories about the circumstances of Jesus' birth? Unfortunately, they never tell us, which is why their accounts have engendered so much debate and discussion. Inevitably, the debate focuses on the virginal conception of Jesus, if only because such a thing is so foreign to human experience. The very notion challenges our basic understandings about what is possible in this world, and highlights in a particularly stark way the role that our own presuppositions inevitably play in the interpretation of the New Testament texts. Those who begin by assuming that anything contrary to our own experience of life cannot exist will inevitably need to question, if not reject, the possibility that these birth stories are reporting anything that has a basis in historical fact. They will also have problems with other aspects of the gospels, notably the stories of Jesus' healings, and of course his resurrection from the dead. Following the arguments of scholars like the eighteenth-century philosopher David Hume, who claimed that there could be no such thing as the miraculous, generations of scholars have sought other ways to comprehend the apparently supernatural dimensions of the New Testament stories. In reaching such conclusions, they were inevitably working within the scientific paradigms of their day, which tended to be based on a mechanistic understanding of the cosmos, in which everything needed to be understood in a strict relationship of cause and effect. That was long before Einstein's articulation of the principle of relativity, not to mention the development of chaos theory, the uncertainty principle and other insights which have all made it plausible to imagine that unique events can, and do, happen randomly without any obvious rational explanation.

In today's more open atmosphere of New Age science and spirituality, the notion of the universe as a closed system has been abandoned, and people are more tolerant of the possibility of events that simply defy logical understanding. Indeed, whereas a century ago serious thinkers would have found it hard to believe anything beyond our own experience, there is an increasing trend in contemporary culture towards believing absolutely anything of an esoteric or unusual nature.

Neither of these approaches is particularly helpful, and a more appropriate way to tackle such questions is to keep an open mind about what is possible, while rigorously checking the alleged evidence in seeking to determine what might actually have happened in any given case. In this particular example, this means that the question of Jesus' conception should be addressed by asking: Does the evidence of the gospels make good sense? This involves examining the evidence on its own merits, scrutinizing its claims and possibilities, and being prepared to listen to its nuances, rather than prejudging its value on the basis of predetermined suppositions, whatever form they might take. Objectivity is notoriously difficult to pin down, but by weighing all the possibilities in this way, and recognizing our own starting points (while being prepared to go beyond them if necessary), we can at least hope to go some way towards a comprehensive appreciation of even the most perplexing issues.

As it happens, the stories of Jesus' virgin conception provide a particularly good example of the kind of concerns that are raised at many points in the New Testament gospels. Even a cursory examination of all the New Testament evidence as it relates to this story will demonstrate that it is not as simple a matter as we might imagine it to be. There are several aspects to be considered here:

● One of the most surprising things is that, apart from those references in the birth stories recorded by Matthew and Luke, there is no explicit statement in the whole of the rest of the New Testament regarding the circumstances of Jesus' conception and birth. There is no mention of it in the accounts of the teaching of the first disciples in the book of Acts. Paul never mentions it, nor is it found in the gospels of Mark and John (though neither of those gospels mentions Jesus' birth at all). It therefore seems certain that it was possible for the earliest Christians to have a complete understanding of the Christian faith without any mention of the virgin birth, and maybe without any knowledge of it. Later Christians have often argued that the virginal conception of Jesus was necessary in order for him to have been both divine and human, but the New Testament writers certainly believed all that without ever basing their arguments on the particular way that Jesus was either conceived or born.

This might appear to be a very strong argument for doubting that the stories in Matthew and Luke were intended to be understood factually. But in fact it is a double-edged argument. Since the idea of a virgin birth was not essential for a complete understanding of the precise nature of Jesus' person, why would Matthew and Luke want to invent it? Neither of them make any theological claims on the basis of their birth narratives: they simply present them as statements about the way Jesus was born.

● In certain passages of the gospels, Jesus is referred to as 'the son of Joseph' (Luke 4:22; John 1:45; 6:42), and the lists in both Matthew (1:2–16) and Luke (3:23–38) trace his ancestry through Joseph. It is therefore sometimes suggested that even within the gospels themselves there is no consistency, and Matthew and Luke have inserted these stories without noticing their incompatibility with other parts of their own narratives. For how could Joseph be Jesus' father if Mary was a virgin when Jesus was conceived? It is worth noting this, but it is not to be regarded as relevant to the issue of Jesus' conception. When Joseph married Mary he would be, in the eyes of both public opinion and of the Jewish law, the legal father of Jesus. Besides, there is no word for step-father in either Hebrew or Greek, and so the gospel writers were probably just recording the common description of Jesus as 'son of Joseph'. Luke certainly thought this was what he was doing (3:23).

● The notion of Jesus' conception by a virgin has sometimes been traced back to Greek or oriental stories about the gods having intercourse with human women and producing children. This notion is not taken so seriously today as it would have been two or three generations ago, not least because the stories of the gospels obviously move in a very different literary atmosphere from the stories told of the Greek gods. In addition, Luke's birth stories as a whole have a distinctive style when compared with the rest of his writings. Though some scholars believe this to be a deliberate device used by Luke in imitation of the style of the Septuagint, others have argued that Luke's Greek is of a sufficiently consistent character to suggest that he is here quoting or depending on an Aramaic source. If that is true, it would imply that he was incorporating traditional stories of Jesus' birth that came to him from the very earliest group of Christians in Palestine itself, who were the only Christians ever to speak Aramaic.

● Matthew's account raises a different set of questions. In support of his story he quotes from the Old Testament: 'All this took place to fulfil what the Lord had spoken by the prophet: "Behold, a virgin shall conceive and bear a son, and his name shall be called Emmanuel"' (1:22–23). A significant fact to note in this connection is that this passage from Isaiah 7:14 has a different meaning in the Septuagint (from which Matthew quotes) than it had in the original Hebrew text. Whereas the Greek version quite specifically uses the term for 'virgin', the Hebrew text calls the mother of Emmanuel a 'young woman'. In the past, it has been suggested that the whole idea of Jesus' conception by a virgin arose out of this apparent mistranslation of a passage from Isaiah in the Septuagint. Three things need to be noted in this connection:

In the first place this argument can apply only to Matthew since Luke does not quote this passage in his birth narratives. So, even supposing this argument is correct, it can only account for Matthew's account, and not Luke's.

Then it is undoubtedly true that Matthew's sole reason for accepting and using the Greek version instead of the Hebrew text was that it was appropriate to his purpose in a way that the Hebrew was not. But this is a common feature of Matthew's Gospel, and he often selects Old Testament texts and says they have been fulfilled in Jesus' life and ministry in a way that to modern readers seems irrelevant and trivial. This was almost certainly because he was writing mainly for Jewish readers: since the Hebrew scriptures were especially authoritative for them, it was particularly important for Matthew to use them to show how Jesus was indeed the Messiah promised in their pages. This is nothing like so important for the other gospel writers, whose readers were mainly Gentiles, with neither knowledge of nor interest in the Old Testament.

Thirdly, it is quite likely that it was not the actual author of Matthew's Gospel who selected this particular version of the text from Isaiah. There is considerable evidence to suggest that at a very early stage of its existence the church began to gather together Old Testament texts which seemed to them to predict or forecast some aspect of Jesus' life. These are the collections of texts often called *testimonia*, and there were probably several different collections in existence not long after Jesus' death. Again, these texts would have a special appeal to Christians from a Jewish background, but since the concept of a virgin birth was quite unacceptable in any form to orthodox Jews it seems unlikely that they would have gone searching for alleged scriptural references to such a thing unless they had other reasons for supposing it to be an appropriate way to describe Jesus' conception and birth.

In trying to reach a conclusion about the nature of the birth stories in Matthew and Luke, it is important to set them in the context of these gospels as a whole. It is hard to avoid the conclusion that Matthew and Luke treated them in the same way as the other traditions which were handed down to them, and which they incorporated in their own accounts. In terms of their genre, then, there is no reason to suppose they were in any way different from other narratives about Jesus, which probably places them in the context of Hellenistic popular biography. Indeed, some of their most distinctive literary and stylistic characteristics can be understood by placing these particular stories alongside traditional Jewish infancy narratives, such as those attached to Old Testament heroes like Moses, Samuel, and others. Luke's story in particular seems to be almost modelled after the stories of Samuel's conception and birth (1 Samuel 1 – 2), and Mary's song of praise, the Magnificat (Luke 1:46–55) not only parallels Hannah's song of thanksgiving following the birth of her son (1 Samuel 2:1–10), but is full of allusions to many other Old Testament passages. Matthew's story is also structured around many Old Testament texts, though in a completely different way, with subtle allusions and references to passages that Matthew saw as having been fulfilled in Jesus. In framing their accounts like this, Matthew and Luke were following in a long tradition of Jewish exposition of the ancient scriptures, known as Midrash – something that came in many different forms, but which was always loosely focused around an interpretative paraphrase of the scriptures. This is probably the most fruitful place to find literary models for what Matthew and Luke were doing, though not forgetting that the scope for wholly fictional elaboration of the stories must have been limited by the fact that they were both writing not more than a couple of generations after the events they purport to describe, at a time when (even in the 80s and 90s) there were still some who would remember how Jesus' birth had been reported from the very beginning.

John the Baptist and Qumran

In view of the similarities between the work of John the Baptist and some of the most distinctive activities of the Qumran community, it was inevitable that scholars would speculate about some possible connection between them. Two similarities between them are most obviously apparent.

In the Judean desert
Luke depicts John the Baptist living in the desert until he began his public work (1:80; 3:2). Since his baptizing took place in the River Jordan, it is natural to assume that the desert in question was the Judean desert surrounding the Dead Sea, into which the River Jordan flows, which in turn means he was probably living in the same desert as the Qumran people, and at about the same time. Since their monastery must have been one of the few places where it was possible to live in such an inhospitable region, it is suggested that John might well have known them, even that he might have been a member of their community.

It is certainly not difficult to believe that John would know of the existence of the monastery at Qumran, but some have gone much further by suggesting that he was a member of the group, and might even have been brought up by them from an early age. This argument is based on the statement in Luke 1:80 that as a child John 'grew and developed in body and spirit. He lived in the desert until the day when he appeared publicly to the people of Israel.' This statement can be put together with a piece of information given about the Essenes by Josephus, who comments that they often adopted other people's children in order to indoctrinate them with the ideas of their sect (*Jewish Wars* 2.8.2). This notion has many attractions, but in the end it creates more problems than it solves:

● The Greek words used in Luke 1:80 and 3:2 do not necessarily imply that John was actually brought up as a child in the

John the Baptist and
Qumran *continued*

desert. It is certainly the case that he was in the desert reflecting on the nature of his life's work immediately before he began baptizing, but the most natural way to read the story about his birth is that he was brought up at home by his parents.
● It is also doubtful whether his parents would have allowed a group like the people of Qumran to adopt their child. Not only were they longing to have this son, but John's father Zechariah was a priest. One of the distinctive beliefs of the Qumran sect was that the Jerusalem priests were corrupt, and it is difficult to think that John's parents would have given their child to a group who were so hostile to all that they themselves stood for. It might make sense to imagine that John was kidnapped by the sect in order to rescue him from his family, but there is absolutely no evidence for that, either in the New Testament or anywhere else.
● The Judean desert was a big place, and by no means everyone who lived there would need to have been associated with Qumran. The shores around the Dead Sea are full of caves that would make ideal lodgings for hermits, as they did for the Zealots who continued to resist Rome after the destruction of Jerusalem in AD70. Even Josephus records an episode in which he once joined a hermit called Bannus who was living a solitary life in the desert (*Life of Josephus* 2). The appeal of this kind of life has always been strong to people of a particular disposition, and there must have been plenty of individuals living like this in the desert surrounding the Dead Sea.

Baptism

If it is difficult to make any direct connection between John and the Essenes through their style of life, it is certainly no easier to do it through their religious rituals. John and the Qumran people both made use of water in their religious rites, but they had little in common beyond that. There were in fact several striking

Reconstructed pottery jar from Qumran. The scrolls and manuscripts were originally stored in pots like this to hide them from the Roman armies in the period following the fall of Jerusalem.

differences between John's concept of baptism and the ritual washings that were practised at Qumran:
● The recipients of baptism were different. John baptized people who wanted to change their way of life, while the community at Qumran accepted only those who could prove that they had already changed their way of life. An initiate often had to wait for a year or two before being allowed to take part in the ritual washings at Qumran, whereas John was prepared to baptize immediately anyone who was willing to declare their intention to change.
● The character of the two rituals was also different. A person baptized by John was baptized only once, and the rite could not be repeated. By contrast, the ritual washings at Qumran were repeated over and over again. Indeed, 'baptism' in the sense that word is usually understood is not really an appropriate word to describe what went on at Qumran. Essene 'baptisms' were a means of effecting a ritual purification in the lives of those who were members, rather than being a rite of admission to the sect.
● The overall significance of the rituals was different. John's baptisms were carried out as part of the preparations for the arrival of the expected Messiah. But the Qumran washings were not connected with the expectation of a Messiah, or indeed of anyone else. They were more a means of expressing in symbol the moral and spiritual purity which the community hoped to preserve among its members.

If John the Baptist ever had been a member of the Qumran community, he had certainly changed his outlook quite radically by the time he began his public work. But arguments in favour of such a connection are not very strong, and it makes better sense to think of both John and the people of Qumran as offering different forms of response to the growing political, moral, and spiritual crisis that was facing their nation at the start of the first century.

3 Who was Jesus?

After he had met John and been baptized, most of Jesus' life was spent as a religious teacher. It was quite normal for Jewish religious teachers to adopt an itinerant lifestyle, wandering about from place to place, often accompanied by their disciples. Jesus plainly fitted into this pattern. He had his disciples, and the term 'Rabbi' or 'Teacher' was regularly applied to him (John 1:38; 3:2; 9:2). Like other religious teachers he carried out much of his work in the synagogue, the place where Jews met for worship each sabbath day (Mark 1:21; Luke 4:16; 6:6). He also spoke with people wherever he met them (Mark 1:16–20). He called his first disciples from their fishing boats, and regularly taught out in the open countryside where large crowds could gather round him.

It was Jesus' teaching that really caught the imagination of the people. As they listened to him they sensed that this was no ordinary rabbi, not least because he was not just someone else's disciple passing on what he had heard from others. He was saying totally new things about people and their relationship with God, and doing so in an especially provocative way that almost forced his hearers into making a decision about him. All the gospels document the rapid emergence of somewhat polarized opinions about him. On the one hand many ordinary people declared that 'he taught them as one who had authority' (Matthew 7:29), while many religious experts dismissed him as an impostor and a cheat.

The teaching that caused such a sharp division among his hearers focused especially on two subjects. On the one hand the gospels depict Jesus making many bold claims about his own person and significance, and while he never actually claimed in so many words to be the Messiah of ancient prophecy, that is the clear implication of the way the narratives present him. Alongside the various claims about his own destiny and importance, there are also numerous statements about the exact nature and meaning of the 'kingdom of God' whose arrival Jesus announced. The kingdom is a sufficiently significant subject to require a whole chapter to itself. But first we will consider the claims that Jesus apparently made about himself, not least because his teaching about the kingdom is shot through with the assumption, either stated or implied, that he himself was to play a central role in its coming.

The Son of man

It was not long after the death of Jesus that his followers everywhere were openly claiming that he was the long-awaited Messiah of traditional Jewish expectation, and by the time groups of his followers were established in Gentile communities around the Roman world the Greek term 'Christ' – the equivalent of the Hebrew 'Messiah' – was widely used almost as a second name for Jesus. It is therefore surprising how infrequently that terminology is used in the gospels themselves. Mark's Gospel was probably the first one to be written, and the word for 'Messiah' or 'Christ' is used only seven times there. One of them is in the title of the gospel (1:1), and of the other six only three could be taken as a reference to Jesus being the Messiah or Christ (8:29; 9:41; 14:61–62). In only one of these (14:61–62) is Jesus shown making a direct personal claim to be the Messiah, and it is striking that even in that instance Mark shows Jesus immediately going on to identify the Messiah with someone he calls 'the Son of man'.

The meaning of 'Son of man'

The exact meaning of the term 'Son of man' has been one of the most hotly disputed subjects in recent study of the New Testament, and what can be said here is only the barest summary of what some of the experts are saying.

One point on which all scholars are agreed is that the most helpful question to ask is: What would come into the minds of those people who actually knew Jesus when they heard him use the term 'Son of man'? Since his first hearers were Jews, it is natural to look to the Jewish religious tradition for an answer. In the Hebrew Bible, the expression 'Son of man' is typically used in two ways. More often than not, it simply means human beings as distinct from God. In this context, it usually emphasizes the weakness and poverty of ordinary mortals in contrast to God's might and power (Numbers 23:19; Job 25:6; Psalm 8:4; 146:3; Isaiah 51:12). Prophets could on occasion be addressed by God as 'son of man', and this was a means of emphasizing the difference between them and the ultimate source of their message (Ezekiel 2:1; Daniel 8:17).

But the term is also used in a quite different way in Daniel 7:13–14. In this passage, far from indicating the weakness of men and women as opposed to the greatness of God, 'one like a son of man... came to the Ancient of Days and was presented before him. And to him was given dominion and glory and kingdom, that all peoples, nations and languages should serve him.' Moreover, 'his dominion is an everlasting dominion, which shall not pass away, and his kingdom one that shall not be destroyed'. The book of Daniel was an apocalyptic work, which no doubt explains the somewhat exaggerated nature of some of its imagery. But the same character also seems to feature in other apocalyptic writings that might have been current at the time of Jesus. In *The Similitudes of Enoch*, 'the Son of man' again appears as a supernatural figure sent from God as the future judge of humanity (1 Enoch 37–71), while the reference to an individual more cryptically described as 'the Man' in 2 Esdras 13 might also be intended to carry the same connotation. It is not easy to trace more direct connections between the gospels and these usages of the term. There is no certainty that either of these books was actually written by the time of Jesus, and they are only known through

So who was the Son of man? The actual term is used fourteen times in Mark's Gospel; in the longer account of Matthew it occurs no less than thirty-one times. This term is used more often than any other to describe Jesus and his work, and in addition it is only used in sayings actually ascribed to Jesus himself: there is only one clear example of others using it of Jesus (John 12:34, where his listeners are requesting clarification of his own use of it). Moreover, it is only found once outside the gospels (Acts 7:56). The unambiguous testimony of the entire New Testament therefore is that this is a term that Jesus used for himself, and one that was never widely used of him either by his contemporaries or later generations of his followers. So what did it mean?

One commonsense view would be that when Jesus spoke of himself as 'Son of man' he was simply wanting to emphasize that one part of his nature was ordinary and human, while another side of his character could be described in grander terms by epithets such as 'Son of God'. Even if something of that kind might on occasions be included, the term has to mean more than this, however, because the Son of man can be

---

relatively late texts that might in any case have been subject to later emendation and corruption. It is certainly not possible to use them with any confidence to show, for example, that the term 'Son of man' could have been a widely recognized title of any sort in the time of Jesus.

In addition to these uncertainties, it has also been claimed that in Aramaic the phrase 'son of man' would either convey nothing sensible at all, or would at best be some kind of generic way of referring to people in general (like the English term 'humankind'), rather than a specific way of describing a particular individual. This particular consideration is complicated by the fact that, though Jesus must undoubtedly have used an Aramaic term, the gospels were all written in Greek and, though they do occasionally preserve the actual Aramaic words used by Jesus, they do not do so in this case, though scholars generally assume that the Aramaic phrase would have been *barnasha*.

Three factors then need to be considered in trying to decide what the significance of this term 'Son of man' was meant to be when used by Jesus:
● The actual Aramaic words 'son of man' might well have had no specific meaning,

but were possibly just a circuitous way of saying something like 'human being'.
● In the Old Testament, the term 'son of man' had been used to describe human beings and their difference from God.
● In the book of Daniel and other Jewish apocalypses, the 'son of man' was a transcendent, heavenly figure who shared in God's own power.

It is not necessary to choose between these possible backgrounds to the way Jesus used the term: probably all of them are relevant. If the term 'Son of man' had no very clearly definable meaning in the Aramaic that Jesus spoke, then it could easily have been used for that very reason: with no ready-made significance, Jesus would have been free to make it mean exactly what he wanted it to mean. If the term 'Messiah' had featured in his teaching, it would have been far more difficult for him to explain precisely what he understood his role to be, since people had so many preconceived ideas of what the Messiah was supposed to do and say. Though it can hardly have clarified things, the ambiguous term 'Son of man' at least offered the potential for avoiding that particular problem.

described as 'coming in clouds with great power and glory' (Mark 13:26), or 'seated at the right hand of the power of God' (Luke 22:69). Statements like that can hardly have been intended to emphasize Jesus' human character over against his claims to have some special significance in the plans of God!

The Messiah

It is unnecessary to spend long examining Jesus' claims to be the Messiah, for it was not a title Jesus used for himself. In Mark, the first gospel to be written, there is only one instance where he might have been doing so (9:41), though there are four very significant occasions when other people called Jesus 'the Messiah', and he apparently accepted the title:

■ When Peter finally began to articulate his embryonic beliefs about who Jesus might be, and told him 'You are the Christ', Jesus replied that he was 'blessed' to have received such a special insight (Matthew 16:16–17).

The meaning of 'Son of man'
continued

At the same time, for those with the perception to see it, the background of the term in the Jewish scriptures and other religious writings did provide some clues to the things Jesus wanted to say about himself. For it seems that he did want to claim both that he was an ordinary human being, and that in some way not clearly defined he was specially sent from God – and these are both concepts that could be found in the traditional use of the 'Son of man'.

In the first three gospels (Matthew, Mark and Luke) Jesus is shown using the name 'Son of man' in four distinct ways:

● There are some instances where the term 'Son of man' appears as the equivalent of the personal pronoun 'I', simply as a means of describing Jesus' ordinary human existence. Certainly that is how the gospel writers understood some passages, for in places where different gospels have the same sayings, one gospel can use 'Son of man' where another writer uses the pronoun 'I'. Examples can be found by comparing Mark 10:45 and Luke 22:27; or Mark 8:27 and Matthew 16:13; or Matthew 19:28 and Luke 22:30.

● In other places, 'Son of man' is used to emphasize Jesus' claim to have special

authority to speak in the name of God – as, for example, when he claims to forgive sins (Mark 2:10) or assumes the right to set aside the traditional sabbath commandments (Mark 2:28).

● At other times, Jesus uses the title 'Son of man' with reference to a future coming on the clouds of heaven and to his exaltation at God's side where he then plays a key role in a future judgment. This is the same use as in Daniel 7, and features particularly in Matthew (for example, 10:23; 13:41; 19:28; 24:27, 37), though it is also found in Mark (8:38; 13:26; 14:62) and Luke (17:30; 18:8; 21:36; 22:69).

● Most often, however, the term is used with some reference to the suffering and death that was to be part of Jesus' experience. In nine out of the fourteen uses in Mark, 'Son of man' is used to refer to Jesus' coming death. This characteristic use might appear to be all but incompatible with the previous reference to triumph and glory. But, in fact, the precedent in Daniel 7 had identified the 'one like a son of man' as a representative of 'the saints of the Most High', who in the context were clearly undergoing great suffering and persecution. Some passages (for example, Mark 9:12;

■ Another occasion was during his trial before the Jewish authorities, when Jesus acknowledged to the high priest that he was the Messiah (Mark 14:61–62).

■ There is also the story of how Jesus healed someone who was thought to be possessed by demons. Not only did he allow this man to address him as 'Son of the Most High God'; he also told him, 'Go home to your friends, and tell them how much the Lord has done for you' (Mark 5:1–20).

■ On another occasion Jesus was going along a road near Jericho when a blind beggar called Bartimaeus shouted out and addressed him as 'Son of David'. Though others who were standing around evidently told the man to be silent, Jesus did not do so, and therefore by implication seems to have accepted this title for himself (Mark 10:46–52).

From these four instances it is clear that the gospels do not consistently show Jesus expressing the same attitude towards the claim that he was the Messiah, 'the Son of David', on every occasion. By the time he appeared before the high priest it was obvious that he was to be

10:45) use 'Son of man' language alongside allusions to suffering persons in the Old Testament (for example, Psalms 22; 69; 118:22; Isaiah 52:13 – 53:12), thereby combining different traditional images to show Jesus as the one foretold in the ancient promises, who would achieve glory and vindication through suffering and service.

The phrase 'Son of man' also occurs in John's Gospel, with some of the same connotations as in the others, though here there is additional emphasis on the Son of man as one who came from heaven to earth and will return thence (3:13; 8:28), as well as a connection between his suffering and the celebration of the Christian eucharist (6:53). It is also used to refer to Jesus being 'lifted up', a term that is used in John to refer to suffering (in the crucifixion, 3:14; 8:28; 12:34) as well as to glory and exaltation (12:23; 13:31).

The Last Judgment, woodcut by Albrecht Dürer (1471–1528).

condemned anyway, and so he apparently had no qualms about claiming to be the Messiah (though even on that occasion he at once went on to redefine the concept of 'the Messiah' in terms of the more nebulous 'Son of man'). But when Peter confessed that he was the Messiah, Jesus told him and the other disciples to keep it secret and not to tell anyone else about it. On the other two occasions he apparently accepted a messianic title from other people without making any further comment – and in the case of the man possessed with demons he told him to share his experience with his friends and relatives. Jesus' attitude to letting people believe he was the Messiah apparently varied according to the circumstances, and was partly dependent on the question of whether or not this claim should be publicized. How is such apparent inconsistency to be understood? Two possible explanations have dominated discussion of this issue:

JESUS NEVER CLAIMED TO BE THE MESSIAH

One way to solve the problem is to say that Jesus never in fact claimed to be the Messiah at all, and that Mark and the other gospel writers have written their stories of Jesus' life and teaching with an eye more to what they believed about Jesus than to what he might have claimed for himself. In the light of all they had learned from Jesus, and especially after his death and resurrection, it seemed only natural to conclude that he was indeed the Messiah who had fulfilled the prophecies contained in the Old Testament. When they came to write their gospels, they knew that Jesus himself had been ambivalent about claiming to be the Messiah, but by then it was more important for the church's mission that it should be made perfectly clear just exactly who Jesus really was. So Mark (the writer of the earliest gospel, and who was followed by Matthew and Luke) bridged the gap between his own beliefs and the reality of Jesus' more cautious self-perception by creating the literary motif of a 'messianic secret'. This phrase was first coined by W. Wrede to explain why it is that whenever Jesus is depicted talking to his disciples about his position as Messiah he always tells them to keep it a secret.

The difficulty with this notion is that although it fits in with some of the evidence, there are other pieces of information which do not fit. There are, for example, the incidents involving the demon-possessed man at Gerasa and Bartimaeus at Jericho. Then there is also the undeniable fact that, while different people no doubt understood it in different ways, Jesus was actually condemned to death because he claimed to be 'king of the Jews', that is, their Messiah. It is difficult to see how Mark could have left these stories in his narrative in this form if he had been so intent on making the idea of the 'messianic secret' convincing.

JESUS BELIEVED HE WAS, BUT NEVER CLAIMED TO BE THE MESSIAH

We seem to be left with the implication that Jesus thought he was the Messiah, but that he did not explicitly claim he was. This idea itself

raises some awkward questions, though three facts are particularly
relevant to any consideration of such a possibility:

■ It needs to be remembered that, while the preservation of the story
of Jesus' life and teaching for posterity was undoubtedly one reason
why the gospels were written, it was not the only one. Indeed, a more
important purpose was to provide a resource for Christians at the time
(mid to late first century) that would facilitate their own spiritual
nurture as well as their mission in calling others to join them. Like
today's readers, those who first received the gospels had a broader
perspective than those who were with Jesus during his lifetime. Their
starting point was their own experience of faith, their reception of the
Holy Spirit, and behind that their knowledge of the end of the story in
Jesus' death and resurrection. They had no difficulty in recognizing that
Jesus must be the Messiah, sent by God to inaugurate that new way of
being which he called 'the kingdom of God', for they knew their own
lives had been so changed by following him that they believed
themselves to be already living according to the new standards and
values which Jesus had announced. The more time that passed, the
more certain they were of this fact, which perhaps explains why the
word 'Christ' is used so many times in John's Gospel, whereas it is hardly
ever used in the other three, for it is generally thought that John was
writing later than the others, by which time Jesus' messiahship was so
self-evident that he could simply be called 'Christ' (Messiah) without the
need for further definition or qualification.

■ Another relevant consideration is that the gospels themselves make
it clear that Jesus and his contemporaries were at cross-purposes when
they spoke of the Messiah. To most people, the Messiah was to be a
political king, something that Jesus constantly sought to deny and
redefine; for him being the Messiah meant humble service and
obedience to God's will. Arguably therefore for Jesus to have spoken
openly of being the Messiah, far from being a clarification of his
message, would actually have concealed the real significance of what
he was trying to say. It would certainly have brought about an early
encounter with the Romans. Even the disciples, including Peter who
declared his belief that Jesus was the Messiah, seem not to have fully
understood all the ramifications of that until much later. Despite their
close relationship with Jesus, they displayed their ignorance of his
intentions on more than one occasion (Mark 8:14–21; 9:30–32;
10:35–45). There can be no doubt that this is an accurate picture of
their faith, or lack of it, for by the time the gospels were written these
same disciples were the church's heroes, and no one would have made
up stories that gratuitously portrayed them in a bad light.

■ It makes overall sense to conclude that Jesus' attitude did in fact
vary, and that his whole life and work was a mixture of revelation and
secrecy. This comes out in the way he liked to call himself 'the Son of
man', which had no ready-made meaning. To those who were not

prepared to think very deeply about it, it was a name that could only confuse, and conceal Jesus' claims rather than reveal them. At the same time, many incidents in Jesus' life – including the miracles, but also occasions such as his baptism (Mark 1:9–11), his temptations (Luke 4:1–13) and his entry into Jerusalem (Mark 11:1–11) – would lose their meaning if Jesus was not claiming to be the Messiah.

Many of the things he did and said were exactly the things that the Messiah was expected to do and say when he came.

The most satisfying overall conclusion seems to be that Jesus did not use the word 'Messiah' of himself because of the way it would have suggested to his hearers an earthly king and a new political state. Jesus certainly had no intention of being that kind of 'Messiah', as Matthew and Luke highlight by showing that possibility being so decisively rejected right at the start of his ministry in the temptations. So he cast his whole ministry in a mould that would conceal his claim to be Messiah from those who did not want to understand it in the same way as he did, but that would provide enough clues to his identity as Messiah for those who were prepared to think about it more deeply.

The Son of God

The belief of the Christian church from the very earliest times has always included the statement that Jesus was 'the Son of God'. This too was an expression that would be familiar to the people of Jesus' day. In Hellenistic culture, it was often used to refer to some heroic human figure, and this is probably the way it was used by the Roman centurion at the cross who said of Jesus, 'Truly this was the son of God' (Matthew 27:54). That is certainly how Luke understood it, for in his account he has the centurion say, 'Certainly this man was innocent' (Luke 23:47).

Like the terms 'Son of man' and 'Messiah', the term 'Son of God' had also been used in the Hebrew scriptures. It could be applied to the nation of Israel (Exodus 4:22; Jeremiah 31:9; Hosea 11:1), to leading individuals within the nation (for example, Deuteronomy 14:1; Isaiah 1:2; Jeremiah 3:22), to angels and other heavenly beings (Genesis 6:2–4; Job 1:6–12; Psalm 29:1), and to the king (2 Samuel 7:14; Psalm 2:7). Partly as a result of the way this title was applied to the kings, especially those descended from David, it came to be applied to the Messiah as well (2 Esdras 7:28, and in the Qumran texts at 1QSa 2:11–12; 4QFlor 1:10–13; 4QPsDan A). Within the Jewish context, this phraseology did not indicate a divine figure descending from heaven as the bearer of salvation, except insofar as angels were thought of as messengers from God. The status of 'son of God' was more often understood as a recognition by God of some particular achievement by the individual who received the title.

In the gospels, however, the notion of Jesus' divine sonship is quite explicitly used to indicate that Jesus enjoyed a special relationship with

God. Notwithstanding all the debates about the authenticity of various sections of Jesus' teaching, one thing on which virtually all scholars are agreed is that Jesus consistently used parent-and-child language to refer to his relationship with God. Even at the early age of twelve, Luke depicts him referring to the temple at Jerusalem as 'my Father's house' (2:49), and the story about the wicked tenants of the vineyard makes it clear that he himself was the heir whom the owner had sent to put things in order (Mark 12:1–11).

Jesus clearing the temple – an episode that clearly implied some claim to special authority (Mark 11:15–19; John 2:13–22). Illustration by a 19th-century artist.

The claims implied by such stories are also made explicitly on the lips of Jesus, most strikingly in a statement recorded by both Matthew and Luke: 'All things have been delivered to me by my Father; and no one knows the Son except the Father, and no one knows the Father except the Son...' (Matthew 11:27; Luke 10:22). It is clear that Jesus was understood to be claiming a unique relationship with God, with very little room for misunderstanding.

So what did it mean for Jesus to be spoken of in this way? This is, of course, one of the great questions that theologians have thought and talked about for centuries, and it is only possible here to give a very sketchy response to it.

■ In any discussion of the nature of God, it should never be forgotten that to describe Jesus as 'the Son of God' is to invoke a familiar analogy to describe something that is, by definition, indescribable. When Jesus took the human relationship of child to parent, and said, 'My relationship with God is a bit like that', this was never intended to be a literal statement about the being of God. Talk of God as 'father' is not to be understood as a claim that God is male, though generations of Christians have uncritically made that assumption. Nor indeed is even the parent–child image meant to be applied inflexibly. There is no suggestion that every aspect of human family relationships can be matched to relationships with God, not least because many people have unhappy relationships with their parents. The gospels themselves warn against this kind of literal understanding, for though children might on occasion be able to say in a normal family that 'Whoever hates me hates my Father also' (John 15:23), no human could ever say 'I and my Father are one' (John 10:30).

■ Like the other titles reviewed here, this one had also been used in the Old Testament. The term 'son of...' was a common idiom of the Hebrew language. For example, the Israelites could be called 'sons' or 'children' of Israel, though modern translations often disguise the wording (Deuteronomy 1:1; Judges 1:1). Wicked people are regularly referred to as 'sons of wickedness' or 'sons of Belial' (Deuteronomy 13:13), while the Hebrew word equivalent to 'human beings' is 'children of men' (1 Samuel 2:12).

Though we would not now use the exclusively male-oriented language of the Hebrew Bible, if we described ourselves as 'children of our parents' we would be saying that we share precisely the same characteristics and nature as our parents before us. So when the New Testament says that Jesus is 'the Son of God' it is stating that Jesus shared the actual characteristics and nature of God. He was claiming to be really and truly divine; to make a narrow distinction between the nature of 'God' and the nature of 'the Son of God', as has been done by, for example, the Jehovah's Witnesses, is to disregard the way that the analogy is being used here, as well as to ignore the natural idiom of the linguistic context in which the New Testament was compiled.

■ In John 1:1–18 and Revelation 19:13, this relationship between Jesus and God is expressed in another way. There Jesus is called the 'word' or *logos* of God. God's word is, of course, the way that God communicates. But when the New Testament calls Jesus 'the word' it says something more than that. For John says that 'the Word was God' (1:1) – that is, God's message to humankind was not just written in a book, it was displayed in the very person of God. He also says that 'the Word became a human being': God was personally embodied in 'the Word', in Jesus (1:14). Moreover, because of the way the concept of the 'logos' had been used in circles inspired by Greek philosophy to denote the fundamental principle of the universe, it seems likely that some cosmic claim about the significance of Jesus was also being made when such language was used.

Whether Jesus is described as 'the Son of God' or 'the Word of God', the implication is the same: the earliest Christians were all saying that through Jesus it is possible to gain a perfect image of what God is like. That is why it is worthwhile giving careful attention to uncovering the nuances of what Jesus was actually saying and doing, for the New Testament claims that in his life and teaching it is possible to see and hear what God is really like.

The servant

The way Jesus depicts God is challenging and disturbing to conventional views, most of which owe a great deal to images inherited from the Greek philosophers, in which 'God' was portrayed as a being of great splendour, majesty and, above all, power. This final title – 'the servant' – overturns that conception, and it seems to be the image that Jesus most readily applied to himself and his work. It is true that nowhere in the gospels do we find Jesus actually calling himself 'the servant of God', yet it is hard to get away from the impression that Jesus' perception of himself was so very different from current expectations precisely because he understood his mission in terms of the suffering servant of the book of Isaiah (Isaiah 52:13 – 53:12).

The gospels make many references to Jesus' conviction that it was to be his lot to suffer, not least in the distinctive use of the term 'Son of man' in that connection. From the time he was baptized, and perhaps before that, Jesus saw that the course of his life was to be one of suffering. The voice at his baptism, echoing words from one of the passages in Isaiah about the suffering servant (Mark 1:11; Isaiah 42:1), made it clear to him that his life's work was to consist of humble self-denial, and this conviction was vigorously reiterated in his responses to the temptations. According to Mark, Jesus warned his disciples at a very early stage in his ministry that the day was near when he, the bridegroom, would be taken away from his friends (2:20). Immediately after Peter declared his belief that Jesus was the Messiah, Jesus again repeated that 'the Son of man must suffer many things' (Mark 8:31), something reinforced by the further statement that 'the Son of man also came... to give his life as a ransom for many' (Mark 10:45).

Most of the titles applied to Jesus are difficult to understand in detail, largely because they all had varied meanings and implications within their original Jewish context. But all have one very clear implication. There is no doubt that by applying them to Jesus, the gospel writers were wanting to claim that he had a unique relationship with God, and a unique authority. This authority was expressed in his claim to forgive the sins of other people, which the religious teachers of the day correctly recognized as a claim to exercise power that belongs only to God (Mark 2:1–12). But Jesus also demanded from his followers a loyalty and devotion that no ordinary human being could ever have the right to claim. He told would-be followers: 'Whoever does not bear their own cross and come after me, cannot be my disciple' (Luke 14:27). This claim to a unique relationship with God is expressed in John's Gospel in terms of a complete identification between Jesus and God: 'I and the Father are one... whoever has seen me has seen the Father' (10:30; 14:9), and a virtually identical claim is found also in the gospels of Matthew (11:27) and Luke (10:22).

There continues to be a good deal of discussion about the extent to which these elevated claims go back to Jesus himself. There is no question that the full significance of who Jesus was, and how that significance might best be articulated, only emerged as his followers reflected on their own experience of him, in the light of the total picture of his life and ministry that was only possible after his death and resurrection. In the past, scholars have often attempted to distinguish some core tradition consisting of the actual words Jesus might have used from the further reflections on him that emerged as the gospel writers and others worked through the wider consequences of his life and teaching. Such an enterprise is not altogether misguided, and in a later chapter we will need to give some further consideration to this matter. But when all is said and done, the gospels are the only portrayals we have of the life and teaching of Jesus, and it is ultimately a pointless exercise to try to find within them a simple religious teacher who had no awareness of his own possible significance in the divine scheme of things. Who would wish to crucify such a harmless person? It is a waste of time trying to separate the supposedly human figure, the 'Jesus of history', from the Christ and risen Lord who was soon regarded as equal with God in early Christian theology. Jesus is depicted making grand claims for himself in the very earliest records about him, and it is not possible to find in the New Testament a Jesus who did not make supernatural claims for himself, without in the process so discrediting the overall reliability of the texts that it would scarcely be worth reading them for any purpose at all. If Jesus' followers later made new claims about his importance, these were all firmly grounded in his own teaching about himself and his understanding of his place in the plans of God.

4 Understanding Jesus' Death

Why did Jesus die? Of all the questions that might be asked about Jesus, perhaps no other can be answered in so many different ways. To a certain extent, the answer given will depend on the way the question is approached. We can see this quite clearly, even in books written as long ago as the first century AD.

Josephus, for example, says very little about Jesus, but he does say that 'he was the Messiah; and when Pilate heard him accused by the most highly respected men amongst us, he condemned him to be crucified' (*Jewish Antiquities* 18.3.3). He was obviously convinced that Jesus died as a result of political intrigue and collaboration between Pilate, the Roman prefect of Judea, and the religious establishment in Jerusalem. This is also clearly stated in the stories of Jesus' death in the gospels. But if we look at some other parts of the New Testament and ask the same question, 'Why did Jesus die?', we find a somewhat different emphasis in some of the answers. According to the book of Acts, Peter said on the day of Pentecost that though Jesus was 'crucified and killed by the hands of lawless men', he was also 'delivered up according to the definite plan and foreknowledge of God' (Acts 2:23). Paul expressed a similar understanding when he explained his most deeply held convictions to the Christians in the Greek city of Corinth by saying that 'Christ died for our sins in accordance with the scriptures' (1 Corinthians 15:3).

The New Testament itself then answers the question, 'Why did Jesus die?' in two different ways. One answer is based on the historical facts that led to Jesus' crucifixion, while the other is based on the claims Jesus made about himself, and on the beliefs of the early church about his significance in God's plan for humanity. Jesus' death can be understood as a simple matter of history, but at the same time the very nature of his death, executed in the company of criminals, raises its own questions when placed alongside the claims made for him. For how could someone who was God's own representative have come to meet his end in such a way? Surely if Jesus was in some way divine, it would be a contradiction in terms for him to die at all, let alone on a cross.

Opposition and conflict

All the gospels are unanimous in showing that, from the very start, Jesus' actions and words created divisions among those who met him. John explains this in a theological way by saying that when Jesus came, God's light had come into the world, and this fact itself demanded that people make some kind of decision about him, to be with Jesus on God's side, or against him (John 3:16–21). Elsewhere in the gospel traditions, Jesus himself makes the same strident demands: 'No one can serve two masters; for a slave will either hate the one and love the other, or be devoted to the one and despise the other. You cannot serve God and wealth' (Matthew 6:24). There are many stories about Jesus which show how he enjoyed great popularity as a teacher and healer, but was also opposed by the religious and civil authorities of the day.

The Jewish and Roman calendars.

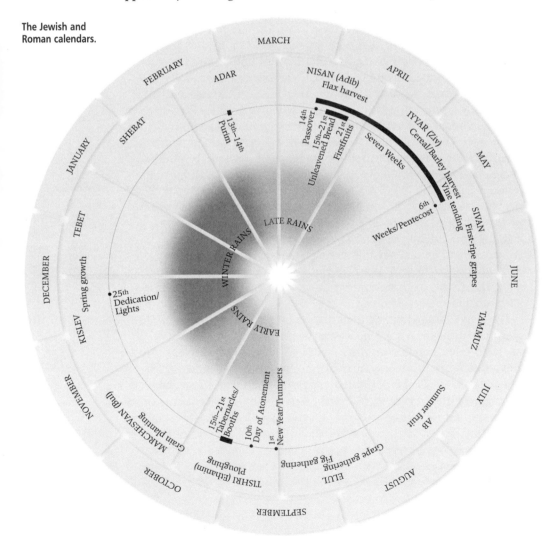

The Roman rulers of Palestine were always suspicious of anyone who became too popular, just as people today are often suspicious of politicians who appear to be too successful. According to Josephus, Herod Antipas got rid of John the Baptist because he was afraid of political revolts, and it must have been difficult for the authorities not to think of Jesus in the same way. After all, he attracted very large numbers of people, and on at least one occasion a crowd of 5,000 wanted him to become their king and lead a revolt against the Romans (John 6:15).

The gospels show Jesus resisting such political power time and again. But they also show that he had no such qualms about getting on the wrong side of the religious authorities. Right from the very start, the crowds declared that his teaching was different from that of their own religious experts, and Jesus evidently accepted this. What is more, he had no hesitation in condemning the Pharisees and Sadducees outright, describing them as 'blind leaders of the blind', who had perverted and denied the word of God (Matthew 23:16–24). Though they appeared to be very religious and holy, he said that deep down inside they were as rotten and worthless as a grave full of old bones (Matthew 23:27).

What is more, Jesus' criticism of these people appears to have been a deliberately planned policy. Though Jesus is portrayed spending a short time in more remote areas teaching his disciples, all the gospels suggest that there was a specific moment at which he decided the time had come to confront the authorities in Jerusalem itself. Different explanations have been given of this step:

■ The oldest view is that Jesus realized the time for his death had come, and so he set himself to go to Jerusalem to fulfil God's will. This is clearly implied in what Jesus said to his disciples according to Luke's account: 'Behold, we are going up to Jerusalem, and everything that is written of the Son of man by the prophets will be accomplished' (Luke 18:31).

■ It was at one time fashionable to think that Jesus made a deliberate gamble that did not pay off. According to this view, which was popularized by Albert Schweitzer (1875–1965), Jesus expected God to intervene in history in a dramatic and more or less immediate way, and his visit to Jerusalem was an attempt to force God's hand. When God did not act, Jesus found himself unexpectedly dying on the cross.

■ Others have suggested that Jesus went to Jerusalem simply because he had been to most other parts of Palestine and he wanted to continue his teaching in the religious capital of the nation. The fact that he became involved with the political authorities there was just an unexpected and unfortunate miscarriage of justice.

We will return to the views of Schweitzer in a later chapter. The other two explanations of Jesus' visit to Jerusalem probably both have some truth in them. No doubt Jesus did want to share his teaching with the people of Judea as well as those in other parts of Palestine – though according to John's Gospel, he might well have done so on more than one occasion before his final visit there. But if we allow for the possibility that Jesus was in any way at all conscious of some kind of special relationship with God, it is inevitable that he cannot have been totally ignorant of the growing opposition he was arousing among the religious leaders of his people. A visit to Jerusalem was bound to bring him into direct confrontation with them.

If there had previously been any doubt as to who Jesus was claiming to be, his entry into the city of Jerusalem made it plain, for the manner of his arrival brought to a focus several underlying messianic themes in his lifestyle and teaching. In effect, Jesus entered Jerusalem in a way that amounted to an open declaration that he was the Messiah. He came on an ass, in accordance with a prophecy in Zechariah 9:9, and the crowd acclaimed him as their king entering his capital city. Immediately after this he went to the temple, the place from where the Messiah was popularly expected to begin the task of expelling Gentiles from Jerusalem (Mark 11:10; John 12:12–19). Jesus hardly fulfilled that particular expectation, for instead of putting the Gentiles out he made a symbolic attempt to restore to them the only court of the temple in which they were allowed to worship, and in the process banished the Jewish bankers who had turned it into a place of business (Mark 11:15–17).

Jesus obviously knew what he was doing, and he can hardly have been surprised to discover that the religious leaders soon put a price on his head. He does not even appear to have been surprised when one of his own followers, Judas Iscariot, picked up the money offered by the high priests (Mark 14:43–52), and he found himself betrayed, arrested, and put on trial for his life.

Jesus on trial

The gospels appear to report two different trials of Jesus. One was before the religious authorities, when of course he was charged with a religious offence. The other was before the Roman prefect Pontius Pilate, where he was naturally charged with a political offence. It is widely believed that the religious authorities had no power to carry out a death sentence themselves, which was why they needed the support of the Romans, though there are different opinions about this, and also about the precise relationship of the different trials to one another. It certainly makes good sense to suppose that Jesus' enemies would make much of the charge of blasphemy before a religious court, and then change to a charge of political revolt as the one most likely to secure some action by the civil authorities.

John's Gospel shows the trial beginning in the house of Annas, father-in-law of Caiaphas, the high priest (18:12–14). Annas had no official position, but as a former high priest and a leading Sadducee he was obviously someone of great influence. Perhaps this trial was an informal investigation held to formulate proper charges. The supreme religious court of seventy members, the Sanhedrin, could not officially meet until daylight, but as soon as it was morning the members were summoned to Caiaphas' house (Mark 14:53 – 15:1; John 18:15–27).

After Jesus had refused to answer questions about his teaching, and the witnesses had failed to agree in their evidence, Caiaphas asked Jesus a direct question under oath: 'Are you the Christ, the Son of the Blessed?' To this Jesus not only replied 'I am', but added, 'and you will see the Son of man sitting at the right hand of Power, and coming with the clouds of heaven' (Mark 14:61–62). This confession apparently convinced the Sanhedrin that Jesus was guilty, though not all of them can have been opposed to what Jesus stood for. Many of them would certainly have welcomed a messianic leader who would strike a blow against the Romans, while Joseph of Arimathea, who subsequently arranged for Jesus' body to be interred in his own tomb, is specifically identified as a member of this Council (Mark 15:42–47). But for others, Jesus had already shown that he was ready to challenge too many of their inherited religious traditions, including not only ritual matters but even central institutions such as the sabbath. By the time Jesus was brought to trial, the ultimate outcome was a foregone conclusion no matter what was said.

The next step was to bring Jesus before Pilate. Here the charge of blasphemy was dropped, for a charge based on religious scruples would never have appealed to a Roman official. It appears that Jesus' accusers first tried to get Pilate to confirm their own sentence without stating a charge at all, but when Pilate then insisted on a charge, three accusations were made:

■ Jesus was perverting the Jewish nation. The religious leaders, of course, thought of this in terms of perverting the nation from their own brand of Judaism. But they no doubt wanted Pilate to think of it in terms of undermining the nation's loyalty to the emperor.

■ Jesus had forbidden the payment of taxes. This was the usual charge made against Zealots.

■ Jesus had claimed the title 'king' – something that only the Roman senate could give.

After Pilate had interviewed Jesus, he realized that, though Jesus might have upset the sensitivities of some religious leaders, he was scarcely guilty of any crime under Roman law. If he had claimed to be a king, he was obviously not the kind who could rob Caesar of his power (Luke 23:13–16). But Pilate also realized that to upset the Jerusalem establishment was a very serious thing. He was caught in a cleverly contrived trap. On the one hand he could acquit Jesus and risk a riot – something which would be looked upon very seriously by his own superiors. On the other hand, he could condemn Jesus, and have to live with a guilty conscience for the rest of his life. It was the fear of riots that eventually forced his hand, as the crowd told him: 'If you let this man go you are no friend of Caesar's' (John 19:12). The last thing Pilate could face would have been bad reports of his conduct going to Rome.

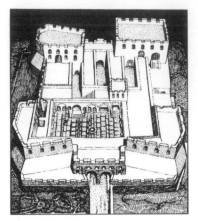

A model of the Fortress Antonia, the place where Jesus appeared before Pilate. It abuts and overlooks the Temple wall.

So Jesus was crucified, and as often happened in such cases, a placard was nailed to the cross to show his offence. In this instance the inscription read: 'Jesus of Nazareth, the King of the Jews'. No doubt that satisfied Jesus' religious opponents, who could understand kingship in terms of a claim to be the Messiah, while the Romans for their part would be satisfied that Jesus was worthy of death as a revolutionary opposed to their own power. None of this would be exceptional or noteworthy. Jesus died in the same way as many other messianic claimants and Zealots. The only difference noted by the gospels is that Jesus' death took a little less time, only six hours, something that facilitated the religious systems that had opposed him so effectively, for the sabbath day was fast approaching and in order to be ritually pure in time it was necessary for his accusers to see his body disposed of as fast as they could.

In purely historical terms there is little more to be said about the crucifixion of Jesus. But for the earliest Christians, the true significance of this event went well beyond the apparently straightforward happenings of that day.

Understanding the death of Jesus

The first generation of Christians, like all Christians ever since, were convinced that Jesus' death on the cross had a meaning that affected not only their own experience, but also had consequences for the whole of the cosmos. Their starting point was the knowledge that their own lives had become meaningful in a new and fresh way because of what Jesus did on the cross. They expressed it in many different ways: some said their sins had been forgiven, others that they had found peace of mind, or that they had been reconciled to God. But all of them were convinced that what had happened to them as a result of Jesus' death was real – as real as the fact that Jesus had died. Indeed, in one way they knew it better. For whereas their knowledge about Jesus' death came from hearing the reports of other people, each one of them had personally experienced this dynamic change in his or her own life.

But how could such a thing be explained in terms that other people would understand, and that would bear some relationship to the reality of what had actually taken place on the cross? The one thing that was clear from the outset was that this was not something that could easily be expressed in logical, analytical terminology. If its meaning could be encapsulated in words at all, they would need to be symbolic and pictorial words, language that would use the familiar and ordinary to describe a reality that was quite extraordinary. The New Testament uses many different figures of speech to describe what Jesus was actually doing when he died on the cross. He was sacrificed (1 Corinthians 5:7); he took the punishment for human sinfulness (1 Corinthians 15:3); he paid the ransom for the human race (1 Timothy 2:6); he justified believers (Galatians 2:16). Each of these statements, and many others, brings out some of the things the early Christians understood about Jesus' death. But in using such statements, two things should never be forgotten:

■ They are all pictures, or analogies. Just as it was important not to press too literally the metaphors and images that were used in talking about Jesus' personal claims, so it is important to bear in mind the essentially illustrative nature of the language used in the New Testament to describe his death. Failure to do that can lead to absurdity, if the details of a particular analogy are used in ways that the early Christians never contemplated.

■ In pictorial terms, the theology of the New Testament can more usefully be compared to a landscape than to a portrait. Just as a landscape is made up of any number of different items, so the New Testament's explanation of Jesus' death consists of many different images. It is possible to consider certain parts of the landscape separately and in greater detail than others, and in some circumstances it might be both necessary and legitimate to do so. But it is always important that the details are not isolated from their overall context as components in the bigger picture. Every one of the metaphors used in the New Testament to describe Jesus' death played an indispensable part in the early church's articulation of its meaning. But no one of them by itself was believed to contain the whole truth. For that it is necessary to consider them all, and place them within the context of the entire experience and theological understanding of the early church.

Five particular images seem to be central to what the New Testament says about Jesus' death on the cross.

Jesus' death as a battle

The gospels show the whole of Jesus' life and ministry as a battle against those forces that might oppose God's will. Sometimes (as in the temptations) these forces can be imagined in dualistic fashion as embodied in the figure of the devil, who represents the opposite force to God. At other times particular individuals can be identified with the forces opposing God, even Jesus' own closest friends (Peter, in Mark 8:33). Jesus' miracles were often described in terms of releasing people from the power of evil, while Jesus appears to have regarded his whole life as an effort to win a victory over the kind of negative influences represented by unjust suffering, sin and death. Paul regarded the cross as God's final and decisive struggle against the powers of evil, believing that in spite of Jesus' apparent defeat, his resurrection actually signalled a complete victory over sin and death (Colossians 2:8–15). The same view is found in the gospels (John 12:31), and the image of the cross as a battle with the forces of evil is one that has regularly appeared in the Christian tradition ever since, not least in its Easter hymns.

To understand Jesus' death only in these terms leaves unanswered a very obvious question. If Jesus triumphed over sin in his cross and resurrection, why is there still so much evil in the world today? One set of images that has been used to explain this was taken from the events of the end of World War II. The decisive moment that settled the outcome of the war came on D-Day, but the final day of victory (V-Day) came some time later. The day of Jesus' crucifixion can be thought of as the D-Day of God's warfare against sin – but the V-Day is still to come, in the future when evil is finally conquered. This is by no means the full answer to the problem of evil, but it is a partial answer to it when Jesus' death is understood in terms of a battle. Of course, viewing Jesus as a military leader is a very one-sided image, not least because he went out of his way to redefine messiahship in completely different terms. Ultimately, Jesus did not see the way to the world's salvation through power and control, but through love and humility. This particular metaphor has often been given more importance than it deserves, as it has had a natural appeal to those generations of Christians who were also empire builders and conquerors. Arguably it has led to some of the worst atrocities ever committed by Christians, from the medieval Crusades against the Muslim world to the colonialism of more recent times.

Jesus' death as an example

Many well-known Christian hymns describe Jesus' death as an example. This stems from the belief that on the cross Jesus revealed God's love for the world. Jesus himself never spoke of the cross as a revelation of God's love, but both Paul and John did (Romans 5:8; 1 John 4:10). They also suggested that as Christians consider Jesus' sufferings, they ought to be challenged to share such sufferings themselves. The writer of 1 Peter used this as a powerful motivation to encourage Christians who were being persecuted for their beliefs: 'to this you have been called, because Christ also suffered for you, leaving you an example, that you should follow in his steps' (1 Peter 2:21).

This is a concept that is easier to understand, for there are many examples of people who have selflessly given their lives for a good cause. Others admire and respect them, and might even be moved to take up the cause themselves. This particular image has been especially inspirational to those who suffer, either for their faith or from the effects of economic and political oppression. Many Christians of the developing world find it speaks to them in a way that the military image of power never can, reminding them that the Jesus who found the most acceptance among the poor and the marginalized also died among the same people, at the hands of the rich and powerful. Again, this metaphor does not exhaust all that the New Testament wants to say about Jesus' death, for he was not simply an innocent man dying at the hands of his oppressors – and if it was in some sense God who was there on the cross, there is a correspondingly limited sense in which people can take up and share that experience.

Jesus' death as a sacrifice

One of the most natural images for people with a Jewish background was the picture of sacrifice. Animals were sacrificed as part of the regular ritual in the temple, as they were more generally in the ancient world. Sacrificial language is used to explain and comment on the death of Jesus throughout the New Testament. When John the Baptist saw Jesus he exclaimed: 'Behold the lamb of God...' (John 1:29). Paul wrote of 'Christ our Passover lamb' (1 Corinthians 5:7), while 1 Peter described Jesus as 'like a lamb without blemish or spot' (1:19), and the book of Hebrews went to extraordinary lengths to compare Jesus' death with the sacrificial rituals of Judaism and to present it as in some way the fulfilment of them all.

This image raises particular questions for today's readers of the New Testament, largely because it is so alien to their experience of either religion or life. Reflecting on two questions might help to explain it:

WHAT WAS 'THE LAMB' TO WHICH JESUS WAS COMPARED?

The New Testament writers generally connect Jesus' death as a sacrifice with the consciousness that their sins had been forgiven, so the most obvious connection of the imagery is likely to be with the various sacrificial procedures of the Old Testament that were designed to procure forgiveness from sin. These sin offerings are documented in Leviticus 5:17–19. There was also, however, the well-known event of the first Passover, at which the people of Israel were delivered from slavery in Egypt, and in which the sacrifice of a lamb played a large part (Exodus 12). In the context of the last supper, Jesus himself seems to have made a deliberate connection between his own death and the annual death of the Passover lambs, reminding his disciples that what he was to do on the cross was to be as great a turning-point in their own lives as the Passover had been in the experience of their forebears (Mark 14:22–25). There is no need to choose between these two somewhat different sacrificial images. When the New Testament describes Jesus' death in terms of a lamb being sacrificed, either or both of them could be in view at different times. The lamb of the sin offering and the lamb of the Passover were each regarded as relevant images for the death of Jesus.

WHAT DID THE ACT OF SACRIFICE MEAN?

Relatively few people today have seen an animal sacrifice, even in those cultures where it is still practised. The majority probably tends to think of it as a rather barbarous ritual from an uncivilized past. But in sacrificial contexts, its real importance is generally located not so much in the physical brutality as in what the action as a whole can be understood to represent or symbolize.

Worship in ancient Israel was based on a strong concept of difference between ordinary people and God. This difference could be understood in both spatial and moral terms. Spatially, 'uncleanness' disqualified people from dealing with the 'holiness' that was equated with religious shrines, so that only certain specially equipped people (usually priests) could touch, or even come into close contact with, the presence of God. Morally, 'sin' – whether deliberate or accidental wrongdoing – similarly disqualified a person from acceptance by God. Both forms of alienation could be dealt with by the offering of appropriate sacrifices. Not all sacrificial procedures were exactly the same, but a typical sacrifice might begin with the worshipper approaching the altar (representing God's presence) with the sacrifice, hand placed on the animal's head. This identified the worshipper with the animal, indicating that what happened physically and outwardly to the animal was understood to be happening to the worshipper inwardly and spiritually.

After that, the animal was killed, usually according to carefully laid-down regulations. In the context of sin offerings, this action itself reflected the seriousness of sin, reminding the sinners that they too deserved to die. The priest would then take the blood of the sacrifice (which now symbolically represented the sinner's life given up to God) to the altar. This act of reconciliation, or 'atonement', indicated that the sin had been dealt with, and God and the sinner had been reconciled to each other. At this point the animal's body could be placed on the altar in the temple, signifying that the forgiven worshippers were offering their whole being to God. Finally, much of the meat would be eaten in a meal shared with others, thereby showing that sacrifice not only reconciled people to God, but also to one another.

This, in general terms, is what the New Testament writers had in mind when they described Jesus' death as a 'sacrifice'. The book of Hebrews in particular goes further, however, and argues that there was some intrinsic connection between the inherited Jewish understanding of sacrifice and the death of Jesus, with Jesus' death being the actual fulfilment of the Old Testament rites. His death was the reality, the sacrifices the picture. Other writers applied the imagery in a looser way, comparing the beneficial effects of the cross (reconciliation to God) with the outcome of animal sacrifices, but without necessarily drawing detailed parallels between them.

Jesus' death as a ransom

One of the few statements about the cross and its meaning in the gospels is found in Mark 10:45, where Jesus himself is reported as saying that his intention was to be 'a ransom'. This figure of speech is much easier to understand, for the idea of kidnappers demanding the payment of a ransom in exchange for the safe release of their victims is well understood. The background to this picture in the New Testament was not, of course, the hijacking of planes or the kidnapping of diplomats, though the general concept was the same. The 'ransom' in this case would be the price paid to set a slave free. In the Roman world, this ransom was often paid by a third party, who would accompany the slave in an act of worship at the shrine of their local god. There the ransom was paid to the slave's owner in a religious ceremony. The legal explanation of what took place was that the slave had been bought by the gods, and so could no longer be owned by another human.

When the emphasis is on the resulting freedom, this is a very appropriate way of describing Jesus' death. The New Testament frequently affirms that a person set free by Jesus is redeemed in order to belong to God. So Peter could speak of Christians as 'ransomed from... futile ways' (1 Peter 1:18), and Paul reminded his readers: 'you are not your own; you were bought with a price, so glorify God in your body' (1 Corinthians 6:19–20). He even linked this image to sacrificial language by exhorting those who were set free 'to present your bodies as a living sacrifice, holy and acceptable to God' (Romans 12:1).

Crucifixion, engraving (1511) by Albrecht Dürer.

However, like all the other images used to illustrate the meaning of Jesus' death, this one is open to misunderstanding, even reduction to absurdity, when it is understood in a literalistic way, for example by asking to whom Jesus paid the ransom. But accepted in the way that the New Testament presents it, it is perhaps the most comprehensive of all the pictures used in the New Testament to describe what Jesus did on the cross: he set free those who were oppressed.

Jesus in the place of others

To say that Jesus died as a sacrifice, or to pay a ransom, is basically to say that he died in the place of other people. On the cross he did something that the human race could not do for itself. This representative nature of Jesus' death is expressed in 1 Peter 2:24, by the statement that Jesus 'bore our sins in his body... that we might die to sin and live to righteousness'. The statement in Mark 10:45 that Jesus came 'to give his life as a ransom for many' also conveys the same idea. It is a powerful image, but once again it is important to clarify what is meant by saying that Jesus suffered in the place of others, if this picture is not to end in absurdity.

It is not difficult to imagine a legal scene like a law court, in which the judge is God the Father, a harsh, authoritarian figure demanding that justice not only be done, but be seen to be done. Instead of the human race as a whole being on trial for the way the values and standards of God's kingdom have been disregarded, Jesus finds himself there. Even though he is guilty of nothing, and certainly not worthy of the death penalty, he is to become the unfortunate victim of God's harsh and unbending demand for justice. From time to time, the imagery has indeed been understood in this way, but if that is the picture then it is very difficult to see how it can be an adequate account of early Christian convictions about the death of Jesus. It implies, for example, that God is actually less just than a human judge, for how many of us would consider justice to be satisfied if an innocent person were punished in place of a guilty one? It suggests that God has a perverted sense of justice and moral responsibility – for how many of us would agree that it is always good for a repenting sinner to escape all the consequences of their wrongdoing? In addition, how can this view be reconciled with the fact that God does seem sometimes to allow people to suffer the consequences of their misdeeds – indeed, that they can on occasion suffer for no apparent reason at all?

What is really wrong with this caricature is its image of God. In the Hellenistic world, it was not difficult to find people who thought of God as a terrible and awesome figure, remote from the everyday concerns of ordinary people, and generally more interested in punishment than in forgiveness. The idea that God is like that has been perpetuated by more recent generations of Christians. The use of exclusively male language to refer to God has often created the impression that God behaves like the worst sort of macho warrior, and this secularization of the biblical image has in turn made it all too easy for the values of Jesus' teaching to be corrupted and replaced by an essentially unchristian world-view. If there is anything distinctive about the teaching of Jesus, it has to be in the way he redefined God, replacing the harsh confrontational image of judgment and condemnation with the language of family love and acceptance. It might place question-marks against some deeply held inherited beliefs, even among Christians, but there is no escaping the fact that the image of God offered by Jesus is not about domination, power, control, and exploitation, but has at its centre vulnerability, weakness, and affirmation of the human condition. This is the point at which incarnation and cross come together, for when the New Testament speaks of Jesus suffering on behalf of others, those others have already been redefined as members of Jesus' own family. His suffering for the wrongdoing of others was not something imposed by a stern judge to fulfil the demands of some abstract notion of justice, it was suffering in the way that a person might suffer for the wrongdoing of a member of their own family. In that context, the reality of evil is certainly not diminished: indeed its long-term consequences need to be taken

This unusual rock formation in Jerusalem has often been compared to 'the place of a skull' (Golgotha, John 19:17). Though it is unlikely that this was the site of the crucifixion, it perhaps gives an idea of the kind of terrain in the area.

much more seriously than might be the case in an exclusively legal context. But when it is addressed in the context of a family, it is always going to be with a view to unconditional acceptance of those who have done wrong, and a progression towards forgiveness and new life in the context of a supportive group.

Each of these ways of talking about Jesus' death has its inadequacies, for they are all only pictures, and even to the writers of the New Testament the cross remained a great mystery. But two aspects of God's relationship with the human race run through all these images:

■ One of the most pressing problems in life is the problem of evil. If God is really loving and forgiving, why is there so much evil in the world? If God is a forgiving God, then surely the universe should be arranged differently so that the stupidity of people will not cause so much suffering? There is no easy answer to such questions. In biblical terms they are part of the frustration of a world that has been so spoiled by sin that Paul could speak of 'the whole creation... groaning in travail' as it waits to be released from its suffering (Romans 8:18–25). The cross shows that, even if the suffering so endemic in human experience is not removed, God shares it with us. If Jesus was divine, as the earliest Christians believed, then in the cross God personally was somehow sharing the final and extreme consequence of human sinfulness.

■ The cross highlights the cost of forgiveness and, therefore, of discipleship. Forgiveness is often costly, especially when it involves relationships within a family. It is often more demanding to forgive a close friend than someone who is otherwise a stranger. Grace does not come cheap. Forgiveness is not an arbitrary thing, and its price is seen in the crucifixion.

Of course, ultimately all these statements are figures of speech, pictures, metaphors, analogies. Some of them seem remote, even irrelevant to the images we would most naturally adopt today. It is natural to ask ourselves why the first Christians found it necessary to reflect on Jesus' death in such complicated terms. Could they not have contented themselves with regarding him as a good man dying a bad death? Was it really necessary to turn a sad story into a theological analysis of the meaning of life? The answer to questions like that is to be found in what they believed to have happened three days after the cross. For they were convinced that Jesus came to life again. If they had not believed that, then the cross would have meant nothing to them. But because of their belief in the resurrection and their experience of the risen Christ at work in their own lives the earliest Christians were totally convinced that Jesus really was who he had claimed to be, and that meant his life must have consequences that went well beyond the few years of his own ministry on the fringes of the Roman empire. But were they right? That is perhaps the most crucial question of all, and one to which we must turn our attention in the next chapter.

Palestinian politics and justice under the Romans

When Herod the Great died in 4BC, both the country and his own family were left in chaos. The semi-independence of Judea was at an end, for though Herod left a will, it was subject to the approval of Augustus, who naturally divided the country up as he pleased. Behind the scenes, Rome had always been the real ruler of Palestine since Pompey's invasion in 63BC, but with Herod's death it asserted its sovereignty more directly. Herod's son Antipas disputed the terms of the will, and along with his brothers Archelaus and Philip was called to Rome to see the emperor. While this consultation was taking place, the whole country was torn apart by revolts, all of which were crushed by Roman troops. Augustus decided that, in the circumstances, it made sense to divide Palestine between the three of them. Archelaus got Samaria, Judea and Idumea, while the rest was split between Philip and Antipas.

This was a compromise arrangement. Had Augustus given the kingdom intact to any of the three, it could easily have provoked all-out war. Yet to introduce direct Roman government would have incensed the Zealots and other nationalists. In the event, Archelaus proved to be so incompetent that even the long-standing rivalry between Jews and Samaritans was laid aside so they could present a united complaint about him to Augustus. As a result, in AD6 Archelaus was recalled to Rome, and sent off into exile in Gaul. Augustus could have appointed one of the other two brothers in his place, but he knew that whoever was not appointed would almost certainly plot the downfall of his brother. In any case, he really trusted neither of them, and so Quirinius, the imperial legate of Syria, was sent to take a census of the taxable property of Judea, as the first stage in its organization as a province within the Roman empire.

Judea became one of the imperial provinces of the empire, and was governed by a procurator of equestrian rank, a man called Coponius. We know very little about how these procurators were allowed to govern their provinces. Indeed, there is some doubt as to whether they should be called 'procurators' at all. Tacitus certainly applied this title to Pontius Pilate, but there is some evidence that 'prefect' was the correct title at the time. In *The Jewish War*, Josephus states that Coponius 'was entrusted by Augustus with full powers and authority to inflict the death penalty' (2.8.1) – which seems to imply that the governor had the equivalent of the *imperium* exercised by the proconsuls in other parts of the empire. There is no ancient definition of what this *imperium* amounted to, but it apparently conferred supreme power in administration, defence, the dispensation of justice, and the maintenance of public order.

The maintenance of order would certainly be a major concern in a province like Judea, with such a volatile population in a strategic position on the edge of the empire. As a judge, the procurator had absolute authority in matters of life and death within his province, and even Roman citizens could appeal to Caesar only in special circumstances. Very few cases would actually come to the procurator. Most minor affairs would be settled in the various local courts, or in the Jerusalem Sanhedrin where traditional religious law was properly understood and dispensed. Only crimes involving capital punishment would be referred to the procurator, since he was the only one with power to prescribe the death sentence. The Sanhedrin was concerned with matters relating to traditional Jewish law, in civil and criminal cases, as well as matters relating to religion. In Judea, it could make arrests, try, and condemn criminals to any punishment apart from death, without any recourse to the procurator – though on occasion this prescription was ignored, and mobs took matters into their own hands by lynching criminals after only a Jewish trial.

The procurator's court was formally run, with charges being presented against the accused by any private parties with an interest in the case. There was no inquisition by the court, and cases were heard by the holder of the *imperium* on his tribunal, generally assisted by his *consilium* of friends and officials, who constituted a panel of reference rather than a jury. All these features can be found in the trial of Jesus.

There was a whole network of local courts to deal with other matters. Judea was divided into eleven toparchies, or districts, and each village within a toparchy had its own council, presided over by a village clerk. They would deal with civil cases and certain less important criminal ones. Since this was the official structure of the land, it is surprising to find no reference to it in the gospels. Neither village clerks nor the commandants who controlled each toparchy feature in them, though the tax collectors who do would be part of the same system of administration. At a time when their independence was suspended, it was natural for Jews to want to use their own ancient procedures, even if it had only a theoretical significance. As a result, the authority of the village congregation, the rulers of the synagogue, was widely respected, even though it had no officially recognized jurisdiction.

Little is known of the way that Philip and Antipas organized things, except that their territories did not fall under the jurisdiction of the procurators. They had the right to mint their own coins, and Philip went as far as to put his own head on them – a thoroughly un-Jewish action. But the area he ruled was well away from the mainstream of Jewish life. Antipas was the local ruler of Galilee, which is why Pilate sent Jesus to him for trial (Luke 23:6–12). Maybe he hoped that there would be some loophole in the law of Galilee that would enable Antipas to take responsibility for a citizen of his own territory. But Jesus had already described this same Antipas as a 'fox' (Luke 13:32), and he was certainly far too crafty to allow himself to be duped in this way. As a result of his clever manoeuvring on this and other issues, he managed to stay in power until AD39, long after Pilate had been removed from office.

Did the Jews condemn Jesus?

Who was it who actually conspired to bring about the death of Jesus? What was the precise relationship between the various Jewish leaders who feature in the gospel stories, and the Roman Pontius Pilate who eventually condemned Jesus? That might sound like the sort of historical conundrum that would interest only a minority of people. But in reality it has been one of the hottest subjects in discussion of Jesus' death for many generations. Down through the centuries, the belief that the Jews were responsible for the crucifixion of Jesus has led to the most horrific persecution of that nation. Even the Nazi holocaust can, in some respects, be traced back to religious roots. Reading many of the books written by leading Bible scholars in pre-war Germany, it is not difficult to see how their apparently abstruse historical and theological theories actually gave encouragement to those who for political and racial reasons already hated the Jewish people. The claim that Judaism was a dead and lifeless religion, designed only to keep people in bondage rather than setting them free to live life to the full, can only have fuelled the fires of anti-Semitism that swept across Europe in the 1930s. And the certainty that Jewish leaders were in the vanguard of the opposition to Jesus merely fanned the flames to even greater intensity.

In point of fact, the New Testament nowhere suggests that either Jews or Romans should carry all the blame, in any absolute sense. At one time, it can seem as if 'the residents of Jerusalem and their leaders' were instrumental in Jesus' death (Acts 13:27), while at another it is attributed to Judas or Pilate, or the devil, or other cosmic forces (1 Corinthians 2:7–8). The fact is that, for the earliest Christians, the precise identity of the players in this drama was not all that important, though it is absolutely clear that the death of Jesus was not an ethnic issue,

**Did the Jews
condemn Jesus?**
continued

and the arguments about his teaching did not have a racial basis, but were concerned with the kind of religious attitudes that have surfaced frequently in both religious and non-religious societies. The kind of bigotry, narrow-mindedness, and intolerance that Jesus opposed is by no means an exclusively Jewish trait, and never has been. The kind of goodness represented by Jesus makes us all uncomfortable, and many others would have reacted to him in exactly the same way as some of his contemporaries did.

In addition to these general matters, however, there has been a good deal of discussion about historical issues related to the trials of Jesus. In what sense can it be claimed that there ever was a Jewish trial at all, in the sense of a formal legal procedure conducted by a group such as the Sanhedrin? The problem is that there is no contemporary evidence about Jewish customs and practice at this time. Our only knowledge of the subject comes from the Jewish law book, the *Mishnah*, which dates in its present form from about AD200. This contains traditions that are much earlier than the time when it was written down, but it is impossible to know how far these regulations were in force at the time of Jesus.

Judged according to these later standards, a trial such as that which the gospels describe would certainly have been very irregular. The leading members of the Sanhedrin were the prosecution as well as the judges, and they had already been involved in the plot to have Jesus arrested. The trial appears to have begun with no definite charges, and no evidence was called for the defence even though the key prosecution witnesses contradicted each other. Moreover, two very important rules of later Jewish law were ignored completely. These laid down that twenty-four hours had to elapse between a death sentence being passed and carried out; and that a trial should not be held on the day before the Jewish holy day, the sabbath.

Because of these irregularities many Jewish writers — often motivated by their understandable concern to undermine the kind of anti-Semitic propaganda that regarded them as Christ-killers — have insisted that there is no historical truth in the gospel narratives at this point. In terms of the social dynamic of Palestinian society at this time, however, it is hard to find convincing reasons for regarding this trial as fiction. Though the Jews had very little real influence over their political society, their leaders were always keen to apply their own law whenever they could. This was not only a kind of psychological prop to nationalist aspirations: it was also a useful means of gaining the support of the mass of the Jewish people for their policies. A death sentence passed on Jesus under traditional Jewish law by a religious court would certainly have influenced ordinary people against him, and it might even have been expected to exert a certain moral pressure on the Roman judge who was to have the final word.

It is, however, not very likely that this Jewish trial was as illegal as it can be made to appear if compared with the rules of the *Mishnah*. Quite apart from the doubt over whether these procedural rules were in operation at the time, it is especially significant that, of all the charges made by the first Christians against the religious establishment, they never accused them of breaking the law in order to have Jesus executed. In addition, there is no reason to imagine that the members of the Sanhedrin were anything other than people of high moral ideals, some of whom had considerable sympathy with Jesus' message. Perhaps a majority of them met with their minds already made up, and to that extent were unable to give Jesus a fair hearing. But even these people were genuinely convinced that their view of things was right, and that Jesus was nothing but a messianic pretender and a troublemaker.

Pontius Pilate

Pontius Pilate was the fifth Roman prefect of Judea, coming to power in AD26 in succession to Valerius Gratus. He ruled for ten years. Little is known of him before he received this appointment, though legend has it that he was born at Fortingall, a remote spot in the highlands of Scotland which his father allegedly reached while serving with the legions on the northern edge of the empire. As procurator of Judea, Pilate's normal residence would be in Caesarea, and his name has been found there on an inscription, which confirms that he was known by the title of 'prefect'. Pilate was accompanied by his wife (Matthew 27:19), which was a relatively recent innovation introduced by the Roman senate only five years before his appointment.

Pilate's only claim to any sort of fame relates to his involvement in the death of Jesus. The Roman author Tacitus (*Annals* 15.44) only mentions him in this connection, though the Jewish writers Josephus and Philo both supply more information about his general disposition. They had a low opinion of him, and describe him as a brutal and callous man who cared little either for Jewish religious scruples or for common human values. One passage in the gospels refers to an occasion when he ordered the death of certain Galileans, and 'mingled their own blood with their sacrifices' (Luke 13:1). This was probably the occasion described by Josephus, when Pilate had raided the temple treasury for cash to build an aqueduct, only to face demonstrations from crowds of outraged believers when he made a visit to Jerusalem, presumably for one of the festivals. In retaliation, Pilate sent his troops into the crowd in disguise, and a considerable number were killed while he himself sat and watched the gory spectacle (Josephus, *The Jewish War* 2.10.4). It could well be that this was why Antipas never had much time for Pilate (Luke 23:12), and it might have been

This inscription from Caesarea mentions the rule of Pilate as 'prefect' of Judea.

sensitivity to this situation that led Pilate to send Jesus to him for trial.

Eventually, Pilate's cruelty and careless disregard for religious sensitivities led to him being summoned to Rome to give an account of himself. What happened then is unknown. Some traditions claim that he and his wife later became Christians, and the Coptic church honours them both as saints and martyrs. But Eusebius reports more plausibly that he eventually committed suicide during the reign of Gaius (AD37–41). His rule was the second longest of all the procurators, which suggests he might well have been an efficient administrator. But the gospels present him as a weak man, and an opportunist who condemned Jesus to death, not out of any respect for the Jews, but only as a means of preserving his own reputation with the authorities back in Rome who had already had to endure enough problems during his rule in Judea.

The last supper

All four gospels give an account of what is generally called the 'last supper' of Jesus. They relate how Jesus acted as host to his disciples in a room loaned by a friend in Jerusalem, on the evening before he was crucified (Matthew 26:20–30; Mark 14:12–26; Luke 22:7–39; John 13:1–30). The first written account of this meal is contained not in the gospels but in the writings of Paul in 1 Corinthians 11:23–26, though his account of it agrees in its main details with the stories told in the synoptic gospels (Matthew, Mark and Luke). John's Gospel gives a fuller account of some aspects of the meal, and includes the story – not mentioned by the others – of how Jesus washed his disciples' feet. At the same time, John omits to mention the central feature of the other accounts, the institution of the Lord's supper, or eucharist.

At this last meal with his disciples, Jesus followed the normal Jewish custom and gave thanks to God for the meal. He then proceeded to break the bread that was on the table, and handed it to his disciples, saying, 'This is my body which is for you. Do this in remembrance of me' (1 Corinthians 11:24; compare Matthew 26:26; Mark 14:22; Luke 22:19). After this, he handed them a cup of wine, telling them: 'This cup is the new covenant in my blood. Do this, as often as you drink it, in remembrance of me' (1 Corinthians 11:25; compare Matthew 26:27–28; Mark 14:24; Luke 22:20).

Times and dates

The disciples, like all other Jews, would be quite familiar with the idea of a 'covenant'. The last supper took place at about the same time as the Jewish people were preparing to celebrate one of the most important religious festivals, the Passover. The Passover festival celebrated and recalled the inauguration of God's 'covenant' with their ancestors. They remembered how, long ago, God had delivered Israel from slavery in Egypt, and in gratitude for this deliverance Israel had given their obedience and devotion to God (Exodus 12 – 23). Ever since that time they had regarded themselves as 'the people of the covenant', and the 'covenant' was simply the fact that God had done something for the people as an act of undeserved love, and they had responded in love and obedience.

When Jesus compared his own death to the inauguration of a 'new covenant', he was suggesting to his disciples that through him God was performing a new act of deliverance, and that a similar promise of loyalty and devotion would be required of those who would share in its benefits. God's new kingdom makes demands of those who would be part of it, and Paul says that Christians ought to repeat this meal regularly as a constant reminder of the fact that their new life of freedom was won by Jesus on the cross. Because of that, they owe him their unfailing loyalty and obedience.

Paul, of course, was not intending to give an historical account of the last supper; he mentions it more or less incidentally. His main intention was to emphasize that the eucharist (as it came to be called) was a continuing reminder to Christians of how much they owe to God. But in the case of the gospel accounts of the last supper, the matter is much more complex. They were clearly intending to give some sort of historical account of the last supper, and it is therefore legitimate to ask historical questions of them. The most important question is whether the last supper was a celebration of the Jewish Passover, or whether Jesus was observing some other kind of feast with his disciples.

This in turn resolves itself into two further questions:

Do Jesus' actions at the last supper suggest that he was observing the Passover with his disciples?
Here we shall restrict our discussion to what Jesus and his disciples actually did.

The traditional 'Passover plate' contains foods symbolizing different aspects of the story of Israel's deliverance from slavery as told in the book of Exodus.

The question of what the gospel writers *thought* he was doing is dealt with separately. Within the gospel stories it is possible to find arguments both for and against the idea that Jesus was observing the Jewish Passover. The following facts seem to favour the view that it was a Passover meal:

● The meal of the last supper was eaten in Jerusalem, and not at Bethany where Jesus was staying at the time (Mark 14:13; Luke 22:10). With growing opposition from the religious leaders, this can hardly have been a sensible time for Jesus to make unnecessary excursions into Jerusalem. But if Jesus was intending to share in the Passover festival, he would have to do so, since the Passover feast could only be eaten within the walls of the city. This could explain the emphasis on the disciples' concern to find a room in a suitably located house (Matthew 26:17–19; Mark 14:12–16; Luke 22:7–13).

● According to John 13:23–25, Jesus and the disciples took their meal reclining on couches. This was not the invariable Jewish custom, but it was obligatory at the celebration of the Passover. The instructions for celebrating Passover (the Passover *Haggadah*) say: 'On all other nights we eat and drink either sitting or reclining, but on this night we all recline.' The *Mishnah* adds that even the poorest person in Israel must not eat the Passover feast except while reclining (*Pesahim* 10:1).

● The meal took place at night. This was also a distinctive custom associated with the Passover. The usual custom was to eat the main meal of the day in the late afternoon. But the Passover was always at night, the time when the events it commemorated had taken place.

● The dipping of pieces of food into a sauce (Mark 14:20; John 13:26) was definitely a custom used only at the Passover. The Passover *Haggadah* does not refer to bread being served in this way, but it does say: 'all other nights we do not dip... even once, but on this night twice'.
● The disciples sang a hymn before they left the room (Mark 14:26). The singing of the so-called 'Hallel' psalms (Psalms 113–118) was a special feature that marked the end of the Passover meal.

Despite all these similarities between the last supper and the Passover, however, there are other aspects of the gospel narratives that suggest the last supper was not a regular Passover feast:
● It is most unlikely that Jesus would have been judged, condemned and crucified in the middle of such an important feast as the Passover. In particular, it is unlikely that a Roman governor would have been so foolish as to take the great risk involved in the public execution of a popular figure at a time when Jerusalem was crowded with pilgrims. To have done so would have defiled the day of the great festival, and could easily have sparked off a riot among the Jews.
● It would have been against Passover laws for Jesus to be tried in the middle of a festival. All forms of work were prohibited on the Passover, and that included the work of the Sanhedrin. In addition, religious leaders would have risked ritual defilement by having anything to do with Pilate at this time (John 18:28). The whole business of the trials, and especially the element of urgency about them, is better explained if the Passover was to begin shortly than if it was already taking place.
● A number of circumstantial details do not easily fit with the assumption that Jesus was observing the Passover. There is, for example, no mention of a lamb or of unleavened bread, though these were the single most important items of the

traditional Passover meal. It would also have been surprising to find Simon of Cyrene coming in from the fields at the height of such an important festival when work was strictly forbidden (Mark 15:21). It is also surely significant that the earliest Christians observed the Lord's supper once a week and not annually, as they might have been expected to do had it originally been a Passover celebration. Taken by themselves small details like this would not prove very much. But when considered along with the other evidence they can be given some weight in the argument.

Faced with these apparently conflicting pieces of evidence, equally reputable scholars have made different judgments. Many have argued strongly in favour of the view that Jesus was actually keeping the Jewish Passover, though a significant minority have argued just as strongly that he was not. They suggest that what he was celebrating was a *Kiddush*, a type of feast with which committed believers would often prepare for the beginning of the weekly sabbath. It has also been understood as a feast of a more general nature known as a *Haburah*. Such feasts are well known in later Judaism, and still form a part of modern Jewish observances, but there is little evidence to show that they existed at the time of Jesus, and even less to show what might have taken place at them.

Did the gospel writers think Jesus was observing the Passover with his disciples?
Judged purely on the basis of the evidence reviewed so far, there is much to be said on each side of the argument. But the really awkward questions begin here, for the three synoptic gospels say quite definitely that the last supper was a Passover meal – though, as we have seen, not every detail of their description of the meal fits in with this assumption (Matthew 26:18; Mark 14:12; Luke 22:15). On the other hand, John says equally clearly that

	Synoptics	John
Thursday		
evening	Passover	Last supper
	Last supper	Arrest
	Arrest	
Friday		
morning	Trials and	Trials and
afternoon	crucifixion	crucifixion
evening	Beginning of sabbath	Beginning of sabbath and Passover
Saturday	Sabbath	Sabbath and Passover
Sunday	Resurrection	Resurrection

The relationship of Passover to the last supper, according to the synoptics and John.

the last supper was not the Passover, but took place on the day before the Jewish festival – yet here also, not every part of his description of the occasion matches that statement (John 13:1; 18:28).

At one time, it would have been easy to solve this problem by assuming that John, in particular, made a mistake in his story. There are some scholars who still take that approach today, but it is now generally recognized that this is too simplistic a solution, and even if John's Gospel was one of the latest books of the New Testament to be written, it is by no means a later fabrication of the life and teachings of Jesus. On the contrary, though the fourth gospel does present its own problems of interpretation, the accounts preserved by John are clearly based on authentic, reliable and early traditions.

In order to grasp the precise nature of the difficulty, some knowledge is necessary of the way times were calculated in Jewish culture. Ancient Jewish chronology is notoriously difficult to understand, and in this case the matter is made more complex by the fact that the Jewish day begins at sunset, whereas the Roman day (like our own) began at midnight. So, for example, while for the sake of convenience the weekly Jewish sabbath might be referred to as Saturday, it actually lasts from sunset on Friday evening until sunset the next day (Saturday).

The gospels all agree that Jesus was crucified on a Friday afternoon, and his empty tomb was discovered on the Sunday morning. In between this was the sabbath, which was always a holy day – but on the particular week in question, the Passover was also being celebrated, and this was an even more holy day. Putting this calendrical information alongside what is reported in the gospels, it seems that the synoptic writers thought that the Friday was the Passover festival, whereas John believed that the Passover fell on the sabbath in that particular year. On this understanding, there is no problem with the statements made about Jesus: the difficulty rather is concerned with the chronology of these various religious festivals.

This is one of those matters on which caution is probably the wisest course. There is certainly no one answer that could claim to be the generally accepted consensus of opinion. But one possible way of understanding the awkward distinction between John and the synoptics is to suppose that the two traditions were using different calendars, and that what was in one calendar the day of the Passover would be another day in a different calendar.

Nowadays we would find it impossible to believe that there could be different opinions about something as basic as the date, but in the context of first-century Judaism this is not such a far-fetched explanation as it sounds. There was constant speculation on such matters, and the existence of the various sectarian

The last supper
continued

movements within first-century Judaism was to a large extent related to differing opinions on this very subject.

One of the most striking differences between the Essenes of Qumran and the Pharisees in Jerusalem, for example, was on the question of their religious calendar. The mainstream Jewish calendar was based on calculations related to the movements of the moon, whereas the Qumran people appear to have used another calendar as well, based on calculations about the movements of the sun. This same calendar features in the *Book of Jubilees*, and according to it the Passover meal was *always* on the day that began on the Tuesday evening. If Jesus used this same calendar, then he could have celebrated a real Passover with his disciples on the *Tuesday* evening, but still have been crucified as the official Passover was about to begin on the Friday evening. This ingenious solution, however, still leaves unanswered a number of vital questions:

● There is no reason to suppose that Jesus did in fact use anything other than the official calendar. He appears to have moved in the mainstream of Judaism rather than in any sectarian movements, and is often depicted taking part in the regular worship of the synagogue. If, as John suggests, he had often attended the great temple-based festivals in Jerusalem, it would be more natural to suppose that he kept the same calendar as the Jerusalem authorities, otherwise he would not have attended the festivals at the same times as everyone else (John 7:1–39). In addition, we know that Jesus was often in conflict with the Pharisees about the observance of religious festivals, and was regularly accused of doing things that were not allowed on the sabbath – yet he never claimed that he did them because he used a different calendar. He explained his actions by reference to the fact that he believed himself to be 'lord even of the sabbath' (Mark 2:28).

● The Passover lambs had to be ritually slaughtered in the temple, and this would obviously be done according to the official calendar. It is therefore difficult to see how the disciples could have had a lamb available in Jerusalem on the Tuesday evening – yet without the lamb, there could be no Passover meal.

● This alternative calendar would mean that Jesus was held in custody for two days before his crucifixion, which is difficult to reconcile with the unanimous testimony of all four gospels that the trials took place in a hurry so that Jesus could be condemned and executed before the beginning of the sabbath.

Despite its attractions, this theory rests on rather shaky foundations, though it is not impossible to imagine that new evidence to strengthen it could be discovered in the Qumran texts or elsewhere. In the present state of our knowledge, however, it is difficult to accept it as a sufficient explanation of the difference between the synoptic gospels and John. A more likely possibility is that these dating indications were inserted into the narratives by their respective authors consulting the calendar at the time and place when they were actually writing. John's Gospel was written from the perspective of the Jews of Palestine: could it be that on the year in question, they celebrated the Passover on the sabbath, while Mark (followed by Matthew and Luke) followed the customs of the Jews of the Dispersion, and on their reckoning the Passover was held on the Friday in the year that Jesus died? Many more speculative theories have been advanced from time to time, all with something to commend them. Perhaps this is one of those topics on which the wisest approach is to admit that we simply do not know for certain – though the explanation is highly likely to be related to calendrical confusion. In any case, this one detail should not be allowed to hide the fact that all four gospels are in complete agreement on everything else. Nor can it be concluded that because there is no obvious answer at present, that means there is no answer. But if an explanation lies in the arcane speculations of religious experts on their calendar, it will be a long and tedious process before a widely acceptable answer is found.

The New Covenant

In any case, we will never find a full explanation of the last supper if we only ask what sort of Jewish feast Jesus was keeping. What Jesus was doing at the last supper fits in with many Jewish customs. That is hardly surprising, since he and his disciples were Jewish believers. But the precise nature of what he was doing cannot be fitted exactly into any specific occasion in the Jewish religious calendar. It seems unlikely, for the reasons already given, that the disciples were celebrating the Jewish Passover, though at the same time it seems obvious that their last supper with Jesus followed fairly closely the formal setting of the Passover meal.

Perhaps a little more room should be allowed for the creative originality of Jesus himself. In the nature of the case the Passover lamb was absent, but in this supper that was of little importance. By this point, Jesus had a pretty clear idea of what would happen next, and was bold enough to claim that God was already providing a lamb, and he was here offering himself in symbol to his disciples as 'the Lamb of God who takes away the sin of the world' (John 1:29). It was no coincidence that he was crucified at the very same time as the symbols of God's past deliverance were being sacrificed in the temple courts.

At the same time, there was a strong sense that Jesus' death was not to be just a reinterpretation of an ancient ritual, but would usher in something quite different and revolutionary, that would both sum up and supersede the events associated with the first Passover. This was the inauguration of the kingdom of God and in the last supper, surrounded by those who would become the nucleus of this new way of being, Jesus was symbolically offering himself for their freedom in the bread and the wine. This is why these things became within the church the external symbols of that freedom from sin and its consequences which Jesus had announced, and which his death and resurrection were about to bring to birth.

5 The Resurrection

All the New Testament writers agree that Jesus was raised to life on the third day after his death. The reactions of other people to this claim will of course depend to a large extent on their basic presuppositions about the supernatural. Those who begin from the assumption that anything beyond our normal experience is impossible will obviously have to find some other explanation for what the first Christians thought was the resurrection of Jesus. Those who accept the possibility of unique occurrences which seem to go beyond regular human experience will no doubt find it worthwhile to pay serious attention to some of the claims of the New Testament. With the general collapse of the rationalist-materialist world-view in recent years, and the emergence of so-called 'New Age' postmodern spirituality, the dominance of an unbridled scepticism in Western culture has gradually been eroded, so that there is probably a greater openness about such matters at the start of this new millennium than has been the case for some time. That should not be used as a substitute for critical consideration of the evidence, such as it is, though it certainly changes the atmosphere in which such examination can take place.

There can be no question that the earliest Christians were completely convinced that the resurrection event, or complex of events, was a real, historical happening that had taken place in their own world, and which had exercised a profound influence on their own lives. Whereas it is unclear just how widespread was belief in the conception of Jesus by a virgin, the resurrection was a different matter altogether. Paul spoke for the whole of the early church when he declared that, if the reality of Jesus' resurrection was denied, the Christian faith would be emptied of its meaning: 'If Christ has not been raised, your faith is futile and you are still in your sins' (1 Corinthians 15:17). By way of unpacking that conviction, Paul proceeded in the same passage to give a list of people who could verify that Jesus had come to life again, so he obviously thought of the resurrection event as something that could be attested by witnesses – an outward, public happening rather than a private, mystical experience. At the same time, one of the other dominant features of the New Testament accounts is that nowhere do they provide an account of the actual act of rising again, only of the results of that act as demonstrated through the appearances of the risen Jesus, and the fact that his tomb was found empty.

The belief of the early church

The earliest evidence for the resurrection almost certainly goes back to the time immediately after it is alleged to have taken place. This is the evidence contained in the summaries of Christian faith found in the first part of the Acts of the Apostles. Of course, these are now contained in a document that was compiled in its present form at least thirty years after the death of Jesus, and perhaps as much as fifty years later, but there is a widespread consensus that the first few chapters of Acts preserve material from very early sources. The language used in speaking about Jesus in the early speeches in Acts is quite different from that which was in common use when the book was compiled in its final form. It is even quite different from the letters of Paul, which were certainly written long before the book of Acts. So we may be reasonably confident that here we have very early sources.

The Resurrection of Christ, woodcut (1510) by Albrecht Dürer.

These early speeches indicate a largely Jewish type of Christianity, showing a set of simply expressed beliefs about Jesus, and providing a generally believable account of what life might have been like in the first days of the church. According to this picture, the central feature of the early Christian church's message was the story of Jesus himself – how he had come to fulfil God's promises, how he had died on the cross, and how he had come back to life again. This message was so consistently expressed that it has been possible to discern a regular pattern of statements that were apparently made about Jesus from the very earliest times. C.H. Dodd, who first identified this pattern of statements, called it *kerygma*, a Greek word meaning 'the declaration'. Every authentic account of the Christian message contained these statements:

■ Jesus has fulfilled the Old Testament promises;
■ God was at work in his life, death and resurrection;
■ Jesus has now been exalted to heaven;
■ The Holy Spirit has been given to the church;
■ Jesus will soon return in glory;
■ All who hear the message must respond to its challenge, showing a willingness to change their lifestyle and follow Jesus.

If the resurrection was to be removed from this *kerygma*, then most of it would no longer make sense. The whole existence of the early church was based on the belief that Jesus was no longer dead, but was alive.

It also seems likely from the evidence in Paul's letters, as well as from Acts, that the recognized qualification for an apostolic leader was that he or she had seen the risen Jesus. This was explicitly made a condition when the apostles came to appoint a successor to Judas Iscariot (Acts 1:21–22), and Paul also claimed that his own vision of Jesus on the road to Damascus gave him the same status as those who had been apostles before him (Galatians 1:11–17).

The evidence of Paul

The second main piece of evidence regarding the resurrection is provided by Paul himself in 1 Corinthians 15. If there is room for differing opinions on the importance of the evidence of Acts, there is no such room in the case of Paul's evidence. He was certainly writing his letter no more than twenty-five years after Jesus was crucified, and his statements might well form the earliest piece of documentary evidence for belief that Jesus had risen again. It is obvious, both from the contents of 1 Corinthians and from its context, that Paul's main intention there was not to give a reasoned argument for believing in the resurrection of Jesus. He was, rather, trying to help his readers to overcome a specific set of problems that had arisen in their local faith community. The information he included about how Jesus rose from the dead is more or less accidental, which in itself makes it all the more impressive, for he reminded the Corinthians that what he was saying was something they had always known and believed. Even though he sketched the details in just a few sentences, his account shows that at a very early date Christians, even in Greece, were quite familiar with the full story of how Jesus had died and come back to life again.

In this account Paul refers to an occasion when the risen Jesus was seen by more than 500 disciples at one time, most of whom he

says were still alive when he wrote and could confirm what he said
(1 Corinthians 15:6). He also mentions an appearance to James, the
brother of Jesus, and includes his own conversion encounter with the
risen Lord among these resurrection appearances (1 Corinthians 15:7–8).
Though they were all written later than Paul's letters to Corinth, the
gospels never mention these appearances of the risen Jesus at all, which
suggests that the fact of Jesus' resurrection was so widely believed
among the first generations of Christians that the people who wrote
the gospel stories did not even think it important to marshal *all* the
evidence for it. As with the rest of the narratives, they used only a small
selection of the material that was at their disposal.

The gospel traditions

The stories found at the end of each of the four gospels are of course
the main source of information about Jesus' resurrection. There are
certain distinctive features about these stories:
■ They all emphasize two main facts: that the grave of Jesus was found
empty, and that the risen Jesus was seen by different people on several
different occasions. Both these pieces of
evidence were important. By itself, the fact
of the empty grave would prove nothing
except that Jesus' body was not there.
Without the empty grave, the visions
would prove nothing objective, though
they might reveal something about the
mental state of the disciples. But the
combination of the two facts, if they are
indeed correct, would be strong evidence in
support of the claim that Jesus was alive.
■ When the resurrection narratives are
compared with many of the other stories
about Jesus, they are told in a relatively simple and uncomplicated way.
For example, they contain no symbolism requiring special insight to
understand, nor are there many subtle allusions to the Old Testament,
nor any real attempts to bring out the theological significance of the
events they describe. If they are compared in this respect with, say, the
accounts of how Jesus was baptized, the contrast is very marked indeed.

After his
crucifixion, Jesus
was placed in a
tomb carved
from the solid
rock. Tombs of
this kind often
had a heavy
stone which
could be rolled
across the
entrance.

The disciples

The fourth and final piece of evidence relating to the resurrection event
is the indisputable fact that a thoroughly disheartened band of disciples,
who should by all the rules of historical probability have been depressed
and disillusioned by their leader's crucifixion, was, in the space of seven
weeks, transformed into a strong band of courageous witnesses, and the

nucleus of a constantly growing church. The central fact of their witness was that Jesus was alive and active, and they had no hesitation in attributing the change in themselves to what had happened as a result of his rising from the dead. They themselves were obviously convinced that this was what had actually happened, for the resurrection was not just something they talked about: it was something they were willing to die for. It is beyond doubt that no one dies for something unless they are totally convinced of its truth.

Facts and faith about the resurrection

So much, then, for the various pieces of information supplied by the New Testament. What can be made of them? Firstly, three general observations are worth making:

Why do the accounts differ?

Despite the fact that the information given in the gospels is narrated in a simple way, the gospel accounts are not easy to reconcile with one another. Though many people have tried, no one has been completely successful in producing an 'agreed version' of how the New Testament says it all happened. It is unlikely that anyone ever will. Throughout their work, the gospel writers were selective. They used only those stories and teachings of Jesus that would be helpful to their first readers. This is one of the reasons there are four different gospels:

An ossuary. After a body decomposed, the bones were gathered together and placed in this kind of container.

because people in different parts of the empire had their own varied concerns. This process of selection was clearly applied to the resurrection stories, as can be seen from the fact that Paul preserves some pieces of information not mentioned by any of the gospels.

At first sight, this might appear to be an argument against the resurrection having happened at all, but it can also be claimed as a strong argument on the other side. Eye-witnesses often give very different accounts of what they have seen, especially when they see things that do not fit in with their expectations of how things should be. The disciples themselves had no expectation at all that a dead person might come to life again. Mark 9:9–10 suggests they had no idea what 'resurrection' could possibly mean; it was something quite alien to their way of thinking. It is not surprising then that the disciples did not tell a logical and coherent story. The story of someone rising from the dead would be much more difficult to believe if all four gospels had given exactly the same account. Yet, despite minor discrepancies in detail, all the

■ There is no evidence that the risen Jesus appeared to anyone apart from his own followers, though it is possible that he might have done so. Those who wrote the gospels were writing for a specific readership, which was either a Christian readership or people who were already sufficiently interested in the Christian faith to want to know more about it. In this context, the first concern of the gospels was to describe what it might be like when disciples encounter the living Jesus.

■ Evidence about somebody who appeared and disappeared in a room with closed doors is obviously quite a different kind of evidence from that historians normally deal with. That is not to say it should be inadmissible, but it certainly does not fit into the ordinary rules of evidence.

■ The fact that Mary Magdalene, the married couple on the road to Emmaus, and the disciples in the boat on Lake Galilee all failed to

---

accounts are agreed on the main parts of the story. In all of them the tomb is empty and Jesus appears to the disciples.

In Mark, the earliest gospel, the account ends at 16:8, and what follows in some English versions as 16:9–20 is generally considered to be a later addition. In this account, some women who came to the grave on the Sunday morning to finish the process of embalming Jesus' body found that the stone slab used as a door to the rock tomb had been rolled back, and were terrified by the sight of a young man in white sitting inside. This 'young man' (who is clearly intended to be understood as an angel) said, 'Do not be amazed; you seek Jesus of Nazareth, who was crucified. He has risen; he is not here, see the place where they laid him. But go, tell his disciples and Peter that he is going before you to Galilee; there you will see him, as he told you' (Mark 16:6–7). At that, the women ran terrified from the graveyard, and because of their fear they told no one of what they had seen and heard.

Luke includes the story of a couple returning to their home in the village of Emmaus, who met the risen Jesus without recognizing him. They spoke of women visiting the grave and seeing a vision of angels, who assured them that Jesus was alive (Luke 24:22–24). But no reference is made here to Jesus going to Galilee. Many sophisticated explanations have been proposed for this, though it is not inconceivable that the women did not deliver this message for the simple reason stated by Mark: they were afraid to go back there, for they thought that the king of that area, Herod Antipas, would now be ready to get rid of any of Jesus' followers who were found there.

Matthew repeats Mark's account, though with some additional details, mostly directed towards heightening the supernatural trappings of the event. He speaks of a great earthquake on the Sunday morning, and also mentions the terror of the guards at the tomb (Matthew 28:1–4). In this account, the women are still central but left the grave in a mixed mood of fear and joy, and were met by Jesus himself, who repeated the message about going to Galilee (Matthew 28:5–10). Matthew includes a story showing how the disciples followed this instruction at once, and describes how they met with the risen Jesus on a mountain in Galilee, where they were commissioned to take his message to all nations and invite others to join them in a life of discipleship (Matthew 28:16–20). This appearance of Jesus seems not to be the same as the ascension story told by Luke. Though Jesus is reported as making

recognize Jesus, though they knew him well and had seen him only a few days before, suggests that his physical appearance must have changed in a way that would certainly be confusing to any ordinary witness in giving evidence.

What, then, can be said on the basis of these various pieces of evidence? There can be no question that the earliest church believed that Jesus had come back to life again. The disciples and their followers knew that something had happened to change their lives after the crucifixion of their master, and they explained this change by the fact that he had risen from the dead. But to speak of this kind of 'resurrection faith' is one thing; to speak plausibly of a 'resurrection fact' is quite another. Obviously there must have been something that can be called the 'resurrection fact' which called forth the disciples'

Why do the accounts differ? *continued*

some similar statements on each occasion, the ascension took place not in Galilee but in or near Jerusalem (Luke 24:44–53; Acts 1:6–11). In effect, Matthew brings the story begun by Mark to its logical conclusion: Jesus' appearance in Galilee and commission to the disciples to proclaim the good news about him.

Luke's story has certain differences from Mark's: there were two angels in the tomb, and Galilee is mentioned not as the location where Jesus would meet the disciples later, but as the place where he had originally foretold his death and resurrection (Luke 24:1–11). When the women told the disciples their story, it was not believed. In some old manuscripts of Luke, there is at this point a story of how Peter and John visited the tomb to confirm what the women reported, but this is probably a later effort to harmonize Luke's story with the incident recorded in John 20:1–10. After telling of how Jesus met the couple on the road to Emmaus, and then appeared to all the disciples in a room in Jerusalem (Luke 24:13–43), Luke goes on to record the ascension on the road to Bethany, as if it followed immediately after the resurrection (Luke 24:44–53). But in Acts he makes it clear that the ascension took place after an interval of forty days (Acts 1:3). He does not mention an appearance in Galilee.

John's Gospel, on the other hand, describes appearances of Jesus both in Jerusalem and in Galilee. Of the women named in the other gospels as having discovered the empty grave, only Mary Magdalene is mentioned here, though the fact that she uses the plural pronoun 'we' in reporting the event to Peter implies that others were with her (John 20:1–2). They found the tomb empty and returned to tell the disciples, whereupon Peter and John then went to the tomb and found the grave clothes lying undisturbed – proof that the tomb had not been robbed (John 20:3–10). At this point Mary saw two angels in the tomb and was greeted by Jesus, whom she mistook for the gardener (John 20:11–18). An account then follows of two appearances to the disciples in Jerusalem. During the first of these Jesus breathed on them and gave them the Holy Spirit (John 20:19–29), while the last chapter of John, which is almost certainly a later addition, albeit by the same author, describes Jesus' appearance to the disciples on the shore of Lake Galilee, and how he had breakfast with them before recommissioning Peter (John 21:1–25).

The 'Garden Tomb'. Though this is certainly not the actual place where Jesus was buried, it gives an idea of what his tomb might have looked like.

'resurrection faith'. But what was it? It does not have to begin with the actual rising of Jesus' physical body from death, and it is not difficult to think of alternative explanations:

The 'resurrection fact' was a subjective experience

A natural reaction to the evidence about the resurrection is to suppose that the so-called 'resurrection appearances' were purely subjective. The pious might call them visions; psychologists would be more inclined to call them hallucinations. If we could assume that this is what happened, it would solve the problem. But it is not quite so simple:

■ The fact that the tomb was empty, and that neither friend nor enemy produced the body of Jesus is so strongly emphasized in the gospels that it must be accounted for. Both the Romans and Jesus' religious opponents had an obvious vested interest in producing a body, for that would have squashed the Christian movement once and for all. It is therefore safe to assume that neither of these groups had removed it. The disciples, on the other hand, were prepared to stake their lives on the fact that Jesus was alive. Many of them were brutally murdered for their faith, including Peter and other members of Jesus' inner circle, who would be prime suspects for removing the body. It is highly improbable, if not impossible, to imagine that they would have willingly suffered in this way, if all the time they knew where they themselves had hidden Jesus' body.

■ Although an individual experience like that of Peter or James might be reasonably regarded as subjective, and an appearance to a crowd of 500 might sound like a mass hallucination, an encounter such as that on the road to Emmaus, with the absence of excitement and the gradual recognition of the stranger by two people, has all the marks of an authentic account. The statements that the risen body could be touched, that the risen Jesus ate food with his disciples, and that he breathed on them, show the disciples were convinced they were in contact with a real physical body and not a vision.

■ Unlike the other disciples, Paul was what might be called 'psychically experienced'. He writes of having had visions and revelations of a mystical nature on several occasions (1 Corinthians 14:18; 2 Corinthians 12:1–4), but he placed his Damascus road experience in a different category altogether. For him it was quite distinctive, to be compared only to the appearances of the risen Jesus to the other disciples. All the accounts describe encounters with the risen Jesus as an apparently unique kind of experience – neither purely subjective like dreams, nor purely objective, but with some of the characteristics of both.

The 'resurrection fact' was a theological creation

It has been argued that the 'resurrection faith' arose because the disciples saw some theological reason that required it. Because they believed Jesus to be God's Messiah it would be natural for someone who claimed this position to rise from the dead. This explanation, however, raises more questions than it answers:

■ There is no evidence from any source at all to suggest that the Messiah was expected to rise from the dead. On the contrary, the Messiah was popularly expected to kill other people and, if he suffered and died himself, by definition he was not going to be regarded as the Messiah.

■ The Old Testament expresses a very negative attitude to the idea of resurrection, and many Jews simply did not believe it was possible. The disciples themselves appear not to have known what it was earlier in the ministry of Jesus (Mark 9:9–10).

■ It is also difficult to see how the idea of resurrection can have come from an interpretation of Old Testament expectations, since the resurrection stories are completely lacking in scriptural quotations. In this respect there is a sharp contrast with the stories of the crucifixion, which are full of such allusions. In addition, there was no consistent expectation of life after death in the Hebrew tradition, let alone any preconceived notion of what it might be like.

The 'resurrection fact' was a later belief

It has also been argued that belief in Jesus' resurrection was a late idea, only coming to prominence after the Christians had been forced to leave Jerusalem at the time of the Jewish revolt against the Romans (AD66–70). Up until then, they regularly met for worship at the tomb of Jesus. But what could they do once they had been barred from entering the city? To answer that question, the story of the empty tomb was put together to explain why, after all, they did not need to worship there.

Worship at the tombs of heroes is a common practice. It happened in Jesus' day (see Matthew 23:29), and Christian pilgrims of later generations have certainly visited Jesus' traditional burial site in the Church of the Resurrection, or its rival, the so-called 'Garden Tomb'. But to suggest that the discontinuation of such a practice in the first century led to belief that Jesus was alive is completely far-fetched. For one thing, there is no evidence that anybody at all was interested in the place where Jesus was buried, earlier than the fourth century. In addition, there are the statements made by Paul in 1 Corinthians, written at least ten years before AD66. By that time, one gospel had certainly been written and, furthermore, the gospel accounts were undoubtedly based on stories that went right back into the earliest days of the church. It makes no sense at all to suppose that belief in the resurrection was a late development. The fact is that Christians did not venerate the tomb of Jesus because they believed there was nothing in it – and they held this belief right from the start.

Many other more fanciful suggestions have been made from time to time to account for the 'resurrection fact'. But the overwhelming weight of all the evidence suggests that, however it might be described in cognitive abstractions, the 'resurrection fact' was a real, historical event. No other hypothesis gives an adequate account of so much of the evidence.

What does the resurrection mean?

To talk of describing the 'resurrection fact' in abstract terms, not to mention the language of scientific enquiry, moves well beyond the categories of thought of the first disciples. One of the most striking things about the evidence of the New Testament is that the disciples appear to have had no interest at all in probing the whys and wherefores of the 'resurrection fact'. They knew it was a real fact, because of their own experience of Jesus Christ and the evidence of the empty tomb – and that was all they needed to know. This no doubt helps to explain why there is no description anywhere in the New Testament of how the resurrection actually took place. Some Christians in the second century regarded this as a deficiency in the New Testament, and produced their own vivid descriptions of what the body of Jesus looked like, how it came out of the grave, and how those who saw it were affected by the experience. But for the first witnesses such details were not the main focus of interest. For them, the resurrection was not just a happy ending to the story of Jesus; it was the natural climax of the whole of his life, and the vindication of the high claims made for him during his ministry. It was also a guarantee that the life and teaching of Jesus was not just an interesting chapter in the history of human thought, but was the way through which men and women could come to know God. This is why the proclamation of a living Jesus became the central part of the message the disciples declared throughout the known world.

But why was it so very important? Why did Paul claim that without the resurrection of Jesus the whole of the Christian message would be meaningless? A good way to answer this question is to put it the other way round: rather than asking negatively what would be lost if the resurrection could be disproved, asking what positive place the resurrection held in the beliefs of the first Christians. Three claims are made in this respect:

The resurrection and Jesus' identity

Jesus' claims to be the Son of God were shown to be true. Peter said on the Day of Pentecost that the resurrection was a clear proof that 'God has made this Jesus, whom you crucified, both Lord and Messiah' (Acts 2:36). Paul wrote to the Christians of Rome that Jesus was 'declared Son of God by a mighty act in that he rose from the dead' (Romans 1:4). In spite of Jesus' authority displayed in his teaching and actions, and the implied claims about his central role in God's plan, without the resurrection he might have been thought of simply as a great and good man. But after he had risen from the grave, his followers knew for certain that he was who he had claimed to be. They could now see and appreciate his whole life on earth in a new and fuller way, as the life of God personally lived out among ordinary mortals.

The resurrection and new life

The resurrection was more than just a new light on the crucified Jesus. It is emphasized throughout the New Testament, and especially by Paul,

---

The ascension

The ascension as such features only in Luke's story of Jesus' life. It is unclear whether Luke 24:50–53 tells of it, for in some ancient manuscripts the crucial words 'and was taken up into heaven' are missing. But Luke certainly documents it in more detail in Acts 1:6–11. This story marks the point at which the regular resurrection appearances of Jesus ceased. As such, it is merely the culmination of several occasions when Jesus had disappeared from his disciples' gaze in the forty days following the resurrection. From the time of the resurrection itself, Jesus was understood to have been exalted into the presence of God. When he left the couple at Emmaus, he did not return to some kind of earthbound limbo, but to the heavenly glory which, as the risen Son of man, he had now entered. The actual story

of the ascension presumably reflects some particular occasion when he left the disciples in a dramatic and memorable way – and after which, they saw him no more. Though the ascension story itself is only recorded by Luke, the idea is referred to in several passages in John (20:17; 13:1; 16:10; 17:11), while Matthew's Gospel concludes with the conviction that Jesus had received precisely the kind of universal authority that the ascension story seems to imply.

The notion that Jesus was taken 'up into heaven' has sometimes been problematic for modern readers of the gospels. Certainly, we no longer share the perception of ancient people, that the universe is a three-tiered construction, with the earth sandwiched in the middle between the heavens and the underworld. In this frame of reference, it would be natural to think of Jesus being taken 'up to

that the resurrection, as well as the cross, was an indispensable part of the arrival of God's kingdom and all that entailed. The first Christians were practical people rather than theorists. What they wanted was something that would work in real life. They were longing for some kind of personal empowerment that would enable them to be the best people they could possibly be. They understood this in terms of living at peace with God, and being delivered from their self-centredness to live in harmony with other people and, indeed, with the natural environment. They realized that this was unlikely to be achieved either by formal religious observance or by their own efforts at self-improvement, and what was needed was some fresh, energizing life-force that could transform the human personality.

Paul found this new life-force in Jesus, and expressed it in a mystical way as a union between the deepest recesses of his own person, and the Jesus who had been crucified and raised from death. It was such a striking reality for him that he could even write, 'It is no longer I who live, but Christ who lives in me' (Galatians 2:20). This was not just conventionally religious language, for Paul seems to have meant what he said in the most literal sense: Jesus was now living in him in such a way that even the details of his life were determined not by him but by this living Christ. In trying to express all this, Paul used imagery in which he compared the baptism of Christians to the death and resurrection of Jesus (Romans 6:1–10). In baptism, Christians were covered with water as a physical symbol of something that would also happen inwardly and

---

heaven'. But even today, that could easily be a natural, common sense way to describe such a disappearance. Acts 1:12 seems to place the ascension on the Mount of Olives, and Constantine subsequently built a church there, around a cave that he believed marked the spot. Later tradition identified an open space as the more likely site of the ascension. In AD384, Egeria joined in a celebration of the ascension on a small hill a little further up the Mount of Olives, and some six years later a pilgrim called Poemenia had a shrine constructed there – around a rock which bears a mark allegedly made by Jesus' right foot as he said farewell to his disciples.

The New Testament's concern, however, is not with spatial definitions as such, but with the fact that Jesus himself had returned to be exalted in glory with God. This was always implicit in the 'Son

of man' title, for in the book of Daniel this character received 'authority, honour, and royal power' (Daniel 7:14). In the context of imagery depicting the cross as Jesus' final battle with the forces of evil, and his resurrection as the proof that he had triumphed, then the ascension demonstrated that this victory was absolute. It was a way of affirming the cosmic dimensions of Christian salvation, declaring that the life, death and resurrection of Jesus were good news not only for people, but also for the world of nature, and indeed for everything in the entire universe. It brought order out of chaos and, in theological terms, represented the reversal of all that had gone wrong in the primeval fall, and both declared and inaugurated the possibility of renewal and rebirth.

spiritually, so that being drenched with water was like being buried, as Jesus was, and coming out of the water was like being raised again, as Jesus was. The essence of Paul's understanding of these events was that becoming a Christian involved a willingness to 'die', in the sense of shedding a self-centred existence, in order to be 'raised' again and receive a new existence, the life of Jesus Christ himself living within.

So the resurrection of Jesus was crucial, for if Jesus had only died on the cross, he might well have been understood to have set an example, or offered a sacrifice, or paid the price of human freedom – but his suffering would have had no power to affect everyday living. Without the resurrection, the cross might have been an interesting theological talking point, but would have been powerless to have any lasting effect on the lives of ordinary people. Because of the resurrection, however, Paul had discovered a new life: 'For to me, life is Christ' (Philippians 1:21). Moreover, he was confident that this was to be the normal experience of everyone who was a Christian: Jesus Christ actually living in those who commit themselves to him.

The resurrection and future hope

The resurrection of Jesus has a further implication for those who already have Christ's life within them. An important part of Jesus' teaching in John's Gospel was that his followers would share in 'eternal life' (John 3:15; 4:14; 17:3). This 'eternal life' included two things. On the one hand, the phrase indicates that Christians were expecting to enjoy a new quality of life: 'eternal life' is 'God's life' and, when Paul wrote of his own Christian experience of Christ living within him, he was reflecting a similar conviction.

On the other hand, to have the kind of life that God has does not just mean that Christians have a new dynamic for life in this world; it also implies that their relationship with God inaugurated by faith in Christ will never end. This distinctive aspect of Jesus' teaching was reinforced and emphasized by Paul when he wrote that the resurrected Jesus should be regarded as 'the firstfruits of those who have fallen asleep' (1 Corinthians 15:20). He understood this to mean that Jesus' rising again was a pledge and a promise that his disciples, too, would survive death. Those people who shared in Christ's sufferings and resurrection in a spiritual sense had the assurance of a life beyond the grave which, like their present lives, would be infused by the personal presence of God. But it would also be distinctive and new, for this resurrection life takes its character from the fact that Jesus is risen, and therefore shares the incomparable nature of that kind of renewed existence now enjoyed by Jesus – a life in which suffering, death and oppression are gone for ever and replaced by the new ways of God's kingdom (1 Corinthians 15:57).

To understand more fully what the implications of that might be, we now need to move on to consider Jesus' teaching about God's way of doing things, that different way of being which is called 'the kingdom of God'.

6 What is God's Kingdom?

The kingdom of God is the major theme of Jesus' teaching in the gospels of Matthew, Mark and Luke. This concept, expressed in various ways, had been a central part of Jewish religious aspirations for generations. At the time of Jesus, it was popularly anticipated as a time when the promises of the Hebrew scriptures concerning the place of Israel in God's plan would be fulfilled in a dramatic way: the hated Romans would once and for all be driven out of their land, and the people would enjoy a new period of political and religious freedom, and self-determination.

It is no wonder, then, that when Jesus emerged as a travelling prophet after his baptism and the temptations, and declared that 'the time is fulfilled, and the kingdom of God is at hand' (Mark 1:15), people of all kinds showed great interest in what he had to say. This was what they were waiting for: a new kingdom of God that would finally crush the old kingdom of Rome. Moreover, they fully expected that they, the Jewish people, would have a prominent part in this coming kingdom under the leadership of their long-awaited Messiah.

From the very beginning of Israelite history, God had always been regarded as 'king' of the people (Psalms 96:10; 99:1; 146:10). The Hebrew Bible declared that the whole world belonged to God, because God made it – and Israel as a nation belonged to God because God had rescued its ancestors from slavery in Egypt and led them to a new land. When they wanted to appoint Saul as their own king a century or two later, some people opposed the move on the grounds that God was the only true king the nation should ever have (1 Samuel 8:1–18). Subsequently, when David became king in Jerusalem, the two ideas were brought together: David and his successors were the rightful rulers of the nation, because God had chosen them (2 Samuel 7:1–17). Their duty was to do God's will, so that the kingdom would reflect the standards of God's law. In reality, things were rarely that simple. As one king succeeded another, it was painfully obvious that many of them were interested only in power and self-fulfilment, and the earlier ideals gradually disappeared. They certainly disappeared as practical politics, though they never quite vanished altogether, for they were transformed into a hope for the future: that at some time God would step in to put things right and establish a kingdom of justice and righteousness. The prophet Zechariah was only one of many who fervently looked for that time to come, a day on which 'the Lord will become king over all the earth' (Zechariah 14:9). By the time of Jesus, there was a widespread expectation that the arrival of the Messiah would herald the coming of this kingdom.

The kingdom of God

But what did Jesus mean in speaking of 'the kingdom of God'? Today, the notion of 'kingdom' most obviously denotes a state or territory that, if not actually ruled by a king, is nevertheless a political entity of some kind. In the ancient world, things would have been no different, and there can be no doubt that it would have been perfectly understandable for Jesus' contemporaries to conclude that he was announcing the establishment of a new state which, in contrast to the countries around, would somehow be ruled by God in person.

That idea is so obviously contrary to what Jesus taught about the kingdom of God that, right from the beginning, it is clear that he must have been using the phrase in some other way. If Jesus was talking about a new state, then he must have seen himself as the agent of a new political dynasty, in effect a Zealot. Yet both his words and his actions seemed to deny that. So what was Jesus really talking about? Some Christians have concluded that, in spite of all the indications to the contrary, Jesus must have been mainly concerned with starting a society that was to be ruled by God, distinct from those ruled by ordinary mortals. Many theologians of the Middle Ages, for example, followed St Augustine in identifying the kingdom of which Jesus spoke with the organized society they knew in the church. Throughout the days of Christendom, the concept that the church was a legitimate successor to the Roman empire, with a political mandate to expand its own empire, motivated Western exploration of other parts of the world, and played its part in the emergence of colonialism. Even today, it is not difficult to find Christian leaders who will speak as if 'the kingdom' is just another word for 'the church', while many more are prepared

Augustine of Hippo (AD354–430). Unattributed engraving copied from a 15th-century

to talk of it as if it is a kind of political manifesto. Here, we will suggest that Jesus' use of the term 'the kingdom of God' cannot be limited to any of these things, but is in fact more comprehensive than all of them. A good definition of it is 'God's way of doing things'. It begins from those values and standards that most adequately reflect God's own character, though as Jesus expounds the significance of that, he inevitably provides insights into how all this might be applied in practical terms to different life situations. That means that we can expect to find models for how discipleship might impact politics, economics, or other tangible social realities. But these things do not exhaust the meaning of 'God's kingdom', which is both wider and deeper than that: wider because it is a way of being that was to be applied to the whole of life, both private and public, and deeper because it would address not only material but also spiritual realities, giving those who committed themselves to it a fresh understanding of true freedom and justice, and the renewed experience of God's presence in their lives.

A new way of being

There were already clues pointing in this direction in the actual words that Jesus probably used to articulate his teaching. Though Jesus might well have been able to speak two or three languages, it is very likely that most of his teaching was given in Aramaic, for that was the language that most people in Palestine knew best. The gospels were written in Greek, of course, like the rest of the New Testament, and we therefore have no direct record of the actual Aramaic words used by Jesus. But even the Greek word that is translated into English as 'kingdom' (*basileia*), more often means the activity of a king rather than the territory over which a sovereign might rule. The Aramaic word that most scholars think Jesus himself would have used (*malkutha*) certainly had that meaning. So we are justified in supposing that Jesus was talking about what might be called 'the kingship of God', rather than 'God's kingdom'. 'Kingship' would be about God's style, the way that God operates, and the example that God sets to others. This helps to explain why Jesus was concerned more than anything else about the quality of human life, and the nature of meaningful relationships, rejecting attitudes of power and control in favour of love, acceptance and mutual service. For him, these qualities were to characterize the life of his disciples because he perceived them as central to the person of God.

This helps to explain some of the apparently more difficult things that Jesus said. For example, he told the Pharisees, 'The kingdom of God does not come in such a way as to be seen... because the kingdom of God is within you' (Luke 17:20, 21). On another occasion he told his disciples, 'whoever does not receive the kingdom of God like a child shall not enter it' (Mark 10:15). It would have been nonsensical to speak of a political territory existing in the lives of individual people: there is no sense in which a person could 'receive' a state, nor could it be 'within them'. But Jesus was saying that from the moment God is recognized as sovereign in someone's life, then the 'kingdom of God' has really arrived. He could say this kingdom was already 'among' his hearers, because he himself was there, and he was completely committed to exploring and putting into practice the values and standards that God represented.

In a similar way, Jesus compared 'entering the kingdom' to 'entering into life' (Mark 9:43–47). Those people who 'inherit the kingdom' also 'inherit eternal life' (Matthew 25:34–46), and the gate leading to the kingdom is 'the way that leads to life' (Mark 10:17–23). The well-known story of the son who ran away from home also emphasized the fact that to be a member of the kingdom is to share in God's family life, and to experience God as a loving parent (Luke 15:11–32). In the same way, Paul reminded his Christian readers in Corinth that 'the kingdom of God does not consist in talk but in power' (1 Corinthians 4:20), the empowerment of God that enables those who wish to change to live in ways that will truly reflect God's ways of doing things.

At the same time, it would be wrong to understand the kingdom exclusively in terms of an individual relationship between people and God, for there are many statements in the gospels which show that Jesus regarded the kingdom of God not only as the inward rule of God in the lives of his followers but also as some kind of tangible reality. For example, he spoke of people who would 'come from east and west, and from north and south, and sit at table in the kingdom of God' (Luke 13:29). At the last supper Jesus told the disciples, 'from now on I shall not drink of the fruit of the vine until the kingdom of God comes' (Luke 22:18). Matthew records him saying that his followers would 'inherit the kingdom prepared... from the foundation of the world' (Matthew 25:34).

Jesus seems, therefore, to have understood this idea of God's kingdom in at least two ways: on the one hand, as God's guidance in the lives of those who would be disciples, and on the other hand, as something that God would somehow display to the world at large. Both these concepts were already found in the expectations of the Old Testament writers. Though it is true that certain parts of ancient Judaism had expected God's sovereignty to be displayed in the form of an organized kingdom, which would replace the empires of the world, not all previous generations had seen God's future intervention in human affairs in the same nationalistic terms as some of Jesus' contemporaries. Circles inspired by apocalyptic thinking had a tendency to magnify the material aspects of 'the kingdom of God'. In Daniel, for example, 'the saints of the most high', represented by 'a figure like the Son of man', receive the kingdom of God and possess it for ever (Daniel 7:13–18), and this kind of expectation was heightened and magnified by later apocalyptic writers, some of them contemporaries of Jesus. It was an outlook expressed by some of Jesus' own followers when they wanted to make him their king after the miraculous feeding of the 5,000 (John 6:15) and it was by no means absent from the inner circle of his closest disciples. When James and John tried to claim the chief places on either side of Jesus' throne they were obviously thinking in crudely political terms (Mark 10:35–45).

Though Jesus rebuked them on that occasion, he never denied that God's kingdom would in some way affect society in a political sense. He sometimes suggested that it would do so in relatively undramatic ways, comparable to the way yeast makes bread rise, or a mustard seed quietly grows into a large tree (Matthew 13:31–33). But he was also quite convinced that God would act decisively and directly, not just in the lives of individuals, but also in the public affairs of nations and empires (Mark 13).

At the time of Jesus, many of the rabbis were emphasizing that God's kingship over Israel was already in existence, even under the Roman rule, and that it operated through the Torah, or Law. The rabbis sometimes referred to people 'taking upon themselves the kingdom of God', and by this they meant accepting and obeying the Torah as the instrument of God's rule over his people.

This tension between what God can do now in those who are prepared to order their lives according to God's standards, and what God will ultimately do through them in society at large, is found elsewhere in the New Testament, so that there is a constant balancing act between what God is accomplishing now, and what God might be expected to bring to pass in the future. Paul, for example, says that 'the kingdom of God is not concerned with material things like food and drink, but with goodness and peace and joy in the Holy Spirit' (Romans 14:17), thereby linking it inseparably with moral choices and personal spirituality. Elsewhere, however, Paul easily connects the arrival of God's kingdom with the events surrounding the end of the world: 'The end comes when Jesus delivers the kingdom to God... after destroying every other rule and authority and power' (1 Corinthians 15:24), making it clear that he also believed God would break into history and alter its course, and that this too was part of the coming of God's kingdom. This was made quite explicit in Revelation, in which 'The kingdom of the world has become the kingdom of our Lord and of... Christ, and he shall reign for ever and ever' (Revelation 11:15). It was also an important element in the teaching of Jesus himself, which needs to be considered alongside the more personal aspects of his message, in order to produce a rounded account of what he wanted to say.

'Eschatology' and the kingdom

This whole question of the different things that might be meant by 'God's kingdom' is generally called 'eschatology'. The actual word 'eschatology' is derived from the Greek words *eschaton* and *logos*, and means 'ideas about the end'. But eschatology is not just concerned with what might happen at the end of the world: it is essentially concerned with God's sovereignty, and with all the different means by which God's ways of doing things can make themselves felt, whether in the lives of individual people, in society, or in the ultimate meaning of the entire cosmic process. Over the last century or so, three main perspectives have dominated discussions about the meaning of Jesus' teaching on the kingdom of God.

'Futurist eschatology'

The first of these views Jesus' teaching as part of a 'futurist eschatology'. Used in this context, the word 'futurist' means in the future from Jesus' point of view, and not from the standpoint of the present

Albert Schweitzer was a doctor in Africa. His ideas about the kingdom have been widely influential.

day. There are many contemporary Christians who have a 'futurist eschatology' in the sense that they expect God's kingdom to come in a tangible, material form at a time that is still in the future from now, and they often further identify the coming of God's kingdom in this way with beliefs about the second coming (or *parousia*) of Jesus himself. But when scholars talk of the gospel traditions, they normally reserve the term 'futurist' for Jesus' own expectations about the kingdom, and not the expectations of modern Christians.

Albert Schweitzer (1875–1965) was a German musician and theologian who became a medical missionary in Africa, and

in the early days of his career he did a great deal to promote the idea that Jesus was obsessed with a futurist eschatology. By that, he meant that Jesus held roughly the same expectations as the apocalyptic writers of his day, and that he believed God was about to intervene immediately and dramatically in the affairs of humanity, and his own life's work was to be the decisive climax of history. By definition, therefore, that climax would have to come within Jesus' own lifetime. On the basis of this perception, Schweitzer suggested that when, for example, Jesus declared that 'the kingdom of God is at hand', he really expected the cataclysmic end of the world to come almost immediately. More than that, Jesus also imagined himself to be 'the Messiah designate' who would assume a position of full authority once the kingdom had actually arrived. Like many other visionaries both before and after him, Jesus found the reality of life rather different from these idealistic dreams, and as life went on very much as before it began to seem as if the dream had been only an illusion.

Early in the course of his work, said Schweitzer, Jesus was sufficiently confident to announce to his disciples that the Son of man was about to appear in glory – so soon that they could expect his arrival in the course of a few days (Matthew 10:23). When it failed to happen, Jesus decided to try to force God's hand by going to Jerusalem and pressing his claims with the authorities there, and it was this move that resulted in him being arrested, tried and tragically sentenced to death. However, even this astonishing display of blind faith did not produce the desired result, but ended with defeat and a cry of despair from the cross, as Jesus realized that the God he served had abandoned him.

Surprisingly, perhaps, the fact that Jesus' ministry so evidently ended in failure did not invalidate his teaching, for Schweitzer claimed that an even greater power resulted from this incredible act of misplaced confidence than would have been the case if the hoped-for apocalyptic kingdom had actually arrived. The example of Jesus is something that can still exert a dynamic moral and spiritual influence over those who are willing to be obedient. Schweitzer himself certainly put into practice the lessons he saw there, though ironically his overall perspective on Jesus prevented him from taking his actual teaching very seriously, for he regarded even the Sermon on the Mount as an 'interim ethic', valid only for the very short period of Jesus' own ministry. Instead, he attached the greatest importance to Jesus' faithfulness to his convictions, even when those convictions were apparently seriously inadequate.

Schweitzer's views were published in a remarkable book that first appeared in English in 1909, under the title *The Quest of the Historical Jesus*. It is still regarded as one of the great theological classics, not least because of its comprehensive presentation of the course of scholarly debate over the decades preceding its publication, and the fact that Schweitzer put his finger on some key aspects of Jesus' life and teaching. The way he placed Jesus' teaching about the kingdom of God in the same frame of reference as the work of the apocalyptic writers opened up many new possibilities for understanding the impact that Jesus must have had in the cultural context of his day. He was also certainly correct in seeing that Jesus' style of life, and especially his death, could not easily be separated from his message, and that it was inappropriate to try to understand his teaching without also taking account of his personality.

But taken as a whole, Schweitzer's view failed to convince as a comprehensive account of the whole of Jesus' life and teaching. For one thing, he consistently underrated the claims made in the gospels about Jesus' own significance, preferring instead to confine his attention almost exclusively to the statements about the kingdom of God. But for a holistic view that takes account of all the evidence, these two parts of Jesus' teaching must be understood together, for what is said about the kingdom of God is complementary to the teaching about Jesus' self-claimed special relationship with God.

Unless we are prepared to deny all historical credibility of the gospel narratives, it is hard to believe that Jesus realized the importance of dying at Jerusalem only after the failure of all his previous efforts to bring about the kingdom. Nor is it necessary to believe with Schweitzer that Jesus' death also failed in its intended purpose, and left only a vague spiritual influence to affect the lives of those who take time to think about it.

Schweitzer made much of statements such as Jesus' words to his disciples just before his transfiguration: 'there are some standing here who will not taste death before they see the kingdom of God come with power' (Mark 9:1), something which, on Schweitzer's understanding, never happened. But he was able to reach this conclusion only because of his generally sceptical attitude to the evidence of the New Testament. The whole conviction of the early church, however, was that God *did* intervene in human affairs in a powerful and dramatic way with the resurrection of Jesus and the gift of the Holy Spirit to his followers – and that both of these were the direct outcome of Jesus' death on the cross. Since much of the New Testament was written less than a generation after these events took place, its evidence cannot be brushed aside quite as easily as Schweitzer thought.

'Realized eschatology'
The exact opposite of Schweitzer's theory was C.H. Dodd's idea that Jesus had what he called a 'realized eschatology'. According to Dodd (1884–1973), what Jesus was really saying was that the kingdom had already arrived in his own person. We could say, therefore, that the coming of Jesus was itself the beginning of God's reign; though the kingdom might need to grow and develop, the ultimate and decisive act has already taken place.

This proved to be an attractive view, especially to people of the mid-twentieth century who were still optimistic that the

'Eschatology' and the
kingdom *continued*

world could gradually be made into a better place, and generally saw this coming about through a scientifically inspired evolutionary process of moral improvement and education. Whereas the thought patterns familiar to first-century Jewish apocalyptists seemed bizarre and unbelievable, this image of the kingdom naturally commended itself to middle-class social activists in the Western world. Moreover, the idea that Jesus saw his own life and work as the coming of God's kingdom did actually shed new light on some aspects of the gospel narratives. The miracles, for example, are much easier to understand when they are viewed as signs and demonstrations that God was at work in bringing the kingdom to birth through the life of Jesus than they would be with the more traditional view that had regarded them as 'proofs' of Jesus' divine nature.

Dodd was a sufficiently careful scholar to recognize that not all the gospel materials can be easily understood in the context of a realized eschatology. What could be made, for instance, of those parables that appear to be concerned with the last judgment and some kind of future winding up of things – parables like the story of the ten bridesmaids or the sheep and the goats (Matthew 25:1–13; 31–46)? Dodd proposed that these should be interpreted not as images of a final judgment that would come at the end of the world, but as pictures of the kind of challenge that presents itself to anyone whenever they are confronted with the message about Jesus and God's kingdom. There is certainly plenty of evidence that Jesus regarded the declaration of his message as, in some sense, a judgment on those who heard it and did not respond. The terms in which he condemned the Pharisees often seem to imply that they had placed themselves beyond the possibility of salvation (Mark 3:28–30; Matthew 23),

C.H. Dodd, the English theologian who developed the idea of 'realized eschatology'.

and the author of the fourth gospel is surely giving an accurate representation of at least part of Jesus' message when he comments that 'Whoever believes in Jesus is not condemned; but whoever who does not believe is condemned already, because they have not believed in the name of the only Son of God. And this is the judgment, that the light has come into the world, and people loved darkness rather than light, because their deeds were evil' (John 3:18–19).

It is not difficult to find passages in Jesus' teaching that can give some support to most aspects of Dodd's theory. But the theory ultimately proved incapable of accounting for all the evidence. There were two major stumbling-blocks:

● Although there are many passages in Jesus' teaching which are consistent with a 'realized eschatology', there are a good many more which are not. In many cases Jesus refers to the Son of man coming 'with the clouds of heaven', and his whole outlook was undoubtedly coloured by the kind of apocalyptic imagery to which Schweitzer so strikingly drew attention.

● It is also necessary to consider what the rest of the New Testament reflects about the beliefs of the first Christians, and there can be no doubt that other writings reveal a mixture of a 'futuristic' type of eschatology and a 'realized' type alongside one another.

In the letters Paul wrote to the church in the Greek city of Thessalonica in the early 50s of the first century, there is a considerable emphasis on the expectation of the early Christians that Jesus would return in glory. Paul himself obviously shared this expectation, though not in the same extreme fashion as the Thessalonians (1 Thessalonians 4:13 – 5:11; 2 Thessalonians 2:1–12). In Corinth, on the other hand, the same Paul knew people who believed that the conventional descriptions of the end of things were to be taken as symbols of their own spiritual experience – and to them he again emphasized his own belief that Jesus would return in the future (1 Corinthians 15:3–57). At the same time – and paradoxically, perhaps – Paul himself was not totally one-sided in the matter, for in Galatians, one of his earliest letters, he suggested that in a very real sense the fullness of God's kingdom had come and was already at work in those who were Christians.

If Dodd's theory was completely correct and Jesus did actually think that the kingdom had already arrived in its final form, it is hard to see how and why the first Christians should have forgotten this emphasis so soon and turned instead to speculations about the future. This is an especially important question, since so many of these Christians were not Jews, and they would not naturally have thought of the future in terms of traditional apocalyptic teachings. We should also bear in mind that the gospel traditions themselves were preserved in the churches, and for the churches' use, and it is surely unlikely that such a glaring inconsistency between the teaching of Jesus and the actual beliefs of the church would have gone unnoticed.

'Inaugurated eschatology'

Because of the difficulties involved in both the futuristic and the realized views of Jesus' eschatology, there has been considerable support for a view that would take the best from both of them, recognizing that in a sense God's kingdom did actually come in the person of Jesus, but that its complete fulfilment was still seen in the future. Thus Jesus' teaching is what might be called an 'inaugurated eschatology'.

This is probably the best explanation of the matter. It is essential to recognize with Schweitzer that Jesus' background was that of first-century Judaism, and his teaching included a complete view of the future course of events, including last judgment and final resurrection, as part of the consummation of God's kingdom. But it is also important to recognize that Jesus claimed that the kingdom had arrived already in his own person, and so people

must make their own response to God's demands upon them here and now. If, as has been suggested here, 'the kingdom of God' is a way of speaking about 'God's way of doing things', then there is no intrinsic difficulty in bringing these apparently diverse understandings into dynamic relationship with each other: they are simply different aspects of the same divine will.

This rather complex subject can be summarized by noting four points which seem basic to understanding what Jesus had to say about the coming of the kingdom:
● Jesus certainly used the language and, perhaps to some extent, shared the views of those who expected the kingdom's imminent arrival through a direct intervention of God in human affairs.
● Jesus believed that the fundamental nature of the kingdom of God was being revealed in his own life and work. It is clear from the gospels that this proved to be very different from what most of his listeners had expected, for the kingdom was revealed not as a tyrannical political force that would take over from Rome, but as a loving community of those whose only allegiance was to God, whose values in turn were quite different from the norms of conventional society.
● God's direct intervention is to be seen not only in the life and teaching of Jesus, but also in his death, resurrection and gift of the Holy Spirit to the church. It might well have been in these events that some of Jesus' own predictions about the last things were fulfilled – for example, the statement that some of his disciples would see the kingdom coming with power before they died (Mark 9:1).
● Since there is so much variety in the language used by Jesus to describe the kingdom, its full understanding also requires a similarly broad and comprehensive interpretative framework. The kingdom can arrive secretly, like the yeast working in the dough (Matthew 13:33), or it can come by the sudden appearance of Christ in glory, as at the expected second coming (Mark 13).

The kingdom of God and the kingdom of heaven

One of the striking facts about Matthew's Gospel is that it consistently uses the term 'kingdom of heaven' to describe the subject of Jesus' teaching. The only exceptions to this are in Matthew 12:28; 19:24; 21:31 and 21:43, where we find the term 'kingdom of God', which is used throughout Mark and Luke.

On the basis of this distinction, some interpreters have thought they could differentiate two quite separate phases in Jesus' teaching. But, in fact, there can be no doubt that the two terms refer to the same thing. This can be demonstrated quite easily by comparing the same statements in Matthew and in the other two synoptic gospels. For example, whereas Mark summarizes Jesus' message as 'the kingdom of God is at hand; repent' (Mark 1:15), Matthew has, 'Repent, for the kingdom of heaven is at hand' (Matthew 4:17). The two statements appear in exactly the same context (the beginning of Jesus' teaching ministry), and it is obvious that they are different versions of the same saying. There are many other examples of the same thing.

The most obvious explanation of this variety of expression is the fact that Matthew was writing for Jewish readers, whereas Mark and Luke were both writing for a predominantly non-Jewish readership. The Jewish tradition had always avoided direct use of the name of God in case people should unwittingly find themselves breaking the commandment, 'You shall not take the name of the Lord your God in vain' (Exodus 20:7). To minimize the possibilities of this happening, they often used other terms instead, and 'heaven' was a favourite substitute for 'God'. Matthew, therefore, speaks of 'the kingdom of heaven' in order to avoid offence to his readers. Gentiles, however, had no such reservations, and to them a term like 'kingdom of heaven' would have been unnecessarily complicated, if not altogether meaningless, so Mark and Luke use the term 'kingdom of God' instead.

It might be thought that since 'kingdom of heaven' was the most natural term for Jewish believers to use, this would be the one originally used by Jesus himself, and later adapted for non-Jews by Mark and Luke. But the likelihood is that Jesus actually spoke of the 'kingdom of God', and Matthew has adapted this to 'kingdom of heaven' for his own purposes. There are two reasons for thinking this:

● In general, Jesus never showed any reticence in speaking about God. Not only did he claim to know God in a close and personal way, he also dared to place relationships with God in the intimate context of family imagery, thinking of himself as a child and God as a parent.

● There are, as we have seen, four instances in Matthew where the term 'kingdom of God' is actually used. This can readily be understood if we suppose that Matthew overlooked these four occurrences of the word, but it is really impossible to think that in just these four cases he changed an original 'kingdom of heaven' into 'kingdom of God' for the benefit of his Jewish readers.

7 Jesus the Teacher

In the ancient world, teachers were always given a place of special importance. Roman and Greek cultures had a long tradition of philosophical schools, going back to the time – centuries before Jesus – when eager students had sat at the feet of intellectual giants such as Plato or Socrates, hoping to discover the meaning of life. Though times had changed, when the earliest disciples of Jesus took their message out into the great cities of the Roman empire, there was still no shortage of people who were happy to spend time listening to a good teacher.

Jesus himself never set foot in ancient Greece or Rome, but he, too, was brought up in a culture that placed great value on the spoken word. There were books, of course, predominant among which was the Hebrew Bible, the subject of intense study by professional students of the Law (scribes), who devoted themselves to becoming familiar with the ancient scriptures, and then sharing their learning with the rest of the people. But most ordinary people had to learn by listening, not reading. They heard the scriptures as they were read in worship each sabbath – a process that would be accompanied by a translation from the original Hebrew into the Aramaic they normally spoke (and which eventually led to the production of written Aramaic versions, the Targums). And, above all, they listened to the exhortations of the rabbis as they sought to explain what the requirements of the Law meant in terms of everyday life and behaviour.

Everyone recognized Jesus as a religious teacher. Not only his disciples, but also his opponents, and people in general, referred to him as a rabbi. He had the opportunity to teach in the local synagogues, and in the temple at Jerusalem, as well as speaking in fields and market places wherever he went. People came to ask Jesus for his opinion on points of law and religion, in much the same way as they did with the other rabbis. In response to questions, he dealt with matters such as divorce and marriage (Mark 10:1–12), adultery (John 7:53 – 8:11), family quarrels (Luke 12:13–15), and paying taxes (Mark 12:13–17), as well as more theological matters such as the commandments (Mark 12:28–34), belief in resurrection (Mark 12:18–27), or the reasons for undeserved suffering (John 9:2–3).

The Jewish people had a long tradition of such teaching. The Hebrew Bible itself was no doubt handed on by word of mouth for many generations before it was eventually written down, and much of it consists of teaching that was originally delivered orally. The prophets of the Old Testament were predominantly speakers, not writers, while the pithy sayings contained in a book like Proverbs were obviously the sort of everyday wisdom that would be passed on verbally, in the home, from one generation to another. The spoken word was always held in high esteem, and even in the second century we find Papias, leader of the Christian community at Hierapolis in Asia Minor, writing that 'what was to be got from books was not so profitable to me as what came from the living and abiding voice' (reported in Eusebius, *Ecclesiastical History* III.39). Perhaps this explains why it took the early Christians so long to get around to writing the gospels: apart from the fact that many of them were illiterate, they actually preferred to listen than to read.

Jesus' teaching was characterized by memorable stories and sayings. To hold people's attention, a teacher must be interesting, and Jesus was an expert at this. His style did not centre on abstract theological truths, but on the living experience of his hearers. As a creative thinker himself, he recognized the power of storytelling. Stories seize the imagination. But they also create an open space in which people can reflect, and draw their own conclusions. No two people take exactly the same lesson out of a story. Jesus obviously had this art of communication highly developed, for people immediately recognized that he was different from other teachers (Mark 1:22). Other rabbis often insisted their disciples should learn their teachings off by heart. But Jesus gave people freedom to think for themselves, and encouraged them to work out what God was saying to them personally, in their own particular circumstances of life.

The extended stories that Jesus told are generally referred to as parables. But much shorter sayings are also referred to in the same way. A popular proverb such as 'Physician, heal yourself!' (Luke 4:23) could be called a 'parable', as could the saying, 'Can one blind person guide another?' (Luke 6:39) – and the same terminology was applied to the more or less factual statement (perhaps originally some kind of riddle) that 'there is nothing outside a person that by going in can defile, but the things that come out are what defile' (Mark 7:15–16). There are many other places where Jesus used words to conjure up a vivid mental image that would help to communicate his message. In the Sermon on the Mount (Matthew 5 – 7) he spoke of salt, light, a city, birds and flowers, while in John's Gospel he described himself as 'the good shepherd' (10:1–18), 'the true vine' (15:1–11), 'bread of life' (6:35), or life-giving water (7:37–39), and talked of the disciples being called to reap a harvest (4:31–38). By using this kind of graphic language, Jesus ensured that his teachings would be remembered without difficulty. Instead of speaking in abstractions, as Western religious teachers have tended to do, Jesus always spoke of concrete situations and people.

The parables and their meaning

Though there is considerable diversity in Jesus' teaching style, even at those points where he is said to be teaching 'in parables', it is usual and convenient to reserve the word 'parable' for actual stories that Jesus told.

Parable or allegory?

For centuries, the usual way of understanding these story parables was to think of them as 'allegories'. An allegory is a detailed account of one subject, written in such a way that it appears to be about something altogether different. John Bunyan's *Pilgrim's Progress* is a well-known example of this kind of writing. In this book Bunyan seems to be telling the story of someone on a journey, but as the narrative unfolds the journey is so extraordinary, and the characters so much larger than life, that it soon becomes obvious he is not writing about a journey at all, but actually describing the things that might happen in the life of a Christian, from the beginning of discipleship right through to the end of life.

There are some examples of this kind of teaching in the New Testament. In John's Gospel, for example, there is the allegory of the vine and its branches (15:1–11). In this story Jesus is ostensibly explaining the means by which a vine bears grapes on its branches, but when he begins to talk about the branch of a vine deciding to cut itself off from the main stem of the plant, it becomes obvious that he is not really giving a lesson on how to grow grapes, but talking about what it might mean to be one of his disciples.

Though there are a few examples of allegories in the gospels, in most cases this method of understanding the parables is neither faithful to the original intention of Jesus' teaching, nor particularly enlightening. A good example of the dangers of such interpretation can be found in the parable of the good Samaritan (Luke 10:25–37). According to Luke, this story was told by Jesus in answer to the question, 'Who is my neighbour?' and at the end, Jesus told his questioner to behave as the Samaritan had done in the story. Yet, within a very short time, Christians were applying an allegorical interpretation to the story, totally losing sight of the fact that it was an answer to a practical question.

According to St Augustine (AD354–430), the traveller who went down from Jerusalem to Jericho was Adam. Jerusalem represented the heavenly city of peace from which he fell, and Jericho was the human

A shepherd leading a flock. Jesus often told stories based on things that would be familiar to his hearers in rural communities.

Where to find Jesus' parables in the gospels

	Matthew	Mark	Luke
Salt	5:13		
Light under a bushel	5:14–16	4:21–23	8:16–17
			11:33–36
Houses on rock and on sand	7:24–27		6:47–49
New cloth on an old garment	9:16	2:21	5:36
New wine in old wineskins	9:17	2:22	5:37–39
Sower and soils	13:1–23	4:1–20	8:4–15
Weeds in the field	13:24–30, 36–43		
Mustard seed	13:31–32	4:30–32	13:18–19
Yeast	13:33		13:20–21
Hidden treasure	13:44		
Pearl of great value	13:45–46		
Drag-net	13:47–50		
Lost sheep	18:12–14		15:1–7
Unforgiving servant	18:23–35		
Workers in the vineyard	20:1–16		
Two sons	21:28–31		
Wicked tenants	21:33–41	12:1–9	20:9–16
Wedding feast	22:1–14		
Fig tree as herald of summer	24:32–33	13:28–29	21:29–31
Ten maidens	25:1–13		
Three servants	25:14–30		
Sheep and goats	25:31–46		
Faithful servant	25:45–51		12:42–48
Seedtime to harvest		4:26–29	
Creditor and the debtors			7:41–43
Good Samaritan			10:25–37
Friend at midnight			11:5–8
Rich fool			12:13–21
Alert servants			12:35–40
Fig tree without figs			13:6–9
Places of honour at the wedding feast			14:7–14
Great feast			14:15–24
Counting the cost			14:28–33
Lost coin			15:8–10
Prodigal son			15:11–32
Unjust servant			16:1–8
Rich man and Lazarus			16:19–31
The master and his servant			17:7–10
Unjust judge			18:1–8
The Pharisee and the tax collector			18:9–14
Gold coins			19:11–27

Some of the 'I am' sayings of John's Gospel are similar to parables:

Bread of life	6:35–40
Light of the world	8:12–13
Door	10:7–10
Good shepherd	10:11–18
Resurrection and life	11:17–27
Way, truth and life	14:1–7
True vine	15:1–11

mortality that he inherited as a result of his fall. The robbers were the devil and his angels, who stripped him of his immortality, while the priest and the Levite who passed by on the other side were the priesthood and ministry of the Old Testament, which could not save him. The good Samaritan was Christ himself, and his binding of the traveller's wounds was the restraint of sin. The oil and wine that he poured in were the comfort of hope and encouragement to work hard. The beast was the flesh in which Christ came to earth. The inn was the church, and the innkeeper the apostle Paul. The two pence he was paid were the commandments to love God and neighbour (Augustine, *Quaestiones Evangeliorum* 2.19).

This is undoubtedly an ingenious account of Augustine's understanding of the story of Christian salvation, but it has little connection with the story of the good Samaritan. These 'spiritual meanings' are read into the story rather than coming out of it, and in Augustine's version, the original question of Jesus' hearer is not even addressed, let alone answered!

The point of the parables

It is surprising that this method of interpretation was not seriously challenged until the end of the nineteenth century. When scholars began to read the New Testament as a historical document, they realized that Jesus probably used parables in much the same way as other teachers in the ancient world. After comparing Jesus' methods of teaching with the way parables were used in Greek literature, Adolf Jülicher suggested that Jesus used them in much the same way as a modern teacher might use an illustration. Far from being intended to convey a hidden meaning in every detail, they were simply meant to illustrate and drive home a particular point.

In the parable of the good Samaritan, for instance, the main point was that the person who proved to be a real neighbour was not a religious Jew, but a member of a despised and hated social group, the Samaritans. All the other details in the story, about the ass and the inn, the oil and the wine, were an imaginative description of the scene to make the story realistic and interesting, but they had no intrinsic connection with the main point of what Jesus was trying to say.

Once this fact was appreciated, it soon disposed of some real problems of interpretation, for in some parables the main characters are not the kinds of people whose actions Christians have ever felt they ought to copy. There was the unjust steward, for example, who gained his employer's approval by manipulating the accounts to his own advantage (Luke 16:1–8). Was Jesus really commending this sort of behaviour? Of course not. The main point of the parable was that people should copy this steward's far-sighted determination to be prepared for a crisis in life, and the other details in the story were there just to give a realistic portrayal of an imaginary situation.

Following on from this important insight by Jülicher, other scholars went back to the parables of Jesus, in an effort to see what difference this new approach might make to the recovery of their meaning. Notable among these scholars were C.H. Dodd in England and Joachim Jeremias in Germany. They both agreed with Jülicher that a parable generally had only one lesson to teach, though they also argued that the subject of the parables was not generalized moral truth (as Jülicher had thought) but the arrival of the kingdom of God. However, some of the other assumptions that Dodd and Jeremias adopted from Jülicher have not been so widely upheld in subsequent study:

■ Though it is true, in general, that each of the parables of Jesus has only one main point, it can be misleading to insist that no parable can ever have more than one. Some of them quite obviously do have a number of lessons to teach.

In the parable of the talents, for example, at least two simple points seem to be made (Matthew 25:14–30; Luke 19:11–27). The story tells of a householder who is going away and divides the family fortune among the servants for safe keeping. On the householder's return, the servants are rewarded in different ways, depending on the uses to which they have put the money entrusted to them. The main point of this story is to emphasize the connection between individual responsibility and final accountability, but there is another emphasis that might be just as important: the householder far exceeded any known legal or moral obligations by generously entrusting the property to the servants in the first place. The parable of the wedding feast seems to make exactly the same two points (Matthew 22:1–14; Luke 14:15–24), and in the overall context of Jesus' teaching, both points correspond to significant statements that Jesus wished to make about generosity and accountability in relation to God.

■ Again, while most parables are not to be given an allegorical interpretation, this does not apply to them all. As it is reported in the various gospels, the parable of the sower incorporates an allegorical explanation of its meaning, for the different kinds of ground are said to correspond to different types of people hearing Jesus' message (Matthew 13:1–23; Mark 4:1–20; Luke 8:4–15). It has often been argued that this allegorical application does not go back to Jesus himself, but originated with the earliest Christians at a time when they were trying to understand why only a few people responded to their preaching. There is no doubt that this parable could be used to help answer a question like that. But if this interpretation of the parable is rejected as being only a secondary meaning, perhaps added later (and therefore, by implication, of lesser value), there is still a need to explain what the main point might have been as Jesus first told it. A survey of the various attempts that have been made in commentaries on the gospels reveals that it is very difficult to

Parable of the Sower, woodcut by Albrecht Dürer from a series published in a prayer book in 1503.

imagine a different meaning for it, and many commentators follow a tortuous route to end up back where the gospel writers started.

There is an even more striking example of the apparent need for some allegorical understanding in the parable of the wicked tenants (Matthew 21:33–45; Mark 12:1–12; Luke 20:9–19). The story here concerns a vineyard owner who let the property out to some tenants for a rent that included part of the annual crop of grapes. Yet, when the owner's servants arrived to collect the agreed share of the crop, they were beaten up and killed. After this had happened several times the owner's son was sent, in the hope that he might be given more respect – but exactly the same thing happened to him. In the end it was inevitable that, when the owner was forced to pay a personal visit, the tenants would be thrown out of the vineyard and punished. In this story, an allegorical interpretation seems to be the only meaning possible; if Israel was not the vineyard, if the prophets were not the servants, if the owner who sent them was not God, and if Jesus was not the son, then the whole parable loses its point.

It seems wise, therefore, to adopt a more flexible approach, and recognize that, though the parables do not normally need an allegorical interpretation, some of them might.

■ Dodd and Jeremias emphasized the importance of understanding the parables in their original historical context. Because of their insistence on this point they invested a lot of energy in trying to uncover the original meanings of the parables for Jesus' hearers, then later for the Christians who first wrote them down. This was a natural procedure for them to adopt, as they were both committed to the value of the historical-critical method, believing it to be the most reliable way of interpreting these ancient texts. The strengths and weaknesses of this methodology are discussed in more detail in a later chapter. There is no doubt that much can be said in support of the view that in order to understand what the New Testament might mean today, it will help to know what it meant to those who first read it. But in terms of their literary style or genre, the parables are quite different from most other sections of the New Testament. Though the descriptive language they embody finds its fullest significance in the social context in which they were formulated, the reader does not need to understand every nuance of their imagery in order to grasp the core of the message. Stories like those in Luke 15, describing the shepherd who had lost a sheep, the woman who had lost a precious coin, and the parent whose child ran away from home, speak to human experience in any culture. They do not need particular acquaintance with first-century Palestine before their implications can be understood. The parables of Jesus are more like works of art than discourses on religion, and like all art their characters and situations have a correspondingly universal quality that can be understood by anyone, for they deal with the basic condition of what it means to be human. Their meaning and challenge is self-evident to all who read or hear them.

The parables and their message

What is the message and the challenge of the parables? In the widest sense, the subject of the parables is the coming of 'God's kingdom'. This is clearly indicated by the many parables which start with the words, 'The kingdom of God is like...'. Because of this, different interpreters have seen various meanings in the parables, in accordance with their particular understandings of what they have believed the kingdom to be. Those like Albert Schweitzer, who thought the spectacular and immediate intervention of God in the affairs of human society to be the most important characteristic of the kingdom, have naturally been inclined to understand the teaching of the parables in that context. On the other hand, those attracted to the views of C.H. Dodd have found no difficulty in finding traces of a realized eschatology in the parables.

But the real message of the parables is rather more complex than either of these alternatives suggests. When they are all considered as a group, their message can be seen to focus on four main subjects, each of them emphasizing some particular aspect of 'the kingdom of God' and its impact on the lives of those who are a part of it.

The kingdom and its ruler

Most communities are strongly influenced by the character of their leader or leaders. Harsh, authoritarian rulers will have little difficulty in persuading their people to adopt the same attitudes, while the example set by liberal, humane rulers will usually encourage their people to share a similar viewpoint. The kingdom of God is no exception to this: it takes its character and form from the God who is its sovereign.

Several parables, therefore, illustrate significant aspects of God's own nature. The story of the lost sheep underlines the fundamental fact of God's love for the undeserving ('grace'): God takes the initiative in finding those who, for whatever reason, have lost their way and need personal restoration. God is concerned when even a single person loses their way in life, and has an irresistible urge to go after that lost one. The other parables in Luke 15, of the lost coin and the lost son, also stress the same theme of God's unconditional love for all humanity. Even when people get themselves into a mess, like the lost son, they will not be abandoned by God, who cannot rest until they have been brought home to a place of safety.

The precise extent of God's generosity is illustrated by the story about the workers in the vineyard (Matthew 20:1–16). In this parable, Jesus told of an employer who hired workers for a vineyard. They started work at different times of the day, so that when the time came for them

Sarcophagus of Livia Primitiva, inscribed with early Christian symbols: fish, the good shepherd and an anchor. It was found in Rome and dates from early in the 3rd century.

to receive their pay, some had only worked for an hour, while others had worked the whole day. But they were all given the same amount of money! Because they had all agreed in advance what they were to receive, the employer was not cheating anyone, and those who started early in the day got the level of pay they had negotiated before they began. But the difference was that the employer was unexpectedly generous to those who began work late in the day, by giving them as much as if they had been there from the start. This, said Jesus, is what the kingdom of heaven is like: God is overwhelmingly generous, and those who scramble into the kingdom at the last minute receive as warm a welcome as those who were first through the door.

This parable could, of course, be read to imply that God is unfair, for surely those who arrived early *did* deserve more than those who came to work late in the day. This was the kind of question Jülicher was trying to answer when he suggested that a parable normally has only one point. In the case of this parable he was undoubtedly correct, for there are many other sayings of Jesus which show God is overwhelmingly responsive to all human needs. There is, for example, the story of the friend who requested food at midnight, which is used by Luke to emphasize that God is only too willing to answer prayers: 'ask, and you will receive; seek, and you will find; knock, and the door will be opened to you' (Luke 11:5–9). Another example would be the story of the unjust judge, which makes a similar point (Luke 18:1–8). Then there are the

statements in the Sermon on the Mount which, though not story
parables, are certainly parables in the wider meaning of the word. 'Look
at the birds of the air: they neither sow nor reap nor gather into barns,
and yet your heavenly Father feeds them. Are you not of more value
than they?... And why are you anxious about clothing? Consider the
lilies... how they grow; they neither toil nor spin... if God so clothes the
grass of the field... can you not expect God to give even better clothing
to you – you of little faith?' (Matthew 6:26, 28, 30). God cares about
people, even down to the smallest details. In the course of his ministry,
Jesus met many people – religious ones among them – who were
actually incapable of accepting his message because this emphasis on
God's generous love did not match their preconceived expectations of
how God should work. Many felt that God's love should be dispensed
on a *quid pro quo* basis, and those who were the most righteous should
have the first claim on it. But Jesus turned such ideas upside-down and,
as a result, those who were apparently the least righteous frequently
found his message easier to accept.

The emphasis on the close, personal relationship that exists between
God and those who commit themselves to doing things God's way is
one of the most strikingly original parts of Jesus' teaching. Jesus himself
addressed God as 'Father'. In John's Gospel, this way of articulating Jesus'
relationship to God is often used to explain Jesus' nature as divine (John
1:14, 18; 5:43; 8:19). But the other three gospels more often accentuate
the character of the relationship, implying that God can be addressed
and known in the same intimate way that a human father might be
addressed by a child. Jesus used the word 'Abba', the Aramaic term for
father that would be used in the home, and he encouraged disciples to
do the same when speaking to God in prayer (Matthew 6:9; Luke 11:2).
This way of addressing God was apparently unique: though in Jewish
tradition God could on occasion be referred to as 'Father', that title
would generally be qualified by some reference to God's holiness and
majesty, thereby distancing the image from the familiar family language
that Jesus used. Jesus' parables repeatedly portray a God who is not
remote and out of contact with the real world, but a God with whom
ordinary people – even sinful people – can enjoy a close, personal and
loving relationship. Like the best kind of parent, God watches over and
cares for all those who commit themselves to living by the standards of
the kingdom.

The continuing appropriateness of this terminology can be
questioned on the basis of its apparent endorsement of a patriarchal
world-view, and there is certainly no denying that the notion of God as
the male parent has been utilized by power-hungry men, even in the
church, as a way of asserting their sexual dominance over women. This
is one of those instances in which it is important to recall that we are
dealing with a human metaphor to express something that can only be
described through analogy and pictorial language. To imagine that Jesus

was implying God is actually male is to misunderstand the purpose of the text. God is beyond human categories of experience and, therefore, in a significant sense, is without gender. But if God is relational, then it is inevitable that images from human relationships will be used to describe God, however inadequate they might eventually turn out to be. Jesus does, of course, assume a particularly perfect form of family relationship between parent and child, which was not the experience of everyone in the ancient world, any more than it is today. But one of the key elements of his teaching on God is the way in which it challenges even the most perfect human relationships imaginable. In reality, the attributes of God as portrayed by Jesus are very far removed from the image of a patriarchal male wanting to control and dominate in a macho way. The relational qualities of which Jesus spoke regularly challenge traditional male stereotypes – and, in addition, Jesus was not averse to applying female imagery to himself on occasion (Matthew 23:37).

People in God's kingdom

To be a part of God's kingdom not only gives people the privilege of knowing God in an intimate and personal way, but also imposes certain responsibilities on them. A number of the stories Jesus told stress the kind of response required if people are to 'enter the kingdom'.

At the beginning of Mark, the main thrust of Jesus' teaching is summed up in the slogan, 'repent, and believe in the gospel' (1:15), and many of the stories told by Jesus underline the importance of being prepared for a radical change in lifestyle ('repenting') in order to become a member of God's kingdom. The story of the lost son, already mentioned, not only emphasizes the goodness and generosity of the loving parent, but also the importance of the child realizing his foolishness and being willing to change his way of life (Luke 15:11–32).

Repentance has never been a popular idea, for it involves the recognition of inadequacy and wrongdoing. It means a certain loss of face and moral credibility. But Jesus made it quite plain that being honest about personal failures is the starting point for any kind of meaningful relationship with God. There is the story of the Pharisee and the tax collector, who went to pray in the temple at the same time. The Pharisee prided himself on his moral and religious attainments – and told God so. The tax collector, however, was so conscious of his own unworthiness to speak to God at all that he could only cry out, 'God, have pity on me, a sinner!' But, said Jesus, 'the tax collector, and not the Pharisee, was in the right with God when he went home', because he recognized his own sinfulness and came to God with no spiritual pretensions (Luke 18:9–14). A similar point is made in the story of the rich fool, who thought that his wealth would place him in good standing with God (Luke 12:13–21). Moreover, Jesus made the teaching of these parables quite explicit in his statement that living God's way is not a matter for negotiation, but is something to be accepted in an attitude of childlike trust: 'Whoever does not receive the kingdom of God like a child will never enter it' (Luke 18:17; Mark 10:15).

Willingness to change, and forgiveness for the past, are not the end of the matter, however: they are only the beginning of a life lived according to the way God does things. In the kingdom, there is to be found a new kind of life, 'eternal life' or 'abundant life' as it is called in some of the sayings recorded in John's Gospel (3:15; 6:54; 10:28; 17:3). Life in the kingdom means a life that is empowered by God. Those who have chosen to live by God's values commit themselves to putting them all into practice on a daily basis, and this has unmistakable repercussions for their lifestyles:

■ It means they will be far more concerned with what God thinks about them than what other people might think. This comes out especially in their attitudes to spirituality. Though some might accept God's standards rather reluctantly, struggling to fulfil their own best aspirations, their devotion is preferable to that of others who make a great show of serving God, but in reality are unprepared to change in any profound way (Matthew 21:28–32). God's people must live in the spirit of the widow who secretly put her last coins into the offering box at the temple (Mark 12:41–44; Luke 21:1–4). They will not behave ostentatiously so that others will applaud their much-publicized goodness, but will work and live quietly, and without self-advertising, knowing that God – the only one who truly matters – will reward them (Matthew 5:4–6, 16).

■ This requirement is not, however, to become an excuse for doing nothing. Those who want to adopt God's way of doing things for themselves must make good use of God's provision for them. They must act responsibly, using the resources God has given them and, like the unjust steward, they should always be ready to account for their actions (Matthew 25:14–30; Luke 16:1–8; 19:11–27).

■ Those who imagine they have arrived in some moral or spiritual sense have scarcely begun to comprehend God's ways, for being a part of the kingdom is about journeying with God in the expectation that new possibilities will be discovered all the time. Two of the shortest parables illustrate this: the stories about the hidden treasure and the pearl (Matthew 13:44–45). Someone who finds a field full of treasure will have no hesitation in selling all they possess in order to be able to buy that field. Or, similarly, a merchant looking for fine pearls who comes across an especially good specimen will sacrifice everything to be able to own it. God's kingdom is like that: the journey might be demanding and difficult, but it is always worthwhile in the end.

The kingdom and the community

Though Jesus was clearly offering personal empowerment to those who would respond to him, it would be wrong to imagine that his message was confined to a purely personal or individualistic spirituality. A large part of his teaching concerns the relationship of disciples to the wider

community, and to one another. Indeed, in the parable of the
unforgiving servant, Jesus seems to suggest that the way God deals
with us will in some way depend on the way we deal with other people
(Matthew 18:21–35). Then there is also Jesus' statement that loving our
neighbour is the second most important duty after loving God (Matthew
22:39; Mark 12:31).

Those who accept God's standards must behave like God, and since
God's generosity extends even to the outcasts of society, Jesus' disciples
should be the same. The good Samaritan in the parable is not just an
imaginary person to be admired, but a role model for real-life situations
(Luke 10:25–37). Jesus put this into practice himself, by taking his
message to the outcasts of society. This was such an unexpected reversal
of the role of religious teachers that the disciples could hardly have
failed to realize the kingdom of God was indeed present already in this
person they had chosen to follow. Not only did the kingdom mean a
new relationship with God, but it also bound them to one another in
a new community of caring service and mutual love.

Future aspects of the kingdom
Finally, a number of parables refer to the coming of God's kingdom in
the future. They depict Jesus returning as the heavenly, supernatural
Son of man, and speak of the final judgment of men and women.

Some have thought this was just a picturesque way of presenting
the challenge of Jesus' message as it came to his first hearers. But, in
view of the strongly apocalyptic tone of much of the language used, it is
hard to escape the conclusion that it would have been understood by
Jesus' hearers as relating to a future time, when God's authority and
sovereignty would be made visible in some kind of tangible way.

Some parables depict a great day of reckoning, when those who
merely profess to serve God, but do not actually do so, will be sorted out
from those who really carry out God's will. This is the main lesson of the
parables about the corn and the weeds, the fishing net, and the sheep
and the goats (Matthew 13:24–30, 47–50; 25:31–46). In other parables,
the future climax of the kingdom is depicted as a feast. This kind of
imagery had often been used to describe the coming blessings of the
messianic age. But Jesus' pictures make it clear that not everyone will
gain admission. Indeed, the parable of the great supper suggests that the
conventionally religious will have no place in it at all, and those who
share in its blessings are more likely to come in from the streets than
from the sanctuaries (Matthew 22:1–14; Luke 14:15–24).

Matthew's Gospel emphasizes the responsibilities that all this places
on those who profess to be trying to live in God's way. Since no one
knows the day or the hour when the final accounting will take place,
they must be in a state of constant readiness, like the attendants of a
bride waiting for the bridegroom to arrive at a wedding (Matthew
25:1–13).

This element in Jesus' teaching transcends the sharp distinctions conventionally drawn between what is future and what is present. Because Jesus has come, the kingdom of God, understood as God's way of doing things, has already arrived. Those who are willing to follow that vision are, even now, a part of the kingdom, which means that whatever else might be revealed in the future will be not so much a new start, as the final working out of all the implications of something that, in its essence, is already here. Though the new way of being that will emerge from all this might seem to have a small and insignificant origin, it is the kind of beginning that must inevitably produce spectacular growth – like that of the mustard seed, 'the smallest seed in the world' which grows into one of the biggest plants of all (Matthew 13:31–32; Mark 4:30–34; Luke 13:18–19).

Why did Jesus teach in parables?

There is a statement in Mark 4:11–12 which seems to suggest that Jesus told parables with the deliberate intention of making his teaching obscure to those who were not already his disciples, so that, echoing the words of Isaiah, 'they may indeed see but not perceive, and may indeed hear but not understand; lest they should turn again, and be forgiven'. Such an idea is so contrary to all we know of Jesus that some explanation seems to be required. Many suggestions have been put forward, of which we mention two:
● The most popular explanation is that this was not a genuine saying of Jesus, but reflects the conclusions of the early church as they tried to explain why Jesus' message had been rejected by the religious establishment within Judaism. It was, they said, a part of the providential wisdom of God, who had always intended this to happen. There are, however, two arguments against this view.

Firstly, it was probably only the first generation of Christians who were deeply concerned that the Jews had rejected Jesus. The church was Jewish only at a very early stage of its development, and after the destruction of Jerusalem by the Romans in AD70 Jewish Christianity almost ceased to exist. It certainly had little

influence on the church at large. This means that the problem was most acute not long after the events of Jesus' own lifetime – and the nearer we are in time to Jesus himself, the less room there must be for the church making additions and alterations to his teaching.

Secondly, Matthew's Gospel has a similar saying, quoting the same passage from Isaiah. Since we know Matthew was especially interested in the relative status of Jews and Christians, we would expect him to have preserved exactly the same words as Mark, if this statement was indeed concerned with the Jewish rejection of Jesus. But in fact the statement in Matthew's Gospel has a slightly different implication. There Jesus says, 'This is why I speak to them in parables, because seeing they do not see, and hearing they do not hear, nor do they understand' (Matthew 13:13).
● A second possible explanation takes its starting point from this statement in Matthew. On this understanding we need to suppose that the word translated '*so that... they may see*' in Mark is actually meant to be the beginning of a factual statement, much as it is in Matthew. Evidence for this view can be drawn from a comparison of the Greek that Mark wrote with the Aramaic statements that most probably lay behind it. Thus the statement describes not the *purpose* of teaching in

The parables and their hearers

Some scholars have spent a lot of time trying to discover the exact 'life situation' (*Sitz im Leben*) of the various parables, thinking that by doing so their immediate meaning will be easier to grasp. But, in most cases, it is not possible to discover the precise situations in which Jesus told particular stories; like the other parts of the gospels, the parables have been recorded not as part of an exhaustive account of Jesus' life, but as a message explaining Jesus' teaching and its continuing relevance to the needs of the world and the church.

Very occasionally the parables have a story attached to them, and this perhaps gives some indication of their original life setting in the ministry of Jesus. There is, for example, no good reason for doubting

parables, but the inevitable *consequences* of doing so. Jesus was pointing out that the parables will inevitably separate those who listen to them with spiritual insight from those who are spiritually blind.

This explanation is the more likely. It fits in with what we saw in a previous chapter about Jesus' attitude to keeping his messiahship secret. It also fits well with the nature of Jesus' teaching, in particular the centrality of storytelling. Indeed, the way in which this alleged 'problem' has been defined highlights one of the weaknesses of Western scholarship and its over reliance on cognitive, analytical approaches to understanding truth. In the context of abstract philosophical discourse, there would indeed be a contradiction between saying that a set of propositions both revealed and concealed something at one and the same time. But storytelling is a completely different form of communication, which allows more flexibility in the exploration of meanings, and deliberately creates space for different possible responses in a way that the methods of traditional philosophical argument do not. Almost by definition, truth is both hidden and revealed when it is embodied in story. This phenomenon is found throughout all cultures and in all periods of history. On one hand, stories can be understood as simple narratives, told exclusively for their entertainment

value. On the other hand, they generally invite those who hear them to engage at a different level in order to see them as reflections of life and its challenges. Jesus' parables fit this model exactly: many people could listen to what Jesus was saying and see nothing in it but a simple tale. In that sense, the core of his message was 'hidden' by the story form. But for those who were committed to the search for spiritual meaning, the very same stories could open up new spaces in which to explore the implications of his message, and to reflect on the nature of God and the kingdom, which Jesus had come to announce.

that the parable of the good Samaritan was given in answer to the question 'Who is my neighbour?' addressed to Jesus by a religious leader. Similarly, the parable about the unforgiving servant makes perfect sense when reported in the form of a reply to Peter's question about how often he should forgive someone who was offending him (Matthew 18:21–35). Likewise, it is hard to imagine a more appropriate setting for the story of the rich fool than as part of the answer to a question about the best way of dividing a legacy (Luke 12:13–21).

Some of the parables appear in different contexts in different gospels. The parable of the lost sheep appears in Luke along with the parables of the lost coin and lost son as an answer to the Pharisees' complaints about the bad company Jesus was keeping (15:1–7). In Matthew the same parable is told as an encouragement to the disciples

---

Did Jesus intend to found a church?

People have often asked whether Jesus intended to found a church. There are two statements in Matthew's Gospel that seem to suggest that he did (16:18–20; 18:17). But some scholars believe these statements come from Matthew himself, and not directly from the teaching of Jesus. Albert Schweitzer, for example, found it impossible to think that Jesus intended to found a church, for he believed that Jesus expected the immediate end of the world. But even those who do not share this opinion have often rejected the notion that Jesus was intent on starting any kind of organization. The theological liberals of the early twentieth century viewed Jesus as a simple ethical teacher and, because they regarded the concept of a church as inconsistent with this, they concluded that it was a later, alien intrusion into the originally simple gospel.

Though very few people today would agree with this point of view, it does highlight two important facts that need to be borne in mind in any discussion about Jesus and the idea of 'church':
● 'The church' need not imply the kind of religious hierarchy that evolved in the second century and is familiar in institutionalized Christianity today. Jesus

spoke of two or three people gathered in his name (Matthew 18:20).
● In the strict sense it is probably anachronistic to speak of the existence of 'the church' in the lifetime of Jesus. The church in the New Testament saw itself as more than just a social grouping of like-minded people organized as a religious society. Its own self-consciousness was of being a group of people who shared in a common life because of the events of the life, death and resurrection of Jesus himself, and their participation in the empowerment that came from the Holy Spirit. In this specific sense, therefore, the church could only have come into existence after the foundational events of Jesus' death and resurrection, which is why the New Testament depicts the pouring out of the Holy Spirit on the Day of Pentecost as the real 'founding' of the church (Acts 1:8; 2:1–4).

Clearly, then, any statement about Jesus as the church's founder needs to be carefully qualified. But, at the same time, there are strong indications in the gospels that he certainly intended to form a community of those who followed him:
● All the gospels show Jesus as the person in whom the messianic promises of the Old Testament had been fulfilled. The Messiah had come in Jesus, and a significant element of traditional

to be faithful 'shepherds' of the church (18:12–14). Given what we know about the respective aims and objectives of Matthew and Luke, it seems likely that it was these writers who chose the appropriate context for the parables within their own narratives – though it is, of course, not inconceivable that Jesus might have told the same story more than once, and drawn different lessons from it on each occasion. Storytellers regularly do so.

But the fact is that these parables are exceptional in having any background information at all attached to them, and nothing is known about the circumstances in which most of the parables were first recounted. This is accentuated by the way they are collected together in blocks in the various gospels. Matthew has a complete section of his gospel devoted entirely to parables (chapter 13); Mark contains a similar

---

expectation was the belief that the Messiah would set up a new community, in which people could enjoy a close relationship with God as well as with one another. No matter how vaguely Jesus might have seen himself as a messianic figure, it would be a natural part of such an image for him to envisage the foundation of a community among his followers. In addition, Jesus' favourite name for himself, Son of man, also contains a corporate dimension. It is probably incorrect to say, as some have done, that every time Jesus used this name he meant to include his disciples along with himself, but there is no doubt that in the book of Daniel the Son of man was not simply an individual, but a representative member of 'the saints of the most high' (Daniel 7:13–18).
● When Jesus describes his own work and the work of God's kingdom, his words often suggest that he is talking about a group of people linked not only to God, but to one another. For example, he speaks of himself as a shepherd, implying that there would be a flock of sheep under his care (Luke 12:32; John 10:1–18). In comparing himself to a vine and his disciples to its branches, he must have been meaning to suggest that the branches would have some kind of connection with each other as well as with the main stem (John 15:1–11). Many of

the things Jesus says about the kingdom would be difficult to understand without assuming that he had a visible group of followers in mind (Matthew 23:13; Luke 16:16), while his ethical teaching is invariably concerned with life in a community (Matthew 5:22; 7:3–5).
● There is also the striking fact that some of the parables suggest the kingdom of God is to be a visible entity. Parables like the mustard seed (Mark 4:30–32), the corn and the weeds (Matthew 13:24–30), the fishing net (Matthew 13:47–50), the workers in the vineyard (Matthew 20:1–16), and the wedding feast (Matthew 22:1–14) clearly imply some kind of organized structure.

While it might be doubted whether Jesus ever expected the church to become the sort of establishment it did in the days of Christendom, it is certainly reasonable to conclude that he did expect there to be a continuing community of his followers, and that the kind of churches his disciples later founded were an attempt to give tangible expression to that.

(though not identical) collection (chapter 4), while Luke also has a long section predominantly composed of parables (13:18 – 16:31).

In the end, the real meaning of the parables must always be bound up with the challenge they bring to those who read or hear them. They offer a series of pictures of what life might be like when God's ways of doing things are taken seriously, and they invite their hearers to commit themselves unconditionally to living this way. It is only as the readers identify themselves with the lost sheep, the wicked tenants, or the person who discovers a field of hidden treasure, that their full impact is felt. In the last analysis, the parables – like most stories – are an invitation into new territory, an opportunity to reimagine the world as we know and experience it, in the light of Jesus' portrayal of God's character.

8 Signs of the Kingdom

Some of the most striking parts of the gospels are the stories about Jesus performing miracles, as they are usually known. He healed the sick (Mark 1:29–34), exercised authority over the forces of nature (Mark 4:35–41), and on occasion even raised the dead (Mark 5:21–43; Luke 7:11–17; John 11:1 44). Of all the subjects related to Jesus, this is the one that has presented most problems for readers of the gospel stories in recent centuries. It is generally not difficult to understand Jesus' teaching about God and the kingdom, and even people who are unable to accept the truthfulness of what he said still frequently respect his ideals, and might even make a genuine effort to put some of them into practice. But when it comes to the miracles, many people, including some Christians, have found it hard to imagine that these stories recorded in the gospels could actually have taken place.

Influenced by the scientific rationalism that has permeated Western culture for the last 200 or 300 years, there has been a tendency to put the miracle stories down to the ignorance and superstition of ancient people. As the twentieth century progressed, this opinion became much less credible than it had seemed in the days of colonialism and empire building, when Western people were still generally convinced by the scientific-materialist world-view that enabled them to imagine their way of doing things was the most advanced form of understanding there could ever be. For people who held a low opinion of all cultures except their own, it was not difficult to dismiss the perceptions of ancient people as due to ignorance and superstition. Today, however, that kind of opinion can be seen for what it was: ethnic arrogance and a form of intellectual colonialism. There is plenty of evidence to show that ancient people were no more gullible or naïve than their modern counterparts. In addition, the more science has discovered, the more mysterious many things have turned out to be, illness and its cures being prominent among them. As knowledge of cultures outside the West has increased, it has become obvious that it is rationalism, with its insistence on 'logical' explanations of cause and effect that is the aberration, not the belief in a spiritual world that is beyond what we normally see and handle. When the majority of the world's people at all times and places have never had any hesitation in accepting the reality of such things, it is only an outmoded and defensive form of intellectual and cultural imperialism that will question it, which is why the rise of New Age spirituality, with its universalistic agenda, has so easily put the miraculous and the supernatural very firmly back onto the Western agenda.

It is all too easy to make our own presuppositions an excuse for failing to take serious account of the nature of the actual evidence for remarkable events. The question posed by the miracles of Jesus can hardly be given an adequate answer simply by reference to our own disposition not to believe in such things. Of course, in seeking to understand what was going on, we cannot return to a first-century mentality either, for believers can no more prove the truth of the miracles simply by reference to their presuppositions than unbelievers can disprove them by reference to their own rather different preconceptions. It is essential to take full account of whatever evidence might be available.

It is also important to have a reasonably clear understanding of what we understand a 'miracle' to be. Someone in a remote tribe might see a modern invention like television and regard it as a miracle. Another person will know how it works, and describe it differently. A mother with a long history of miscarriages and stillbirths may have a healthy baby, and she regards it as a miracle – while someone else can point to the statistics, and say it was bound to happen sooner or later. People can look at the same event and, depending on their perspective, make rather different assessments of what has taken place. For example, it is now known that there is a close link between mind and body, and even ailments that are very physical can, on occasion, have psychological roots. It would be surprising if some of the illnesses cured by Jesus were not psychosomatic, as we would say nowadays. Some gospel stories seem to hint as much – for instance, the account of how Jesus healed a woman with a haemorrhage merely by her touching his clothes (Mark 5:25–34) – or when he cured a blind man by mixing clay and placing it on his eyes (John 9:1–11).

The gospels themselves set the

Jesus healing the paralytic (Mark 2:1–5). From a 19th-century engraving.

miracles in a distinctive context right from the outset. In his sermon at the synagogue in Nazareth, Jesus referred to a passage from Isaiah which celebrated the fact that the messianic age would bring 'good news to the poor... liberty to the captives and recovery of sight to the blind' (Luke 4:18). Words were an important part of Jesus' message. But they were not the only element, and his deeds (including the miracles) played a significant role both in his popular appeal and the opposition that he encountered. It is not hard to discover some reasons for this. For part of the distinctiveness about Jesus' miracles was not so much what he did, but when he did it – and to whom. It is striking that the kind of people Jesus healed – the deaf, dumb, and lame – do not feature at all in contemporary stories of Jewish healers, though in Isaiah 35:5–6 (which was widely regarded as a messianic prophecy) these were the very things that were singled out as signs of the coming kingdom. The coincidence would not be lost on those who were suspicious of Jesus' intentions. Nor would it escape their attention that the circumstances in which he cured people often infringed traditional laws. Not only did Jesus heal people on the sabbath, but he also healed those who were non-people by conventional definitions of ritual purity: people of the wrong racial origins (such as the Gentile woman in Mark 7:24–30), or those who lived in the wrong kind of places (like the man in the Gentile graveyard in Mark 5:1–20), and others who by any definition were ritually impure (such as the woman with a permanent menstrual flow, Mark 5:25–34).

How could anyone of goodwill possibly be opposed to the healing of those who were suffering? That was the common sense question asked by Jesus when he cured a man with a paralysed hand in the synagogue (Mark 3:4). When expressed that way, any opposition would seem particularly perverse. But Jesus did not primarily heal people because he was sorry for them. He saw disadvantage of any kind as a sign that the power of Satan was at work – and so, for example he was 'filled with anger' at the sight of a man disfigured by leprosy (Mark 1:40–45). He did not however identify suffering with personal sin, or suggest that sufferers were somehow responsible for their own misfortune. On the contrary, when the Pharisees proposed that to him he categorically denied it (John 9:1–5). But if God's kingdom was to displace 'the kingdom of this world', then it had to take seriously the problem of disease. There was, therefore, a very strong theological underpinning to Jesus' miracles, and it was this to which his opponents took exception; for close scrutiny of the miracle stories uncovers the same underlying themes as we have noticed in Jesus' lifestyle. God is presented as a loving parent, who cares for all people without exception. Just as Jesus taught in words and attitudes that God loves all kinds of people, so his miracles regularly involved the outcasts of society – showing that his declaration of God's care and concern was not just talk, but demanded action (Matthew 8:1–4; Luke 17:11–19; Mark 5:21–43). Healing and

Where to find Jesus' miracles in the gospels

	Matthew	Mark	Luke	John
Healing a leper	8:2–4	1:40–42	5:12–14	
Healing the centurion's servant	8:5–13		7:1–10	
Healing Peter's mother-in-law	8:14–15	1:29–31		4:38–39
Many demon possessed	8:16–17	1:32–34	4:40–41	
Calming the storm	8:23–27	4:35–41	8:22–25	
The Gerasene demoniac healed	8:28–34	5:1–20	8:26–39	
Healing a paralysed man	9:2–8	2:3–12	5:18–26	
Jairus' daughter healed	9:18–19, 23–25	5:22–24, 35–43	8:41–42, 49–56	
Woman with a haemorrhage healed	9:20–22	5:25–34	8:43–48	
Healing of two blind men	9:27–31			
Healing of man dumb and possessed	9:32–34		11:14–15	
Man with a withered hand healed	12:10–13	3:1–5	6:6–10	
Healing of man blind, dumb and possessed	12:22–23			
Feeding the 5,000	14:13–21	6:30–44	9:10–17	6:1–14
Walking on the water	14:22–33	6:45–51		6:16–21
Healing Canaanite woman's daughter	15:21–28	7:24–30		
Feeding the 4,000	15:32–38	8:1–9		
The epileptic boy healed	17:14–21	9:14–29	9:38–43	
Coin in the fish's mouth	17:24–27			
Blind Bartimeus healed	20:29–34	10:46–52	18:35–43	
Fig tree withered	21:18–22	11:12–14, 20–25		
Healing of a possessed man		1:23–26	4:33–35	
Deaf and dumb man healed		7:32–37		
Healing a blind man at Bethsaida		8:22–26		
Miraculous catch of fish			5:1–11	
Widow's son raised from the dead			7:11–17	
Healing of woman bent double			13:11–13	
Man with dropsy healed			14:1–4	
Healing ten lepers			17:11–19	
Malchus' ear healed			22:50–51	
Turning water into wine				2:1–11
Healing of official's son at Capernaum				4:46–54
Healing of sick man at Pool of Bethesda				5:1–15
Healing a man blind from birth				9:1–41
Lazarus raised from the dead				11:1–44
Another catch of fish				21:1–11

forgiveness also went hand in hand (Mark 2:1–12), while faith could be called for on the part of those who would be healed (Mark 5:32–34; 9:14–29), and at least one story implies that the absence of faith was a hindrance to the work of healing (Mark 6:5–6).

The miracles and the evidence

It is obviously important to look critically at all our sources of information before we even begin to consider the more general problems involved in understanding these stories of 'miracles'. For if it can be shown that there is no good evidence for the belief that Jesus did in fact perform these deeds, we can forget all our other questions about the miracle stories.

When we delve into ancient history it is striking to find that its evidence unambiguously supports the belief that Jesus was widely thought to have performed remarkable deeds of the kind mentioned in the gospels. This evidence comes not only from the gospels themselves, but also from non-Christian historical sources.

Jewish history

Josephus makes the following statement about Jesus: 'About this time arose Jesus, a wise man, if indeed it be lawful to call him a man. For he was a doer of wonderful deeds, and a teacher of those who gladly receive the truth. He drew to himself many both of the Jews and of the Gentiles. He was the Christ; and when Pilate, on the indictment of the principal men among us, had condemned him to the cross, those who had loved him at the first did not cease to do so, for he appeared to them again alive on the third day, the divine prophets having foretold these and 10,000 other wonderful things about him. And even to this day the race of Christians, who are named from him, has not died out' (*Antiquities of the Jews* 18.3.3).

This passage is not without its own difficulties, and scholars have different opinions as to how much of it was written directly by Josephus himself. The problem is that the passage says explicitly of Jesus that 'he was the Christ'. But of course Josephus was not a Christian, and it would have been remarkable for a Jew – even a renegade one – to have made such an unequivocal statement. Perhaps this phrase has been inserted into Josephus' work by a later Christian editor, or Josephus might originally have written that Jesus was 'called the Christ', and the text has subsequently been amended to make his reference more specific. But, in spite of this, most scholars have no doubts about the authenticity of the rest of Josephus' description of Jesus, which contains the statement that he was 'a doer of wonderful deeds'.

More evidence from a Jewish source is contained in the Babylonian Talmud (*Sanhedrin* 43a) which reports that Jesus was executed because he practised 'sorcery' and misled the people. This is an interesting parallel

Josephus (c. AD37–100), the Jewish author who wrote histories of his people to commend them to the Romans.

to the evidence from the gospels, which suggest that the religious leaders had no quarrel with Jesus over the fact of his miraculous power to heal, but only over the source of it. It was not so much that people regarded the miracles as a hoax; rather, they were not considered indicators that God was at work in Jesus' life. There were prophets, and false prophets – and Jesus was one of the latter. In Mark 3, certain scribes offered the opinion that Jesus was inspired by 'the chief of the demons', which is why he found it so easy to drive them out (3:22), and this appears to have been a popular opinion at least among religious people. His opponents believed he was operating under the control of 'Beelzebub' (a name for the devil) – but they apparently had no reason to doubt the reality of what he was doing (Matthew 12:22–28; Luke 11:14–23).

Miracle stories in the gospels

The gospel narratives themselves raise some significant questions about Jesus' miracles.

● Some form critical studies, exploring how the gospels were written, have suggested that in their literary form the miracle stories of the gospels are often similar to stories found in Hellenistic literature. Attention has been drawn in particular to alleged parallels between the gospel accounts and the stories of a first-century Cappadocian seer and wonder-worker found in the *Life of Apollonius*, written by the third-century author Philostratus. This is not especially surprising, for the stories of Jesus' miracles were first written down by Greek-speaking people, who would naturally use the literary forms and conventions that were most familiar to them, and authors writing about the same kind of incidents in the same cultural situation might be expected to use similar language.

The 'parallels' drawn between Apollonius and Jesus favour the originality of the gospel traditions. Not only are the Hellenistic stories of much later date than the New Testament, but they were published with the express purpose of disputing the Christian claims about Jesus. If there is any question of 'dependence' by either account on the other, it could more easily be supposed that later writers consciously modelled their stories on the gospel accounts than the other way round. In any case, similarity of literary form can really tell us nothing at all about the historical facts. (See the fuller discussion of form criticism in chapter 10.)

● It is a well-documented fact that, as time goes on, remarkable deeds do tend to be accredited to people who are highly regarded for other reasons. This tendency can be found in the legends that have been gathered around the lives of so many of the medieval saints, and it is undeniable that the same thing happened to the stories of Jesus. Many of the so-called 'apocryphal gospels' which were written in the second century are of a similar nature, and relate all kinds of bizarre miracle stories about Jesus. From time to time, certain miracle stories in Matthew and John have been compared to the stories in these apocryphal gospels, but on the whole there is no compelling evidence to suggest that this is the origin of the miraculous element of the New Testament gospels.

The date of writing of the gospels is much closer to the events described than is usually considered necessary for the development of such mythological accretions. The earliest traditions of the life of Jesus developed into some kind of fixed form as early as the late 40s, which was only fifteen years after his death, while the gospels themselves began to be in their

Early Christian teaching

A secondary source of information is the evidence provided by the *kerygma* of the early church. One of the consistent elements of this early summary of Christian belief was that the promises of the Hebrew scriptures had come true in the life, death and resurrection of Jesus, and in several places the ministry of Jesus is explicitly described in terms of miracle-working. On the day of Pentecost, for example, Peter is reported as speaking of the 'mighty works and wonders and signs which God did through Jesus' (Acts 2:22). Again, in the sermon to Cornelius and his household, there is a mention of how Jesus 'went everywhere, doing good and healing all who were under the power of the devil, for God was with him' (Acts 10:38).

final written form by about AD65–70, which takes us only thirty-five years beyond the lifetime of Jesus. A conscious mythologizing process would certainly need longer than that to develop, and at the time the gospels were taking shape there must have been many surviving eyewitnesses of the events they describe, who could no doubt have corrected any stories that were out of character with Jesus as they remembered him.

There is also a striking difference between the miracle stories of the New Testament gospels and the stories told about Hellenistic 'divine men', or medieval saints, or even about Jesus himself in the apocryphal gospels. There is, for example, nothing in the New Testament to compare with the grotesque tale told in the *Arabic Infancy Gospel*, according to which Jesus produced three children out of some goats he found in an oven. Even the story found in the *Infancy Gospel of Thomas* about Jesus turning twelve clay birds into real sparrows on the sabbath is of quite a different character from the stories contained in the New Testament. Legendary tales of miracles are almost always concerned with the ostentatious display of special powers. But in the four gospels there is none of this, indeed they make it clear that the miracles Jesus performed were not concerned with satisfying idle speculation about the supernatural. When the Pharisees asked

Jesus to perform a miracle to satisfy their curiosity, he told them in no uncertain terms that this kind of spectacle was quite alien to his work (Matthew 12:38–42; Mark 8:11–12; Luke 11:29–32).

It is also significant that Jesus is portrayed as a worker of miracles in even the very earliest strands of the gospel

The miracle of the loaves (Mark 6:30–43), portrayed on a 3rd-century sarcophagus from the Via della Lungara, Rome.

We need not enter here into the complex subject of the authenticity of these sermons attributed to Peter, for regardless of whether they come directly from him or were the creations of Luke, the author of Acts, they still provide evidence that at an early stage Christians believed that Jesus had performed miracles, and that they expected an appeal to non-Christians on the basis of these miracles would not be rejected out of hand. If this indication is taken together with the evidence from Jewish sources, it seems clear that most people who knew anything at all about Jesus' ministry believed that he had done remarkable deeds – and this belief was quite independent of whether or not they were themselves Christians.

Miracle stories in the gospels *continued*

traditions that can be traced. The gospel source Q (see chapter 10) is generally thought to have been an early collection of Jesus' sayings, but this material also reports one miracle, the healing of the Roman centurion's servant (Matthew 8:5–13; Luke 7:1–10), and it also states that Jesus was in the habit of doing miracles. It is in Q that John's disciples are told to report the miracles they have seen (Matthew 11:1–19; Luke 7:18–35), and the cities of Galilee are condemned because they have not repented in spite of the repeated miracles done in them (Matthew 11:20–24; Luke 10:13–15).

● It is often pointed out that in at least two of his temptations Jesus decisively rejected the temptation to perform miracles (Matthew 4:1–11; Luke 4:1–13). He was tempted to turn stones into bread and to throw himself from the temple without injury, and he refused to do either. Is it then likely that he would perform in the course of his ministry such a miracle as the feeding of the 5,000, which apparently resulted in the crowd trying to make him their king (John 6:1–15)?

This is not such a significant question as it perhaps appears at first sight. Indeed it only arises if Jesus is regarded first and foremost as a wonder-worker. The ancient world was full of magicians who practised their art as a means of displaying their own special powers and significance. But the whole tone of the gospel stories is quite different, and Jesus' work is characterized not by a quest for power, but by humble service of God and loving actions among other people. The miracles, like his teaching and preaching, were a call for faith and obedience from those who experienced or witnessed them.

It is impossible to avoid dealing with the clear consensus of all the various pieces of evidence regarding Jesus' miracles. Both Jewish and Christian sources contend that Jesus did perform remarkable deeds, and though there is obviously room for making different judgments about individual miracle stories, it would be unreasonable to remove the miraculous element from the gospel traditions. At the same time, the gospels never allow us to regard the miracles as an end in themselves: like so many other parts of Jesus' ministry, their real importance lies in the way they assist the communication of his essential message about the kingdom of God, for they themselves exemplify God's way of doing things.

The miracles and their meaning

To understand fully what the miracles mean, they should be set in
their wider context in the whole of Jesus' ministry. The gospels view
the life and work of Jesus against the background of Old Testament
expectations, aiming to show how these prophecies were fulfilled in
Jesus, and how through him the long-awaited kingdom had arrived. To
understand the many nuances of the miracles, it is necessary to set them
in this frame of reference. Just as Jesus' self-designation as 'Son of man'
would be difficult if not impossible to understand without reference to
its Old Testament background, so it is with the miracles.

In the Hebrew Bible, miracles invariably meant something. What
God said was often associated with what God did. Indeed, in Hebrew the
single word *dabar* could mean both a word and an action, and the two
were very closely linked together in Hebrew thought. God's actions
might be understood as an extension of God's words. What God does is
essentially identical with what God says. So, for example, at the time of
the exodus the remarkable deeds performed by Moses before Pharaoh
were not just wonders performed for effect, but were themselves
perceived as the vehicle of God's message, living signs of the truth
of God's words (Exodus 10:1–2).

This idea was taken up and developed especially by the prophets, who
often included mimetic actions as part of their message. Isaiah, for example,
walked round Jerusalem naked and barefoot as an indication of his belief
that Judah's allies would soon be destroyed by their enemies (Isaiah 20:1–6).
Ezekiel drew a picture of a besieged city on a tile, to indicate what was
going to happen to his own city of Jerusalem (Ezekiel 4:1–3). Actions such
as these were regarded as more than just symbols or illustrations: they were
an actual part of God's message through the prophets, and were closely
bound up with the meaning of God's activities in the history of the nation.

When John's Gospel called Jesus' miracles 'signs', it was probably
this kind of 'dynamic illustration' that was in mind. The English word
'sign' implies merely a symptom or an indication, which might imply
that miracles as signs were nothing more than artificially contrived
indications to prove that Jesus was the Messiah, or that the kingdom
had arrived. But they were more than that, for like the 'signs' given by
the prophets, the miracles were actually a part of Jesus' message. They
were an extension in actions of the teaching given in the parables, and
like that teaching, they describe God's kingdom and present its
challenge to those who witness them.

When they are examined in this light, the miracles can readily be
seen to be drawing attention to three aspects of the kingdom of God.

The arrival of the kingdom

When Jesus began his teaching ministry, the main content of his
message was the declaration that 'the kingdom of God is at hand'

(Mark 1:15). The precise meaning that is given to the phrase 'at hand' will depend on how Jesus' eschatology is understood. But most scholars agree that at least one implication of the statement was that the kingdom had already come into existence with the coming of Jesus himself. This is brought out quite clearly in Jesus' miracles, where the arrival of God's kingdom is both declared and explained.

On one occasion John the Baptist sent some of his disciples to ask Jesus whether he was indeed the Messiah who was to inaugurate the kingdom. The answer that Jesus gave was as follows: 'Go and tell John what you hear and see: the blind receive their sight and the lame walk, lepers are cleansed and the deaf hear, and the dead are raised up, and the poor have good news preached to them' (Matthew 11:4–5; Luke 7:22). These words in which Jesus addressed John were a quotation from Isaiah 35:5–6, and were generally believed to be a reference to the future messianic age. Jesus was telling John that his miracles were a sign that the ancient promises were coming true.

John's Gospel suggests that the miracles not only announced the arrival of the kingdom, but also showed Jesus to be its central figure. In the first miracle recorded in John (the changing of water into wine) Jesus 'revealed his glory, and his disciples believed in him' (2:11). Later on, the raising of Lazarus is 'the means by which the Son of God will receive glory' (11:4). Yet Jesus did not use miracles for personal gain, for the prologue to John points out that Jesus' glory was not his own but was the glory of God, which he shared as God's Son (1:14). The same theme occurs in other miracle stories, where Jesus requires praise to be given to God and not to himself (Luke 17:11–19; John 11:4). In the miracles, God's power was demonstrated in such a way that those who witnessed them would realize that the kingdom had arrived with the coming of Jesus.

The scope of the kingdom

A large water pot of the type used for rites of purification.

The miracles not only announce the arrival of the kingdom in a general sense: their message also parallels Jesus' explicit teaching in many more detailed ways. It is not difficult to see how the various types of miracle that Jesus performed were meant to emphasize in a striking way the different things he said in the parables about the kingdom of God. The miracles can be grouped into three sections, each of which expresses a different aspect of Jesus' teaching. They declare the meaning of the kingdom for individuals, for the world as a whole, and its future consequences and consummation.

THE KINGDOM AND THE INDIVIDUAL

In one of the temptations, the devil had claimed that he was the master of the world's kingdoms, and many people in the time of Jesus would have agreed with that (Matthew 4:8–10; Luke 4:5–7). As they looked at their own lives and the lives of other people, they saw suffering, illness and death as signs that their lives were influenced by the operation of evil forces in the world. It was commonly believed that disease was caused by the demonic members of an evil spiritual world operating in the natural, physical world. Sin and evil caused disease – not in the personal sense implied by those Pharisees who suggested that because a man was blind he and his family must be great sinners (John 9:1–12), but in a cosmic sense, so that human illness was seen as a part of the total fallenness of God's creation.

An important part of Jesus' teaching was that people could be set free from the domination of sin over their lives, not only in terms of any wrongdoing that individuals might commit, but also as it was expressed through their experience of being sinned-against by other people or by circumstances. In the casting out of demons and in the other healing miracles, Jesus made this announcement in the most dramatic way possible. He also underlined another part of his teaching, for the miracles more often than not involved those who were the outcasts of society – lepers, whom no one would touch for fear of religious impurity (Matthew 8:1–4; Luke 17:11–19); a Roman centurion, whom many Jews must have hated (Matthew 8:5–13; Luke 7:1–10); those who were past helping themselves (Mark 5:21–43). Those were the people to whom Jesus' message and miracles were of most value.

THE KINGDOM AND THE WORLD

If the healing miracles show Jesus releasing individual people from the power of sin, the 'nature miracles' show Jesus doing the same for the whole of creation. The power of evil had affected not just the lives of individuals, but the life of nature as well. There was a real sense in which Satan was the ruler of the world, and Jesus had come to cast him out of every part of his dominion (John 12:31). So he 'rebuked' the wind and the waves in the same way as he 'rebuked' the demons that had such a harmful effect in the lives of people (Mark 1:25; 4:39).

It was an important part of Jesus' message that he had come to save people in their whole environment, and the nature miracles were intended to provide a striking declaration of the global scope of Jesus' work.

THE KINGDOM IN THE FUTURE

It is interesting that the future dimension of Jesus' teaching about the kingdom of God is also reflected in the miracles. In Jewish thought the future kingdom was often pictured as a meal, and Jesus himself described it in terms of a banquet (Matthew 8:11; Luke 14:15–24; 22:30). The miraculous feedings of the 5,000 and of the 4,000 are an acting out of this picture, in which Jesus showed himself as God's Messiah feeding God's people (Matthew 14:13–21; 15:32–39; Mark 6:30–44; 8:1–10; Luke 9:10–17). According to one account of the feeding of the 5,000, the people were so impressed by what took place that they thought

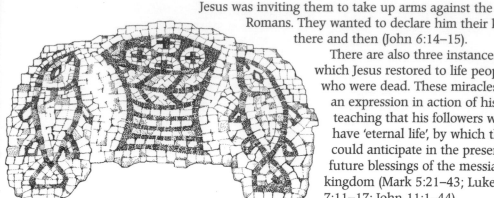

Jesus was inviting them to take up arms against the Romans. They wanted to declare him their king there and then (John 6:14–15).

There are also three instances in which Jesus restored to life people who were dead. These miracles are an expression in action of his teaching that his followers would have 'eternal life', by which they could anticipate in the present the future blessings of the messianic kingdom (Mark 5:21–43; Luke 7:11–17; John 11:1–44).

Mosaic of loaves and fish from the Church of Multiplication at Tabgha, Galilee.

The challenge of the kingdom

In dealing with the parables, we observed that they were a way of inviting people to think out the full implications that God's kingdom might need to have for their own lives, and it was commented that without a willingness to engage with the message of the parables on their own terms as stories, the full meaning of many of them would remain hidden. The challenge of accepting God's values and standards is presented in similar terms in the miracle stories.

Faith regularly features as an important element in Jesus' cures. On three occasions he says, 'Your faith has made you well' (Mark 5:34; 10:52; Luke 17:19), and according to Mark the absence of faith was a hindrance to performing miracles (6:5). Indeed without faith it was not possible to realize that the miracles were a sign of God at work, and unbelief led to the conclusion that Jesus was in league with Satan (Matthew 12:24).

In the complex set of interactions between mind and body, 'faith' is often an important part of a cure, and there is no intrinsic reason to suppose that Jesus, who 'knew what was in everyone' (John 2:23–25) could not have understood that. But the faith of which the gospels speak went beyond a requirement merely to trust the healer. What Jesus demanded was not a predisposition to be healed, but an unconditional acceptance of the need for personal change, and a willingness to adopt God's ways of doing things. To ask Jesus for healing was a sign of this kind of faith, whose further implications were more fully spelled out in the parables. In this sense, the purpose of the miracles was not so different from the purpose of the parables: to those who were willing to trust God they could become a vehicle of revelation, while those whose minds were closed to such a possibility might easily dismiss them as trivialities.

9 The Kingdom of God in Action

Society has always needed rules and regulations to govern the conduct of its members. Often these are simply the result of what experience has taught about the best ways of doing things. Sometimes, as in a few of the law codes of the ancient Middle East, the rules stem from a system of religious beliefs. Occasionally, as in the Old Testament, there is a mixture of both. The relationship between inherited ways of doing things and the actual needs of people can easily become complex and problematic. By the time of Jesus many, if not all, of the specific laws of the Hebrew scriptures had been rendered obsolete by cultural changes taking place in Palestinian society. The Torah envisaged a fundamentally different form of social organization than was generally allowed for by the Roman empire, which in itself required that it be adapted and reinterpreted in order to meet the changed circumstances. The updating of the Law had been undertaken with some enthusiasm by the Pharisees, who saw the need for change if the traditional ways were to continue to be held in respect by people struggling with new challenges to their entire lifestyle. They had generally done a good job and, from all the available evidence, it seems they were highly regarded by other people, even if their stringent requirements were not always easy to observe.

Jesus' conflicts with Judaism

The Pharisees were the people with whom Jesus most often found himself in conflict. Modern readers of the gospel stories may be forgiven for supposing that these people were personally responsible for all that was corrupt in Jewish society, and that Judaism was so far removed from the original intentions of the Old Testament faith that Jesus would of necessity be in conflict with it. That is how it sometimes looked to the Christians for whom the gospels were written, later in the first century, for in cities like Rome or Ephesus the Jewish communities often went out of their way to make life difficult for the church. It is not hard to understand the historical and sociological reasons for such antagonism. But theologically, things were not so simple. Most religious Jews had a strong personal trust in God, and faithfully tried to keep the Torah as part of their response to what God had done in the life of their nation. They were not legalists, trying to blackmail God by their own moral goodness, but honest and straightforward people with a high level of commitment.

Jesus himself was apparently quite happy to share in the worship of local synagogues on a regular basis, something that he presumably would not have done had he been fundamentally disillusioned with what went on there. It is perhaps surprising, therefore, that he should so soon have found himself locked in acrimonious conflict with the very people who might have been expected to be his natural allies. Ostensibly, it was arguments about religion and law that were at the root of all this. But disagreements on religious matters only became so controversial because they also highlighted issues of social stratification within the community. The extent to which a person was able to observe the various religious rules had become a way of determining his or her intrinsic worth, and those who were scrupulous in keeping all the rules wanted little or nothing to do with those who were lax in their observance of the Law. The Law-keepers looked down on the others as 'people of the land', who were in effect second-class citizens. There was little direct dealing between the two groups, and the more religious people generally despised those whom they considered spiritually corrupt and inferior.

As a result of earlier Jewish history, various racial and economic tensions were also involved in all this, with Samaritans and Galileans among the leading offenders in this respect. Centuries before, the Samaritans and Jews might have had some common racial ancestry, but by now they were implacably opposed to each other. As far as orthodox Jewish believers were concerned, they were no better than Gentiles, claiming a temple they had built for themselves on Mount Gerizim was of equal status to the temple in Jerusalem. In some respects they were regarded as even worse than Gentiles, for they had had the chance to accept orthodox Judaism, and had refused. The Galileans were, likewise, despised as mere opportunists, who had been willing to side with anyone if it was to their advantage. Sociologically, the religious people most opposed to Jesus were probably middle-class town dwellers, who were inclined to regard all others as inferior to themselves. When Jesus crossed swords with the cultural establishment in Jerusalem, certain Pharisees dismissed his followers with the comment that 'This crowd does not know the Law of Moses, so they are under God's curse!', adding for good measure that 'no prophet ever comes from Galilee' (John 7:49, 52). The writings of the later rabbis contain similar statements declaring, for example, that a faithful believer 'may not be the guest of one of the people of the land nor may he receive him as a guest in his own raiment' (*Desai* 2.8–10). In dealing with such sweeping prohibitions and implied condemnation, it is hard to distinguish purely religious considerations from social and racial prejudices.

If this was the way country people were treated by religious town dwellers, then it is no surprise that they were attracted to Jesus. Their only previous experience of religion was to be put down by it. They

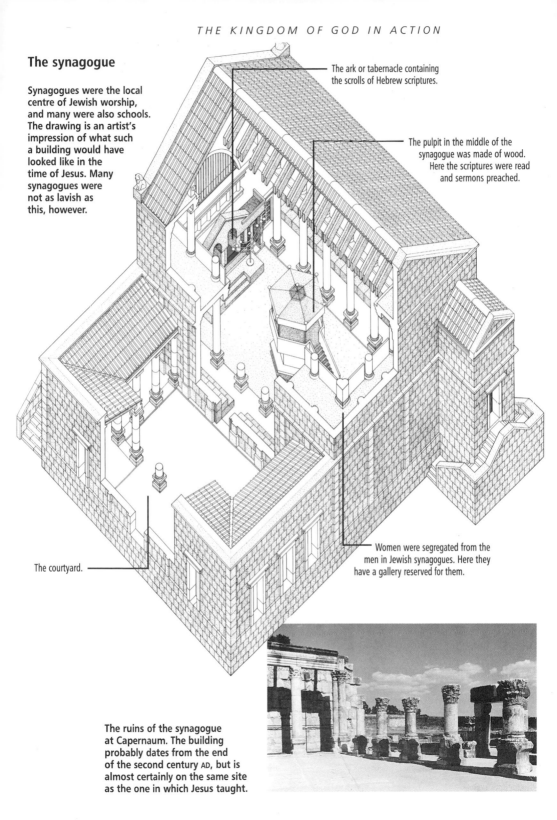

The synagogue

Synagogues were the local centre of Jewish worship, and many were also schools. The drawing is an artist's impression of what such a building would have looked like in the time of Jesus. Many synagogues were not as lavish as this, however.

The ark or tabernacle containing the scrolls of Hebrew scriptures.

The pulpit in the middle of the synagogue was made of wood. Here the scriptures were read and sermons preached.

Women were segregated from the men in Jewish synagogues. Here they have a gallery reserved for them.

The courtyard.

The ruins of the synagogue at Capernaum. The building probably dates from the end of the second century AD, but is almost certainly on the same site as the one in which Jesus taught.

were routinely disadvantaged and abused by those in positions of power – but Jesus turned the tables by treating them as people of value to God, and to their fellow human beings. Others would find a place for them in the system if they came grovelling and broken, confessing their sins and seeking forgiveness (and they sometimes did: the famous Rabbi Akiba began life as one of the 'people of the land'). But Jesus actively went out to mix with such people, to share their oppression – and in the process to open them up to new understandings of God. They might have been the 'wrong' sort of people, but they were the ones whom God would welcome. The short parable of the Pharisee and the tax gatherer says it all: 'all who exalt themselves will be humbled, but all who humble themselves will be exalted' (Luke 18:14).

It was never going to be difficult to interpret Jesus' habit of mixing with unsuitable people in terms of a failure to keep the traditional laws of his people, but his insistence on challenging the establishment's ways of doing things more directly highlights the extent to which he was genuinely out of sympathy with customary approaches to spirituality. In one of the first stories in John's Gospel, Jesus went to the temple in Jerusalem, took a whip, and drove the merchants and bankers out (2:13–21). They had a right to be there, of course, though it was probably a recent concession granted to them not long before by the high priest Caiaphas, as a means of undermining other markets set up outside the temple walls on the Mount of Olives. Most temple worship

The Pharisees criticizing the disciples for plucking heads of grain on the sabbath (Mark 2:18–22). From a 19th-century engraving.

involved offering sacrifices, which meant that urban worshippers needed to buy animals when they got there, and since anything related to Rome was banned from the temple precincts – including its money – they needed to obtain the ritually approved currency before making a purchase. Both the merchants selling animals and the money changers were, therefore, providing a useful service. Jesus, however, chased them out, challenging a form of religiosity that would turn faith into a commodity to be bought, sold and controlled by self-opinionated experts. The other gospels describe him doing this towards the end of his ministry (Matthew 21:12–13; Mark 11:15–18; Luke 19:45–48), but John places it at the beginning because it highlighted so clearly the nature of the conflict between Jesus and the establishment. Jesus was convinced that anyone, no matter how ordinary, could have direct access to God, which meant that people must come before procedures, regardless of how hallowed and venerable they might be. Even when a woman was caught in the very act of committing adultery, Jesus refused to condemn her, at the same time challenging her accusers with the words, 'Whichever one of you has committed no sin may throw the first stone at her' (John 8:1–11). For people who were socially excluded, valued by religious people at much less than the birds and animals they offered in sacrifice, it was good news indeed to be told that 'you are worth much more than many sparrows!' (Matthew 10:31).

Not only did Jesus challenge underlying attitudes about the nature of true spirituality, he also challenged some of the central provisions of the Old Testament Law itself. The question of sabbath observance surfaces within the first two or three pages of Mark's Gospel, and is never far from the centre of the action thereafter. Jesus was roundly condemned by religious leaders when he insisted on healing people on the sabbath, or allowed his disciples to pick ears of grain as they walked through a cornfield (Mark 2:23–28; 3:1–6).

This was more than an argument about social convention. Observance of the sabbath as a day of rest was enshrined in the ten commandments, which in turn claimed it went back to creation itself. According to the Old Testament, the people were to rest on the seventh day because 'I, the Lord, made the earth, the sky, the sea, and everything in them, but on the seventh day I rested' (Exodus 20:11). In Jesus' day, defining the sabbath was a major preoccupation of some religious experts. What does it mean to rest or, for that matter, for it to be the sabbath? As in the Jewish reckoning, a day ran not from midnight to midnight, but from sunset to sunset, who could tell precisely when any given sabbath would begin and end? This last debate led to all sorts of bizarre arrangements, to ensure that people were not caught out, still at work if the sun went down unexpectedly. Reference has been made in a previous chapter to the rule defining the nature of 'a sabbath day's journey' as 2,000 cubits, but even that was less clear-cut than it might seem, for legal experts had worked out ways of going further without actually breaking the Law. This was done by designating a point 2,000 cubits from one's normal residence as 'home' for the sabbath day, maybe by storing some food there in advance. Since a 'sabbath day's journey' was reckoned to begin from 'home', that gave a legal entitlement to travel at least 4,000 cubits, if not more!

The same kind of perverse ingenuity could be applied to other laws as well, so that for those in the know it was possible to break the law, while still theoretically keeping it. In the light of practices like this, Jesus had good reason to ask why it was considered wrong to heal someone on the sabbath (Mark 3:4). What was supposed to be a day of rest had all too often become an excuse for upper-class people to use the system to their own advantage, while finding fault with others whose understanding of it differed from their own. People were being strangled by their own rules. But Jesus reversed this, insisting that in God's way of looking at things people come first, and institutions second: 'The sabbath was made for humankind, and not humankind for the sabbath' (Mark 2:27).

This kind of thing was not an isolated example. The same happened with rituals for washing and eating food. Centuries before, the high priest had been required to wash his hands before entering the tent of worship (Exodus 30:19; 40:12), but by the time of Jesus many devout people had adopted this practice as part of everyday life, and they regularly washed their hands first thing in the morning, and before meals. This was done not for reasons of hygiene, but for religious purposes, to ensure their ritual purity. None of this had actually been required by the Old Testament laws, but that only left more scope for later rule-makers, who had even developed regulations prescribing exactly which parts of the hands should be washed to preserve ritual purity. When all this was combined with the already complex dietary rules of the Old Testament itself, then even a simple thing like eating food had the potential to spark off lengthy

---

Jesus meeting people

In all four gospels, Jesus is presented as someone who was more interested in people than ideas. He was impatient with the theological hair-splitting of religious experts, and he did not care to engage much in abstract debates, nor was he particularly interested in intellectual knowledge for its own sake. His whole life was focused on people and their needs.

The gospels paint many vivid thumbnail sketches of Jesus at work among people – dancing with them, drinking with them, in casual conversations in fields and market places – but always with a view to bringing healing and renewal into their lives, as he pointed them to God and the kingdom. The fact that Jesus engaged in so many 'ordinary' things at once marked him out as different from other religious teachers. But that was not his only attraction for people who were normally considered well beyond the pale of respectable religion. Any one of a large number of stories could be chosen to illustrate why Jesus was so captivating. But there is one in particular that combines so many themes it provides a more comprehensive model than most. This is the story in John 4 of how Jesus met a woman by a well, in the most unpromising circumstances, how he invited her to discipleship, and how she not only

accepted the challenge, but also went off to share it with others from her village.

One of the most surprising features of this whole encounter is the simple fact that Jesus was there at all. In terms of the conventions of the day, everything was out of joint. Women were not typically considered capable of receiving religious teaching from a rabbi, and even a relatively enlightened teacher like the second-century rabbi Jose ben Johanan, who readily welcomed to his home the homeless and destitute, still advised, 'Talk not with womankind... He that talks much with womankind brings evil upon himself and neglects the study of the Law and at the last will inherit Gehenna' (*Aboth* 1.5). It was unusual enough that a religious teacher like Jesus should take a woman seriously. But this one was a Samaritan, a member of a group who were hated more than most by Jewish people.

There is some dispute as to who exactly the Samaritans of New Testament times were. They might have been the descendants of half-Jewish people who opposed the introduction of strict religious laws after the Jewish exiles returned to Jerusalem from Babylon, back in the third and fourth centuries BC. More probably, they were a new sect that had emerged in the days just before the beginning of the Christian era. In any event, Samaritans were not highly regarded by devout Jews.

religious debate. When Jesus was challenged about his own failure to keep all these regulations, he did not enter into discussion on the issue. He simply stated (quoting Isaiah) that, as far as he was concerned, rules of this sort were unnecessary additions to the scripture: 'You abandon the commandment of God and hold to human tradition' (Mark 7:8). As if to reinforce his indifference to such things, he went on to talk about the things that, in his opinion, really make a person unclean – like 'greed, deceit, indecency, jealousy, slander, pride and folly' (Mark 7:22). A person could appear exceedingly righteous by observing various minor rules and regulations, while side-stepping the central challenge of the Old Testament to 'Love the Lord your God' and 'love your neighbour as you love yourself' (Mark 12:30–31). If, as was suggested in an earlier chapter, some members of Jesus' own family were Pharisees, that might easily explain how he came

---

They had their own customs – religious and civil – and their own place of worship. Their land was located between Galilee and Judea, and to get from one to the other rigorous Law-keepers would have made a long detour, east of the Jordan river, rather than risk contamination by travelling through Samaria. But Jesus had no such inhibitions. He did not require that people should meet him on territory where only he felt safe, where he was in control and could determine the outcome. Jesus went out to where people actually were, and willingly made himself weak and vulnerable in order to communicate.

The circumstances of this particular story show just how far Jesus was prepared to extend his own vulnerability. The well was on a remote hillside, it was a hot day, Jesus was desperately thirsty – and the woman was the only one with the means to get water! She was a woman with a lot of experience with men and, as the story unfolds, it emerges that she had been married five times, and was cohabiting with a sixth man. She had suffered much abuse at the hands of men, and the last thing she wanted, in this remote spot, was to be exploited yet again. Jesus knew he was speaking with a doubly disadvantaged person. So where did he begin? Right from the start, Jesus got alongside her. First of all, he revealed that he had a need: he was desperately

thirsty. More than that, it was a need that she could meet, and so he asked if she would share her water with him. This certainly placed him in a position of weakness, but by doing so he was able to affirm this woman as a person of value. Right away she recognized something unusual was happening: instead of the lecture she might have expected, complaining about all that was wrong with her, this was to be a two-way conversation. Moreover, here was a rabbi who would actually listen – to a woman, and a Samaritan – and who was prepared to ask questions, and pay attention to another person's answers. One of the secrets of Jesus' appeal to disadvantaged people was that he was a listener: he had time to hear what they wanted to say.

Not only that, but Jesus was also prepared to follow the woman's own agenda. He did not focus on communicating a set of abstract ideas, but on the questions the woman herself was asking. Jesus always addressed people at their point of need, and began where they were. When he met fishermen by the Sea of Galilee, he talked about fish. With a rich man, the subject was money. With this woman at the well, he began with the water. He followed an adaptive strategy. Jesus was not primarily message-centred, but people-centred. Christians have often felt uncomfortable with the fact that Jesus'

to be so well acquainted with this kind of devious behaviour, even though it was not, as far as is known, official Pharisaic policy.

There can be no doubt that Jesus challenged some fairly central aspects of Jewish practice in his day. The Torah certainly did lay down the death penalty for adultery; it certainly encouraged keeping the sabbath day; and it insisted that food should be eaten only within certain prescribed limits. When Jesus apparently set aside all of these, and more, it was natural that those who were trying to remain faithful to the old traditions saw him simply as a heretic. In terms of traditional religious practice, Jesus *was* a heretic, for at the bottom of all these differences of opinion was a different theology as well, with a fundamentally different picture of God. Jesus did not understand God as an abstract force, requiring the observance of stringent regulations, but as a personal being with whom

---

Jesus meeting people
continued

message was not expressed in the same terms for everyone. It can come as a surprise to learn that only once did Jesus mention being 'born again' (John 3:3), or require a person to 'sell all you have' (Mark 10:21). Jesus knew his message would only be taken seriously if it was relevant to each person and situation.

As it happens, the woman did not immediately express her deepest needs to Jesus. Perhaps she still felt too threatened by her previous experiences to do so. But Jesus had some unusual insights. An earlier passage in John states that 'he knew all people and needed no one to testify about anyone; for he himself knew what was in everyone' (2:24–25). The other gospels make similar claims. Luke frequently reports not only Jesus' openness to all sorts of outcasts from society (a Samaritan even makes it as one of the heroes of the parables in Luke 10:25–37), but also the fact that Jesus consciously relied on his own intuitive insights to apply his message to the concerns of his hearers. This is what happened here. Jesus had no prior knowledge of the woman's home circumstances, but when he revealed them to her in such detail, she knew for sure that he was 'a prophet' – maybe even 'the prophet' foretold by Moses.

Having moved the woman on in her understanding, Jesus was in a uniquely credible position from which to challenge her about discipleship. This was always Jesus' style. Though willingness to change and accept God's forgiveness were central to his understanding of the kingdom, he never put people down. Just as he had done with Peter by the shore of Galilee, so with this woman he never spoke of her sinfulness. She was already well aware of her own inadequacy, but precisely because Jesus gave her time and space to come to terms with it in her own way, she was happy enough to go back to the village to share her experiences with her friends. For such a person – a woman (maybe even a prostitute) and a Samaritan – this was good news indeed. Jesus' habit of dealing in this sort of way with people who were despised by other religious teachers was one of the things that eventually brought him into serious conflict with the authorities. Not only did his teaching threaten some cherished religious ideas, as when he challenged strict sabbath keeping, or laid aside the traditional food laws – but his behaviour also undermined the accepted norms of social segregation, valuing outcasts with the same vigour with which he opposed religious teachers. But, for ordinary people, it was not difficult to believe that someone like this, who lifted them up and left them feeling affirmed and valued, must have a special place in the purposes of God.

people could have a loving and empowering relationship. We have seen the implications of all this in the parables that Jesus told, and – because Jesus had a holistic approach to spirituality – we have also already touched on some of the ethical consequences of his teaching. Those who claim to have a living relationship with God must also love their neighbours. They must care for the outcasts of society, and be concerned for one another's welfare. In Jesus' teaching, social concern follows on from personal spirituality as certainly and as naturally as night follows day.

The style of Jesus' ethical teaching

It is easy enough to see the outcome of Jesus' ethics. But why should God's people act like this? What is the basis for Jesus' ethical teaching, and how can it best be understood? It is, of course, not very easy to speak of Jesus' ethics in isolation from the rest of his teaching. All his teaching about God and the kingdom has an ethical dimension to it – while the Sermon on the Mount (Matthew 5 – 7), which is generally taken to be the most comprehensive collection of ethical teachings in the gospels, is also full of theology. Nevertheless, this so-called 'sermon' does give us a good idea of the place of ethics in the new society that Jesus had come to inaugurate.

Before looking at the actual content of the Sermon on the Mount, we first need to consider the best way of understanding what Jesus says in it. This is an important question, for it is obvious that the way Jesus gives his teaching here is quite different from the approach of modern ethics textbooks, and even quite different from the ways ordinary people might express the same ideas. As a good teacher, Jesus naturally used forms of language and expression that would most easily inspire those who first heard him to put his teaching into practical operation in everyday life. At least three distinctive devices feature in the teaching contained in the Sermon on the Mount:

■ Much of the sermon is poetry, though not the sort of poetry with which most of today's readers of the gospels would be familiar. English poetry depends, for its effect, on rhyme or stress, whereas Hebrew poetry depended on a correspondence of thought. There could be two basic kinds of poetry depending on whether the correspondence was one of similarity or of difference. Take, for example, the following statement from Matthew 7:6, which can be arranged poetically as follows:

> *Do not give dogs what is holy;*
> *and do not throw your pearls before swine.*

This is genuine Hebrew poetry, in which the second line repeats the thought of the first line, but using different imagery. This particular form is called 'synonymous parallelism', and there are many examples of it in the Psalms and other poetic sections of the Old Testament.

Another type of Hebrew poetry is known as 'antithetical parallelism', and again there is an example of this in Matthew 7:17:

Every sound tree bears good fruit,
but the bad tree bears evil fruit.

A similar lesson is being taught in each line, but the thought is expressed by the use of exactly opposite concepts. This technique also occurs frequently in the Old Testament.

Even the Lord's prayer (Matthew 6:9–13) can be arranged poetically, as follows:

Our father in heaven	*hallowed be your name,*
Your kingdom come;	*Your will be done;*
on earth	*as it is in heaven.*
Give us today	*our daily bread*
And forgive us our debts,	*as we have also forgiven our debtors;*
And do not bring us to the time of trial,	*but rescue us from the evil one.*

■ Another common feature of Jesus' teaching is the constant use of pictorial imagery. On some occasions this can take the form of story, as in the parables; on other occasions it can be a single, vivid illustration chosen from everyday life. This is quite different from the way people tend to make ethical statements in a culture dominated by propositional forms of expression, where ethics would be spoken of in an abstract way. By contrast, Jesus always dealt with concrete things. Instead of saying 'Materialism can be a hindrance to spiritual growth,' he said, 'No one can be a slave of two masters... You cannot serve both God and money' (Matthew 6:24).

■ Jesus also had a tendency to state things in an exaggerated way, using hyperbole to make a point. For example, he said that it would be better for his disciples to pull their eyes out than commit adultery, or better to cut their hands off than displease God (Matthew 5:29). He was obviously not meaning to suggest they should do either of those things literally, but used this extravagant language to impress on his hearers the seriousness of his message.

In considering Jesus' ethical teaching, it is important to look out for these different techniques, for recognizing the different forms will often help to illuminate exactly what Jesus was meaning to say.

God and the moral imperative

Jesus' ethical teaching cannot be separated from his teaching about God's kingdom, and the demands and opportunities offered to those who wish to identify with God's way of doing things. It is very difficult to make sense of the Sermon on the Mount without an appreciation of this God-related foundation of all its precepts.

All ethical systems have a basic premise from which everything else is developed. Jesus' ethical teaching is based on the declaration that the God who created all things, and who acted in history in the experience of Israel, can be known in a personal way, and the behaviour of those who commit themselves to such knowing is then a natural outcome of their familiarity with God's ways.

In essence, this was not as new as it can be made to seem, for the Hebrew scriptures had promoted two simple moral premises that were also basic to Jesus' teaching in the New Testament.

Human goodness takes its character from God

At the central part of the holiness code in the Old Testament is the statement, 'You shall be holy; for I the Lord your God am holy' (Leviticus 19:2). The ethical standards to which God's people were expected to aspire were nothing less than a reflection of the character of God. Biblical morality was to take its models from divine conduct: people should behave as God behaves.

In the experience of ancient Israel, one of the most characteristic of God's activities had been the expression of an undeserved and unconditional love for them. The traditional national story told how Abraham had been called from Mesopotamia and given a new homeland, not because of any moral or spiritual superiority that he might have possessed, but simply because God's affection was centred on him. Israel subsequently emerged from the shattering experiences of the exodus and what followed, not because of their own moral perfection but simply through the care of a loving God, and it was on the basis of these undeserved acts of kindness that God had made certain demands of the people.

This is made clear in the opening statement of the ten commandments: 'I am the Lord your God, who brought you out of the land of Egypt, out of the house of bondage' (Exodus 20:2). This was the foundational principle on which all the other commandments were based: the people were exhorted to respond in love and obedience to what God had already done for them. The same pattern can be found elsewhere in the Torah: 'You shall remember that you were a slave in the land of Egypt, and the Lord your God redeemed you; *therefore* I command you this today' (Deuteronomy 15:15).

The 'therefore' was central, and forged a clear link between beliefs about the character of God and expectations about the behaviour of people. The ethic of the New Testament continued this same pattern as the basis of moral action. It is striking, for instance, that when Paul wanted to stop the quarrelling that was going on in the church at Philippi, he appealed not to ordinary common sense to solve the problem, but to this same concept of God's behaviour supplying the pattern for human behaviour (Philippians 2:1–11). In that particular instance, he drew attention to the way the incarnation represented a sacrifice for God, who was born into this world in the person of Jesus of Nazareth. He then proceeded to make this the basis of a moral appeal to his readers: because Jesus had given up everything for them, they ought to be willing to sacrifice their own self-centredness in order to please him.

The fact that God's character as a holy God and a loving parent underlies all the Bible's teaching on behaviour then has several important practical consequences for Christian behaviour:

■ It has given Christians a great sensitivity to the seriousness of sin. When people are faced with a holy God who is willing to express unconditional love for the benefit of those who neither cared for nor respected God's standards, they recognize how different their own character is from the character of God. In the history of the Christian tradition, this consciousness of human failure to live up to God's ways has on occasion become a way of heaping guilt on people. But for Jesus, the recognition of sin was not restricted only to personal wrongdoing. Indeed, it most typically did not begin with personal wrongdoing at all, but with the plight of those who were wronged by the unjust situations in which they found themselves. Time and again, Jesus met people whose lives had been blighted by the effects of sin and, instead of demanding that they be held accountable for their predicament, he had compassion on them – recognizing that people frequently encounter the evil that is in the world not when they themselves do wrong, but when they are sinned against. For Jesus, sin was a bigger matter than personal wrongdoing. Following the insights of the traditional Hebrew story of the fall, he saw it as something that affected the entire cosmos, and required a correspondingly comprehensive approach in dealing with it. That is not to say that Jesus played down personal accountability. But, in pointing people in a new direction, his message was more often an assurance that, with God's help, they could be empowered to take responsibility for their lives, rather than condemnation for the fact that their lives had been damaged by sin and its consequences.

■ Following on from that, Christian goodness has a numinous, other-worldly quality that regularly goes beyond the demands of common sense. The kind of self-giving love that Jesus saw as characteristic of God was recommended as a basis for practical action over and over. A rich person might be told to 'go, sell what you have, and give to the poor' (Mark 10:21), while the disciples were encouraged to go two miles if the Roman troops forced them to carry their bags for one, and to 'turn the other cheek' and return good for evil (Matthew 5:38–42). These things would be quite unreasonable, even absurd, in most conventional views of ethical responsibility. But when viewed in the light of God's generosity, they take on a different appearance and become the only possible response to such love.

■ Ultimately, therefore, the ethic recommended by Jesus is grounded in theology. These apparently ridiculous moral standards are to be adopted 'so that you may be true children of your Father in heaven... for if you love those who love you... what more are you doing than others?' (Matthew 5:45, 46, 47). Being like God, then, becomes the prime motivation for disciples to follow Jesus' advice.

Christian goodness and the community

The central theme of the Old Testament was the belief that God had acted decisively in the history of Israel, and had entered into an intimate relationship with them through the making of a covenant. This meant that the individual Israelite was never simply an individual, but a member of the people of God. As a result of this, the goodness that God required was to be demonstrated not only in pious individuals, but also in the institutions of national life.

Jesus laid the same emphasis on the importance of community, and all his teaching on the kingdom had both an individual and a corporate dimension to it. In replying to a question about spirituality, he used the book of Deuteronomy to affirm that he was concerned both with self-fulfilment and service of others, and neither of these had priority over the other (Mark 12:28–34). In John's Gospel, which arguably has more emphasis than the others on the personal aspects of discipleship, he gave his followers a 'new commandment' that was to be the basis of the Christian community: 'that you love one another; even as I have loved you, that you also love one another. This is how everyone will know that you are my disciples, if you have love for one other' (13:34–35).

Behaviour and discipleship

Jesus' teaching was intended as a way of life only for those people who subjected their lives to God's rule. This is the point at which Jesus' ethic has most frequently been misunderstood. Those who claim to be able to accept the Sermon on the Mount, but not the other claims made about Jesus in the New Testament, have failed to recognize the essential character of Jesus' teaching. It is impossible to isolate his theology from his ethics, and to do so destroys the integrity of them both.

In his introduction to the Sermon on the Mount, Matthew informed his readers that it was the disciples who formed the audience for the sermon, and the various elements of it were directed to certain committed people, not to all and sundry. This was clearly understood by the earliest Christians. Indeed, as we shall see in a later chapter of this book, the sermon was constructed in the form it now has for the purpose of instructing new converts in the churches with which Matthew was associated in the first century. Both in the context of Jesus' life and in that of the early church, the ethical teaching of the sermon was preceded by the communication and acceptance of the Christian message.

Wild flowers in
Galilee.

C.H. Dodd demonstrated that two strands of early Christian teaching can be distinguished in the New Testament, and it is instructive to discover that they correspond to the overall pattern we have noticed in biblical ethics more generally. Underlying everything else, there is the kind of teaching that he called *kerygma*, which was essentially a declaration of what God had accomplished through the life, death and resurrection of Jesus. In terms of its function in New Testament ethics, this was comparable to the telling of the story of Abraham and his descendants' calling in the Hebrew scriptures. Now, through Jesus, God had acted not because of any moral value in those people who became his disciples, but purely as an act of undeserved love – what Christians came to call 'grace'. In the same way as Israel had been summoned to obey the Law on the basis of God's loving actions, the early Christians could be given moral and spiritual exhortations because of what Jesus had accomplished for them in his life, death and resurrection.

This moral advice has been called the *didache*, or 'teaching', and the connection between it and *kerygma* comes out especially clearly in some of the letters of Paul, which often deal with theological matters first and then make practical appeals to Christians on the basis of those theological arguments. But the same pattern – ethics following teaching – is also found in the various sayings of the Sermon on the Mount. When Jesus says to his disciples, 'forgive others the wrongs they have done to you', it is because they themselves are receiving God's forgiveness (Matthew 6:14–15). When they are called to love their enemies, the reader naturally calls to mind the dynamic of God's own undeserved love (Matthew 5:44), and even the missionary work of the disciples was to be carried out on the same basis, as Jesus told them that 'You have received without paying, so give without being paid' (Matthew 10:8).

Freedom and the ethic of Jesus

One of the greatest temptations for readers of the Sermon on the Mount has always been to try to interpret it as a set of rules and regulations – a new law for Christians, which would replace the old law of the Old Testament. This tendency emerged very early in the church's history, and some scholars believe that even Matthew himself considered it to be a 'new law' delivered by Jesus on a mountain in Galilee, comparable to the 'old law' delivered by Moses on Mount Sinai.

Did Jesus abolish the Old Testament Law?

Given the many ways in which Jesus clearly not only challenged, but also set aside key requirements of the Old Testament Law, one statement found in the Sermon on the Mount presents some difficulties. This is the saying in Matthew 5:17–18: 'Think not that I have come to abolish the law and the prophets; I have come not to abolish them but to fulfil them. For truly, I say to you, till heaven and earth pass away, not an iota, not a dot, will pass from the law until all is accomplished.'

Several explanations of this statement have been proposed:

● The simplest is to argue that this saying is not, in fact, original to Jesus, but has come into the sermon later and reflects a situation in the Jewish Christian churches for whom Matthew was writing his gospel. Matthew might have had in mind the chaos that had been caused in some churches as a result of misunderstanding Paul's teaching about freedom from the restraint of the Law, and perhaps he wished to pre-empt any similar movement among the Christians he knew. This might sound like a drastic solution, but these verses are so out of character with the whole of the rest of Jesus' teaching that many scholars believe it to be the best answer.

● It has also been suggested that, when Jesus spoke of 'fulfilling the law', he might have meant something rather different from what we imagine him to mean. The kingdom of God spoken about by Jesus is usually depicted as the fulfilment of the Hebrew scriptures and, though Old Testament spirituality had been overloaded with legalism, especially in the immediate post-exilic period, the central core of Judaism did emphasize the place of the Law not as an awful burden, but as a delight and a joy. Could Jesus, therefore, have been referring not to what the Law had become to many people in his day (notably the social outcasts and 'people of the land'), but to its original intention, which called for a person's life to be right before God: 'what does the Lord require of you but to do justice, and to love kindness, and to walk humbly with your God?' (Micah 6:8)?

● It is also possible that what Jesus says about the Law's permanence is not to be taken literally. This could be an example of the kind of exaggerated hyperbole that he frequently used and, understood in this way, it might be saying no more than that he saw his mission and message as being firmly grounded in the Old Testament revelation.

But the ethical teaching of Jesus was never intended to be a 'law' in any sense at all.

The way Jesus expressed his teaching was quite different from the style in which law would be formulated. Law needs to be based on a calculation regarding how the majority of people can reasonably be expected to behave. A law that cannot easily be kept is a poor law, and it is no use making a law to put pressure on people to become what they are not. Yet this, of course, is exactly what Jesus' teaching does: it invites people to be different from how they would naturally be. It is, therefore, inadequate to regard it as a 'new law', because its requirements are not the kind that anyone could keep simply by 'making the effort'.

Throughout the course of his ministry Jesus was in conflict with the Pharisees, the guardians of the ancient traditions of his people. They were concerned with actions that could be governed by rules. There was nothing actually wrong with that: not only was it a faithful reflection of the demands of the Old Testament, but it was also a way of organizing society that had been well tried and tested, in ancient Israel as well as in many other social contexts. But Jesus had a different approach altogether to human behaviour. His primary concern was for people, and for him the secret of goodness was not to be found in obedience to rules, but in the spontaneous activities of a transformed character: 'A sound tree cannot bear evil fruit, nor can a bad tree bear good fruit' (Matthew 7:18).

Jesus' teaching was not a law, but an ethic of freedom. Consequently, Jesus did not burden his followers with rules and regulations, but gave them principles and guidelines by which to structure their lives. These principles were more concerned with what people are than with what they do, not because actions were unimportant to Jesus, but because he realized that the way people behave depends on their inner motivation and self-understanding. The principles were clear enough, and consisted of the images of God and the kingdom that are set out, both in parables and miracles. They give glimpses of 'God's way of doing things', which is what we suggested the concept of 'the kingdom' really amounts to. But Jesus' storytelling style of communication, opening up spaces in which people were invited to reflect for themselves exactly what might be the appropriate means of 'doing things God's way', in any given set of circumstances, ensured that it would always be incredibly difficult to turn his advice into a detailed set of moral prescriptions. Here, as in most other aspects of his teaching, Jesus provided his disciples with a compass from which they could get their bearings, rather than a map, which would provide them with specific directions. For those who like to have everything laid down in detail, Jesus will always remain a frustrating enigma, though others regularly find his open-ended approach empowering and inspirational. Either way, his refusal to legislate for human spirituality has ensured that people have found him a source of endless fascination over the last 2,000 years, and the trend looks set to continue.

10 Understanding the Gospels

Up to this point, we have said a great deal about the life and teachings of Jesus, but very little about the sources of information through which he may be known. Naturally, what has been said about Jesus has been mostly based on those parts of the New Testament which tell of his life and work – the four gospels, according to Matthew, Mark, Luke and John. In using them, several assumptions have been made about their character as literature, assumptions that have inevitably coloured the picture of Jesus presented here. For example, it has been assumed that, though they display some characteristics of biographical writing, they are not comprehensive chronicles of his entire life but rather are selective presentations of those aspects of his life and teaching which seemed most important to the people who first wrote them down. In addition, we have assumed that there is a good deal of overlap and repetition in their various accounts, so that one gospel may legitimately be used to elaborate or clarify the teaching contained in another. Then we have also taken it for granted that it is actually possible to know something about Jesus from the study of the gospels – that, although they are indeed the products of the early church and therefore reflect the concerns and interests of their writers, it is still possible to distil from them a core of hard information about Jesus as he actually was. In this chapter and the two which follow, some of these assumptions will be examined in greater detail, as we seek to understand the reasons for holding them, and to explore their implications.

What is a gospel?

Discussion of this question dominated scholarship throughout the twentieth century. For most of the century, the gospels were regarded as unique documents, a distinctive form of literature created by the early church for the specific purpose of sharing their own faith in Jesus, and used in the celebrations of Christian worship as well as in the missionary endeavour of inviting others to follow him. By the end of the century, however, a strong case was being presented for understanding the gospels in the context of other literature of the Hellenistic world, and in particular for seeing them as a form of Graeco-Roman biographical writing.

It is obvious that the gospels are not 'biography' in the modern sense of that word. A contemporary biography usually begins with an account of the subject's childhood years, and progresses consecutively through adolescence and adulthood to show how the mature person has developed in response to the various influences of early life and environment. By contrast, the main emphasis in the gospels is not on the course of Jesus' life, but on the events of the last week or so. This is prefaced by reports of Jesus' teaching and accounts of a few incidents from the three years immediately preceding his death, with virtually no mention at all of his childhood and adolescence.

The gospels and Graeco-Roman biography

Applying today's standards to the gospels is not likely to be particularly enlightening, for questions about the style or genre of a piece of writing need to be addressed in relation to the actual context in which it was written, and what possible models might have been current in that time and place. In assessing the genre of a particular piece, among other things we need to take account of the structure and style in which it is written, the stated intentions of the author (if any), the process whereby the writing has been put together, the way the author expected or intended it to be used, and the contents. Knowing what kind of writing we are dealing with – even in the most general terms – can make a difference to the way in which we read it.

An example taken from a world perhaps more familiar might help to illustrate this. Television is a major source of information for most people today, and in that medium the same subject might be treated in several programmes that belong to different genres. The topic of world debt, for example, might be considered in a news bulletin, or in a documentary investigation, or in a piece of drama. Depending on which genre the viewers believe a particular programme belongs to, they will view it differently. The genre of a news bulletin creates an expectation that this will be a factual account of the subject, whereas if a programme is perceived as a documentary viewers will expect it to be more wide-ranging, probing the subject from different perspectives, and constructing an argument that requires viewers to form some assessment of what is being claimed. More often than not, there will be an accompanying expectation that, no matter how personally detached the programme makers might try to be, they will have their own angle on the subject, and to a greater or lesser extent they will be crusading for the wider acceptance of their conclusions or recommendations. A piece of drama, perhaps illustrating the impact of debt on poor countries by telling the contrasting stories of life for a typical family in the West and in the developing world, might easily combine features of the news bulletin and the documentary, but viewers would instinctively look at it with yet different expectations, and a major purpose might easily be seen as entertainment, even though it deals with some very serious issues. In each case, the viewers' expectations of a particular genre will shape the way they understand and interpret what they are watching. Things are not always quite so clear-cut, of course, as programme-makers can make subtle changes to their basic genre, thereby confusing the audience about what they are seeing. In some TV programmes it can be hard to distinguish fact from fiction, for the two are either deliberately combined (as in drama-documentaries), or (as in science fiction movies) the visual effects make even the most unbelievable possibilities seem factual. But the general point still stands: genre affects how we approach a programme, and at what level we seek to understand and respond to it.

The same is true of literature. The genre within which the New Testament gospels are placed determines to a significant extent how the reader will process and understand what is in them. As long ago as 1915, C.W. Votaw proposed that in the world of the Roman empire, the gospels could best be understood as part of the genre of popular biography. The emergence of form criticism, however, moved discussion in a different direction, and two form-critical insights in particular seemed to undermine the possibility that the gospels should be understood in this way:

■ Form critics generally saw the gospels as collections of traditions about Jesus' life and teaching that emerged from the life of the earliest Christian communities, rather than being the creative work of particular authors.

■ Form critics viewed the gospels as 'kerygmatic' documents, written to proclaim the primitive Christian message (*kerygma*), and if they provided any sort of portrait of Jesus as he might have been that was an unexpected bonus and not the primary purpose.

Further study – and in particular the emergence of redaction criticism (which is dealt with in more detail in the next chapter) – called these presuppositions into question. In particular, the gospel writers ('evangelists') came to be regarded as creative writers, not merely collecting traditions that were handed onto them, but actually shaping and presenting them in ways they believed would be most appropriate to their readership. In that light, the need to define what kind of literature they thought they were writing once again emerged as a key question. After several false starts, in which the gospels were occasionally compared to what turned out to be non-existent genres of literature in the Roman world, the popular biography now seems to be the category into which they might most easily be fitted. It is not difficult to find similarities between the gospels and such works:

■ In some instances, the gospels share particular stylistic characteristics of popular Graeco-Roman biographies. Luke's preface, for example (Luke 1:1–4) follows a common literary practice of ancient writings, while both Matthew and Luke provide genealogies of their subject, and Luke also includes some time indications placing Jesus in the context of events in the wider Hellenistic world (2:1–2; 3:1–2).

■ The continuous nature of the gospel narratives, albeit generally encompassing only a short period of time, places them in the category of biography, as distinct from the so-called apocryphal gospels of the second century, which contain disconnected sayings or stories, without any overall framework.

■ Though the early Christians wanted to say much more about it, the way in which the gospels portray Jesus' death as a heroic martyrdom was another regular feature of traditional biographies of the time.

■ The gospels regularly use some literary devices that were popular with biographers: for example, the placing of key events or significant teaching within the context of meals, or the descriptions of private conversations and discussions between Jesus the teacher and his disciples.

■ Though there are exceptions, both gospels and ancient biographies generally displayed no interest in the personal psychological growth and development of the subject (something which readily distinguishes them from modern biography).

At the same time, some features of the gospels serve to set them apart from Graeco-Roman biographies:

■ All four gospels were anonymous pieces of writing (the names of Matthew, Mark, Luke and John were attached to them only later, probably to distinguish them from one another once they were all circulating together). This was highly unusual among traditional Greek or Latin authors.

■ Luke is the only one who shares any significant stylistic characteristics with classical authors, though his gospel also raises other issues in relation to the fact that it is only the first part of a two-volume work, which included Acts. While it is not impossible to regard Acts as a continuation in the form of a biography, that is neither the most obvious nor the most plausible literary genre for it. It might be, though, that Luke (and, to a lesser extent, Matthew) represents a stage of gospel writing at which Christians were becoming more aware of the possibility of commending Jesus to educated Romans by conscious adoption of the literary conventions of the day.

■ All the gospels include extensive references to the Old Testament as a way of explaining their subject matter. This would not generally recommend them to the literary élite of their day, and might actually have prevented their recognition in such circles, where examples from the Greek and Latin classics would have been considered more appropriate, and also more widely known. At the same time, it perhaps indicates that a better place to search for literary antecedents for the gospels might be the Jewish tradition, if not the Old Testament itself.

■ While traditional biographers would have portrayed their subjects as models of particular virtues that were admired by society at large, the gospel writers say very little about Jesus' personal characteristics, and when they do it is not to affirm some existing assumptions, but to present Jesus as the originator of a new set of values altogether.

■ The gospels appear to have been written not for general circulation in the literary market place, but for the benefit of Christian groups who would use them in the context of their own worship and mission.

■ An additional complicating factor in this attempt to place the gospels within a literary context in the Hellenistic world, is the ongoing disagreement among experts in Graeco-Roman literature about the actual extent to which authors would follow the allegedly typical characteristics of a particular genre. There is some evidence that there was not necessarily a rigid demarcation between different genres, and that any given author might actually choose to combine a variety of styles in a particular piece of writing, for example by incorporating into a biographical narrative features that would have been more at home in a novel, especially in elaborating the details of private conversations or in describing events that took place behind closed doors.

In the light of all these considerations, the best conclusion still seems to be that, while the gospels show a much greater acquaintance with the conventions of ancient literature than was once believed – especially with the category of popular biography – they have too many distinctive features for it to be plausibly concluded that their authors were self-consciously compiling works of literature that would take their place alongside the writings of classical authors. It is more likely that the evangelists had an awareness of the styles in which others were writing about their own heroes at the time, and were influenced by the conventions of the day only in the general sense that they were themselves part of Hellenistic culture, and had a general familiarity with the way in which literature might be constructed. Though their works undoubtedly display some of the characteristic features of biography, they are rooted within a distinctive set of purposes that more closely related to the needs of the evangelists and the Christian communities for which they wrote.

Gospel writers on the gospels

In the end, we are still left with the necessity of turning to the gospels themselves in order to ascertain their nature. What did their authors think they were doing as they wrote? The obvious place to begin is with Mark, which is commonly thought to be the earliest of the four, and therefore to a large extent provided a model for the others, especially Matthew and Luke, which in different ways may be regarded as revised versions of Mark. Mark 1:1 describes this work as 'The beginning of the gospel of Jesus Christ', a statement which stands as a kind of title or heading to what follows. Two words are relevant here in relation to understanding the purpose of the gospel: the words 'beginning' and 'gospel'. 'Gospel' is simply the English equivalent of Mark's Greek word *euangelion*, and it was originally chosen because the two words had the same meaning: 'good news'. Mark, then, was writing about 'the beginning of the good news', which was not something detached or distant from Mark and his readers, but could actually be a way of referring to their own spirituality.

Mark and the other gospel writers had heard the 'good news' about Jesus, and their own lives had taken a totally new direction as a result of their acceptance of it and their decision to follow Jesus. For them, an important part of discipleship was the need to make known to others the message that had changed their own lives. Their preaching and teaching did of course have a cognitive element within it, along the lines of those basic statements of faith identified by C.H. Dodd as the earliest *kerygma* (chapter 5). But for Mark and his contemporaries this message was far more than just a bare statement of propositional truths about Christian belief: it was also in an important sense the 'good news' of their faith, which had expressed itself in their own lives as they opened themselves to the possibility of changing values and standards, and experienced the empowerment which came to them as they sought to follow Jesus and put into practice God's ways of doing things.

When Mark described his gospel as 'the beginning of the good news', he was therefore saying that his purpose was to describe the first stage in the development of the message to which he and others had responded. The story he told was not a historical curiosity, but was an integral and important part of their own story and experience as Christians. Luke had a similar intention, and in his preface informed his readers that his narrative was designed to enable them to know the full implications of the Christian message which they had heard so often (Luke 1:4). Indeed, Luke felt an even greater compulsion than Mark to emphasize the continuity of the life of the church with the life of Jesus by writing a second volume (the Acts of the Apostles) to bring the story more fully up to date.

When the writers of the gospels are called 'evangelists', therefore, this is a very precise definition of their intention. For they were primarily concerned to deliver the message about Jesus to their own contemporaries, and the normal interests of a biographer were very much a secondary consideration. This observation has at least three important consequences for our understanding of the gospels they wrote:

■ The gospels must be regarded as *selective accounts* of the life and teachings of Jesus. On occasion, incidents from Jesus' life and teaching might have been used as illustrations to explain more abstract theological points, though we may be sure that the stories would also be told for their own sake, as self-contained presentations of the Christian message requiring no further explanation. Indeed Papias, a leader of the church at Hierapolis in the early second century, claimed that Mark's

Gospel consisted of summaries of the stories told by none other than Peter himself (Papias, quoted in Eusebius, *Ecclesiastical History* III.39.15).

The fact that the information contained in the gospels was first presented in this way goes some way towards explaining the apparent incompleteness of the gospel accounts. All four of them put together would hardly contain enough information to document three years of anyone's life, let alone someone as active as Jesus. But when we realize that the information they contain has been preserved because of its relevance to the life of the earliest churches, we can readily understand why so much that we would like to know has been left out. This probably explains why the New Testament has no mention of the early childhood of Jesus, nor for that matter any descriptions of what he looked like, or the kind of person he was. Had the evangelists been writing merely to satisfy people's curiosity about Jesus, they might have included that sort of information. But that was not their intention. They were primarily concerned to nurture the faith of their Christian communities, and to invite other people to follow Jesus, and for these purposes such details were quite irrelevant.

■ If the gospels are illustrations of the apostolic preaching, this means that their contents cannot be regarded as simple stories about Jesus. They must be closely related to the beliefs of the evangelists. At one time it was fashionable to suppose that it was possible to recover from the gospels a picture of a simple Galilean teacher which had later been altered by Paul and others into a theological message about the Son of God. But it is now widely recognized that the gospels are themselves among the most important theological documents of the early church, and we can never in fact discover a picture of Jesus as a simple Galilean teacher. As far back as it is possible to go, the Jesus found in the pages of the New Testament is always a person who is at the centre of great claims about his significance and who utters definitive pronouncements on the relationship of people to God. All his teaching and every incident recorded in the gospels has a specifically theological dimension to it.

■ If, as we have suggested, the authors selected their materials to serve their own purposes in writing, then it follows that we can probably discover something about them and their readers by comparing their relative selection and use of information about Jesus. In the case of the first three gospels this can be done quite easily, for they tell roughly the same story in the same order, and each of them repeats large sections of the material that is found in the others. By comparing the different ways that Matthew, Mark and Luke have used the deeds and teaching of Jesus in their narratives, it is possible to learn something about them and the situation in which they lived and worked.

So to understand the gospels fully is a rather complex business. We need to know why the evangelists wrote as and when they did. Then we need to try to understand the way they assembled their material, and why they used it in one particular way rather than another. In addition, we must always bear in mind that their gospels were intended to serve the ongoing purposes of the church, which means that in the final analysis they were not written as biography, history, novels, or even theology in the usual sense.

Preaching and writing

Where did the evangelists get their information, and what did they do with it? This question has occupied much scholarly attention since about the mid-nineteenth century. It has at times led investigators down many tedious blind alleys, though that should not be allowed to conceal its usefulness and relevance to developing a considered understanding of the nature of the gospels. The way authors use their sources can provide helpful clues to the purpose of their writings, and to know what a writer is doing can be an essential part of grasping his or her message. Method and message are more closely connected than many readers appreciate.

Since the gospels developed in the context of the mission and worship of the early church, we can expect to find clues to their origin by examining the church's message, which typically centred around three major themes: the promises of the Old Testament, information about Jesus and his significance, and a personal appeal to those who heard about these things to respond by choosing to follow Jesus for themselves.

Old Testament texts

A major underlying assumption of the beliefs of the early church was that the promises of the Old Testament had been fulfilled in the life of Jesus. In the New Testament summaries of the church's message, this statement is often made in a rather generalized way, but in real-life situations it must have consisted of a more specific declaration, whether in a predominantly Jewish or a mainly Gentile context. Anyone who was already familiar with the Old Testament would not have been content to know that, in some general way, Jesus was the fulfilment of the ancient scriptures: they would have wanted a clear explanation of precisely which prophecies Jesus was supposed to have fulfilled, and on what evidence such a claim might be based. At the time, a favourite preoccupation of several groups within Judaism was the compilation of lists of Old Testament promises which the Messiah would fulfil when he came. Several such lists have been found at Qumran, but they were not the only people who had such an interest. These lists are generally referred to by scholars as *testimonia*, referring to their function in providing scriptural testimonies to the coming of Christ.

The New Testament contains several indications that suggest these text-lists were probably in regular use among Christians from the earliest times. Matthew and John both refer to a considerable number of texts from the Old Testament, with an indication that they were fulfilled in some particular incident in the life of Jesus. The passages they quote are often relatively obscure, and it is striking that Matthew and John hardly ever used the same ones – perhaps because they were using different collections of *testimonia*.

Some of Paul's letters also string Old Testament texts together in continuous passages in what often seems to be a rather arbitrary fashion, and here again it is reasonable to think that Paul must originally have found these grouped together under the same headings in a collection of Old Testament texts to which he had access. It could easily be that the collection of these texts from the Old Testament was the very earliest form of literary activity in the Christian church. They would be assembled for the convenience of those who were engaged in sharing the Christian message so that they could give specific examples to support their claim that Jesus had fulfilled the traditional expectations concerning the Messiah.

Words of Jesus

The central element in the *kerygma* was a series of statements about Jesus himself. No doubt in the very earliest days of the church's existence it would be possible to proclaim the message with no more than a passing reference to Jesus' life and teachings, particularly in Palestine in the years immediately following the death of Jesus himself, for many could be assumed to know something about Jesus and his teaching, even if they had no personal experience of him. But, before long, Christian missionaries were spreading out far beyond Palestine and carrying their teaching to parts of the Roman empire where Jesus was quite unknown. In this different environment it would have been essential for the Christian message to include some kind of information about Jesus himself, if only a skeletal outline of the most significant events such as death and resurrection.

Once people had become Christians they would require further instruction in their new faith, which would presumably include the kind of information about Christian beliefs and behaviour that could also be found in the various New Testament letters. One obvious and important source of such teaching must have been the remembered statements of Jesus himself. This would not necessarily be separately identified as information about Jesus, but would be incorporated into the developing tradition of the churches. For instance, in Romans 12 – 14 Paul gives advice that is so reminiscent of some of the most distinctive aspects of Jesus' teaching in the Sermon on the Mount that it is most natural to

Paul's use of only small sections of Jesus' teachings known from the gospels raises many questions. However, this diagram highlights the fact that it is only possible to trace the exact source of a particular passage when it occurs in more than one text. In other places, Paul could have been using Jesus tradition, but we have no way of recognizing it as such.

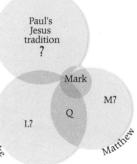

suppose that the two derive from the same source, even though Paul never actually says that he was quoting from, or alluding to the teaching of Jesus. Other parts of Paul's writings also show that traditions related to Jesus' life and teaching were familiar to the early Gentile churches (1 Corinthians 7:10–11; 11:23–26; 15:3–11).

It is therefore quite likely that long before the gospels were written in their present form the sayings of Jesus had already been collected together to form the basis of teaching for new converts in the early church. No doubt there would be a number of such collections of Jesus' teaching (generally referred to as *logia*, a Greek word meaning 'sayings'), compiled for different purposes and occasions.

In addition to these general considerations, other indications also support the belief that this would be one of the earliest types of Christian writing about Jesus:

■ There certainly were later collections of this kind, even long after the writing of the New Testament gospels. A number of papyrus fragments dating from the third century AD, found at Oxyrhynchus in Egypt, contain sayings of Jesus, some of them different from those found in the gospels, while the various Gnostic gospels also generally consist of sayings, as distinct from narratives. They were all compiled for different purposes than the New Testament gospels, and contain sayings of Jesus not found there, which might or might not be authentic. But quite apart from arguments about their genuineness, the existence of such documents shows quite clearly that the collection of sayings of Jesus was an ongoing activity in Christian circles.

■ The organization of the material in the gospels often seems to suggest that Jesus' sayings had been grouped together before they were placed in their present context. There are many groups of sayings which are only loosely linked together and do not form any kind of consecutive argument. For example, the sayings about salt in Mark 9:49–50 appear to have no intrinsic thematic connection with each other apart from the fact that they all mention salt: possibly they had already been gathered together on that basis alone before Mark incorporated them in his gospel. The same can probably be said for even quite extensive sections such as the Sermon on the Mount. Here too, there is no very obvious consecutive argument running through these chapters (Matthew 5 – 7), and it seems certain that the sermon as such was gathered together by Matthew, as the same sayings appear in quite different contexts in Luke's Gospel. No doubt the fact that these particular teachings of Jesus all deal with issues of Christian behaviour was a major reason why they were put together in this way, to provide a compendium of ethical teaching that would be easily accessible to new converts.

■ A strong reason for assuming the existence of collections of Jesus' sayings early in the church's history has been the fact that Matthew and Luke have a large amount of material that is common to both their gospels, but which is altogether absent from Mark's Gospel. This material consists almost entirely of Jesus' teachings, but it also includes the story of his baptism and temptations (Matthew 3:13 – 4:11; Luke 3:21–22; 4:1–13) and the story of one miracle, the healing of the centurion's servant (Matthew 8:5–13; Luke 7:1–10). The generally accepted explanation of this common material is that Matthew and Luke both used the same collection of Jesus' sayings and incorporated it into their respective gospels.

This sayings collection is referred to as 'Q', a convenient abbreviation of the German word *Quelle*, meaning 'source'. It is widely believed to have been a written document, whose original order has been generally preserved by Luke when he incorporated its material into his own gospel. For this reason, it has become conventional to refer to Q material by using the symbol Q followed by the chapter and verse reference from Luke. So, for example, the original Q story of the healing of the centurion's servant (as distinct from the edited versions of it contained in Matthew and Luke) might be referred to as Q 7:1–10. A few scholars argue that Q did not exist in written form, but was a looser collection of traditions existing in oral form. Its existence in some more or less fixed form is certainly credible, not least because its alleged contents are quite similar in their arrangement to the collections of prophetic oracles that we find in

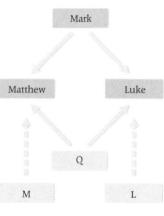

Synoptic gospels

the Old Testament. Prophetic books generally contained predominantly the prophet's spoken messages, gathered together and edited by disciples, but supplemented by an account of the prophet's call and just one or two representative incidents from his life. The tradition called Q seems to have adopted the same literary model: an account of the baptism and temptation of Jesus (which can reasonably be equated with his call), and an illustration of the most typical of his activities (a healing miracle), but with the main emphasis on his teaching.

The synoptic gospels and their sources.

From the evidence assembled so far, it may be concluded that from the very earliest times the church's main interest was in two kinds of literature: the *testimonia*, and the *logia* of Jesus. They might also have had a commonly agreed outline of the course of Jesus' life and teaching, though that is less certain. In any event, it was not long before it became necessary to gather all this material together in a more permanent form, perhaps in the first instance by the rewriting of *logia* in the light of the *testimonia*, supplemented by an outline narrative to give coherence and form to the enterprise. It is difficult to be sure for how long this process continued, but the end product was to be the four documents we now know as the gospels of Matthew, Mark, Luke and John.

Putting the gospels together

The first three gospels are referred to as the synoptics because they are so much alike: when they are set out in columns alongside one another, it is obvious that much of their material is a variation on a common theme shared by the others, though each of them is too distinctive in its emphases for the relationship between them to be understood merely as different editions of the same information. The precise way in which these three gospels are related to one another is at the centre of the 'synoptic problem'.

Many of the resemblances between these gospels could be explained by imagining that their authors had used the same collections of sayings, which had been circulating in slightly different forms among different groups of Christians, but a close examination of them shows that this would be too simplistic a solution. There are so many instances where the three synoptics use precisely the same language, vocabulary and grammatical constructions in the same contexts that the only reasonable conclusion is that they must have shared written sources.

As early as the fourth century, Augustine was proposing that Matthew must have been written first, Mark then made a summary of Matthew's work, and eventually Luke came along and wrote his gospel on the basis of both Matthew and Mark. This view was widely held until the late nineteenth century, though from time to time variations on it were proposed – most notably by J.J. Griesbach (1745–1812) who accepted Augustine's view on the priority of Matthew, but argued that Luke came next, and Mark eventually abbreviated both of them to write his own gospel.

With only a very few exceptions, no one today would accept any of that. To suppose that Matthew or Luke was the first gospel raises more questions than it answers:

■ Why would anyone have wanted to condense Matthew and Luke in order to make a gospel like Mark? Compared with the two longer gospels, Mark's short narrative can hardly be regarded as comprehensive. It has no mention at all of Jesus' birth or childhood, comparatively little about some of his most distinctive teaching, and only a very abbreviated account of the resurrection. Since the gospel writers selected their materials according to the interests and concerns of their readers, we must allow that in principle there would be no reason why an abbreviated version of Matthew and Luke should not have been produced. But given the absolute centrality of precisely those elements which are either missed out or underplayed in Mark, it is virtually impossible to envisage any Christian group that would have been satisfied with Mark's account of Jesus if they already had access to Matthew and Luke. Indeed, it was not long before Christians almost universally ignored Mark and preferred Matthew and Luke for this very reason. If Mark was written last, in full knowledge of the other two synoptic gospels, it is very difficult to explain why it was written at all.

■ Much of Mark's language seems to point to the same conclusion. If Mark used the polished accounts of Matthew and Luke, why did he so often write Greek that is virtually unintelligible? The parable of the mustard seed is a good example: Matthew and Luke are similar to each other, and both contain eloquent Greek expressed in a sophisticated style (Matthew 13:31–32; Luke 13:18–19). Mark 4:30–32, by contrast, contains a very complicated Greek sentence which is lacking any verb, and which makes imperfect sense as it is. If Mark was copying Matthew's or Luke's account, then it looks as if he went out of his way to avoid using their grammatically correct words, substituting a construction that is all but meaningless. It is very difficult to think of a good reason for doing that.

■ It is almost as difficult to believe that Luke read and used Matthew's Gospel. If he did, then here again he seems to have adopted some unexpected literary procedures. From a literary standpoint, Matthew contains one of the greatest masterpieces in any of the gospels, the Sermon on the Mount. If Luke had that before him as he wrote, why did he break it all up, using some of its content in his own Sermon on the Plain, but scattering the rest of it in small sections all over his own gospel?

There are many other examples of similar problems at other points in these three gospels, which is why most scholars have preferred a rather different explanation of their relationships to one other. The more generally accepted explanation of the resemblances between the synoptic gospels is that Matthew and Luke both used two source documents in writing their own accounts of Jesus' life and teaching. These were the sources we now know as Mark's Gospel and the hypothetical document Q. It is, of course, certain that Luke, at least, used a variety of sources in composing his gospel, for he explicitly says that he had sifted through the work of other people, selecting those parts of their record that were suitable for his own purpose in writing, and in view of its close literary connections with Mark and Luke, it seems highly likely that the author of Matthew must have used the same method in his work.

Five major considerations point to the conclusion that Matthew and Luke used Mark.

WORDING

A comparison of the words used in different texts is a very simple way of determining their literary connections. More than half of Mark's actual vocabulary is contained in Matthew and Luke, and both of them have identical sections not found in Mark. So it seems that there was one source known to them all, and another source used only by Matthew and Luke.

ORDER

If the order of events in a narrative contained in more than one gospel also corresponds with those sections that have the same wording, it is reasonable to go a step further and assume that a common source lies behind them, whose order as well as wording has been substantially reproduced by all three evangelists. Again, there is much evidence for this. Matthew, Mark and Luke all follow the same general order of events, beginning with John the Baptist's prophetic ministry, followed up by a time when Jesus taught in Galilee, all the while provoking increased opposition from the religious authorities. During this period, Jesus is shown making journeys to remote northern areas to give teaching privately to his disciples, before finally they go to Jerusalem, and Jesus' last days, his trials, crucifixion and resurrection. It is not just that the same general narrative framework appears in all three synoptics, for within this framework particular incidents are also often recorded in the same order.

This feature of the synoptic gospels is easiest to explain if Matthew and Luke were using Mark, and not the other way round. For it is striking that when Matthew departs from Mark's order, Luke has the same order as Mark; and when Luke departs from Mark's order, Matthew follows Mark (for specific examples, compare Mark 3:13–19 with Matthew 10:1–4 and Luke 6:12–16). There is only one incident which both of them place differently from Mark: the appointment of the twelve disciples. Sometimes Matthew or Luke will leave the pattern of Mark's narrative in order to add something new, but after their addition they usually return to the point in Mark at which they left off. This is one of the strongest arguments to support the conclusion that Matthew and Luke must have copied Mark, and not the other way round.

CONTENT

An analysis of the content of the narratives also reveals the use of different sources. If one writer records the same story in the same words and order as another author, then it is reasonable to suppose either that both have used the same source, or that one has used the work of the other. This is what happened in the case of the synoptic gospels: of the 661 verses in Mark, 606 are found in Matthew in a virtually identical form, and about half of them are also contained in Luke.

STYLE

This is a very difficult criterion to use satisfactorily, for an author's style can depend on so many things: the situation in which he or she is writing, the readership that is in mind, whether a secretary was used, and so on.

There certainly are some marked stylistic differences between Mark and the other two synoptists, and on the whole Mark's Gospel is written in a poorer Greek than the others. For example, he very often describes incidents in the historic present tense (using the present tense to speak of something that happened in the past). Even in the same passages, however, Matthew and Luke always have a past tense, which is, of course, the correct literary form. This argument for dependence of Matthew and Luke on Mark is not as strong as it is sometimes imagined to be, for it relies on the assumption that the evangelists would of necessity use their sources in a rather wooden way, simply copying out word for word what they had before them. In reality, not many authors would follow a source closely enough for its style to obscure their own, and if Mark was poor at writing Greek, then his grammar would tend to be poor whether or not he was copying from some other source. But other considerations all point to Matthew and Luke having used Mark, not the other way round. For example, in eight cases where Mark records sayings of Jesus in Aramaic there is no trace of this in Luke, and only one example in Matthew. It would certainly be more likely that Matthew and Luke would have omitted the Aramaic sayings than that Mark would have deliberately introduced them.

IDEAS AND THEOLOGY

If it could be shown that one gospel narrative contains a more developed theology than another, then it might seem reasonable to regard it as the later of the two. There are certainly some discernible differences of emphasis in the gospels. For example, Matthew and Luke appear to have modified or omitted certain statements in Mark that could be thought dishonouring to Jesus. The blunt statement of Mark 6:5, that in Nazareth Jesus 'could do no mighty work' appears in Matthew 13:58 as 'he did not do many mighty works there', while Luke omits it altogether. Similarly, Jesus' question in Mark 10:18, 'Why do you call me good?' appears in Matthew 19:17 as, 'Why do you ask me about what is good?'

Surely, then, the more primitive a statement, the earlier it must be? This can be made to seem like a simple test, but it is not so simple to apply in practice. It is not always easy to determine whether an apparent difference in attitude is a real one, nor is it altogether straightforward and self-evident how a particular view should be described as 'developed' as opposed to another view that is characterized as 'primitive'. Even supposing it might be possible to make such a differentiation with some degree of certainty, why should a 'developed' theology be regarded as chronologically later than a more 'primitive' outlook? Throughout the history of the church – and still today – simplistic beliefs have existed alongside more sophisticated and complex ones, and the acceptance of one or the other is more clearly related to personal choice and temperament than it is to any kind of time considerations. In terms of the first century, the theology of Paul (highly 'developed' by any standards) was certainly in existence long before the gospels were written, and there is also some evidence to indicate that there was considerable diversity of theological expression in all the major centres of Christianity at the time. Had there not been, most of the rest of the New Testament would never have been written at all! The question of theological diversity will be taken up in a later chapter; here it is simply important to note that equating theological difference with an extending timeframe is, at best, a very subjective business.

Not all these five factors are of equal importance, and it is not hard to pinpoint real or imaginary difficulties with some of them. But taken together, the cumulative effect of their evidence is most easily explained if we suppose that Matthew and Luke used Mark's account, rather than that Matthew was the original gospel which Mark summarized and from which Luke made selective extracts.

New light on old problems

Much of the emphasis in New Testament scholarship is now moving away from a mechanistic analysis of the gospels, towards a more holistic effort to understand their origins in the total context of the social

Two sources or four?

What has been said so far about the way the gospels came to be written represents the broad consensus among New Testament scholars; though there might be differences of opinion on points of detail, this solution to the synoptic problem is, in general outline, universally held by virtually everyone.

But in addition to the idea that the synoptic gospels depend mainly on the two sources Mark and Q, it has been suggested that these are not the only sources that can be discerned behind these gospels. Perhaps the classic statement of this solution to the synoptic problem (certainly in the English-speaking world) was set out by B.H. Streeter in his 1924 book, *The Four Gospels*. He not only proposed that Matthew and Luke used Mark's Gospel and Q, but suggested that in addition it was possible to trace two further sources which he called M and L. In effect this material was simply what is left of the accounts of Matthew and Luke once the Marcan and Q material has been removed, but Streeter's identification of them was important, because he believed that these two collections of material were themselves separate and coherent sources of independent origin, and therefore could be used alongside the others when it came to matters of the historicity and value of the traditions.

Streeter began his observations from the fact that Matthew and Luke each seem to have used Mark in rather different ways. Matthew followed Mark's order and general framework very closely, though at the same time he frequently rewrote the actual material, and often condensed material from Mark to make more room for additional information. The result is that Matthew's Gospel looks rather like an enlarged edition of Mark. But Luke is different, for whereas Matthew made use of almost all the material contained in Mark, Luke's Gospel contains only about half of Mark's material. What is more, Streeter discovered that if all the Marcan material is removed from Matthew, what is left has no coherence and the book simply falls to pieces. But if the same thing is done with Luke, what is left is a reasonably consistent and continuous story. This is particularly true of the stories of Jesus' death and resurrection in Luke, which seem to have a different underlying shape than the stories in Matthew and

experience of the early Christian communities. Though the two-source theory of gospel origins is still widely accepted, new angles are constantly being explored, some of which might well have a decisive influence on future understandings of the way the New Testament came to be written.

Did Q really exist?

Questions continue to be asked about the two-source hypothesis itself. Debates that seemed to have been settled in principle almost 100 years ago are now being reopened, and much of the evidence for the two-source theory is being looked at again. Was Mark really the first gospel to be written? Did Q ever exist independently as yet another 'gospel'? If so, why was it originally written, and what was its distinctive message? Is it really necessary to suppose that Q represents a fixed collection of *logia* rather than just a looser collection of traditions known by both Matthew and Luke? Several reasons have been advanced for doubting the existence of Q:

Mark, and appear to have been supplemented by information from Mark, rather than being based on Mark's story.

In the light of these observations Streeter suggested that, before Mark was written, Luke must have compiled a first draft of his gospel, based on the sayings collection Q and the material labelled L, which he had obtained from the church at Caesarea where he stayed while Paul was in prison (Acts 23:23 – 27:2). Streeter called this first draft of the gospel 'Proto-Luke'. Then, he suggested, when Luke was living in Rome at a slightly later date he got to know of Mark's Gospel, which had been written in the intervening years, and he fitted extracts from it into his own already existing Proto-Luke. At the same time, he might also have added the preface (Luke 1:1–4) and the stories of Jesus' birth in chapters one and two.

Several considerations certainly give plausibility to this theory. For example, Luke often contains a different version of a story from Mark's. The story of Jesus' rejection at Nazareth is a good example (Mark 6:1–6; Luke 4:16–30), in which it is obvious that both evangelists are reporting the same incident, but Luke's account is so much fuller that it seems likely that he

must have had a different source of information. Streeter also drew attention to the way that small sections of Mark's narrative, often in Mark's exact wording, appear to have been inserted into the middle of other material in Luke, creating the impression that they were later additions. It is also striking that a great deal of information contained in Mark is simply omitted in Luke, and Streeter argued that if Luke had known of Mark's Gospel when he first wrote his own, he would have included more of Mark's material in it.

Another feature of Luke's Gospel which Streeter's theory seemed to explain is the way in which Luke appears to have two beginnings. The preface at 1:1–4 is followed by the stories of Jesus' birth, but then the flow of the narrative is interrupted at 3:1, which reads like another beginning, with its careful dating of the opening of Jesus' ministry, followed by the list of his ancestors in 3:23–38. If 3:1 was the original beginning of Proto-Luke, to which Luke later prefaced what is now chapters 1 and 2, that could provide a credible explanation of this unusual feature.

The importance of Streeter's theory about the way Luke wrote his gospel lies

■ There is no hard evidence of its existence. In spite of the confidence with which scholars have reconstructed Q, and even claim to be able to give an account of its own literary history and development, no one has ever seen it. There is not even a fragment of any ancient manuscript of Q, nor is there a single reference to its existence anywhere in ancient literature. Nineteenth-century scholars believed that Papias was referring to Q in his statement that Matthew 'compiled the *logia* in the Hebrew language, and each one interpreted it as he could' (quoted in Eusebius, *Ecclesiastical History* III.39). But Papias used the very same word *logia* to describe the whole of Mark's Gospel, so there is no reason to imagine he was referring to a collection of the sayings of Jesus rather than the completed Gospel of Matthew – still less that Q could have been the specific sayings collection he had in mind.

■ There are no other ancient documents that look like Q. Though some Gnostic gospels (especially the *Gospel of Thomas*) provide a kind of parallel for interest in collecting sayings of Jesus, and though such interest seems inherently likely among his followers, Q is not actually like

---

Two sources or four?
continued

in the fact that if there ever was a Proto-Luke, this would form another independent and early source of knowledge of the life and teachings of Jesus. It has not, however, commanded anything like universal assent, though it continues to have its advocates. One of its major weaknesses is the assumption that Streeter made about the nature of the gospel traditions in the early churches. He assumed that the gospels were written in a neatly defined, linear way, and tended to think of the evangelists as if they had been newspaper editors, sitting down with reports from several sources and extracting various sections from different written documents. This was a popular concept in the early twentieth century, and was widely applied to the study of both Old and New Testaments, often combined with an evolutionary perspective on literary development which supposed that tradition develops from more or less primitive forms to more sophisticated ones. Subsequent research has shown that this was a considerable over-simplification of the matter, at several different levels. It could well have been, for example, that Luke was familiar with the Marcan material, but not through Mark's Gospel in its present form.

This is also a weakness in other suggestions that Streeter put forward. He argued not only that four identifiable sources can be traced behind the synoptic gospels, but that each of them represented the traditions of the life and teaching of Jesus as they had been preserved in the four most important centres of early Christianity: Mark was written in Rome, Q in Antioch, M in Jerusalem and L in Caesarea. If it could be demonstrated, this would be a neat way to understand not only the gospel traditions, but also some aspects of the life of the early Christian communities. But it was based on flawed assumptions, not least the idea that what Streeter called M and L were coherent documents. In reality, however, this is hardly the case: when the Marcan and Q material is taken away from Matthew, what is left is not a coherent collection at all, and the same is true to a lesser extent of L, which is just Luke's Gospel minus the Q and Marcan material.

Thomas in that it contains some narrative material as well. It is therefore difficult to identify a specific genre to which Q might belong. This is not a conclusive argument, as the early Christians do seem to have been remarkably creative in the way they produced their literature. For people who actually invented a new type of book (the codex) by fastening single pages down one edge, in place of the more cumbersome use of lengthy scrolls, departing from literary and stylistic norms would hardly be an adventurous move. Yet it would still be surprising that there should only be one single example of a Q-style writing, especially when we know that the early church was not embarrassed to preserve multiple diverse accounts of Jesus, as for example in the finished gospels themselves.

■ In a considerable number of passages, Matthew's and Luke's texts agree over against Mark's, in either wording or order. This can generally be explained by the assumption that, at some points, there was overlap between Mark and Q, and that Matthew and Luke preferred the fuller version generally believed to be contained in Q. However, some of these agreements of Matthew and Luke against Mark are found in the story of Jesus' death (compare, for example, Matthew 26:67–68 / Luke 22:63–64 with Mark 14:65), and since every account of the scope of the hypothetical Q has concluded that it did not contain a passion narrative, some scholars want to argue that this phenomenon can more easily be explained on the assumption that Luke used Matthew than by reference to the traditional view that both of them used Q.

■ The existence of Q has also been questioned on the basis of considerations related to the way in which ancient authors might have operated. It has been claimed that when a writer is using a source, while the information might be sharpened up and reshaped at the beginning of the day, as tiredness sinks in there will be a tendency to revert to the underlying patterns of whatever source is being used – and that in the case of the so-called Q material, such evidence always shows Luke reverting to Matthew's forms of expression. For example, in the parable of the talents (Matthew 25:14–30; Luke 19:11–27) Matthew has three servants, and Luke has ten. But as the story is told, Luke mentions 'the first', 'the second', and then 'the other' servant (19:16, 18, 20), which is easier to understand if Luke knew Matthew than if both of them were using the hypothetical Q. Those who wish to dispose of Q also argue that the very notion of gospel writers using sources in this way is a legacy from a previous generation which adopted a 'scissors and paste' approach to literature, which can no longer be sustained – and if M and L as separate written sources should be jettisoned, then so should Q.

In spite of all this, the consensus still favours the two-document hypothesis, according to which Mark was written first and Q had a more or less fixed form, in which it was used by Matthew and Luke independently. A major reason for this is that, while some of the arguments against Q carry some weight, the traditional view still seems to be more capable overall of answering more questions than the view that Luke used Matthew. Given the nature of the argument, there will always be room for disagreement on the details, but for the present at least, most scholars are still prepared to believe that the balance of probability lies in believing that Q was a real gospel source, whose existence solves more problems than it creates.

Who were the gospels for?

Ever since the rise of form criticism in the early part of the twentieth century, a major assumption on the part of scholars was that the four gospels were each written for quite specific readerships, and emerged within particular Christian communities. The reason for there being four gospels, rather than just one, has been explained in terms of the different challenges faced by Christians in different social and religious contexts, and the need for these diverse questions to be addressed using the stories and teachings of Jesus. Just as Paul and other Christian leaders

---

Form criticism

Once the two-source theory had been widely accepted as the most likely explanation of the 'mechanics' of gospel writing, a whole series of new questions began to present themselves. For the isolation of the various sources used by the evangelists in composing their accounts of Jesus' life and teaching only answers the question, where did the gospels come from? But there is also the further question, where did their sources come from? What was happening to the traditions about Jesus between his death and resurrection and their preservation in writing in the gospels?

These questions had occurred to a number of scholars in Germany even before B.H. Streeter had published his classic work on gospel origins – The Four Gospels – in 1924, and in trying to answer them, they came up with a new method of analysing the Bible literature. This was largely the creation of Hermann Gunkel (1862–1932), who began his academic career as a professor of New Testament, though his most lasting reputation has been as a scholar of the Old Testament. His interests, however, also included the study of other traditional literature, as well

as psychology and other emerging social science disciplines. He realized the Bible was not written in a cultural vacuum, and concluded it would be worthwhile to compare the way its authors worked with what was known of the way other similar writings came into being. In particular, he observed that the literature of nations and movements always develops not in a self-conscious literary way, but as a natural part of everyday life. That means the lifestyle (not to mention the temperament and disposition) of those who write and read it plays a key role in its formation. Gunkel studied literary forms in the hope of being able to reach beyond the text to see how the books had been used in real life, and in the process to shed new light on the history of the text itself. This procedure was reflected in the term he used to describe his work, Formgeschichte, which literally means not 'form criticism', but 'form history'.

Gunkel's application of this method to the Psalms broke new ground, and New Testament scholars soon began applying it to the gospels, most notably K.L. Schmidt, Martin Dibelius, and Rudolf Bultmann. Two well-established conclusions on the writing of the gospels seemed to make it natural to explore this new methodology:

wrote letters to inform and inspire faith in their readers, and to address their questions about lifestyle and beliefs, so the evangelists wrote their gospels for roughly the same purposes. Therefore, while their main intention might not have been to document the experiences of the various communities to which they belonged, it is nevertheless possible to discern within the nuances of the different gospels the distinctive concerns of the churches for whose use they were written. These assumptions arose from the form-critical belief that social function can be read out of the literary form of a narrative, and this in turn encouraged the development of redaction criticism as a discipline which would try to give a coherent account of the communities which produced the gospels in their final form.

This way of understanding the gospels has been questioned, on several grounds:

■ It is argued that the gospels are a different kind of literature from the New Testament epistles, and that to apply the same methodology

---

● Before the rise of critical study, the gospels had been understood as straightforward lives of Jesus, written to preserve a historical account of his deeds and words. That position had been abandoned at an early stage in critical study, to be replaced by the view that the evangelists wrote for essentially pragmatic purposes, to meet the needs of the early Christian communities. These needs mostly related to evangelization (sharing the Christian message with others), liturgy (regular worship), catechesis and paranesis (the teaching of Christians about their faith), and conflict resolution (on such topics as Christian attitudes to observance of the Jewish Law). On this understanding, the gospels were not comprehensive accounts of either Jesus' deeds or his words, but were selective recollections about him extrapolated from a much larger pool of available material – and the sole basis on which the stories about Jesus were selected and preserved was their relevance to significant questions and debates in the life of the early Christian communities. Two of the gospel writers actually said this (Luke 1:1–4; John 20:30–31;

21:25), but the full implications of that had never previously been noticed.

● Within this frame of reference, creating a continuous story of Jesus' life from start to finish was neither necessary nor appropriate. This is the sense in which it might be said that the early Christians had no particular interest in the 'historical Jesus'. To claim, as some have done, that it would have made no difference to their faith whether or not Jesus ever existed is absurd. But the evangelists were less interested in constructing a 'life of Jesus' than in saying something to demonstrate his relevance to the everyday experience of his followers. Again, Luke and John spelled this out clearly and there is no reason to suppose Matthew and Mark operated in any different way. This practical purpose had repercussions for the way the evangelists (particularly the synoptists) arranged their material in short paragraphs or sections (*pericopes*), with no obvious continuity of either narrative or argument running from one to the other. The apparent lack of connection from one *pericope* to the next is so striking that K.L. Schmidt could refer to the individual sections as 'pearls on a string'. Even where stories seem to have been gathered together in blocks prior to their inclusion in

to understanding them is a fallacy. In order to understand the epistles, it is undoubtedly necessary to have at least some knowledge of the various communities to which they were addressed, even if the epistles themselves may then be used to develop even more detailed perceptions of the concerns of those same communities. But in the case of the gospels, no such prior knowledge seems to be required.

■ The idea that the evangelists would write only for other Christians implies a parochial mentality that other evidence does not support. Roman society as a whole was remarkably mobile, and Christian leaders travelled extensively, seeing the church as a worldwide movement and encouraging the various Christian communities not to remain separate, but to communicate regularly with one another in order the more effectively to encourage one another's faith.

■ It has also been argued that the only reason why scholars would have wished to identify the gospels so closely with specific communities was

---

Form criticism
continued

the gospels, the basis of such collation was invariably topical rather than historical or biographical. So, for example, the material in Mark 2:1 – 3:6 consists entirely of stories about controversy, while Mark 4:35 – 5:43 is a collection of miracle stories and Matthew 5 – 7 is a block of teaching (the Sermon on the Mount). The only possible exception seems to be the story of Jesus' death, which has an internal argument and organization that might imply it was always preserved as one continuous story – though even that was probably related to apologetic concerns, namely the need to explain how a respected teacher could meet such an unexpected end.

The forms

Building on these established results of scholarship, form critics speculated that individual stories would be preserved in different 'forms', depending on their context and purpose. This 'life situation' (in German, *Sitz im Leben*) would then determine the way in which things were expressed. The term 'form' referred to features such as the length of a particular *pericope*, its structure, way of organizing material and so on. This methodology had already been well tested in relation to the

traditional folk literature of northern Europe, but form in this sense is still a familiar part of modern life. Think, for example, of the difference between a TV documentary and a game show. They might easily deal with the same subject (say, sport), but their approach is quite different. In fact, just by observing the structure of each programme, viewers can instantly distinguish between the two, without needing to know anything at all about sport. In the same way, form critics suggested it is possible to identify the context in which particular sections of the gospels had been used in the life of the early church just by looking at their form.

If this could be done reliably, it would of course be an invaluable aid to understanding the gospels, for if it were possible to know the use to which the various traditions were put in the early church, that would in turn illuminate their relevance to the church's life, and potentially reveal new dimensions of their essential meaning. Unfortunately, however, the form critics have failed to agree on this essential point, and though Martin Dibelius gave what has come to be regarded as the classic analysis of gospel forms in 1919, his five main forms have by no means been universally accepted by others.

A fragment of the Egerton papyrus (first half of the 2nd century), containing scraps of the text of a non-canonical gospel.

However, it is worth reviewing them here as they illustrate the kind of things that form criticism looks for.

Paradigms

Different scholars gave different names to these stories. Rudolf Bultmann called them 'apothegms', while Vincent Taylor more prosaically called them 'pronouncement stories'. Whatever they are called, they certainly do form a distinctive group of stories, distinguished by the way they all culminate with a punch-line. Some of them contain narrative, but the key thing is the pithy statement that comes at the end, and all other details are secondary. Several examples are found in the early chapters of Mark (see 2:1 – 3:6). This literary form was common in both Greek and Jewish literature of the time, and provided Christians with memorable slogans to describe significant aspects of their beliefs. Dibelius believed that this form originated in the earliest Christian preaching, in which such stories would be used as examples and illustrations. In addition to the use of a striking saying as the culmination of such stories, they were also characterized by their tendency to minimize pictorial description in order to focus attention on the most important element, which was the saying of Jesus. When a story is handed on orally, two things may typically happen to it. Either it can be worn down by frequent repetition, so that little remains apart from the most essential facts expressed in as succinct and striking a way as possible – or the opposite can happen, with extra details being added to make it more realistic and interesting. Most form critics regarded the paradigms as having been worn down to their bare essentials, rather than being elaborated as they were handed on.

Tales

Dibelius defined these as stories told for the sake of being a good story, and he included many (though not all) of the miracle stories in this group. Vincent Taylor actually called this form 'miracle stories'. Again, there were similar forms elsewhere in the first-century milieu, and it is not hard to imagine Christians utilizing them to highlight Jesus' own powers as a means of authenticating his message. In these stories Jesus' deeds are much more important than his words. Dibelius believed they were the work of professional storytellers in the early church, whose job was to cast stories about Jesus into the same form as the

related to a loss of confidence in them as historical sources for the life and teaching of Jesus himself. This topic is dealt with in a later chapter. But, the argument goes, if the gospels tell us little or nothing about Jesus, they must still contain information about something – and that something must therefore be the life of their own communities, presented in quasi-allegorical form through the narratives about Jesus. If such scepticism was rejected, there would be no reason to suppose that the gospels were written for other Christians in specified locations: instead, they can be understood as general literature written for the same reasons as anyone might write a book, to communicate a message to as many people as possible.

Arguments like this have caused a stir in the world of New Testament scholarship, though the idea that the evangelists saw themselves as literary artists writing for anyone who would read their books raises its own questions:

Form criticism
continued

stories of the Greek gods, in order to win converts to the Christian faith by demonstrating that Jesus was superior to other deities. The New Testament never explicitly mentions storytellers in the early Christian communities – perhaps because this way of sharing faith was so common that its existence could be taken for granted. Certainly, given the general popularity of storytelling in the ancient world, not to mention the fact that Jesus' own most characteristic method of communication was in the telling of stories, it would be surprising if his followers did not self-consciously use the same approach. To suppose that the stories of Jesus were carefully crafted by professional storytellers is not to imply any particular view of the reliability of their picture of Jesus. In view of the fact that the gospels themselves were written down in something less than a generation after the events they describe, there cannot have been too much scope for the free creation of fictitious details about him. But there can equally be little doubt that the stories of the gospels have, for the most part, been carefully crafted so as to capture the imagination of those who would read or hear them.

Legends
Dibelius chose this term because of its common use (in his day) to describe traditional stories about the lives of the saints, the main point of which was typically to provide a moral example for others to follow. By using this terminology, he was not intending to make any value judgment about the historical reliability or otherwise of these stories, though he was of the opinion that they would often be fictitious. Their main function was to glorify the person they describe, rather than to report any factual information about him. Examples of this 'form' in the gospels would be Matthew 14:28–33; 16:13–23; 27:3–8; Luke 2:41–49.

Myths
For Dibelius, this term indicated stories in which a human person interacted with some other spiritual or supernatural world. He included only three gospel stories here: Jesus' baptism (Mark 1:9–11 and parallels), temptations (Matthew 4:1–11 and parallel in Luke), and transfiguration (Mark 9:2–8 and parallels).

Exhortations
By exhortations Dibelius meant teaching. There is of course a lot of teaching in the

■ The suggestion that the evangelists saw themselves as producing literature for wide circulation depends to some extent on the view that their gospels fit neatly into the category of Graeco-Roman biography – which was usually composed for general circulation. But, as we have already noticed, the gospels do not represent a pure form of this genre. They are more accurately described as religious works written with some of the style of biography than as biographical works written about a religious subject. In the case of the only two evangelists who explicitly spell out their purposes in writing, both of them quite specifically say they were writing to encourage and nurture Christians in their already-existing faith (Luke 1:1–4; John 20:31).

■ The gospels for the most part do not actually speak a language that would automatically have been accessible to any readers who cared to pick them up. They assume a community of common understanding, whose ways of expressing things was in many respects very different from the wider Hellenistic world. For example, the extensive use of the

gospels, and there are very many diverse forms of it. But since he believed it was all used in the same context in the life of the church (i.e. the instruction of converts) Dibelius lumped it all together. The parables would obviously belong here, along with other sayings.

Criticisms of form criticism

Throughout the twentieth century, the methodology as well as the conclusions of form criticism have been subjected to extensive appraisal. In the process, the method has been refined to meet some of the objections. The following are the main points of debate:

● Some have questioned the appropriateness of the entire method. They point out that the early development of form criticism owed a great deal to theories about the compilation of north European folklore, which was not only separated by time and distance from the biblical writings, but also originated in a very different cultural context which was arguably alien to the Semitic mindset. How relevant is it to extrapolate principles and theories from one culture and apply them to another at a different period of history? Rudolf Bultmann addressed this concern by drawing attention to what he considered

parallels to New Testament 'forms' in the works of Jewish rabbis – but virtually all his examples suffered from the same weakness, dating from a time much later than the New Testament. However, subsequent research has shown that the concept of literary forms was indeed known in Hellenistic writing both before and after the first century, and though some earlier claims might have been exaggerated, the general models provided by form criticism are still of value, provided their limitations are recognized.

● Even supposing that forms were a common device, have form critics sometimes been over-enthusiastic in their assumption that the biblical writers were so consistently and exclusively influenced by convention and custom in the way they spoke and wrote that a particular genre (or *Gattung*, the German term) always had the same terminology, style and *Sitz im Leben*? While this is in general a safe assumption, form criticism did not always make enough allowance for the distinctive and particular. In reality, passages that clearly share the same general form often also show considerable variation in detail, and by emphasizing the common elements it is all too easy to miss the distinctive intention of particular speakers or writers. One of the

Hebrew scriptures, not only in general terms but through the citation of specific quotations, presupposes some prior knowledge on the part of readers. The many nuances in the descriptions of Jesus, in which he can be compared to Old Testament characters, not to mention the use of technical terms, all implies an original readership with some knowledge of such matters. When, as in John's Gospel, the Jewish background is explained, it is done in a self-conscious way that implies it was not normally necessary – and, indeed, in the case of John was quite likely done at a time when the gospel was being reissued for somewhat wider circulation than it had originally enjoyed.

■ Though it was a worldwide network, with many of its leaders travelling regularly around the churches, who must therefore have known of each other's existence, the early church was also a threatened minority group. In such circumstances, the preservation of the story of its own origins for its own internal support would have been a perfectly natural thing to do. With the likely exception of Luke, at least one

---

Form criticism continued

few things that all sources seem to testify to is Jesus' difference from other teachers, not his similarity to them.

● Form and content cannot be separated as easily as some form critics have supposed, and to concentrate on form alone can be misleading. In theory, once the 'pure' version of a form has been identified (by, for example, comparative study of Greek, Latin or Jewish literature), it should then be possible to check the extent to which any particular New Testament example departs from it, and thereby to identify some of the distinctive aspects of the New Testament's message. In practice, it is not at all easy to identify such pure forms. Dibelius and Bultmann both argued strongly in favour of using pure forms as the starting point, but in practice their categories were often not based on form at all, but on content. Dibelius' legends, myths and exhortations were all classifications of content, not of form, and it is arguable that tales were as well (they are all miracle stories, though in this case the content does seem to be accompanied by a distinctive form). The only category which was unambiguously based on literary form was the paradigm. To take account of the obvious diversity of forms found in the New Testament,

scholars today operate with a much more elastic definition of forms than Dibelius or Bultmann. But this raises a different set of problems, because the more flexibility there is, the less useful the whole analysis of forms becomes.

● Form criticism has sometimes become a circular and self-validating form of study. A scholar's prior understanding of how forms develop does affect exegetical judgments on particular passages. Dibelius and Bultmann believed that over time the forms became more complex, while Taylor argued the exact opposite – that the stories and teachings were worn down with much repetition so that what is left now is the bare essentials. To see the difference these different assumptions can make, we might think of study of the parables. It has generally been assumed that the parables all follow one form, and only ever make one single point. If so, it is a foregone conclusion that any additional points or 'explanations' of a parable's meaning must be later additions to the text. But if there was diversity in the forms, or if the evangelists were creative writers and not merely collectors of traditions, then this understanding would be at least questioned, and might be undermined completely. Self-validating arguments like

purpose of the gospels was to provide reassurance and support to groups who were either suffering persecution or were feeling threatened in some way by others, and who would value the specific support that could be given to them by the writing of their own gospel, which would show how their particular predicament was rooted in the origins of their group, and might be addressed by resources drawn from the experience of their founder, Jesus himself.

No doubt the gospels, like other Christian literature, did circulate among communities other than those for whom they were first compiled. There is evidence for the exchange of epistles, though only within local areas (Colossians 4:16), and it was not until nearer the end of the first century that wider collections of Christian writings were made. Of course, if the two-source theory of the origins of the synoptic gospels is correct, it also assumes that the evangelists had access to the writings of other people. But it is important to remember that though travel in the Roman empire

---

this are not intrinsically without value: the formulation and testing of a hypothesis is a proven procedure in many fields of research. But the constant challenging of the hypothesis is important, and this is what has often been lacking in New Testament study. In its original version, form criticism depended on the accuracy of Schmidt's notion that the evangelists were only stringing pearls together. Redaction criticism has now shown that the string is at least as significant as the pearls, and that needs to modify the method.

● Form criticism has also been criticized for paying too little attention to other kinds of evidence, notably historical commentary. For example, it was too easy to move from the observation that exhortations were preserved in a catechetical context in the early church, to the conclusion that much of the teaching of Jesus was invented by early Christians to answer their own ethical or theological questions. Ernst Käsemann went as far as to comment that form criticism 'was designed to show that the message of Jesus as given to us by the synoptists is, for the most part, not authentic, but was minted by the faith of the primitive Christian community in its various stages.' Moreover, it is not as easy as it seems to identify particular forms

with specific life contexts. Klaus Berger has questioned whether life settings do actually give rise to literary forms, and insists that it is rarely possible to correlate individual *pericopes* with particular life situations. Even granting that such an enterprise is possible, how can we be sure that we have identified the most useful parallels? For example, what assurance can there be that stories of Jesus' miracles had the same function as Hellenistic stories of divine wonder workers that share the same literary form? How do we know that the forms of the Jewish world operated in the same way – particularly given the traditional Jewish concern for the accurate transmission of the teachings of the rabbis? In the hands of Birger Gerhardsson, this Jewish concern for accuracy in preserving the teaching of rabbis became a powerful reason for rejecting form criticism altogether. He clearly overstated his case: the mere fact that the early church preserved four different gospels shows that they were able to live happily with some diversity in the traditions about Jesus. The form-critical quest is still worth following, but with greater sensitivity to the nuances of the cultural context than has been the case in the past.

was relatively easy, it would still only be the upper classes who were easily mobile, and that itself is probably sufficient to explain how Matthew or Luke could have laid hands on Mark's work or the hypothetical Q. The majority of Christians were unlikely to have been literate, and when they discovered the stories of the gospels, it would be as they heard them read out in their own church community. If others beyond the churches learned these stories, most of them would do so by being introduced to such reading and storytelling sessions by their Christian friends in the places where they lived, which itself underlines the likelihood that, as the stories developed, they would be told in ways that had direct local relevance.

Study of the gospels does not stand still for long. The assured results of one generation are constantly being probed and questioned, if not abandoned, by those who come after them. Whether today's questions will continue to be as important as they seem to be right now, remains to be seen. No doubt new questions will present themselves, many of

---

Form criticism
continued

The value of form criticism

● At the time of its development, form criticism was a corrective to the findings and attitudes of historical and literary criticism. There were some questions that these methods had been unable to address. They could not construct a literary history of the New Testament, nor were they able adequately to understand all the diverse contours of New Testament faith. The picture painted by historical and literary criticism turned out to be too simple and unilinear, partly because it studied the early church in isolation from its wider cultural and religious context, and partly because it tended to impose a rigid evolutionary framework in which theological ideas could only develop in one direction, from simple to complex. Form criticism at least identified the right questions that would give access to the pre-literary period of the gospels, even though it now seems that time might have been much shorter than was once imagined.

● Form criticism highlighted the fact that serious study must begin with understanding the kind of literature we are reading, the literary category to which it belongs, and its characteristic features. This is particularly important when we recall that Jesus was operating in a cultural context with its own long literary history and traditions.

● Form criticism set out to discover the function of literary genre in the life of the community or the individual, how and when it was used and for what purpose. This is one of its features that is both a weakness and a strength. There will certainly always be room for legitimate disagreement on this, as it is inevitably a circular argument to use our present understandings of the forms to determine the needs that existed in the churches, and then to use these needs as a way of understanding and interpreting the forms. But as long as we remember such conclusions are tentative, there is nothing wrong with this. In any case, the rest of the New Testament gives at least some glimpses into what was going on in the early church, and can be used as a check.

Those who want to reject form criticism out of hand are being too extreme. On the other hand, if form criticism is applied as if it were the only possible way to understand the gospels, then it can lead to unreliable — even absurd — conclusions. Past generations have sometimes made that mistake, and it is not for nothing that

them of a different kind from those asked by earlier generations. One of the major shifts during the course of the twentieth century was a recognition that, wherever the evangelists obtained their own information, each of them has written what is essentially an original composition, distinctive in important respects from the work of any of the others. Much of the interest is now focused on what the evangelists were doing, rather than on revealing the mechanics of how they were doing it. As a result, theological insights need to be used to supplement the earlier findings of the literary critics.

---

more recent scholars have supplemented it with redaction criticism, rhetorical criticism, and other reader-oriented methods of understanding texts. No one method by itself can possibly answer all our questions in relation to the writing of the gospels. But that is not a reason for rejecting it outright. Form criticism is an important part of the jigsaw – but it is the whole picture that is ultimately significant, not merely the individual pieces. When combined with other methods of investigation, form criticism's positive outcomes far outweigh whatever weaknesses it might have. Understanding just how a form is being used and reshaped gives important clues to a writer's purpose – but a satisfactory analysis and evaluation of those clues will only emerge out of a more comprehensive investigation, in which form criticism is just one of several possible methods that must be used.

11 Four Portraits of Jesus

Mark

Mark's Gospel is considered first because it is now recognized as a basic source for the other two synoptic gospels. It is, however, only in fairly recent times that Mark has received careful attention. It was generally neglected by the church in earlier centuries, in favour of the longer accounts of Matthew and Luke. This is hardly surprising, for they contain most of Mark's information and a lot more as well, and so Mark soon came to be regarded as an abbreviated version of Matthew. But the situation has now changed and, with the knowledge that Mark's Gospel was almost certainly the first to be written, it has achieved an eminence it has probably never enjoyed since the time of its first compilation.

Ancient evidence

There is, however, some evidence to show that it was valued in certain Christian circles not long after its composition. Papias (c. AD60–130) identified Mark as 'Peter's interpreter', and reported that 'he wrote down accurately, but not in order, as much as he could remember of the things said and done by Christ' (quoted in Eusebius, *Ecclesiastical History* III.39.15). Irenaeus (*Against Heresies* I.1.1) and Clement of Alexandria (in Eusebius, *Ecclesiastical History* VI.14.6ff) also associated Mark's Gospel with Peter's preaching, and in more recent times the contents of the gospel have often been thought to support the belief that Peter was the source of much of it.

A number of stories are told with such vivid details that it is natural to regard them as first-hand accounts of the events they describe. The story of Peter's call (1:14–20) and of Jesus' first sabbath in Capernaum, when Peter's mother-in-law was healed (1:29–34), are good examples of this. In addition, some of the references to the disciples, and to Peter in particular, are highly unfavourable. The disciples are consistently portrayed as ignorant and obtuse, repeatedly failing to understand what Jesus was trying to teach them (4:35–41; 5:25–34; 6:37–38; 8:14–21, 31–33; 9:2–6, 32; 10:35–45). In Mark's Gospel the disciples are not at all the kind of people the later church liked to think they were, and it is unlikely that they would have been depicted in such an unfavourable light had Mark not had good information, perhaps coming from Peter himself, to support such a picture.

The author

Mark, or Marcus, was a very common name, and he could have been anybody. In considering matters of authorship, our starting point has to be the fact that none of the gospels actually names its writer. John's Gospel comes nearest to doing so, but even then it is only an enigmatic reference to a witness to the crucifixion (John 19:35), and though this person is often identified with the 'beloved disciple', it is far from clear who that might have been. In this respect the gospels are quite different from most of the rest of the New Testament, for they are presented as anonymous writings. The traditional ascriptions to Matthew, Mark, Luke and John were of course added at an early stage, but they represent the opinions of the early church about the authors of the gospels, rather than any sort of claim by the authors themselves.

It is clear from the evidence that the author of the second gospel was generally associated by the early church with a person called John Mark who is known from other parts of the New Testament (Acts 12:12). According to Acts, a group of Christians regularly met in his mother's house in Jerusalem, and John Mark himself is named as the companion of Paul and Barnabas in their earliest missionary work (Acts 12:25; 15:37–41). Though Mark deserted them, Paul mentions him favourably in two of his later letters (Colossians 4:10; Philemon 24), so they must have patched up their differences. He is also spoken of with affection in 1 Peter 5:13 and that (depending on one's view of the authorship of 1 Peter) may be taken as evidence for associating him with Peter as well as with Paul.

It is more difficult to be certain that this same Mark was actually the author of the gospel, though in view of the tendency of second-century Christians to associate books of the New Testament with key figures in the early church, it might well be that the tradition connecting Mark with the second gospel is not altogether untrustworthy. John Mark was a comparatively insignificant person, and not the kind of individual who would be credited with writing a gospel unless there was good reason to believe that he did in fact do so.

The readers

It is generally thought that Mark's Gospel was written in Rome, to serve the needs of the church there. Irenaeus and Clement of Alexandria disagree on the precise circumstances of its composition, but both agree it was written in Rome. If the author of the gospel was indeed John Mark, then references to him in the New Testament also place him in Rome.

The gospel was certainly written for a non-Jewish readership. Aramaic phrases such as *talitha, koum* or *ephphatha* are translated into Greek for the benefit of Mark's readers (5:41; 7:34). Jewish customs are also explained in a way that suggests they were unfamiliar (7:3–4). There are also a number of Latin technical terms in Mark, which suggests that the gospel originated in a part of the Roman empire where Latin was spoken (4:21; 12:42; 14:65; 15:19). In view of all these pieces of evidence Rome certainly seems to be a plausible place of composition.

The date

Dating the gospel, however, is not so easy, for a number of reasons:

■ The evidence of the church fathers is contradictory. Clement of Alexandria says that Mark wrote the gospel under Peter's dictation, and that the final draft of it was approved by Peter himself. But Irenaeus places the writing of the gospel after the deaths of both Peter and Paul. This means that we have to try to decide from the evidence of the gospel itself when it might have been written, which is no easy task.

Peter dictating the gospel to Mark. From an 11th-century Italian ivory relief.

■ It is often thought that the many references to trials and persecutions in Mark suggest that his readers were suffering for their faith in Christ (8:34–38; 10:33–34, 45; 13:8–13). If this is so, it could date the gospel somewhere between AD60 and 70, during which period Nero tried to blame the Christians for problems in the city of Rome. But of course, persecution was such a common feature of church life in the first century that it is not essential to connect Mark's Gospel with one of the more well-known persecutions. There must have been many local persecutions that have left little trace in literary sources, though they would be real enough to those who had to suffer them.

■ Then there is the question of whether the apocalyptic section in Mark 13:1–37 presupposes that Jerusalem had already fallen to the Romans when it was written. Since this took place in AD70, an answer to this question would at least date the gospel on one side or the other of that event. Here again opinion is divided, though a majority of scholars place the gospel's composition between AD60 and 70, or even a little later.

Mark's purpose in writing

Mark's intention in writing is revealed in the key themes which appear in his gospel:

■ If, as the early traditions suggest, this gospel had some connection with Peter, one reason for its composition could well have been the desire to preserve Peter's reminiscences as a lasting testimony for the church. This would be especially easy to understand if Mark wrote at a time immediately preceding, or just after, Peter's death. To this extent,

Mark probably did have some kind of biographical purpose in view. The theme of persecution also features in several passages relating to the nature of discipleship. The disciples and their faith, or lack of it, form a significant literary motif in the structure of Mark's narrative. Stories about them are used to introduce new aspects of Jesus' ministry in the main section of the gospel (1:16–20; 3:13–19; 6:7–13), and in the second half of the narrative the disciples are the focus of continual attention, playing a key role even in the final enigmatic paragraph of the entire gospel (16:7–8).

■ The failure of the disciples to appreciate that following Jesus would involve suffering is related to the way Mark presents Jesus as Messiah. The opening sentence confirms the importance of messiahship for Mark's presentation of Jesus (1:1), and this theme is expounded in different ways throughout, sometimes in association with the title 'Son of God' (1:1; 1:11; 3:11; 5:7; 15:39), while at other times the 'Son of man' terminology is more prominent (occurring no fewer than thirteen times between 8:31 and 14:62). Mark's understanding of Jesus' divine significance ('Christology') is always related to the themes of suffering and the cross: ultimately, it is through the cross that Jesus' true nature as Messiah is revealed.

■ Alongside the elevated descriptions of Jesus as Messiah, Son of God, and Son of man, Mark also presents Jesus as a very human figure: he can be angry on occasions (1:43; 3:5; 8:12; 8:33; 10:14); he is unable to perform miracles if the appropriate conditions of faith are absent (6:1–6); and he suffers physically in a way that might be thought incompatible with his position as the Son of God (8:31–33; 9:31). At one time these things were thought to be signs of Mark's 'primitive' theology, though that is not the only possible explanation. A better one might be to place it in the context of first-century debates about what it meant for Jesus to be regarded as both human and divine. Under the influence of a metaphysical dualism inherited from Greek philosophy, many Christians struggled to understand how God (a spiritual being) could have any contact at all with this material world, and resolved their problem by supposing that the divine Christ-spirit only entered the human Jesus at his baptism, and left him again before the crucifixion. Such people came to be known as Docetists, because they held that Jesus only seemed to be human (from the Greek verb *dokeo*, 'to seem'). The writer of 1 John was certainly concerned to correct such people, and John's Gospel might have been as well. But Mark could also have been intended as a corrective to this idea: in response to those who were asserting that Jesus' humanity was illusory, Mark emphasized its reality by depicting him as the divine Messiah whose origin and significance was both hidden and revealed in the life of a truly human person.

Mark's ending

The best ancient manuscripts have Mark ending at what is now designated 16:8, which appears to be part-way through a sentence, and

therefore an odd way to conclude a book. There is no evidence that Mark's narrative was originally longer, though there have been suggestions that the final page was torn off at an early stage and lost, which would explain the efforts of later writers to make good the omission by adding either what is now known as the 'longer ending' of 16:9–20, or a somewhat shorter one which is indicated in the footnotes of most Bible versions. Mark 16:8 is certainly a dramatic and unexpected ending, especially since it means there are no resurrection stories in Mark, and indeed the resurrection is only hinted at in the most general way possible. This certainly cannot have been because Mark did not either believe or expect a final glorification of the crucified Jesus, for there are several passages elsewhere which point forward to precisely such an outcome for his ministry (9:2–8; 13:26–37; 14:62). It might be that the explanation is to be found in the secrecy motif that pervades Mark's narrative, alongside the many stories that show the disciples failing to comprehend the full meaning of all that Jesus was saying, though some have argued that Mark was influenced by the classic structure of Greek tragedy, and this conclusion was intended to be a particularly striking form of the *denouement* that regularly ended such literature, after catastrophe had befallen the hero.

Was Mark influenced in writing his gospel by the classic structure of Greek tragedy? The scene shown on this vase is from the tragedy *Choephoroi* by Aeschylus.

Luke

Traditions associating the third gospel with a person called Luke date from as early as the second century. The Muratorian Canon and the anti-Marcionite Prologue to Luke, as well as Irenaeus, Clement of Alexandria, Origen and Tertullian, all identify Luke as its author. The exact value of these traditions is, however, uncertain, since most of what they contain could just as easily have been deduced from the New Testament itself, and so they are not necessarily of any independent worth. The evidence of the New Testament is in fact more useful in identifying the author.

■ A distinctive feature of Luke's Gospel is that it is not complete in itself: it is the first volume of the two-volume history of early Christianity which is continued in the Acts of the Apostles. The style and language of these two books is so similar that there can be no doubt they were both the product of one writer. Both are addressed to the same person, whose name is given as Theophilus (Luke 1:1–4; Acts 1:1).

■ In Acts there are certain passages known as the 'we passages'. They are given this name because at these points the narrative changes from using 'they' and 'he' to the pronoun 'we' (Acts 16:10–17; 20:5–15; 21:1–18; 27:1 – 28:16). Though it is never clearly stated who the 'we' are, the use of this pronoun clearly implies that the writer was present on these occasions, and therefore was a companion of Paul. Since the style of these passages is the same as that of the book as a whole, it seems likely that the author has used his own travel diary as a source of information, and a careful scrutiny of the narratives shows that Luke is the person who best fits the evidence.

■ This Luke is identified as a doctor by Paul, and it has occasionally been proposed that the author of Luke and Acts displays a particular interest in the diagnosis of illness – though it is likely that the limited medical terminology used would be familiar to any intelligent person in the Roman world. But there are one or two points in the gospel at which Luke seems to show himself to be more sympathetic than Mark to the work of doctors. This comes out very noticeably in the story of how Jesus healed a woman with an incurable haemorrhage. Mark 5:26 records that she had been treated by many doctors, and then comments, somewhat cynically, 'She had spent all her money, but instead of getting better she got worse all the time,' while Luke 8:43, on the other hand, simply comments that 'no one had been able to cure her'.

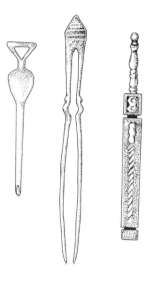

Part of a collection of instruments used by a Roman doctor.

Luke is mentioned three times in the New Testament. On each occasion he is said to be a companion of Paul, and in Colossians 4:14 Paul says that he was not a Jew (see also Philemon 24; 2 Timothy 4:11). That would probably make him the only Gentile writer of the New Testament. The Greek style of Luke–Acts certainly suggests that their author could have been a native Greek speaker.

According to Eusebius (*Ecclesiastical History* II.4.6) Luke came from Antioch in Syria, and one ancient manuscript of Acts 11:28 implies that he was in Antioch when the church there received news of the impending famine. But the generally accepted text of Acts has Luke join Paul when he entered Europe for the first time. He also accompanied Paul on his final journey to Jerusalem, and then on to Rome itself. According to Streeter and others, Luke might have collected some material for his gospel during this period from the church at Caesarea – though his final version of it might well have been written in Rome.

The date

It is not possible to be certain of the exact date when Luke finished his gospel. Since he incorporated in his own account some material from Mark, he must have written the final draft of his own book after Mark's

Gospel was written and in circulation, so the date given to Luke will depend to some extent on the date we assign to Mark. It has been suggested that Luke 21:5–24 displays a knowledge of the fall of Jerusalem to the Romans in AD70, and if so the finished gospel would need to be dated sometime after that.

Luke's purpose in writing

Why did Luke write his gospel? There has been extensive discussion of this, in relation to Luke in particular, and some key themes can be identified:

■ Luke articulates his purpose in the prologue to the gospel (1:1–4), where he indicates that he was writing for a person called Theophilus, 'so that you will know the full truth about everything which you have been taught'. Moreover, he states that he undertook this work in a consciously literary manner, studying the accounts written by other people, and then on that basis compiling what he describes as 'an orderly account'. While Luke was not solely motivated by biographical concerns, he emphasizes his concern for historical record more clearly than any of the other evangelists.

■ Partly arising from this, Luke continually emphasizes that the events he describes are part of a much larger divine plan for the whole of history. The notion that God has a plan is repeated many times (1:14–17, 31–35, 46–55, 68–79; 2:9–14, 30–35; 4:16–30; 13:31–35; 24:44–49, and in many other places). Luke makes explicit connections between his story of Jesus and the history of Judaism, and goes out of his way to demonstrate the continuity of Christianity with the Old Testament, while also insisting that Jesus was the fulfilment of all God's promises, and so the old ways had been superseded. Right from the outset, he makes it clear that those who follow Jesus do not first need to become Jews in order to be Christians, but that Jesus had come to be 'a light... to the Gentiles' (2:32). By the time Luke was writing, there were many more Gentile Christians than Jewish ones, and the relationship of Judaism and Christianity had become a significant issue. Luke portrays them both as part of a much bigger picture: in his account, the story of salvation (often referred to by the German term *Heilsgeschichte*) spans the whole of time, though the life, death and resurrection of Jesus is presented as the mid-point of all time: the event to which the Old Testament was pointing forward, and from which all subsequent human life could take its meaning (2:11; 4:21; 5:26; 13:32–33; 23:42–43).

Luke used this observation to bridge the gap between the events of Jesus' life and the concerns of the Christians for whom he was writing. He stressed this connection especially by his emphasis on the role of the Holy Spirit as a key player in the entire drama of salvation. The Spirit features at significant points in the story (1:35; 3:15–18, 21–22; 4:1, 14, 16–18), and by underlining the way in which the Spirit operated both in the life of Jesus and in the ongoing life of the Christian community

(24:49), Luke links together the two volumes of his writings, and in the process assures his readers that though Jesus the Messiah might seem to be dead, and therefore absent from the scene, he is very much present through the continuing work of the Spirit. It might be that Luke emphasized the continuing presence of Jesus with his followers as a corrective to some of his contemporaries who were becoming impatient because the second coming of Jesus, the *parousia*, had not yet taken place. He reminded them that although his final appearance in glory is yet in the future, Jesus is with his people in a real way through the presence of the Holy Spirit in their lives.

■ Another notable feature of Luke's Gospel is its emphasis on the nature of the community that was established by Jesus, and continued through to his own day. In particular, he stresses the inclusive nature of that community of disciples: the Christian message is for everyone. In recounting the story of the infant Jesus, Luke included the statement that he was to be 'a light to reveal God's will to the Gentiles' (2:32). In tracing Jesus' ancestry, Luke 3:23–38 went back to Adam, the common ancestor of all, in contrast to Matthew 1:1–17, which traced it back only to Abraham, the forebear of the Jewish race. In Luke's account of the sermon in the synagogue at Nazareth, Jesus' message was concerned with the Gentiles (4:16–30), and Luke also tells of Jesus' special interest in the Samaritans, whom the Jews hated even more than the Romans. Throughout this gospel Jesus is characteristically presented as the friend of the outcasts of society (9:51–56; 10:25–37; 17:11–19). These are the people whom God is happy to welcome, an attitude that is also recommended to Jesus' followers. The happiness of being a Christian is emphasized over and over again. Luke's account begins with the angels telling 'glad tidings of great joy' (2:10), and ends with the disciples returning to Jerusalem after the ascension 'with great joy' (24:52). In between these events, many of the most appealing of Jesus' parables end on the same note of happiness. The parables about lost things (15:1–32), and many others, emphasize the joy that is given to Jesus' disciples, while at the same time encouraging them to show the same openness to others as God had shown to them when they were themselves outside the kingdom.

Matthew

Matthew's Gospel is very different from either Mark or Luke, and there are a number of special characteristics that need to be considered before we can say anything about its origin, date or authorship.

The structure of the gospel

The one thing that is immediately obvious about Matthew's Gospel is that it is much more carefully crafted as a piece of literature than either of the other two synoptics. Its structure presents a very well-organized arrangement of the material, which is generally set out in topics. That

much is agreed by all interpreters. However, there is nothing like a
consensus on what the structure might be, or even on the actual nature
of the topics which are used to give it shape. Several suggestions have
been put forward.

One particularly popular way of understanding Matthew's structure
was proposed in the early part of the twentieth century by B.W. Bacon,
who identified a series of five blocks or 'books' of material, arranged
between the prologue of the birth stories and the epilogue of the
passion narrative. Each of these sections of the gospel concludes with
the statement that 'when Jesus had finished these things...', and they
were characterized by a well-balanced combination of narrative and
teaching material which Bacon suggested was intended to present Jesus
as the new Moses, with the five central sections corresponding to the
five books of the Law in the Old Testament (ascribed to Moses in Jewish
tradition). On this understanding, the structure of the gospel would be
as follows:

Introduction	1:1 – 2:23
Book 1 The new law: following Jesus	3:1 – 7:29
Narrative (Galilean ministry)	3:1 – 4:25
Teaching (Sermon on the Mount)	5:1 – 7:29
Book 2 Discipleship and Christian leaders	8:1 – 11:1
Narrative	8:1 – 9:34
Teaching	9:35 – 11:1
Book 3 The revelation of the kingdom	11:2 – 13:53
Narrative	11:2 – 12:50
Teaching (parables)	13:1–52
Book 4 The church and its administration	13:54 – 19:1a
Narrative	13:53 – 17:27
Teaching (order, discipline, worship)	18:1 –19:1a
Book 5 Judgment	19:1b – 26:2
Narrative (controversies in Jerusalem)	19:1b – 22:46
Teaching (judgment on the Pharisees, apocalyptic teachings)	23:1 – 26:2
Conclusion	26:3 – 28:20

The main weakness with this proposal is that the story of Jesus'
death and resurrection does not feature as a central part of the gospel's
message, and appears only as a concluding postscript, as it were, to the
major part of the book. The idea also failed to convince others because,
though it does correspond to what appear to be natural divisions in
Matthew's work, there is no compelling reason for adopting it other than
the fact that it is possible to find a plausible understanding of the gospel
on this basis. Nowhere does Matthew say that Jesus is the 'second

Moses', nor do the individual sections of the gospel correspond in any very exact way to the five books of the Pentateuch: arguably the only thing common to both is the number five.

Others have made different suggestions, pointing out that if the gospel is analysed not on the basis of literary style, but of content, quite different conclusions may be reached. By using the statements of 4:17 and 16:21 ('From that time on, Jesus began to...') as structural markers, it has been suggested that Matthew has not five divisions, but only three. J.D. Kingsbury accordingly proposes that Matthew's main concern was to show how Jesus was God's Son and Messiah, and that the gospel is arranged topically around this theme as follows:

■ The person of Jesus as Messiah and Son of God (1:1 – 4:16).
■ The proclamation of Jesus' messiahship (4:17 – 16:20).
■ The suffering, death and resurrection of the Messiah and Son of God (16:21 – 28:20).

This has the advantage of understanding the passion narratives as a central element in Matthew's Gospel, though it is open to question whether the statements in 4:17 and 16:21 are intended to bear the structural weight thereby placed upon them, while there is also the fact that they are not specifically unique to Matthew, for both of them are taken over from the Marcan account. In the absence of other evidence that Matthew accorded them particular significance, it does not necessarily follow that they reflect a particular Matthean emphasis, as opposed to just being a part of the tradition that Matthew inherited.

A number of more speculative attempts have also been made to explain the structure of the gospel by means of Jewish lectionaries, or various linguistic and mathematical formulas. It is of course true that the gospel's teaching is often grouped in series of threes and sevens, but this might have been intended as an aid to Christians who wished to memorize Jesus' sayings, rather than as a cryptic clue to the organization of its material.

Matthew's purpose in writing

While the exact nuances of Matthew's structural procedures might be elusive, there are several clear and unequivocal emphases that are distinctive to this gospel.

■ When compared with the other gospels, Matthew has a clear orientation towards the Old Testament and its relationship with the Christian message. This is of course true in general terms of just about the whole of the New Testament. But Matthew presents the life and teaching of Jesus as the fulfilment of the ancient promises made to Israel, not just in the general sense that Jesus is 'the son of David', but with extensive and specific reference to Old Testament texts. It seems that Matthew wanted to assert that Jesus had fulfilled in his experience all that happened to the nation of Israel, and to prove it he often quotes scriptural passages in ways that can seem to stretch credulity. For example, when Matthew reports Jesus' return from Egypt to his homeland as a baby, he quotes Hosea's statement about the exodus of Israel from Egypt: 'Out of Egypt have I called my son' (2:15; see Hosea 11:1). The methodology whereby the Old Testament is being used might be unclear (in fact, it reflects typical Jewish exegetical practices of the time), but the message is clear: everything that was central in the relationship of God with the people of Israel has now found its true and final expression in the life of Jesus.

■ It is therefore rather surprising to find that alongside this strong Jewish interest there is a great emphasis on the universality of the Christian message. The faults of Judaism are not passed over in silence. Indeed Matthew contains the most scathing criticisms of the Pharisees found in any gospel (23:1–36), while there are other passages indicating that Israel's day as God's people has now passed (8:10–12; 21:43). But this is all balanced by a striking emphasis on the missionary work of the church. This becomes most explicit in the great missionary commission given by Jesus to his disciples in 28:16–20, but it is implied from the very beginning, in the story of eastern rulers travelling to pay homage to the infant Jesus (2:1–12).

■ There is also a distinctive interest in eschatology here, and the teaching on this subject in Matthew 24 and 25 is considerably fuller than the corresponding sections of the other synoptic gospels. Matthew has a number of parables on the subjects of the second coming and last judgment that are not found elsewhere, most of them concerned to encourage Christians to live in a state of constant readiness for Jesus' return, because 'you do not know the day or the hour' (25:13). Perhaps some of Matthew's readers were beginning to doubt that Jesus would return, and for them parables like that of the ten bridesmaids would emphasize that such an attitude could lead to even those who thought they were disciples being unexpectedly excluded from the kingdom.

■ Another striking characteristic of Matthew's Gospel is its concern with Christian community and discipleship. It is the only gospel where the actual word church (Greek *ekklesia*) occurs (16:18; 18:17), and this fact alone probably contains the clue to the purpose of the whole gospel.

Matthew was making a collection of Jesus' teachings in a form that could be directly utilized in the ongoing life of the church. It was a compendium of authoritative advice for both new converts and older believers as they tried to put their Christian faith into practice in their everyday lives. It undoubtedly succeeded in this last aim, for it was not very long before Matthew's Gospel was the most widely used and respected. It contained Jesus' teaching in a form that could easily be understood by new converts, and would provide the basis of their instruction in the Christian faith. It also demonstrated the continuity between Jesus and the Old Testament in a very direct way, and so could be a useful handbook for dealing with questions raised by enquiring Jews, as well as helping Christians from a Jewish background to integrate their new faith with their heritage. Though it is not the longest of the gospels, it had the added advantage of being the most comprehensive of the synoptics: since it contained almost all of Mark, and much of Luke, its position as the most important gospel was soon assured in the early church.

The author

There is no widespread agreement on who wrote the gospel, and when. Many scholars today find no difficulty in accepting the early Christian traditions that identify Mark and Luke with the other two synoptics, but with Matthew the position is rather different. For the Matthew whose name was associated with this gospel by later church leaders was a disciple of Jesus, and therefore an eyewitness of the events described. It is not easy to see why one of the twelve disciples should have relied so heavily on Mark's Gospel, which was written by someone who was not a witness of the events of Jesus' life, especially when Matthew's own call to discipleship is told in 9:9–13 in a version that is largely copied from Mark 2:13–17. Other arguments against Matthean authorship are less substantial. For example, it has been claimed that, as someone obviously steeped in Jewish ways, Matthew would not have known enough Greek to compose such an impressive work in that language. But he was a tax collector, and therefore a close partner with the Romans – and in any case Greek was much more widely known and spoken even in Palestine than was at one time thought likely. Others have proposed that Matthew must have been written by a Gentile, because of its universalism and a handful of apparent misunderstandings of Jewish practices. However, the complaints against traditional Jewish attitudes are very much in line with statements made by the Old Testament prophets, while the kind of mistakes allegedly found here (misunderstanding of the nature of Hebrew poetry in 21:5–7, the idea in 18:34 that torture was a Jewish practice, which it was not, and others like them) are hardly evidence for a Gentile author.

Though some leading scholars continue to believe that the apostle Matthew was the author, it is worth pointing out that, as with all the other gospels, knowing the exact identity of the author is not going to be crucial for understanding it. The book itself is anonymous, and makes no claim at all about its author. We can be fairly certain it would be a man, but whether he was associated with the apostle Matthew, and at what stage or in what way, is impossible to say with certainty.

The date

The date of the gospel is also in doubt, and depends on the answers to a number of other questions.
■ If the two-source hypothesis about synoptic origins is correct, then Matthew must have been written after Mark, and after the collection of sayings known as Q was in existence.

■ It is widely believed that Matthew was written later than Luke,
because 22:7 and 24:3–28 appear to contain direct references to the fall
of Jerusalem in AD70. This presumption of course depends on the belief
that there can never be such a thing as genuine predictive prophecy,
and therefore if Jesus appears to have foretold an event in the future
this means the early church must have rewritten the tradition in the
light of later circumstances. Even if the possibility of such foresight is
allowed, though, Matthew was clearly an intentional literary stylist of
some skill, and might easily have formulated the actual phraseology to
reflect the details of what happened when the temple was destroyed in
fulfilment of an earlier prediction.

■ It has also been argued that the type of church organization
envisaged in Matthew is well developed, and therefore reflects a stage
towards the end of the first century. Like all arguments based on the
notion of 'development', this one is easier to put forward than it is to
substantiate. When the details of this gospel's teaching on the church
are compared with, say, Paul's letters to the church at Corinth in the
mid-fifties of the first century, it is very difficult to find any substantial
differences between the two.

The majority verdict is that, taking all these factors into account,
Matthew is probably to be dated sometime in the period between about
AD80 and 100.

John

John is quite different from the other three gospels. Its style of writing is
more reflective than the immediacy of the others, while its presentation
of Jesus is distinctive. Instead of spending most of his life in the relative

obscurity of Galilee, Jesus is a regular visitor to the festivals in the temple at Jerusalem, where he continually debates and discusses with the religious authorities the finer points of Jewish scriptural interpretation and spirituality (2:13; 5:1; 6:4; 7:2; 10:22; 11:55). Instead of speaking about his possible identity as Messiah in a hesitant way, he makes openly messianic claims from the outset, and in a series of seven sayings introduced by the words 'I am' he appears to take for himself the traditional authority that was reserved in the Old Testament for God alone (where God's personal name *Yahweh* had been defined as meaning 'I am who I am'). Instead of speaking in parables about the kingdom of God, he talks in extended discourses about 'eternal life' – discourses in which (since ancient Greek had no equivalent of modern quotation marks) it is incredibly difficult to decide where the speech of Jesus is meant to end and the reflections of the evangelist himself might begin. Some familiar synoptic episodes such as the casting out of the money changers from the temple are placed in a different context, while others are not mentioned, though the meaning of them seems to be referred to.

So, for example, the last supper is dominated by the washing of the disciples' feet by Jesus (13:1–20), while the idea that bread and wine are the body and blood of Christ is expounded in a discourse following the feeding of the 5,000 (6:25–58). The other gospels to varying degrees present the cross as tragic, albeit inevitable, but in John it is depicted as Jesus' final glorification, the one thing above all others that demonstrated his oneness with God and his place in God's plans for the cosmos – a universal aspect of his significance that is also emphasized in the opening paragraphs, where Jesus is identified with the universal *logos* (word, or reason) of Greek philosophical speculation (1:1–14).

Structure

All this is set out in a carefully constructed narrative, with three easily recognizable sections sandwiched between a prologue and an epilogue, as follows:

THE PROLOGUE (1:1–18)

In which the scene is set, perhaps with references taken from some early Christian hymn or confessional formula, but certainly with allusions to the story of creation in the book of Genesis, to the Old Testament figure of Wisdom as a mediator of God's presence on the earth, and drawing connections between these themes and the concepts of Greek philosophy – all of them designed to highlight the universal significance of the person of Jesus.

THE BOOK OF SIGNS (1:19 – 12:50)

Within which the key events of Jesus' ministry are organized by themes and topics, highlighting in particular his growing conflicts with the religious establishment in Jerusalem, and in the process affirming the fact that as Son of God he was the fulfilment of all the expectations of the Old Testament.

THE BOOK OF GLORY (13:1 – 20:31)
Where through a series of private meetings with his disciples, including extensive discourses, he prepares them to be leaders of the infant church, nurturing their own faith and entrusting them with guidelines for the future life of the Christian community. As the culmination of all this, the stories of Jesus' death and resurrection gather up the other themes of this gospel, and whereas sacrificial overtones are present in the synoptic accounts of the cross, here it becomes yet another manifestation of Jesus' divine nature.

EPILOGUE (21:1–25)

The character of the fourth gospel
The striking nature of the differences between this gospel and the others has, not surprisingly, led to heated debates about the relative value of their respective accounts of the life and teaching of Jesus. In his monumental study of gospel origins, B.H. Streeter described John as deriving 'not from the original authorities, but from the vivid picture... reconstructed by [the author's] own imagination on the basis of contemporary apologetic'. For him this could lead to only one possible conclusion: John must be a second-century theological interpretation of the life of Jesus – a kind of extended imaginative sermon, based on a muddled misunderstanding of the synoptic traditions, and therefore of no value at all as a reliable account of Jesus as he might actually have lived and taught.

This verdict has now to be regarded as a most inadequate account of the matter, for several reasons:

FACT AND FICTION IN THE TRANSMISSION OF STORIES
To suppose that, if the synoptics give a 'true' picture of Jesus, John's picture must be 'false' is to set up an artificial dichotomy between the two that, if it ever did have validity, would have been more appropriate to the mechanistic view of science popularized by the rationalist-materialist philosophy of the European Enlightenment than to the understanding of literary compositions. We have already seen that the New Testament gospels cannot be simply categorized as ancient biography – though John undoubtedly has more of the characteristics of that form than the other three – but they are certainly carefully crafted narratives aiming to tell the story of Jesus' life and teaching. As such, they are to be judged not by the standards of scientific enquiry, but according to the practices of storytelling, in which the 'truth' of a narrative is to be judged as a whole on its own terms, rather than in relation to notions of truth and falsehood drawn from some other sphere of human endeavour. The early Christian communities clearly had no problem in accepting that within the gospel

traditions there would be a subtle combination of factual and fictional elements. Had they not done so, they would certainly not have tolerated the existence of four gospels which, for all their similarities, are sufficiently different from one another as to defy all attempts at producing one harmonized, 'factual' version of the life and teaching of Jesus from them. They knew what more recent interpreters have often forgotten, that both artists and historians operate under similar constraints as they seek to balance bare fact with fictional elaboration, and that the telling of a good story that will speak to the hearts and minds of its hearers or readers depends on the coherent combination of both these elements. While all four gospels contain both factual and fictive elements, the fourth gospel appears to have a greater preponderance of the latter. Perhaps, it might be suggested, this is one reason why, of all the gospels, it seems to have had the power to speak more profoundly to a greater variety of people in different times and places than the other three – because it presents its subject matter from more angles than the synoptics. We return to this topic in the next chapter, when we discuss more extensively the reliability of the gospel traditions.

John and the synoptic gospels

At one time, it was widely assumed that the author of John's Gospel knew the synoptic gospels, because a number of stories are common to both. The story of how Jesus fed the 5,000 (6:1–15; see Mark 6:30–44 and parallels) and the story of his anointing at Bethany (12:1–8; see Mark 14:3–9 and parallels) are examples. Even in the earliest centuries it was therefore supposed that John was writing a kind of 'theological' interpretation of the 'factual' stories of the synoptic gospels. Clement of Alexandria, for instance, characterized John as a 'spiritual gospel' in comparison to the 'physical' or 'bodily' accounts of the synoptics (quoted in Eusebius, *Ecclesiastical History* VI.14.7). This inevitably led to the conclusion that the fourth gospel must be late in date and inferior in quality to the synoptic gospels.

This assumption has, however, been questioned at two points. In the light of more recent study it is obvious that it is too simplistic to set the 'history' of the synoptics over against the 'theology' of John, for the synoptic writers were themselves theologians and did not write their gospels for purely biographical reasons but because they had a message for their readers. It is also now widely (though not universally) believed that the fourth gospel is not dependent on the other three, and it might well have been written without any knowledge of them.

Closer examination of the stories found in all four gospels shows that though there are similarities, there are also a number of differences, and these differences are not the kind that can easily be explained on theological or ideological grounds. John's variations are much easier to understand on the assumption that he had access to different reports of the incidents known also to the synoptists. When this hypothesis is

Some of the great scholars of the early church who wrote about the Gospels:

Irenaeus, Bishop of Lyons (from AD175–195), known for his writings against Gnosticism.

Origen (AD185–254), one of the Fathers of the Greek church.

Tertullian of Carthage (c. AD160–215), whose writings had a strong influence on the church in Western Europe.

tested in detail, it can be seen not only that John's account comes from a different source, but also that there are a number of pieces of information in John which can be used to supplement the information of the other gospels in such a way as to make the whole story of Jesus' life and ministry more understandable.

For example, John 1:35–42 mentions that some of Jesus' disciples had previously been followers of John the Baptist, an observation that can help to explain the exact nature of the Baptist's witness to Jesus in the synoptics, and especially the emphasis placed there on his role in 'preparing the way of the Lord'. John's account also helps to answer the question (not obvious from the synoptics) of what Jesus was doing between his baptism and the arrest of John the Baptist. The synoptics report that Jesus began his ministry in Galilee after John's arrest (Mark 1:14; Matthew 4:12; Luke 4:14–15). This is the only ministry recorded in the synoptic gospels, though during his last visit to Jerusalem Matthew and Luke (Q) report that Jesus said of its inhabitants, 'How often would I have gathered your children together...' (Matthew 23:37; Luke 13:34), which suggests that Jesus had visited Jerusalem on a number of previous occasions. John 2:13 – 4:3 tells of just such an occasion, right at the beginning of Jesus' ministry, when he worked alongside John the Baptist in Judea before going back to Galilee when John was arrested.

John 7:1 – 10:42 fills out the synoptic material at a later point, when it records another visit by Jesus to Jerusalem some six months before his entry on Palm Sunday. John records how Jesus left Galilee and went to Jerusalem for the Feast of Tabernacles (September) and stayed there until the Feast of Dedication (December) after which, because of growing hostility, he returned to the area where John the Baptist had worked (10:40), only making a brief visit to Bethany when he heard that Lazarus had died (11:1–54). A little later, six days before the Passover (April) he returned for his final visit to Jerusalem (12:1, 12). This is the only one recorded in any detail in Mark, though the others are perhaps implied by Mark's summary statement: 'he left [Galilee] and went to the region of Judea and beyond the Jordan' (Mark 10:1).

John also provides a number of smaller details which help to explain and clarify some points in the synoptic narratives. At the end of the feeding of the 5,000, Mark 6:45 records that Jesus compelled his disciples to escape on a boat while he himself dismissed the crowd, while John 6:14–15 fills in some of the detail, explaining that Jesus had to take this action because the crowd were eager to kidnap him and make him their king. We have already noticed in an earlier chapter how the stories of the last supper and of Jesus' trials can be fully understood only in the light of information contained in John's Gospel.

In view of evidence of this sort, it is now coming to be realized that John's Gospel is a source in its own right. The information it contains is independent of that in the synoptic gospels, but at many crucial points John complements the other three.

THE BACKGROUND OF JOHN IN JUDAISM

It is also now recognized that the background of much of John's Gospel is Jewish, and not exclusively Greek. Early traditions place the origin of this gospel in Ephesus, which made it inevitable that scholars should look for an exclusively Hellenistic background, especially in view of the prologue (1:1–18) which explains the incarnation in terms of the word or *logos*. Apart from the fact that Hellenism is now known to have been all-pervasive throughout the Roman empire, even in Palestine, it is interesting to note that if the prologue is removed from John there is little in the rest of it that demands a Greek background. Not only is there an emphasis throughout the gospel on the fulfilment of the Old Testament, but the evangelist states his purpose in a very Jewish form: 'these things are written that you may believe that Jesus is the Christ [Messiah], the Son of God' (20:31).

This impression is confirmed by a closer analysis of the actual language of the gospel, for at many points the Greek shows a close connection with Aramaic sources. The writer often uses Aramaic words – for example, *Cephas* (1:42), *Gabbatha* (19:13), or *Rabboni* (20:16), and then explains them for the benefit of Greek readers. Even the meaning of the word Messiah is given a careful explanation in 1:41. There are also places where the Greek of the gospel follows the rules of Aramaic idiom. Though the distinction is not generally made in modern translations, such an instance occurs when John the Baptist says of Jesus, 'I am not worthy *that I should untie* the thong of his sandals' (1:27; the other gospels have a different and correct Greek expression, meaning 'to untie').

Jesus' sayings in John are also on occasion expressed in the typical parallelism of Semitic poetry (12:25; 13:16, 20), while other sections of his teaching can be retranslated into Aramaic to form completely realistic Aramaic poetry (for example, 3:29–30). It is not likely that John is a direct translation of an Aramaic document, though some have suggested this. But these facts do suggest that the teaching in John has the same Palestinian background as the material of the synoptic gospels, while the curious use of Aramaic grammar in Greek writing might well suggest that Aramaic was the author's native language.

NEW DISCOVERIES

There is now a considerable and important body of evidence drawn from archaeology which has rendered the idea that John was a late Hellenistic gospel untenable:

■ The Dead Sea Scrolls have shown that the apparently odd combination of Greek and Jewish ideas found in John was current not only in Greek cities like Ephesus in the second century AD, but also in Palestine itself, in strict Jewish circles, in the pre-Christian era. Many phrases familiar from John are also found in the scrolls, such as 'doing the truth' (3:21), 'walking in darkness' (12:35), 'children of the light'

(12:36), or 'the Spirit of truth' (14:17). Moreover, the contrasts made in John between light and darkness, truth and error, are also typical of the Qumran scrolls – and in both contexts this dualism between light and darkness, truth and error is an *ethical* dualism, in contrast to the metaphysical emphasis of most Greek and Gnostic philosophies.

■ The discovery of Gnostic gospels has had a different kind of impact on study of John. Prior to the discovery in the late 1940s of the Coptic Gnostic library at Nag Hammadi in upper Egypt, knowledge of Gnosticism was based largely on information given by a number of church historians and theologians who wrote books to refute it, and from their statements it was not too difficult to imagine that John's Gospel could have been written in the second century as a part of the

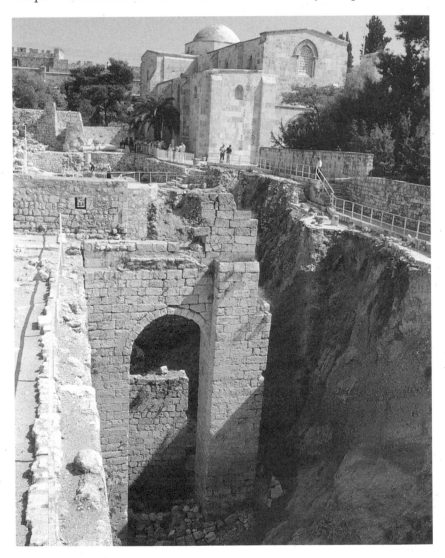

The author of John's gospel is now known to have had personal knowledge of the city of Jerusalem in the period of Jesus' lifetime. Some have identified this site near St Anne's Church as the location of the Pool of Bethesda (or Beth-Zatha) mentioned in John 5:1–18.

battle between Gnostic and 'orthodox' Christians. But the knowledge derived from the writings of Gnostic teachers themselves has demonstrated quite categorically that there was a vast difference between the world of John's Gospel and the world of classical Gnosticism.

■ Archaeological excavations in Jerusalem have also provided evidence to illuminate the traditions of John's Gospel. One of the unusual features of this gospel is its proliferation of names and descriptions of places, and it was widely thought at one time that these names were introduced either as a theological device (as symbols), or to give the impression of authenticity in otherwise fabricated accounts. But it is now clear that most of this geographical information rests on real knowledge of the city as it was before AD70. Since the Romans completely destroyed Jerusalem at that time, a later visitor to the city would not have been able to observe the ruins and imagine what it must have looked like beforehand. Excavations in Jerusalem have now shown that descriptions of the Pool of Bethesda (John 5:1–15), for example, or 'the Pavement' where Jesus met Pilate (John 19:13) are based on intimate knowledge of the city at the time of Jesus.

John's purpose in writing

In one sense this is an easy question to answer, for 20:31 spells out the purpose: 'that you may believe that Jesus is the Christ, the Son of God, and that believing you may have life in his name'. Though that can be understood as a statement of some evangelistic purpose, which would mean the gospel was written for those outside the church, the first clause could also be translated 'that you may continue to believe', and other factors also seem to indicate that it was written with the needs of Christians in view:

■ There are extensive references to the concerns and interests of second-generation Christians who were not eyewitnesses of the events described (20:26–31), with specific mentions of persecution (15:18–25; 16:1–4), mission (14:12–14; 15:26–27; 17:15–19), the need for continued faithfulness (15:1–11; 17:11–12), unity and love within the community (15:12–17; 17:20–23), as well as extensive teaching throughout chapters 14 – 16 on the role of the Holy Spirit in the ongoing life of the church.

■ There is a strong emphasis on the distinction between 'Jews' and Christians here, which is not so much an ethnic distinction as a religious one ('Jews' are not contrasted with Gentiles). In view of the lack of racial overtones and the emphasis on religious differences, it is going too far to describe this as anti-Semitism, though the acrimony of a passage such as 8:42–47 is unmistakable, while 9:22, 12:42 and 16:2 clearly imply a total break between Judaism and Christianity, and some believe they reflect the situation around AD85–90 when Christians were expelled from the synagogues as a consequence of a prayer against heretics formulated by Rabbi Gamaliel II. If so, this experience was clearly in the past at the time the gospel was written, though its recipients (who seem to have included Gentiles as well as Jews) were still living with the painful memories of such an event.

Author and date

The question of authorship has always been rather confused. Early church traditions mention two Johns in connection with the gospel: the apostle, and a John whom they call 'the Elder'. In the gospel itself, the 'beloved disciple' seems to be portrayed as a source of some of the information, though it is never made clear who this person was. Irenaeus identified the beloved disciple with John the apostle (*Against Heresies* I.1.1), though

---

Redaction criticism

Whereas source and form criticism are concerned to uncover the very earliest beginnings of the stories about Jesus, and to trace the history of the material before it was incorporated into the gospels themselves, redaction criticism sets out to discern how the individual authors actually used the materials that were handed down to them, and from which they constructed their gospels. All the claims about the aims, purposes and special interests of Matthew, Mark, Luke and John that are outlined in this chapter are based on the conclusions of redaction criticism.

Redaction criticism begins from the assumption that it is possible to distinguish between the traditions that the evangelists used, and the way they themselves actually shaped and wrote up those traditions in the process of compiling their own distinctive accounts of the life and teaching of Jesus. It then assumes that the way the individual evangelists have used their materials can reveal something about their own concerns, insights and theological perspectives.

The ability to compare how different evangelists have used the same material is obviously an important part of this process, which is why it is much easier to discern the redactional concerns of Matthew and Luke than it is of Mark or John, because we know that Matthew and Luke were working with the same sources (Mark and Q). By identifying changes of wording, and

analysing which materials an evangelist has included, and which have been left out, as well as the editorial connecting phrases that are used to link it all together, it is possible to discern patterns and then to conclude that those patterns must correspond with some particular concern of the author. For example, Luke not only contains more material on prayer than the others, but he also inserts references to prayer in passages which in Mark make no mention of it (compare, for example, Mark 3:7–19 with Luke 6:12–19). When such features keep on recurring, it is reasonable to suppose that they reflect a particular theme which the evangelist wanted to emphasize (as Luke does with prayer).

It is obviously easier to be certain of some conclusions than others. For example, discerning trends in how Matthew and Luke have used Mark will always be easier than doing the same for their use of Q, since there is no independent access to what Q might have been in its original form, as there is for Mark. But that should not be used to question the method, which when judiciously applied has often led to significant and creative insights into the evangelists and their overall concerns. Far from being the kind of wooden 'scissors-and-paste' editors that Streeter imagined them to be, all four of them were obviously creative literary artists, carefully constructing their narratives so as to have maximum impact on their readers.

some interpreters believe he might just be an ideal figure, symbolic of the true follower of Christ, while others have pointed out that Lazarus is the only person of whom it is specifically and consistently said that Jesus loved him (John 11:5, 36). In addition, 21:24 appears to distinguish the final editor of the gospel from this 'beloved disciple', while implying that he was the source of much of its information.

One way of explaining all this is to suppose that John has gone through two editions. Apart from the prologue, it does focus on issues related to the Jewish background and heritage of Christianity, whereas with the prologue it takes on the appearance of a book more suited to the wider Greek world. Could it be that the prologue was added after the completion of the original work, to commend the gospel to a new readership, facing relational issues with the synagogues, but well beyond the original context of Palestine?

This possibility might be supported by the odd connection between chapters 20 and 21. The last verse of chapter 20 appears to be the logical conclusion of the book, though it is then followed by the post-resurrection instructions of Jesus to Peter in chapter 21. This final chapter could perhaps have been added at the time when the book was adapted to serve the needs of a new group of people, though its style and language is so close to that of the rest of the gospel that it must have been added by the same person or persons. It seems at least possible that the gospel was first written in Palestine, to demonstrate that 'Jesus is the Christ' (20:31), perhaps over against the views of sectarian Jews influenced by ideas like those of the Qumran community, and then when the same teaching was seen to be relevant to people elsewhere in the Roman empire, it was revised, with Jewish customs and expressions being explained, and the prologue and epilogue added. The advice to church leaders in chapter 21 suggests that the final form of the gospel might have been directed to a Christian congregation comprised of both Jews and Gentiles somewhere in the Hellenistic world, perhaps at Ephesus.

The date of the gospel is not easy to ascertain, partly because (unlike the case of Matthew and Luke) there is no other evidence against which to set it. Traditions from the second century onwards suggest that it was written by John the apostle at the end of a long life, and most scholars continue to date it somewhere between about AD85 and 100, though opinions differ regarding the possible connection of it all with the apostle John. He cannot have been the final author, for that was a group of people who identify themselves as at least second-generation Christians (21:24). Nor are there are any specific indications that he was the 'beloved disciple', though a plausible case can be made out for that. However, there is no widely accepted opinion on the author's identity, and the consensus at this point in time can best be described as an open-minded agnosticism, with many scholars willing to allow some direct connection between John the apostle and the fourth gospel, though few wish to be more precise than that.

12 Can We Trust the Gospels?

In our study of the life and teaching of Jesus, we have taken it for granted that we can actually learn something about him from the gospels of the New Testament. We have suggested that, though the gospels share some of the characteristics of ancient biographies of Jesus, their ultimate purpose was not to give a comprehensive account of all that could be known of him, but rather to provide selective presentations of aspects of his words and actions that would assist Christians in addressing key concerns within their own communities, while at the same time providing resources that would equip them for their mission in the wider world. We have not taken that fact as a reason to question the general reliability of their accounts of Jesus' life and teaching, but have assumed that the traditional stories and sayings that were handed on to the evangelists, and from which they constructed their own narratives, can be trusted to provide an authentic picture of Jesus as he actually was, rather than regarding them as imaginative creations dreamed up by those who first wrote about Jesus.

It must be frankly admitted, however, that this assumption has been called into question from a number of different directions. We do not need to take seriously those writers who occasionally claim that Jesus never existed at all, for there is clear evidence to the contrary from a number of Jewish, Latin and Islamic sources. But when people who have studied the New Testament for a lifetime claim that the gospels reveal nothing of importance about Jesus, then we need to take serious account of their arguments. One of the most radical expressions of this viewpoint was associated with the name of Rudolf Bultmann, who in a book first published in 1934 made the remarkable statement: 'I do indeed think that we can now know almost nothing concerning the life and personality of Jesus.' Not even his own students were generally as negative as that, and indeed that statement itself has to be set against the fact that, in reality, Bultmann argued elsewhere that significant elements of teaching as found in the gospels were indeed original to Jesus himself. But in the mid- to late-twentieth century, whole generations of scholars adopted a generally sceptical attitude towards both the possibility and the value of knowledge about 'the historical Jesus', to such an extent that in some instances the gospels themselves were treated almost in an allegorical sort of way, as if they were really intended to be pictures of the life of early Christian communities, dressed up to look like accounts of the life of Jesus.

Our knowledge of Jesus is obviously going to be different from our knowledge of Paul, for he can be known through the letters that he wrote, and these can be compared and contrasted with the New Testament's narrative accounts of his doings in order to produce a coherent account of his life and thinking. Jesus, however, did not write a book, and he spent his brief life as a wandering teacher, working in a more or less remote corner of the Roman empire, among people who were probably not especially interested in literary matters. For that and related reasons, it is quite unlikely that Jesus' words and actions had ever been written down by those who actually heard him speak.

Furthermore we know that Jesus lived in a society whose common daily language was probably Aramaic, while our knowledge of his teaching comes from documents written in Greek. Though Greek would certainly have been familiar to the people of Galilee, there is no compelling reason to suppose Jesus normally taught in that language, which means the gospels are, at best, a translation of the words of Jesus from Aramaic into Greek. One of the consequences of the transmission of Jesus' sayings in Greek is that there are now variant accounts of what is obviously the same basic tradition. The similarities between the synoptic gospels are so close that there can be no doubt they are variants on the same themes, though the differences are too striking to be explained merely as variant translations from Aramaic into Greek. These are the underlying considerations which have given birth to source, form and redaction criticism. No matter which explanation of gospel relationships is adopted, it is obvious that something has happened to the traditions of Jesus' teaching and deeds in the process of their being handed on from one group to another.

It is important not to exaggerate the potential problems raised by all this. For generations, gospel readers who had never heard of the synoptic problem have had little difficulty in dealing with such matters. For all the distinctiveness of the various stories about Jesus and the reports of his teaching, there is clearly an inner coherence in the gospels as a whole. It is not difficult to gather together an account of what the gospels collectively present as 'the teaching of Jesus', and the fundamental elements of that teaching are the same in all four gospels. However, that should not absolve us from giving some attention to the question.

Oral culture and literary culture

Modern readers of the gospels are often surprised to learn that there is no conclusive evidence to show that any of the four New Testament gospels was written by a direct disciple of Jesus, and that two of them (Mark and Luke) certainly were not. That, combined with the fact that

the earliest gospel was written something like thirty to forty years after
Jesus' death, can seem a definite weakness to people living in an age of
instant electronic communications. But today the spoken word is still
the main method of communication for most of the world's people,
while even in the West the continued relevance of oral history for a
proper understanding of the past is being reasserted. All over the
Western world, projects have been initiated to save in more permanent
form the unwritten recollections of older people before their memories
fail, and in cultures where this type of memorizing has been
encouraged and promoted for generations it is amazing how
comprehensive a power of recall an older person can have, even for
events in the dim and distant past. Oral reminiscences can provide an
exceedingly accurate way of recording history, and those whose history
has been deliberately disrupted, by events such as the forcible
enslavement of Africans in America or the Nazi Holocaust, have
regularly been surprised at how easy it can be to piece together the
story of their forebears on the basis of traditional stories handed on in
their own families, sometimes (as in the case of African Americans) over
centuries. By contrast, the oral period for the New Testament stories
about Jesus covers something like fifty years at most, and some of it a
lot less. For instance, Paul mentions some eyewitness evidence about
the resurrection of Jesus (1 Corinthians 15:1–5). While he actually
wrote this down in about AD55, he says he had known the information
since he first became a Christian, which happened not more than a
year or two after Jesus' death.

It is a well-established fact that the rabbis took great pains to ensure
that their sayings were actually learned and passed on word for word by
their followers. From time to time scholars have proposed that Jesus
adopted the same methods, formulating his teaching with a view to his
disciples learning it by heart, so that they could transmit it to their own
followers in the same easily memorized form, and that the gospels
therefore represent the writing down of accurately transmitted traditions
going right back to Jesus himself. There is absolutely no evidence at all
to support this suggestion: not only do the gospels themselves highlight
how different Jesus was from other religious teachers (Mark 1:22), but
there is nothing to suggest that the early Christians ever regarded
themselves as the transmitters of tradition, rather than interpreters
of the message of Jesus to the needs of their own people. At the same
time, theories of this kind have drawn attention to the fact that Jesus'
teaching did originate in a cultural context where the teaching of an
authoritative leader was treated with great respect, and even if the
earliest disciples did not learn Jesus' sayings by heart, they would
certainly have had a high regard for them and would not readily have
corrupted or altered them.

There is also ample evidence for the reliable oral preservation of
stories in the wider Hellenistic world. The *Life of Apollonius of Tyana*

has often been viewed as a possible literary model for the gospel genre. Apollonius was a contemporary of Jesus, though he lived on into old age and died towards the end of the first century. But the account of his life was not written down until the beginning of the third century. Its author collected the stories of his life from a number of different sources, and was certainly not an impartial and detached biographer, but there are no serious doubts about the reliability of the main outline of his account. Compared with this and other written accounts about persons and events in the Roman world, the New Testament gospels were compiled very close in time to the events they describe, and still within the lifetime of eyewitnesses.

Presuppositions

Another relevant consideration relates to the attitudes that readers themselves bring to the gospels. What do we expect to find in them? History? Biography? Chronologically structured journals of Jesus' life? Word-for-word precision in reporting what he said? Or something else? Such terminology was alien to the evangelists themselves, who used quite different language to describe their books. The only thing they all consistently claim is that they were writing 'the good news'. But to describe anything as 'good' news is to make a value judgment on it – to commend it, and to imply that those who read it will be glad that they did. We have already given extensive consideration to the way in which the gospel writers have carefully selected the materials they include in order to fulfil this overall purpose. But this understanding is not merely concerned with the literary style and origin of the gospels: it also has repercussions for an appreciation of the nature of the 'truth' about Jesus as the evangelists present it.

In the light of the clearly stated purposes of Luke 1:1–4 and John 20:31 (implied in the other gospels), there can be no question that the gospel writers were biased. They all believed in Jesus. Through his teaching they had discovered new purpose for their own everyday existence, and they wanted to share that with other people. They were convinced that Jesus was not dead, but alive, and was now continuing to work through the supernatural power of the Holy Spirit in his people. The evangelists were certain that the absolute truth about life's meaning was to be found in Jesus – and if they had not been, they would never have bothered to write about him at all.

No doubt some readers will be thinking this proves what they have long suspected, for how can people so biased possibly present an objective picture? But the idea that only supposedly 'unbiased' people can ever tell the truth belongs to a way of understanding reality that no longer stands up to critical scrutiny. The philosophical notion developed through the European Enlightenment, that merely by the exercise of human reason it is possible to step outside our own experience of life and judge things in some kind of 'objective' way entirely detached from our own perspectives, is now seen to have been just wishful thinking on the part of self-opinionated white Westerners who wished to justify their own ideas over against what they regarded as the 'irrational' understandings of people of other times and places. We now know that even the outcome of scientific experiments can be affected by the presence or absence of the investigators in the laboratory, and a moment's thought about how we all receive information in everyday life is sufficient to question not only the existence, but also the value, of a truly 'unbiased' person.

To know anything at all about events we have not witnessed ourselves, we must depend on the accounts of those who did, and those accounts are invariably 'biased'. Moreover, in dealing with things like news reports, we actually expect people to explain to us the significance of what they report. This is what distinguishes news reports and 'proper history' from bare data. Mere records may contain 'facts', but in an abstract and incoherent way, and before they become even remotely interesting they need to be interpreted, and that means asking relevant questions, identifying possible opinions, and presenting some kind of considered value judgment, which will invariably be related to the personal perceptions of those who are processing the information.

In everyday life, all this is taken for granted, and most people generally place more value on the kind of impressionistic account of events given by those who have reflected on their possible significance than they do on mere reporting of 'brute facts'. Of course, that means that choices sometimes have to be made between different accounts of the same episodes. Lawyers and judges do this all the time, for the recollections of different individuals about what they have seen naturally differ. In describing a car crash, for example, there might be any number of detailed differences in the accounts provided by witnesses. We expect judges to reached a decision by taking account of them all. A judge would be unlikely to conclude that because a crash was described in different ways, it probably never happened, or even that the cars and the roads – the city where the alleged incident took place – did not exist. One who did would not keep the job for long, because these would be absurd conclusions. Yet this is exactly the sort of crazy logic that otherwise intelligent people seem prepared to apply when talking about the New Testament. The four gospels are not identical, their writers were biased and they make value judgments about what they report – so the only safe conclusion must be that these things never happened, and maybe Jesus never existed!

Intellectual imperialism

One of the reasons why such a line of argument can seem to make sense is that Western thinkers have often imagined that only people like them are capable of making rational assessments of such matters. Many modern theologians (though not as many historians) speak so disparagingly of the historians of the Roman world that it is easy to get the impression that the concept of accurate history writing was quite unknown to them. We need hardly be surprised at the emergence of this form of intellectual imperialism towards ancient authors, for it is just another version of the sort of ethnic arrogance that in recent centuries has motivated white Western people to regard themselves as superior to all the rest of the world's people. It is of course true that ancient historians did not have at their disposal all the aids that might be available today, but ancient people were just as conscious of the need for proper research as their modern counterparts. They used different tools and procedures to verify their information, but they did not make things up. Latin and Greek historians set themselves high standards for sifting and assessing their information, and developed their own sophisticated procedures for doing so. The principles outlined by authors like Lucian and Thucydides make it quite clear that they operated within guidelines that would not be out of place even today. Luke and John both indicate that they thought they were using the same procedures, and there is every reason to think the others did as well.

Lucian (AD117–180) came from Syria, but settled in Athens. In his *True Histories,* he poked fun at the imaginative stories of other writers.

A good example of their literary sophistication can be found in the work of Luke, whose gospel was part of a two-volume work which also included the book of Acts, linking the story of Jesus to the story of his early disciples. One of the more striking features of the book of Acts is that it tells the story of Paul's dramatic conversion three times, in 9:3–19, 22:6–16, and 26:9–23. All three versions are different. Is this because Luke had no idea what actually happened, or because he was making it all up? If he had been doing that, he would have been more likely to create just one account rather than preserving three distinctive versions. As it is, the most obvious explanation is that Luke adapted the same story at different points in his narrative in order to present varied aspects of the meaning of what he was reporting. If one writer could do that within a single book, and see no inconsistency about it, there can be no grounds for complaint when different writers are found to have utilized the stories about Jesus in diverse ways, to suit the needs of their audience. The early church certainly had no problems with this, as they quite happily preserved all four of the canonical gospels alongside each other and not until the second century was there any attempt to create one single harmonized account from them.

If modern readers find this hard to accept, it is because they are imprisoned by their own presuppositions about how the gospels should have been written. The evangelists were not interested in preserving the words of Jesus merely as souvenirs from the past: they were not primarily annalists, but evangelists and pastors. For them, Jesus' teaching was a living message, with the power to bring new light into the lives of those who read and reflected on it. It was something to be used, not merely recorded. Even something as important as the Lord's prayer was used in different forms when Christians met for worship – and so Matthew's version (Matthew 6:9–13) was not quite identical with Luke's (Luke 11:2–4), and after both their gospels had been written, continued use changed it a bit more, adding the ascription of glory with which all modern versions now conclude. Those who question the reliability of the gospel accounts on the basis of their diversity are imposing unfair standards of logical consistency that would never be applied to any other literature.

Not unrelated to this is a more general philosophical scepticism towards any document, whether ancient or modern, that appears to give credence to the possibility of the occurrence of unique, or apparently miraculous happenings. Academic biblical study still generally operates within a mechanistic world-view, according to which the universe is understood as a closed system, operating according to rigidly structured 'laws of nature' which are entirely predictable and never deviate. By definition, therefore, the unpredictable cannot happen, and on this view it is inevitable that the gospels should be seen as something other than history, for they do contain accounts of a number of unique happenings which appear to violate the 'laws of nature' as set out by Newtonian science. Physics, of course, no longer operates on that paradigm, and the work of more recent theorists has led to the emergence of a far more flexible understanding of what might be possible within the physical universe. Philosophers and theologians frequently have a lot to say about the emergence of so-called postmodernity, but on the whole they have yet to accept its implications, not least because it would put their own work in a wider context, as just one possible way among many others of understanding the nature of reality. This is not the place for an extensive engagement with this narrow-minded philosophical stance, except to observe that it is part of the legacy of Western imperialism and colonialism, which has already been superseded by cutting-edge science and which will need to be jettisoned by theologians if they are to be capable of engaging creatively with the wider experience of the human race. To say that unique events cannot happen, or that the supernatural does not exist, when most people of most ethnic groups at most points in history have claimed otherwise, is merely to perpetuate the intellectual arrogance of previous generations of Western thinkers, and far from providing an answer to the questions raised by history it merely begs larger and more important questions about the nature of Western intellectual culture.

Sir Isaac Newton (1642–1727) laid the foundations for much Western science.

Positive evidence

In addition to these general factors, the case for the overall authenticity of the gospels can be made in relation to a number of specific positive considerations as well.

Inscriptions and artifacts

The gospel stories show direct and specific knowledge of life in Palestine at the time of Jesus, and give a generally authentic image of life in that culture, even though some of their writers were certainly not at home in Palestine, and one (Luke) was not a Jew at all. They were all writing after the events they describe, most of them at a time when the face of the country had been irreversibly changed by the devastation of a major war between Romans and guerrilla fighters (AD66–70), and they compiled their books in places geographically far removed from the scene of Jesus' ministry. They must have been relying on information that went back much further in time and which was based on actual knowledge of the places and people mentioned, for archaeological finds have regularly shown the gospel writers to have been correct even in cases where they were once thought to be mistaken.

Language

There is also the fact that behind the teachings of Jesus (recorded in the gospels in Greek) it is possible to trace clear echoes of the language of rural Palestine: Aramaic. Even the gospels written in Greek occasionally preserve Aramaic expressions – like the words from the cross (Matthew 27:46), or the call to Jairus' daughter (Mark 5:41), or the name of 'the Pavement' in Jerusalem (John 19:13). At other points, notably in the Sermon on the Mount (Matthew 5 – 7), when sayings of Jesus are translated back into Aramaic they display literary features that would only have made sense in that language. Much of Jesus' teaching is preserved in the form of Aramaic poetry, recognizable even in an English translation, which at times displays features such as alliteration and assonance that could have had meaning only in Aramaic. Such facts do not of course 'prove' that Jesus spoke these words. Strictly speaking, the most they can show is that they go back to a form in which they were preserved by Aramaic-speaking Palestinian Christians. But for that reason they favour the authenticity of the gospel accounts of Jesus' teaching, for they link them with a time shortly after the events of Jesus' life, death and resurrection, when many eyewitnesses must still have been alive to challenge any accounts which did not present an authentic image of him.

Distinctiveness

Another striking fact is that the gospels are different in every way from the rest of the New Testament. They are of course different in literary genre, for much of the rest consists of letters written by various

Christian leaders to their friends. But their fundamental concerns are also very different from what is known of the life and circumstances of the early Gentile churches. It is wrong to imagine that, because the gospels were written to serve the needs of the churches, they are little more than a mirror reflecting the life of those early communities, for the rest of the New Testament shows that the church had many needs that are not even remotely addressed in the gospels.

There is, for example, no real teaching on the church itself, something that is so obvious a gap that we found it necessary to ask in an earlier chapter whether Jesus had been interested in founding a church at all. Even baptism, which from the start was the rite of initiation into the Christian community, is never mentioned by Jesus, apart from one isolated instance (Matthew 28:19). Jesus himself did not baptize, nor did he make baptism a central part of his teaching, yet this was a matter of great importance to the early church, and if they did indeed make a regular practice of manufacturing 'sayings of Jesus' to meet their needs, it is difficult to understand why they would not have chosen to do so on such a significant topic.

We find the same lack of specific guidance on other crucial subjects. Very soon after Jesus' death there was a wide-ranging controversy over the relationship between Jews and Gentiles in the Christian community. This was a major practical issue, for the two groups needed to get along with each other in the church, and their habits were often quite different. But it was also a theological question, for if Jesus was the Messiah, then how did being one of his followers relate to those who were part of the people of God in the faith tradition to which the Hebrew scriptures bore witness? Church leaders wrestled with that question for a long time, and if only Jesus had said something on it, much heart-searching and acrimony could no doubt have been avoided. There must have been great pressure for somebody to invent a 'saying of Jesus' that would provide the definitive answer, and yet there is no sign at all of that happening.

In other respects also the gospels preserve their own distinctive emphasis when compared with the rest of the New Testament. Whereas the term 'Son of man' is the most widely used name for Jesus in the gospels, it hardly appears anywhere else, and the same is true of 'the kingdom of God', which was the heart of Jesus' teaching, but virtually never features in the rest of the New Testament. The fact is that if we were to try to reconstruct the church's life situation from the gospels, we would never produce the kind of picture that is painted in the New Testament letters, for there are so many features of the gospel stories about Jesus that are quite different from the life and concerns of the early church.

Taken overall, facts such as these seem to suggest that, at the very least, the burden of proof must be with those who wish to deny the accuracy of the gospel accounts of Jesus, rather than with those who wish to assume that the gospels preserve a generally authentic picture of Jesus as he actually was. That is not to say they contain something akin to a photographic record of his life, but then they never claimed to do so. Nor does it entail the belief that the gospels contain an exact word-for-word account of all Jesus' teaching – but they do not claim that either. The evangelists were not mere recorders of tradition, but were interpreters of the facts handed on to them. The gospels are more like portraits than photographs, for they present Jesus through the eyes of those who knew his teaching and admired his example. Far from invalidating their stories, this very fact makes what they have written more true to life, and more accessible to their readers, because it enables these narratives to speak in the common language of humanity, addressing the issues that have concerned people searching for the meaning of life at all times and in all places. It is this quality that has ensured the adaptability of the gospels to many different cultures, and that will guarantee that future generations continue to be fascinated by the person who is their central character.

The quest for the historical Jesus

One of the great movements in New Testament scholarship, lasting for a century and more, has been the search for an accurate way of describing Jesus as he really was ('the historical Jesus'), that would take account of all the emerging insights into the nature of the gospels and their presentations of his person and teaching.

The quest begins

The search for a 'historical Jesus' had its origins in the European Enlightenment of the seventeenth and eighteenth centuries. Up to this point, the Bible had traditionally been regarded as the supernatural gift of God, and therefore beyond rational scrutiny. Likewise Jesus had been regarded as the Son of God, and therefore by definition he could not be revealed or understood as a human figure, because he was not one. But as principles of rational enquiry began to be applied to all aspects of human life and experience in the effort of providing a final, objective account of the meaning of it all, secular historians also wondered what would happen if the gospels were to be subjected to the same scrutiny as they were beginning to apply to the classics of ancient Greece and Rome, or the stories of medieval saints? What would Jesus look like when viewed as just one historical figure among many?

The first person to give an answer to that question was Hermann Samuel Reimarus (1694–1768), though his views were not published until after his death by his friend Gotthold Lessing. Reimarus proposed that the real Jesus was quite different from the one portrayed in the gospels, and whereas Jesus had been a simple Jewish teacher, the disciples wrote the gospels to promote their own new religion – a religion that they themselves had deliberately founded on a deception, by stealing Jesus' body and then claiming he was still alive. This view, especially the

element of conscious deception by the disciples, was by no means universally accepted, but the very fact that it could be expressed at all gave confidence to others to continue asking purely historical questions about Jesus. By 1836, David Friedrich Strauss (1808–1874) had published his monumental *Life of Jesus Critically Examined*, in which he dismissed the supernatural elements of the gospels as incredible and argued that the gospels as a whole were best understood as mythological stories embodying the beliefs of the early Christians rather than historical information about Jesus' life.

If Jesus was not as the gospels showed him, then what was he like? The following decades saw the publication of many books attempting to answer that question. Most of the 'lives of Jesus' published in this period depicted him as a moral reformer and ethical teacher, though there were some dissenters, most notably Johannes Weiss (1863–1914) who believed Jesus to have been an apocalyptic prophet expecting the end of the world, and Alfred Edersheim who argued in his *The Life and Times of Jesus the Messiah* of 1896 that the gospels present a reliable picture of Jesus as he truly was.

By the beginning of the twentieth century, this quest for the historical Jesus had provoked such interest that Albert Schweitzer (1875–1965) wrote his classic account of its development: *The Quest of the Historical Jesus* (1906). As it turned out, Schweitzer's book not only catalogued the achievements of the quest, but also undermined its credibility, for he convincingly demonstrated that the various portraits of Jesus that had emerged from it really owed more to the optimistic liberalism of those who created them than they did to anything that Jesus might be imagined to have been. The scholars who wrote so confidently about the 'historical Jesus' were actually describing themselves. Insofar as Schweitzer had a view on the matter, he agreed with Weiss that Jesus was an apocalyptic prophet, who had obviously been mistaken. But he further argued that in fact the quest was not possible anyway, not only because of the lack of objectivity of those scholars who were engaged in it, but also because he believed that the gospels simply do not contain enough biographical information on which to base any kind of solid judgment.

The quest is suspended

Following Schweitzer's exhaustive analysis, it no longer seemed worthwhile to continue searching for that elusive picture of the historical Jesus. Schweitzer's work was not the only reason for this suspension of the quest, however. At the same time as some were confidently writing their lives of Jesus, others were more painstakingly investigating the nature of the gospels as literature. In 1863, the fundamental principles of the two-document hypothesis of synoptic origins were first expounded by Heinrich Holtzmann (1832–1910), and he and others began the task of trying to ascertain the relative historical value of the various early accounts of Jesus' life and teaching that this theory had uncovered. During this period, Mark was reinstated as a source of unexpected value, while John was dismissed as a relatively worthless source of actual information about Jesus, and Q was also identified as a source of independent (and therefore, by implication, reliable) information about Jesus. These findings had in turn encouraged those who were trying to describe the historical Jesus to think that they had a more or less objective set of criteria with which to identify the real Jesus and separate him out from the church's fantasies about him: anything found in Mark and Q was likely to be factual, while the rest of the gospel traditions were more open to question. William Wrede (1859–1906), however, put an end to that idea with his 1901 book, *The Messianic Secret*, in which he argued that even Mark was inextricably bound up with the early church's efforts to project its own faith in Jesus as Messiah back into the traditions of Jesus' own lifetime. With one of its major sources of the history of Jesus thus dismissed, the quest could not go on.

For the next forty years, roughly up to the end of World War II, the dominant opinion was that it was impossible to disentangle the Jesus of the church's faith (the gospels) from the historical Jesus of Nazareth. During this period, the findings of form criticism seemed to make historical reconstruction even more problematic, for if the gospels were basically constructed out of otherwise unrelated units of tradition, with the framework within which the units were placed being the creation of the evangelists, that meant that even Mark did not provide any sort of reliable chronological or geographical – let alone biographical – context within which to imagine what the historical Jesus might actually have been like. Moreover, at the same time Rudolf Bultmann (1884–1976) was arguing that the quest was methodologically impossible, not only because of the difficulty of breaking through the theological images overlaid by the evangelists, but also because it was theologically futile, since Christianity was based on faith in Christ rather than the historical person of Jesus of Nazareth. Incorporating an understanding of Christianity derived from the existentialist philosophy of Heidegger, he argued that it really made no difference at all who the historical Jesus might have been, for what really mattered was not what Jesus of Nazareth might have said or done during his lifetime, but what God did through the cross and resurrection.

Rudolf Bultmann (1884–1976).

The quest resumes

Ironically, the quest resumed among a group of Bultmann's own students, most notably Ernst Käsemann (1906–1998) in a lecture delivered at Marburg in 1953. Their aim was simple. Using the tools of form criticism, and the emerging discipline of redaction criticism, the gospels would be examined to see if there was not some irreducible minimum of reliable tradition about Jesus that could have given rise to the more extensively developed beliefs about him that were held by the early church. An underlying supposition here was that the beliefs of the church could hardly have arisen in a vacuum, from nowhere, so there must have been aspects of the teaching of the historical Jesus that, while not as sophisticated as the later beliefs of the church, could have been the starting point for subsequent reflection. This was the context in which the various criteria for distinguishing authentic Jesus tradition were developed. Foremost among these was the so-called criterion of dissimilarity, or distinctiveness – the assumption that teaching could be traced back to Jesus only if it could not have derived from either the beliefs of the early church or from Judaism.

These criteria are discussed separately in more detail, but it has to be said that the effort to distance Jesus from Judaism was not always motivated by a concern for detached objectivity, and it is not a coincidence that the idea that the most authentic Jesus was not Jewish emerged at a time when Europe – Germany in particular – was in the grip of an anti-Semitic ideology, inspired by the Nazis. Another element that shaped this resumed quest for the historical Jesus was also the strongly held conviction that anything in the New Testament that seemed to reflect the beliefs of the Roman Catholic church was a secondary corruption of the pure apostolic faith, which in radical Lutheran terms was represented by Paul. These aspects of scholarly enquiry are discussed in more detail in later chapters of this book, but they are mentioned here because this obvious ideological agenda was a key reason for the replacement of this particular phase of the quest for the historical Jesus by a rather different emphasis, which brings us up to the present day.

The third quest

This period, which began in the 1970s, is generally referred to as the third quest to distinguish it from the first one (nineteenth century) and the second, or new one that we have just mentioned. Unlike its predecessors, this quest is rooted not in Germany but in the English-speaking world, both Britain and north America. Three main concerns characterize it so far.

Interdisciplinary

While every generation imagines its methods to be not only the latest word, but also the final word, on any given subject, it is certainly the case that today's scholars have at their fingertips a greater variety of methodologies and approaches than has been the case for any previous generation. The use of sociological and anthropological insights into the first-century world in which Jesus lived and the gospels were written has added important new dimensions to the quest for the historical Jesus. By trying to set Jesus in the context of his day, and examining what is known of his life to see to what extent the narratives reflect an authentic portrayal of what was going on in Palestinian society, it has been possible to compare Jesus with itinerant charismatic preachers within Judaism, and to establish a plausible social context within which he operated, and which also influenced the style of his followers in the early church.

Jesus and Judaism

Jesus has been reclaimed for Judaism, and in a complete reversal of the approach of the second quest, a major criterion of authenticity is now the extent to which his lifestyle and teaching would have made sense within a Jewish context, rather than (as before) the extent to which he differed from his Jewish compatriots. Given the New Testament's extensive use of imagery from the Hebrew scriptures to articulate the significance of the life and teaching of Jesus, it might seem odd that such a comparison should be noteworthy, for it would seem obvious to test the gospel presentations of Jesus against this background. But such has been the desire of past generations of Christian (and, more generally, Western) scholars to distance Jesus from Judaism that this is indeed a new departure – and one which, in the process, is affirming the gospel accounts as generally credible portrayals of Jesus.

Other gospels

The third quest is also characterized by a recognition that early Christianity was itself a diverse movement, and that in order to make the picture of the historical Jesus as comprehensive as possible, all the gospel-type traditions that can be identified should be used in the effort. Probably the most high-profile example of this approach is represented by the Jesus Seminar, established by Robert Funk in 1985, which has taken the view that non-canonical gospels such as the Gnostic *Gospel of Thomas* represent an early, independent perspective on Jesus' teaching, and are therefore of equal value to the synoptics and John. Q has often been included in this, as evidence for the existence of a different way of understanding Jesus within mainstream Christianity, with apparently no need for the inclusion of his death and resurrection. On this basis, it has been proposed that the historical Jesus was a 'wisdom' teacher, a kind of Jewish Cynic, influenced by similar trends within Hellenistic culture – and that this explains his gradual marginalization from Judaism. However, this is based on a particular understanding of the way in which Q came to be written, and others find it more plausible to see Jesus as an apocalyptic teacher in a more traditional Jewish context.

The outcome of this current phase in 'historical Jesus' research is not so clear-cut as previous stages of the quest have been, though (notwithstanding the continuation of a generally sceptical stance through the Jesus Seminar in particular) it is probably true to say that overall it has led to more positive evaluations of the gospels, particularly among those who have compared them with Jewish spirituality. The fact that Jewish scholars have played a leading role in this 'third quest' has been an added bonus, which has highlighted many more connections between Jesus and Judaism than previous (largely German) scholars had been prepared to allow.

Identifying the authentic words of Jesus

Jesus spoke Aramaic, and some Aramaic words are retained in the gospels. But they were largely written in Greek. This 1st-century Greek letter opens 'Prokleios to his good friend Pekysis, greetings'.

How can we be sure that the gospels contain the teaching of Jesus, and not the impressions of the early church about him? Through all its stages this has been one of the central questions within the quest for the historical Jesus, and some of the techniques that have been developed to try to answer it are sufficiently important to merit a separate discussion here. In particular, in the period of the so-called second or new quest (roughly 1950–70), a series of criteria were devised which are still often claimed to be a reliable means of identifying the authentic teaching

of Jesus in the gospels. These criteria were most comprehensively expounded in a 1967 book by Norman Perrin, *Rediscovering the Teaching of Jesus*, which outlined three separate tests, or criteria, on the basis of which it was concluded that at least three areas of Jesus' teaching in the gospels could be shown to be authentic: the parables, the teaching on the kingdom of God, and the themes mentioned in the Lord's prayer.

The criterion of dissimilarity, or distinctiveness

This criterion had already been recommended by Rudolf Bultmann, in his book *The History of the Synoptic Tradition* (1921), and was based on the assumption that anything in Jesus' teaching that might be paralleled in either Judaism or the theology of the early church must be of doubtful authenticity for it could have come into the gospels from either of those two sources rather than from an authentic reminiscence of Jesus. So the only points at which we may be sure that we are in direct contact with Jesus himself is in places where Jesus' teaching is totally unique and distinctive. Typical examples might be Jesus' use of the word *Abba* in his address to God, or his characteristic way of beginning important statements with the word *Amen*, which as far as we know were devices used neither by the Jewish rabbis nor by the early church.

It can scarcely be denied that, in Perrin's words, information retrieved from the gospels by this means would represent 'an irreducible minimum of historical knowledge' about Jesus. But on closer examination, it is doubtful whether even this modest claim can be fully justified on the basis of this particular method. For its successful use depends entirely on the further assumption that our present knowledge of both Judaism and the early church is more or less complete. The fact is, however, that very little is known about the form of Judaism at the time of Jesus, and the New Testament itself is one of the few contemporary accounts of Jewish practice in the early first century. New information is constantly being discovered and assessed, and with it new parallels to the teaching of Jesus are certain to emerge. As a method, therefore, the criterion of distinctiveness is a counsel of despair, and by using it, it could only be a matter of time before the logical outcome was reached: that nothing certain could be known about Jesus. This, together with the intrinsic implausibility of the notion that Jesus would be completely isolated from his environment, led to the emergence of the third quest. A Jesus who was unique in the sense that his teaching was totally detached from both Judaism and the church was unlikely ever to be the real Jesus.

In addition, though, there are large and important areas of the gospels where this method is of no use at all even within its own presuppositions. Using it to analyse the major titles ascribed to Jesus ('Messiah', 'Son of God', 'Son of man') could only ever have led to the conclusion that Jesus gave no teaching about his own destiny and person, for all of them were used by someone in the early church. The outcome would be the same on Jesus' eschatology, for that can also be paralleled in Jewish and early Christian sources. Even the distinctive teaching of the Sermon on the Mount would have to be jettisoned for the same reasons, for Paul shows a clear knowledge of that in Romans 12 – 14, as also does the epistle of James. There was always therefore a basic fault in the whole concept of this approach: it must inevitably lead, both theoretically and practically, to the claim that nothing useful can be known about Jesus from the gospels.

The criterion of 'coherence'
Those who still use these criteria are not unaware of the problems involved with the principle of dissimilarity. Perrin therefore put forward another one which could be used in conjunction with it: the criterion of coherence. This is based on the assumption that any material in the gospels that is compatible with the teaching which passes the dissimilarity test can also be counted as a genuine statement of what Jesus said and did.

On the face of it, this further criterion seems promising, but of course it is very heavily dependent on a successful application of the first one. We have already seen the difficulties involved in this, and if it leads to no sure results then this second test is also useless. In any case it is very difficult to judge what is 'coherent' and what is not: what seems coherent to us would not necessarily have seemed so to the early church.

The criterion of multiple attestation
This one goes back to the earliest stages of the quest for the historical Jesus, and has been widely used by scholars of many different persuasions, not only those who adopted a form-critical methodology. On this criterion, teaching mentioned in the gospels is genuinely from Jesus if it is found in more than one gospel source. This is a useful test as far as it goes, for if Mark and Q give a similar impression of the content of Jesus' teaching then it is reasonable to believe that it is an authentic impression. But this criterion also faces a number of difficulties, though they are not as great as the problems involved in operating the other two:

● It is not possible by this means to say anything about specific statements attributed to Jesus, for there are very few stories or sayings that are contained in more than one of the gospel sources. Indeed this fact is one of the foundations of the whole source-critical approach to the gospels. If the same teaching was found everywhere, there would have been no need for any explanation of the relationships between the various gospels. This means that the most this method can discover is the general tone of Jesus' teaching, rather than a detailed account of it.

● It also has another built-in limitation, for it would presumably dismiss as inauthentic those parts of Jesus' teaching that are found in only one gospel source. Yet this is the case with some of the most distinctive parts of Jesus' teaching. Using this test, stories such as the good Samaritan (Luke 10:25–37) or the lost son (Luke 15:11–32) would be excluded altogether from an account of Jesus' life and teaching, because they are found only in Luke's Gospel.

● To be applied convincingly, this criterion needs to assume the existence of a fairly rigid distinction between the various gospel sources, such as Burnett Hilman Streeter (1874–1937) proposed in 1924 in his classic presentation of the four-document hypothesis. But more recent study has shown that the question of the relationships between the gospels and their sources is far more complex than that, and the traditions underlying the gospels in their present form must have been both more diverse and more fluid.

A basic flaw

The problems involved in using these criteria to identify the authentic words of Jesus within the gospels highlight a more fundamental flaw in the whole method represented by them. For they all begin from the basic assumption that the gospels mostly contain the beliefs of the early church and only a very little, if anything at all, that comes directly from Jesus himself. Perrin himself gave two main reasons to justify this built-in pessimism:

● 'The early church made no attempt to distinguish between the words the earthly Jesus had spoken and those spoken by the risen Lord through a prophet in the community, nor between the original teaching of Jesus and the new understanding and reformulation of that teaching reached in... the church under the guidance of the Lord of the church.' An alleged model for this might be found in the first three chapters of the book of Revelation, where the Christian prophet John delivers messages from the heavenly Christ to seven churches in Asia Minor. Paul also mentions prophets working in the church (1 Corinthians 12:27–31), and it is often argued that their main function was to issue 'sayings of Jesus' to meet some specific need

in the church's life. Though this argument has been quite widely accepted, a number of significant objections can be made against it.

Firstly, it is based on very precarious evidence. Though it is often confidently stated that the role of the Christian prophet was to invent sayings of Jesus, there is in fact very little hard evidence to show what the prophets did in the early church. The messages to the seven churches in the book of Revelation are quite irrelevant, for a clear distinction is made there between the experience and words of the writer of the book and what is reported as a message from the risen Christ. The only episode where prophets are shown at work is in Acts 13:1–3, where they give instructions regarding the missionary work of Paul and Barnabas. Even these instructions, however, are not said to have been given in the name of Jesus, but with the authority of the Holy Spirit. This kind of evidence is so slight that it can provide only the vaguest indication of what prophets might most typically have done in the context of the church.

Secondly, the assumption that prophets could freely invent 'sayings of Jesus' also assumes that the first Christians made no clear distinction between Jesus' teaching and their own. Again, there is no hard evidence for this. Paradoxically, such evidence as there is comes most clearly from the writings of Paul, who is the New Testament writer most often accused of showing a disregard for the teachings of Jesus, and who also claimed more than once to have a greater measure of charismatic endowments than most of his contemporaries (1 Corinthians 14:18–19; 2 Corinthians 12:1–10). These two facts alone would make him an ideal candidate to have been a purveyor of 'sayings of Jesus', and it might be expected that his letters would be full of such sayings, manufactured by himself under the influence of the Holy Spirit for the purpose of giving advice to his readers. In fact, the opposite is true, and in 1 Corinthians 7, for example, he goes out of his way to distinguish between his own opinions and the teaching of Jesus.

Thirdly, another problem with the assumption that the early church freely manufactured sayings of Jesus is the self-justifying nature of the argument. The only 'evidence' that prophets regularly formulated such sayings is the notion that the gospel traditions had their origin in the early church and not in the ministry of Jesus: a hypothetical life setting has been imagined for the gospels, which is then used to interpret the meaning of the gospels. It is not surprising that on this basis the gospels can be demonstrated to be products of the pious imagination of the early church for, like the liberal nineteenth-century 'lives of Jesus' which portrayed him in the image of their authors, the evidence has been put into the gospels rather than emerging as the end-product of the investigation.

● Perrin's second reason for scepticism has a firmer foundation. He asserts, quite correctly, that the primary aim of the gospels was not to give historical or biographical information about Jesus, but to edify readers. Everything in the gospels is there because it served a particular purpose in the church's life – and on that basis it is stated that the gospels are unlikely to contain historical reminiscences of Jesus as he actually was. This is another argument that is often asserted but seldom supported. There is no reason at all for a story or piece of teaching that conveys a practical or theological message of necessity to be historically false. That would be absurd. It is simply not a valid historical argument to propose that because the gospels and their contents were relevant to life in the middle of the first century, they can have had no historical context in the times of Jesus himself.

Sayings of Jesus outside the New Testament

At various points reference has been made to traditions about Jesus' life and teaching that are not found in the New Testament. Apart from Josephus and the rabbis, Jesus is also mentioned in the Latin authors Suetonius and Tacitus, as well as in the Qur'an. Some of the church leaders in the early centuries preserve a few fragments of teaching which they say was first given by Jesus, and in other parts of the New Testament itself there are occasional references to sayings of Jesus not found in the gospels (see, for example, Acts 20:35). But most attention has focused on a number of so-called 'infancy gospels' written in the second century and purporting to tell of the early childhood of Jesus, and the various Gnostic gospels, typified by the *Gospel of Thomas*.

The material preserved in these second-century sources is of a remarkably varied character. Much of it, especially in the infancy stories, is clearly legendary and was written to fill in the gaps that are left by the New Testament gospels. Many of the stories of these apocryphal infancy gospels are so unreal and pointless that they can immediately be seen to be of a quite different character from the New Testament accounts of Jesus.

Other questions are raised, however, by the collections of Jesus' sayings found in such documents as the gospels of *Philip* and *Thomas*, or the various papyri discovered at Oxyrhynchus in upper Egypt. Most of these documents were written for sectarian purposes, and many of them emanate from the various Gnostic groups that were prevalent in the second century and later. The *Gospel of Thomas* in its present form seems to date from about the f.ourth century, and was compiled for the purpose of supporting the life of an esoteric group in the church, almost certainly a Gnostic group. It consists entirely of sayings of Jesus, not narratives about him, and many of its contents are obviously derived from the New

235

Sayings of Jesus
outside the New
Testament *continued*

Fragment of
the *Gospel of
Thomas*, in a
Coptic version
found at Nag
Hammadi.

Testament, but presented with a Gnostic slant, while others have probably come in direct from some other Gnostic source.

Besides these, there are some others which appear to be of independent origin. For example, logion 82 of *Thomas* reads as follows: 'Jesus said, "He who is near me is near the fire, he who is far from me is far from the kingdom."' This particular saying was also known to Origen (AD185–254), and there might be allusions to it in other early Christian writers. It is certainly characteristic of the type of saying attributed to Jesus in the New Testament and, in addition, it has the form of Aramaic poetry, which again is a regular feature of Jesus' teaching in the four canonical gospels. There are a number of such sayings scattered about in the literature of the early church. When they do not teach any specially sectarian doctrine, and when they are in general agreement with the teaching of Jesus found in the New Testament, there seems to be no real reason for doubting that they could go back to authentic traditions about Jesus. If, as in the example we quoted, they also have the form of Semitic poetry, that is a further indication of their primitive character.

The fact that such information should have been preserved outside the New Testament is consistent with all that is known about the writing of the gospels. The author of John, for example, mentions many accounts of Jesus' life and teaching which he knew of but chose not to use in his own gospel (John 20:30–31). They must have existed somewhere, and perhaps some of them ended up in the various documents mentioned here. But it is important to notice that, by comparison with the vast number of extra-canonical traditions about Jesus, only a tiny proportion have even a slight claim to being genuine. The vast majority of the material is quite worthless as a historical source for knowledge of Jesus, and their real value lies more in highlighting the quality of information preserved in the canonical gospels themselves.

13 Engaging with the Wider World

After the resurrection of Jesus, his followers were faced with some hard choices. The previous two or three years had been the most exciting time of their lives. They had been captivated by his teaching, and watched with growing expectancy as Jesus' actions made it plain that God's kingdom had really and truly arrived. Then came the crucifixion, and with it all they had hoped for seemed doomed to certain failure. Even the resurrection left them afraid and disillusioned, and when they realized that Jesus would no longer be physically present with them they must have been under intense pressure simply to forget him, or at least to regard those three years as a temporary interlude, and to return home to pick up the threads of their working lives where they had left off before they joined Jesus. By doing that, they would still be able to share their memories of him, and perhaps even try to put some of his teaching into practice in the local synagogues of rural Palestine – but their lives would no longer be dominated by him in the way they had been before.

Yet the more they thought about it, the more they knew how impossible such a reaction would be. Jesus had demanded their radical and wholehearted obedience when they first met him, and his final message to them was just as challenging and uncompromising: 'Go, then, to all peoples everywhere and make them my disciples... you will be witnesses for me in Jerusalem, in all Judea and Samaria, and to the ends of the earth...' (Matthew 28:19; Acts 1:8).

Back to Jesus

Jesus had never really been an establishment figure. People who met him often recognized him as a 'rabbi', and gave him that title (e.g. Matthew 26:25; Mark 9:5; 10:51; John 1:49; 4:31), but right from the very beginning they all knew that he was different and that his message was distinctive. In his very first report of Jesus' public teaching, Mark comments: 'The people who heard him were amazed at the way he taught, for he wasn't like the teachers of the Law; instead, he taught with authority' (1:22).

That does not mean to say that his teaching was completely new and unique. It has been rightly pointed out that almost everything in Jesus' teaching had been said before him by the Jewish rabbis. Since both he and they were setting out to explain the significance of the Hebrew scriptures for their own generation, it is hardly surprising that they discussed the same issues, and even on occasion reached similar conclusions. But what was so different about Jesus – and what was to set his followers radically apart from Judaism – was the framework in which he set his teaching. For on two crucial matters Jesus adopted a fundamentally different stance from other religious teachers of his day.

Keeping the Law

The Law, or Torah (the first five books of the Old Testament), was central to Judaism, as keeping the Law in all its details was the way that faithful believers could demonstrate their obedience to God and commitment to the covenant with Israel. It is often difficult for a non-Jew today to understand the almost mystical significance of the Law for a faithful Jewish believer in the time of Jesus, and no doubt that is part of the reason why some of the most influential Protestant biblical scholars of the last 100 years or so have found it easy to misrepresent Jewish spirituality as a harsh and unforgiving legalistic system. Jewish believers in the time of Jesus must have had a far more positive attitude to faith than the kind of blind obedience credited to them by some Christian writers in more recent times. But no matter what their motivation, keeping the Law and its precepts had always been a central plank of Judaism, and it would have been unthinkable that anyone might please God without also observing the many detailed requirements of the Torah.

There had always been more than one way of understanding what might be entailed in keeping the Law, of course. The prophet Amos, 700 years before the time of Jesus, had condemned his contemporaries for their eagerness to keep the minute details of the ritual and ceremonial regulations, while ignoring the central moral requirements that were also laid down in the Torah (Amos 5:21–24). The same tendency could be found in Jesus' day, and his strongly worded condemnation of the Pharisees was not so very different from Amos' complaints: 'You hypocrites! You give to God a tenth even of the seasoning herbs, such as mint, dill and cumin, but you neglect to obey the really important teachings of the Law, such as justice and mercy and honesty' (Matthew 23:23). Such behaviour was presumably not uncommon, for when Jesus was asked why his disciples did not keep every detailed requirement of the Law, he pointed out to his questioners their own inconsistency in avoiding moral obligations to their parents by using a legal loophole that would allow them to use their wealth for more 'religious' purposes (Mark 7:1–13).

The adoption of such double standards is of course by no means an exclusively Jewish problem, and to label it as such is to import an ethnic dimension into Jesus' teaching that was never there. Jesus never actually questioned the validity of the Law, nor did he deny that it had been given by God, though he did suggest that with his own coming, it was no longer relevant (Luke 16:16). More than that, in a series of remarkable statements he contrasted his own teaching with that of the Torah, and elevated his own authority to a higher status than that of Moses, the traditional Hebrew Law-giver: 'You have heard that people were told in the past [by Moses] but now I tell you...' (Matthew 5:21–22, 27–28, 31–47). It is also significant that, according to Mark's account of his trial by the religious authorities, Jesus was first charged with blasphemy against the temple (Mark 14:57–59). The charge failed, but from the authorities' viewpoint it was not totally without foundation, as can be seen from his statement in Matthew 12:6, 'I tell you that there is something here greater than the temple.'

It is therefore not surprising that, though he seemed to be an ordinary rabbi, Jesus was soon outlawed by the religious establishment. This radical teaching about the Law and the temple struck at the very foundations of their most firmly held convictions. Other rabbis had asked awkward questions before, but generally in the context of polite debate about points of interpretation of the Law. If Jesus had been content to do the same, perhaps the system could have assimilated him more easily. It was not totally inflexible, and had survived many changes before and would undergo many others after the time of Jesus. But Jesus was above all an activist, and detached scholarly argument was not his style.

The way he behaved was, if anything, even more scandalous than his teaching. Mark 2:23–28 tells how he and his disciples picked grain as they walked through the fields, an action that was forbidden because it was regarded as harvesting by the legal experts of the day, and therefore an infringement of the law about not working on the sabbath. Jesus' reply to their criticism of this behaviour was to justify his disregard of the Law with the declaration that 'the sabbath was made for humankind, and not humankind for the sabbath'. On another occasion when he was asked why his disciples ignored the conventions about ritual washing before eating a meal, he also dismissed that criticism by appeal to a higher principle: 'whatever goes into a person from outside cannot defile... it is what comes out of a person that defiles... it is from within, from the human heart, that evil intentions come, leading people to do immoral things, to rob, kill, commit adultery, be greedy...' (Mark 7:18–22).

Not only did Jesus challenge the precepts of the Law in this way, but he also insisted on taking his message to all sorts of people who were regarded as unclean. Lepers, prostitutes, tax gatherers (Roman collaborators) and others feature regularly and prominently in the gospels, and Jesus himself was described as 'a glutton and a drinker, a friend of tax collectors and other outcasts' (Matthew 11:19). Instead of making his friends among the conventionally religious, Jesus chose those who were despised for their inability to keep the Law. Indeed, he made a virtue out of it, reminding his questioners on one occasion that, 'I have not come to call respectable people, but outcasts' (Mark 2:17).

A number of stories in the gospels explain why Jesus felt like that, but perhaps none sums up his attitude more succinctly than the parable of the Pharisee and the tax collector who went to pray in the temple at the same time. The Pharisee prided himself on his moral and religious attainments – and told God so. The tax collector, on the other hand, was so conscious of his own unworthiness to speak to God at all that he could only cry out, 'God, have pity on me, a sinner.' 'But,' said Jesus, 'the tax collector, and not the Pharisee, was in the right with God when he went home', because he recognized his own sinfulness and came to God with no spiritual pretensions (Luke 18:9–14). The Pharisees were emphasizing the importance of showing commitment to the covenant by faithful observance of the Law, whereas Jesus believed it was possible to keep all that was in the Law – and more besides – and still not please God. Whereas the religious establishment was concerned with actions that could be assessed and regulated by rules (as religious establishments always are), Jesus was much more concerned with what a person is than with what he or she does. Paradoxically, perhaps, he did not go on to dismiss behaviour as unimportant, but he emphasized that how people behave depends on their inner nature, and for him the secret of goodness was therefore to be found not in obedience to rules, but in the spontaneous activities of a transformed character: 'A sound tree cannot bear evil fruit, nor can a bad tree bear good fruit' (Matthew 7:18).

Religion and race

There was another element in Jesus' conflicts with the religious establishment. Many people in the Roman empire admired the moral precepts of the Old Testament, and the principles enshrined in the ten commandments and other parts of the Torah commanded the respect of many upright Romans and Greeks. But admiring the Law was not quite the same thing as pleasing God, and before they could be fully incorporated into the people of God, Judaism demanded that Gentiles must be circumcised and accept the various detailed regulations of the Law. In effect, Gentiles had to become Jews before they could be accepted by God: there was no salvation outside the Jewish nation. This stringent requirement of converts did not stop the Pharisees and others from engaging in missionary activity among non-Jews, and Jesus himself commended them for their enthusiasm (Matthew 23:15). But he evidently did not approve of their insistence that in order to please God such people should accept all the detailed regulations of the Torah.

The precise extent of Jesus' own involvement in a mission to those Gentiles is somewhat unclear. He certainly made no concerted effort to preach the good news to them, though all four gospels show him accepting and respecting the faith of such people whenever he met

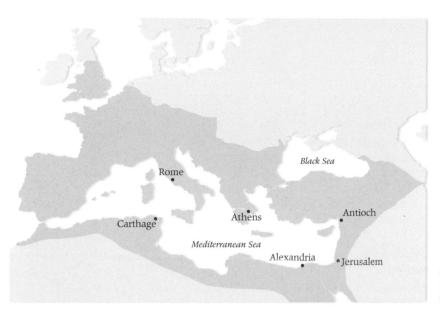

The extent of the Roman empire at the time of Jesus.

them. He was not unwilling even to assist a Roman officer, remarking in the process that, 'I have never found anyone in Israel with faith like this' (Matthew 8:5–13). A number of incidents show his acceptance of various non-Jewish groups within Palestinian society (Mark 5:1–20; 7:24–30), while one of his best-known parables praised the virtues of a Samaritan, the one race that was despised perhaps more than any other by religious Jews (Luke 10:25–37).

In the light of this, some readers of the gospels have found a contradiction in Jesus' instruction to his disciples in Matthew 10:5–6, 'Do not go to any Gentile territory or any Samaritan towns. Instead, you are to go to those lost sheep, the people of Israel.' But this advice was given in respect of a limited mission tour which the disciples were to undertake for a short period only, during Jesus' own lifetime, and Matthew himself certainly did not regard it as more widely applicable, for he is the only gospel writer to record the great commission of Jesus, exhorting his disciples to 'Go... to all peoples everywhere and make them my disciples...' (28:19). Other passages such as Matthew 8:10–12 and 21:43 make the same point, as do many passages in Luke's Gospel. The best way to understand the advice of Matthew 10:5 is to set it alongside another commission given, according to Luke, after the resurrection: '... you will be witnesses for me in Jerusalem, in all Judea and Samaria, and to the ends of the earth' (Acts 1:8). It was natural that the first followers of Jesus should take their message in the first instance to the Jewish community, for they were themselves Palestinian Jews, but Paul later adopted the same strategy in cities far removed from Palestine, and regularly gave the Jewish community the opportunity to respond to his message before he took it to Gentiles. In Romans 11:13–24 he insisted there was a theological basis for this priority, related to the ancient history of Israel as the recipients of the Law and people of God's covenant.

The church is born

As they met behind closed doors in Jerusalem in those early days after Jesus' resurrection, the disciples knew that it was easier to talk about changing the world than it would be to go out and do it. But it was not long before something happened that not only altered their thinking, but gave them a courage and boldness to share their faith that was to send shockwaves throughout the Roman world.

Only fifty days after the death of Jesus, Peter found himself standing before a large crowd in the streets of Jerusalem, fearlessly proclaiming that God's kingdom had arrived, and that Jesus was its king and Messiah. At the time Jerusalem was full of pilgrims who had come from all parts of the empire for the Festival of Pentecost – and as Peter spoke they not only understood his message, but, when he invited them to become disciples of Jesus themselves, 3,000 accepted his challenge and declared their willingness to live according to the values and standards of God's kingdom (Acts 2:14–47).

What had happened to bring about such a transformation in the lives of Jesus' followers? The answer to that is contained in the opening

Peter's audience on the Day of Pentecost had travelled from far and wide, indicating the extensive spread of Jewish people throughout the ancient world.

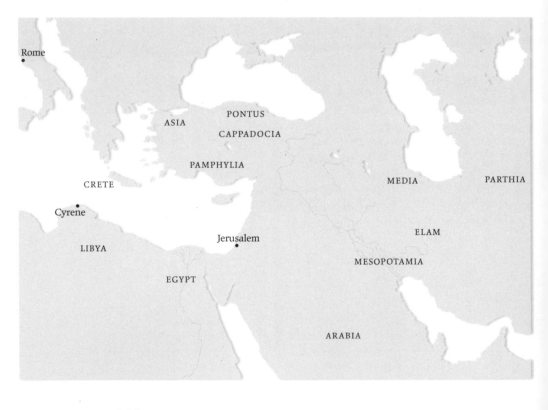

section of Peter's address. For as he stood up to speak with the crowd, he reminded them of an Old Testament passage that had described the coming new age as a time when God's Spirit would work in an exciting new way in the lives of men and women. As the Hebrew prophets had looked to the future, some of them realized that the human predicament would never be resolved until a new relationship was set up between people and God, in which God would not just ask for obedience but would actually give people a new moral power that would enable them to be what they were intended to be (Jeremiah 31:31–34). In Joel 2:28–32, this new power for living had been associated with the gift of God's Spirit, and Peter took that passage as his text and claimed that it was now coming true in the experience of Jesus' disciples. Through Jesus' death and resurrection, ordinary people could enjoy a new level of personal relationship with God. Peter was prepared to testify to that on the basis of his own experience.

For Peter and the others, that day had begun like any other. But as they faced the enormity, and the apparent impossibility, of the task Jesus had left them, they were taken by surprise as a new life-giving power burst into their lives. It was a moral and spiritual dynamic that equipped them to bear witness to their new faith – a power that would make them like Jesus. It was not easy to describe in words exactly what they experienced, but they identified it as the power of the Holy Spirit. As a consequence of what happened to them, their hesitating and uncertain trust in Jesus and his promises was remarkably confirmed and from that moment onwards they had no doubt that God's promises to previous generations were actually coming true in their own lives. The church was in the process of being born. More than that, they themselves were being reborn for, in addition to Peter's new-found ability to speak in a powerful way to the crowds gathered in Jerusalem, he and the others discovered that they now had the ability to carry out remarkable deeds in the name of Jesus. If they had ever entertained any residual doubts, the power that swept over them was so overwhelming that they needed no further argument to persuade them that Jesus was alive and at work in their lives in a unique way.

As a result of all this, the apostles and their converts were so totally dominated by their love for the living Jesus and their desire to serve him that the humdrum concerns of everyday life were forgotten. Instead, the Christians 'spent their time in learning from the apostles, taking part in the fellowship, and sharing in the common meals and prayers' (Acts 2:42). As a first step towards beginning to live the way Jesus had spoken of, they even sold their goods and pooled the proceeds. Making money was no longer the most important thing in life: the only things that really mattered were serving God, and taking their life changing message to other people.

The church grows

During these early days in Jerusalem, the open friendship and simple lifestyle of the early church must indeed have seemed like the dawning of a new age. But it was not long before other more complex questions reminded Peter and the others that God's kingdom had not yet arrived in all its fullness. Their newly established community of mutual acceptance and sharing was itself proof that the new society had begun but, as time passed, the tension between present and future that was so fundamental in Jesus' teaching was to have disturbing repercussions for the ongoing life of the embryonic Christian church. During the lifetime of Jesus, the new messianic movement which he founded was for the most part a local sect within Palestinian Judaism. All the disciples were Jews and, though both the logic of Jesus' message and the example of his own practice made it clear that Gentiles were not to be excluded, the issue simply did not arise to any great extent. Those Gentiles whom Jesus encountered were isolated individuals, few in number, and in any

The Day of Pentecost

The precise nature of the disciples' experience on the Day of Pentecost has been much discussed. It has sometimes been suggested that it never happened, and that the whole of the story in Acts 2 was intended by Luke to convey some theological lesson rather than to report an actual incident. A typical explanation along these lines would be to seek a background for the narrative in the fact that the festival of Pentecost was traditionally connected to the giving of the Old Testament Law at Mount Sinai. According to the late second-century Rabbi Johanan, the one voice of God at the giving of the Law had divided into seven voices, which had then spoken in seventy different languages. That, together with the fact that wind and fire were present both at Sinai and at the events of Pentecost, is said to be enough to explain the picturesque language used by Luke.

This kind of explanation seems far less plausible today than it would have done in the nineteenth or twentieth centuries, when the rationalist-materialist world-view of the Enlightenment was still dominant, with its underlying assumption that there

is no such thing as religious experience, and therefore phenomena like speaking in tongues, visions or other mystical manifestations can only be explained by being reduced to categories of psychology or anthropology. But even on its own terms it is possible to challenge the idea that the Acts narrative is a gloss on traditional Jewish beliefs. There is no evidence at all to show that the rabbis linked Sinai and Pentecost before the second century, which was long after the particular day of Pentecost to which Luke refers, and indeed much later than the lifetime of Luke himself. The narrative presents a realistic account of what the disciples might have been expected to do under the circumstances, and it is perfectly believable that after the unexpected events of the previous Passover they would have gathered in the way Luke describes, apprehensive about what might happen next. It is probably unlikely that their expectations included what did actually take place, and they might well have been naïvely thinking that, after the death and resurrection of Jesus, there was nothing else left except the end of the world. If so, they were in for a surprise, for the new age of which Jesus had spoken did indeed

case many of them were probably either God-fearers or actual converts to Judaism, and so not totally outside the boundaries of traditional Jewish spirituality (Mark 7:24–30; Luke 7:1–10).

But it was not long before the church was forced to give considerable attention to the whole question of the relationship between Jewish and Gentile followers of Jesus. Though they did not realize it at the time, the events of the Day of Pentecost recorded at the beginning of the book of Acts were to be a watershed in more ways than one. For when Peter stood up to explain the Christian message to the crowds in Jerusalem, he faced a very cosmopolitan audience of 'religious people who had come from every country of the world' (Acts 2:5). Naturally, they must all have been interested in Judaism, or they would not have travelled to Jerusalem for a religious

A typical street in old Jerusalem.

dawn, but not in the way they imagined it might, even if Peter did later connect it with what the prophet Joel had expected in 'the last days' (Acts 2:17–21).

Like all mystical happenings, their experience defies neat classification. It certainly had some of the common features of visions, as the disciples saw 'what looked like tongues of fire' (but were not fire), and heard 'a noise from the sky which sounded like a strong wind blowing' (but was not the wind). But the result of this experience was clear for others to see: 'They were all filled with the Holy Spirit and began to talk in other languages, as the Spirit enabled them to speak' (Acts 2:2–4). The most natural understanding of this is that they were speaking in tongues, or 'glossolalia' as it is sometimes called. This phenomenon is mentioned elsewhere in the New Testament as one of the gifts of the Spirit (1 Corinthians 12:10; 14:5–25), and is also widely known and practised today in churches of many traditions. It is generally agreed that such speaking in tongues is not the speaking of foreign languages otherwise unknown to the speaker, but a kind of ecstatic speech, quite different from the form and content of actual languages. Paul certainly

perceived a difference, for he contrasted the speaking of ordinary languages with tongues, which he called 'the language of angels' (1 Corinthians 13:1).

Some still argue that the experience of the Day of Pentecost was not the speaking of tongues, but the speaking of foreign languages. But if that was the case, it is hard to see why some who heard it should have concluded that the disciples were drunk (Acts 2:13), while others heard God speaking to them quite clearly in terms that they could understand. No doubt the explanation for this lies in the fact that what Luke reported he had learned from others who had been there, and whose lives had been changed as a result of what they had heard. Whatever kind of inspired speech the apostles were using, those who were present found themselves caught up by what the followers of Jesus called the power of the Spirit, and the message they heard came to them as clearly as if it had been expressed in their own everyday languages.

festival. But not all the Gentiles among them would be full converts who had accepted the whole of the Law, while even those who were from Jewish families in various parts of the Roman empire must have had a rather different background and outlook from those who had been born and bred in Palestine itself. Most of those listening to Peter's address were probably Greek-speaking Jews who had made a pilgrimage to Jerusalem for this great religious festival. Many of them would have been visiting Jerusalem for the first time. Though their homes were far away, such Jews of the Dispersion always had a warm regard for Jerusalem and its temple. This was the central shrine of their faith, just as it was for their compatriots who lived much nearer to it. Peter and the other disciples had no doubt that the good news about Jesus must also be shared with people like this. Indeed, they had much in common. The disciples themselves were regular supporters of the synagogue services. They too observed the special festivals, and on occasions they could even be found teaching within the temple precincts (Acts 3:1–26). This was something that Jesus himself had not been able to do without fear of the consequences, and though Peter and John were subsequently arrested and charged before the religious authorities, they were soon released and the only restriction imposed on them was that 'on no condition were they to speak or to teach in the name of Jesus' (Acts 4:18). Apart from their curious belief in Jesus, their behaviour was generally quite acceptable to the Jewish authorities.

The conflict begins

It was not long before all this was to change, when an argument arose between some Jews who spoke Greek ('Hellenists') and others whose main language was Hebrew or Aramaic ('Hebrews'). They had all become Christians, perhaps on the Day of Pentecost itself, and some of these 'Hellenist' Christians were probably visitors to Jerusalem from other parts of the Roman empire (Acts 6:1) – though many Jews in Palestine also spoke Greek, and some of them might have been permanent residents. At any event, those whose main language was Greek felt they were getting an unfair deal in the distribution of funds within the church, and as a result of their complaints seven people were appointed to supervise the arrangements for these Hellenistic Christians, in addition to the apostles who had the care of the more conservative Hebrew Christians. Though most of those who are named are otherwise unknown, one of them – Stephen – soon demonstrated that he was at least as gifted in theological argument as he was in the administration of funds (Acts 6:2–6).

According to Acts, it all started as an argument within the 'synagogue of the Freedmen' in Jerusalem. It is not

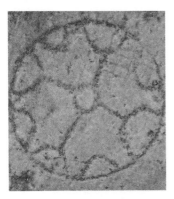

A Christian symbol carved on the steps of the Hellenistic Temple of Apollo at Didyma in modern Turkey.

certain just who these 'Freedmen' were, but it is a fair guess that they would have been Jews who had come from other parts of the Roman empire, released from some form of slavery, and had then formed their own synagogue in Jerusalem. Acts says that this synagogue congregation 'included Jews from Cyrene and Alexandria', and that they sided with others 'from the provinces of Cilicia and Asia' in debates with Stephen. Stephen himself was presumably a member of this synagogue, and no doubt he supposed that by sharing his new insights into the scriptures with other members of it he would be able to influence them to recognize Jesus as the promised Messiah. But it was not to be. Far from persuading his fellow Hellenists of the truth of the Christian claims, all he managed to do was to convince them that he was himself a heretic, and before long he found himself accused before the court of the Sanhedrin.

The narrative in Acts suggests that in order to bring effective charges, Stephen's accusers had to tell lies: 'This man', they said, 'is always talking against our sacred Temple and the Law of Moses. We heard him say that this Jesus of Nazareth will tear down the Temple and change all the customs which have come down to us from Moses!' (Acts 6:13–14). This accusation has a familiar ring about it, for according to

---

Stephen's speech

The address of Stephen before the Sanhedrin (Acts 7:1–53) is one of the longest speeches reported anywhere in the New Testament, and at first sight it seems hardly to be a response to the charges that had been made against him. Because of this, some have suggested that what is contained in Acts 7 was a free composition by the author of Acts to provide an appropriate theological explanation for why the Hellenist Christians began to move away from Jerusalem and to loosen their allegiance to Judaism. This question is not of course restricted to the story of Stephen: it is also relevant to the speeches reportedly delivered by Peter, Paul and others in later sections of Acts. Were these speeches based on verbatim reports that were handed down to the author of Acts? Or did he follow the example of a writer like Josephus, who seems to have inserted speeches at will into the mouths of those whose exploits he describes? A number of points may be made:

● Obviously, none of the speeches reported in Acts can be verbatim accounts. They are far too short for that, and in any case people in the ancient world were not obsessed with the desire for accurate quotation which is so important today. This can be seen quite clearly in the way some New Testament writers refer even to the Old Testament scriptures. Though they had supreme authority for them, they often quote from no known version, but refer to them from memory, regularly introducing inaccuracies as a result. In the case of Stephen's trial, it is unlikely that anyone would have taken down extensive notes of what was actually said. The narrative gives the impression that the whole thing took place with great urgency.

● At the same time, it should be borne in mind that not all ancient historians were like Josephus, and the Greek tradition of history-writing would be better represented by an author like Thucydides. He also felt that the inclusion of speeches

Thucydides (460–400BC).

Mark 14:57–59 it was one of the charges brought against Jesus at his trial. But whereas on that occasion the false witnesses failed to agree, and so other charges had to be found, in the case of Stephen he went on to condemn himself out of his own mouth.

In his long speech before the Sanhedrin, Stephen not only admitted the truthfulness of the vague accusations made against him by the witnesses; he also went on to make very specific statements about the subjects in dispute (Acts 7:1–53). With a carefully detailed survey of the history of Israel, he argued that the temple ought never to have existed at all. Illustrating his case with copious quotations from and allusions to the Hebrew scriptures, he pointed out how Moses had received instructions for the construction of a simple tent as a place of worship in the desert, and this had continued in use long after the time of Moses. Things had begun to change only with the accession of Solomon to the throne, when increased wealth and a new international political stature had inspired him to build a central sanctuary in Jerusalem (1 Kings 5:4–5). The Old Testament suggests that Solomon had divine approval for his actions, though strenuous religious and moral conditions were also imposed to ensure the continued existence of the temple (1 Kings 9:1–9). But quoting Isaiah 66:1–2, Stephen argued that the temple had

---

Stephen's speech
continued

at appropriate points in his narrative would help to highlight the important points, but he was not in the habit of simply inventing such speeches, as he explains in the beginning of his *History of the Peloponnesian War* (1.22.1): '… some speeches I heard myself, others I got from various quarters; it was in all cases difficult to carry them word for word in one's memory, so my habit has been to make the speakers say what was in my opinion demanded of them by the various occasions, of course adhering as closely as possible to the general sense of what they really said.'

● On more general grounds, Acts would appear to fit into the Thucydidean mould rather than following the traditions of a person like Josephus. Though its story of early Christianity is undoubtedly selective, when it can be tested against external evidence from other sources, it appears to be generally trustworthy.

● All the speeches in Acts at least have the appearance of authenticity. In subject matter, language and style they are varied

to suit the people who make them. Certainly, as far as the Stephen speech is concerned, the content of the speech does fit in admirably with the kind of occasion that is described. Whenever dissidents of any kind are on trial for their lives, they often choose to defend not themselves, but the ideals for which they stand, and that is precisely what Stephen did. No doubt he had argued like this many times before within the synagogue itself, and others would likely repeat the same arguments on many subsequent occasions. To that extent, his speech was a confession of faith. It is not unrealistic to imagine that he would be determined to take his own last chance of standing before the highest religious authority and making sure his message was heard there too. It is certainly the sort of thing one can imagine having taken place, and in this respect it is quite different from the verbose and often irrelevant speeches which Josephus inserted into the mouths of many of his characters.

been a mistake from the start, for 'the Most High does not dwell in houses made with human hands' (Acts 7:48). He then went on to accuse the religious leaders of wholesale disobedience to the very Law that they professed to uphold (Acts 7:53).

Not surprisingly, all this was too much for them, and when Stephen committed what they regarded as the final blasphemy by asserting that he could 'see heaven opened, and the Son of man standing at the right hand side of God', he can hardly have been taken aback when he was dragged out of the council chamber and stoned to death (Acts 7:56–60).

Stephen's speech is almost unique in the New Testament. With the exception of the book of Hebrews, no other New Testament person or book has much to say about the temple and its services. But outside the New Testament there is evidence of others who disapproved of what was going on there. At a much later date, the *Epistle of Barnabas* adopted a

Stephen's death

The manner of Stephen's trial and death raises some of the same questions as we have already dealt with in relation to the conviction and crucifixion of Jesus. Indeed, it seems likely from the way Luke describes the two episodes that he was consciously intending to draw some connections between the two, maybe to remind his readers that, whatever their undoubted successes, the followers of Jesus could expect to share in the same rejection at the hands of the religious establishment as Jesus himself had suffered. But whatever the literary motif behind the story might be, the same underlying historical issue arises, namely whether or not the Sanhedrin had the right to execute Stephen in the way Luke describes. At the time, Judea was a Roman province, and in Roman provinces generally the right to execute even convicted criminals was reserved for the Roman governor and no one else. This point was brought out quite clearly in the stories of Jesus' trials and execution in the gospels, and according to John 18:31 the same religious leaders who were implicated in Stephen's death had been forced to admit earlier to Pilate that 'we are not allowed to put anyone to death'.

This was not the full story, however, for there seems to have been one circumstance in which the Sanhedrin was allowed to carry out a death sentence without reference to the Roman authorities. This was in the case of a person who violated the sanctity of the temple at Jerusalem, and Josephus reports that anyone, even a Roman, who entered the temple unlawfully could be executed on the orders of the Sanhedrin (*Jewish Wars* 6.2.4). But this has all the appearance of having been a special arrangement, which simply serves to emphasize the weak position of the religious court, for if it already had general powers of jurisdiction in such cases, it would not have required this kind of special dispensation.

In view of the way that Stephen had spoken, it is always possible that he might have been deemed to have violated the temple and its rights in some way, though it is more likely that his death was not the result of a formal sentence, so much as a mob lynching. Acts 7:54–60 does not suggest that any legal verdict was given, but rather that his accusers spontaneously stoned him in their fury. There is evidence of at least one other example of such behaviour, namely the execution of James of Jerusalem in AD62.

very similar radical position on the temple, and some of its strongly anti-Jewish sentiments could easily have been inspired by the story of Stephen (there can be no question of the influence being the other way round, for *Barnabas* was not written until the early second century).

But some scholars have suggested that Stephen's thinking could have been influenced by two religious groups in Palestine who did exist at the same time as him, and who also rejected the temple in Jerusalem. These were the people of Qumran, who wrote the Dead Sea Scrolls, and the Samaritans, neither of whom took part in the worship at the temple, though they each had their own reasons for not doing so, neither of which coincided with the convictions that Stephen apparently held.

The Qumran community had imposed on themselves an enforced isolation from Jerusalem. Believing the temple and its priesthood to be corrupt, they had moved out to establish their own monastic community by the shores of the Dead Sea. But they fervently believed that this state of affairs was only temporary: they looked for the messianic age to dawn very soon, and believed that when it did they themselves would be able to return to Jerusalem and restore the temple and its worship to its original purity. Unlike Stephen, though, they did not despise the temple as an institution, but deplored what they regarded as its temporary corruption.

The Samaritans were also unable to take part in the temple worship at Jerusalem, though for rather different reasons related to their status as a renegade group within Jewish culture, with their own sanctuary on Mount Gerizim and their own version of the scriptures, which was substantially shorter than that used by the Jews themselves. There are obvious points of contact between the thinking of the Qumran community, the Samaritans and Stephen, and the way that Stephen expounded the Old Testament is not unlike the way some of these other sects would have used it. But it is problematical to suppose that Stephen had ever been a member of either group. If he had been, it is hard to see how and why he could have been in Jerusalem in the first place. It is more likely that his thinking on the temple, which was derived from the Old Testament, developed spontaneously as a result of the events of the Day of Pentecost and what followed. Through the presence and power of the Holy Spirit in the church, Christian believers felt they now had direct access to God in person, and for them that was a major reason why the temple was redundant. It had at best been an indirect means of worshipping God, and once people had direct access for themselves then the temple and its rituals became an unnecessary encumbrance for those who were following Jesus.

In Luke's narrative, the story of the death of Stephen plays a pivotal role as one of the crucial events in the life of the early church, with repercussions for the church and its development that were not restricted to Jerusalem, or even Palestine, but ultimately throughout the Roman empire.

Moving beyond Jerusalem

One of the immediate consequences of Stephen's death was a widespread persecution of the Christians in Jerusalem. There is no evidence that a majority of them had adopted the same radical attitude towards the temple as Stephen, but it was perhaps inevitable that people should suppose that most, if not all Christians would share his opinions. It was entirely predictable that the religious establishment should resist this kind of teaching, for Stephen was striking at the very heart of their power base. But the persecution that followed was counter-productive, for it led to the dispersal of Christians from Jerusalem itself, especially those elements who were perceived as the most liberal. Caesarea, Antioch and Damascus – not to mention other, more far-flung cities from which the Hellenist Christians had originally come – all witnessed a considerable influx of these people, who were not just the first Christian refugees, but turned out also to be the first Christian missionaries. This can hardly have been what their opponents intended, but the oppression of the church in Jerusalem only encouraged it to spread to other parts of the land.

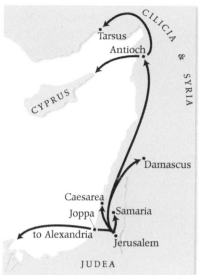

The spread of the early church.

Not all Christians felt they had to leave Jerusalem, and the Acts narrative suggests that those who continued in faithful observance of traditional religious practices were able to stay, even in the face of such intense opposition. Luke mentions by name only the apostles, but it is certain that others must have stayed behind too, all of them characterized by their commitment to uphold the Jewish faith, while incorporating within it their belief in Jesus as the Messiah. This inevitably meant that the church in Jerusalem became more conservative and more conventionally Jewish, a fact that in due course led to its demise and the extinction of all Judaistic forms of Christianity.

But Acts has very little to say about the church in Jerusalem at this time. Instead the attention shifts to the exploits of various Christian leaders elsewhere in Palestine.

Into Judea and Samaria

Philip is one of the Hellenist Christian leaders singled out for special mention in Acts, and he was no doubt typical of many others. Relatively little is known about him, but he was obviously very successful in communicating the Christian message, especially in Hellenistic cities like Caesarea. Some years later, he and his daughters were leading figures in a prosperous Christian community there (Acts 21:8–9), but before settling in Caesarea he had a successful mission among the Samaritans too. From this period, Luke includes the story of how Philip met and baptized an African, an Ethiopian government official who was presumably an adherent of Judaism, since he was on his way home from visiting the temple in Jerusalem when Philip met him in the desert. After an extended conversation about the meaning of the Hebrew scriptures, the man declared his faith in Jesus as the Messiah, and was baptized there and then (Acts 8:26–40).

Philip had been a member of the same group as Stephen, appointed to oversee the funds for Hellenist Christians, and his close association with Stephen might have been the reason he left Jerusalem. But it was not long before some of the original disciples of Jesus also began to tour the countryside of Palestine with their message. People such as Peter and John would probably never have felt at home in Jerusalem anyway, for they were themselves from the country, and the urban culture was foreign to them. Moreover, though Jesus had no doubt visited Jerusalem on several occasions during his own lifetime, the main centre of his activity was not among the conventionally religious people there, but among the marginalized 'people of the land' in rural Palestine, so it would be natural for the remaining disciples to follow his example.

Luke tells of Peter and John together visiting the Samaritans who had come to believe in Jesus as a result of Philip's mission (Acts 8:14–17). Whether or not they initially went as some kind of official delegation to check out what Philip was doing, they found themselves making a public affirmation of his work. Not only did they recognize his Samaritan converts as true disciples, but they also engaged in teaching among the Samaritans themselves (Acts 8:25). Before long Peter had become involved in an itinerant ministry over a wide area of the Palestinian countryside, visiting Lydda, Joppa and even Caesarea (Acts 9:32 – 10:48).

Widening horizons

It was in the course of such travelling that Peter was to become convinced of the importance of non-Jewish people for the future of the Christian church. Of course, he himself had probably never been as religiously conservative and traditional as some of the church members whom he left behind in Jerusalem. The very fact that he was prepared to take his message to the more Hellenized parts of Palestine is itself evidence of that. It is also significant that in the course of this tour, 'Peter stayed in Joppa for many days with a leather-worker named Simon' (Acts 9:43) – something that no strictly orthodox Jew would have been prepared to do, for workers in leather were generally regarded as being ritually unclean, since they were in constant contact with the skins of dead animals (Mishnah, *Kelia* 26.1–9). But in this case, Peter was simply following the example of Jesus himself, who had never had much time for such prohibitions, and was not afraid to have close dealings with all kinds of outcasts of Jewish society (Luke 15:1–2).

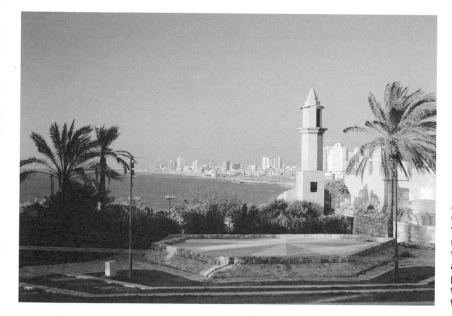

Joppa, modern-day Jaffa, was the scene of a radical about-turn in Peter's attitude to preaching the gospel to non-Jews.

While staying with this man, Peter had an experience that was to change his life. In a dream, he saw a large sheet full of 'all kinds of animals, reptiles and wild birds', many of them ritually unclean by the standards of the Old Testament food laws (Acts 10:1–23). When a voice told him to help himself to a meal from some of these creatures, all his religious instincts told him not to do so – until he was rebuked by the voice (which he now recognized to be God's) telling him, 'Do not consider unclean anything that God has declared clean' (Acts 10:9–16). This was another lesson that Peter must have heard from the lips of Jesus himself (Mark 7:14–23), though in the tense atmosphere of Jerusalem after the death of Stephen he had adopted the more expedient course of following the normal practices of the culture. But he was about to become caught up in something far larger than arguments about food, and what followed eventually had far-reaching implications for the rest of his life's work.

No sooner had Peter woken from his dream than messengers arrived at the door of the house asking that he accompany them to their master, Cornelius (Acts 10:17–22). This man was a Roman centurion in Caesarea, which was the main garrison town and the headquarters of the Roman procurators. Peter must have realized the serious implications of going there, both politically and religiously. But after the vision he had little choice, and so not only did he see Cornelius, but he entered his home and accepted the Roman's hospitality – something that would have been quite unthinkable to the Christians back in Jerusalem. Moreover, as Peter spoke with Cornelius and the members of his household the seriousness of their spiritual search was too obvious to ignore. They not only heard what he had to say, but they responded warmly to his message and when they began to speak in tongues just as the apostles themselves had done on the Day of Pentecost, Peter knew he could not deny the reality of their commitment to Christ. As a result they were baptized and welcomed into the community of the church and – as if to underline his own acceptance of them – Peter stayed in their home for a few days more, no doubt instructing them further in their new faith (Acts 10:24–28).

This was a turning-point for Peter. On his return to Jerusalem, the more conservative Christians were not at all pleased, and though his own account of the affair gave them some reassurance, the rest of Acts shows that this incident had a deep and lasting effect on Peter's relationship with the church at Jerusalem (Acts 11:1–3). Peter would never be leader of the Jerusalem church, but before long was displaced by someone who had not even been one of the original twelve disciples: James, the brother of Jesus. In addition, it was not long after Peter's visit to Caesarea that Herod Agrippa I, the ruler of Palestine at the time, instituted an official persecution of the Christians in Jerusalem. As a result of this, James, the brother of John, was martyred, and Peter himself put into prison (Acts 12:1–5). Peter's willingness to reach out to Gentiles with the Christian message might have given Agrippa the opportunity he was looking for to gain the sympathetic support of the religious establishment for his actions against the church, and if so, that would be an added reason why Peter soon fell from prominence among those Christians who also wanted to maintain their traditional Jewish allegiances.

Very little of a specific nature is known about Peter's activities after this point, but what evidence there is connects him not with the Jewish churches in Palestine, but with the Gentile churches that were soon to emerge all over the Roman empire. Paul provides evidence of an occasion when Peter visited Antioch in Syria (Galatians 2:11–14), and he also seems to have had some kind of contact with the church at Corinth in Greece (1 Corinthians 1 – 4). He seems to have travelled extensively, often accompanied by his wife (1 Corinthians 9:5), and according to well-attested traditions he had strong connections with the church at Rome, and it was there that he was put to death during the persecution of Christians by Nero in about AD64.

The church in Galilee

Apart from occasional visits to Jerusalem, Jesus spent almost all his life in Galilee. The majority of his followers lived there – many thousands of them, according to the gospels – and yet Galilee hardly ever features in the remainder of the New Testament. The story of Acts deals exclusively with the exploits of the followers of Jesus in Jerusalem and in the Gentile cities of the Roman empire, while the New Testament letters mostly relate to the same set of circumstances and none of them can unequivocally be connected with continuing communities of disciples in Galilee.

It is not difficult to see the reasons for this. Luke is the only New Testament writer to have produced anything like a history of the church, and he himself was a Gentile which ensured that his main interest – and that of his readers – would be in the work of Paul and others like him who had been instrumental in spreading the gospel to the major centres of Hellenistic population. For these people, Palestine was a little-known remote outpost of the empire, and small internal distinctions such as the difference between Galilee and Judea must have been relatively insignificant to Gentiles who scarcely knew the location of either of them. In his gospel, Luke did not always distinguish the two areas with as much precision as the other evangelists, and in Acts the only real distinction that he makes is between Jewish Christians and Gentile Christians. A native of Palestine would not have seen it like that. The Judeans had little time for the people of Galilee: it was too open to Gentile influences for their liking, and the fact that Jesus originated there was to many people a good reason for paying no attention to him (John 1:46).

In spite of the fact that followers of Jesus in Galilee would tend to be ignored by Gentile Christians and despised by those from Jerusalem, it is reasonable to assume that they must have continued to flourish. Popular movements like that built up by Jesus do not vanish overnight, especially in a rural area. But what happened to his thousands of followers in Galilee? Some have suggested that they simply dissipated and eventually went out of existence altogether. Some of them had certainly accompanied Jesus to Jerusalem, convinced to the very end that he was about to set up a new nationalist government that would overthrow the Roman rule. Judas Iscariot seems to have thought that way, and when Jesus died in apparent defeat such people probably just went back home to look for another leader. But not all Jesus' followers went with him on his last journey to Jerusalem, and not all of them had an exclusively political view of his message. These others presumably continued the work that Jesus had started in Galilee, and might easily have developed their own continuing communities of his followers independently of what was going on in Jerusalem. There are certainly some indications to support such a view:

● Galilee had always been quite different from Jerusalem, with its own ways of doing things, and its own religious traditions, most of which were despised by the more orthodox and conservative religious leaders in Jerusalem. In view of this background, it is not especially likely that the church in Jerusalem would have wanted any involvement with affairs in Galilee, and still less probable that the Galilean followers of Jesus would automatically have been prepared to accept the authority of the Jerusalem church and its leaders.

● The very character of these leaders must have been an influential factor in the development of the Galilean church. After the expulsion of the Hellenists, the church in Jerusalem seems to have taken a very conservative direction. Members of some of the very same religious groups that had been so strongly opposed to Jesus actually rose to positions of influence in the church itself (Acts 6:7; 15:5), and there are compelling reasons for thinking that James, the main Jerusalem leader, was himself a Pharisee. Presumably in aligning themselves with the Christian cause they had acknowledged Jesus as the Messiah, though that seems to have made little difference to their general outlook and behaviour. They were still firmly committed to upholding traditional rituals and customs, as can be seen from the reception they gave Peter after he had stayed with Cornelius (Acts 11:1–4). It can have been no coincidence that Peter and the other original disciples did not stay long in Jerusalem. Persecution from the authorities and resistance to their more liberal ways from within the church itself soon forced them to leave the city: did most of them return home, to Galilee?

● The assumption that they did fits neatly with the evidence relating to Peter, and provides a plausible explanation for what he might have been doing between the time when he left Jerusalem and the slightly later stage at which there is evidence for him travelling the Roman empire as an itinerant evangelist. Was it in the familiar surroundings of Galilee that he worked out his own approach to the questions raised by the admission of Gentiles to the church? If there is any truth at all in those traditions which have connected Peter to Mark's Gospel, then it is noteworthy that one of Mark's essential themes is the way in which the people of Galilee are depicted giving a warm welcome to the Christian message, while the inhabitants of Jerusalem consistently reject it. Could this emphasis reflect Peter's thinking about the development of the church at Jerusalem during this period?

● Two other New Testament books have from time to time been connected with the Galilean churches: James and Hebrews. Both of them have clear Jewish connections, and both are difficult to identify with what is known of the kind of beliefs that were held in the church at Jerusalem. James has a very uncomplicated understanding of the Christian message, with many connections in both style and

substance to the message of Jesus himself as it is reported in the gospels, while Hebrews not only seems to show some acquaintance with the traditions about Jesus, but also sets out to demonstrate the irrelevance of Jerusalem and its temple – something that would be welcomed by Galileans. Both these books are discussed in more detail in chapter 23.

No one will ever know for sure exactly what happened to the followers of Jesus in Galilee, for their story was never written down. There does however seem to be enough evidence to suggest that the movement started there by Jesus did not die out, but probably grew and flourished, at least for the lifetime of his original disciples.

The Acts of the Apostles

The book of Acts is the sequel to Luke's Gospel. The two books obviously belong together: they were both written to the same person, 'Theophilus', with the gospel intended to tell the story of the life and teaching of Jesus while Acts continues the story to describe how his small band of disciples had developed into a worldwide Christian movement.

Despite its title, Acts does not in fact tell the story of all the apostles. Only some of them are mentioned extensively, and the book has most to say about Peter and Paul, together with a few incidents from the lives of other early Christian leaders such as Philip, John, James the brother of Jesus, and Stephen. The story is told in two parts. The first is concerned mainly with events in Jerusalem and elsewhere in Palestine, and here Peter is the leading character (chapters 1 – 12). The second section of the book tells the story of Paul (chapters 13 – 28), though there are some integrating features in the narrative: Paul makes his first appearance at the stoning of Stephen (Acts 7:58), while Peter is still a major player in Luke's story of the Council of Jerusalem, which is essentially a part of the story of Paul (Acts 15:7–11).

The author

Who wrote the book of Acts? Or, to put the question more accurately, who wrote the two volumes, Luke and Acts? There is no doubt they were both written by the same person. They are both addressed to Theophilus, and their style and language are identical. Other considerations have already been outlined in the earlier discussion of Luke's Gospel, where it was concluded that all the evidence points to the author being Luke, the Gentile doctor who accompanied Paul on some of his travels.

The date

The date of Acts is a more complicated matter and three main suggestions have been put forward:

The second century

Scholars of the nineteenth-century 'Tübingen School' believed that Acts must have been written sometime after AD100, and though this view has by no means won a majority following it still has some supporters. Two main considerations are usually advanced:

● Acts 5:36–37 refers to two individuals called Theudas and Judas, and 21:38 mentions an Egyptian troublemaker. Since Josephus' *Antiquities of the Jews* 20.5.1 seems to describe the same events, and since this was not published until AD93, Acts, it is claimed, must have been written later than that. But there is no textual or stylistic evidence to support the idea that Luke used Josephus' account as a source for his own, and his description of these people actually has significant differences from what Josephus says, which means it is only possible to connect the two by making the further assumption that Luke misunderstood Josephus' story when he read it.

● It is also suggested that Acts was written in about the middle of the second century to counteract the influence of Marcion. Among other things, Marcion was suggesting that the first disciples of Jesus had misunderstood the point of his teaching, and that Paul was the only true interpreter of Jesus. It is certainly true that Acts was read with renewed interest at the time of Marcion, for its story shows little sign of the kind of misunderstanding that Marcion emphasized. But there is no real trace of second-century concerns in Luke's writings, while there are plenty of indications to connect it with the period that it purports to describe.

AD62–70

At the opposite extreme of what is historically plausible, other scholars have suggested that Acts was written almost at the same time as the events it describes – either immediately after the arrival of Paul in Rome (AD62–64) or shortly after his death (AD66–70). The following

The Acts of the Apostles *continued*

The Roman emperors exacted heavy taxes both from their own people and those in subject provinces. In this 3rd-century relief from Germany, the collector sits with his ledger and heaps of coins.

arguments are said to favour such an early date:

● By any standards, Acts ends very abruptly. Paul has arrived in Rome, and the last we see of him he is 'teaching about the Lord Jesus Christ quite openly and unhindered' (Acts 28:31). This is not as odd as it can be made to seem, for from another viewpoint it is the natural climax of Luke's narrative. The prologue of Acts 1:8 indicates that Luke's intention was to explain the progress of the Christian message from Jerusalem to Rome, and that is what he does by ending the book once Paul has arrived there. It was no doubt inevitable that some readers would be curious to know what eventually happened to Paul: did he appear before the emperor's court, and what was the outcome? Eusebius supplemented Luke's story with the

information that 'after defending himself the apostle was sent again on his ministry of preaching, and coming a second time to the same city suffered martyrdom under Nero' (*Ecclesiastical History* II.22), and *1 Clement* 5 (written about AD95) suggested that Paul visited Spain during this short time of freedom, which has convinced some that it was during this period that Paul penned the 'pastoral epistles' of 1 and 2 Timothy and Titus. Whether or not Paul went on such further travels, all the evidence indicates that he was beheaded during Nero's persecution in about AD64.

In view of all this, it is argued that if Acts was written after Paul was dead, then the statement about him preaching openly and unhindered is an odd note on which to finish the story of his life. This is the kind of argument that can be turned

on its head, though, for since Paul was obviously Luke's hero it is just as likely that he would want to show his life ending in triumph rather than the apparent defeat of martyrdom.

● A more substantial argument is that the book of Acts adopts a generally favourable attitude to the Roman authorities. Paul's Roman citizenship is constantly highlighted as an invaluable asset which gave him freedom to travel in peace all over the empire. When he meets Roman officials they are always on his side: Sergius Paulus, the proconsul of Cyprus who became a Christian (Acts 13:6–12); Gallio, the proconsul in Corinth who gave him a fair hearing (Acts 18:12–17); even the Roman commander in Jerusalem who rescued him from a hostile mob (Acts 21:31–40). They all look favourably on Paul's mission, and

Acts gives the impression that, if the empire was not exactly supporting the church, it certainly was not its sworn enemy. All that changed in AD64, with the persecution started by Nero, and official persecution of one sort or another continued spasmodically right through to the end of the first century. On this basis it is argued that Acts must have been written prior to AD64. Like the other one, this proposition ultimately depends on a more or less subjective estimate of what an ancient writer might have been expected to do in the circumstances. In reality, there is no way of telling whether or to what extent any author might allow his or her perception of historical events to be affected by what later took place, and if Acts can be regarded as a reasonably faithful presentation of the period it describes, then its apparent pro-Roman bias might simply reflect the facts of the situation. It might also reflect Luke's own experience as a member of the Roman upper classes.

● Acts does not seem to contain any hint of the fall of Jerusalem in AD70, and if Jerusalem had been destroyed before the work was written, it is claimed that we would have expected a mention of the fact, for it would have been a striking vindication of Luke's viewpoint on Judaism and indeed on Jewish Christianity. Again, this argument depends on the assumption that it is possible to know precisely what was in the mind of an ancient author, and what he or she might be expected to write in given circumstances.

● Another relevant fact is that Acts makes no mention at all of the letters that Paul wrote to his churches. This almost certainly implies that Acts was written before the letters were collected together and circulated more widely, which certainly would date Acts earlier than a writing like 2 Peter, which mentions Paul's letters as a part of the Christian scriptures (2 Peter 3:16).

AD80–85

The consensus would be to reject both a very late second-century date for Acts and a very early date in the sixties of the first century. On this understanding, it was probably written sometime between AD80 and 90. Two substantial reasons have been put forward for this:

● Acts 1:1 begins with the words: 'In my first book I wrote about all the things which Jesus did and taught', and this 'first book' was Luke's Gospel. When he wrote the gospel, Luke incorporated stories and sayings of Jesus derived from Mark, which seems to have been written between 60 and 65. On this reckoning, Luke's first volume can hardly be placed much earlier than about 65–70, which in turn means that Acts, as the second volume, cannot have been written as early as 62–64. This is a persuasive argument though it is not the final word, for it has at least two weak spots.

Firstly, it depends on the date assigned to Mark, which to some extent is a matter of scholarly guesswork, though good reasons can be put forward in support of the generally held view.

Secondly, it is also possible that the prologues of both Luke and Acts were added last, when the two books were in their final form. If Luke's Gospel existed in some other form before its final one (whether or not that can be identified more specifically as Streeter's 'Proto-Luke'), then maybe that reflected Luke's way of working, and Acts also might have been written in stages. The passages where Luke uses 'we' rather than 'they' could have been just the first of several editions of Luke's story of the early church, an original account that was later expanded to include stories about the early Jerusalem church, perhaps brought to Luke's attention during his stay in Caesarea while Paul was in prison there. It is therefore always possible that the basic core of Acts could have been written before the gospel, with only the prologue being added later to commend it to Theophilus.

There is however a more substantial reason for dating Acts later than the lifetime of Paul. Luke's writing often seems to show signs of attitudes and beliefs which were common in the post-apostolic age. Indeed, Luke and Acts together have been regarded as a kind of manifesto of what scholars refer to as 'early Catholicism'. This subject is dealt with in some detail in chapter 22, where it is argued that the emergence of so-called 'Catholic Christianity' was a natural, almost imperceptible development of certain elements within the teaching of the apostles themselves. Whatever the outcome of that debate, however, Luke does have a distinctive outlook that in many respects corresponds to a form of church life that was more prevalent in the late first century.

For instance, by reading only Acts it would be quite easy to get the impression that the early church had a largely uncontroversial existence, whereas Paul's letters (all of them borne out of controversy) paint a different picture. No doubt it was a part of Luke's intention to stress that there was fundamental agreement between all sections of the early church, and up to a point Paul himself wanted to argue as much, for he went out of his way to emphasize his own continuity with the earliest disciples. But that is only a part of the picture, and Paul's letters more typically reveal him as a person who had profound disagreements not only with his enemies, but on occasion with his friends as well. Of course, Paul's letters also show him as a very impulsive person, and it is quite possible that some of the issues he wrote about with such passion turned out to be less serious than he thought at the time, and Luke, writing some time later, could take a more detached view of these things, and see them in their proper perspective, both in the life of Paul and in the ongoing experience of the church.

This does not mean that Luke was any less a friend or even a disciple of Paul, for good teachers do not turn out students who are clones of themselves, but encourage them to develop their own distinctive thinking. In any case, as we shall see below, the positions that Luke adopts in Acts differ from Paul in the details rather than on the fundamentals.

The real choice for the date of Acts is between the sixties and the eighties of the first century. The evidence on the one side is just about as problematic as that on the other, though the balance of probability seems to favour a date in the eighties, perhaps around AD85.

The value of Acts

What sort of book is the Acts of the Apostles? We have occasionally referred to it as a history of the early church, but of course it is not a comprehensive history: there are so many things it does not include that it is clearly not the full story of early Christianity. Instead, it is a selective story, drawing attention to those people and movements which Luke believed to be especially significant. In writing his gospel, Luke had adopted exactly the same procedure, selecting those aspects of the life and teaching of Jesus which would be most relevant to the concerns of his readers, and in Acts he covers those incidents which for him typified the trend of events among the first generation of Christians. He wanted to show how Christianity spread from Jerusalem to Rome, and everything that he included was intended to illuminate that transition. In the process, he omitted many things that today's readers might have wished to know about. What happened to Peter? How did James get on in the church at Jerusalem? What became of Jesus' other disciples? Luke simply ignores these questions because they were not relevant to his purpose.

This means that his story is also an interpretation of the progress of the early church. All history, of course, is an interpretation of past events, and the book of Acts therefore raises many of the same questions as we have already dealt with in connection with the gospels. Much of what has been said in chapters 10 and 12 can also be applied to the understanding of the historical nature of Acts, and there is no point in covering the same ground again here. It is however worth repeating that by characterizing Acts as a Lukan interpretation of early church history nothing is being either said or implied that would not be true of any kind of second-hand knowledge we might have. It is not to suggest, for example, that Luke simply invented his stories: indeed, if nothing had happened, there would have been nothing for him to interpret. Acts, however, reflects the way that Luke, from his own presuppositions and background, saw the history of the earliest church.

There are in fact a number of reasons for thinking that the picture which he painted was an essentially authentic reproduction of life in the period which it describes:
● In the prologue to his gospel (Luke 1:1–4) Luke gives some indication of his procedures: he read all that he could find, sifted through it and then wrote his own considered account of what had happened. In the case of the gospel it is possible to see pretty clearly how he went about it, for the end product can be directly compared with Mark, which was one of his major source documents. The way he has used Mark shows that Luke was a very careful writer, aware of the need to reproduce his sources accurately and without distortion. There is no comparable direct access to whatever sources he might have used in the writing of Acts, though it is widely surmised that he relied on written information for at least the stories of early events in Jerusalem and Samaria (chapters 1 – 9). The natural assumption would be that he would have exercised the same care in compiling the narrative of Acts as he had previously taken with the gospel.

The Acts of the Apostles *continued*

The inscription from one of Thessalonica's gates mentions the rulers of the city as 'politarchs' – the term used in the account of Paul's visit in Acts. It helps reinforce the authenticity of the account in the Bible.

In addition to that, he was himself personally present for at least some of the events in Acts (the 'we' passages).

● The picture Luke paints of life in the earliest Palestinian churches is consistent with what might be expected. Much of the theology which he attributes to those earliest Christian believers has a far less sophisticated character than the theology either of Paul or of the church later in the first century. For example, Jesus is referred to as 'the Messiah' (Christ) in Acts 2:36; 3:20; 4:27, and he can be called 'the servant of God' (Acts 3:13, 26; 4:25–30), or even in one instance 'the Son of man' (a title much used by Jesus himself but found nowhere in the

and its officials. He always uses the right word to describe Roman administrators, and sometimes uses terminology that would only be familiar to people living in particular cities. Sergius Paulus and Gallio are correctly designated 'proconsuls' (Acts 13:7–8; 18:12). Philippi is accurately described as a Roman colony, ruled by the *Strategoi* (Praetors), which is an unusual word to find in a literary source, but has been discovered on inscriptions which show that it was the colloquial term used in Philippi itself (Acts 16:12, 20–22). At one time, Luke was believed to have been mistaken in using the term 'politarchs' to describe the rulers of Thessalonica (Acts 17:8), because it

rest of the New Testament except Acts 7:56). The Christians are called simply 'disciples' (for example, in Acts 6:1–7; 9:1, 25–26), and the church itself is 'the Way' (Acts 9:2; 19:9, 23; 24:14, 22). Norman Perrin, whose scepticism about the reliability of the gospels was reviewed in chapter 12, describes all this as 'extraordinarily realistic… the narratives of Acts are full of elements taken directly from the life and experience of the church'.

● This same realism can be seen in Luke's description of the Roman world

is found nowhere in the rest of Latin or Greek literature. However, subsequent archaeological discoveries have shown that Luke was quite right to describe the authorities at Thessalonica in this way, though only someone who had actually been there would have been likely to do so, for it was a local term not common elsewhere. There are also many other points at which Luke's stories can be shown to depend on direct and reliable knowledge of the Roman world as it actually was at the time he purports to be describing.

● The same concern for authenticity can also be seen in Luke's representation of the problems of the early church. The only real controversy that appears in Acts is concerned with the relationship of Jewish and Gentile Christians. This argument rapidly diminished in importance, and after AD70 was of no significant concern at all, except as a theological debating point. At the time when Luke was writing, other issues were far more prominent – efforts to define heresy and orthodoxy, and various power struggles between different factions within the church – though these later concerns are never incorporated into the Acts story.

● There is just one point which may at first sight appear to undermine confidence in Luke's general trustworthiness as a historian, and this is his treatment of Paul. Paul's letters do seem to present a somewhat different angle on Paul's life and teaching from the picture of him in Acts – indeed, Acts does not even mention the fact that Paul wrote letters at all! A number of points are relevant in explaining this apparent discrepancy.

Firstly, Luke's failure to mention Paul's letters is not all that serious. He might quite possibly have regarded them as personal letters, and therefore of no great importance for his own purpose. We must also remember that though we rightly regard Paul's letters as primary evidence for his activity, they are to some extent evidence without a context and it is therefore easy for us to overestimate how their significance would be seen at the time of their composition.

More seriously, however, it is pointed out that the sort of things Paul concerns himself with in Acts are usually significantly different from his normal concerns in the letters. Again, this is not specially surprising. When Paul wrote letters, he was writing to Christians, whereas when he speaks in Acts he is usually addressing non-Christians. There has been plenty of speculation about the content of Paul's initial preaching to the Galatians, Corinthians, Thessalonians and others, but it is impossible to know for certain what he would typically have told them. One thing we can be sure of is that he would present his message in a different way to engage the attention of the unconverted than he would when trying to correct the errors of those who were already Christians. It is noteworthy that in the only instance where Acts reports an address to Christians by Paul (Acts 20:17–38), the substance of his message is not materially different from the typical content of his letters. Even his message at Athens (Acts 17:22–31) is not significantly different from what he wrote on the same subject in Romans 1:18 – 2:16.

A third consideration, however, is that significant differences are said to emerge in relation to what many believe to have been the central feature of Paul's thinking: 'justification by faith'. But this is not a strong argument, for it depends on the prior assumption that 'justification' was in fact the centre of Paul's thinking. For scholars of the Lutheran tradition (German Lutherans in particular), this assumption is beyond question. But it is equally plausible to argue that, far from being the central core of Paul's theology, this topic assumed such large importance in letters like Galatians and Romans only because, either really or potentially, a particular kind of Judaizing opposition was in view. In any case, where 'justification' does feature in Acts (for example, 13:39, the sermon in the synagogue at Antioch in Pisidia), the way it is used is not at all inconsistent with Paul's arguments in Galatians or Romans, even though it might be less comprehensively worked out. Luke was generally less interested in theological matters than Paul was, and though it has become fashionable to speak of Luke as a 'theologian', he was not a professional and he would not have had the same concern for detail that Paul himself no doubt had. The kind of theology Luke attributes to Paul is exactly what we would expect in the circumstances, and he shows his knowledge of key phrases and ideas that Paul used, while displaying less interest in the detailed arguments that could be brought out in their support.

The purpose of Acts

Though he does not address their problems directly, Luke must have hoped that his first readers would learn something from his story to help their own Christian thinking. He might therefore have had at least three primary aims in view:

● Perhaps the main thing that comes out clearly from Acts is the conviction that Christianity is a faith with the potential to change the world. Indeed, through Paul and others it *did* change the world, and the secret of its success was the endowment of the Holy Spirit bestowed on them by the risen Jesus Christ. Luke sought to encourage his readers to follow the example of those who had been Christians before them, and to do for their generation what Paul had achieved in his.

● Luke also seems to go out of his way to emphasize that Christianity could enjoy good relationships with the Roman empire. On the one hand, he commended the Christians to Rome itself, by his emphasis on the fact that their faith was the true successor of Judaism – and Judaism, of course, was a recognized religion within the empire. But he also encouraged his readers themselves to take a positive attitude towards the empire by stressing that its officials were good, honest people, and implying that a maniac like Nero was the exception rather than the rule.

Nero (AD37–68). Roman emperor from AD54 until his suicide.

● In view of the claim made at the beginning of his gospel, we must also take seriously the position of Luke as the first historian of Christianity. His two books were addressed to Theophilus in order that he might be informed about the facts of the Christian faith, and the procedure that Luke adopted for compiling his story suggests that he had a historian's interest in finding out about the past for its own sake. As the church developed into a significant community within the Roman world, it was important for its members to know their origins and history, and Luke was perhaps the first person to set some of it out in a systematic form.

The missing apostles

All three synoptic gospels, together with Acts, list twelve special disciples of Jesus, yet apart from Peter, James, John and Judas Iscariot, none of them feature prominently in the gospels, and they are not mentioned at all in the rest of the New Testament. We do not really know what happened to these people but there are a number of stories about them in early Christian writings outside the New Testament.

Thomas supposedly went to India, where he died as a Christian martyr, though not before he had persuaded a notable Indian ruler and his family to believe in Jesus. The Mar Thoma church in southern India claims that he was its founder, but it is more likely that it was established by other missionaries from the church in Edessa, by the banks of the River Euphrates. Eusebius says that Thomas himself went to India, and perhaps that is why the Indian Christians regard him as their patron saint (Eusebius, *Ecclesiastical History* III.1.1).

Andrew is said to have travelled extensively throughout Greece and Asia Minor, even crossing to the northern shore of the Black Sea. His life was allegedly characterized by miraculous deeds, including the resurrection of thirty-nine dead sailors washed up from a shipwreck! However, when the proconsul's wife in the Greek city of Patrae became a Christian, her husband was so enraged that he had Andrew crucified on a cross shaped like the letter X. Other legends claim that sometime between the fourth and ninth centuries, his arm-bone was taken by Regulus to Scotland, where Andrew became the patron saint and his cross the national flag.

Thaddaeus is mentioned in the New Testament only by Matthew and Mark. According to Eusebius (*Ecclesiastical History* I.13), a person of that name was connected with the establishment of the church in Edessa. The story tells how

Agbar, king of Edessa, had written a letter to Jesus asking that he be healed of a disease, and in his reply Jesus said that after his ascension, Thaddaeus would be sent to heal him. But other traditions connect Thaddaeus with Africa.

Philip and *Bartholomew* feature in stories about their travels around Asia Minor, accompanied by Philip's sister Mariamne. The *Acts of Philip* tell of encounters with dragons and beasts who speak to them, with Philip finally being martyred in Heirapolis, though Clement of Alexandria suggests that he lived to old age. Bartholomew has also been connected with a mission to India.

Matthew is said to have preached in Judea for eight years after the ascension, before going off to Ethiopia and Arabia. According to Papias, he had something to do with Matthew's Gospel.

James, the son of Alphaeus is mentioned in Spanish traditions that tell how Theodorus, Bishop of Iria, discovered his tomb at Santiago in 835, apparently guided there by a star.

Simon the Zealot travelled to England, according to some stories, together with Lazarus and Joseph of Arimathea.

We cannot trust any of these traditions about the 'unknown' apostles. Some of them might conceivably be based on vague recollections of their exploits, but on the whole their stories are just designed to fill in the gaps in the New Testament story, and have no independent historical value.

14 Introducing Paul

After the early chapters of Acts, the centre of interest moves away from Peter and the other disciples of Jesus to another important figure in the life of the early church: Paul, the Pharisee. He was not the only Pharisee to become a Christian (Acts 15:5), but he was certainly the best known of them. Unlike the first generation of Christians, Paul was not born in Palestine, though he was a Jew. His home was in the city of Tarsus in the Roman province of Cilicia, and he was also a Roman citizen (Acts 22:3, 27).

Paul's early life

There were probably two distinct periods in Paul's early life: his childhood, spent in Tarsus, and his adolescence and early adult years, which were spent in Jerusalem. The words translated 'brought up' in Acts 22:3 could indicate that Paul was only a baby when he moved from Tarsus to Jerusalem, though it is more likely that they refer to the period of his formal education, which would mean he was resident in Jerusalem predominantly during his teenage years, or perhaps a little earlier. Since he returned to Tarsus after he became a Christian, this seems the most obvious meaning of the expression.

First and foremost, Paul was a Jew, and incredibly proud of it – as he was of the reputation of Tarsus, which was a notable university town and centre of government and trade. Though efforts have been made, from time to time, to discover the influence of formal Greek rhetoric behind the structure of some of his letters, there is little evidence that he had any specialized Hellenistic education, and the general cultural ethos of this kind of city is probably sufficient to explain the three references to Greek literature which are contained in Paul's letters and sermons: references to the poets Epimenides (Acts 17:28), Aratus (Titus 1:12), and Menander (1 Corinthians 15:33). Since Paul's parents were Roman citizens, they must have been fairly liberal in their attitude towards non-Jewish culture, and Paul's letters reveal a similar outlook on his part. Though he did not necessarily find all aspects of the lifestyle of Hellenistic culture equally appealing, Paul had a robust appreciation for life in the urban centres of the empire, and a sympathetic understanding of the pressures faced by those who became Christians from such a background.

Quite early in his life, Paul's parents decided that he should become a student and teacher of the Jewish Law. As a small child in Tarsus, he would have learned the traditions of his people through regular instruction at the local synagogue, though as a Jew of the Dispersion his first Bible was probably the Septuagint rather than the Hebrew Bible. Paul also learned the art of tent making, for all students of the Torah were expected to have a practical trade as well as doing their studies. This skill played a significant part in Paul's mission strategy later in his life, for not only did it enable him to live in financial independence of the churches he founded, but it also gave him an opportunity to share his message in the market place while plying his trade.

As a young man, Paul was soon sent away from Tarsus to the centre of the Jewish world, Jerusalem, where he became a student of the learned Rabbi Gamaliel, who was the grandson and successor of Hillel, one of the greatest rabbis of all time. Hillel (60BC – AD20) had taught a more advanced and liberal form of Judaism than his rival, Shammai, and many interpreters believe that what Jesus said about divorce might have been provoked by arguments between the followers of these two rabbis (Mark 10:1–12). Hillel was of the opinion that a man could divorce his wife if she displeased him in any way – even if she burned his dinner – whereas Shammai took the view that divorce was justified only in the event of some serious moral sin. What Paul himself later wrote on this subject suggests he must have changed his mind after he became a Christian. Paul gained at least one great benefit from his education in the tradition of Hillel. Shammai had refused to see any place for the Gentiles in the purposes of God,

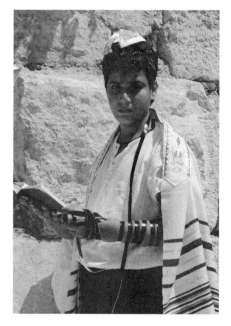

This Jewish boy has portions of the Law in a tiny leather 'phylactery', in literal obedience to the instruction in Deuteronomy 6:8 to tie the commands of the Lord 'on your arms and wear them on your foreheads'.

whereas his rival had welcomed them, positively setting out to invite them to consider the Jewish faith. No doubt it was through Gamaliel that Paul first came to appreciate the enormous spiritual potential for introducing the God of the ancient scriptures to the Gentile population of the Roman empire.

Paul progressed well in his studies at Jerusalem, and by all accounts was a highly successful student (Galatians 1:14). Though the exact position to which he rose in Judaism is never clearly spelled out, he had sufficient influence that when Christians were being tried for their faith he found himself in a position to 'cast his vote' against them, either in a synagogue assembly, or even possibly in the supreme religious council, the Sanhedrin (Acts 26:10).

Significant influences in Paul's life

Like that of any other young person, Paul's character was formed by many diverse influences in his early life, and their complex interaction with his inherited, temperamental disposition and his religious upbringing hold many clues to the person he became, both as a Jew and as a Christian.

Paul and Judaism

Paul himself never explicitly mentions Hellenistic influences, but he makes many statements about his Jewish background and upbringing. In particular, until the end of his life, he remained proud of the fact that he was a good Pharisee, and his many letters reveal that, even as a leading Christian, he never rejected the fundamental world-view and beliefs of his teachers. The differences of opinion on matters of faith between the Pharisees and the Sadducees appear at several points, both in the narratives of Acts and in his own letters, and on every point of dispute between these two groups, Paul always took up, and often elaborated upon, the viewpoint of the more liberal Pharisees.

A key Pharisaic belief seems to have been the conviction that history had a goal and a purpose, and the Pharisees held that God was ordering events according to a specific plan which would culminate with the coming of the Messiah to lead the people. Paul warmly embraced this view as a Christian, and used it in Romans 9 – 11 to deal with one of the things that caused him considerable personal pain – the rejection of Jesus as Messiah by the mainstream of the Jewish world. He argued that God was ordering the course of history with a view to the ultimate salvation of both Gentiles and Jews, who would be incorporated into the one community of God's people.

Pharisees also had distinctive beliefs about a future life, and Paul stressed this to his own advantage when on trial before the Sanhedrin (Acts 23:6–10), and again before Herod Agrippa II (Acts 26:6–8). But, as a Christian, Paul went further, for he wanted to add that no one could guarantee there would be a resurrection without acknowledging the fact that Jesus Christ had risen from the dead.

Pharisees believed in the existence of angels and demons, while the Sadducees did not. Again, Paul retained the Pharisaic belief as a Christian, but transformed it in the light of his experience of Christ by linking it to the cross, on which he claimed Jesus had vanquished the powers of evil. Because of this, he could describe Christians as 'more than conquerors through the One who loved us' (Romans 8:37). Though Paul had a developed angelology, he always understood angels to be heavenly beings serving as God's messengers: they could never rival the living Christ, in whom 'all the fullness of God was pleased to dwell' (Colossians 1:19).

It was not only in terms of specific beliefs that Paul continued to respect and celebrate his Jewish heritage. The very way he wrote and

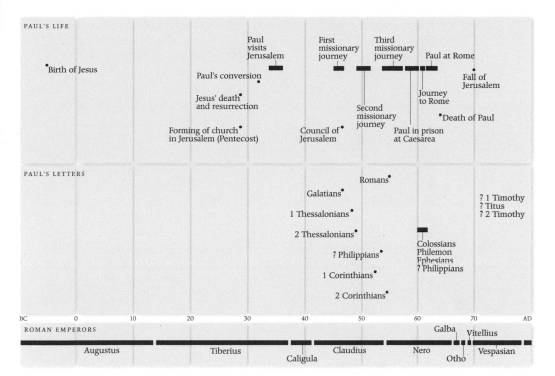

PAUL'S LIFE

Birth of Jesus

Paul's conversion

Paul visits Jerusalem

First missionary journey

Third missionary journey

Paul at Rome

Fall of Jerusalem

Jesus' death and resurrection

Journey to Rome

Death of Paul

Forming of church in Jerusalem (Pentecost)

Council of Jerusalem

Second missionary journey

Paul in prison at Caesarea

PAUL'S LETTERS

Romans

Galatians

1 Thessalonians

? 1 Timothy
? Titus
? 2 Timothy

2 Thessalonians

? Philippians

Colossians
Philemon
Ephesians
? Philippians

1 Corinthians

2 Corinthians

BC 0 10 20 30 40 50 60 70 AD

ROMAN EMPERORS

Galba Vitellius

Augustus Tiberius Claudius Nero Vespasian

Caligula Otho

Paul's life and letters.

reasoned, using the Hebrew scriptures to 'prove' his theological points, was taken directly from his training as a Pharisee. No one who reads his letter to the Galatians can fail to be amazed, and sometimes surprised, by the way Paul draws what can seem to be very unusual meanings from apparently quite straightforward Old Testament passages. For instance, he was arguing like a Jewish rabbi when he claimed that the promises made to Abraham referred to a single person, Jesus Christ; the Greek word for 'offspring' (like its English equivalent) is a collective singular word and not plural in form (Galatians 3:16). Like the rabbis, Paul argued from single isolated texts, and could link up texts taken from completely different, and unrelated, parts of the Old Testament.

These specific points of agreement between Paul's upbringing as a Pharisee and the beliefs he continued to hold as a Christian are, however, relatively trivial compared with what Paul appears to have regarded as a major break between his own original beliefs and his convictions as a Christian. In recent years there has been very considerable discussion of the nature of Paul's relationship to Judaism, all focused on his attitude to the Torah. Put simply, when Paul compared and contrasted Christianity with Judaism – as he did especially in Galatians and Romans – was he being fair to Jewish beliefs about the Law, or was he setting up a misleading caricature which was then predictably easy for him to dismiss? The overall impression that Paul gives is that Jews in general, and the Pharisees in particular, were narrow-minded legalists who insisted on detailed observance not only of the actual Law of the Hebrew scriptures, but also of traditional laws and customs for which there was no biblical authority. What is more, Paul can be understood as implying that it was claimed those who did not observe all of these regulations in every particular could never attain to full salvation, and that he himself had been all but destroyed as he vainly tried to do so.

The problem is that Jewish sources themselves tend to present a rather different picture – not of oppressed people struggling hard to keep a Law that was always beyond their moral grasp, but of committed believers joyfully observing the Law as part of their total response to the love of God as they had experienced it. We take a longer look at this matter in a later chapter. Here, it is worth making three general observations:

■ Direct and specific information about Judaism in the first century is very limited, and the most comprehensive accounts of Jewish theology come from the period of the Mishnah (mid-second century onwards) and even later. After the fall of Jerusalem in AD70, Judaism was forced to reimagine itself without the temple, and underwent a considerable period of uncertainty and radical change. All the evidence relating to Jewish thinking dates back to this time. Of course, it would be unreasonable to conceive of the second-century rabbis inventing their views from nothing, and we can be certain that, to a large extent, the structure of the faith that emerged then would have been largely a systematic reordering of traditional beliefs that went back much further. Nevertheless, the lack of hard evidence that is itself contemporary with the New Testament should at least introduce a note of caution into the debate, for Paul's evidence is indisputably first-hand.

■ When we enquire about Paul's overall attitude to his Jewish heritage, the picture that emerges is more complex and more carefully nuanced than it can be made to look on the basis of some of the texts. Paul never actually stated that Judaism had not worked for him as an intellectual system; indeed, in more than one place, he claimed that he was very satisfied with it (Galatians 1:14; Philippians 3:6). Moreover, he never abandoned the belief that, somehow, the Jewish people would remain central to God's plans right to the end, and though he expressed considerable anguish that his compatriots refused to recognize Jesus as their Messiah, this did not prevent him from remaining committed to them (Acts 21:17–26), and anticipating that they would ultimately share in the benefits of God's kingdom (Romans 9 – 11). It is too simplistic to portray Paul as having abandoned Judaism, still more so to imagine that he could be described as anti-Semitic. The thing that really made a difference, as we shall see in the next chapter, was his personal encounter with the living Christ on the Damascus road. This was the ultimate source of his Christian faith, and the rest of his life was spent struggling to understand how, if Judaism was based on a revelation of God's will, it could be reconciled with what happened to him on that day.

■ Since Paul had a personal vested interest, not in seeing Judaism undermined, but in seeing it transformed as a result of the new insights he believed had been entrusted to him, it is inherently unlikely that he would have deliberately misrepresented it. Regardless of what the rabbis thought Judaism ought to be about, it is hard to get away from the conclusion that Paul himself did actually know Jewish believers who were self-righteous legalists. In any book-based religion there will always be a problem with narrow-minded bigots who pervert the spiritual essence of the faith in order to establish their own power base. The Christian church has had its fair share of such people: one need only think of the Crusades, and much of what followed them, to appreciate that, while the clearly stated essence of Christian faith in the teaching of Jesus allows no place for the imposition of the 'kingdom of God' by militaristic means, this has not deterred those who claim to follow him from making the effort to do just that. If there were first-century Jews who similarly corrupted some central aspects of their own faith, this should hardly be a cause for surprise. More unusual would be the fact that, later, rabbis were able to make a break with this and rediscover something of the more generous spirit that had always pervaded their traditional scriptures.

Paul and the philosophers

Of the many philosophical schools of the time, Stoicism was probably the most congenial to Paul. One or two of the great Stoics came from Tarsus, and Paul might have remembered something about their teachings from his youth.

Some scholars have suggested that Paul's acquaintance with Stoic philosophy was closer than this. Paul's style of debate and argument sometimes resembles the Stoics' procedures: both use rhetorical questions, short, disconnected statements, an imaginary opponent to engender debates, and frequent illustrations drawn from athletics, building, and urban life in general. It is even possible to find phrases in Paul's teaching that are not inconsistent with Stoic doctrine, even if they do not overtly support it, for example, the description of the cosmic Christ in Colossians 1:16–17: 'all things were created through him and for him. He is before all things, and in him all things hold together.' There is also the fact that, in his address at Athens, Luke reports that Paul had actually quoted from Aratus, who was a well-known Stoic poet (Acts 17:28). Some of Paul's letters also often reflect Stoic terminology, as when he describes morality in terms of what is 'fitting' (Colossians 3:18; Ephesians 5:3–4). No doubt Paul would know and sympathize with many Stoic ideals, but at a deeper level there are outstanding and quite fundamental differences between Paul's world-view and Stoicism:

■ Stoicism was based on philosophical speculation about the nature of the world and its people. Insofar as there was one, the real 'god' of Stoic thinking was abstract human reason. By contrast, Paul's faith was very firmly based on the notion of direct revelation coming from God to humankind, most notably (though not exclusively) through the life, death and resurrection of Jesus Christ (1 Corinthians 15:3–11).

■ The Stoic 'god' was an ill-defined abstraction, sometimes associated with the whole universe, sometimes with reason, and sometimes even with the element of fire: 'What god we know not, yet a god there dwells' (Seneca, *Letters* 41.2, quoting Virgil). Paul, however, always regarded God as a personal being, definitively – though not exclusively – revealed in Christ.

■ Stoics found 'salvation' in self-sufficiency. They sought to win mastery of themselves so they could live in harmony with nature: 'The end of life is to act in conformity with nature, that is, at one with the nature which is in us and with the nature of the universe... Thus the life according to nature is that virtuous and blessed flow of existence, which is enjoyed only by one who always acts so as to maintain the harmony between the daemon within the individual and the will of the Power that orders the universe' (Diogenes Laertius, *Lives of the Greek Philosophers* vii.1.53). Paul's understanding of salvation and personal fulfilment was completely different from this, and was to be found not in dependence on himself, but in a mystical identification with Jesus Christ: 'I have been crucified with Christ, it is no longer I who live, but Christ who lives in me; and the life I now live in the flesh I live by faith in the Son of God, who loved me and gave himself for me' (Galatians 2:20).

■ Stoicism had no future hope or expectation. It was a philosophy of hopelessness, in which most people were considered incapable of reaching any moral maturity, but would be destined to be destroyed as one cycle of the world's history followed another, only to be reborn, or reincarnated, again so that the whole cycle could be repeated. Paul's theology was quite different, for he believed that the world as it now is would end decisively with the future, personal intervention of Christ himself, after which he expected a completely new world order to emerge (1 Corinthians 15:20–28).

The influence of the Stoics on Paul must be reckoned to be minimal. No one can avoid using words and phrases, even religious ones, with which they are familiar in other contexts, and on those occasions when Paul used the language of the Stoics, it was because it had a wider currency in Hellenistic culture. He certainly endowed it with new meanings, for his own message of salvation through Christ was a long way from the Stoic message of salvation through self-discipline.

Paul and the mystery religions

There are several superficial resemblances between the mystery religions and the Christian faith: both came to Rome from the east, both offered 'salvation' to their followers, both used initiation rites (Christian baptism) and sacramental meals (the Christian communion), and both referred to their saviour god as 'lord'. Undoubtedly, the two often became intertwined as converts from the mysteries entered the church and, naturally enough, used the familiar categories of their mystery beliefs as a vehicle for articulating their new faith. It was probably this tendency that was the cause of much of the trouble in the church at Corinth, about which Paul wrote in his letters to the Corinthians.

Because of these resemblances between Christianity and the mysteries, some scholars of the late nineteenth and early twentieth centuries proposed that Paul changed the simple, ethical teaching of Jesus into a kind of mystery religion. This view was rejected by the scholarly community because there is no real evidence in its favour, though it still surfaces occasionally in more popular presentations of Paul. What evidence there is tends to show quite the opposite:

■ The mysteries were always syncretistic – ready, and even eager, to combine with other religions. This was something that Christians always rejected, believing that they alone had the full truth revealed to them by Christ.

■ Much of the evidence that was claimed to show Paul was a mystery adherent is now known to have been either false or misleading. For instance, when the title 'lord' was applied to Jesus it certainly did not come from mystery religions, but from the Old Testament. The Christian

The dining room or *triclinium* in the 3rd-century Temple of Mithras under the church of San Clemente in Rome. The small altar in the foreground has a carving of Mithras killing the bull.

confession of faith, 'may our Lord come' (recorded in 1 Corinthians 16:22 in its Aramaic form, *Maranatha*) shows that the very earliest church in Jerusalem, the only one to speak Aramaic, must have given Jesus that title long before Paul came on the scene.

■ What always impressed the Graeco-Roman world was not the similarity of Christianity to other religions, but its difference from them. The accusation most often made against Christians was of atheism, because they would not admit even the possibility that other gods might exist.

No doubt Paul knew of the mystery religions and their resemblances to Christianity. They told of deities coming into the world in the guise of humans; of salvation as 'dying' to the old life; of a god giving immortal life; and of the saviour god being called 'lord'. It is possible that Paul, who was ready to be 'all things to all people' (1 Corinthians 9:22), sometimes deliberately used their language. But, as with Stoicism, it is more likely that he used it unconsciously, for the terminology of the mystery religions was widely known, and would be used as easily and uncommittedly as people today might use the language of the New Age. Paul shows no detailed knowledge of the mystery religions, and makes no clear reference to any of their ceremonies.

Paul's background included three worlds of thought: the Jewish, the Greek and the mystery. Each one of these can shed a certain amount of light on his personality and his teaching. But Paul cannot be regarded as merely the natural product of his cultural surroundings. He understood himself primarily in terms of his faith relationship to Jesus Christ, and whatever he might have gained from these other sources, the consciousness of having found new direction on the Damascus road was always dominant in his thinking.

Paul and the earliest church

But what about Paul's relationship to the other leaders of the early church? In reading the New Testament, it is not difficult to get the impression that only two people really mattered in the early church: Jesus himself, and Paul. The stories of Jesus in the gospels and the writings of Paul together account for something like three-quarters of the whole New Testament, and though we occasionally meet Peter, James, and other lesser characters such as Silas or Timothy on the pages of Paul's letters, even in the book of Acts they take a back seat to Paul himself. Of course, there are reasons for this, no doubt connected with the purpose for which Acts was written in the first place. It is, by any account, a selective story of the beginnings of Christianity: for example, if we only had Acts to go by, we might suppose that Paul was the first Christian to take the gospel to Rome, though his own letter to this church demonstrates that a large and thriving Christian fellowship existed there long before he ever visited Italy (Romans 1:6–7). Paul's work, though of fundamental importance, was clearly complementary to that of many other figures in the early church, whose names and exploits have not been recorded in any detail.

But is 'complementary' the most appropriate way to describe Paul's relationships with Peter and other early Christian leaders – or was he instead establishing a different brand of Christianity altogether, different from the original church at Jerusalem not just in character, but in belief as well? That suggestion was first put forward in the middle of the nineteenth century by the members of the 'Tübingen School' in Germany, orchestrated by Ferdinand Christian Baur. They argued there was a vast difference between Paul's type of Christianity and that of churches founded by more self-consciously Jewish Christians such as Peter, or James of Jerusalem. They understood the whole of the first generation of Christianity as a conflict between these rival forms of Christian belief – a conflict that was resolved only with the emergence of the Catholic Church in the second century. This was not a new idea and, even in the second century, the anonymous authors of *Clementine Homilies* and *Clementine Recognitions* had suggested there were irreconcilable differences between Paul and the original apostles.

Is this a fair picture, either of Paul or of the others? Was he really independent of the original base of the church in Jerusalem? Or did that become a convenient conclusion for twentieth-century scholars to reach because, on the whole, they found his open-minded view of the gospel more congenial, or even – as has been suggested – because their anti-Semitic bias required them to marginalize Jewish elements in the early church, while their Protestant bias naturally inclined them to reject anything that could be made to resemble Roman Catholicism? There is a good deal of truth in such suggestions, as we shall see in later chapters when we return to these themes. Here, it is appropriate to point out that, when the New Testament is examined more closely, whether Paul's own writings or the stories of Acts, it soon becomes clear that Paul was much more conscious of his own Jewish origins and background than the majority of early twentieth-century scholars were prepared to allow. At a number of points Paul went out of his way to establish some sort of continuity between his own Gentile churches on the one hand, and the earliest Jewish churches – even Judaism itself – on the other.

Christians and the Old Testament

It is significant that whenever Paul defined Christian faith, he consistently did so in relation to Judaism. In his letter to the Galatians, for example, the argument of which is also closely followed in Romans, the interpretation of the Old Testament is a crucial element in what he says. In one way, this is understandable, for the Galatian churches were being infiltrated by people claiming that, before being admitted to the church, Gentile believers in Jesus first needed to become Jews. Paul found this argument unacceptable for, he claimed, a living relationship with God through Jesus Christ depended on simple trust (Galatians 2:15–21). Yet, instead of merely stating this, he still held the Old Testament in sufficiently high regard to feel it was important to demonstrate the position he was taking was fully in accord with the teaching of these ancient scriptures. He argued that, long before the Old Testament Law had even come into existence, Israel's ancestor Abraham had trusted God's promises, and had found acceptance with God on that basis. Therefore, anyone who now wished to be a member of God's covenant people need only to follow the example of Abraham, and trust God, for the Law was in some ways an aberration from the original simplicity of the relationship between Abraham and God (Galatians 3:6–9).

Modern readers can find the argument of Galatians somewhat convoluted and unnecessarily complicated, but that is only due to Paul's insistence on taking the Old Testament seriously. Though he disagreed with the argument that, in order to please God, a person needed to accept the Jewish Law and customs, he accepted without question the more fundamental premise that, in order to please God, a person must become a part of the covenant nation which traced its historical origins back to the Old Testament stories of Abraham's calling. Far from dismissing those who were saying that Gentiles must become Jews in order to be Christians, he was agreeing with them. But, while they supposed that obedience to the Law was the hallmark of the real Jew, Paul redefined 'Jewishness' to lay all the emphasis, instead, on continuity with Abraham. For him, to be a child of God was to be a member of Abraham's family and, to join that, faith in God was the only required qualification (Galatians 3:6–25; 4:21–31).

This line of argument was continued in his letter to the church at Rome, in which he added the comment that 'the real Jew is the person who is a Jew on the inside... and this is the work of God's Spirit, not of the written Law' (Romans 2:29). In saying this, Paul stood in the same tradition as Stephen, and the Old Testament prophets before him, who had consistently tried to restore the covenant faith to what they believed its original position to have been, namely that obedience to God's will, and not ethnicity, was its core value. No matter how he redefined the Old Testament faith in relation to the Judaism of his own day, Paul always felt it was important that Christians, whatever their ethnic origins, understood their own spirituality within the context of the continuing actions of God in history, which had begun with Abraham, and would receive their final fulfilment and consummation at some unspecified future time (Galatians 3:29). Unlike some of his later admirers, Paul never suggested that the Old Testament was irrelevant for the Christian, but instead viewed even Gentile Christians as part of a great line of faith stemming from Abraham himself, and insisted that this was what qualified them to be a part of 'the Israel of God' (Galatians 6:16).

The church and Israel

One of the most difficult passages in the whole of Paul's writings makes all this even more explicit (Romans 9 – 11). There is no consensus on how this section of Romans relates to its context, with some commentators arguing that this is the key that unlocks the door to the rest of the letter, and others believing it was an afterthought, representing Paul's uncertain speculations on the fate of the Jewish people, rather than any kind of carefully developed thinking on the subject. Whichever view is correct, what Paul actually says is clear enough: that in his understanding, to be born a Jew still carried a distinct advantage. The whole 'people of God' (ancient Israel and their descendants, together with the Gentile Christians) can be compared to an olive tree, whose roots extend deep into the Hebrew scriptures, and onto which Gentile Christians have been grafted like a new branch (Romans 11:13–24). In the meantime, it might seem as if some of the original – Jewish – branches have been broken off, but this is only a temporary situation and they will be restored. Though it might seem to some that 'the people of God' now comprises only Gentile Christians, God had allowed them to enter the covenant only to encourage the further obedience of those who belonged to it by birth: 'Because they sinned, salvation has come to the Gentiles, to make the Jews jealous of them... the stubbornness of the people of Israel is not permanent, but will last only until the complete number of Gentiles comes to God. And this is how all Israel will be saved' (Romans 11:11, 25–26).

Paul uses the imagery of an olive tree to describe the Jewish naton, onto which Gentile Christians have been 'grafted'.

Paul concludes discussion of the subject on that somewhat cryptic note, and there are many difficulties in understanding precisely what he meant. But however he thought this was all to be accomplished, Paul clearly believed the Jews had an important part to play in the whole history of salvation, something which in itself suggests he was by no means as implacably anti-Jewish as some have suggested.

To the Jews first

Paul's missionary practice reveals the same emphasis, for whenever he went to a new town in some hitherto unvisited part of the Roman world he always went first to the Jewish synagogue (Acts 13:14; 14:1; 17:1–2). Of course, there would be good tactical reasons for doing so: since he was concerned to declare that Jesus was the Messiah, it was only natural that he should speak first to people who had some notion of who and what the Messiah might be. The fact that they had rather different expectations from Paul himself usually became clear fairly quickly, and he found himself thrown out of one synagogue after another. But that did not prompt him to abandon the strategy, for in addition to its practical advantages he also had a strong

Orthodox Jewish
boy with teacher.

theological reason for operating this way: 'the gospel... is God's power to save all who believe, first the Jews and also the Gentiles' (Romans 1:16).

Jews and Gentiles

Despite this, Paul believed he was specifically called to take the gospel to Gentiles rather than Jews. According to his letter to the Galatians, this special commission was recognized by the Jewish church leaders in Jerusalem: Paul would go to Gentiles, they to Jews (2:7–9). Obviously this was not a hard and fast rule, for Paul often met and spoke with Jews, while Peter in particular was to become involved in missionary activity among Gentiles. But as a rough arrangement, it was a satisfactory division of labour. Its origin could well have been in social and economic considerations rather than purely theological ones, for Paul was a single person and therefore had more freedom to engage in long and arduous journeys than the Palestinian apostles, who had dependent families and needed regular financial support from the churches. Paul, by contrast, probably had inherited wealth from his family, and could easily stay long enough in a place to take casual employment to support himself as the need arose (Acts 18:3; 2 Thessalonians 3:8).

There are many complex problems involved in understanding the accounts of Paul's dealings with the leaders of the Jerusalem church. But the fact remains that Paul evidently had regular and not unfriendly contacts with the leaders of the church there.

Paul and Jerusalem

But was it more than that? Was Paul, as some have argued, almost under the control of the Jerusalem leaders? Do his letters not conceal the truth, by making him appear much more independent than he actually was? This suggestion has gained some support from the fact that, towards the end of his third missionary tour, Paul put a great deal of effort and energy into taking a collection among the Gentile Christians of Greece and Asia Minor, which was to be for the benefit of the church in Judea (1 Corinthians 16:1–7). Hellenistic Jews throughout the empire sent an annual tax to the authorities in Jerusalem, to support the temple and its services there – so does this collection imply that the Jerusalem church exercised a similar central control over the whole Christian movement?

It seems unlikely, for Romans 15:26–27 describes the collection in the following terms: 'the churches in Macedonia and Achaia have freely decided to give an offering to help the poor among God's people in Jerusalem. That decision was their own'. Paul added that 'as a matter of fact, they have an obligation to help them. Since the Jews shared their spiritual blessings with the Gentiles, the Gentiles ought to use their material blessings to help the Jews.' In other words, conscious of his own deep indebtedness to the Jewish Christian church, Paul had organized this collection as a kind of thank offering and spontaneous expression of love for the Christians in Jerusalem (2 Corinthians 8:8–14). That would not necessarily prevent some of the Christians in Jerusalem seeing it in a different light, of course, and it has been suggested that they might have regarded it as the fulfilment of the ancient prophecies of Isaiah 60:11 in which 'the wealth of the nations' would be brought to Jerusalem by Gentile messengers 'bowing down to show their respect'.

If that were the case, however, we might expect them to have received Paul and his Gentile Christian companions with open arms. In fact it is not at all clear what happened to the collection when it finally arrived in Jerusalem, and it has been plausibly suggested that the Christians there actually refused to accept it. It is certainly notable that when Paul was subsequently arrested in the temple, it was not the Christians who sprang to his defence, but a Roman officer (Acts 21:27–40). Perhaps the more conservative Christians there had not gone as far as to lead him into a trap, but still they were not sorry to see the last of him. The same cannot, however, be said of Paul's attitude to them, and the very fact that he had made the effort to return to Jerusalem at this time shows his deep and lasting indebtedness to the leaders of the first Christian church.

Paul and the teaching of Jesus

This indebtedness also comes out in the way Paul's letters often display knowledge of and familiarity with the teachings of Jesus himself. One of their most intriguing features is the complete absence from them of any direct references to the life and teaching of Jesus. At one time it was fashionable to suggest that Paul had no time for Jesus, and that his own brand of Christianity was based instead on Greek and Roman concepts. But there are just enough references to Jesus to make that proposition unacceptable.

Occasionally, Paul says explicitly that he is quoting from or referring to 'words of the Lord' (1 Corinthians 7:10; 9:14; 1 Thessalonians 4:15), but there are many other places where his own advice is so close to the teaching of Jesus, as it is known from the gospels, that Paul must have been referring to it. An example is in the practical advice given to the church in Rome, where some key gospel themes recur:

Love your enemies	Matthew 5:43–48	Romans 12:14–21
Love God and your neighbour	Mark 12:29–31	Romans 13:8–10
'Clean' and 'unclean' foods	Mark 7:14–23	Romans 14:14
Responsibility to state authorities	Mark 12:13–17	Romans 13:1–7

Paul's knowledge of the words and deeds of Jesus had not come from personal contact with Jesus, but from those who had been Jesus' first disciples – especially, perhaps, from Peter with whom Paul spent two full weeks after his conversion (Galatians 1:18). Paul must have known a great deal more about Jesus' teaching than can be inferred from his letters, but there are probably good reasons for his apparent silence on the matter. For one thing, his letters were all occasional writings rather than considered and carefully worked out accounts of his whole theology. In addition, his readers would have been likely to know a lot about the life and teaching of Jesus already, for it is reasonable to suppose that such information would have been included in the initial communication of the Christian message. It is certainly improbable that Paul could have spoken meaningfully about Jesus either to Gentiles or to Hellenist Jews without at the same time giving them some explanation about who Jesus was. To be able to do that with conviction, he needed the cooperation and friendship of the original Jewish disciples.

Taken together, these six points suggest that, far from being an eccentric individualist, Paul was fully integrated into the Christian movement as it began among the first Jewish disciples of Jesus. But, in addressing some of these matters, we have already anticipated the course of much of Paul's life, and before going further it will be necessary to pause and consider how and why Paul the Pharisee became a Christian in the first place.

15 Paul the Persecutor

One of the most cherished beliefs of Judaism, and one that Paul no doubt shared, was that God would soon intervene in history to rescue the chosen people of Israel from the domination of alien political forces. A popular expectation was that at this time God would re-establish them as one of the great nations of the world; the Messiah would arrive in dramatic fashion, march on Jerusalem with his followers, enter the temple, and drive the hated Romans from the land. According to the gospels, Jesus had fulfilled all this and more, though not along the lines of the traditional expectation. Far from being royal, he was of obscure origins (Luke 1 – 2; John 1:46), with no army, and an obvious contempt for physical violence (Matthew 5:38–42). Though his entry into the temple (Mark 11:1–19) could be depicted as the fulfilment of the prophecy of Zechariah 9:9, it heralded not victory over the Romans but humiliation and death at their hands.

Paul felt an intense contempt for this crucified 'Messiah' and, if anything, he despised even more the activities of the followers of this pseudo-Christ who were soon claiming that after his degrading execution he had risen from the dead, and God had recognized him as the true Messiah by giving him a place of high honour (Acts 2:22–24). Paul might conceivably have had some respect for Jesus himself, for he had been an ethical teacher and said many things with which other rabbis could agree. But his followers were ignorant and uneducated and had nothing at all to commend them (Acts 4:13). What right had they to tell the religious leaders of the day that they had been mistaken, and had done nothing to prevent the death of God's own son?

Persecution

When Stephen dared to say in public that the days of the temple and its traditional religious practices were over, Paul and other religious leaders knew that the time had come for action (Acts 7:2–53). It was no longer acceptable to dismiss these followers of 'the Way', as they called themselves, as if they were amiable eccentrics, for they were beginning to pose a dangerous threat to the whole religious system. No doubt it was this fear that led to Stephen being stoned to death by a Jerusalem mob while, according to Acts 7:54 – 8:1, Paul himself stood by guarding their coats.

This is how the reader of Acts is introduced to Paul, but as the narrative unfolds it becomes obvious that he was more than just a coat minder. When he saw that the Christians were beginning to move out of Jerusalem to other places, he realized that, far from having solved the problem, the way Stephen and others were being persecuted was only helping the Christian cause to spread to other parts of the Roman empire more remote from Jerusalem and where, if it took hold, it would be correspondingly more difficult to restrict or control.

One of the places where the Christians were congregating was Damascus, an independent city within the Nabatean kingdom. At this period Aretas IV (9BC–AD40) ruled over the Nabatean kingdom, though he had no direct authority over Damascus itself (2 Corinthians 11:32–33). This was not the first time that Damascus had served as a haven for religious refugees from Judea. According to the *Zadokite Fragments* (documents that stem from a Jewish sect associated with the Essenes) a large number of Jews had fled there just before 130BC. Since these people had been able to live independently of the authorities in Jerusalem, the early Christians probably thought they could do the same. In addition, the faith communities formed by these earlier migrants might be expected to provide an ideal audience, which would be interested in hearing the Christian claims that Jesus was the awaited Messiah. Without Paul's astute mind, they might have got away with it. But he remembered that, at an earlier time in the nation's history, the Romans had given the high priest in Jerusalem the right to have Jewish criminals extradited from other parts of the empire (1 Maccabees 15:15–24), and so he went to the high priest to ask for a letter that would authorize him to pursue the Christians to Damascus, and bring them back to Jerusalem for trial and sentence (Acts 9:1–2). It was while doing so that Paul had a remarkable experience which was to alter the course of his whole life.

The Damascus road

This experience is described in detail in three different places in the book of the Acts, which shows just how important it was not only in Paul's life, but in the entire history of the early church. In Acts 9:3–19 there is Luke's summary account of what happened, then 22:6–16 presents a personal account given by Paul when defending himself before a Jewish mob in Jerusalem, and finally in 26:9–23 there is yet another account given by Paul, this time in his defence before Herod Agrippa II.

The three accounts do not agree precisely in every detail, and it is clear that Luke used them to build up a composite picture, exploring the different nuances of the experience that would be specially relevant to the concerns of the different circumstances depicted in his narrative.

In all essential points, the three accounts tell the same story. Paul was travelling along the road to Damascus, intent on wiping out the Christians there, when 'a light from heaven, brighter than the sun' (Acts 26:13) shone down on him, and he was challenged by the voice of the risen Christ asking, 'why do you persecute me?' (Acts 9:4; 22:7; 26:14). Paul's life was to take a radical about-turn, as he was presented with the possibility of understanding the world in a way more different than he had ever imagined. His inherited assumptions were not only challenged, but also shown to be false, as he realized that what was happening was, in his own words, 'a revelation of Jesus Christ' (Galatians 1:12). The one whom Paul had so despised, and whose followers he was bent on punishing, was standing before him, thereby revealing his identity as Messiah, and inviting Paul to believe in him. Though the narratives are unclear as to the precise moment of Paul's conversion, they leave no doubt that he became a new person as a result of what happened both on the roadside and, subsequently, in Damascus itself. From this moment onwards, the Pharisee who had hated the Christian faith was to be one of its greatest advocates, and he was to place his traditional faith in a different perspective altogether as a result of what happened that day.

Like most notable events, Paul's conversion did not spring from nowhere. Unquestionably, he already knew a great deal about the life and teachings of Jesus of Nazareth – indeed, on the basis of what he later wrote in 2 Corinthians 5:16, some have concluded that he might have been personally acquainted with Jesus during his lifetime. That seems unlikely, but what is certain is that he must have taken a considerable interest in the kind of interpretation that was being placed on the scriptures by Hellenist Jewish Christians like Stephen. By depicting him as a bystander, watching the coats at the stoning of Stephen, Luke was probably intending to suggest that, even at that time, Paul had a hesitating sympathy with what was being said. Either way, there can be little doubt that such thinking had an enormous and profound influence on his own life for, in many respects, the later teaching of Paul on the place of Old Testament Law and covenants in the Christian life was but a logical extension of the teaching of those Hellenist Jews who were Christians before him.

Paul gives several accounts of the decisive events on the Damascus road, when the risen Christ spoke to him. The encounter meant a radical change in Paul's life.

Though Paul's letters show him to have been mostly concerned about the Law as a source of morality, and not much interested at all in its ritual and ceremonial aspects, much of what he later wrote about the temporary and passing nature of the Law bore a striking similarity to Stephen's arguments about the Law and the temple (Galatians 3:1–25).

When Paul arrived in Damascus after his remarkable experience, he was unable to see, and was overwhelmed by it all for three days, during which he neither ate nor drank. But when Ananias, a Christian living in Damascus, went to visit Paul his sight was restored, Paul was baptized, and then introduced to the Christians in the city (Acts 9:10–19; 22:12–16). Like Peter at the household of Cornelius, Paul discovered that, within the community of the church, he would find acceptance among people who, on any other ground, would have been abhorrent to him. In many ways, his experience was even more radical than that of Peter, for the people who welcomed him so generously were the very ones he had been intent on hounding to death. In the light of this, it is hardly surprising that, when he wrote to advise the Galatian Christians, who were struggling with the consequences of ethnic diversity, he should have emphasized his conviction that people of different social and religious backgrounds could come together only through living a shared commitment to Jesus Christ: 'there is no difference between Jews and Gentiles, between slaves and free men, between men and women; you are all one in Christ Jesus' (Galatians 3:28).

The different accounts of Paul's conversion

There are three main differences in points of detail between the accounts of Paul's conversion:

● In Acts 9:7 Paul's companions heard the voice of the risen Christ, but saw no *person*. They might have seen the bright light. In 22:9 Paul says they 'saw the light but did not hear the voice of the one who was speaking to me'. What they heard was presumably a sound, but not an intelligible voice. The account in chapter 26 does not refer to the companions either seeing or hearing.
● In Acts 9:4 and 22:7 the only person mentioned as falling to the ground is Paul, the central figure in the drama, though this need not exclude the possibility that the others fell to the ground, as in 26:14.
● In Acts 9:6 and 22:10 Paul is told to go on to Damascus, where he will be instructed what to do, whereas in 26:16 his commission to be an apostle is given at the time of the vision. As he reflected on it later, Paul generally identified the entire experience as the occasion of his call, and Galatians 1:11–12 seems to imply that the actual content of his message was given to him on the Damascus road.

These distinctions are not of great importance and can be easily explained by reference to the different purposes of the narratives in each case. Indeed, the fact that these variations in emphasis have been preserved by Luke instills greater confidence in his abilities as a credible historian. If he had invented the story he would have been more likely either to have told it only once, or to have made sure that each account of it was identical with the others in form and language.

It was this burning conviction that inspired Paul to carry the Christian message not only to the cities of Palestine – places like Damascus itself, Antioch, and even Jerusalem – but also to the furthest corners of the world as it was known to him. In doing so he displayed an amazing vitality and, through his many letters, he has provided an invaluable series of snapshots of what it was like to be a Christian in the wider Roman world of the first century AD. It was not all easy going, even for an apostle, and Paul's long journeys must have been physically exhausting and highly dangerous. But Paul was undaunted for, from the time of his conversion, he was quite convinced that he was not alone in his endeavours, but the Christ whom he had encountered on the Damascus road was living within him and empowering him for this work. Paul's references to his achievements in Judaism show him to have been a fanatical believer, and, from that moment onwards, all his energy was redirected into serving Christ. Writing towards the end of his life, he put it like this: 'I count everything as loss because of the surpassing worth of knowing Christ Jesus my Lord' (Philippians 3:8).

Paul did not forget his original purpose in coming to Damascus, which had been to visit the Jewish synagogues of the city. He went straight to the Jewish community, where his arrival was undoubtedly expected. But his message was not what they expected, for instead of denouncing the Christian faith he proclaimed it, and made known his new allegiance to Jesus the Messiah (Acts 9:20–25). In Galatians 1.17 Paul mentions a brief visit to a place he refers to as 'Arabia' (probably an area near Damascus) before returning to Damascus for three years. Though Luke never mentions it, this is not inconsistent with the narrative of Acts, where it is stated that he remained in Damascus for 'many days' (9:23). He might have retreated to 'Arabia' immediately after meeting Ananias, or he might have gone there after some initial teaching in the synagogues.

Eventually, Paul found it impossible to stay any longer in the city of Damascus. Religious and civil authorities were both eager to get rid of him, so his friends secretly let him down over the city wall in a basket (Acts 9:23–25; 2 Corinthians 11:32–33).

Paul and the Jerusalem Christians

At this point, Paul paid a visit to Jerusalem, which was probably the one described in Galatians 1:18–24. Not surprisingly, his arrival struck terror into the disciples in Jerusalem until Barnabas, one of the leaders of the church, told them of Paul's conversion and witness in Damascus (Acts 9:26–30). After this, Paul went out and shared his new message with such boldness in Jerusalem itself that the apostles sent him away to Caesarea for his own safety, and from there he returned to his original home in Tarsus. Paul later explained that his main motive for visiting Jerusalem at this time had been to meet Peter, with whom he stayed for fifteen days. He also met James, the brother of Jesus, though he did not meet many of the other Christians, and most churches in the area only knew of him by reputation (Galatians 1:18–24). He then spent the next eleven years in Cilicia and Syria, probably still unknown to many of the original believers in Jerusalem and the surrounding area.

Though the Christians in Jerusalem might justifiably have forgotten Paul, Barnabas did not and, when he found himself becoming involved in the work of the church in Antioch, in the Roman province of Syria, he sent for Paul to come back from Tarsus to help (Acts 11:19–26). Paul and Barnabas had been working together for about a year in the church at Antioch, when a prophet named Agabus arrived from Jerusalem and declared to the church that a great famine was coming, which would adversely affect the well-being of the Christians in Jerusalem (Acts 11:27–30). The largely Gentile church in Antioch decided to send aid to their fellow believers, and delegated Barnabas and Paul to take the relief fund in person. Luke's narrative places this visit to Jerusalem in AD43, when the persecution of Christians in Jerusalem, begun by Herod Agrippa I in AD42, was still continuing. It was probably this visit that Paul referred to in Galatians 2:2; the 'revelation' of which he speaks was presumably the prophetic message of Agabus about the famine. Paul added the further information that, on this visit, he only saw the church leaders in private, which would be easy to understand if there was persecution going on at the time.

Antioch, on the River Orontes, was the third largest city in the Roman empire. It was the capital of the Roman province of Syria, and an important centre of commerce. The church at Antioch was fast-growing and dynamic. The town is now Antakya in south-east Turkey.

Paul and the Gentiles

Paul's own account of all this makes it clear that his meeting with
the leaders of the Jerusalem church was crucial for the emergence of
his own ministry, for at this time the original apostles indicated their
willingness to recognize his mission to the Gentiles as a valid extension
of the Christian message (Galatians 2:1–10). This was an important issue
for the early church.

Some Jews, mostly those living in the Dispersion and Pharisees of
the more liberal school of Hillel, had shown considerable missionary
zeal in winning converts to Judaism. But their converts were required to
obey the traditional law in its entirety, both ritual and moral. Though it
was possible to join in Jewish worship as 'God-fearers', without taking
upon themselves the whole burden of the Jewish Law (like Cornelius), a
central requirement for those who sought full admission to the Jewish
faith community was the rite of male circumcision. The church leaders
in Jerusalem, who were all practising Jews and probably regarded
themselves as a reforming movement within Judaism rather than a
separate faith, naturally took it for granted that any Gentiles who wished
to become Christians would first become Jews, by being circumcised.

The experience of Peter with Cornelius had convinced them that it
was possible for a Gentile to be converted and receive the power of the
Holy Spirit (Acts 10:1 – 11:18), but when Paul and Barnabas inaugurated
a mission among the Gentiles in Antioch it raised different questions
altogether. For one thing, Cornelius had been an adherent of Judaism
and, though he was a 'God-fearer' and not a full proselyte, his case was,
therefore, somewhat different from that of converts with no previous
connections to Jewish spirituality. In addition, there does not appear to
have been a widespread Christian movement connected with Cornelius
at the time of Peter's visit, whereas in Antioch a church of Gentile
believers was formed. The Jerusalem leaders were willing to recognize
that Paul and Barnabas were engaged in a commendable enterprise,
but they refused to accept any responsibility for it.

When Peter visited Antioch afterwards, he at first followed the
custom established by Paul, and ate with the Gentile converts. Peter
himself had previously eaten a meal in the home of Cornelius, but this
would not normally have been an acceptable practice for an orthodox
Jewish believer. When less liberal Christians arrived in Antioch from
Judea, Peter was easily persuaded to abandon the practice, and Barnabas
joined him. This inconsistency led to a severe rebuke from Paul, and the
evident tensions running through this episode provide the first example
of something that was to trouble Paul throughout his ministry. Although
he knew that his own special mission was to Gentiles, Paul could never
forget his people. He was proud of having been born into the Jewish
faith community, and constantly went out of his way to affirm the
advantages it had given him. Yet, in his heart, he believed the religious

leaders had been mistaken in not recognizing Jesus as the Messiah. He felt so passionately about it that in Romans 9:3 he went as far as to declare, 'I could wish that I myself were accursed and cut off from Christ for the sake of my own people, my kindred according to the flesh'. But he never quite came to terms with the extent to which the issue of Gentiles becoming Christians would divide the church. As Paul began to fulfil the terms of his calling, inviting Gentiles to follow Jesus without ever considering the long history of the faith tradition they would enter, it took only a short time for the rumblings of discord first heard in Antioch to develop into a full peal of thunder.

Who were the prophets?

When Paul was giving advice to the Christians at Corinth about the use of spiritual gifts within their church, he advised them to desire all the gifts that had appeared among them, but especially 'prophecy' (1 Corinthians 14:1–5; 12:4–11). What was this prophecy, which is mentioned not only in 1 Corinthians, but also throughout the book of Acts?

It is clear that there was, in the early church, an important group of men and women known as prophets. They are regularly listed immediately after the apostles (1 Corinthians 12:28–29; Ephesians 2:20; 3:5; 4:11), while the tasks of evangelist, pastor and teacher, to which later Christians have always given a high priority, are regularly placed after the prophets in order of importance (1 Corinthians 12:28–29; Ephesians 4:11; Acts 13:1; Romans 12:6–8).

These prophets seem to have been people with particularly close access to God's will, which enabled them not only to forecast certain specific events in the future (as Agabus did, Acts 11:28; 21:10–11; see also Revelation 22:6), but also to deliver other authoritative guidance for situations that arose within the church. In Acts 13:1–4 the prophets of the church at Antioch, inspired by the Holy Spirit, gave directions that Paul and Barnabas should be 'Set apart for... the work to which I have called them,' while the four daughters of Philip the evangelist regularly acted as prophets in the church at Caesarea (Acts 21:8–9). The deliverance of prophecy was also involved in the appointment of Timothy (1 Timothy 1:18; 4:14), while at other times prophets could be found rebuking Christians who were lazy, or encouraging those whose faith was under attack (see for example Acts 15:32; 1 Corinthians 14:3).

In addition to such practical activities within the Christian community, prophets also had an important theological task. 1 Corinthians 13:2 equates being a prophet with understanding 'all mysteries and all knowledge', while Ephesians 3:5–6 indicates that the prophets had a particular part to play in explaining how Gentiles could be incorporated within the community of God's people, which had its beginnings in Old Testament times. At the same time, however, prophets could get things wrong, and Paul laid considerable emphasis on the need for prophetic utterances to be scrutinized by the further gift of 'discernment' whereby the true and the false might be distinguished (1 Corinthians 12:10).

Nevertheless, the prophets were highly regarded in the churches of the New Testament period, as charismatically inspired individuals who enjoyed particular insights into the Christian message, and through whom God's will could be made known to the church.

What happened after Paul's conversion?

In describing what happened after Paul's conversion on the Damascus road, we have taken information from Acts and Paul's letter to the Galatians and, by combining these two sources, it has been suggested that the order of events was as follows:

Paul's conversion (Acts 9:3–19; 22:6–16; 26:9–18; Galatians 1:11–17).

A brief stay in Damascus (Acts 9:19b).

A visit to 'Arabia' (Galatians 1:17–18).

Work in Damascus for something like three years (Galatians 1:17; possibly Acts 9:20–22).

Paul's first visit to Jerusalem after his conversion (Acts 9:26–30; Galatians 1:18–20).

Paul's stay in Tarsus (Acts 9:30; 11:25; Galatians 1:21).

● Barnabas joins the Christian movement among the Gentiles in Antioch (Acts 11:20–24).

Paul joins Barnabas in Antioch (Acts 11:25–26).

● Paul and Barnabas visit Jerusalem with famine relief for the church there, fourteen years after Paul's conversion (Acts 11:29–30; 12:25; Galatians 2:1–10).

This interpretation is by no means universally accepted, and is only one possible way of understanding the various time references provided by Acts on the one hand, and by Paul himself on the other. There is a major dispute concerning whether Paul's own account of his contact with the Jerusalem apostles can be reconciled with Luke's narrative in Acts.

From Galatians 2:1–10 it is obvious that Paul regarded the visit he describes there as absolutely crucial for his entire ministry to the Gentiles. In trying to connect this with Acts, it is natural to look for an account of a visit which had the

same kind of far-reaching significance for Paul's ministry to the Gentiles, and the occasion that most obviously appears to meet this requirement is depicted in Acts 15:1–29. This is the occasion often known as 'the Council of Jerusalem' when Paul and Barnabas, sent to Jerusalem as official delegates from the church in Antioch, met in some kind of formal session with the other apostles and church leaders to try to decide once and for all what was to be required of Gentile Christians in relation to

Paul's movements between his conversion and the Council of Jerusalem.

the Jewish Law. While the traditional view has, therefore, been to regard Acts 15:1–29 as an account of the same meeting as Paul describes in Galatians 2:1–10, this identification raises two major problems:

● According to Acts 15:1–29, this visit resulted in a thorough and wide-ranging discussion of the very issues with which Paul was dealing when he wrote Galatians, namely the question of the status of Gentile Christians, whether they should be expected or required to observe the Torah, and if so whether they needed to keep the Law in its entirety, or only certain aspects of it. Acts 15:23–29 records the details of a compromise

What happened after Paul's conversion? *continued*

worked out by the Council, with the agreement of Paul and Barnabas, which was apparently accepted by all concerned as an appropriate basis for the admission of Gentiles to the Christian church. Yet, in Galatians 2:1–10, Paul makes no reference to any such agreement having been made, even though it would have been crucial in this defence of his own position. In Galatians 2:6 he confidently declares that the Jerusalem church leaders 'added nothing to me', which is a very different story from that in Acts 15:1–29, where they insisted that he should stick to the

same position as everyone else, which he evidently agreed to do.

● If Acts 15:1–29 refers to the same events as Galatians 2:1–10, there is a further historical discrepancy between the two accounts. Between Paul's conversion and the Council visit, Acts tells of two earlier visits to Jerusalem (Acts 9:26; 11:30; 12:25), while Paul mentions only one (Galatians 1:18). It is virtually unimaginable that Paul could have been mistaken, for the whole of his argument in Galatians depends for its validity on the assumption that he was describing every

The church at Antioch sent Paul and Barnabas with relief funds to help the Christians in Jerusalem. This early Byzantine structure in Antioch has been claimed as the first Christian church building.

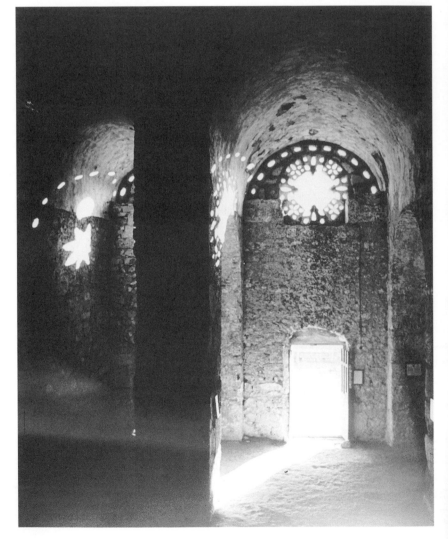

single meeting he had ever had with the Jerusalem leaders. To have omitted one of them – especially such a significant one – would have undermined everything he was arguing for. It would, therefore, be necessary to suppose that Luke was mistaken in his account in Acts, either by describing the same incident twice, or out of sheer ignorance of what really happened.

Besides these difficulties in correlating Acts 15:1–29 with Galatians 2:1–10, several smaller points of detail can also be interpreted to suggest the alternative possibility that, in fact, these two accounts are not describing the same meeting:
● In Acts 15:2, Paul and Barnabas were 'appointed' by the church at Antioch to go to Jerusalem and meet with 'the apostles and the elders'. In Galatians, however, Paul quite specifically uses different language, saying that he 'went up by revelation' (Galatians 2:2).
● The conference of Acts 15:1–29 seems to have been a semi-public, and certainly formal event with the apostles and elders and 'the whole church' involved in it (Acts 15:22). In Galatians, however, Paul makes a special point of mentioning that the meeting was held in private (Galatians 2:2); and only James, Cephas (Peter) and John are mentioned by name in connection with it (Galatians 2:9).
● The outcome of the meeting of Acts 15:1–29 was a decision ('the Apostolic Decree') allowing Gentile converts to remain uncircumcised, while also insisting that they ought to observe certain traditional dietary customs, which would make it easier for Jews to eat meals alongside them (Acts 15:28–29). The outcome of the Galatians conference, on the other hand, was a mutual recognition of Paul and Barnabas as apostles to the Gentiles, and of Peter and the others as apostles to the Jews (Galatians 2:9–10), with no mention at all of the relational complexities between the two groups within the church.

In view of these differences between Acts 15:1–29 and Galatians 2:1–10, it seems better to suppose that Galatians 2:1–10 records the same events as Acts 11:29–30 and 12:25. There are at least four factors in favour of this:
● The claim that Paul went to Jerusalem 'by revelation' (Galatians 2:2) would be a natural way to refer to the prophecy of the famine by Agabus, which was the immediate occasion of the Jerusalem visit of Acts 11:28.
● Galatians 2:2 suggests that the meeting with the church leaders was a private one, and Acts dates the famine either during, or shortly after, the persecution of Herod Agrippa I, which could easily explain the need for such secrecy. The absence of James and other Christian leaders from the meeting mentioned in Acts 12:17, which took place during this visit, is also consistent with this reconstruction.
● It is possible to translate Galatians 2:10 as follows: 'Only they asked us to go on remembering the poor, and in fact I had made a special point of doing this very thing.' On this understanding, Paul could have been making a direct allusion to some such visit as is recorded in Acts 12:25, when he took famine relief to the Jerusalem Christians.
● Since Paul obviously intended to recount every visit he made to Jerusalem, from the time of his conversion to the time he was writing, and if Acts 11:29–30 refers to the same event as Galatians 2:1–10, this provides a simple explanation for his silence regarding the terms of the Apostolic Decree: the Apostolic Council had not yet taken place.

On this interpretation, Paul's letter to the Galatians must have been written sometime between the events of Acts 12:25 and Acts 15:1–29, though this in turn raises other important questions about the date of Galatians which will be dealt with in the next chapter.

16 Into All the World

Not long after they had returned from Jerusalem to Antioch, Paul and Barnabas entered a new phase of their work, as the Gentile church there, following guidance from its prophets, set the two friends apart and sent them off on their first real missionary expedition (Acts 13:1–3).

From Antioch to Cyprus

When they left Antioch, they firstly went to Cyprus, which was Barnabas' home country. In the story of Paul's meeting with the Roman proconsul, Sergius Paulus, in the capital, Paphos, Luke introduces one of the central themes of the book of Acts, namely the warm acceptance of Paul's message by representatives of the Roman empire (Acts 13:6–12). Significantly, too, from this point in his narrative Luke abandons the use of the Hebrew name Saul, and exclusively refers to him by his Roman name, Paul. This narrative also introduces another theme, in the form of Elymas, or Bar-Jesus, a Hellenistic magician who attempted to thwart Paul's efforts to convince Sergius Paulus of the truth of his message about Jesus. Just as the gospels depict Jesus himself as confronting the power of alternative spiritualities, so throughout Acts, Paul is faced with the same kind of challenge.

After a promising start, Paul and Barnabas left Cyprus and sailed to the south coast of Asia Minor, then crossed the mountains into Pisidia, to another town called Antioch (Acts 13:13–14). From there they pressed on eastwards to the region of Lycaonia, which was part of the Roman province of Galatia and, after successful missionary work in several towns of that region, they returned to Antioch in Syria by roughly the same route, except that they did not visit Cyprus

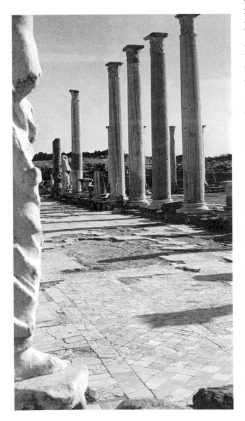

Paul and Barnabas' first stop on Cyprus was at Salamis. They preached initially at the synagogue, a strategy repeated elsewhere. The ruins include a gymnasium, pictured here.

again (Acts 14:21–28). In each town, the apostles began their work in connection with the Jewish synagogue. Probably they felt that in this context they were likely to meet the kind of Gentile 'God-fearers' who would be most open to their message. On the return journey, Paul and Barnabas made a point of revisiting each new congregation of Christians that had been formed, encouraging them in their new faith and helping their leaders to understand what might be required of them (Acts 14:21–23).

At some stage during this trip Paul seems to have fallen ill, for in writing to the Galatians he referred to a disease which gave him a repulsive appearance when he was with them (Galatians 4:13–15). He also mentions elsewhere that he suffered from a 'thorn in the flesh', which might well have been the same ailment (2 Corinthians 12:7). The way it is described in Galatians suggests it must have been some kind of eye disease.

The first Gentile churches

As a result of Paul's visits to these cities, many Gentiles came to believe in Jesus Christ. Besides Jewish proselytes and God-fearers, there were many others with no previous connection at all with Judaism. Paul began to realize how much potential there was for sharing the gospel with Gentile people, and the significance of his own calling in that respect. His experiences at this time also convinced him that Gentile believers should be admitted to the Christian community on the basis of their faith in Christ, and with no further obligation to be circumcised, or to observe other conditions derived from the Jewish Law. One of the first discoveries Paul made after his own conversion had been that his new understanding of Jesus Christ helped him establish a new relationship with other people, including those whom he might previously have looked down on. In the same way, he now found that, though he himself continued in his Jewish observance, a shared belief in Jesus enabled him to enjoy a new level of meaningful relationship with Gentiles of all sorts. This was what Paul had come to expect, following his experience on the Damascus road, for it had been made clear to him then that he was to fulfil a very special role in spreading the Christian message through the wider Roman empire. When he and Barnabas returned to Syrian Antioch, they were welcomed by the church there, who agreed with their strategy of taking the gospel directly to Gentile people, and celebrated their success in evangelizing the inhabitants of southern Asia Minor.

Judaizers

But this happy situation did not last for long. Emissaries from the Jerusalem church soon arrived in Antioch with a very different attitude. What was worse, from Paul's point of view, they also visited the new groups of Christians which he and Barnabas had just established in the course of their first missionary expedition (Galatians 2:11–14). Their arrival created havoc among the new Christians as they told them that Paul had only delivered to them a very deficient account of the Christian message. According to Paul, if Gentiles were willing to accept the claims of Christ over their lives they would be given power by the Holy Spirit working within them to live the kind of life that was pleasing to God. To many more conservative Jewish Christians, this idea was blasphemous. Their understanding was that God's will had been revealed in the Old Testament, where it had been clearly taught that, in order to be a part of the community of God's people, a person must be circumcised and observe many other regulations. So how could Paul claim that these Gentiles were proper Christians when they had never even considered the full implications of God's ancient revelation? How dare he suggest that an acceptable standard of Christian morality could ever be attained by any means other than careful observance of the rules clearly laid down in the Torah?

Mediterranean Sea

Paul's first missionary journey.

The new converts were thrown into confusion by such teaching. All they knew was that they had accepted the message Paul declared, that their own experience of Christ matched what had happened to Paul on the Damascus road, and that they could expect to be empowered by the Holy Spirit to live in a way that would be pleasing to God. The majority of them had never been followers of Judaism, and had no idea what was in the Old Testament. Paul had given them no indication that it was necessary for them to find out in order to be acceptable to God.

But when these new Christians began to read the Old Testament under the guidance of the Judaizers who had now visited their churches, they found themselves faced with a mass of rules and regulations, many of which seemed irrelevant to the reality of life in the average Hellenistic city, and which they had no real inclination to fulfil, even if it was necessary to do so for salvation. Some of them decided to make a brave attempt, and began by keeping the sabbath and possibly certain other traditional festivals as well (Galatians 4:8–11). A number of them even started thinking seriously about being circumcised, in order to fulfil what seemed to be the requirements of the Old Testament (Galatians 5:2–12). But the great majority simply did not know what to do.

This was the point at which news of the situation reached Paul, and he was infuriated by what he heard. It was not practical for him to visit these new converts again just at that particular time, so in the heat of the moment he decided that he must write them a letter. This was the letter known to us as the epistle to the Galatians.

Paul the letter writer

When Paul wrote letters to the Christians who were under his care, he naturally followed the common style of the day. An ancient letter usually had a more or less set pattern, and Acts 23:26–30 contains a typical example of such a letter in the form of the message sent by Claudias Lysias to Felix at the time when Paul was committed for trial. Paul always adopted the same structure in the letters he wrote to churches:

■ Unlike a modern letter, an ancient one would always begin with the name of the writer, and only then would it name the person to whom it was sent. Paul follows this quite closely.

■ Then followed the greeting, usually a single word. Paul often expanded this to include the traditional Hebrew greeting, *shalom* ('peace') together with a new, Christian greeting ('grace' – in Greek very similar to the normal everyday greeting).

■ The third part of a Greek letter was a polite expression of thanks for the good health of the person addressed. This was usually expanded by Paul into a general thanksgiving to God for all that was praiseworthy in his readers.

■ Next followed the main body of the letter. In Paul's letters this was often divided into two parts: doctrinal teaching (sometimes in response to questions raised by his readers), followed by advice on aspects of the Christian lifestyle.

■ Personal news and greetings came next. In Paul's case this was more often news of the churches and prominent individuals in them, though occasionally there might be news of Paul himself.

■ There was often also in Paul's letters a note of exhortation or blessing in his own handwriting, as a kind of guarantee of the genuine and personal nature of the letter.

■ Finally, ancient letters often ended with a single word of farewell, a feature which Paul almost always expanded into a comprehensive expression of blessing and prayer for his readers.

Paul writes to the Galatian churches

A quick look at Galatians reveals just how closely Paul kept to this pattern, even when he was writing what must have been a very hurried letter. He began by giving his own name, 'Paul an apostle', and he also associated with his letter 'all those of God's family who are with me'. He then named the people to whom he was writing, in this case a group of churches: 'the churches of Galatia'. The greeting followed, 'Grace... and peace', and was expanded into a brief sentence of praise to God (1:1–5).

Antioch in Pisidia, high in what is now central Turkey, was a Roman city with a strong Hellenistic Greek and Jewish culture – just the sort of place Paul chose for his visits. The aqueduct once carried by these arches provided Antioch's water supply.

One very significant omission is to be noted at this point. Nowhere in Galatians did Paul give thanks for the spiritual condition of his readers. There was nothing to be thankful for: they had not been Christians long enough for Paul to be able to refer to praiseworthy deeds done in the past (as he did, for example, in Philippians 1:3–11), and their condition at the moment of writing certainly gave Paul no cause for thanksgiving.

After that, the main body of the letter follows, divided roughly into a doctrinal and a theoretical section (1:6 – 4:31) and a practical description of Christian living (5:1 – 6:10). No personal news and greetings finish this letter, perhaps because of the haste with which Paul was writing, or because he had no time for such pleasantries with people who had so readily disregarded his teaching. He did, however, include a final appeal in his own handwriting, which contained the interesting information that his own writing was much larger than that of the secretary who had written most of the letter – an observation which, incidentally, gives added probability to the suggestion that Paul might have suffered from bad eyesight (6:11–17). Paul then drew his letter to a conclusion with a blessing which was also a prayer for his readers, assuring them that a power greater than their own was ready to their hand: 'The grace of our Lord Jesus Christ be with your spirit, brothers and sisters, Amen' (6:18).

The letter and its argument

That has covered only the bare bones of the letter. But what was Paul actually saying? Though Galatians is not an especially long and involved letter, it is not always very easy to understand Paul's meaning. This is partly because the letter was written hastily in the middle of a raging controversy, and in such circumstances people do not express themselves in the ordered way they would in calmer moments. But the complexity of his expression also stems partly from the subject matter, for Paul was very much at home in the Old Testament and was able to quote it with great freedom as he set out to expound the twin principles of liberty and equality within the Christian community.

Paul's letter falls conveniently into three main sections, as he deals in turn with what he regarded as three false ideas that were being propounded by the Judaizing teachers, who had visited the Galatian churches.

Where did Paul get his authority?

The first thing the Judaizers had said was that Paul was not a proper apostle, and because he was not one of the original twelve, nor had he been accredited by the original apostles in Jerusalem, he had no right to give any directions to new Christians, so they ought to pay no attention to what he said. Paul's reply to all this is in 1:10 – 2:21, where he argues strongly that he needed no authorization from Jerusalem or anywhere else, since he himself had met with the risen Christ on the Damascus road. Far from being inferior to the others, he had encountered Jesus face to face – indeed, he was in the same situation as James, the Jerusalem leader, who had a very similar experience to Paul (1 Corinthians 15:7). This was where he got his accreditation as an apostle (Galatians 1:11–12) and, though he had visited Jerusalem on several occasions, he had never felt it necessary to obtain the permission of the original disciples to carry on his work, nor had they suggested that he needed such permission (1:18 – 2:10). In fact, quite the opposite was the case, for 'when they saw that I had been entrusted with the gospel to the uncircumcised [i.e. Gentiles]; just as Peter had been entrusted with the gospel to the circumcised [the Jews]... and when they perceived the grace that was given to me [by my encounter with the risen Christ], James and Cephas and John... gave to me and Barnabas the right hand of fellowship; that we should go to the Gentiles and they to the circumcised' (Galatians 2:7, 9). Subsequent events at Antioch had proved conclusively that Paul was in no way inferior to Peter (Cephas), who was commonly reckoned to be the greatest of the apostles. When Peter had broken off eating with Gentile Christians merely because some Jewish believers arrived from Jerusalem, Paul had no hesitation in opposing him 'to his face' (Galatians 2:11). Paul implies (and we have no evidence to the contrary) that Peter accepted the rebuke delivered to him on this occasion, thereby implicitly recognizing Paul's apostolic authority.

Christians and the Old Testament

After dealing with this malicious attack on his own credentials, Paul went on to appeal briefly to the Galatians' own experience before proceeding to deal with the second piece of false teaching propounded by these Judaizing intruders. What they knew of Christ ought to have shown them that they had received the Holy Spirit (the mark of the true Christian, Romans 8:9) not because they had obeyed the Old Testament Law, but because they had exercised faith in Jesus (3:1–5). This then led straight into an attack on another part of their teachings. In the Hebrew scriptures the promise of the messianic kingdom had been given to Abraham and his descendants (Genesis 17:7–8), and this was the basis on which the Judaizers were arguing that anyone who wished to be in the messianic kingdom must become members of Abraham's family by circumcision and continued obedience to the Old Testament Law (Genesis 17:9–14). Paul addressed this contention in three ways, by appealing to the Old Testament itself:

■ He pointed out (3:6–14) that the blessings promised to Abraham apply to 'all who believe'. Abraham had faith in God, and this faith was the basis of his acceptance by God (Genesis 12:1–4; see also Hebrews 11:8–12, 17–19). At the same time, 'all who rely on works of the law are under a curse'. Human experience and scripture both proved that, in practice, it was impossible to be justified in God's sight by keeping the Law, because this was so hard to do.

■ But was not the Law God's highest revelation, surpassing all that had gone before it? No, says Paul; since the Torah only came into effect long after Abraham's time, it could not possibly alter a direct promise made to him by God. The 'inheritance' promised to Abraham could not be obtainable by both Law and promise (3:18). The Law had a different purpose in God's plan:

Firstly, it served to show up sin as a transgression against God's will (3:19; see also Romans 4:15; 5:13). Before the law was given, the only moral guidance that humankind had was the 'law of nature', expressing itself through their own conscience. But after the Law was given by Moses, people were able to understand wrongdoing for what it really was: defiance of God's will.

Secondly, the Law was given to be a teacher 'until Christ came, that we might be justified by faith' (3:24). Paul suggests that, as people tried to gain salvation by their own efforts at keeping the Law, they realized it was an impossible task, and so the way was prepared for God's new act of grace in Jesus Christ.

■ Paul then proceeded to take this argument to its logical conclusion (3:25 – 4:7). The Old Testament Law was only effective 'till the offspring should come to whom the promise had been made' (3:19) and, since this 'offspring' had come in Jesus Christ, that inevitably meant the era of the Law was ended and, to those who had faith in him, Christ would give freedom from the Law and its demands. Before, they had been slaves to 'the elemental spirits of the universe' (an expression which includes the Law, but is not restricted to it, 4:3), but now they were children and heirs of the promise made to Abraham (4:4–7).

Freedom and legalism

By placing themselves under the Law and keeping traditional Jewish holy days, the Galatians were trying to undo what God had already done for them in Christ. Paul was fearful that if they did this, he had wasted his time ministering among them (4:8–11). By way of explaining why, he went on to deal with another argument put forward by the Judaizing teachers, who had given 'scriptural' reasons to show that even Gentile Christians ought to keep the Torah and be circumcised, reasons which Paul counteracted in three ways:

■ Paul returned again to examine the status of the Law (4:21 – 5:1) Once more he appealed to the story of Abraham, this time using the incident of Sarah, a free woman, driving out Hagar, the slave. This, he said, was an allegory of the superior position of the good news in Christ over and against what might be perceived as the legalism of the Jewish Law.

A Jewish or Christian bronze stamp of Byzantine origin and dating from the 3rd or 4th century, showing traditional imagery: a seven-branched candlestick, a palm frond, and a cluster of grapes.

■ Paul also answered the queries about circumcision (5:2–12), making it clear that, in his view, circumcision was of no value either way to Christians: it simply made no difference whether Christians were circumcised or not. Their standing before God must depend not on such external signs, but on 'faith working through love' (5:6). In the case of people like the Galatians, he believed that to submit to circumcision would actually be a denial of what Christ had done for them (5:2). In any case, being circumcised also obliged people to observe the whole of the Jewish Law (5:3) – the very thing that Paul had just rejected, and which experience showed to be impossible. The freedom brought by Christ was clearly incompatible with the 'yoke of slavery' (5:1) associated with circumcision and the Law.

■ After this, Paul dealt with the question of Christian behaviour (5:13 – 6:10). One thing that marked Jews off from other people in the ancient world was their very high moral standards, which resulted from their close adherence to the Old Testament Law. The Judaizers who visited Galatia had argued that if Christians discarded the Law, they would have no guide for their conduct and be indistinguishable from other people around them. This was an important question, and one that was not easy to answer.

It seems Paul had told the Galatian Christians that, if they trusted Christ, the Holy Spirit would empower them to live as Jesus lived. This is the kind of thing he indicates in 2:20: 'I have been crucified with Christ, it is no longer I who live, but Christ who lives in me; and the life I now

Who were the Galatians?

In discussing the order of events following Paul's conversion, it was suggested that the letter to the Galatians can be dated about AD48, just before the visit of Paul and Barnabas to Jerusalem for the Apostolic Council. The arguments already set out provide good reasons in favour of this date and, if they are correct, Galatians would be the first letter that Paul ever wrote and probably, therefore, the first book of the New Testament to be written. But what has been said so far is not the complete story.

In addressing the letter, Paul says he is writing 'to the churches of Galatia' (1:2), and later calls his readers Galatians (3:1). The mention of people who could be called 'Galatians' would most naturally suggest the Celtic people of that name who lived in the region of Ankara in present-day Turkey, and who gave their name to an ancient kingdom there. But if these are the people referred to, then Acts indicates that Paul did not visit them until his second and third missionary expeditions (Acts 16:6; 18:23), which in turn means that he could not have written to them as early as AD48. It has also been argued that, since Paul's teaching in Galatians closely resembles what he says in Romans, which certainly was written towards the end of his third missionary tour, it would make more sense to suppose that this letter was written to the people of north Galatia some time between AD56 and 58. The scholarly consensus, in fact, favours this later date, and the view put forward here is a minority opinion, albeit one that has been, and continues to be, held by some very eminent scholars.

Sir William Ramsay was the first scholar of any importance to advocate this view of the matter. At the beginning of the twentieth century, he conducted extensive archaeological investigations in the very areas of Asia Minor of which we are speaking, in the course of which he revealed that the *Roman province* of Galatia included not only the ancient kingdom of the Galatians in the north of Asia Minor, but

also the southern region of Lycaonia ('south Galatia'), in which Paul worked during his first missionary expedition, and where he had established churches at Lystra, Derbe and Iconium. This, at least, eliminates the argument that Paul did not visit a place that could be called 'Galatia' until much later, and makes it possible that Galatians could have been written about AD48 to the churches Paul had visited on his first missionary expedition.

The other argument often put forward to support a later date for the letter, that it is similar to Romans, is weak, and the evidence can be interpreted in more than one way. There are subtle distinctions between Galatians and Romans, with Romans certainly being a more sophisticated and rounded presentation of what are fundamentally the same arguments. The more detached tone of Romans suggests that it was written at a time and place when Paul was able to set the passion and acrimony of the Galatian situation in a wider context, which might suggest a longer period between them, rather than some immediate connection.

There are still many unanswered questions about the date and setting of Galatians, but on balance the early dating has the ability to answer more questions than a later date (including other issues previously discussed concerning the integration of the accounts of Paul's visits to Jerusalem in Acts), and therefore can plausibly be advocated as the most satisfactory option.

live in the flesh I live by faith in the Son of God, who loved me and gave himself for me.' But would it work? Paul dealt with the accusations of the Judaizers on this score by making four important statements:

Firstly (5:13–15), 'freedom in Christ' does not mean a freedom for Christians to do as they like. It is a freedom to serve one another in love and, since the Holy Spirit's purpose is to reproduce in Christians a Christ-like character, their freedom should obviously be demonstrated in ways that are consistent with this.

Secondly (5:16–26), though the Christian gospel does not prescribe particular actions, 'those who belong to Christ Jesus have crucified the flesh with its passions and desires' (5:24). That means the Christian's life will be marked out by the fruit of the Spirit. The demands of Christ are far more radical than the external imposition of ethical rules: the Christian's whole personality should be transformed, as attitudes and behaviour have been changed from within. This was the same lesson that Jesus himself had taught: 'A sound tree cannot bear evil fruit, nor can a bad tree bear good fruit' (Matthew 7:18).

Thirdly (6:1–6), Christians should beware of judging others. They ought to recognize that they themselves could have no moral strength to do what is right, apart from the power of the Holy Spirit. Insofar as they have a duty, it is to 'fulfil the law of Christ' by bearing 'one another's burdens' (6:2), which is something very different from the observance of a restricted collection of externally imposed rules and regulations.

Fourthly (6:7–10), Paul sums up his advice: in order to reap the harvest of eternal life, his readers must not cultivate the 'flesh' (their own self-gratification), but the 'Spirit' (their new life given by Jesus Christ).

Then, finally, in 6:11–18, Paul makes one last appeal to his readers, which includes two further points against his opponents, followed up by two balancing statements of his own belief and practice.

His opponents, in spite of their high pretensions, were in fact spiritually bankrupt (6:12), wanting to 'make a good showing in the flesh', the very thing that Paul had denounced in the previous section of his argument (6:8, 'those who sow to their own flesh will from the flesh reap corruption'). They are also inconsistent, even with their own starting points for, though they emphasize the outward sign of circumcision, they are not willing to accept the spiritual discipline involved in keeping the Old Testament Law.

After preaching in Perga, Paul and Barnabas completed their first missionary journey by sailing back from Attalia to Syrian Antioch. There they recounted their experiences to the church which had commissioned them. Attalia is now the modern resort of Antalya in southern Turkey.

Paul was driven by the conviction that what had been revealed to him by the risen Christ was of supreme authority, and so he concluded by affirming that the only real cause of boasting before God must be that the Christian is crucified to the world, through the cross of Christ. Talk of a cross in the first century meant only one thing: death, and that is what Paul meant when he wrote of Christians sharing in the cross of Christ (Galatians 2:20). He was not urging them to be martyrs, but was indicating in a more mystical, inner sense that Christians should die to themselves, by giving up their claims to final jurisdiction over their own lives and destinies, and applying the gospel and its values to every aspect of life. This kind of 'new creation' would be the only thing of any value in the sight of God, and constituted the sole qualifying mark of membership in 'the Israel of God' (Galatians 6:14–16). Paul himself may be criticized for being a traitor to Judaism, but as far as he was concerned he bore the mark of true spirituality before God: 'I bear on my body the marks of Jesus' (6:17).

This, then, is how Paul dealt with the problems of the churches of Galatia. One slogan used here neatly summarizes it all: 'in Christ, it is not circumcision or uncircumcision that counts, but the power of a new birth' (Galatians 6:15).

The Apostolic Council

No doubt it was in this fashion that Paul set out his arguments at the Council of Jerusalem in AD49. According to Acts even James, probably the most traditional of the Jerusalem leaders, had to agree with the main part of Paul's argument (Acts 15:6–21). The Jerusalem apostles accepted that there was no great doctrinal principle involved, though there was still the pressing practical problem of how Jews and Gentiles could meet together and share food at the same table.

In order to make this possible the Jerusalem leaders suggested that Gentile converts should abstain from those activities particularly offensive to Jewish Christians: things like eating food that had been offered in pagan sacrifices, eating meat from which the blood had not been drained, and sexual habits which did not accord with accepted Jewish Law and custom (Acts 15:19–21, 28–29). This arrangement was accepted by Paul, but it was a compromise, and it appears not to have been a very successful one, for when Paul faced the same problems again in Corinth, he never referred to the terms of the Apostolic Decree at all, but argued once more from the basic principles involved in the matter (1 Corinthians 8:1–13; 10:18 – 11:1).

There is, however, another question raised by Luke's account of the Apostolic Decree. If we are correct in thinking that Paul wrote Galatians just before he went to the Council, then the narrative of Acts 15 depicts him accepting something he had just vehemently rejected in Galatians, namely the application of some sort of 'law' to Gentile Christians.

Various explanations might be possible:

■ One solution is to suppose that the Apostolic Council never actually happened, and that it was invented by Luke for the purpose of showing that both Jewish and Gentile sections of the church were united in the early years of its history. This explanation is largely the result of supposing that the narrative of Acts cannot be reconciled with Galatians 1 – 2, whereas if the alternative correlation between the two proposed here is accepted, that difficulty largely disappears. There is also the more general consideration that, since Luke usually emerges as a trustworthy historian at those places where his story can be tested against external evidence, in the absence of specific indications to the contrary, there is no reason to suspect his overall reliability at this point.

■ Another possibility is to suppose that the Apostolic Decree was in fact addressed to just a small and relatively local group of churches, namely those specifically mentioned by name in Acts 15:36 – 16:5. If this was the case, there would be no difficulty over the fact that Paul did not quote the Decree in 1 Corinthians, for it would never have been intended to apply there.

■ Perhaps a better explanation still is that Paul was, at heart, a conciliatory and pragmatic sort of person. Having said his piece in Galatians, and having won the theological debate in Jerusalem, he was content to accept that, regardless of theological difficulties, Jews and Gentiles had to live together within the local church, and the acceptance of these guidelines was a straightforward means of achieving this.

■ As we proceed now to consider Paul's experiences in other churches, it is noticeable that, time and again, he bent over backwards to accommodate people whose viewpoint was different from his own (1 Corinthians 9:19–23). He realized that a divided church was a poor witness to the non-Christian world, and at this stage of his ministry the Apostolic Decree perhaps seemed the best solution to a pressing problem.

17 Paul the Missionary

Back to Galatia

After his crucial meeting with the leaders of the Jerusalem church, Paul went off again into the Gentile world, fired with a new enthusiasm. In the course of his earlier mission work, he had come to realize just how attractive the Christian message could be to the populations of the great urban centres of Asia Minor, and he could now see the potential for moving even further afield to invite others to follow Jesus Christ.

Paul's second missionary journey.

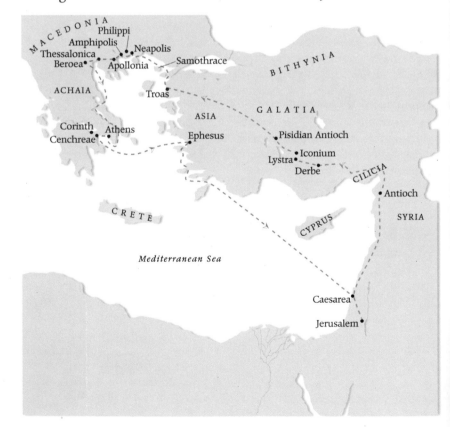

He began this second expedition with a new companion. Barnabas did not join him on this occasion because Paul was unwilling to give a second chance to John Mark (Barnabas' cousin) who had apparently let them down during their earlier trip (Acts 15:36–40). But Paul found a keen helper in Silas, one of the messengers who had been sent to Antioch to explain the decisions of the Jerusalem Council to the church there (Acts 15:30–33). In the course of their journeying, Paul was joined by two others in addition to Silas: Timothy, who met them at Lystra (Acts 16:1–3), and Luke who attached himself to them at Troas (Acts 16:10–12).

The first thing Paul wanted to do was to revisit some of the communities that he had founded in south Galatia during his first expedition from Antioch. He had been hoping to see them ever since he heard of the consternation created by the interference of the Judaizers, and during this further visit he no doubt explained that, although as Christians they were not required to fulfil all the detailed requirements of the Torah, it would nevertheless be desirable if they could agree to accept the arrangement that had been worked out in Jerusalem, because that would create an environment in which Christians from a Jewish background could feel free to meet with them (Acts 16:4).

After this, Paul and Silas went on with Timothy, who had joined them in Lystra, through Phrygia and Galatia – perhaps this time north Galatia. Paul had planned to go to the Roman province of Asia, which was the area round Ephesus in the west of Asia Minor, and also into Bithynia, the province to the north which adjoined the Black Sea (Acts 16:6–7). Neither of these intentions worked out, and indeed Luke specifically comments that they were 'forbidden by the Holy Spirit', though he gives no indication as to how this instruction might have been received. Paul and his companions, therefore, went on into Troas, ancient Troy, in the part of Asia Minor nearest to Europe.

During the night Paul had a dream of a Macedonian appealing for help, something which he recognized as a mandate directly from God inviting him to cross the Aegean Sea and enter Europe (Acts 16:9–10). In the context of the narrative of Acts, Paul's entry into Europe at this point is portrayed as a pivotal point in Luke's purpose to document the spread of the gospel from Palestinian beginnings to the centre of the empire in Rome itself. In terms of the expansion of the church, however, it was certainly not the first time that Christian missionaries had entered Europe, for at a later date Paul wrote to a large and flourishing church at Rome, which had not been founded by his own efforts.

The great Roman roads were of vital military and commercial importance. The stone slabs of the Egnatian Way were worn down by the heavy traffic. Paul's group used this route to travel from Philippi to Thessalonica.

Philippi

The first town the missionaries visited was Philippi (Acts 16:12). This was a Roman colony in the north-east corner of Macedonia, largely populated by retired soldiers from the Roman army. Although the city had such a large Gentile population, Paul still followed his earlier custom of first going to the Jews at their usual meeting place, which in this case was 'a place of prayer' by the riverside; there were so few Jews in Philippi that they did not even have a synagogue building.

Paul was summoned to Europe by a dream in which a Macedonian (a person from northern Greece) appealed to him. This Latin inscription from Philippi includes the name of the Roman province of Macedonia.

Converts

Among Paul's hearers at this place of prayer was Lydia, and she was the first to become a Christian in Philippi. If Paul had any lingering doubts about the wisdom of abandoning his earlier plans and moving instead into Europe, they must have disappeared with the conversion of this woman, for she was a native of Thyatira, a city located in the very area of Asia Minor where Paul had originally been intending to go (Acts 16:14–15). She might well have been the one who first took the Christian message to her home town, where there was soon a large Christian community (Revelation 2:18–29). In any event, her discovery of Jesus as the Messiah brought about an immediate and revolutionary change in her life, for though she was a woman of some importance, her own home was soon opened to Paul and his friends and became the headquarters of their activity. Once again Paul was learning that the gospel created a unity of friendship between men and women that could overthrow all normal social and racial barriers.

One thing that happened at Philippi provides a good illustration of why the Christian faith began to arouse so much antagonism in many parts of the Roman empire at this time. As he was going about his evangelistic work, Paul was continually pestered by a slave girl who, by means of some kind of clairvoyance exercised in a trance state, had brought a large income to her owners. Like Jesus before him, Paul had a keenly developed sense of both social and spiritual injustice, and could not pass up the opportunity to help this person find freedom from the spirit of divination, which was believed to possess her, as well as from the exploitation of those who owned her. Predictably this action was not well received, and her owners were so angry that they accused Paul and Silas of creating a public disturbance, by recommending customs that were unlawful for Roman citizens (Acts 16:16–21).

Imprisonment

Accusations of causing a public nuisance could always be guaranteed to arouse a Roman official to some sort of action, and the town officials responded swiftly. Paul and Silas were beaten and thrown into prison, where they spent the night singing praises to God. During the night an earthquake broke open the prison doors and, though they could have escaped, they chose to remain, along with the rest of the prisoners. The local jailer was ready to take his own life, assuming that in such circumstances all his prisoners would get out, and when he found they were still there he was amazed, and challenged by the realization that these prisoners were at peace with themselves in a way that he was not. On learning of the secret of their power, he became a Christian himself, along with his entire household. After the conversion of his jailer, Paul was determined to leave prison. In fact, he ought never to have been there in the first place, for he was a Roman citizen. He, therefore, claimed his rights as a citizen, and demanded an apology from the embarrassed city authorities, before leaving the city of Philippi altogether (Acts 16:22–40).

Luke stayed behind in Philippi to help the new Christians become established in their faith. They were drawn from all levels of society and included a prominent local trader, a spiritual healer and astrologer, as well as the city jailer and his family. Paul's reputation travelled fast and, at one of the next places they visited, he and his friends Silas and Timothy were described as 'people who have turned the world upside down' (Acts 17:6). The next towns to be visited were Thessalonica and Beroea. There were significant synagogues in each place, and many converts were made. In both places, however, there was also serious opposition stirred up from within the Jewish community, opposition which seems to have been directed specifically at Paul himself, as a former Pharisee, since Silas and Timothy were able to stay on there when Paul went to Athens (Acts 17:14–15).

Athens

Athens had for centuries prided itself on being the intellectual centre of the ancient world. By the time of Paul it was no longer an important political centre, but it was still a city of learning to which many young Romans were sent to study philosophy, or to be initiated into one of the many oriental mystery religions which found a home there.

Communicating his message in Athens was bound to require a very different approach from that used in most of the places Paul had visited up to this point. The people there had no Jewish or biblical background at all, therefore to introduce Jesus as the Messiah would have meant little or nothing to them. With ethnic Jews and Gentile proselytes or God-fearers, Paul could begin from the Hebrew scriptures and point out how the promises made there had been fulfilled in the life, death and resurrection of Jesus. At Athens, he was conscious of his own relative ignorance regarding the nature of the Hellenistic spiritual search, so his mission began not by speaking, but by observing what was going on there, and listening to the debates that were already in progress. It was only a matter of time before he was invited to go and address the court of the Areopagus. The Athenians had always enjoyed a good debate, and the city leaders believed that taking an interest in philosophy and religion was part of their job.

In speaking with them, Paul began from the Greek view of God as creator, benefactor and invisible presence within the universe, talking of the universal human search for God, who is 'not far from each one of us', and referring in the process to statements made by the Greek poets Epimenides and Aratus (Acts 17:27).

Athens symbolized the tradition of classical learning. The Acropolis, on which the Parthenon was built as a temple to the goddess Athene, served as both a focus of worship and a defensive stronghold.

He also spoke of the many shrines and altars which were located all round the city. This was fairly typical of Greek cities, which generally had an abundance of small statues and icons at strategic locations, to provide an opportunity for people to pay homage to the deities as they went about their daily business. The status of these gods and goddesses had been thrown into some doubt as a result of the thinking of previous generations of philosophers, and some of the language employed by Paul might have been alluding to arguments used to question this form of traditional observance since the days of Xenophanes in the sixth century BC. Paul was not specially concerned with condemning the traditional spirituality of his hearers, but with using it as an opening to present his own message. Since he had observed an altar 'to the unknown god', he identified Jesus with this unknown deity, and proceeded to explain the gospel from this perspective. Paul had a strong belief in a creation-centred spirituality, shared by all people by virtue of their common humanity, quite independently of their formal religious traditions (Romans 1:18 – 2:10), and this was his starting point in Athens. Of course, he also shared those aspects of Christian belief which were unique and distinctive, including belief in one God whose nature had been revealed in the life, death and resurrection of Jesus Christ.

A stone altar discovered at Pergamum. The top line reads, 'to unknown gods'.

His message was given a mixed reception, and Athens was not one of the cities where Paul immediately established a thriving Christian community. Nevertheless, this narrative plays a central part in the book of Acts, for while other stories can give the impression of a somewhat triumphalist progress of the gospel, this one reminds its readers that even Paul's mission work was not guaranteed instant success. It also – and more importantly – provides a model for contextualizing the Christian message in cultures where the salvation history of the Old Testament story was unknown. In doing so, Paul is shown affirming the spiritual starting points of his audience, and being prepared to journey alongside them, while at the same time challenging them to see things from the new perspective of belief in Jesus. In the process, he drew on resources that were already in his own Jewish tradition, particularly the creation-centred theology of the book of Genesis, and its developments in later Judaism.

Corinth

After this, Paul pressed on to Corinth, an ancient Greek city that had been rebuilt as a Roman colony in 46BC. Corinth had a unique location, at the narrowest point in the mainland of Greece, and therefore provided easy access to the Aegean Sea on the east and the Adriatic Sea on the west. Though the Romans had opened up extensive seagoing trade routes, and navigational methods were well advanced, ancient sailors still preferred to travel close to the coastline whenever they could, and Corinth took advantage of this to establish itself as one of the foremost centres of trade and transportation. Though there were plans to build a canal from the Aegean Sea to the Adriatic, even in New Testament times, it was many centuries later before the project was carried through. At the time when Paul visited the city, it had two separate harbours on each of its coasts – Lechaeum and Cenchreae – and between the two was an intricate construction like a conveyor belt, along which vast numbers of slaves would haul ships from one harbour to another. Corinth became an important transit point at which ships could pass from the Aegean to the Adriatic, without navigating the dangerous southern tip of Greece. Because of its strategic position, roughly midway between the eastern end of the Mediterranean and Italy, there was always a constant stream of traffic passing through.

Corinth had become a major interchange not only for commerce, but also for the many cultures of the empire. On the streets of Corinth, people of many different ethnic origins and religious convictions mingled naturally, and the city was a vibrant microcosm of the life of the entire empire. As a staging post for sailors, it was also home to one of the largest numbers of prostitutes anywhere in the empire, and its name became a byword for sexual experimentation of every imaginable kind.

Paul clearly recognized the strategic importance of Corinth, staying there for the next eighteen months (Acts 18:11), and even after that he took more interest in the nurture of the church there than he normally did with other Christian groups he founded. In Corinth, Paul made friends with Aquila and his wife Priscilla who, like himself, were Hellenistic Jews and tent makers. He followed his previous pattern of beginning his work in the synagogue, but he was forced to leave when he met the usual opposition. He then moved next door, to the home of one of his new converts, Titius Justus, and used that as the base for his mission to the city. Many citizens became Christians at this time, including Crispus, one of the synagogue leaders (Acts 18:8), and a very large and influential Christian community began to be established in the city.

After Paul had been there for about eighteen months, the synagogue authorities decided to make a concerted effort to have him chased out of town. This move coincided with the arrival of a new Roman magistrate, the proconsul Gallio, who was the brother of the well-known poet and philosopher, Seneca. The charge against him was that 'this man is persuading people to worship God in ways that are contrary to the Law' (Acts 18:13). Predictably, it came to nothing because Gallio would not judge Paul under the Jewish Law, and according to Roman law he had done nothing wrong. The major significance of this episode is that it is the only incident in Paul's life which can be given a fairly precise date. Gallio's period of office in Corinth is recorded in a copy of a letter sent from the emperor, and preserved on a stone inscription, which shows that he must have been proconsul either in AD51–52 or AD52–53.

Paul writes more letters

At an early point during Paul's stay in Corinth, Silas and Timothy (who had remained behind in Thessalonica) arrived with news of the Christians there. Their report was most encouraging for, though it had been little more than six months since their conversion to Christ, the example of their changed lifestyle had made such an impact on the surrounding area that others had also been attracted to Christian faith. However, there were also some problems in the church. The people in the synagogue had stirred up opposition, including physical violence, and several matters were leading to tensions within the Christian community itself. Questions needed to be answered about sexual relationships, about the nature of leadership, and about the fate of Christians who had died. On hearing of all this, Paul wrote to encourage them and to give them guidance on these particular problems. The letter he wrote was 1 Thessalonians.

However, the Thessalonians were soon diverted away from following Paul's advice in this letter, as what he had said about the state of Christians who died, and the expected *parousia* of Jesus became the occasion for apocalyptic speculation. It was not long before Paul had to write another letter to help sort out the difficulties which, to some extent, the Thessalonian Christians seem to have invented for themselves out of certain parts of his first letter, and so he penned 2 Thessalonians.

It was in Thessalonica that Paul had been accused of 'turning the world upside down', and the Christian community that he left behind him there continued this activity. As we read the letters Paul wrote to them, it is easy to conclude that the Thessalonian church was in serious difficulties, but we must not allow a few trivial criticisms to obscure the fact that this was one of the very few churches that Paul commended so warmly for its Christlike character. The encouragement he received from these people must have been a great help to him as he faced the next big test of his life's work.

1 Thessalonians

After his usual introduction, Paul begins by commending his readers for their faithfulness to the Christian message. They had worked carefully to follow all that Paul had taught them, with the result that a strong church had been established and, by the example of their changed lives, the claims of the gospel had been advanced within their wider social context. In Galatia, it had been suggested that Paul's message of freedom from the Law would lead to low moral standards, whereas the exact opposite seemed to have happened here, as the whole of Macedonia and Achaia saw the difference the Christian faith made to the way of life of these believers (1 Thessalonians 1:2–10). The way Paul describes all this raises some questions about the exact nature of his mission in Thessalonica, for he refers to his converts as having 'turned to God from idols' (1:9), which would imply they were predominantly Gentiles, whereas Acts 17:1–9 only mentions converts from within the synagogue community. But later sections of this letter cover apocalyptic concerns that are more likely to have been raised by converts from within Judaism, so perhaps the reality is that Paul's mission appealed to a broad cross-section of the Thessalonian population, including those of Jewish ancestry as well as Gentiles previously associated with the synagogue, and those with no such connection.

Paul and his converts
Paul goes on to reflect on his own mission strategy when he and his friends first arrived in the city. He reminds his readers that the apostles had been careful not to advertise themselves, but to draw attention to the essentials of their message; though they had been sent out with the personal authority of God, and with the backing of the earliest churches, in their attitude towards the people they were serving they followed the example of Jesus: 'we were gentle among you, like a nurse taking care of her children... we were ready to share with you not only the gospel of God but also our own selves' (2:7, 8). They felt they had been well rewarded for their efforts, for the Thessalonians had responded to the message, and had recognized its life changing potential: 'when you received the word of God that you heard from us, you accepted it not as a human word but as what it really is, God's word, which is also at work in you believers' (2:13). This knowledge, together with the news conveyed by Silas and Timothy, proved a great encouragement to Paul as he worked in difficult conditions in Corinth (2:17 – 3:8). Nevertheless, there was something lacking in their faith (3:10), and so Paul set out to try to give good advice on the various matters which Timothy had reported to him.

How should Christians behave?
The Judaizers were right when they suggested the one thing that would present the biggest challenge for Gentile converts was the question of personal morality. Hellenistic culture was generally very permissive, and few kinds of sexual activity were prohibited outright. Paul's hope had always been that, by relying on the empowerment of the Holy Spirit, converts would align their lifestyles with accepted Christian values and, in a majority of cases, that was what had happened among the Thessalonians. But

it was still necessary to reinforce what he had no doubt told them when he founded their church (4:1–8), and in doing so Paul naturally reflected on what he had written earlier in Galatians on the same matter: 'you were called to freedom... only do not use your freedom as an opportunity for the flesh, but through love be servants of one another' (Galatians 5:13). The Thessalonians had learnt this lesson well: 'you yourselves have been taught by God to love one another; and indeed you do love all the brothers and sisters throughout Macedonia' (1 Thessalonians 4:9–10). It was a lesson that could never be overemphasized. In a world in which the established order was rapidly changing, and in which people were frantically grasping at whatever spirituality came their way, one of the most important things the church could do was to display the love of Christ (4:9–12). Jesus himself had taught, 'By this everyone will know that you are my disciples, if you have love for one another' (John 13:35), and the advice is here repeated and reinforced by Paul.

What about the future?

One thing above all appears to have been troubling the church at Thessalonica. They understood well the relationship that ought to exist among the members of their community, but what about those Christians who had died shortly after Paul's departure from the city? Perhaps Paul's teaching on the *parousia* had been misunderstood, as some of these converts seem to have had the idea that no Christians would die at all before Christ returned in glory. Paul corrected this by providing a clear statement spelling out his beliefs on the matter, and emphasizing that, though Christ's presence was already operative in the church through the work of the Holy Spirit, Jesus would one day come back openly and in glory (4:13–18). Meanwhile, the Thessalonian Christians should not worry unduly about loved ones who had died: 'since we believe that Jesus died and rose again, even so, through

Jesus, God will bring with him those who have fallen asleep' (4:14).

Paul appreciated the potential pitfalls in emphasizing what God would do in the future, so he went on to remind the Thessalonian Christians that their belief in the future return of Jesus was no excuse for inactivity in the present. Though some people would not be prepared for 'the day of the Lord', Christians ought to be. Their business was not to try to calculate 'the times and the seasons' (5:1), but to 'encourage one another and build one another up' (5:11).

Living the Christian life

Finally, Paul gave some advice to his readers on a number of topics, summarizing all that he had said before (5:12–21).
- In the church, the Christians should:
  - respect those who laboured among them, that is the leaders;
  - be at peace among themselves (a repetition and reinforcement of what he had said in 4:9–12);
  - encourage one another in their faith in Christ (5:14).
- In their everyday lives, Christians should:
  - return good for evil (5:15), one of the most characteristic marks of the Christian (see also Matthew 5:44);
  - 'rejoice always' (5:16).
- In their relationship to God, Christians must:
  - live in an attitude of prayer (5:17);
  - allow the Holy Spirit to direct their lives (5:19–20).

Paul signed off with his usual blessing and greeting, making a last appeal and promise to his readers. He reminded them that the secret of successful Christian living was to be found in the work of the living Christ continuing to operate through the lives of his followers, and 'the one who calls you is faithful, and will do this' (5:24).

2 Thessalonians

In this second, shorter letter to the Thessalonians Paul clarified three main points.

The church and its enemies
From what is said in 2 Thessalonians 1:5–12 it appears that the church had faced increasingly fierce opposition. He explained that this was to be expected, for the more widely known their love and Christian character became, the more their enemies would make life difficult for them. No one would ever bother about a religious faith that meant nothing to those holding it; but the revolutionary character of the life of the Thessalonian church naturally drew the attention of others to what was going on. It would be impossible to turn the world upside down without provoking some reaction from that world. Paul reminds these Christians that, though for the moment things might be difficult, God is on their side and will ultimately vindicate them.

The church and the future
A more subtle form of 'persecution' had also come into the church, with the appearance of forged letters claiming to have been written by Paul and his associates (2 Thessalonians 2:1–12). Apocalyptic enthusiasts of some kind had taken advantage of Paul's mention of the *parousia* of Jesus in his earlier letter, and used the occasion to put across their own point of view on the subject. Paul had to warn the Thessalonian Christians 'not to be quickly shaken in mind or excited, either by spirit or by word, or by letter purporting to be from us, to the effect that the day of the Lord has come' (2:2). The exact connotation of the claim that 'the day of the Lord has come' is difficult to establish. In 1 Corinthians there is a mention of people who thought that the resurrection (which was generally associated with the end of things and the *parousia* of Christ) had already taken place,

on the basis of which belief they indulged in what Paul deemed to be unacceptable sexual practices (1 Corinthians 15:12–58). It is difficult to make any specific connection between the two groups of people, but in any event Paul goes on to emphasize here that, in his view, the *parousia* and all it entails was not an event that could take place invisibly or mystically (which would need to have been the case if it had already happened). On the contrary, he places his own expectation firmly in a context of actual events by mentioning certain historical occurrences connected with 'the lawless one' (2:3–12) that would herald the return of Christ.

The church and society
The outcome of the interest in future events that had arisen in Thessalonica was that some of the Christians had stopped living a normal life. They had opted out of society and were idly waiting for Christ to return, an attitude which Paul criticized severely. For him, authentic Christian spirituality was unlikely to be demonstrated by becoming a religious hermit, but required people to play their full part in the life of the wider culture. People who did not do this, however 'spiritual' their motives, should be disciplined by the church. It was not very often that Paul instructed a church to take disciplinary action against one of its members, but this was one such case. Of course, the other Christians were not to do this with a judgmental spirit, but in a way that was calculated to lead to restoration: 'Do not regard them as enemies, but warn them as believers' (3:15).

Even with all their problems, however, the Thessalonians had learnt the true secret of the Christian way of life that Paul had shown them. They were rapidly becoming the kind of congregation of which Paul could be proud: 'your faith is growing abundantly, and the love of every one of you for one another is increasing' (1:3).

Did Paul write 2 Thessalonians?

In our analysis of 1 and 2 Thessalonians, we have assumed that Paul wrote them both, the second one in response to problems that had arisen subsequent to his first letter. There is room for debate regarding the actual order in which they were written, and some have proposed that 2 Thessalonians was actually written first. Not only does it seem to be addressing a circumstance in which persecution was an immediate concern, whereas 1 Thessalonians implies it was in the past, but it is also possible to understand the questions about eschatology in 1 Thessalonians as having developed on the basis of what is said in 2 Thessalonians, rather than vice versa.

There is no way to be sure of the order of the letters, but of more importance is the suggestion that the two letters are so individually distinctive that if Paul wrote one of them, he cannot have written the other. Since 2 Thessalonians is the shorter

and less comprehensive, this one has most often been questioned, for a number of reasons.

A different eschatology

In 1 Thessalonians 4:13 – 5:11, Paul writes of the coming of Jesus as an imminent event, and Christians are warned not to be taken by surprise when it comes. But in 2 Thessalonians 2:1–12, Paul lists a sequence of events that will take place before the *parousia* and this, it is argued, removes the element of immediacy from it. Paul can hardly have held both views at once. But this argument is not as impressive as it seems, for two reasons:

● Though 'signs of the end' are not listed in 1 Thessalonians, they are implied in 5:1, where Paul writes, 'There is no need to write to you, brothers and sisters, about the times and occasions when these things will happen.' This statement seems to suggest that Paul thought they already knew about such matters, and when he proceeds to warn his readers not to be taken by surprise, it is precisely because

The Arch of Galerius, an impressive Roman structure, straddled the Egnatian Way at Thessalonica.

**Did Paul write
2 Thessalonians?**
continued

they, of all people, should have been able to recognize when Jesus was about to return.

● The two letters deal with different issues. In the first place, Paul had been asked a personal question about the fate of Christians who died – and he gave his answer on an appropriate personal level. But the question behind 2 Thessalonians is quite different, and concerns people who were saying that the 'day of the Lord' was there already. This was a quite different kind of argument, and it demanded a different sort of answer, not this time from a personal perspective, but on a broader cosmic level.

A different tone

2 Thessalonians is said to be more formal than 1 Thessalonians. Here again, the alleged differences are nothing like as great as some seem to think. The writer of 2 Thessalonians still has a deep concern for his readers and if, as we have suggested, 1 Thessalonians had been wilfully misunderstood by some people, it is hardly surprising that Paul should have been sterner with them the second time. Exactly the same change of tone can be traced in the later correspondence between Paul and the church at Corinth, and for the same reasons.

Too many similarities

This is almost the opposite argument – not that the two letters are different, but that they are too much alike! Some similar words and phrases are used in both, and this has been interpreted as an indication that 2 Thessalonians is just a rewritten form of 1 Thessalonians – rewritten, presumably, by someone else, later than the time of Paul. Again, this is a very slender basis on which to reach such a conclusion, for three reasons:

● Why would anyone wish to produce such a rewritten version of one of Paul's letters? The only plausible possibility would be to try to contradict, or correct, what was later seen as an erroneous idea

in 1 Thessalonians. If the eschatological perspective of 1 and 2 Thessalonians was different, then that could perhaps provide an explanation. But we have already seen that this is not the case.

● Why should an author not repeat himself or herself? Even today, someone engaged in a long correspondence will often refer to previous letters in the process of compiling later ones, and there is no reason to suppose that Paul could not have done the same. We certainly know that was the practice among other Greek letter writers. Especially when giving personal advice in a continuing situation, it is often necessary to say the same things more than once.

● The actual verbal similarities between 1 and 2 Thessalonians are not very extensive. At least two thirds of 2 Thessalonians is quite new, and much of the rest consists of standardized terminology which was part of the stock-in-trade of the letter writer – the equivalent of our 'Dear sir', or 'Cordially yours'.

All these problems are more apparent than real. Distinctions of this kind can be made to look significant when viewed as objects of detached analysis, but such variations and repetitions make good sense when placed in a wider social context, and are the sorts of things that happen every day in real life, especially in dealing with situations such as these letters presuppose.

Paul's strategy for evangelism

Paul was perhaps the most successful Christian missionary there has ever been. In less than a generation he travelled the length and breadth of the Mediterranean world, establishing growing and active Christian communities wherever he went.

What was his secret? Paul, of course, was always conscious that he was only a messenger, and that what really brought a change to the lives of those whom he met was the power of God's Holy Spirit. As he considered the many hardships that he had to endure, he described himself as a 'common clay pot', just a temporary container for the renewing power of God (2 Corinthians 4:7). But Paul was also a sophisticated strategist. His route was never haphazard, and his methods of communication were based on considerable insight into the ways people think and take decisions.

Paul was a frontier evangelist, but he himself never visited a geographical frontier! He could have spent months, even years, trekking through uncharted territory, or making his way laboriously across country paths to reach remote places. He did neither of these things. Instead he took advantage of the major highways the Romans had built across their empire. Combined with regular sea routes, they gave ready access to all the major centres of population, and these were the places Paul visited. He knew that he could never personally take the gospel to every man and woman throughout the empire, but if he could establish enthusiastic groups of Christians in some of the key cities, then they in turn would spread the good news into the more remote areas. Moreover, residents of rural districts often had to visit the nearest city, so they too could be reached with the gospel, which they could then take home to their own people. This was what had happened on the Day of Pentecost in Jerusalem, and Paul was well aware of the great potential that such a strategy offered. At least one of the churches to which Paul later wrote a letter – that in Colossae – was founded like this.

Paul was also aware of the need for variety in his presentation of the Christian message. The great secret of Jesus' success had been his ability to speak to people wherever he found them. When he was in the fields, he spoke of growing crops (Mark 4:1–9). With families, he spoke of children (Matthew 19:13–15). With fishing people, the subject was fish (Mark 1:14–18). Paul was the same. He went to people wherever they would listen – in the Jewish synagogues, in the market places, even in the shrines of traditional Greek deities. In the synagogue at Thessalonica, he began with the Old Testament (Acts 17:2–3); at Athens, he started from the 'unknown god' for whom the Greeks were searching (Acts 17:22–31); in Ephesus, he was prepared to engage in public debates about the meaning of the Christian gospel (Acts 19:9).

Readers of Paul's letters have often sought to understand them by reducing his message to a collection of abstract propositional statements about the human condition, but that was not how Paul communicated. He began where his hearers were, and was prepared to engage with their needs. Sometimes it might have been appropriate to deliver a formal address; at other times that would have been entirely the wrong method of approach. Paul and his associates were always ready to get alongside people to help them find new direction for their own spiritual journeys. This was part of the secret of success in Thessalonica: 'we were gentle when we were with you, like a mother taking care of her children… ready to share with you not only the good news from God but even our own lives' (1 Thessalonians 2:7, 8).

It was this sensitivity to people, and flexibility in his evangelism, that Paul was later to encapsulate by saying, 'I make myself everybody's slave in order to win as many people as possible… all things to all people, that I may save some of them by whatever means are possible' (1 Corinthians 9:19, 22).

18 Paul the Pastor

When Paul left Corinth he paid a short visit to Ephesus, and then returned directly to Caesarea in Palestine, from where he went straight to Antioch in Syria (Acts 18:18–22). After a short stay there he began what is often called his 'third missionary journey', which was not at all a missionary expedition in the same way as his two earlier tours had been.

This third expedition was more in the nature of a pastor's ministry, and centred on two main places, Ephesus and Corinth. Paul began with a short trip through Galatia and Phrygia (the districts where he had been during his second expedition), but instead of going north to Troas, as before, he went directly to Ephesus.

Paul's third missionary journey.

Ephesus

Ephesus was the capital of the Roman province of Asia and was, therefore, a centre from which, by road or sea, Paul could easily keep in touch with most of the young churches he had already established in Asia Minor and in Europe. It was also a location from which he and his colleagues could reach out into the whole province of Asia. His stay there resulted in churches being established in such places as Colossae and Laodicea, which Paul himself had not yet visited.

Ephesus was a large and cultured city. After the riots protesting at Paul's teaching, the citizens gathered at the theatre, which held 25,000 people. In the distance is the harbour, which has long-since silted up.

In the course of his three years' stay at Ephesus, Paul seems to have paid a short visit to Corinth. When he finally left Ephesus he went on to revisit the churches in Macedonia – probably those of Philippi, Thessalonica and Beroea (Acts 20:1–2). This might have been the occasion on which he went 'as far round as Illyricum', the region of Greece on the Dalmatian coast of the Adriatic Sea (Romans 15:19). For a further three months he stayed in Achaia (probably mostly in Corinth), then went back to Macedonia (Acts 20:3). There representatives of several churches, including Luke, joined him to take a gift from the Gentile congregations to the church in Jerusalem (Acts 20:4–6; cf. 24:17).

The impact of the gospel

Paul's long stay in Ephesus was undoubtedly the most important part of this period of his ministry – perhaps even the most significant time of his entire life's work. In addition to being the geographical centre of all the places Paul had previously visited, Ephesus was also a prominent centre of spiritual traditions, at the heart of which was the great temple of Artemis (Diana) which was renowned as one of the wonders of the ancient world.

Paul's ministry in Ephesus was so successful that the two mainstays of Ephesian religious life were seriously challenged. One of the things for which Ephesus was well known was its great number of magicians and astrologers, many of whom became Christians and actually burnt their books of magic spells. The silversmiths of the city found that their trade in selling small replicas of the temple of Artemis to pilgrims began to decline, which led Demetrius and some others to start a riot against the Christians in the city (Acts 19:23–41).

Prison again?

In spite of such successes, however, Paul endured great hardships at Ephesus – something he had come to expect when his ministry led to large-scale conversions to Christ. In 1 Corinthians 15:32 he states that he fought with 'wild beasts' there, which might suggest he was thrown into the Roman arena, though it is probably a figure of speech. In 2 Corinthians 1:8 Paul speaks of the afflictions he endured in Asia, and in Romans 16:7 (probably written just after he had left Ephesus) he describes Andronicus and Junias as 'my fellow prisoners'. References such as these are often taken to indicate that Paul was imprisoned during this stay in Ephesus. The evidence for such an imprisonment is considered in more detail in chapter 19.

Advising the churches

This third period of Paul's ministry is of most interest to us because it is the period when three of Paul's greatest letters were written: 1 and 2 Corinthians and Romans. They have often been interpreted as if they were theological tracts written in the form of letters but, like Paul's earlier letters, they follow the normal pattern of ancient letters, and each arose out of a specific historical situation.

Paul and the church at Corinth

The letters to Corinth in particular confront us with one of the most complicated historical puzzles of the entire New Testament. Galatians and 1 and 2 Thessalonians were fairly easy to fit into the picture of Paul's activities recorded in Acts. But in the case of 1 and 2 Corinthians we have no information at all from Acts, and in order to piece together the historical situation behind this correspondence we depend entirely on the vague hints and allusions that Paul made as he wrote. Since it was not his main purpose to give a consecutive account of his own movements, or of the state of the Corinthian church, any reconstruction of what was going on must be more or less imaginative. But there is general agreement among most scholars that Paul's dealings with the church in Corinth at this time can be summarized in six stages:

Bad news from Corinth

During his three years' stay at Ephesus, Paul received bad news of the state of the Corinthian church, in response to which he wrote a letter warning them of the dangers of immorality. This letter is referred to in 1 Corinthians 5:9, 11, where Paul says: 'I wrote to you in my letter not to associate with sexually immoral persons... but now I am writing to you.' Some scholars think that part of this previous letter could be preserved in what is now known as 2 Corinthians 6:14 – 7:1, since that section seems to be out of character with its context in 2 Corinthians, and it begins, 'Do not be mismatched with unbelievers.'

Paul writes 1 Corinthians

Members of Chloe's household also brought reports that the Corinthian church was dividing into different parties, and Paul's own authority as an apostle was being challenged (1 Corinthians 1:11). These reports had later been confirmed by Stephanas and two others (1 Corinthians 16:17), who brought with them a letter from Corinth asking certain definite questions. 1 Corinthians was probably Paul's reply to this letter.

Paul visits Corinth

After this, Paul learned, perhaps from Timothy who had returned from Corinth to Ephesus, that his letter was having no effect. At that point he decided to pay a short visit to Corinth to see for himself what was happening. No such visit is mentioned in Acts, but it is certainly implied in 2 Corinthians 2:1; 12:14 and 13:1. On this visit he must have come, as he had threatened in 1 Corinthians 4:21, 'with a rod', for he later referred to it as a 'painful visit' (2 Corinthians 2:1).

Another letter

After his return to Ephesus, Paul sent Titus with a much stronger letter, written 'out of much affliction and anguish of heart', as he puts it in 2 Corinthians 2:4. Some think this letter is now preserved in 2 Corinthians 10 – 13, where Paul launches a vigorous counter-attack on those who were questioning his apostolic authority, something which was almost certainly the subject of this third letter.

Good news from Corinth

Paul then left for Macedonia, having been forced out of Ephesus (Acts 20:1). In Macedonia he met up with Titus again, who brought welcome news of a change of attitude in the Corinthian church. He also carried an invitation for Paul to go to Corinth (2 Corinthians 7:5–16).

Paul writes 2 Corinthians

Paul sent back to Corinth with Titus a more compassionate letter, expressing his great joy. This letter is probably what we now know as 2 Corinthians 1 – 9. He also took this opportunity to write on other subjects: the relation of teachers and hearers; the hope of a life after death; the general theme of salvation; and the collection which he was organizing for the Jerusalem church. If 2 Corinthians 10 – 13 belongs to this same letter, Paul must have heard news of a further revolt against his authority at Corinth while he was actually in the process of writing to them, which led him to defend his own position as an accredited apostle of Christ. Some scholars think that 2 Corinthians 10 – 13, rather than being earlier than 2 Corinthians 1 – 9, or written at the same time, was actually sent later, when Paul's authority was again being undermined.

So much for the circumstances in which these letters came to be written. But what was Paul actually saying in them? In trying to answer that question, it will be best to pick out certain features of what Paul said, from which it will be possible to gain a picture of the situation in the church at Corinth. 1 Corinthians provides most information about this, and so we will focus particularly on that letter.

1 Corinthians

Life in Christ (1 Corinthians 1:10 – 4:21)

One of the things that characterized the city of Corinth was the diverse nature of its society. Its position as an important seaport on one of the busiest routes in the Mediterranean ensured this. In the streets of Corinth, military personnel from Rome, mystics from the east, and Jews from Palestine continually rubbed shoulders with the philosophers of Greece. When Paul had proclaimed the good news about Jesus in this city, it was a cross-section of people from this cosmopolitan society who responded and came together to form the Christian church in Corinth.

Not surprisingly, men and women from such different spiritual and intellectual backgrounds brought with them into the church some very diverse concepts and ideas. While Paul was there the various sections of the young congregation were held together, but on his departure these new Christians began to work out for themselves the implications of their Christian faith, and naturally began to produce different answers.

A DIVIDED CHURCH

As a result the church at Corinth had, for all practical purposes, been divided into four different groups, to which Paul refers in 1 Corinthians 1:10–17. Some were claiming that their spiritual allegiance was to Paul, others to Apollos, others to Cephas, while yet others claimed only to belong to Christ (1:12–13). These four parties clearly reflect the diverse backgrounds of the Corinthian Christians:

■ The 'Paul party' would consist of libertines. They were people who had heard Paul's original preaching on the freedom of the Christian and concluded from it that, once they had responded to the Christian gospel, they could live as they liked. This was exactly what the Judaizers, who opposed Paul in Galatia, had said would happen when the Christian message was declared without making people obey the Old Testament Law. Paul, in fact, always emphasized that, far from relieving Christians of moral obligations, his message actually made deeper demands of them. But this danger of lawlessness ('antinomianism') was always present in his churches.

■ The 'Cephas party' were undoubtedly legalists. They were people like the Judaizers, who believed that the Christian life meant the strict observance of traditional Jewish practices, both ritual and moral. Many of them had probably been members of the synagogue when they heard of Jesus the Messiah.

■ The 'Apollos party' were probably devotees of the classical Greek outlook. Apollos is mentioned in Acts 18:24–28, where he is described as a Jew from Alexandria, 'an eloquent man, well versed in the scriptures'. Alexandria in Egypt had a large Jewish population, and several influential and gifted teachers lived and worked there, both before and after the New Testament period. The best known among these was Philo (about 20BC–AD45), a Hellenistic Jew who specialized in interpreting the scriptures, in accordance with the concepts of Greek philosophy, to demonstrate that Moses and others had already anticipated what the philosophers said centuries later. As an educated Alexandrian Jew, it is likely that Apollos would have been steeped in this kind of scriptural interpretation. He would naturally be an acceptable teacher to those Christians at Corinth with a Greek philosophical background.

■ The 'Christ party' probably consisted of a group who considered themselves to be above the parties that had developed around the personalities of ordinary mortals. They wanted a direct contact with Christ, in the same way as they had experienced direct mystical contacts

Corinth was a city placed at a major junction of trade-routes. Prominent among its ruins is the Temple of Apollo, behind which rises the rock acrocorinth.

with gods in the mystery religions. If Serapis could be called 'lord', so could Christ. But Paul made it clear to them that in fact, 'no one can say "Jesus is Lord" except by the Holy Spirit' (1 Corinthians 12:3). What they were trying to do was exchange one mystery god for another. Since this kind of belief often led to libertinism in practice, these people might well have found themselves aligned alongside the 'Paul party' on some important ethical issues.

THE CONFUSION AT CORINTH

As we read through 1 Corinthians we can see how each of these groups was at work, spreading its own ideas and emphases. *The libertines*, who claimed to follow Paul, encouraged the whole church not to worry about moral norms (5:1–13). *The legalists*, claiming to follow Cephas' example, raised the old question of what kind of food Christians should eat, though this time the argument was over food that had been offered in sacrifice to traditional deities before being sold to the public (8 – 9). *The philosophers*, followers of Apollos, were insisting that they had a form of wisdom that was superior to anything Paul had spoken about (1:18–25). *The mystics*, claiming they were following Christ, were inclined to argue that the sacraments of the church acted in a magical way, and therefore they need not worry about any possible consequences of their lifestyle (10:1–13). The resurrection had already come, they claimed, and they knew it had because they themselves had been raised in a mystical way with Christ (15:12–19). They claimed they were now living on a super-spiritual level of existence, far beyond the grasp of the followers of Paul, Cephas or Apollos (see also 4:8).

Various strands in these different types of extremism led, in the second century, to the emergence of Gnosticism, and here in Corinth we can see the first stirrings in that direction. But at the time, Paul was not concerned with giving a name to this movement; all he saw was one of his largest churches being thrown into a state of considerable confusion by fanatics operating from at least these four different directions.

This was completely contrary to all that he understood the Christian message to be. He had told the Galatians that belief in Christ would create a new community of equality and freedom for all Christians, something that he had himself experienced as he moved from city to city, and found new friends among the unlikeliest of people simply because they had been united in Christ.

THE ANSWER IN CHRIST

He knew, therefore, that the answer to the Corinthian situation must be found in Christ. Neither Paul himself, nor Cephas, nor Apollos, nor the kind of 'Christ' that was being followed in Corinth, could achieve any lasting result. When he had first visited Corinth, Paul declared the cross of Christ and his resurrection to be 'of first importance' in the understanding of the Christian faith (1 Corinthians 15:3–7; 1:18–25). Whatever Paul, Apollos or Cephas had done in their own name was of no lasting consequence, for this was the only basis on which men and women of diverse cultures could be reunited. So Paul repeated his basic message as the answer to the problems of the Corinthian church: 'no other foundation can anyone lay than that which is laid, which is Jesus Christ' (3:11).

Having set out his own starting point, Paul went on to look at some of the specific problems of the church at Corinth – problems concerned with their attitudes to secular standards and institutions, and to one another in the gatherings of the church.

Life in the world (1 Corinthians 5:1 – 11:1)

Though Christians enjoyed certain privileges by virtue of their new life in Christ, they still had to live in the same social context as everyone else. In Corinth, three main areas posed problems concerning the Christian's relationships with non-Christians.

CHRISTIAN BEHAVIOUR

At least two of the 'parties' in the Corinthian church claimed to have a theological reason for ignoring the accepted Christian standards of morality and, in the central part of his letter, Paul mentions three specific matters which had come to his attention in this context:

■ **Permissiveness** One thing that particularly worried him was the report that 'there is immorality among you... of a kind that is not found even among pagans; for a man is living with his father's wife' (5:1). Paul was never one for taking drastic action against people with whom he disagreed, but this kind of behaviour was so serious that he felt he had no alternative but to instruct the church members not to associate with the individual concerned until he was prepared to change his lifestyle. He told them, 'When you are assembled, and my spirit is present, with the power of our Lord Jesus, you are to deliver this man to Satan for the destruction of the flesh, that his spirit may be saved in the day of the Lord Jesus' (5:4–5). The precise meaning of this instruction is not especially clear, but the main point is obvious: this kind of wrongdoing was, in Paul's view, so serious that it must be completely eradicated, and if the person concerned was not prepared to change, then he must leave the Christian community – though his final spiritual fate was not the business of the local church, but would be revealed 'in the day of the Lord Jesus'.

■ **Freedom** Once again Paul had to emphasize that freedom in Christ does not mean the freedom to be immoral (6:12–20). Christians are not free to do as they please, but free to serve God, to whom they belong (6:19–20).

An upper-class Roman couple.

■ **Marriage** One of the questions that the Corinthians had asked Paul was also concerned with marriage and divorce (7:1–40). In replying, Paul permits Christians to marry (7:1–9), though he himself was not married, and could 'wish that all were as I myself am' (7:7). He forbids divorce (7:10–11), except in a case where a non-Christian partner deserts a Christian (7:12–16), and he recommends that the Corinthian Christians should remain in their present condition, either married or single (7:17–24), though he recommends celibacy as the preferable state (7:25–40).

This was clearly advice given for a specific situation that had arisen in Corinth, and it is interesting to note the way Paul separates his own advice and opinion from what he believed to be the teaching of Christ. He felt that he had Jesus' authority for saying there should be no divorce among Christians (7:10–11), but of the other issues with which he deals, in one case he makes it plain that it is 'not the Lord' who is speaking (7:12), and in another he merely says, 'I think that I have the Spirit of God' (7:40).

This is the sort of passage that has given rise to much discussion, for Paul says some exceedingly odd things here. Why does he seem to place so little value on marriage? No doubt Paul's own experience has played its part, for as a rabbi he must have been married himself at one time (all rabbis had to be), though he clearly was not at this point. The most likely explanation of his own situation is that he was divorced, possibly as a result of becoming a Christian. But there was a more fundamental reason behind his advice here, and what he recommends was based on pure pragmatism: given the precarious and unstable state of the Corinthian church at the time (7:26), there were many more important things to be done than making arrangements for weddings.

Jesus himself had said something not altogether different: 'If any one comes to me and does not hate his own father and mother and wife and children and brothers and sisters, yes, and even his own life, he cannot be my disciple' (Luke 14:26), and there is a striking similarity between this and 1 Corinthians 7:29–31. Jesus was certainly not against marriage and family life, and other passages in Paul's writings demonstrate that he also held marriage in high regard. Here, it was a question of practical priorities and, in dealing with what he perceived to be a desperate situation, drastic action was called for.

CHRISTIANS AND THE CIVIL LAW

Another thing that concerned Paul was the way Christians in Corinth were quarrelling with each other, and then going to the civil law courts to sort out their grievances. Paul had to condemn this practice out of hand. For one thing, it was quite absurd that Christians, who claimed to be brothers and sisters, should go to secular courts at all; when a quarrel arises in a family, it should not be necessary to go to court with it, and surely some member of the church community ought to have been wise enough to sort out these problems (6:1–6). But what disturbed Paul even more was that such acrimonious quarrels were arising in the first place. Christians ought to follow the example set to them by Christ, and 'suffer wrong' rather than create division in the Christian community (6:7–8). In the light of what God has done for them in Christ, their petty bickerings fade into insignificance (6:9–11).

EVERYDAY LIFE

It was possible for Christians to live independently of the secular courts, but it was more difficult to avoid other religiously charged aspects of life in a city like Corinth. For the Corinthian church, this focused on the question of food, particularly meat. It became an issue because Corinth, in common with other Hellenistic cities, had no regular butchers' shops. No matter what its source, the purchase of meat almost always had religious connotations. The best and largest source of meat would be the traditional Greek shrines, where animals were sacrificed to honour the deities. In those cities with a substantial Jewish population, meat butchered according to the rituals of the Hebrew scriptures would also be available. Either way, some Christians found themselves with a problem. Relationships with the Jewish community were often difficult so, for the most part, Jewish butchers would not wish to supply them – nor, for their part, would Gentile Christians wish to buy from them, since that would look as if they were accepting the validity of the Torah's dietary prescriptions. But what about meat from Greek temples? Insofar

as they might have considered the possible religious ramifications of buying meat from this source, most Christians argued that, since the deities honoured there did not exist, the fact that animals had been offered to them in sacrifice was of no consequence. Others, however, were less certain, and felt that by buying meat of this kind they were somehow encouraging and sharing in the worship associated with it. What, then, were they to do? Paul took up this matter in 1 Corinthians 8:1 – 11:1, in which the following four points are central to his advice:

Some of the Christians at Corinth had scruples about eating the meat available, since it may have been offered at pagan temples. This inscription is from the meat market (*macellum*) in Corinth.

■ Christians are, of course, free to eat food that had been offered to honour Greek deities, since such gods do not exist. But those who understand this must also be sensitive to the concerns of those who might see the matter differently. Those Christians who are 'enlightened' should occasionally be prepared to forgo the freedom to eat food bought from local shrines, out of consideration for those others who might be offended by such behaviour (8:1–13).

■ This was the kind of concession that Paul himself had made, in a different context. As an apostle, Paul had the right to be supported by God's people, and he even alludes to the teaching of Jesus to prove it: 'the Lord commanded that those who proclaim the gospel should get their living by the gospel' (9:14). However, he reminds the Corinthians that he had given up his right to be maintained in this way, and instead had been willing to place himself under restrictions so that his message might be accepted by all kinds of people: 'though I am free with respect to all, I have made myself a slave to all, so that I may win more of them' (9:19).

■ Christians should also recognize that there could be real dangers in adopting an essentially magical attitude to spirituality. Some of the Corinthians apparently took the view that the Christian sacraments provided them with some sort of immunity from traditional Greek rituals, so that they could take part without necessarily endorsing all that was going on. Paul drew attention to several episodes in the history of Israel that showed this was not so, and argued that it was naïve to

imagine they could share in the Lord's supper one day, and honour the local deities the next, without compromising their integrity (10:1–22).
■ The general principle to be followed in reaching practical decisions on all these matters was not to do anything that would lead others astray, even things that might be right in themselves, but to 'do all to the glory of God' (10:23 – 11:1).

Life in the church (1 Corinthians 11:2 – 15:58)

Paul had been asked the answer to several specific questions that were puzzling the church at Corinth. Some of them we have already considered, questions concerning marriage and divorce, and food bought from local shrines. But there were others, concerned with the church's worship (11:2 – 14:40) and beliefs (15:1–58).

THE CHURCH'S WORSHIP (1 CORINTHIANS 11:2 – 14:40)

As the Christians in Corinth met for worship, trying to put into practice what Paul had taught them, three practical difficulties had arisen:
■ **Freedom in worship** It seems that Paul had taught them very much the same things as he had passed on to the churches of Galatia. Two of the basic points of this message had been that in Christ there was to be no distinction of race, class or sex (Galatians 3:28); and that Christ had given Christians a new freedom (Galatians 5:1). In practical terms of the church's worship, this meant that Paul, contrary to the Jewish custom of the day, allowed women to play a full part in the Christian ministry. He had passed on 'traditions' to that effect to the Corinthian church (1 Corinthians 11:2), traditions which the church members had observed. But they misunderstood the character of Christian freedom, and some women, who were taking a leading part in the church's services, were doing in God's presence things they would not have done in front of their neighbours.

The prevailing social custom of the time laid down that respectable, modest women did not appear in public with their heads uncovered. The Corinthian Christians, however, argued that they were set free, even from the norms of their culture, and that they should be able to express this freedom before God in the church. For Paul, this was a similar situation to the one which had arisen over buying meat, except that in this case it was not other Christians who were being offended, but the wider community. Since Paul saw a major aspect of the church's responsibility to be calling others to follow Christ, he invited the Corinthians to adopt the same strategy as he himself had outlined previously: 'To the Jews I became as a Jew, in order to win Jews... To those outside the law I became as one outside the law... that I might win those outside the law... I have become all things to all people, that I might by all means save some' (9:20, 21, 22). Within this frame of reference, he advised that women taking a public part in the church's worship ought to follow the prevailing social custom and do so with their heads veiled, even if in an ideal world it might have seemed like a limitation of their Christian freedom (11:2–16).

■ **Morals and worship** The way the church was observing the Lord's supper (eucharist) also gave cause for concern (11:17–34). Instead of following the instructions which Jesus himself gave, and which Paul had delivered to them at an earlier stage (11:23–26), some of the Corinthians were making the service into an occasion for feasting and merriment by bringing along their own food, and having private feasts – feasts which they ought to have held in their own homes (11:22).

The party divisions that Paul was so much against were even rearing their ugly heads at the Lord's table (11:18–19), because different groups were happy with eating different foods and, in addition, those who were richer had much more to eat than those who were poor, who were being left on the sidelines. All this division, not to mention the accompanying revelry and drunkenness, was dishonouring both to the purpose of their gathering and to the Christians themselves. They were giving no thought to what they were doing, and some of them had brought upon themselves the judgment which they deserved (11:29–32).

■ **Charismatic gifts and worship** Another very important feature in the Corinthian church was the exercise of spiritual gifts. Basic to Christian experience in the apostolic churches was the conviction that Christians were people empowered by the Holy Spirit. They were 'charismatics', people with *charismata* (a Greek word which literally means 'gifts of grace'). These spiritual gifts included speaking in ecstatic tongues (*glossolalia*), the interpretation of such tongues, prophecy (as in Acts 13:1–2), and the working of miracles by the apostles (Acts 19.11–12).

The Corinthian Christians possessed all these gifts and many more in abundance, and they were so eager to exercise them that several people could be taking part in church worship at the same time. This was clearly an unsatisfactory way of going on, and Paul had to remind them that 'God is not a God of confusion but of peace' (1 Corinthians 14:33), which meant that, when the gifts were being used, it could be taken for granted that, if God was truly inspiring them, this should occur in a way that would lead to the building up of the whole church (12:7).

Paul had no problem with recognizing the validity of all the various charismatic manifestations that had appeared in Corinth. He emphasized that every one of them was God-given and each, therefore, had its rightful place in gatherings of the congregation. Just as the human body has different parts, each of which must make its contribution to the smooth operation of the body, so it is in the church: each of the gifts possessed by different members of the church should contribute to the smooth running of the whole (12:14–31).

Not every Christian would be given one of the more spectacular gifts, such as speaking in tongues, but they were all of value. Over and above this, one gift should be common to all of them, namely love, which was the only basis on which the other charismatic endowments should be either desired or sought after (14:1–2).

THE CHURCH'S BELIEF (1 CORINTHIANS 15:1–58)

Finally, Paul turns to what he regarded as the core of essential Christian belief which, coincidentally, also happened to be one of the most contentious issues engaging the Corinthian Christians: the resurrection of Jesus.

Some members of the church were claiming that, in their mystical experiences, they had already been raised to a new spiritual level above that achieved by more ordinary Christians, a notion that Paul believed to be linked with a fundamental misunderstanding about the resurrection of Jesus. He deals with it in two ways:

■ Firstly he reminds the Corinthians of the firm historical foundation on which belief in the resurrection of Jesus was based (15:3–11). In doing this he provides the earliest New Testament account of belief in the resurrection of Jesus.

■ Secondly, he goes on to show how, if the resurrection of Jesus was a material occurrence (as he and the other apostles believed it was), this must be a guarantee that Christians also will be raised on the last day, in the same way as Jesus was raised from the dead. Therefore, in view of the centrality of Jesus' resurrection to the whole of Christian belief, those who denied its material reality, by re-imagining it as a series of mystical experiences, were actually denying the basis of the Christian faith, for 'if the dead are not raised, then Christ has not been raised. If Christ has not been raised, your faith is futile and you are still in your sins... we are of all people most to be pitied' (15:16–17, 18).

More arguments in Corinth

This was not the end of Paul's correspondence with the Christians at Corinth, though he must have been at least partly successful in persuading them to change their minds, for we hear nothing more of questions about the resurrection, marriage, or things like meat purchased in the local shrines. But there were still problems, this time especially connected with the arrival of messengers claiming to be 'apostles' sent from the church in Jerusalem (2 Corinthians 11:1–15). Paul had already dealt with people like this in the churches of Galatia, but those who came to Corinth were not 'Judaizers' in the strict sense. They were not trying to persuade the Corinthians to become Jews by accepting circumcision and the Old Testament Law. Rather they were aiming to persuade them to transfer their allegiance away from Paul to the more conservatively inclined leaders of the original church in Jerusalem.

Paul had apparently chosen to visit the church at Corinth while these people were in residence there, and this is the 'painful visit' to which he refers in 2 Corinthians 2:1. It was certainly painful for Paul, for he was insulted by these false apostles and their claims that his authority was questionable. He left in a hurry, something he later recognized as a mistake for it seemed to confirm what his opponents were saying about him (2 Corinthians 1:12–22). As a result the Corinthian Christians were left in a turmoil. Who were the real apostles, and how could they tell the difference between true and false? Their loyalty swung from one to the other and, in order to clarify the issues, Paul wrote to them yet again. The letter he wrote this time was 2 Corinthians.

While 1 Corinthians has a clear line of argument from beginning to end, 2 Corinthians has quite a different feel to it, and often reads more like an anthology of Paul's advice on different subjects than the kind of progressive discussion we find in other letters. For this reason, some interpreters think this is just what it is: a collection of two or three letters that were originally written quite independently, and later joined together by an editor. This would not be an unusual procedure in the ancient world and, in principle, there is no reason why a collector of Paul's letters should not have done this. The train of thought in 2 Corinthians certainly does seem to change direction rather abruptly at several points:

■ 2:14 – 7:4 is quite different from what precedes and follows it. Moreover, 7:5 makes quite good sense if it is read as the continuation of 2:13. Even within this section itself, however, 6:14 – 7:1 seems to break the sense of what goes before and after it. Could it be that this section in particular contains what were originally separate letters, perhaps including some of those which we know Paul certainly wrote to Corinth, but which are not separately identified anywhere in the New Testament?

■ Chapters 8 and 9 seem to deal with the same topic (the collection for the church in Jerusalem), but with no reference to each other. In particular, chapter 9 seems to introduce the subject quite independently of what has already been said about it in the previous chapter. Could 2 Corinthians 9:1–15 be another separate letter, this time written before all the troubles began, to recommend Titus and some others to the church at Corinth and to encourage the Christians there to give generously for Jerusalem?

■ Chapters 10 – 13 are in sharp contrast with chapters 1 – 9. At the end of chapter 9, Paul expresses satisfaction that the Corinthians have sorted out their problems, yet at the beginning of chapter 10 he is on the offensive again. So were chapters 10 – 13 originally written as a separate letter at a time when the situation was more desperate?

■ All these suggestions make good sense, especially since we know that Paul wrote more than just two letters to Corinth. The major argument against supposing that 2 Corinthians is this kind of compilation is the somewhat random way in which these other shorter sections seem to be incorporated into the present text. For example, why would a collector of Paul's letters have mixed them all up with each other, inserting separate, shorter letters halfway through longer ones in such a way as to disrupt the sense of both? Would it not have been more natural to have included them in sequence, one after the other? For this reason, a majority of commentators find themselves convinced only that chapters 10 – 13 are a different letter, later than chapters 1 – 9, on the grounds that this is preferable to the only other possible explanation for the change in tone from 9:15 to 10:1, namely that some other information had come to Paul's attention at the very moment when he reached the end of what is now chapter 9. But, because of the apparently illogical juxtaposition of the other material, the consensus is that the apparent changes of subject matter between 2:14 – 7:4, 8:1–24 and 9:1–15 are best understood as digressions in Paul's own thinking.

What, then, does 2 Corinthians have to say about these fresh problems faced by Paul in his relationships with the Corinthian Christians? The letter falls naturally into four main sections.

Facing up to problems (2 Corinthians 1:3 – 2:13)

Paul knew that he needed to explain the turbulent nature of his relationship with the Corinthian church. But there was also the question of true and false apostleship, and he clarifies his position on both these topics in his opening thanksgiving section (1:3–11). Here he draws attention not only to his affection for the church in Corinth, but also to his conviction that suffering and weakness are, in some way, an inevitable part of the true service of God. To cope with persecution, Paul needs to trust wholeheartedly in God, but he also needs the prayerful support of his readers. This is why he appears less self-confident and aggressive than his opponents, for he does not regard his relationship with his converts as a one-sided enterprise: he needs their prayers just as much as they need his guidance.

Paul also needed to reassure the Corinthians that he could be trusted. His unexpected visits and letters, and last minute changes of plan had given them the impression that he was unstable (1:12 – 2:4). They had concluded that he was afraid to visit them because he knew at heart the claims of the 'false apostles' were true. Paul obviously felt these criticisms deeply, and defends himself against the charge that he was acting selfishly. Nothing could be further from the truth: he had written a letter rather than making a visit because he hoped that would be a less painful way of correcting them: 'my purpose was not to make you sad, but to make you realize how much I love you all' (2:4).

Personal animosities must also be put right – and both Paul and the church should be prepared to forgive those who have been particularly offensive (2:5–11). Paul obviously refers here to a specific person – according to some, perhaps the man mentioned in 1 Corinthians 5:5, who was cohabiting with his own stepmother, but more likely someone else who had been especially abusive to Paul himself.

What is an apostle? (2 Corinthians 2:14 – 7:4)

The major point at issue was Paul's authority as an apostle, and he introduces this subject with an expression of his own gratitude to God for his experience as a participant in 'Christ's victory procession' (2:14). Yet, although he is in such a close personal relationship with Christ, this does not allow him to boast in a triumphalist way about his own abilities, for endowment with the Holy Spirit brings great responsibilities, and it is the recognition of this that Paul believed made him different from the other so-called 'apostles' who had arrived in Corinth: 'We are not like so many others, who handle God's message as if it were cheap merchandise; but because God has sent us, we speak with sincerity... as servants of Christ' (2:17).

Unlike those who had come from Jerusalem, Paul did not depend on official letters to establish his credentials, but was content for the validity of his work to be judged by its results in the changed lives of his converts, and the quality of his own personal lifestyle (3:1–18). If Christians are truly serving God, then God's presence should be visible for all to see: 'All of us... reflect the glory of the Lord... and that same glory, coming from the Lord, who is the Spirit, transforms us into his likeness in an ever greater degree of glory' (3:18), something that he identifies as one of the distinct advantages of Christian faith over other spiritual traditions (3:4–17). Even so, this provided no sort of guarantee that apostles could expect to live on a different plane from other people, unaffected by the ordinary problems of everyday life (4:1–15). For though the gospel is a powerful, life-giving message, God chose to entrust it to 'common clay pots', who are 'often troubled... sometimes in doubt... badly hurt' (4:7, 8, 9). Jesus himself had had the same experience, but after the cross had come the resurrection, and this for Paul provided the key to the Christian life. In Galatians 2:19–20 he had emphasized that the secret of his faith was the presence of the living Christ within him, and the same theme recurs here: 'we are always in danger of death for Jesus' sake, in order that his life may be seen in this mortal body of ours' (4:11). For Paul this was where the emphasis ought rightly to be placed: the messengers of the gospel must not be confused with the message itself, and the fact that the 'spiritual treasure' is in 'common clay pots' draws attention to the fact that 'the supreme power belongs to God, not to us' (4:7).

Reflecting on the various physical dangers that he had faced led Paul onto the subject of life after death. This had already been a major topic in 1 Corinthians, but here the perspective has changed and he asks different questions, no doubt as a result of his recent narrow escapes from death (presumably in Ephesus, 2 Corinthians 1:9). What he says in 5:1–10 makes this one of the most complex passages in all his letters, and has given rise to much speculation about the nature of his thinking on the subject. But two things are quite clear: he is still opposed to the views of those Corinthians who had been claiming that 'resurrection' was a matter of a person's inner spiritual experience; and he still clings to the Jewish belief in a bodily existence after death, rather than resorting to the Greek view of an immortal soul that would survive the disposable body. However, he continues to insist (as he had done in 1 Corinthians 15:42–57) that the resurrection existence is continuous with this life, though not identical with it, for he envisages that God will replace 'the earthly tent we live in' with 'a house not made with hands, eternal in the heavens' (5:1).

Throughout, he maintains the tension between present and future that is so familiar from the teaching of Jesus, insisting that even the final resurrection state would only be the final outworking of what God was already doing in the lives of Christian people. This is why the way Christians think, the way they behave, and their standards and values, should reflect here and now the reality of God's living presence: 'No longer, then, do we judge anyone by human standards... When anyone is joined to Christ, there is a new being; the old is gone, the new has come' (5:16, 17).

Looked at in this light, Paul's sufferings could in no way contradict his claim to be an apostle. On the contrary, he regarded them as the clearest possible demonstration of the truth of that claim (6:1–10). By now, Paul felt that he had explained himself in more detail than was necessary, and concludes by appealing to his readers to show the same degree of honesty about their own motivation (6:11–13).

He then moved on to warn them that the Christian lifestyle should be wholly different from a secular lifestyle. Christians must reflect God's own values and standards (6:14 – 7:1) by setting an appropriate distance between themselves and the prevailing values of the culture. It has often been supposed that Paul was here referring to matters of personal morality, especially marriage relationships. These would probably be covered by what he says, but his advice is far more wide-ranging, for he is encouraging his readers to be prepared to put God first in every area of life, not just where they find it convenient.

Looking to the future (2 Corinthians 7:5 – 9:15)

Paul now moves on to the effects of his painful letters, which had apparently led to a change of heart on the part of the Corinthians – a change which Titus had reported (7:5–16). It was presumably on this basis that Paul felt it was now appropriate to invite them to contribute to the collection he was organizing for the financial relief of the church in Jerusalem (8:1 – 9:15). This was not the first time the Corinthians had heard of this (1 Corinthians 16:1–4), but their stormy relationship with Paul had prevented anything being done about it earlier.

Paul urges them to be generous not simply out of a sense of duty, but as a loving response to what God had done for them. The coming of Jesus into their lives had been an unmerited act of God's goodness, and they should meet the needs of others in the same attitude: 'You know the grace of our Lord Jesus Christ; rich as he was, he made himself poor for your sake, in order to make you rich by means of his poverty' (8:9). He also believed that such an act of generosity would improve relations between the purely Gentile churches, which he had established, and the more Jewish congregations back in Palestine (9:1–15).

Authority and charisma (2 Corinthians 10:1 – 13:10)

In this section Paul again takes the offensive. If this was not a separate
letter, it is necessary to imagine that he must have heard of yet further
challenges to his authority, even while he was in the process of writing.
This time it seems he was being criticized because of his personality.
'Paul's letters are severe and strong,' his Corinthian opponents were
saying, 'but when he is with us in person, he is weak, and his words are
nothing!' (10:10). Clearly, he lacked the charismatic appeal of the 'false
apostles' who had come to Corinth. They did not suffer from self-doubt
and persecution as he did, but were always boasting about their own
mystical experiences and spiritual maturity. Paul does not answer these
charges comprehensively. That had already been done in the previous
discussion of the relationship between weakness and power in the lives
of God's servants. He tackles the subject less systematically here,
suggesting that these others only seem so impressive because 'They
make up their own standards to measure themselves by, and they judge
themselves by their own standards!' (10:12). Indeed, they do worse than
that, for Paul accuses the Corinthians of accepting 'anyone who comes
to you and preaches a different Jesus, not the one we preached; and you
accept a spirit and a gospel completely different from the Spirit and the
gospel you received from us!' (11:4).

He then launches into a wide-ranging attack on those who were
questioning his own credentials on this spurious basis – dealing in turn
with his relationship to the Corinthian church (11:1–6), his style of life
(11:7–11), and the ultimate source of his authority (11:12–15). Far from
showing him to be second-rate, his suffering and persecution actually
demonstrate the reality of his calling (11:16–33).

The 'false apostles' also seem to have been claiming more
spectacular manifestations of the Holy Spirit's gifts than Paul. There is
plenty of evidence to show this was a recurring problem in Corinthian
church life (1 Corinthians 12 – 14). Paul recognized that boasting about
such things does no good, but he also needed to set the record straight,
and point out that he too had 'visions and revelations given me by the
Lord' (12:1). Nevertheless, he still returns to the theme of suffering and
weakness as the cornerstone of his apostolic status, arguing that it is
only as people recognize their own weaknesses and trust entirely in
God that they can speak of being truly Christian (12:7–10).

Finally, Paul reminds them that he will be visiting Corinth again, and
they would do well to put their lives in order before his arrival. Despite
what his opponents have claimed, he is prepared to denounce them face
to face, though it would be so much happier for everyone if they would
get back to the basis of the gospel first, and recognize that it is only
when they each acknowledge their human weaknesses that God's power
can work effectively in their lives (13:1–10).

So Paul came to the end of the most complicated correspondence
he ever wrote. Like Galatians, the Corinthian letters were written in the

white heat of controversy, which only adds to our difficulties in understanding them. Paul was under attack from his friends as well as his enemies, something that must have given him considerable reason to pause and think out his gospel again. He wanted to avoid the pitfalls of the past, without in any sense compromising his basic position that in Christ all barriers of race, sex and social standing are removed, and all men and women stand equal in the freedom given to them by the Holy Spirit. It was probably thoughts of this kind that dictated the form of Paul's next major letter, which is quite different from any of those we have looked at so far.

Looking towards Rome

Towards the end of his extended dealings with the Corinthian church, Paul visited the area of Corinth, and spent some three months there. After this, he was intending to go to Jerusalem with the delegates from the Gentile churches, who were taking a gift to the Jewish church. Later, he hoped to visit Rome, before perhaps going further west to Spain. It was natural for Paul to wish to visit Rome, but the Christian situation there was quite different from that in other cities with which Paul had dealings, and would need some careful advance planning. For one thing, the Roman church had not been founded by Paul, which meant he needed to be careful about appearing to meddle in a situation which was none of his business. In addition, the church in Rome did not consist of one single congregation, but of a whole network of smaller groups, meeting in different people's homes around the city. This feature of Roman Christianity could almost certainly be traced back to the Jewish community there, which was similarly fragmented, with many different synagogues ranging from the most conservative to the most liberal. The Christian cause certainly had its origins in these synagogues, and no doubt the spectrum of Christian belief was equally wide, and largely defined along the same lines, except with the additional question of Gentile believers and their responsibility in terms of the Jewish Law and traditions. Though some Christians in Rome admired Paul, others must have been highly suspicious of him, particularly in relation to what they knew of his attitude to Jewish customs. For all these reasons, Paul felt the time was right for him to restate his message in a form that would not easily be open to misinterpretation, either by sympathizers or by opponents, and so he decided to prepare for his visit to the capital by writing a letter to the various factions within the Christian community there, containing a reasoned statement of his own beliefs. This was the letter to the Romans.

Romans

Though Romans has been regarded as a comprehensive summary of the whole of Paul's thinking, this is a misleading and unhelpful way of looking at it. He was certainly in a more reflective mood when he wrote Romans than when he penned Galatians, or any of the Corinthian letters. But there are several important aspects of Paul's thinking that do not feature here at all. In particular there is no mention of his belief in the future return of Jesus, or of life after death – both subjects on which we know he had significant things to say. What he says on the nature of the church in Romans is also very limited when compared with his fuller exposition of the same theme in 1 Corinthians.

Romans is best understood as a more carefully articulated account of some of the major themes of Galatians and 1 and 2 Corinthians (1 Corinthians in particular). As we noted in an earlier chapter, Romans and Galatians cover so much of the same ground that it has often been supposed they must have been composed around the same time as each other. But Romans is more carefully nuanced than Galatians, and Paul takes greater care to spell out his arguments. It is probably more accurate to describe Romans as the argument of Galatians, as it looked when viewed through the spectacles of the struggles he had faced in Corinth. In writing it, Paul was conscious of two audiences. The

It is unclear how the Christian church in Rome began. It included people from different ethnic roots, and even some from the Emperor's household. The forum, seen here, was at the city centre. Rome at this time had a population of over one million.

most obvious one comprised the Roman Christians, to whom he would send it as a summary of his beliefs, to smooth the way for his expected arrival in the city. But before that, he was going to Jerusalem, where he knew he would come under attack from the Jewish establishment, both from those who followed Jesus as Messiah, and those who did not. Though he had forcefully dismissed the arguments of the Judaizers in Galatians, he realized that there was some substance to a few of the claims they had been making. Both in Galatia and Corinth, the way he expressed his beliefs had proved to be easily misunderstood and misrepresented. Now was the time to deal with this, and to refine those aspects of his message that needed clarification, while not watering down the essential elements of his thinking on the place of the Gentiles within the Christian community, and the significance of all that in relation to traditional Jewish observances. He knew that, on his arrival in Jerusalem with the collection, he would need to give a satisfactory account of himself to the church leaders there, and this time he was determined to be more precise than he had previously been in explaining his message. In that context, Romans was a draft of some of the things he intended to say to them.

Because Romans is so closely based on Paul's previous letters to the Galatians and the Corinthians, there is no need to summarize it in such great detail here. The arguments about the Law, and its place in relation to the ancient covenant, are exactly the same in Romans as they were in Galatians, and even the allusions to the Abraham story are repeated. Our discussion is, therefore, deliberately limited to those aspects of the argument that are distinctive or unique to Romans. The letter falls into three major sections.

HOW CHRISTIANS KNOW GOD

The first part of Romans, chapters 1 – 8, is one long theological argument starting with a text from the prophet Habakkuk: 'the just shall live by faith' (Habakkuk 2:4). Here, Paul argues in a way that is already very familiar from Galatians; indeed many of the points he makes are the same. Everyone, whether Jew or Gentile, is under the power of sin. Apart from Christ there is no way of escaping God's judgment (1:18 – 3:20), yet it is possible to receive 'the righteousness of God', that is, release from God's sentence of condemnation and the power to share in God's own goodness. This is something that can be obtained only through faith in Christ, and not by good works (3:21 – 4:25).

As in Galatians, Paul illustrates his theme by reference to the life of Abraham (4:1–25). He then goes on (5:1 – 8:39) to describe the results of this new relationship with God: freedom from God's judgment on sin; freedom from slavery to sin; freedom from the Law; and freedom from death through the working of the Spirit of God in Christ: 'In all these things we are more than conquerors through the one who loved us' (8:37).

These themes had featured before, in either Galatians or Corinthians, but Romans includes several new elements, all of them resulting from Paul's experience of seeing his message misunderstood and misapplied in the churches. This time he deals directly with the problem of antinomianism (6:1 – 8:39) by making it clear that although Christians are set free from the need to observe formal rules, in order to live in ways that would be pleasing to God, this does not mean they have no responsibility for their actions. Though set free from oppressive legalism, they have in fact entered into a new kind of service, not now as 'slaves of sin' (6:17) but 'slaves of God' (6:22). Christians are freed by Christ not so they can do as they please, but so that they may be 'conformed to the image of God's Son', something that is the work of the Holy Spirit empowering them to live in God's way (8:29). All this was already implied in Galatians, but it is spelled out here much more comprehensively, so as to minimize the complaints of the Judaizers against Paul. It is, in effect, the teaching of Galatians as reformulated by Paul after his experiences in Corinth.

ISRAEL AND SALVATION

In chapters 9 – 11 Paul moves on to discuss other aspects of his present understanding of the Law and Judaism more generally. In a very convoluted argument, he reaffirms his pride in his own people and their spiritual heritage, while at the same time struggling to understand why Jesus was not more widely recognized as the Messiah. He goes to some pains to affirm that, while it might seem he is arguing that the Jews as a nation have been completely rejected by God, things are more complex than that, for he still believes in the ancient promises, and also in God's sense of justice and fair play. If Jews seem to be on the sidelines of God's purposes, this is the result of their own choice in rejecting Jesus and the way of 'faith', preferring to stick with the way of 'works'. Even now, though, God's rejection of Israel cannot be final, for there is still a faithful remnant (presumably people like him, 11:1–10), and God's ultimate plan is to bring together people from all races, Jews included (11:11–36).

HOW CHRISTIANS SHOULD BEHAVE

Paul then moves away from strictly theological statements to write about the practical application of God's will in Christian living (12:1 – 15:13). Here, he deals with the Christian's relationship to the church (12:1–8), to other people (12:9–21), and to the state (13:1–10), summing up Christian duty as a whole in the words 'love is the fulfilling of the Law' (13:10). He thereby tried to emphasize again that standards of Christian morality are to be produced not by sets of rules and regulations imposed from outside, but by the power of the Holy Spirit working within the believer. Paradoxically, the outcome of the Spirit's work will be that the Law of God is in fact observed, and the key idea of this law is love. Paul illustrates this by reference to two live issues: the eating of vegetables in preference to meat (14:1 – 15:6) – not for vegetarian reasons, but out of similar concerns to those highlighted in Corinth by the issue of buying meat from Greek shrines; and the general attitude of Jews and Gentiles towards one another within the church (15:7–13).

The final chapter of the letter concludes with many greetings to the various home-based churches in Rome, which in themselves give an interesting insight not only into the diversity of the Roman church, but also into the general mobility of first-century Christians. Paul clearly knew personally many of those he mentions, having previously met them in other cities around the empire.

Paul and his Jewish roots

In recent years, scholars have expended a lot of energy in trying to understand exactly how Paul viewed his faith as a Christian in relation to his ancestral faith within the Jewish tradition. For centuries, it was taken for granted that Paul became a Christian at a point in his life when he was disillusioned with Judaism. Some passages in his letters seem as if they can be understood in that way, and when these were placed alongside strident statements contrasting God's freely given love with human efforts to achieve salvation, it was natural to conclude that Paul was saying dependence on God's grace was the Christian way, while the Jewish way was to try to earn God's approval by doing good things, identified with 'the works of the Law'. This understanding of Paul's thought goes back at least to Martin Luther, the German monk who became one of the leaders of the Protestant Reformation. He himself had been all but destroyed by the legalistic demands of the medieval Catholic tradition, and when he started to read Paul's writings (especially Romans) it was as if Paul was speaking directly to him. It was a truly liberating discovery to realize that achieving God's favour was not a matter of carrying out sufficient good works to merit God's attention, but instead was about recognizing that God had already accomplished all that was necessary for human salvation through the life, death and resurrection of Jesus Christ. As he read further, it almost seemed that Paul was not writing about his own spiritual experiences in first-century Judaism, but was describing with incredible accuracy Luther's own journey of faith many centuries later. For Luther, everything Paul said about Judaism could be read as if it was a detailed comment on the medieval church, and it was inevitable that Luther's own oppressive experiences in that church were in turn read back into the New Testament, so that a detailed correspondence was assumed between the beliefs of the church, and the beliefs of ancient Jews. Just as the church had come to believe that outward ritual by itself was the key to achieving salvation, so it was taken for granted that the Jews must have believed circumcision by itself was an act that could save people. Just as the medieval church leaders had played down God's love and kindness, so too had the Jews, and instead of accepting salvation as a gift from God, they had preferred to rely on external things like circumcision, keeping rules and regulations, and the performance of empty ritual. Since Paul had spoken to Luther's own needs so powerfully, presumably he was wrestling with the same issues himself in ancient Judaism, and therefore the Judaism he knew must have been reduced to the pitiful and pointless effort of trying to earn God's favour by building up religious merit through keeping the law, observing rituals, and so on.

There can be no doubting the profound impact that this insight had on Martin Luther and, through him, on the entire course of subsequent Christian history in the West. It was a correct perception of the problems facing medieval Catholicism. But was it also a true picture either of Paul or of the Judaism with which he was familiar? Protestant – especially Lutheran – scholarship certainly thought so and, for the next 400 years, it was taken for granted that Judaism was based on a very mechanical understanding of God, in which a person's religious duty was defined solely by the keeping of mindless rules and regulations. By contrast, Paul's spirituality was seen as a more spontaneous and immediate response to God, vital and relevant because it broke away from all that. Those sections of the Bible which seem to reflect a more structured approach to faith were questioned, or even rejected, for being secondary interpretations of the core of authentic spirituality. This is what led Luther himself to dismiss the epistle of James as having no value, and inspired more recent Lutheran scholars to draw such sharp distinctions between the life of the truly apostolic church, and what later

Paul and his Jewish roots *continued*

happened as the church became more institutionalized. In the study of the Old Testament also, it led to the prophets being much more highly valued than the priests, who were held to have been responsible for the development of the Law that Paul allegedly found so oppressive in his day.

From time to time, this understanding of Judaism was questioned, not least by Jewish scholars, who were also interested in the origins of Christianity but struggled to recognize their own faith in Paul's letters, as understood through the eyes of Luther. It is not as easy as it might sound to extract a systematic account of Judaism from the disparate writings of the various ancient rabbis – any more than it would be possible to construct a normative account of the whole of Christian belief from the writings of Christians from many times and places. Like the New Testament itself, the writings of the rabbis were addressed to different times and places, and consist of many different styles of literature, ranging from serious exposition of the Hebrew scriptures to jokes told over the meal table. Nevertheless, all the evidence seems to show that ordinary Jews, far from being oppressed by the Law, saw it as God's gift, and regarded the keeping of it not as an unnecessary burden, but as a delight. As the writings of the rabbis were scrutinized, it became obvious that many scholars who had made confident pronouncements about the nature of Jewish beliefs had never consulted any actual Jewish sources at all, but were simply repeating what they had heard from others, much of which was based on Christian opinions which themselves were heavily influenced by Luther's experience. In the early twentieth century, however, such observations were not welcomed. The great social and political upheavals that led to the emergence of the Nazis, and thence to the Holocaust, were already underway in

Carvings of menorah from the synagogue at Corinth.

Europe, and there can be no question that it was politically expedient for Judaism to continue to be portrayed as a primitive and oppressive faith compared with – especially – Protestant Christianity.

By the mid-1970s, the time was right for a reappraisal of these questions, and it came in 1977 with the publication of a book by Ed Sanders, entitled *Paul and Palestinian Judaism*. In it, he reviewed the arguments put forward by earlier scholars, but went on to insist that the most useful way to compare and contrast two faith traditions such as Judaism and Christianity is not so much by asking abstract theological questions about beliefs, but by identifying the inner dynamic of the respective communities through exploration of their 'patterns of religion', which includes two particular questions: 'How do people get into this faith community?' and 'How do they stay in it?' After exhaustive exploration of the Judaism of Paul's day, Sanders suggested that, for all its diversity, there was a common thread in what he called 'covenantal nomism'. This was based on the belief that God's loving actions on behalf of people ('grace') were the foundational starting point, and that the role of people was to respond in obedience to this expression of God's love. In discussing Jesus' ethical teaching in a previous chapter, we have already noticed the significant part played in the Hebrew Bible by this pattern of God's actions followed by human response. The Judaism of Paul's day was fundamentally the same, and on this basis Sanders argued that our starting point for understanding it should be the outworking of God's undeserved love and, therefore, keeping 'works of the Law' was not about 'getting into' the faith community, but was part of what was necessary in order to 'stay in'. On this view, the assumptions of Judaism, far from being diametrically opposed to Paul's Christian faith, were exactly the same.

That being the case, what can we make of Paul? In some passages at least, he does appear to imply that Judaism was about works, and not about faith — indeed, that Israel actively preferred the one to the other (for example, Romans 9:32). If he did not mean what Luther and traditional Protestant interpretation thought he meant, what exactly was he saying? Several possible answers to that question have been proposed:

● Some scholars have sought the answer in the fact that Paul's origins were not with the mainstream of Judaism, as it existed in Palestine, but among Jews of the Dispersion. It has been suggested that Jews living in the wider Roman empire faced different challenges, among which was the influence of Greek ways of thinking, often combined with the ridicule of the traditional Jewish practices that were recommended in the Torah. Under this kind of pressure, Jews had been forced to become more defensive about the centrality of practices such as circumcision, sabbath keeping, food regulations, and so on, which in turn had led to a narrow legalism in which the externals became more important than the faith. If it could be sustained, this would be a neat way of solving the problem, as it would enable both Jewish (Palestinian rabbis) and Christian (Paul) sources of written information to be correct, with the apparent confusion being blamed on a form of Hellenistic Judaism that no longer exists, and was never in any case the mainstream. However, the distinction between Palestinian and Hellenistic Judaism, which this presupposes, is highly problematic, as Palestine was an integral part of the Hellenistic world, and the New Testament itself attests to the presence and influence of Hellenistic Jews, even in Jerusalem.

● Sanders himself proposed a somewhat different way of looking at things, by suggesting that Paul's starting point was not actually Judaism, but Christianity. In other words, Paul looked at all the benefits he perceived himself as enjoying as a consequence of his Christian faith and, in looking back at Judaism, depicted this as the opposite. Since, as a Christian, Paul knew that, for himself, there was no

salvation except through Christ, then by definition there could be no salvation in Judaism. Similarly, if the empowerment given by the Holy Spirit enabled him to live in a way that was satisfying for him, and pleasing to God, then presumably Judaism had not helped him to do either of these

Ruins of the synagogue at Sardis.

things. And if Christ now gave him direct access to God, then the Law must have been unable to deliver this. By adopting this procedure, Paul produced a picture that, by definition, held Judaism up as the exact antithesis of Christianity — a picture that served his purposes in the context of the kinds of debates he became involved in, but which inevitably tended to simplify the relationship between the two, and therefore in the end helped to created a false and misleading caricature of Jewish spirituality. On this view, Paul was not actually reacting to any specific form of Judaism, but was rather meaning to articulate his understanding of Christian faith.

● Others have accepted this somewhat opportunistic view of Paul's intentions, but have argued that, in the end, Paul had an inconsistent and incoherent set of beliefs and attitudes. Yet others, however, have tried to disconnect Paul from actual Jewish practices and beliefs by proposing that his understanding of the Law was based on a bookish reading of the Old Testament, in which it can easily be made to seem that keeping the Law had a salvation-earning quality.

343

Paul and his Jewish roots *continued*

Several points can be made in relation to this debate:

● It is clear that the presuppositions of scholars have played a major part in this debate from start to finish. Luther himself was certainly more influenced by his own circumstances than by a dispassionate understanding of Paul in his first-century context, while much early twentieth-century scholarship was undoubtedly in tune with an anti-Semitic fascism, if not directly created by it. Likewise, Sanders' view is clearly motivated by the perfectly understandable desire to reimagine the New Testament in a form that will not perpetuate anti-Semitism and Christian persecution of Jews.

● In relation to Paul, it is important to remember that all his writings were occasional documents, written to address specific issues in particular circumstances. None of his letters was intended to be a reflective, comprehensive account of his thinking. All the negative references to Jewish practices and the Law were written in the context of acrimonious debates with those who wanted to insist that Gentile believers must first become Jews before being accepted as proper Christians. Though it has been argued that Judaism would never have produced such people as these Judaizers, this is hard to believe, if only because Paul clearly thought his letters were addressing a real group of people. Moreover, he expected the arguments of those people to be answered by what he had to say. Given his pragmatic intent in writing at all, it is difficult to see why he would have done anything other than attack the actual views being put forward by his opponents. His own credibility must have depended on dealing with what was actually being claimed. Since Paul's own letters are, in the end, the primary source material for his arguments with opponents, it is a curious logic that would dismiss their value, but still insist that modern readers of those sources can have accurate insights into what was going on. Whether they were being faithful to Judaism or not, the simple

fact seems to be that Paul did meet people who were legalists in the narrow sense. In that context (represented especially by Galatians, but also in certain sections of Romans), it was inevitable that Paul should play down the importance of the Law, in the face of those who wanted to do the opposite. In point of fact, however, not all of Paul's references to Jewish spirituality are negative, and some (for example, Galatians 2:14; Philippians 3:5–6; Romans 9 – 11) are very positive indeed. It might be that the problem is not so much with Paul, as with those who want to take his letters and distil from them some system of thinking that can be labelled 'Pauline theology'. Do we possess sufficient resources to systematize Paul's thinking in this way?

● Running through much of this debate is an underlying methodological assumption that is sceptical about the possibility of religious experience. In the final analysis, Paul was less against Judaism than for Christianity. In his experience on the Damascus road, Paul discovered that his existing spirituality was deficient: he was wrong in questioning Jesus' messiahship, and that discovery in turn led to further reflection on other aspects of his inherited belief system. His later statements about Judaism and the Old Testament did not emerge as the result of a process of abstract intellectual reflection, but out of his experience. But experience itself has tended to be a problem to theology, ever since the Enlightenment, and consequently there has been a need to reduce anything that seems like religious experience to other categories, usually taken from the discourse of social science. Inevitably, that leads to an exclusively cognitive, analytical perception of Paul's thought, on the basis of which it is impossible to trace a straight line from his Judaism to his Christianity. But if the validity of spiritual experience is allowed, there is no need for such a linear development from the one to the other, and Paul's own accounts of his conversion as well as the narratives in Acts all emphasize the sense of discontinuity between his earlier life and his work as apostle to the Gentiles.

19 Paul Reaches Rome

In Romans 15:23, Paul made the extraordinary statement: 'I no longer have any room for work in these regions'. There is no doubt that the whole of Asia Minor and the Balkan peninsula, where Paul had been working, certainly had not been fully evangelized by this time, but Paul viewed his own missionary task in a slightly different way. He regarded as his responsibility the formation of Christian congregations at strategic points throughout the Roman empire, from where others could reach out into the surrounding regions. At this point in his ministry, he felt he had completed that kind of work in the areas where he had been operating, and he would now set his sights on a different objective. Hitherto, he had worked almost entirely in the eastern part of the empire and, in moving westwards, Italy was the next most obvious place to aim for if he was to fulfil his dream of ensuring that, during the course of his lifetime, the gospel would be spread throughout the major cities of the Mediterranean world. But, since Italy already had churches at its most important centres, including Rome, Paul saw Spain as his next major objective, though he still believed that, as the 'apostle to the Gentiles', he had something to contribute to the church in the most strategic position of all: Rome, the capital of the empire. He was normally reluctant to enter what had previously been the sphere of other missionaries, but he decided to make an exception in this case, and so he planned to visit Rome before moving further west. Firstly, though, he had other urgent matters to deal with.

The collection for Jerusalem

In Romans 15:31, Paul had made what turned out to be a prophetic statement. He asked his readers there to pray 'that I may be delivered from the unbelievers in Judea, and that my service for Jerusalem may be acceptable to the saints'. Paul knew that he was hated in Judea more than anywhere else, even by some of those who were Christians. In the eyes of many, he was just a heretic and a traitor to his Jewish heritage. As a Pharisee he had been entrusted with the priceless privilege of interpreting the Old Testament Law, but as a Christian he had despised this privilege, appearing to regard the Law to be an inadequate channel of salvation, and powerless as a source of moral inspiration. In reality, Paul's view was not quite so straightforward: contrary to what his opponents thought, he held his own Jewish heritage to be very valuable, and in writing Romans he had given powerful expression to his feeling that God had not completely rejected the Jewish people. But he also believed that the whole point of the Old Testament was now summed up in what he had discovered about Jesus Christ, whom he regarded not only as Messiah, but also as the true fulfilment of all that the ancient scriptures had promised.

The collection, which Paul had organized in the Gentile congregations as a gift for the church at Jerusalem, was intended to be a sign of his own continuing care for his people, and an expression of solidarity between Gentile and Jewish believers. He hoped this generosity would show that, whatever theological differences might exist between the Jewish and Gentile Christian churches, they were united in care for one another.

So Paul set off for Jerusalem in the company of Christians from Beroea, Thessalonica, Derbe and Ephesus, along with Luke and Timothy. He must have known that, in some ways, he was taking a foolhardy step, for on the journey he stopped off at Miletus and sent for the elders of the Ephesian church. In the course of his conversations with them he made it clear that, while he hoped to return to them, it was more likely that he would suffer 'imprisonment and afflictions' in Judea. But he was still prepared to take the risk, because he saw the expression of unity between Jews and Gentiles as a fundamental part of his ministry, and something that was an essential witness to the gospel: 'I do not account my life of any value nor as precious to myself, if only I may accomplish my course and the ministry which I received from the Lord Jesus, to testify to the gospel of the grace of God' (Acts 20:24).

When he arrived in Jerusalem, Paul's fears and expectations were fully realized. Reports reaching Judea ahead of him had contained exaggerated accounts of Paul's break with Judaism, making no mention of those concessions he had regularly made to Jewish practices and expectations. James, who was now the leader of the church in Jerusalem, explained the situation to him more fully: 'You see, brother, how many thousands there are among the Jews of those who have believed; they are all zealous for the law, and they have been told about you that you teach all the Jews who are among the Gentiles to forsake Moses, telling them not to circumcise their children or observe the customs' (Acts 21:20–21).

James, like Paul himself, hoped the collection brought by Paul and his friends would pacify these hostile Jewish Christians. He also advised Paul to make a peace gesture to the wider religious culture, by paying the expenses involved in a ritual vow being undertaken by four Jerusalem Christians, and by sharing in their fast (Acts 21:23–24). Paul agreed to do this, for his policy had always been one of fitting in with all kinds of people: 'I have become all things to all people, that I might by all means save some' (1 Corinthians 9:22).

Towards the end of this fast, some Jews from the province of Asia spotted Paul in the temple, and convinced themselves that he had defiled the sacred site by taking some of his Gentile companions into its inner court. To do this was a very serious crime; indeed, it was one of the few misdemeanours carrying the death penalty that the Romans allowed the Jewish authorities to try, and punish, themselves. To ensure that no one committed this crime unknowingly, an inscription stood over the main gate of the temple in Paul's day, reading (in three languages): 'No foreigner may enter within the barricade which surrounds the temple and its enclosure. Anyone caught doing so will have themselves to blame for their ensuing death.' Two such inscriptions, in Greek, have been unearthed on the temple site in Jerusalem.

Under arrest

Those who spotted Paul in the temple wanted to act without the decision of a court by killing him there and then, but the Roman commander arrived and rescued Paul – not because of any sympathy for him or his message, but probably in the hope of avoiding a riot (Acts 21:30–36). This Roman officer assumed that Paul must be some sort of political agitator, and was about to have him beaten to get the truth from him when Paul claimed the immunity from such treatment which was his right as a Roman citizen (Acts 22:22–29). Because the accusation against Paul was clearly a religious matter concerned with the Jewish Law, the Sanhedrin was the proper body to deal with it. But, when they met to hear what he had to say, Paul started a quarrel between the two major groups on the council (Pharisees and Sadducees) by stating that he was still a good Pharisee as he believed in the resurrection of the dead (Acts 23:1–10).

The Romans always felt uneasy in Jerusalem, and when it was learned that a plan was afoot to kill Paul, he was taken under armed guard to Caesarea, the Roman headquarters on the coast of Palestine. There he would escape the direct notice of the Jewish authorities, and the matter could be dealt with under Roman procedures. Paul was again tried before the Roman procurator Felix, and this time the charge was not only that of defiling the temple, but also of provoking civil disorder wherever he went. There is a clear parallel here between the trials of Paul and the earlier trials of Jesus, for in both cases the original starting point was a religious dispute, which was redefined as a political charge before a Roman judge. Though Felix, like every other Roman official, disliked anything that might cause civil disorder, he was convinced of Paul's innocence. He postponed a decision on the case, partly in the hope of receiving a bribe, and partly for fear of arousing yet more trouble among Paul's accusers if he was formally declared to be innocent (Acts 24:1–26).

Anyone could enter the outer court of the Temple in Jerusalem, but Gentiles were forbidden to go through to the inner courts on pain of death. Inscriptions in Greek (like this one) and Latin warned visitors of the penalty.

At this point (about AD59) Felix himself was recalled to Rome to account for his own misconduct in relation to other matters. The new procurator, Porcius Festus, heard Paul's case again, and suggested another trial in Jerusalem. This had no attraction for Paul: he knew the risk of assassination there, and he could also foresee further delays. His imprisonment had already lasted two years, and he was impatient to reach his immediate goal by visiting Rome. If he was forced to go there as a prisoner, that would be better than not going at all, and so he decided to exercise his right of appeal to the supreme court of the Roman empire, the emperor himself (Acts 25:1–12).

Paul's decision to appeal to Rome took Festus by surprise, for he realized the weakness of the case against Paul and was at a loss to know what to write in a report to the emperor. When Herod Agrippa II visited Caesarea, Paul was again called to appear before both men in the hope that Agrippa, who knew more about Jewish affairs, would be able to suggest a solution. Both rulers appear to have been impressed with Paul's message, though they tried to pass it off by joking about it (Acts 26:1–32).

Destination Rome

At last Paul got his heart's desire, and he was sent off to Rome, accompanied by Luke and another of his friends, Aristarchus. He travelled on one of the prison ships that made regular voyages from Palestine to Rome at this time. The Romans imported criminals from elsewhere in the empire, who provided entertainment by fighting with one another, or with wild animals in the amphitheatres of Rome. Though it was a cruel death, many of those who were transported in this way preferred a 'heroic' death, with gladiators or wild animals, to the slow and painful process of crucifixion, which would have been their alternative fate.

Paul was apparently treated as a special case, no doubt related to his status as a Roman citizen, and also the fact that he seems to have been reasonably well off. Like any other rich Roman, he travelled with two companions, and was taken into the captain's confidence, even being consulted about details of the voyage. Luke's narrative account of the voyage to Rome (Acts 27:1 – 28:13), with its graphic descriptions of storms and shipwrecks, is widely perceived as a first-hand account of the journey, and is certainly one of the most gripping of such stories in the whole of ancient literature.

After many adventures on the way, Paul eventually landed at Puteoli in southern Italy, where he was warmly welcomed by the local Christians (Acts 28:14), and then as he got nearer to Rome, Christians from there came out some distance along the road to meet him. For two years, Paul remained a prisoner, under house arrest in a property which he rented for himself, and was protected by Roman guards, whom he would also have had to pay.

Even in such unusual circumstances, however, Luke did not lose sight of the significance of this in terms of his own intention to show the progress of the gospel, from the Palestinian fringe of the empire to its centre in Rome. He portrays this as the fulfilment of Paul's commission to be apostle to the Gentiles, and acknowledges that, though this is hardly

St Paul's Bay, Malta, fits the description of the site of Paul's shipwreck in Acts 27:39–41.

Route of Paul's voyage to Rome.

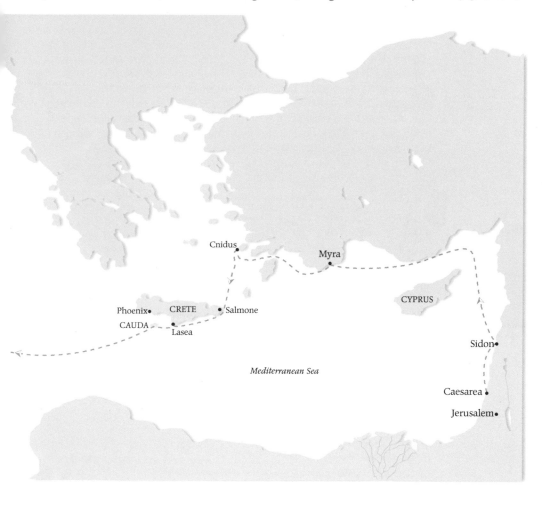

how Paul might have expected to arrive in the capital, this was all part of God's plan that he should have the opportunity to take his message to Rome. Accordingly, Paul soon got in contact with the leaders of the Jewish community there, who (as in many other places) heard his message, with some of them believing but the majority rejecting it. Again Luke portrays Paul turning to the Gentiles and, in spite of the limitations imposed by his house arrest, the final picture of him is 'preaching the kingdom of God and teaching about the Lord Jesus Christ quite openly

After Paul landed in Italy Christians came out from Rome to meet him at the Forum of Appius on the Appian Way. This famous road is still lined with Roman monuments.

When did Paul die?

Luke was more interested in recounting the progress of the Christian message, from Jerusalem to Rome, than in the messengers who spread the gospel, which no doubt explains why the story in Acts ends at the point it does. But all the traditions of the early church say that Paul met a martyr's death at Rome during the persecution ordered by Nero in AD64. We may suppose that, despite the long delays, he was ultimately brought to trial in Rome, and perhaps was sentenced to death immediately after this – though in view of the reluctance of Felix and Festus even to commit him for trial it is unlikely that Paul could have been found guilty on the charges under which he was sent to the emperor's court.

Since this trial would have taken place in about AD62, Paul presumably engaged in other activities until his final trial and death under Nero in AD64. This is certainly the view taken by early church tradition, and so Eusebius, for example, recorded that 'after defending himself the apostle was sent again on his ministry of preaching, and coming a second time to the same city, suffered martyrdom under Nero' (*Ecclesiastical History* II.22). There are two possibilities for his further activities:

● One is that Paul fulfilled his intention of going on to Spain. There is no biblical evidence to support this, though there are local traditions in Spain itself to this effect, and also a statement that he did so in *1 Clement* 5 (a letter written about AD95 by Clement of Rome to the church at Corinth). But it is more likely that the originators of these traditions based their statements on what Paul said in Romans 15:24, and assumed that since he wanted to visit Spain he must actually have done so.

● The other possibility concerning what Paul did after his supposed release arises from the references to Paul's travels in the pastoral epistles (1 and 2 Timothy and Titus). These letters might suggest that Paul revisited some of the places he had been to earlier in Asia Minor and Greece, and also some others of which there is no mention, either in Acts or in the earlier letters, such as Colossae, Crete and Nicopolis.

It is not essential to assume that such visits took place towards the end of Paul's life, for Acts by no means gives a complete account of all his earlier travels. In 2 Corinthians 11:23–27, for example, Paul mentions many incidents not included in Acts, but which had presumably occurred in the course of his pastoral ministry in Ephesus and the surrounding areas. Nevertheless, it would take a considerable degree of ingenuity to fit the travel references that are implied in the pastoral epistles into the Acts narrative. It is certainly easier to suppose that they represent further missionary exploits after his first visit to Rome – though even then it is no simple matter to fit all these references together to reconstruct a plausible journey. There are also other difficulties involved in understanding the pastoral epistles, which we shall come to shortly.

and unhindered' (Acts 28:31). Paul had achieved his objective. On the Damascus road he had been commissioned to be the apostle to the Gentiles, 'to open their eyes, that they may turn from darkness to light and from the power of Satan to God, that they may receive forgiveness of sins and a place among those who are sanctified by faith in me' (Acts 26:18), and Luke leaves him at the point where he had fulfilled the terms of this commission for, by this time, every strategic centre throughout the eastern empire had a Christian community which owed its origins to Paul's unceasing endeavours.

Letters from prison

In four of his letters (apart from 2 Timothy) Paul refers to himself as a prisoner, and it has traditionally been assumed that they must have been written during his period of imprisonment at Rome from AD60–62. These are the letters to the churches at Colossae, Philippi and Ephesus, and the personal letter to Philemon, who lived at Colossae.

The church at Colossae

Colossians and Philemon were written at the same time as each other, the former to the church and the latter to one member of it. Timothy is associated with Paul as the author of them both, and there are greetings in both from the same five people. Aristarchus, Mark, Demas, Epaphras, Luke and Archippus of Colossae are mentioned in both, and so is Philemon's runaway slave, Onesimus.

Though Colossae was not too far from Ephesus, where Paul had worked for three years, he had never visited the town. The church at Colossae had probably been founded by Epaphras, who might have been one of Paul's converts in Ephesus. The fact that such a thriving church had been established at Colossae by this time is striking proof of the wisdom of Paul's missionary strategy of establishing his own work in a central place from which other Christians could reach out to the surrounding areas.

Epaphras visited Paul during his imprisonment in Rome, and gave him a generally encouraging report of the Colossian church. But one thing that was causing him real concern was the emergence of a collection of opinions and practices that has often been labelled 'the Colossian heresy'. This appears to have combined some of the practices that Paul was opposing when he wrote Galatians, with beliefs that seem to have included some elements of the opinions held by the 'Christ party' in Corinth. The kind of ethnic superiority championed by people like the Judaizers had been combined with the intellectual exclusivism that was common in many Graeco-Roman religious cults, and the practical outcome was the emergence of a group of people in the Colossian church who considered themselves better Christians than the rest of the church members. As Paul understood it, these people were proposing that a complete and lasting salvation could not be achieved simply by faith in Christ, but required additional insights into divine things, which were to be obtained through a secret knowledge imparted in a mystical way.

This knowledge could be acquired by taking part in various ritual practices, such as circumcision, not eating certain foods, and observing traditional Jewish festivals and sabbaths. In practice, much of this must have seemed very similar to what was being demanded by the Judaizers in Galatia, who were also promoting the value of circumcision and other rituals, though the underlying ideology among the Colossian Christians was in fact established on quite a different foundation. For the Gentile Christians of Galatia, the issue was whether to observe the requirements of the Torah as an integral part of obedience to the religious covenants of the Hebrew scriptures, whereas in Colossae such observances were being promoted for different reasons. These people seem to have been religious ascetics, and what they were looking for was something that would help them to check 'the indulgence of the flesh' (Colossians 2:23). They were not interested in the arguments raised by those who suggested that, in order to be good Christians, Gentiles should first become Jews, and the fact that they chose to achieve their asceticism by adopting certain practices and attitudes from the Old Testament Law was almost a coincidence. This becomes very clear from Paul's reply to them, for he mentions none of the issues that were so central to his argument in Galatians, but instead opposes them by highlighting the fundamental moral issues that are raised by any kind of ascetic practice.

Colossae stood in the broad fertile valley of the Lycus, near Laodicea. The ancient town is now buried beneath a mound.

The church at Ephesus

Uniquely among Paul's letters, Colossians makes explicit reference to another letter: 'when this letter has been read among you, have it read also in the church of the Laodiceans; and see that you read also the letter from Laodicea' (Colossians 4:16). Laodicea was another town quite near to Colossae, and Paul wanted the churches to exchange letters.

There is, of course, no 'letter to the Laodiceans' contained in the New Testament. Noting this omission, the church of the early centuries lost no time in producing such a letter, and there is indeed a *Letter to the Laodiceans* known in a Latin version. This letter is almost impossible to date accurately and, though it might also have existed in Greek, there is every reason to suppose that it is a very much later composition. It contains no real substance, and consists of a series of bits and pieces from Paul's other letters strung together in an aimless way. A more plausible suggestion regarding the identity of the letter from Laodicea to which Colossians refers is that it was the same as the New Testament letter known as Ephesians. This contains, in a fuller and more carefully argued form, the same kind of teaching about the person of Christ as in

Colossians

In his letter to the Colossian church, Paul deals with this false teaching by emphasizing again that in Christ believers can find all they need. Like the later Gnostics, some of the Colossians had been suggesting that they needed other supernatural agencies, and that Jesus was just one of several possible manifestations of God. Against this, Paul firmly asserted that 'In Christ all the fullness of God was pleased to dwell' (Colossians 1:19). Indeed, he went further than this by reminding his readers that in Jesus 'the whole fullness of deity dwells *bodily*' (2:9).

The Colossians claimed they needed to experience something deep and mysterious if they were to find full salvation, and Paul agreed with them. His own job could be described as the presentation of 'the mystery' – but, far from being something deep and hidden, this 'mystery' was the very thing that lay at the heart of all Paul's preaching, the simple fact of Christ's own life at work within them, empowering them to be the kind of people who could fulfil God's will (1:27). Whatever the Christian might have needed, it could all be found in Christ, for in him 'are hid all the treasures of wisdom and knowledge' (2:3).

Paul then went on to remind his readers of all the things they had as Christians, some of which they were now trying to obtain by other, mystical means:
● Were some of them claiming to be super-spiritual because they were circumcised? All Christians, said Paul, received 'a circumcision made without hands' (2:11) when they fulfilled the true meaning of the old ceremony by 'putting off the body of flesh', that is their old, sinful lives, that they might live a new life in the power of the Holy Spirit given to them by Christ.
● Were some claiming to have a new kind of life that other Christians did not have? Then they should recognize that all Christians have been made alive by God through what Christ did on the cross (2:13–15).
● What about ritual observances, designed to keep 'the flesh' in subjection? These also

were of no real value and, even in terms of their own original purpose, they have been superseded, because they were but 'a shadow of what is to come'. Since the reality has now come in Christ, they are no longer valid. Quite apart from such theological arguments, though, they were a waste of time in practical terms, for though they might have 'an appearance of wisdom in promoting rigour of devotion and self-abasement and severity to the body... they are of no value in checking the indulgence of the flesh' (2:23).

Instead of fixing their attention on these things, Paul advised the Colossians to live up to their true position in Christ. Whoever they might be, and whatever experiences they claim to have, all Christians stand equal before God, all have the same temptations to face (3:5–11), and there is only one way for such temptations to be overcome: 'Set your minds on things that are above, not on things that are on earth. For you have died, and your life is hid with Christ in God... there is no longer Greek and Jew, circumcised and uncircumcised, barbarian, Scythian, slave and free, but Christ is all, and in all' (3:2–3, 11).

Instead of following a false set of values, based on mythological speculation, the Colossians ought again to remind themselves that the true ambition of the Christian must be to become like Christ (3:12–17): 'whatever you do, in word or deed, do everything in the name of the Lord Jesus' (3:17).

By their emphasis on asceticism and speculation those Colossian Christians who had adopted this outlook had actually removed Christian faith from the sphere of real life. But Paul was convinced, as always, that Christianity was essentially incarnational, and its spirituality was not rooted in some other esoteric world, but was to be grounded in everyday life in this one. So he ended his letter by showing how the power of Christ, which operates in the Christian (1:27), might be worked out in the family (3:18–21), at work (3:22 – 4:1), in the church (4:2–4), and in life in general (4:5–6).

Colossians, but without the pointed references to local persons and events. There are certainly indications that Ephesians was intended for a wider readership than just the Christians at Ephesus:

■ The words 'at Ephesus' in Ephesians 1:1 (the only indication that the letter was destined for that city) are not found in the best and oldest manuscripts of this letter. Some modern versions of the New Testament put the words 'at Ephesus' in the margin.

■ There are no personal greetings in this letter, which is especially surprising considering that Paul probably had more friends in Ephesus than anywhere else.

Philemon

Along with the letter to the church in Colossae, Paul also sent a personal note to one of its leading members, Philemon. He must have been quite affluent, for the Christians gathered for their regular meetings in his house (verse 2). Like everyone else in his position in the Roman empire, Philemon had a number of slaves, one of whom, Onesimus, had run away from Colossae, perhaps taking some of Philemon's possessions with him (verses 18–19). While on the run he had met Paul, and as a result he became a Christian himself.

Paul knew it was his duty – both as a citizen and as a Christian – to return Onesimus to his master. There were serious legal penalties in the Roman empire for anyone harbouring runaway slaves and, in addition, Paul appreciated that any other course of action would threaten the bonds of Christian friendship that existed between himself and Onesimus. For all these practical reasons, Paul sent Onesimus back to Colossae, along with this short personal letter. Of course Paul's action in doing this raises other questions about his attitudes to slavery as an institution, and modern readers might reasonably wonder how this episode fits in with Paul's categorical statements elsewhere that freedom is at the very heart of the Christian gospel (for example, Galatians 3:28; Colossians 3:11).

We shall deal with this and related issues in chapter 21. Here it is worth noting that Paul did explicitly express the hope that he was not returning Onesimus to exactly the same position as he was in before, for he sent him back as 'not just a slave, but much more than a slave: he is a dear brother in Christ' (verse 16). Moreover, he instructed Philemon to 'welcome him back just as you would welcome me' (verse 17). There might indeed have been even more than that implied in Paul's request, for it has often been thought that Paul was actually asking Philemon to release Onesimus from his service so that he might return to work full-time with Paul as a Christian missionary (verses 11–14).

There is no way of telling what happened when Onesimus got back to Colossae, as he never features anywhere else in the New Testament. At the beginning of the second century, Ignatius mentioned a person called Onesimus who was leader of the church at Ephesus, describing him as 'a man of inexpressible love' and 'an excellent bishop' (Ignatius, *To the Ephesians* 1). If this was the same person, that could explain why a short personal letter to Philemon should have been preserved and included in the official collection of Paul's letters to churches. Depending on the date when Paul wrote the letter, this identification could be possible, but in any case it makes good sense to suppose that Philemon must have complied with Paul's request, otherwise this note would undoubtedly have been quickly forgotten.

This Roman slave badge reads, 'Seize me if I should try to escape and send me back to my master'. Onesimus' escape was a very risky venture.

Ephesians

In Ephesians, Paul again emphasized the central place of Christ in the plan of God and in the life of the Christian believer. He began by reminding readers of the great privileges they possessed in Christ. Though the people to whom he was writing had previously 'lived in the passions of their flesh' (Ephesians 2:3), God had put them in a new position. They had been 'made... alive together with Christ... and raised... up with him, and made to sit with him in the heavenly places' (2:5, 6). Every individual Christian had become a part of God's new creation in which God's plan was 'to unite all things in Christ, things in heaven and things on earth' (1:10).

Some of the people who read Paul's letter had been told these things before by Paul himself, for this was his special ministry: 'to preach to the Gentiles the unsearchable riches of Christ' (3:8) and to demonstrate how those 'riches' could be received and enjoyed in real life. Some of his readers might have been influenced by the kind of misguided ideas that had circulated in Colossae, but they would only find the true satisfaction they desired if they were willing to be 'filled with all the fullness of God' (3:19), which could be found nowhere else but in Christ.

After setting out this comprehensive and all-embracing description of the cosmic Christ as Saviour of the world, and as the source of all physical, mental and spiritual knowledge and activity, Paul went on to draw attention to its practical implications. If his readers were indeed members of Christ's body, new people and children of God, they must show by their actions who they really were:

● In the church they should be 'eager to maintain the unity of the Spirit in the bond of peace' (4:3). As in 1 Corinthians 12, Paul again claimed that they could expect the unity of the Spirit to be displayed by the giving of 'gifts of grace' to 'the body' for its growth and development (4:7–16). Because of the close relationships enjoyed by believers within the Christian community, any wrong done by one member would inevitably affect the others – something that would 'grieve the Holy Spirit of God' (4:30). In view of what God had done for them in Christ, Christians ought to 'be kind to one another, tenderhearted, forgiving one another, as God in Christ forgave' them (4:32). Paul could even advise them to 'be imitators of God' (5:1), by showing in their dealings with one another the same self-sacrificing love as God had shown to them in Christ.

● In personal morality Christians should 'Take no part in the unfruitful works of darkness' (5:11). What ought to characterize them instead was that they were 'filled with the Spirit' (5:18), the results of which Paul had listed in Galatians 5:22–23.

● In their social lives Christians must again be ruled by the principle of self-giving love, whether the matter at issue was in the family (5:21 – 6:4) or the workplace (6:5–9).

Finally, Paul reminded his readers that they could expect to encounter opposition, 'the wiles of the devil', against which they must 'Put on the whole armour of God' (6:11).

As an ethical theory, what Paul had put forward here would be impossible to carry out. How could anyone hope to be ruled by self-sacrificing love of the same kind that God had shown in Christ? Paul knew, from his own personal experience and his knowledge of the experience of others, that it was possible in only one way: if the Christian was 'strong in the Lord and in the strength of God's might' (6:10). This was one of the constant themes of all Paul's writings: it had appeared in what was probably the first letter he wrote, and a lifetime of work for Christ had only strengthened his belief that 'If we live by the Spirit', we ought also to 'walk by the Spirit' (Galatians 5:25).

■ In the middle of the second century, Marcion referred to Ephesians as 'the letter to the Laodiceans'.

It makes sense to suppose that Ephesians was a circular letter addressed to a number of different congregations. The words 'at Ephesus' in Ephesians 1:1 would have been found in the copy that went to that city, while the copy referred to in Colossians 4:16 would have had the words 'at Laodicea' instead.

The church at Philippi

With the exception of Philemon, Philippians is the most personal of Paul's letters. It was written to acknowledge a gift that the Philippian church had

---

Did Paul write Ephesians?

In most of Paul's letters we are always close to the heartbeat of the apostle, and usually not far from controversy. It takes little imagination to envisage the furious arguments that led to the writing of Galatians or 1 and 2 Corinthians, for example, but in Ephesians things are different. Here the discussion is much more serene and settled, and seems to progress independently of any direct involvement with opponents, or indeed any specific readers.

A number of other arguments can also be presented, which together support the suggestion that perhaps Paul himself was not the actual author of this letter, though its sentiments are not inconsistent with his known positions on any number of matters:

● **Language** A number of words found in Ephesians are not used elsewhere in Paul's writings. This includes some prominent features, such as the references to 'the heavenly world' (1:3; 1:20; 2:6; 3:10; 6:12) which is a key term here but occurs nowhere else.

● **Style** The way Ephesians is put together is also distinctive. Instead of the unplanned – and largely unrestrained – language of the other letters, Ephesians moves from one theme to another in more sedate fashion, generally using more complex sentence structures in the process.

● **Colossians** Ephesians has a close resemblance to Colossians. More than a

third of the actual words of Colossians also occur in Ephesians. Since Colossians has more of Paul's usual personal touch about it, many think this must have been the original letter, which was subsequently copied and adapted by the later author of Ephesians.

● **Doctrine and theology** At a number of points, Ephesians seems to reflect concerns that are known to have been especially typical of church life at a period later than the time of Paul. An example would be the use of the term 'church' to describe a universal movement that included all Christians everywhere (for example, 1:22–23), which is different from Paul's usage, for he generally thought of only local groups of Christians ('the church in Corinth', etc.). Then there is the position of 'apostles and prophets' as 'the foundation' of this church (2:20): does this (along with the list of church officers in 4:11) point to a time when church structures were more fully developed? There is also the apparent absence of any reference to the *parousia* of Jesus, and to the theme of 'justification by faith'.

So was Ephesians written not by Paul himself, but perhaps by one of his close friends, or a later admirer who wished to commend Paul's work to a wider readership? It has been suggested that Ephesians is a compendium of Paul's teaching, written as a concise introduction to the major themes of his theology, perhaps at a time when his letters were being collected together. The problem with this is that Ephesians is not really a summary of the whole of Paul's teaching at all, and it is precisely the absence of some characteristic themes that has cast doubt on its genuineness as a letter by the apostle himself. The same criticism applies if Ephesians is regarded as a synopsis of Paul's theology.

It has also been suggested that both the differences and similarities between Paul's other letters and Ephesians can be explained by his use of a secretary. It is a known fact that Paul regularly asked others to actually put pen to paper, only signing his own name to validate what had been written (for example, Galatians 6:11), and it might be that Luke, or some other person, could have been responsible for the final forms of expression in this letter. There are certainly a number of striking linguistic similarities between Ephesians and Luke–Acts.

Whatever is concluded about the person who actually wrote the words down, we should certainly not miss the weakness of the other arguments put forward against Paul's authorship. The close relationship between Colossians and Ephesians really proves nothing, as authors often base one book on something that they have written previously, and Paul had certainly done this before. The relationship between Galatians and Romans is a useful model here, and is in many significant respects similar to the relationship between Colossians and Ephesians, as both Romans and Ephesians take up points that had previously been made in the heat of debate, and refine and restate them in a way designed to make them more universally applicable to the concerns of a wider readership.

Viewed in this light, many of the apparent theological differences between Ephesians and earlier letters also appear in a different perspective. Nothing in Ephesians actually contradicts previous statements by Paul, and much of it is a logical development of things he had said elsewhere. So, for example, while there is no instance in other letters of the use of the term 'church' to describe all Christians everywhere, the very fact that Paul could apply the term 'church' to Christians in Rome, or Corinth, or wherever, implies that there was something they all had in common and which bound them together. Paul certainly had a profound sense of solidarity between the various local Christian communities, as evidenced by the priority he gave to organizing the collection for Jerusalem – and to talk of all these groups together as 'the church' would simply give theological expression to that reality.

Many of the other alleged doctrinal discrepancies are not as impressive as they can be made to look. It might be true that the *parousia* is not found in Ephesians (though it must surely be implied in 4:30 and 5:26–27), but it is not mentioned in Romans either! The absence of 'justification by faith' would only be remarkable if it was indeed the central core of Paul's thinking, but if (as has been argued in a previous chapter) it only featured in particular situations of controversy, its non-appearance here would mean nothing. In point of fact, one of the major themes of Ephesians is the work of the Holy Spirit in the lives of Christians, a topic which almost certainly has a far stronger claim than justification to be the real centre of Paul's theology.

Ephesians is undoubtedly different, and the conclusions reached by various scholars on its authorship will tend to reflect their opinions on other subjects, most notably their understanding of Paul's temperament (was he the kind of person to engage in further reflection, or was he an impulsive, opportunist thinker?) and their understanding of the part played by pseudonymous writings in early Christianity. Whatever view is adopted, Ephesians represents a significant and mature reflection on some of the key themes in Paul's other letters and, even if it was written by a later admirer, it accurately captures the feel of Paul himself.

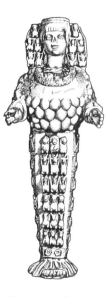

The Temple of Artemis (Diana) at Ephesus was four times the size of the Parthenon at Athens. This larger than life-sized Roman statue of the goddess is in white marble, and is decorated with symbols of sexual fertility.

sent to Paul to help him financially while in Rome. One of the Philippian Christians, a man called Epaphroditus, had brought the gift from Philippi and had been a great help to Paul during his short stay in Rome, and most of Paul's letter, which was sent back to Philippi with Epaphroditus, is concerned with personal matters affecting Paul's possible release, and expressing his warm affection for the generosity of the Philippian Christians.

In what was probably his first letter, one of the central features of Paul's

Philippians

Paul had always been especially close to the Christians in Philippi. It was the first church he established on European soil, and it was also apparently one of the few that had not been torn apart by damaging arguments about Christian faith and behaviour.

Paul's letter begins with an appreciative expression of thanks to God for all that these Christians had meant to him (1:3–11). Unlike some others, they had consistently 'helped me in the work of the gospel from the very first day until now' (1:5), which was why he felt able to accept their financial generosity (1:7) – something that had seemed unwise in the case of more volatile congregations such as that in Corinth (1 Corinthians 9:8–18). Because of their open and friendly attitude, however, he was confident that their Christian living would be marked by 'the truly good qualities which only Jesus Christ can produce, for the glory and praise of God' (1:11).

Paul continued to sound this note as he brought them up to date with his own situation in prison (1:12–30). His main ambition in life had always been to bring glory to Jesus – and even his imprisonment was doing that (1:12). Since Christians already have Jesus Christ living within them, Paul knows that physical death would only deepen that experience (1:21). Death might have been preferable to prison for Paul, but he could see good reasons why God would probably allow him to live a little longer: 'to add to your progress and joy in the faith' (1:25). To suffer for the cause of the Christian gospel

was not a sign of defeat, but of triumph, and so he advised them neither to be sorry for his present plight, nor afraid of persecution themselves (1:27–30).

There was, however, one thing that bothered Paul about the church at Philippi. Some of the Christians were quarrelling with each other, and Paul later named two particularly argumentative women, Euodia and Syntyche (4:2–3), though they were clearly not the only ones. In urging them to 'look out for one another's interests, not just for your own' (2:4), Paul quoted from an early hymn that was no doubt familiar to his readers, and perhaps to Christians in other churches as well (2:6–11). It is obvious that this passage is a quotation: it interrupts the flow of Paul's language; and it has the style of a hymn, with a definite rhythm, carefully balanced lines, and the 'parallelism' that was characteristic of Hebrew poetry. This 'Christ hymn' has been the subject of much scholarly debate. Who wrote it? Where did Paul get it from? How did he use it? And what did it mean? There is no agreed answer to all these questions, though it is clear enough why Paul inserted it here.

This is the only place in any of Paul's letters where he explicitly holds up the example of Jesus as a pattern for Christian behaviour, although 2 Corinthians 8:9 is very similar, and it is striking that the aspect of Jesus' life he chose was not his compassion, care or good works, but his relinquishing of divine status when he became a human person. This idea was very important for Paul, and lay at the heart of much of his thinking. In order to be a Christian at all, people must be prepared to give up their own claims to

self-understanding had been his conviction that 'I have been crucified with Christ, it is no longer I who live, but Christ who lives in me' (Galatians 2:20) and, as he faced the uncertainty of trials and possible death, he again set the dominant note in Philippians 1:21 by a similar statement, just five words in Greek: 'For to me to live is Christ.' From start to finish, Paul was motivated by his experience of the risen Christ, as he saw in his own life what might be possible for those who were willing to commit their time

---

determine their destiny, and instead offer all that they are to Christ for empowerment and transformation. This was a lesson he had himself learned on the road to Damascus, and it runs like a golden thread through the fabric of all his letters.

Paul then moves on to explain, in greater practical detail, what it means for a Christian's life to be infused with the life of the risen Jesus himself. For his readers, it should mean a lifestyle that would be distinctively Christian, shining like stars in a dark sky (2:12–16), while for himself it would eventually lead to a martyr's death. But that, too, was a privilege: 'If that is so, I am glad and share my joy with you all' (2:17–18). Epaphroditus (himself a member of the Philippian church) had recently experienced the same feelings, for he too 'risked his life and nearly died for the sake of the work of Christ' (2:30). He and Timothy would soon be going to Philippi to encourage the Christians there, and perhaps even to prepare the way for a visit by Paul himself (2:19–30).

At this point, Paul seems to digress and to write about troublemakers who were operating in Philippi (3:1 – 4:4). Some have argued that this section was originally a separate letter altogether though, if so, it is hard to see why a later editor would have inserted it at such an odd point in Paul's writing. There are plenty of examples of Paul writing impulsively and changing subjects quite unexpectedly, and it is not difficult to imagine that this is what has happened here. The people he writes about are 'those who insist on cutting the body' (3:2), which is code language for circumcizers. Paul does not spell out the

reasons for their demand for circumcision, whether it was related to keeping the Law (as in Galatia) or as an ascetic practice (as in Colossae), though the former seems more likely, for he replies by reminding them of his own accomplishments in keeping the Jewish Law (3:1–11). This leads him into reflection on his achievements as a Pharisee, in which he was 'without fault' (3:6) – though he was prepared to reckon all that as 'complete loss for the sake of what is so much more valuable, the knowledge of Christ Jesus my Lord' (3:8). This 'knowledge' consisted not primarily in knowing facts about Jesus, but in enjoying a close, personal relationship with him, in which the resurrection life of Jesus himself gave Paul a new and meaningful dynamic for his own daily life: 'All I want is to know Christ and to experience the power of his resurrection, to share in his sufferings and become like him in his death' (3:10).

Even so, Paul was not claiming that he had 'arrived' spiritually, as some of his opponents in Corinth and Colossae believed they had. Unlike them, he was still on his way, like a marathon runner moving steadily towards the finishing line, and those who wanted to be spiritually mature should follow his example (3:12–21).

Finally, he brought to a close this most joyful of all his letters with advice on a number of varied topics, finishing by reminding his readers that, like him, they could have 'the strength to face all conditions by the power that Christ gives' (4:13), for 'my God will supply all your needs' (4:19).

and talents to the empowering presence of the Holy Spirit. Again, the overwhelming significance of the Damascus road experience for his entire world-view is brought out in Philippians, as Paul reflects on the way his discovery of Jesus as Messiah had revolutionized his own career, and invites his converts to join him in affirming that 'I count everything as loss because of the surpassing worth of knowing Christ Jesus my Lord' (Philippians 3:8).

Timothy and Titus

1 and 2 Timothy and Titus are collectively known as the 'pastoral epistles', because they are addressed to local leaders of the early church, Timothy and Titus. Both of them are mentioned elsewhere as Paul's companions, though they also worked independently of Paul, Titus in Crete, and Timothy in Ephesus. In both style and content these three letters are quite different from Paul's other writings, but they are very similar to each other, and were probably written at about the same time.

When was Paul imprisoned?

In our consideration of Paul's life and letters, we have assumed that those letters which indicate Paul was a prisoner when he produced them were written from Rome between AD60 and 62. This is the only imprisonment recorded in Acts, and it has been natural for readers of Paul's letters from the earliest times to assume that they were written at this time. It is not, however, the only possible time and place when they might have been composed, and a significant body of opinion favours the assumption that at least one or two of these four letters were written not from

Junius Bassus was prefect of Rome when he was baptized a Christian on his deathbed in AD359. This carving of Paul under arrest is from his sarcophagus.

Rome, but during an unrecorded imprisonment at Ephesus, which took place during Paul's three-year stay there. There is a considerable amount of evidence that makes such an imprisonment likely.

Imprisonment in Ephesus?

2 Corinthians 11:23, written towards the end of Paul's stay in Ephesus, informs us that by comparison with other Christian workers he had experienced 'far greater labours, far more imprisonments, with countless beatings, and often near death'. In 1 Corinthians 15:32 Paul wrote that he 'fought with beasts at Ephesus', a phrase which was probably not meant to be understood literally, but as a figure of speech could easily describe a trial preceding imprisonment. Again, 2 Corinthians 1:8 speaks of 'the affliction we experienced in Asia', the Roman province of which Ephesus was the capital, while in Romans 16:7, written shortly after he left Ephesus, Paul refers to two people as 'my fellow prisoners'.

Other evidence that Paul was imprisoned at Ephesus is to be found in the Latin introductions to New Testament books that were written in the second century under the influence of the Gnostic Marcion. The second-century *Acts of Paul* includes the account of an imprisonment at Ephesus, followed by an encounter with

They deal with four main subjects.

FALSE TEACHERS

Many of Paul's letters were written in response to threats from various opponents: Judaizers in Galatia, ascetics in Colossae, and Jewish Gnostics of a sort in Corinth. Timothy and Titus were facing similar problems, and were under pressure to abandon the gospel message as Paul had delivered it to them.

This false teaching appears to have consisted of several elements already encountered in earlier letters. The Old Testament Law was certainly involved, for some of the troublemakers are identified as 'converts from Judaism, who rebel and deceive others with their nonsense' (Titus 1:10). It seems that these people were using the Old Testament to support their own sectarian ambitions, for Timothy is reminded that 'the Law is good if it is used as it should be used' (1 Timothy 1:8). The specific

---

lions in the arena, from which Paul was delivered by supernatural intervention. While these last pieces of evidence are of variable quality, the combination of such information with the clues provided by Paul's own writings makes it quite likely that he did suffer a period of imprisonment during his three-year stay in Ephesus.

Were the letters written from Ephesus?
The fact that Paul might have been imprisoned there does not, of course, make it necessary to believe that he wrote the 'prison letters' from Ephesus. But arguments can be advanced to support this view:
● It is claimed that the friends of Paul who are mentioned as having made contact with him during this imprisonment would be more likely to have been in Ephesus than in Rome, which was a long way from their homes. Against this must be set the fact that little or nothing of a specific nature is known about most of these associates of Paul, and the one whose activities are best documented, Luke, was certainly with Paul in Rome though, according to Acts, not in Ephesus.
● It is argued that Philemon's slave, Onesimus, would have been more likely to run away to Ephesus, which was only about eighty miles from his home in Colossae, than to Rome, which was almost 800 miles away.

This, again, is not a convincing argument, for at that time all roads literally did lead to Rome. Arguably a runaway slave would be more likely to try to disappear in the capital of the empire than in a provincial town the size of Ephesus.
● Philippians gives the impression that there was much travelling to and from Paul's prison, and Ephesus was significantly nearer to Philippi than Rome. This is often taken to be a strong argument for supposing that Philippians at least must have been written from Ephesus.
● The strongest argument for an Ephesian origin of these letters is that in them Paul was looking forward to an early release, after which he intended visiting his friends in both Philippi and Colossae. In Romans 15:28, however, he had made it plain that, after his visit to Jerusalem, his intention was not to revisit churches he had founded before, but to go west to Spain.

What, then, can we conclude from these facts? It is almost certain that Paul did have a period of imprisonment during his stay in Ephesus, and quite possible that Philippians at least, with its mention of frequent journeys between Philippi and Paul's prison, might have been written at that time. If this was the case, the letter to the Philippians would need to be dated about AD55 instead of 62.

argument seems to have been about sex and food, with some claiming that true spiritual enlightenment could only be achieved through a life of asceticism in which material bodily existence was denied as far as possible. In contradiction to this, Timothy is urged to remember that 'Everything that God has created is good; nothing is to be rejected' (1 Timothy 4:4).

These people probably had leanings towards a Jewish form of Gnosticism. There is indeed a specific mention of 'the profane talk and foolish arguments of what some people wrongly call "Knowledge" [Greek *gnosis*]' (1 Timothy 6:20). Like the Gnostics of the second century and later, they wanted to deny that this world is really God's world – and so the sooner they could escape from it, the better. Indications that Timothy's opponents were arguing about 'myths and endless genealogies which promote speculations' and had 'lost their way in foolish discussions' also

---

Did Paul write the pastoral epistles?

These three letters are very different from Paul's other letters. They were written not to churches, but to two individuals who were working among recently established Christian communities: Timothy at Ephesus and Titus at Crete. In form, subject matter and style these three letters are very similar to each other, but in all these respects they are quite distinct from Paul's other letters. The differences are so striking that a majority of scholars have concluded that, at least in their present form, they could not have been written by Paul himself.

In considering this question, four main points need to be taken into consideration.

Paul's movements
It is difficult to fit the travels of Paul, implied or described here, into the story of his movements in Acts. Three main explanations have been proposed in the effort to explain the historical references made in these letters.
● *Paul was released after the imprisonment recorded at the end of Acts.* This view supposes that, after his house imprisonment in Rome, he continued his missionary work for a period of about two years before being returned to that city and meeting his death during Nero's persecution. No such release is recorded

in Acts, of course, though in principle this is no problem since Luke's purpose was not to write a biography of Paul, but to tell how the Christian message had spread from small beginnings in Jerusalem to the centre of the empire in Rome. This view that Paul was released and carried on further work has been the traditional view since the earliest days of the church, and is still held today by some scholars. Even within its own frame of reference, however, it cannot solve all the questions, for it is still very difficult to string together all the travel references made in the pastoral epistles to produce any plausible itinerary for further missionary expeditions.
● *These letters were second-century writings.*
On this view, originally popularized in the late nineteenth century, the pastoral epistles were compiled by people who were trying to reinterpret Paul at a time when he had fallen out of favour with the church. The travel references of the pastorals were not based on actual traditions about Paul's journeys, but were created to give a touch of realism to these letters. The difficulty with this view is that some of the historical references here are hardly the kind of thing that anyone would invent. For instance, 2 Timothy 4:13 contains the instruction, 'When you come, bring the cloak that I left with Carpus at

support this identification (1 Timothy 1:4, 6). But, of course, there was more than one way to belittle bodily existence. Asceticism was only one option, and extreme permissiveness was another. At least a section of those with whom Timothy was dealing seems to have chosen this alternative: 'they will hold to the outward form of our religion, but reject its real power' (2 Timothy 3:5). For Paul, the Christian gospel had always been about changing lifestyles, not about provoking arguments.

TRUE BELIEF
In response to all this, Timothy and Titus were being encouraged to reaffirm the basic elements of true Christian faith, especially by continuing to oppose the idea that God does not care about the world we live in. The fact that Jesus himself was both truly human and truly divine clearly contradicted

---

Troas, also the books, and above all the parchments.' It is hard to imagine that a later, self-conscious imitator of Paul would invent such details, for they have no theological content or ideological purpose, nor do they recount anything essential about Paul himself. It is the kind of comment that is more likely to have originated in some real-life situation.

● *These letters were compiled from fragments of genuine Pauline letters.* Though the letters in their present form were written in the second century by someone who was trying to reassert the authority of Paul in the church, pieces of incidental information such as those just mentioned have a ring of authenticity about them. On this basis, it is suggested that five genuine scraps of Paul's writings can be discovered in 2 Timothy and Titus, and that these were incorporated into a later work by a second-century writer. Insofar as there is anything approaching a consensus on the matter, this view has a good claim, even though it has its own difficulties. For example, how or why would five such fragments have survived independently from the time of Paul, in the middle of the first century, to the time of his imitator, almost 100 years later? What kind of person would have been interested in preserving them, since they contain nothing more than scraps of personal information with no theological teaching or pastoral advice?

Church organization
Attention is often drawn to the fact that the type of church organization shown in these letters is much more developed than the structures presupposed in Paul's earlier letters. It is certainly true that the pastoral epistles reflect something much closer to the second-century church, with its ruling bishops and complicated organization, albeit in an embryonic form. Other considerations also need to be taken into account:
● Paul's earlier letters contain no examples of advice directed specifically towards church leaders, and it is therefore difficult to know what kind of advice he might have given such people, or what level of organization he might have assumed in the early Christian communities. 1 Corinthians 5:1–13 advises about church discipline, which itself implies some structure that was able to take responsibility for it, while much of the debate behind other sections of 1 and 2 Corinthians related to the claims and counter-claims of people who, in some way, were jostling for positions of control in the church.
● No functions or positions are mentioned in the pastoral epistles that are not also to be found either in Acts or in Paul's earlier letters.
● The position of Timothy and Titus was certainly not that of the later 'monarchical' or ruling bishop. They are, rather, Paul's personal representatives, and such

Paul dictated his letters to a secretary, often adding a personal greeting at the end. This wooden pen case, dating from Paul's time, contains reed pens and an inkwell half-full of black ink.

such a notion (1 Timothy 3:14–16). Not only did Jesus come into this world to share God's love, but he became personally involved with people in their humanness. The essence of salvation, therefore, is not to be found in philosophical speculation, but in humble acceptance of God's love and mercy as demonstrated in the life, death and resurrection of Jesus (1 Timothy 1:15–17). Those who have their theological priorities right will show it in the way they live, not motivated by making money or empire building, but by 'the true words of our Lord Jesus Christ' (1 Timothy 6:3–10).

CHRISTIAN BEHAVIOUR

This theme keeps arising throughout these three letters. Several passages spell out in more detail how Christians ought to behave: family relationships (Titus 2:1–5), relationships in the church (1 Timothy 5:1 – 6:2), and attitudes to secular governments (Titus 3:1–7) should all reflect

---

Did Paul write the pastoral epistles?
continued

authority as they have stems from the fact that he was an apostle, and they had been sent by him.

● From time to time it has been suggested some sort of Gnostic heresy was in view in the pastoral epistles, which by definition would make them second-century works. But the emergence of Gnosticism and the responses of the church to it were much more complex than that. Whatever was going on in the communities where Timothy and Titus worked, it was quite different from the kind of Gnosticism found in the second century, and has many more obvious points of connection with the kind of arguments that are dealt with in 1 and 2 Corinthians and Colossians.

Doctrinal teaching

The form of teaching in the pastoral epistles is definitely distinctive. Apart from a few statements called 'faithful sayings' (for example, 1 Timothy 1:15), there is very little that connects with Paul's characteristic teaching. The doctrine of the Holy Spirit, for example, hardly features here and, when it does, it seems less related to Paul's charismatic understanding of the Spirit's role in directing the day-to-day life of the church, and more integrated with an organizational structure. These are strong reasons for locating the pastorals in a later stage of church development, though even

here things are not as clear-cut as they can be made to appear:

● Paul's 'charismatic' doctrine has often been portrayed as a free-for-all in the church, with freedom being understood as the opposite of order. But when Paul spoke of the spiritual gifts (*charismata*) in 1 Corinthians 12 – 14, he clearly meant to imply that there should be recognized ways of doing things in the church. Not every person would be equipped by the Spirit to perform the same work, and this was the basis on which some might be recognized as teachers, others as pastors, and so on. This is a different way of identifying and defining leadership, for people are not appointed to 'offices' but recognized by the things they can do well. Nevertheless, while that might be the underlying philosophy of leadership, from an external perspective it was clearly possible, in the early days, to identify those who were in such positions. Philippians 1:1 and 1 Thessalonians 5:12 show that Paul recognized such people and, according to Acts 14:23, he himself appointed some of them. The fact that they were to be Spirit-directed and empowered did not mean there was no formal or visible order about the way in which they operated.

● It is not true to say that the Holy Spirit has no part to play in the pastoral epistles. We find here the same emphasis as elsewhere on the working of the Holy

the best aspirations of the ancient world, 'so that no one will speak evil of the message that comes from God' (Titus 2:5).

CHRISTIAN LEADERSHIP

Given the nature and purpose of these letters, there is much personal advice here for Titus and Timothy about their own conduct. They are to be examples of good behaviour to all whom they serve (1 Timothy 6:11–21; Titus 1:5–9), but they must also have courage to stand firm for the truth (2 Timothy 2:1–26), recognizing that the gospel depends not on personal opinions, but on God's own purposes (2 Timothy 3:10 – 4:8). They must also ensure that those whom they appoint to serve in leadership capacities in their churches have the same qualities, and are the sort of people whom others can admire (1 Timothy 3:1–13; 4:6–16).

Spirit in the lives of believers (2 Timothy 1:14), while Timothy himself is said to have been appointed as God's servant by means of prophecy, which was one of the most characteristic ways of the Spirit's working (1 Timothy 1:18).

Style and vocabulary

The real strength of the suggestion that the pastoral epistles were not written by Paul lies in the style and vocabulary of the letters. There are about 175 words here which are not found in Paul's other letters, many of which would be more characteristic of Christian writers in the second century than the first. In addition to these words, there is a difference of style in what might be called the 'connecting tissue' of these letters, that is the arrangement of conjunctions, participles and similar grammatical features. This is rather different from Paul's other letters, and 112 of his favourite prepositions and particles are missing.

These facts are impressive, and should not be set aside lightly, though again they are open to more than one interpretation. Some linguistic experts think that the pastoral epistles are too short to provide enough material for a reliable literary analysis of this kind. In addition, both style and vocabulary are very often affected by the subject matter that is being discussed, and even the argument from the use

of typical connecting particles is not entirely persuasive, as Colossians and 2 Thessalonians both have considerably fewer of these than Paul's other letters.

What has emerged from all these debates is that there are differences between the language of the pastorals and Paul's earlier letters. These differences could perhaps be explained by reference to the different subject matter, to the fact that Paul was now an older man, that the differences derive from the incorporation of traditional statements or quotations from other sources – even to the fact that he was using a different secretary. It is also possible that a letter written by Paul himself might have been revised later to improve its literary style.

Current opinion is finely balanced. All the evidence of the early church fathers supports the view that Paul had some connection with these letters, and certainly they do not reflect life in the church at a period much later than his lifetime. Some have drawn attention to many similarities between the pastoral epistles and Luke–Acts, and have suggested that Paul's friend and companion Luke could have written them in their present form after the apostle's death, using rough drafts of genuinely Pauline material as a starting point.

20 What Does it Mean to be a Christian?

The story of Paul's life makes exciting reading. By any standards he was a remarkable person. His courage and perseverance were outstanding. He was one of the great visionaries of his age, and his determination to share the Christian message with the whole of the Roman world was surpassed only by his own fervent commitment to Christ. As a writer, he was both prolific and perceptive, and his letters have given us an intimate understanding of the joys and trials of life in the earliest Christian churches.

But Paul was much more than just a brilliant missionary strategist and a devoted disciple of Jesus. He was also one of the church's greatest theologians. His influence was extensive enough during his lifetime, but his writings have inspired many great spiritual movements in every generation since. From Augustine of Hippo in the fourth century to the theologians of fast-growing churches all around the world today, men and women of many times and places would affirm that Paul's writings have spoken to their own situations in new and challenging ways. Historically, Paul stands second only to Jesus himself as an innovative thinker in the developing life of the early Christian communities.

From letters to theology

What then was Paul's understanding of the Christian message? It is easier to ask that question than it is to answer it. Paul's writings account for almost one third of the whole of the New Testament, but not a single one of them can reasonably be regarded as a book of theology explaining how Paul would articulate his Christian beliefs in a systematic form. It is understandable that we should want to produce a comprehensive account of Paul's thinking, but it is important to remember that such an enterprise is something he never attempted for himself – or, if he did, he left no written account of it. Moreover, the literary genre of the writings we do have only increases our own difficulties. Though there are plenty of examples of the letter style being used as a literary device to put across a message, Paul's writings cannot be classified among these 'literary epistles'. They were not just a neat way of presenting arguments about philosophical or theological questions: without exception, they were all real letters, written to real people to deal with real-life situations. If Paul had not come up against the Judaizers in the Galatian churches, we should not have had the letter to the Galatians with its complicated explanations of the relationship of Christian faith to the Old Testament Law. If there had been no 'parties' in Corinth, we would not have the equally important teaching of 1 and 2 Corinthians. If Paul had not been involved in these arguments then perhaps he would never have written Romans in precisely the way he did. Paul's letters were not the product of reflective thinking behind closed doors in the comfort and relative isolation of a study. They emerged out of his experience as a church pioneer, and their contents inevitably reflect that experience.

In reading Paul's letters today, we need to be sensitive to all this. Paul never intended them – either separately or all together – to be a comprehensive account of the Christian faith. He probably never expected anybody to collect them at all, for he generally assumed they would only be read by those to whom they were addressed. Some were detailed replies to other letters that had been sent to him – letters that no longer exist for us to consult. So reading what Paul wrote can be like overhearing one half of a telephone conversation. When that happens, it is often possible to grasp the general meaning of what is being said, but unless the one who overhears has a close knowledge of the people who are talking to each other, the details of their conversation will usually remain obscure. If that is the case with people whose lifestyle and general culture are the same as our own, then it should be no surprise that it is a complex business to come to a full understanding of a person whose letters reflect conditions in a world that was quite different.

To derive a clear and coherent account of Paul's thinking from occasional letters, we need to give special attention to the context in which they were written. In Galatians, for example, Paul argues that it is not necessary to be a Jew first in order to be a Christian, whereas virtually none of those who read his letters today would ever have imagined that it might be – and as a result, his long arguments about Abraham, Moses, and the Old Testament Law can easily confuse rather than clarify. Even ideas that appear to transcend the centuries can pose similar problems. To people today, the word 'church' most often suggests a particular style of building, or a religious organization, whereas for Paul the same word meant something altogether different, and referred neither to buildings nor to bureaucratic structures, but to the quality of relationships that could be found among a particular group of people.

Nevertheless, the problems are far from insoluble and, in spite of differences of opinion over some of the details, there is a remarkable degree of agreement about the readers and general background of most of Paul's letters. Inevitably, the real significance of some things that he mentions will remain elusive. But in spite of all this, it is not difficult to identify those elements that formed the central core of Paul's Christian beliefs.

Back to the Damascus road

The foundation stone of Paul's Christian faith was his experience of the risen Christ on the road to Damascus (Acts 9:1–19; 22:6–16; 26:12–18). The events of that day had changed the whole course of his life. We have already seen what that meant for Paul, as he gave himself wholeheartedly to the service of the one whom he met so unexpectedly. This surprise encounter inspired Paul to share with others the living message of Jesus, who had so radically challenged his preconceptions and changed his own life. But his meeting with the risen Jesus was more than just an internal experience that affected his personal behaviour: it was also the source of his thinking as a Christian evangelist and theologian. He was converted intellectually, as well as emotionally and spiritually.

When Paul left Jerusalem in hot pursuit of the Christians who had fled to Damascus, he was by all accounts a convinced Pharisee. He was quite certain that the most important facts in the world were to be found in the ancient faith of his people, as that was described in their scriptures and interpreted by his own teachers. Paul had no doubt listened with attention to the arguments of people like Stephen, but he believed they were mistaken. The claim that Jesus had in some way superseded the Old Testament – still more the idea that he was alive after his shameful death on the cross – was both incredible and unacceptable. It was because he was convinced that their message was not true that Paul was so energetic in his opposition to the Christians. As far as he was concerned, obeying the Old Testament, not following Jesus, was the only way to please God – and Paul was determined to use every means possible to demonstrate the truth of that.

By all accounts, Paul's own moral and spiritual achievements seemed to back up his thinking, for he later wrote of how 'I was ahead of most fellow Jews of my age in my practice of the Jewish religion, and was much more devoted to the traditions of our ancestors... As far as a person can be righteous by obeying the commands of the law, I was without fault...' (Galatians 1:14; Philippians 3:6). It has sometimes been supposed that by the time he met the risen Christ, Paul was disenchanted with Judaism, but there is no evidence at all for this. On the contrary, it was an expression of his fierce pride in his religion that first motivated him to persecute the Christians, who to him were the arch-enemies of the Law he loved so much.

What followed therefore was totally unexpected. For by the time he reached Damascus, he had changed his mind. As a result of his encounter with the risen Jesus, he knew that he had been wrong, and the Christians were right. It is hard to grasp the full impact that this experience must have had on Paul, but it was natural for him that such a radical about-turn should form the starting point for his subsequent reflections on what it meant to be a Christian. He made that clear in

Galatians 1:11–12 when he wrote that 'the gospel I preach is not of human origin. I did not receive it from a human source, nor was I taught it, but I received it through a revelation of Jesus Christ...'

It was suggested in an earlier chapter that Paul's understanding of the gospel was in all essentials continuous with the message of Jesus, and consistent with the beliefs of those who were Christians before him. But he certainly had an original way of expressing it – and all the most distinctive aspects of his thinking can be traced directly back to his Damascus road experience.

Who is Jesus?

As a Jew and a Pharisee, Paul was looking for the arrival of God's kingdom. Like others of his generation, he was praying for the coming of the Messiah who would inaugurate a new age of justice and peace in which God's will would most truly be done. He no doubt shared the common expectation that when the Messiah came he would be a conquering, all-powerful king, at least part of whose achievements would be to return the land of Israel to the Jewish people and get rid of the Roman troops of occupation. Paul therefore had no time for Jesus. Despite the great personal claims he had implied and his followers had made more overtly, the course of events had proved quite conclusively that he was nothing but a discredited and disreputable messianic pretender. The nature of his death, on the cross, only served to underline that, for the Old Testament had declared that anyone suffering such an end 'brings God's curse on the land' (Deuteronomy 21:23).

But all that was before his conversion. For on the Damascus road, Paul learned not only that Jesus was indeed the expected Messiah, but that he was also the 'Son of God'. This discovery had such an impact on his thinking that it was the major subject of his first Christian preaching in Damascus itself (Acts 9:20). When Paul himself later recalled this experience he described it in terms of God's Son 'revealed in me' (Galatians 1:15–16). Before that, he could never have entertained the idea that anyone else could stand alongside God. As a Christian, he still believed in only one God, of course, but from then on he was convinced that God could only be fully known through Jesus (2 Corinthians 4:6).

More than that, for throughout his writings he gave to Jesus the title that the Old Testament had reserved exclusively for God: Jesus was now 'the Lord'. Paul emphasized more than once that no one could be a Christian without believing that (Romans 10:9; 1 Corinthians 12:3; 16:22). In doing so, of course, he was following the beliefs of the earliest Christians in Jerusalem, who had also expressed their convictions in the simple confession that 'Jesus is Lord'. Paul discovered that later, and in one place he quoted an Aramaic slogan that the first believers had used (1 Corinthians 16:22). But as far as he was concerned, it was on the Damascus road that the essential core of that belief was first communicated to him.

What is the gospel?

How had Paul arrived at this point? What had he done to enable God to break into his life in this way? As Paul reflected on such questions, the answer was obvious, and simple: nothing. Paul became a Christian for no other reason than God's loving concern for him, which had led to his unexpected meeting with the risen Jesus: 'see how much God loves us – it was while we were still sinners that Christ died for us!' (Romans 5:8). On the Damascus road, Paul appreciated that his own salvation depended neither on his ethnic origins as a Jew, nor on his moral achievements. It happened solely because of God's love – love that Paul had never deserved. It was an act of pure 'grace'.

Of course, Paul had done something in response to God's undeserved love. He believed it, and 'belief', or 'faith', became a key concept in Paul's understanding of the Christian life. But what did he mean by it? The queen in *Alice in Wonderland* told Alice that believing needs practice: 'When I was your age, I always did it for half an hour every day. Why, sometimes I've believed as many as six impossible things before breakfast!' Christian faith has often been caricatured in this way, as something essentially irrational, 'a leap in the dark'. But Paul could never have thought of it like that, for two reasons:

■ Paul's word 'faith' does not imply 'blind faith' in impossible things. 'Faith' or 'belief' was a way of describing Paul's response to the revelation of God's love in his life. A more accurate way of describing it would be to refer to it as 'commitment'.

■ But it was not commitment in a vacuum – nor in the private world of Paul's internal spirituality. Some people think that mystery and irrationality are central components of religious experience: if something is easy to understand and seems to make sense, then they doubt whether it can be the real thing! But Paul was not like that. His response to God was based on a holistic perception that began with his direct experience, but was also integrated with the facts. There were people in Paul's day who imagined that feelings were the only important criterion of true belief. Without for a moment playing down the significance of that, Paul also saw faith as something rational, connected to a bedrock of facts that were true, foremost among them the fact of Jesus' resurrection from the dead (1 Corinthians 15:1–8).

These then were the key features in Paul's gospel: God's undeserved love ('grace') shown to humankind through Jesus, to which the appropriate response was 'faith', which included a commitment to God that was based not on wishful thinking, but on the absolute facts of Jesus' life, death, and resurrection, and the arrival of God's kingdom. This was the message that Paul spread so successfully throughout the Mediterranean world. The origin of his missionary zeal was also related to his conversion, for he discovered that God's grace was not for him only, but was to be shared with others – even those who were not Jews. So without seeking the advice of anyone else, he went off almost immediately to 'Arabia' to share the good news about Jesus with the Gentiles he found there (Galatians 1:15–17).

A social gospel

Just as Paul's new-found faith motivated him to share the good news with others by talking of his own experience, so it also gave him new insights into the nature of human relationships and, as his ministry developed, the gospel's impact on such relationships became one of the keynotes of his message. For Paul, commitment was never just a theoretical thing. It was important that his belief should be based on hard facts and experienced in his own life, but he also knew that it must have some practical outworking in the social and cultural realities of the wider community.

Paul had discovered the importance of this shortly after he arrived in Damascus. The Christians there knew he was on his way, and no doubt viewed him with apprehension. But, in spite of his reputation, they also received him as a brother in Christ and a friend. The warmth of their reception challenged all Paul's preconceptions. The social fabric of ancient culture in both the Roman and the Jewish context depended for its stability and survival on the maintenance of appropriate boundaries between different groups of people. Consequently, Jews despised Gentiles, Roman citizens had little appreciation for those whom they considered 'barbarians', masters were implacably opposed to slaves – and even in the family it was often taken for granted that men would exploit their women and children. But Paul discovered that the gospel had the power to change all that.

If people could be accepted and affirmed by God without any preconditions, then those who were Christians must show the same openness in their relationships with others. This became a major theme of Paul's understanding of the Christian faith. It is not a coincidence that he could summarize the message of one of his major letters in social terms: 'there is no longer Jews or Greek, there is no longer slave or free, there is no longer male and female; for all of you are one in Christ Jesus' (Galatians 3:28). Through reflection on that, Paul evolved his distinctive understanding of the nature of the Christian community, which is dealt with in greater detail in the next chapter here. It took him some time to work through all its ramifications, but the centrality of this notion itself was something that Paul first learned on the Damascus road and in what happened immediately after that.

What about the Law?

The relevance of the Old Testament Law for Christian believers is a major subject in many of Paul's letters. As a Jew, Paul believed that careful observance of the Law was an integral part of faithful response to God's love. It was because of his loyalty to the Law that he found it so difficult to believe that Jesus could be the Messiah, for the Law said, 'Anyone who is hanged on a tree is under God's curse' (Deuteronomy 21:23; Galatians 3:13). Since Jesus had been crucified on a cross, then by definition he could not have been the Messiah.

When Paul set off for Damascus he was motivated only by loyalty to the Old Testament Law, and his hatred of the followers of Jesus was based not on personal animosity but provoked by an understandable desire to uphold what he knew to be God's standards. So when Paul encountered the risen Christ and discovered that he was wrong, a large question mark was placed against the whole structure of his inherited spirituality.

From that moment onwards, he knew that the Old Testament Law was no longer the way to please God, because in the very act of keeping it most meticulously, Paul had clearly found himself on the opposite side to God! Paul's Christian life therefore began with the realization that the way to please God was no longer through faithful observance of the Law, and that continuing to do so would be not only irrelevant, but could actually be contrary to the will of God.

Living the Christian life

How then was the Christian life to be lived? Quite simply, said Paul: not by keeping the Law, but by trusting Jesus. Previously the Law had been the centre of Paul's life; now Jesus was at the centre. Before, Paul had seen keeping the Law as an essential part of being good; now, he knew he could be truly good only by allowing God to change his life. This was such a major shift in Paul's moral motivation that he could write of it as a crucifixion and resurrection: a point at which all that he had previously valued became meaningless in the face of his encounter with the God who surprised him by infusing his life with the power to be the kind of person that in his heart he had always most wanted to be.

This was not just a theological theory for Paul. Everywhere in his letters he makes it plain that he had an intense awareness of the power and presence of the living Jesus working in his life to give him victory over failure and to renew his personality: 'it is no longer I who live, but it is Christ who lives in me' (Galatians 2:20). From the moment when he met the risen Christ on the Damascus road, Paul knew that his entire life was to be ruled, guided and directed by this living Lord, and his subsequent experience showed that Jesus could be trusted to do that. Elsewhere, Paul describes the Christian life as a life 'in Christ' (2 Corinthians 12:2). It was by being 'in Christ' that a person could effectively 'die' to a life of sin and receive the power of a new life, reconciled to God. Being 'in Christ' meant that the Christian was filled by Christ, so that at every point the believer could say 'to me to live is Christ... to know him and the power of his resurrection' (Philippians 1:21; 3:10).

Paul used such language in a very literal sense. Christians were intended to 'become like God's Son' (Romans 8:29). Jesus himself had been the only one ever to do God's will perfectly, and Christians could now do the same by the presence of the risen Christ living within them. The way this would happen was by the operation of the Holy Spirit, one of whose tasks was to help Christians to be like Jesus. This too was a lesson Paul learned in the moment of his conversion. Looking back to it some time later, he wrote: 'All of us then reflect the glory of the Lord with uncovered faces; and that same glory, coming from the Lord, who is the Spirit, transforms us into God's likeness in an ever greater degree of glory' (2 Corinthians 3:18).

Explaining the faith

Paul's conversion gave him a new understanding of the relationship between people and God. But Paul was a great thinker, and he soon needed to explain these new beliefs in relation to other aspects of his life. What exactly was it that happened to him on the Damascus road, and what did it all mean?

To answer those questions, Paul naturally began with his own roots in Judaism. If the Old Testament was truly God's word, then how could it be understood in the light of what God was now doing through Jesus? That was an important question for Paul, and for many of those with whom he came into contact. But as he took the good news about Jesus into the wider Gentile world, the same questions needed to be answered in other ways. How did the Christian gospel impinge on the social and moral concerns which had dominated much of the religious and philosophical literature of the Roman world? Paul's thinking on both these matters is clearly reflected in his letters.

The Old Testament

The Old Testament must have been Paul's biggest headache. Starting from the Damascus road, he knew that, through Jesus as Messiah, God had accepted him and changed his life, and had asked only for Paul's wholehearted commitment in return. But the Old Testament had always included observation of the Law as an integral part of what it meant to please God. So if Jesus was God's Son and the Old Testament was God's Law, there was some kind of contradiction here that would need to be resolved. Working out how to address that was a big question, not only for Paul but for every other devoted Jewish person who became a Christian. It was one of the most urgent issues in the life of the early church, which explains why so many of Paul's letters are concerned with it. In looking at Galatians and Romans, we have already noticed briefly how Paul dealt with it.

In effect, he argued that the traditional view and his new Christian understanding were both true, but not at the same time as each other.

The Old Testament was God's word, and Jesus was God's Son. But the Old Testament was only a temporary word from God, 'our custodian until Christ came, in order that we might then be put right with God through faith' (Galatians 3:24). God's gracious love, accepted in faith, had always been the real basis of salvation, as far back as the time of Abraham himself (Galatians 3:6–9).

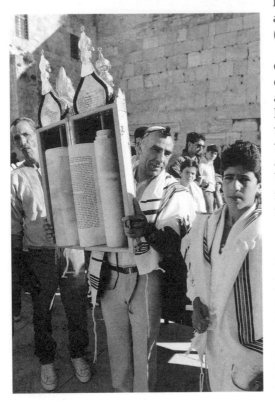

Human experience had shown that even scrupulous law-keeping could not deliver people from guilt, but Jesus could – and did (Galatians 3:10–12). How then did he do it? This further question led Paul to the central facts of Jesus' whole existence: the cross and resurrection. The cross was always at the heart of Paul's preaching, because for him it explained the relationship between Christian faith and the Old Testament Law (1 Corinthians 1:18 – 2:5).

To be in the right with God, a person must be a part of the covenant family of Abraham, and that included observance of the Old Testament Law. Human experience, however, showed that religious observance by itself – whatever the theological explanation behind it – did not always produce a sense of well-being in the human spirit. In spite of all his claims to near-perfection, Paul himself was not flawless, and as he thought honestly about

One of the most urgent issues which had to be resolved by the early church was the conflict of the demands of the Old Testament Law with the new Christian faith. Here, modern Jews parade a copy of the Torah, the first five books of the Old Testament.

the kind of person he was he realized that he was not the kind of person he claimed to be. It was this 'curse' of human failure that Jesus dealt with by his death on the cross. By sharing in that alienation from God which was the result not of his own wrongdoing, but of the wrongdoing of others, he invalidated the effects of human sin, and his subsequent resurrection made the benefits of that available to any who would commit themselves to him (Galatians 3:13–14). Paul never attempted to explain exactly how this could happen. If pressed, he would probably have said that it defied logical explanation, for it was his own experience that had ultimately convinced him of its truth.

The world of experience

Such arguments made sense to people who were steeped in the Old Testament Law. But Paul took the Christian message to non-Jewish people, and for them there were more appropriate ways of explaining the impact of Jesus' coming.

In doing so, Paul began from an idea that was familiar to both Jews and Gentiles. Our present experience of life is not the only one possible, he said. Certainly it is not a total presentation of the ultimate truth about the world, and God, and people. We have already come across one version of this idea in the beliefs of the Gnostics, for whom the truth was to be discovered in a proper distinction between two worlds: the material world where we live now, and the spiritual world where God is. On this view, salvation consisted in escaping from the one to the other. Paul sometimes used their language, but his conceptual framework was provided by a more traditional Jewish idea of 'two ages'.

These 'two ages' are mentioned in many Jewish apocalyptic writings, and also in the teachings of some rabbis. But the distinction between them was an ethical one, and not a cosmological or metaphysical one like the two worlds of the Gnostics. Jewish thinkers had spoken of life in 'this age' as under the domination of sin or the devil, while life in 'the age to come' would be lived under the personal direction of God, or the Messiah. In that context, evil would be defeated and God's will would be supreme. Paul took this notion as a useful starting point to explain how God through Jesus could be related to ordinary everyday life.

Most people's experience suggests that life as we know it is somehow spoiled by evil. However high our ideals might be, it is a simple fact that most of us for much of the time will not actually act in accordance with them. Justice, fairness and equality might seem to be desirable things, but in general the world is not organized that way. On balance, the world seems to have an inclination towards wrong rather than right. Paul accepted this diagnosis, and recognized that, because they are human, Christians are a part of 'this present evil age' (Galatians 1:4).

But alongside that, the Christian gospel presented an alternative possibility. Jesus himself had spoken of the arrival of God's kingdom, offering the possibility of doing things God's way and reflecting God's values and standards. This was the way to create a society whose standards would be the opposite of those which seem to characterize the world as it is now: '... to bring good news to the poor... to proclaim liberty to the captives and recovery of sight to the blind; to set free the oppressed...' (Luke 4:18–19). It is in this rather different way of being that Christians should find their true destiny: they are 'citizens of heaven' (Philippians 3:20).

All this was good Jewish thinking, but Paul's new Christian perspective enabled him to see it in a different light.

■ For Jews, 'the age to come', or 'kingdom of God', was in the future, perhaps a far distant future. But Jesus had announced its arrival, and claimed it was present in his own life and ministry, for he himself was the Messiah and Son of God. He told his disciples that 'there are some here who will not die until they have seen the kingdom of God come with power' (Mark 9:1), and as the earliest Christians looked back at Jesus' life, death, and resurrection and the coming of the Holy Spirit at

Pentecost, they were certain that this promise had indeed come true. Paul agreed with them. Though he did not typically use the terminology of 'kingdom of God', he was deeply conscious of the fact that becoming a Christian meant the transfer of one's allegiance from the standards of the fallen world to the values of God's new creation: 'anyone who is joined to Christ is a new being; the old is gone, the new has come... God rescued us from the power of darkness and brought us safe into the kingdom of God's dear Son, by whom we are set free...' (2 Corinthians 5:17; Colossians 1:13–14).

To be sure, Christians still live in the world that is dominated by sin. But the prevailing influence in their lives must be God's kingdom, and their behaviour should reflect this. This formed the basis of Paul's ethical advice to his readers: 'Do not conform yourselves to the standards of this world, but let God transform you inwardly by a complete change of your mind. Then you will be able to know the will of God...' (Romans 12:2).

That did not imply Christians were already perfect. Like Jesus before him, Paul maintained an eschatological tension between the present operation of God's sovereignty in the lives of Christian people and its full and final unveiling at some point in the future. But the presence of the Holy Spirit in the lives of Christians represented the invasion of this world by God's kingdom – and meant that Christians should live accordingly.

Jesus had spelled out the implications of this both in his teaching and by his way of life. Paul expected his readers to do the same: 'let the Spirit direct your lives... the Spirit produces love, joy, peace, patience, kindness, goodness, faithfulness, humility, and self-control' (Galatians 5:16, 22–23). Paul also believed that God's standards of justice and fairness must apply to the corporate life of society as well as to personal morality. This is why he could declare so boldly that the barriers of the fallen world were meaningless in the presence of God's new creation (Galatians 3:28; Ephesians 2:11–22).

Paul knew well enough that the Christian life would therefore be a life of constant tension, in which the values of the fallen world would be seeking to obliterate the standards of God's new creation (Romans 7:14–25). But he believed it was possible for Christians to triumph over sin and live as God intended, provided they recognized the impossibility of doing so by their own best efforts, and were prepared to trust God to breathe new life into them by the operation of the Holy Spirit (Galatians 5:25). This was the true meaning of Christian baptism, which for Paul was a symbolic expression of a moral and spiritual change that took place in a person's life when they had been committed to Christ (Romans 6:1–4).

■ Paul also altered the traditional Jewish 'two worlds' scheme by suggesting that human experience really encompasses not two worlds, but three. Unlike some of his fellow rabbis, Paul was well aware of the fact that the behaviour of people outside the orbit of Judaism could on occasion reflect God's will. Many Jews wrote off the Gentiles as being quite incapable of pleasing God, but Paul's upbringing in the Hellenistic world showed him that this was wide of the mark. Greek and Roman moralists at their best had expressed the highest ideals, some of them apparently similar to the principles announced by Jesus himself.

The same question often plagues Christians today. Why is it that secularists can sometimes share the ideals and values of Christians? Paul found the answer by referring back to the Old Testament's teaching that all people are created 'in God's image' (Genesis 1:27). One aspect of the meaning of that phrase is that to be human automatically gives a person a built-in capacity for understanding God's will. Of course, in the fallen world that capacity has been limited by the impact of evil. But in spite of that, people do instinctively know the difference between right and wrong, whether alerted to it by conscience or by some other internal moral mechanism.

This has often been referred to as the 'natural law' by theologians, and it undoubtedly played an important part in Paul's thinking (Romans 1:18 – 2:16). It enabled him to explain the relationship between the world as God originally made it, the world in its fallen state as we all know it, and the new creation that God has inaugurated through the life, death and resurrection of Jesus. Christians understand the character of God's kingdom because they themselves are a part of it, while those who have not yet discovered Jesus Christ have a dimmer view of God's standards because they are a part of the fallen world, with its tendency to prevent people from actually carrying out God's will.

We can see from this that Paul had a very comprehensive definition of the meaning of Christian salvation. He has often been criticized for being narrow-minded and introspective. Some of his greatest admirers have often been both, but nothing could be further from the truth as far as Paul himself is concerned.

For Paul, the whole world – indeed, the whole universe – was the stage on which the drama of redemption was to be played out. Personal and individual salvation was important, but could never be separated from social and cosmic salvation. The life, death and resurrection of Jesus was the hinge on which the whole of world history turned: it was the beginning of God's 'new creation'. Like Jesus, Paul looked to a future time when God's kingdom would arrive in its fullness. But Paul never saw the Christian faith as merely a hope for a better future. On the Damascus road, he had experienced the renewing power of God's forgiving Spirit at work in his own life, and he saw all those who committed themselves to Jesus Christ as a channel through which the life of God's kingdom can be directed into life as we know it in the present fallen world.

Through the behaviour of such 'kingdom people', God can demonstrate the meaning of the true freedom for which both the physical world and its people are crying out (Romans 8:18–25). Christians must show this by the way they handle the world of plants and animals, as well as in their own personal spirituality. But for Paul, the greatest opportunity for demonstrating the reality of what life might be like when things were done God's way was through the new relationships which came into being in the church, and in the next chapter we must turn our attention more specifically to that.

Renewing God's world.

	Creation World: 'In God's Image' *(Genesis 1:26–27)* Perfect relationships: free to serve God and one another	Fallen World: 'In Adam' *(Romans 5:12–21)* Broken relationships: bondage and barriers	New Creation/Kingdom of God: 'In Christ' *(1 Corinthians 15:20–28)* Restored relationships: freedom and equality
Physical	**Perfect creation** *Genesis 1:1–2:4; Colossians 1:15–17*	**Ecological crisis – spoiled world** *Romans 8:18–23; Genesis 3:17–19*	**Renewed world** *Colossians 1:15–20; Romans 8:18–23*
Social	**No barriers** **Peace** **Mutual sharing**	**Disharmony: race – class – sex** **War – conflict – injustice – pain – suffering** *Galatians 5:19–21* **Selfishness – disharmony – frustration**	**Freedom and equality** *Galatians 3:28; 1 Corinthians 12:12–31; Ephesians 2:14–18* **Peace and harmony** *Romans 12:17–21; Ephesians 4:1–6; Galatians 5:22–23* **Sharing and love** *Romans 12:8–13; 2 Corinthians 9:6–15; Philippians 2:4–11; 1 Thessalonians 2:1–12; 2 Thessalonians 3:15; 1 Corinthians 13*
Partnership	**Equality of men and women** *Genesis 1:26–31; 2:18* **Permanent marriage** *Genesis 1:27; 2:24* **Sex is God's gift** *Genesis 1:28; 2:25*	**Exploitation of women by men** **Divorce, adultery, etc.** *Deuteronomy 24:1–4; Mark 10:1–12* **Sexual hang-ups and guilt**	**Mutual sharing** *Galatians 3:28; 1 Corinthians 7:3–5; Ephesians 5:21–33* **No breakdown** *1 Corinthians 7:10–11; Mark 10:1–12* **Sex to be enjoyed** *1 Corinthians 7:3–5*
People & God	**'In God's image'** *Genesis 1:26–27; Romans 1:18–23* **Open relationships** *Genesis 3:8*	**God's image tarnished** *Romans 1:18–32* **Guilt – the law – judgment** *Romans 3:9–20*	**New life 'in Christ'** *2 Corinthians 5:17; Galatians 2:19–20* **Forgiveness, reconciliation and love** *Romans 5–8*

Paul's view of death

The background

Paul's thinking was dominated by eschatology, just as the teaching of Jesus had been before him. Jesus and Paul both declared that the kingdom of God, for which devoted Jews had long been waiting, had now arrived. Because of the events of Jesus' life, death and resurrection – and, more particularly, his own encounter with the living Christ on the Damascus road – Paul was certain that the future had now burst into the present, and Christians were truly living in God's kingdom, despite still being a part of the fallen world which so desperately needed salvation.

So is the present spiritual experience of Christians the only thing that really matters? That was the obvious conclusion reached by some members of the church in Corinth (1 Corinthians 4:6; 15:12). It seemed to be the logical outcome of Paul's own teaching, for he had already written of the Christian life as a sort of 'resurrection' (Galatians 2:20). But Paul was unhappy with this idea, and went to great lengths to show why he thought it was mistaken. The present experience of Christians, he claimed, is but a foretaste of the much greater glory that will transform everything when God's kingdom is established in its fullness. Like Jesus, Paul declared the new age to be inaugurated, but not yet fully perfected, which meant his faith must always have a future goal, as well as an immediate objective. For Paul, the future meant the return of Jesus himself in glory (the *parousia*), and the transformation of Christians finally and fully to be like Christ (Philippians 3:20–21).

It has sometimes been suggested that all this was no more than an unhelpful hangover from Paul's Jewish past – and that, in any case, he eventually abandoned such a view. It is certainly true that Paul seems to have retained enough of his Pharisaic theology at this point for him

to have been able to use the fact to his own advantage when the opportunity arose (Acts 23:6–9; 26:6–8). But the resemblance was limited to the bare fact that both Paul and the Pharisees (as distinct from Sadducees and Greeks) believed that death would be followed by a future life, beginning with resurrection. In fact, Paul's view of God's kingdom as 'present but still to come' followed Jesus' own teaching very closely – and belief in a life after death was a necessary and logical outcome of that.

Further developments

But did Paul's view change as he got older? In view of the intensity of Paul's ministry, it is unlikely that his thinking remained absolutely static throughout his Christian life, and so in principle we can expect to find variations in his letters. Some, however, have claimed to be able to detect at this point not simply the natural changes of growing maturity, but quite striking contradictions in his thoughts on Christians and physical death.

It has been argued that, to start with, Paul held a fervent apocalyptic view, and expected all Christians to live until the *parousia* of Jesus. This expectation was challenged by the Thessalonian Christians, some of whose number had actually died – and in response to that, Paul declared they would be raised to life at the *parousia* (1 Thessalonians 4:13–18). Subsequently, he added that the living would also be transformed at the same instant (1 Corinthians 15:51–54), but then only a short time later he described this transformation as a gradual change, beginning with conversion and ending with death, which would lead directly into a new existence in a 'spiritual body' without the need for the *parousia* to come first (2 Corinthians 3:17–18; 4:16 – 5:4). Paul had therefore moved from an original unrefined Jewish view to a more sophisticated position that owed a lot to the influence of Greek philosophy.

This understanding of Paul's statements

draws attention to some important features of his thinking, though it cannot be accepted as it stands:

● Paul's conversion demonstrated to him that his Jewish beliefs were wrong, and it is therefore unlikely that he ever held a purely Jewish expectation as a Christian. No doubt he used familiar concepts from his past to explain his new Christian faith, but we have no evidence to suggest that such concepts were unaltered by his new perspective.

● In dealing with the fate of the dead in 1 Thessalonians, Paul certainly identified himself with those who would be alive at the time of the *parousia*. But the fact that Paul (like Jesus, Matthew 24:43; Luke 12:39) added that the *parousia* would come 'as a thief comes at night' (by definition, unknowable) hardly suggests that he had some kind of detailed timetable in his mind (1 Thessalonians 5:1–11). We should also remember that when Jewish people discussed the future, central themes were often described as 'near' to emphasize their importance rather than to make chronological predictions.

● It is in any case inaccurate to assert that Paul lost his belief in a direct future intervention by God, and viewed the life of the new age in purely individual and spiritual terms. In Philippians, he could still write of Christians dying in terms similar to those of 1 Corinthians (Philippians 3:20–21), while at the same time retaining a clear expectation of the *parousia* (Philippians 4:5).

How then can we understand this apparent diversity in Paul's statements about death? Two factors are especially relevant:

● Paul certainly continued to think creatively about this question when once it had been raised, and we can expect to see the evidence of that in his letters. The passage of time brings change in the way most people contemplate their own death, and in addition, Paul seems to suggest that he received fresh revelations about the subject from Christ himself (1 Corinthians 15:51–57).

● Between the writing of 1 and 2 Corinthians, Paul had an experience which shook him more than most. We do not know what it was, but he writes of feeling that 'the death sentence had been passed on us' (2 Corinthians 1:9). If he was literally sentenced to death, then questions about life after death would inevitably become more urgent – hence his more detailed teaching on the subject in 2 Corinthians 5.

Paul's thinking never changed on the basic issues. He remained convinced that the coming of the new age was not just an internal experience in the lives of Christian people, but something that would come in power, as God transformed not only the world of people but the world of nature too. And since Jesus was God's Son and Messiah, this great 'day of the Lord' must also be the day of Jesus' return in glory.

21 Freedom and Community

What is the church?

A typical dictionary entry defines a church as 'a building for Christian worship'. Such places are familiar features of the landscape of towns and cities around the world. Some are splendid and ornate, others are plain and simple – but just as easy to recognize. Of course the church today is more than just buildings. It is also an organization – indeed, a whole series of organizations, for there are thousands of different 'churches' or Christian denominations throughout the world.

Paul would find all this very mystifying, for to him 'the church' was neither a building nor a sect. When he used the word 'church' he was thinking of people – God's people, followers of Jesus, who were showing by their lifestyle that they were a part of the kingdom of God which Jesus had first announced and which Paul believed had now arrived. 'The church' was therefore not something dreamed up by human imagination, but was the work of God, founded on the Day of Pentecost when the Holy Spirit had breathed new life into a group of disillusioned disciples. Paul himself had shared in that experience on the Damascus road. His conversion brought a consciousness of personal reconciliation with God, but it also introduced him to a new community of love and joy as he found himself part of a large group of Jesus' followers: the church.

Theologically, the church was a microcosm of the transformation that God's new order would bring for the whole world. To be in the church was to have a foretaste of life in God's kingdom. Socially, the church in the Roman empire was an alternative society, based not on selfishness and greed and exploitation, but on the new freedom and fellowship that Jesus had announced: freedom to love God, and to love and serve others (Mark 12:29–31).

This is why the earliest Christians had such enormous success. When men and women asked for proof that God's new way of doing things had truly arrived, Paul and the other apostles could point to the church. Life in the church was indeed a new society – a context in which men, women and children of diverse social, racial and religious backgrounds had been brought together in a new and radical friendship.

Because they had been reconciled to God, they found themselves reconciled to each other. Their whole style of living was totally transformed, and to the honest observer there could be no doubt that something of world-changing proportions had taken place.

Jesus had always resisted the temptation to depict God's kingdom as merely a promise of better things to come in the future. From the very start of his ministry he declared that it was here now, and offered the prospect of renewed lives in the present. In explaining this message in his home town of Nazareth, Jesus had made its social dimension unmistakably clear: 'The Spirit of the Lord is upon me... to bring good news to the poor... to proclaim liberty to the captives... recovery of sight to the blind; to set free the oppressed and announce that the time has come when God will save the people' (Luke 4:18–19). Jesus himself put this into practice, as his own interactions with people demonstrated the reality of God's power to break down the barriers that so often mar human relationships, and the earliest disciples in Jerusalem followed his example.

A major reason for the phenomenal growth rate of the early church was the simple fact that the Christian communities offered a plausible alternative way of life that had the power to fulfil the deepest aspirations of the human personality. As men and women committed their lives to Jesus Christ, they found they were set free to serve God, and incorporated into a new relationship with others who shared their commitment.

Paul had discovered this at the start of his own Christian life. When he arrived in Damascus after his conversion, he found himself united in a new community of love and trust with the very people whom he had sworn to outlaw. After his baptism, Paul spent some time with the Christians in Damascus, and realized that the Christian gospel had within it the power to transform relationships. When he later wrote to the churches in Galatia, he emphasized that faith in Christ should produce reconciliation amongst people as well as peace with God (Galatians 3:28–29). He could be certain of that only because he had experienced it in his own life, as the ignorant and uneducated people whom he had been determined to hound to death now became his closest friends and spiritual companions.

The body of Christ

One of Paul's favourite terms to describe the church is 'the body of Christ'. Sometimes he applies it to a particular local group of Christians, like 'the church in Corinth' (1 Corinthians 12:12–27; Romans 12:3–8). At other times, it can refer to the sum total of all Christians throughout the world (Ephesians 1:22–23), and in yet other places, Paul seems to have both in mind (Colossians 2:18–19; Ephesians 4:12–16).

His readers would not be surprised to find Paul employing this language to describe particular communities of people. The Stoics in particular had often used similar concepts. For them, the universe itself could be thought of as a 'body', characterized by a great diversity in its various parts, and yet all of it working together in harmony, sometimes directed by a supreme deity as its 'head'. Others had written of the ideal democracy in the same terms, envisaging a community which could accept the individual diversity of its citizens, yet at the same time enabling them all to work together for the common good.

When Paul wrote of the church as 'the body of Christ' he was therefore using imagery that many of his readers would readily understand. But it was not the Stoics who had taught him to think of the Christian church in this way. As with other dominant aspects of his thinking, this too was a lesson Paul first learned at the time of his conversion. As he travelled from Jerusalem to Damascus, he was pursuing Christians to put them in prison, but when the voice spoke to him, it asked 'Saul, Saul! Why do you persecute *me*?' (Acts 9:4; 22:7; 26:14). The 'me' was none other than Jesus himself, and Paul was taken aback to learn that in persecuting Christians he was also persecuting Jesus. But he was, and to injure Christians was to afflict their Lord, for they were 'the body of Christ', living extensions of his personality and influence wherever they went.

One of Paul's most comprehensive explanations of all this is found in his correspondence with the church at Corinth. The precise terms in which the subject is expounded naturally owe a good deal to the specific questions which he was seeking to address in that context. But we have no reason to suppose that Paul's basic message would have been any different in another less contentious context. The idea that Christians are a part of 'the body of Christ' must have been a fundamental element in Paul's initial communication of the Christian message, for that is what the Corinthians were arguing about. Paul had spoken to them of 'the body of Christ'. But what exactly did he mean by it – and how should Christians behave in order to demonstrate the new freedom that Paul declared they had within the fellowship of 'the body'?

We have examined the Corinthian letters in some detail in a previous chapter. One of the problems in Corinth was a misunderstanding of the nature of true freedom. 'If Christ has set us free', some were saying, 'then we must be free to do as we please, unrestricted by the inhibitions and hang-ups of others.' As a result, the life of that particular Christian community had come to be dominated by selfishness and discord rather than the mutual sharing and harmony which were the real signs of the presence of the new age. Their regular gatherings were dominated by individuals and small groups who insisted on doing as they pleased. The rich spread social disharmony by having feasts from which the poor were excluded (1 Corinthians 11:17–22), and even their worship had become a spiritual wasteland, as those with the ability to do relatively spectacular things like speaking in tongues insisted on their 'freedom' to do so, even when it rendered the proceedings meaningless for everyone else (1 Corinthians 14:1–4).

There was no way in which Paul could accept all this as a true application of his own understanding of Christian freedom. The church at Corinth had become a denial of the gospel. Its worship was incomprehensible, with meetings that Paul said 'actually do more harm than good' (1 Corinthians 11:13). Its evangelism was ineffective, for such behaviour merely made the church a laughing-stock to ordinary people (1 Corinthians 14:23).

Paul was clearly distressed by what was happening in Corinth. But he was also convinced that in the church true freedom must not be only a subject for discussion: it should also characterize the way the church lives. So he set out not so much to contradict the Corinthians, as to affirm what they had got right, and challenge those things about which he believed them to be mistaken. In the process he provided a unique insight into some of the more distinctive aspects of his own thinking.

Life in the body

The precise point about which Paul had been questioned was the function of 'spiritual gifts' in the church, and it is in the process of answering that question that he explains his understanding of how Christians should relate to one another in the life of the local church (1 Corinthians 12:1–31).

In doing so, he uses the image of 'the body' in its simplest possible form. Even with our more complex understanding of physiology, it is not difficult to see the way Paul's mind worked. He imagines the human body as a complex piece of machinery, with parts of different size, shape and constitution, all required to work together in different locations and in different ways to ensure the smooth operation of the whole organism. A body without an ear or an eye would be impaired, just as would a body with no hands or feet. To ask whether a hand is more attractive or more important than an eye is an absurd question, for both are essential as they are if the human body is to work properly. The unity within diversity that is the key to health in the human body is also a fundamental requirement for proper relationships in the church. Individual Christians are comparable to ears, or hands, or feet, or whatever. They are all different personalities, but they are all vital parts of the whole, and if they are not working properly then the corporate life of the church will be impaired.

This simple imagery introduces us to four decisive aspects of Paul's thinking on the church and its members.

All members are indispensable

In Paul's understanding of the church and its operations, everyone has a part to play. When Christians meet together for worship or fellowship, they all have something to offer and must be given the opportunity to do so (1 Corinthians 14:26–33). This is the opposite of what has actually happened throughout most of the history of the Christian church, for reasons which go well beyond the scope of this particular study. But traditional church

For Paul, being a part of the church was a commitment to a way of life, even when it involved the threat of hostility. As Christians in Rome began to face persecution they gathered in the Catacombs under the city and decorated the walls of their meeting places with biblical scenes. This one from the Via Latina is of Samson routing the Philistines.

structures have generally allowed participation only by a minority (the priest or certain key lay leaders), while the majority have either been expected to be silent spectators, or only occasionally allowed to join in at the specific invitation and under the strict control of the leadership. This was not Paul's expectation at all, for if every Christian was empowered by the Holy Spirit (Romans 8:9), and if the church was the sphere in which God's Spirit was working to demonstrate the reality of God's kingdom, then it was only logical to suppose that all Christians should have a part to play in the life of the church. As a result, Paul asserts that every Christian has their own distinctive *charism*, a ministry that is not restricted by either ordination or some other special experience, but which is given to all by the work of the Spirit in the lives of believers (1 Corinthians 12:7).

All members are different

Paul's understanding of the work of the Holy Spirit in the lives of Christians never becomes mysticism, in which individuals are swamped by a force outside of themselves. Paul affirms in the strongest possible terms that God always respects the individual personalities of people, and this comes out quite clearly in Paul's description of the various functions which different people might be able to perform in order to enhance the life and spiritual development of the church. The list he gives in 1 Corinthians 12:4–28 is by no means exhaustive, and no doubt was determined by the nature of the arguments that were going on in Corinth, for elsewhere he lists rather different functions as being 'gifts from the Holy Spirit' (Romans 12:6–21).

All members are equal

Though individual Christians are not identical in either personality or ability, they are all of equal importance. Though some, such as those who speak in tongues or those who teach, might seem to be more important, they are not – and if some wish to have other functions than those God has given them, they should remember that they can only receive what the Spirit gives them. Any attempt to try to obtain particular gifts for themselves will only lead to the destruction of the whole church – presumably because such activity would undermine the basis of mutual trust and respect on which real spiritual freedom is based (1 Corinthians 12:27–31).

All members are responsible

Paul has a dynamic concept of the church, not a static one. He does not think of it as an organization that holds meetings from time to time, but as an outpost of God's ways of doing things, 'the kingdom'. This means that Christians do not 'go to church', but on the contrary they *are* the church, wherever they are and whatever they happen to be doing. Their responsibility for the condition of the Christian community does not end while they are at work or at home, for everything that happens to them has its effect on the whole body.

This is true of the human body, of course: an injury to one part will inevitably bring discomfort, or worse, to the whole organism. Paul discovered at his conversion that the church is no different: when one Christian suffers, the whole church is injured. But the opposite is also true: 'if one part is praised, all the other parts share its happiness' (1 Corinthians 12:26). For a Christian to be able to opt out of the church would have been unthinkable for Paul. The concept of 'joining the church' (or leaving it) only makes sense in a modern church context, where such joining is a matter of enrolling in a particular sort of organization. But for Paul the church was not a club that could be joined or left: it was a commitment to a way of being, and therefore could be thought of as a living organism, in which Christians were inescapably related to and responsible for one another because of their new relationship with God through Christ.

Leadership in the body

No matter what the theory might be, every social grouping needs adequate leadership, and the church is no exception. How then did Paul cope with the need for competent leaders, while still retaining the flexibility and freedom which are the bedrock on which his thinking about the church was founded?

It is clear that Paul never imagined the church could do without proper leadership. According to the book of Acts, wherever he founded a new Christian community it was his regular practice to appoint leaders in it (Acts 14:23; 20:17–35), something which is confirmed by references in his letters to 'the bishops and deacons' at Philippi (Philippians 1:1) and to 'those who... are over you' in Thessalonica (1 Thessalonians 5:12). Paul himself clearly believed that he had a special position by virtue of being an apostle (Galatians 1:15–19; 2 Corinthians 11), and he was quite prepared to recognize the God-given authority of others in similar positions (Acts 15:4; Romans 16:1–15).

The really distinctive element in Paul's thinking was the model of leadership which he used to explain the functions of these different people. Historically, the church came to model itself on the structures of the Roman empire. Indeed, in many important respects, when the empire collapsed the church took over not only its structures but also many of its social functions throughout Europe. Over the centuries, that has remained the dominant organizational model, amended a little in recent decades by the incorporation of elements taken from organizational strategies developed in the context of business management and marketing. As a result, the contemporary church mostly operates in a hierarchical way, in which authority is passed on from one layer of bureaucracy to the next, and is validated at the top level by various rituals which ensure that what happens there will always be more important than what takes place lower down the structure. Paul however saw leadership in rather different terms. He was working with a 'charismatic' model. The significance of this term has been somewhat narrowed down in recent years by its restricted application to *glossolalia* and other 'charismatic gifts', but Paul used it in a much more comprehensive way. For him, a 'charismatic gift' was not concerned only with the personal experience of individuals: it was a gift that God had given to the entire church, and that had far-reaching repercussions for the whole of its life and relationships.

On this model, the centre of authority is to be found outside the members of the church altogether, and rests with God working through the Holy Spirit. Those who lead are not those who have been appointed to an office by a vote of the congregation, or indeed by their predecessors in office, but those who have been equipped to lead by a personal endowment from God, and whose gifts the other members of the body have recognized. Since God's choice depends on nothing other than the freely given gifts of grace, every single Christian could potentially be the recipient of leadership functions. Several statements made by Paul in writing to Corinth help to explain this concept further:

The head of the body

A good deal of debate has been generated by the fact that in 1 Corinthians 12 Paul does not differentiate between the whole body and its head. In later letters, he clearly identifies Christ as 'the head... from whom the whole body... makes bodily growth and upbuilds itself in love' (Ephesians 4:15–16). But even in 1 Corinthians he never thought of Christ as just the sum total of all Christians, for there he affirms that the whole basis of the church's existence is the confession that 'Jesus is Lord' (12:3), and in another passage, using a different metaphor, he describes him as 'the one and only foundation' of the church (3:11). The church does not belong to people, not even to its members. It belongs to God, and Christ is its head: Christ alone is its true leader, and the ultimate authority belongs to him.

Led by the Spirit

This is why Paul can expect things to happen 'in a proper and orderly way' even without any apparent hierarchical leadership to enforce rules and regulations (1 Corinthians 14:40). If all Christians are guided by the Spirit, he reasons, and if it is God's will that 'harmony and peace' should be the hallmarks of the church (1 Corinthians 14:33) then God will not only equip Christians for different ministries, but will also give others the grace to recognize and accept such Spirit-led leadership where it emerges. Common experience suggests that this is perhaps a counsel of perfection. It is certainly not easy for fallen human nature to cope with such open structures, and at the very least demands extraordinary sensitivity and personal discipline. But Paul simply observed that for people whose lives had been transformed by the power of God, that should be no problem!

Partners in ministry

One reason for Paul's optimistic expectations at this point is the fact that he never supposed just one person would emerge as the sole leader of any given congregation. In the church worldwide, he envisaged the emergence of a number of complementary leaders: 'some to be apostles, others to be prophets, others to be evangelists, others to be pastors and teachers' (Ephesians 4:11). But he also saw such diversity of leadership operating in the context of local congregations as well. In his advice in 1 Corinthians 12:27–31 he mentions apostles, prophets, teachers and several others all working alongside one another in order to build up the whole church. He never for a moment imagined that one person could have a monopoly on the gifts of God's Spirit. It would take the whole church fully to express the greatness of God. For Paul the only thing that determined a person's function in the church was the endowment of God's Spirit. In God's new society gender, race, and social class – all barriers of the fallen world – were quite irrelevant.

This is Paul at his most radical. Even those who have found his understanding of personal salvation most congenial have not often followed him in his thinking on the nature and operation of the church. Yet for Paul the two were inseparable. The heart of the gospel was freedom: freedom from guilt, freedom from the Law, freedom from sin, and freedom from all that would inhibit the development of the human personality to become what God intended it to be. To be set free by Christ was to be released into a new world in which people could find their own true identity, relating to each other in freedom and fellowship because they were related to Christ himself. That final transformation was yet in the future, when 'the glorious freedom of the children of God' would be fully realized (Romans 8:18–25). But in the meantime, the church stands as a testimony to that future hope, and as the context in which people can serve one another most truly as they love and serve God.

Did Paul really believe in freedom?

If not quite the heart of Paul's gospel, 'freedom' is certainly one of its leading motifs. It features prominently in all his major letters, whether he is dealing in a theological way with the nature of salvation (as in Galatians and Romans) or with its practical outworking in the Christian community (as in 1 and 2 Corinthians). But what sort of freedom was Paul talking about? In Galatians, he asserts quite categorically that a true understanding of Christian freedom would lead to the abolition of the major social divisions of the ancient world. Prejudice and discrimination based on race, social class and gender were quite incompatible with the Christian gospel: 'there is no longer Jew or Greek, there is no longer slave or free, there is no longer male and female; for all of you are one in Christ Jesus' (Galatians 3:28). Yet when we look elsewhere in Paul's writings, especially where he gives practical advice to his readers, his specific instructions do not always seem to be consistent with his general statements of policy. This is especially true of his statements about the place of women in the church, and his handling of the issue of slavery. But in order to set these in their proper perspective, we must also see them alongside his attitude to racial issues.

Racism

Some interpreters have argued that the freedom Paul talks of in Galatians is some kind of 'spiritual' freedom, with no social implications at all. On this view, Galatians 3:28 refers to the way God sees people, rather than how people ought to view one another. But this is unlikely to be Paul's meaning. Throughout his writings he makes it plain that his Christian faith was not segregated from the rest of his life, and unless he clearly states otherwise it is natural to suppose that what he says he believed was always intended to affect his

style of living. Moreover, his entire life was dominated by his absolute determination that racial prejudice would have no part in the Christian community. His desire to prove that Jews and Gentiles were equal became almost an obsession with him: he was even prepared to disagree publicly with Peter over it (Galatians 2:11–14), and it was the immediate cause of his final arrest and transportation to Rome (Acts 21:17–36).

It is impossible to believe that Paul thought racism would be abolished only in some ideal world, when he spent most of his life opposing it in human relationships wherever he found it. In principle, therefore, we can only conclude that he did see Christian freedom as defined in Galatians and Romans as something that would affect relationships between people here and now.

Women and men

When we come to Paul's statements about the place of women in the church's life, many passages make exactly the same emphasis. In describing the various 'gifts of grace' in 1 Corinthians and Ephesians, he never suggests that God will give these gifts only to men. In principle, all positions in the Pauline church were open to all Christians, regardless of gender. Paul himself was happy to work alongside women, some of whom were his close friends. His most extensive list of greetings to Christian leaders includes many women (Romans 16:1–15), and he refers to at least one of them as an 'apostle' (Junias, Romans 16:7). Furthermore, when he gives advice to the church at Corinth about the appropriate way to behave, he takes it for granted that both men and women should 'pray and prophesy' in public worship (1 Corinthians 11:4–5). Indeed he reminds them that he had delivered 'traditions' to that effect as part of his initial teaching to them, in much the same way as he had passed on information about the resurrection (1 Corinthians 11:2; 15:1–8 – using the same Greek words in each case).

Did Paul really
believe in freedom?
continued

There are certainly some complex statements made in these contexts, but the whole frame of reference is determined by Paul's insistence that men and women have the same freedom and opportunity to play a full part in the life of the church.

The same point also comes out clearly when he discusses marriage. Here again, some of what he writes is a little obscure, no doubt because of its specific reference to details of the Corinthian situation. But the general principle is clear: men

Women were often influential in bringing the Christian message into Roman homes. This portrait of a Christian family comes from the cross of Galla Placida in Brescia.

and women relate to each other not in a context of male (or female) domination, but in a life of mutual love and service: 'A man should fulfil his duty... a woman should fulfil her duty... A wife is not the master of her own body... a husband is not the master of his own body...' (1 Corinthians 7:3–4).

All this is but the logical outcome of Paul's teaching on the freedom which the gospel brings. The only apparent problem is the fact that in 1 Corinthians 14:33b–35, Paul seems to undermine it by writing that 'the women should keep

silence in the churches. For they are not permitted to speak'. Some have solved this contradiction by suggesting that these verses are not a part of Paul's original letter, but were added later by someone who wished to find Pauline authority for silencing troublesome women. There is a little evidence for this in the ancient manuscripts of the New Testament, but not enough to justify such a conclusion. There are however a number of other clues in Paul's letters that will help us to see the real meaning of what he says here:

● If we can see a contradiction between Paul's advice in 1 Corinthians 11:2–16 and 14:33b–35, then we can be sure that Paul would not have missed it. Presumably he did not think there was a contradiction here, though he might well have thought that in one passage he was stating a general principle, while in another he was giving specific advice to deal with a very particular situation. The whole of the Corinthian correspondence is shot through with this kind of tension, and the volatile nature of the church seems almost to have demanded it. In this particular case, 1 Corinthians 11:2–16, with its appeal to creation, has every appearance of being the general principle.

● In 1 Corinthians 14 it is not only women who are told to be quiet: the whole chapter is full of instructions to various people in the church (some of them certainly men), telling them when it is appropriate to speak and when they should be silent. Worship in Corinth was being continually disrupted by groups of people competing with each other to gain the attention of the rest. It requires no great leap of the imagination to suppose that a group of women was one of them. It is instructive that as an alternative to speaking in church, Paul here tells them to 'ask their husbands at home'. This strongly suggests that the 'speaking' in question was irreverent chattering, that had no real connection with the worship of the church.

● In dealing with the church at Corinth, we have suggested that there was something like what later came to be known as 'Gnosticism' lurking in the background. If so, this could also give us a possible clue to the background and meaning of this passage. The only other New Testament book which contains similar instructions to 1 Corinthians 14:33b–35 was probably written against a similar background of church life (1 Timothy 2:8–15). In the Gnostic heresies of the second century, women often played a conspicuous part that amounted to a kind of 'female chauvinism', and some groups in Corinth might even at this early period have had theological reasons for wanting to assert the priority of female spirituality over against male ways of doing things. If so, it is consistent with Paul's teaching that he should have wanted to curtail their activities. To him, exploitation of men was just as abhorrent as prejudice against women, and both would be a denial of the true meaning of Christian freedom.

Slavery

But what about Paul's attitude to slaves? Was Paul committed to the abolition of slavery too? There is less material available for us to give a precise answer to that question, for nowhere does Paul actually write about the future of slavery as an institution. Of course, Galatians 3:28 implies the end of slavery, just as it spelled out the end of racism and sexism. But there are only one or two hints in Paul's letters of how he would deal with this particular matter:

● In Colossians 3:22 – 4:1 and Ephesians 6:5–9 Paul gives advice to his readers on how to cope with different family circumstances, one of which is the master/slave relationship. Here, he simply takes it for granted that slavery will continue to exist, though his advice contains certain distinctive elements when he reminds masters that they have a personal responsibility for the welfare of their slaves, and for that reason they should treat them generously. The same emphasis on mutuality is found here as in his teaching elsewhere on marriage – and in the culture of the time, the idea that masters had any obligations to slaves would undoubtedly have been a progressive position.

● In Philemon, we have a personal letter sent by Paul with a runaway slave whom he was returning to his master. Here again, his precise intention is ambivalent, as we saw when we discussed that letter in detail. On the one hand, he seems to be asking Philemon to release the slave Onesimus – yet, paradoxically, he sends him back at the same time!

The Onesimus episode seems to suggest that though Paul wanted the slave released, he was not prepared to go outside the law to achieve it, and this perhaps gives us a clue to Paul's thinking on the matter. We cannot reasonably think that Paul would not have realized that the gospel demanded an end to slavery. But his attitude to it was probably influenced by two further considerations:

● In the Roman empire, slavery was the foundation stone on which the whole economic structure of society rested. To abolish slavery would have required a radical dismantling of the very fabric of life – something similar to what happened when communism collapsed in the states of eastern Europe. But neither Paul nor the other Christians were in a strong position politically: 'from the human point of view few of you were wise or powerful or of high social standing' (1 Corinthians 1:26). In any case, the Roman slave revolts of the first century BC had shown that such attempts were doomed to failure. Paul had to make a difficult choice: either challenge

A slave chain dating from Roman times.

INTRODUCING THE NEW TESTAMENT

Did Paul really believe in freedom? continued

the vested interests of the Roman state, and quite probably perish in the process, or accept the situation and seek to exert whatever influence could be achieved through the establishment of a counter-culture in the Christian communities. Paul made the second choice, and we have no reason to suppose that he did not invite slaves and masters to demonstrate their new-found Christian freedom within the Christian community, even though he was forced to recognize his inability to change things in the wider world.

● Paul's personal experience of Roman slaves probably helped him to reach this decision. Modern readers tend to think of slavery in terms of the American experience in the eighteenth and nineteenth centuries. There were of course many pathetic souls who found themselves under the power of such tyranny in Rome, mostly because they were either viewed as criminals or belonged to races that had been conquered by the imperial armies. But the majority of slaves in Roman society were 'household slaves', groups of servants who lived in the homes of their masters in a more or less harmonious extended family. In sociological terms, they were the equivalent of today's ordinary workers, except that their employers gave them the security of housing as well as employment. They might even, on occasion, be adopted by their masters as their own children, and such a slave could inherit the master's property. Onesimus was this sort of slave, and he was probably typical of thousands of the early Christians. This was the type of slavery Paul knew about, and he could no doubt see that unless it was accompanied by a radical revision of the entire Roman economic system, the 'emancipation' of such household slaves would lead not to greater freedom, but less, with enforced homelessness and destitution being the inevitable outcome for large numbers of them.

Paul's attitude to all these issues was no doubt less liberal than modern Christians might wish, and changing circumstances and perceptions of human nature and potential are constantly raising questions that were unheard of in Paul's day. Like other aspects of his advice to his readers, Paul's recommendations on these matters were directly related to the situations in which they found themselves, and cannot therefore be applied across the board to all times and places. Paul would have been among the first to recognize that, which is why he needs to be appreciated within his own context. In that frame of reference, his teaching was radical. But it was a pragmatic radicalism, for Paul realized that there was likely to be a limit to the extent of social reform that one person with no political influence could bring about single-handed. His gospel demanded extensive change to the accepted conventions of human relationships, and where Paul could achieve this – in the church – he sought to do so. But it was left to later generations of Christians, in different social and political circumstances, to realize the full significance of his gospel of freedom, and to act in accordance with it.

392

22 The Spirit and the Letter

The charismatic church

In the previous chapter, we examined at some length Paul's understanding of the nature of the church. But this view was not unique to him. The story of the earliest church in Jerusalem shows that it too began with a charismatic understanding of its own life. These early followers of Jesus were dominated by their experience of the Holy Spirit at work among them, and at the very beginning they gave little thought to the problems of organizing the infant church. It never occurred to them to appoint officials or write a constitution, nor did they find it necessary to establish an army of bureaucrats to direct their worldwide mission from some central headquarters. They believed they already had the only organizing force they needed, in the guidance of the Holy Spirit.

The Spirit told them what to say in their preaching, and gave them the boldness to say it (Acts 4:8, 31; 5:32). When Ananias and Sapphira tried to deceive the church, Peter had no doubt that this was a direct challenge not to himself, but to the Holy Spirit (Acts 5:9). For the church did not belong to the apostles: it had come into being with the arrival of the Spirit, and the ultimate responsibility of its members was to God. We find the same emphasis throughout the later chapters of Acts. When the church at Antioch in Syria sent Paul and Barnabas off as missionaries, it was acting on the instructions of the Holy Spirit, who spoke directly to the congregation through certain Spirit-filled individuals within it (Acts 13:1–3). This sense of dependence on the Spirit's guidance is perhaps the main characteristic of Paul's work, both in the stories of Acts and in his own writings. Indeed, this emphasis is so strong in Acts that some readers of the New Testament have preferred to regard it not so much as the 'Acts of the Apostles', but rather 'The Acts of the Holy Spirit'.

This way of doing things would be quite foreign to modern Western culture, though it is not so different from what has happened in recent decades in the growth of indigenous Christian churches in other parts of the world. This difference of approach underlines a fundamental distinction that must be drawn between the life of the earliest church and the way in which the Christian church subsequently developed within the Western cultural context.

At the beginning, nobody ever sat down and planned to start the church. When Jesus died on the cross, his disciples were for the most part disillusioned and perplexed. This was not what they had expected, and even after the resurrection they were still apprehensive (Luke 24:13–24). The church was not the brain-child of the disciples: it was the work of God. On the Day of Pentecost, God spoke to its founder members and worked among them with such power that they had no option but to respond. Into the deadness of their own frustration, the Spirit breathed the life of God and, as individual disciples experienced the compelling power of the Holy Spirit for themselves, they were drawn together in a community of love and friendship – love for God, love for one another, and love for the rest of the world. Their educational, social, economic and political backgrounds were quite diverse, and the only thing they had in common was the fact that, through the Spirit, God had changed their lives.

They were bound together as a group, not by the fact that they all belonged to the same organization but because they were all inspired by the same Holy Spirit. It is at this point that we can locate the distinctive self-understanding of the early church. Unlike later generations of Christians, they never saw themselves as any kind of bureaucratic organization – indeed, they did not understand themselves as any sort of organization, but preferred to describe their communities as a living

The early church would have regarded itself as a living organism rather than an organization. Paul described the church as the body of Christ. Jesus himself used the picture of believers drawing life from him in the same way that the branches of a vine are attached to the main stem and are fed by it. This mosaic of vines and grapes is from the 6th-century San Prisca Chapel in Capua, Italy.

organism. Paul expressed this idea most explicitly with his use of the terminology of 'the body of Christ' (Romans 12:4–8; 1 Corinthians 12:12–31). For him, what united Christians was not the fact that they were all part of the same organization, but the fact that each and every one of them shared in the life and power of Jesus himself, through the operation of the Holy Spirit in their lives. The Spirit was the 'organizing principle' of the church's life, and because of that it was unnecessary for the believers to organize the church themselves. The same kind of argument had been used by Jesus when he described the relationship between himself and his disciples using the imagery of a living plant, with the same source of life filling and energizing all its parts (John 15:1–10).

We have already seen how this understanding of Christian fellowship became central for Paul, and there is no reason to doubt that it was the view of other apostles, including Peter. The authentic picture of a church in the New Testament is of groups of Christians acting together in a spirit of mutual love and friendship. When Paul wrote to the church at Rome some twenty years after the events of Pentecost, there seems to have been no organized hierarchy. In the final chapter of his letter he seems to imply that there were several groups of Christians there, meeting together in the homes of different individuals in an informal way. Paul mentions a number of people known to him, together with the names of the people in whose homes these house churches met (Romans 16:3–15), but there is no suggestion that any of them had any sort of 'official' position among the Christians. Instead, they are all 'Christian brothers and sisters' – just as the followers of Jesus had always been, not only from the Day of Pentecost, but even from the time of Jesus' own ministry (Mark 3:33–35).

The institutional church

Within the space of about forty years, all this had changed quite dramatically. The next significant piece of evidence from the church at Rome is the early Christian document called *1 Clement*. This was a letter sent from the church at Rome to the church at Corinth in about AD95, and it is especially interesting for New Testament study because it provides some insight into what was going on at that time in two churches that are well documented in the New Testament. The church in Corinth had not changed much at all, and was still being torn apart by controversies and arguments of one sort and another. But the church at Rome used a new argument to try to put things right.

It suggested that certain of its leaders had special authority, which was vested in them by their position as accredited officials in a church hierarchy: 'The apostles have received the gospel for us from the Lord Jesus Christ. Christ was sent forth by God, and the apostles by Christ. Both these appointments were made in an orderly way, according to the will of God... The apostles appointed the first-fruits of their labours to be bishops and deacons for those who would believe. Nor was this a new fashion, for indeed it had been written concerning bishops and deacons from very ancient times...' (*1 Clement* 42).

We can reasonably conclude that by AD95, these local 'bishops and deacons' in the church at Rome were being thought of as the successors of the apostles – not just metaphorically, but quite literally, for they had the confidence to try to exercise the supreme authority of the apostles, even over the church in the Greek city of Corinth. This impression is reinforced when we notice that an earlier chapter of *1 Clement* differentiates between two groups of people within the Christian community. No longer are all members regarded as equals, but instead they are divided into 'clergy' and 'laity'. Indeed, there even seem to be two groups of clergy (both male): 'His own peculiar services are assigned to the high priest, and their own proper place is prescribed to the priests, and their own special ministrations devolve on the Levites. But the lay people are bound by the lay person's ordinances' (*1 Clement* 40).

Of course, *1 Clement* can only tell us how things were moving in the church at Rome. There is no guarantee that the church in Corinth actually accepted all this when it received the letter, still less that it was itself organized in the same way. But as we look at other Christian literature from the same period, we cannot fail to discern a significant change in the church's self-understanding. There was still a certain degree of admiration for the idea that the church could and should be led by the guidance of the Holy Spirit, but Christians were coming more and more to feel that the church must be organized along increasingly institutional lines.

Ignatius, the bishop of Antioch in Syria at the beginning of the second century, also had something to say on this subject. While he was on his last journey to Rome to face execution, he wrote seven letters to various churches. One of the subjects that he discussed was

Ignatius, bishop of Antioch was martyred at Rome in the early years of the 2nd century.

the relationship between a church and its leaders – and it is clear that, in his view at least, the leaders of the church had a special authority that distinguished them from ordinary church members. Three distinct types of clergy are identified in his writings: the elders or presbyters, the deacons and, over them both, the bishop. The word 'presbyter' has given us the modern word 'priest', though at that stage there was no thought of priests who might offer sacrifice on behalf of the people in the Old Testament sense. Both bishop and elders should be given great respect, for a person's attitude to them was regarded as a reflection of their attitude to God (Ignatius, *To the Magnesians* 3). Indeed, in another letter, Ignatius declared that anyone who agreed with the bishop was a friend of God, while those who disagreed with him were God's enemies: '... as many as are of God and of Jesus Christ, they are also with the bishop... but if anyone follows another who creates a division, they shall not inherit the kingdom of God' (Ignatius, *To the Philadelphians* 3).

In understanding the precise significance of all this, it is important to remember that Ignatius was speaking for himself, and it is hard to know to what extent his opinions would be shared by others. He went to such lengths to defend the status of these religious offices that it is a fair guess that their significance must have been in some dispute at the time. Nevertheless, it was not long before Christians throughout the world came to accept that this was what the church should be. Instead of the community of the Spirit to which the early New Testament narratives and letters bear witness, the church came to be seen as a vast organization. Instead of a conscious reliance on the Spirit's direct guidance, it was controlled by a hierarchy of ordained men (never women), following strict rules and regulations which covered every conceivable aspect of belief and behaviour – and when the Spirit featured in this scheme, it was taken for granted that what the leaders decided was what the Spirit was saying.

By the middle of the second century, the change was complete. At the beginning, the only qualification for membership of the church had been a life changed by the power of the Holy Spirit. Indeed, at the very start there had been no real concept of 'church membership' at all, and on the Day of Pentecost, all believers in Jesus were automatically members of the church. There was no need for them to apply to get in, nor could they have opted out, even had they wished to do so. But by the end of the first century things were rather different. Now the key to membership of the church was not to be found in inspiration by the Spirit, but in acceptance of ecclesiastical dogma and discipline. To make sure that all new members had a good grasp of what that meant, baptism itself was no longer the spontaneous expression of faith in Jesus it had originally been (Acts 2:40–42), but the culmination of a more or less extended period of formal teaching and instruction about the meaning of Christian faith (*Didache* 7). In all this, we can see how the charismatic notion of life in the Spirit was being gradually squeezed out of the body of Christ, to be replaced as the church's driving force by the more predictable if less exciting movement of organized ecclesiastical machinery.

The changing church

Why did all this happen? Was it just an accident? Or was it a part of some ancient anti-charismatic plot by subversive elements in the church? Or was it perhaps just a good example of the way that any new movement founded by a dynamic leader will eventually become yet another settled institution in its second generation?

We may trace four main reasons for this change in the style of the early church.

Church growth

One of the most impressive features of the early church is the amazing rate at which it grew. Beginning from a handful of people in rural Palestine, within twenty years or less it spread through the whole of the civilized world. All this was achieved with no real organization at all, and yet the very success of this spontaneous world mission was itself to demand some integrated scheme of operation.

At first, no one gave much thought to such things. They already had the only structure they needed, for most of those who became Christians on the Day of Pentecost were either Jews or Gentile converts to Judaism, and they simply accepted and continued in the forms of worship that they already knew and loved. The early chapters of Acts tell how they regularly met with others who believed in Jesus, but that was an extra, for they also worshipped in the local synagogues, and even in the temple itself (Acts 2:46).

But it was not long before the need arose for some kind of organization, however primitive. Stephen first came to prominence as a leader among the Hellenist Christians of Jerusalem because they felt they were not getting a fair share in the distribution of church funds (Acts 6:1–6). The nature of their complaint implies that the Hebrew Christians were not suffering the same disadvantage, and the fact that the response to the complaint was the establishment of a group of seven to supervise the distribution of funds to the Hellenists suggests very strongly that there was already in existence a similar group dealing with the needs of the Hebrew Christians.

We should perhaps not be surprised that these first church 'officials' were appointed to deal with such a practical matter, for the only 'office' known to us in the small group of Jesus' own disciples was that of treasurer, a function carried out by Judas Iscariot, sometimes with less than complete honesty (John 12:4–6; 13:29). It was not accidental that the very first stirrings of 'organization' within the early church should have been concerned with the same subject, for Jesus himself had taught that after love to God, love to one's neighbour was the next most important thing (Matthew 19:19; 22:39; Mark 12:31, 33; Luke 10:27). It was certainly one aspect of his message that the early church took very seriously indeed, for its members even sold their goods and property and pooled the proceeds. They were determined to be united with other believers not only spiritually, but in other more tangible respects too. They all shared one common purse, as well as serving the same Lord (Acts 2:44–45; 4:32, 34–35).

Though this kind of cooperative use of resources was not to be typical of the church when it spread to other parts of the Roman empire, the sharing of goods to a greater or lesser degree was always part and parcel of the Christian gospel. We have already noticed the generosity of the church at Antioch (Acts 11:27–30) and the Gentile Christians of Greece and Asia Minor, expressed in the gifts they sent to the Jerusalem church (Romans 15:26). Jesus' emphasis on loving one's neighbour was taken seriously throughout early Christianity. The New Testament is full of exhortations to do just that in many detailed ways, while by the end of the first century the church was also acting as an employment agency to help Christians find jobs (*Didache* 12).

Obviously, as the church grew bigger, the demand for such services increased enormously and, as a result, the co-ordination of aid began to require more organization than it had at first. Of course, people performing these jobs were not doing the work of the later 'clergy': they had no control over worship, and their very existence was more a matter of convenience than anything else. Some translations of the New Testament confuse their role by calling them 'deacons', but they were not 'deacons' in any modern sense of the word. They had no authoritative position in the church, but on the contrary were regarded as the church's servants (the real meaning of the Greek word from which 'deacon' is derived).

But were there others who were formally recognized leaders with responsibility for the regulation of worship and belief in the early churches? This is a highly debatable question, though the consensus seems to be that using the language of later church order in relation to, for example, Paul's churches is unhelpful, for in effect there was no 'church order' in that sense. There was certainly no bureaucracy as such, but an individual's usefulness in the church was determined directly by his or her endowment with the Spirit. The whole notion of people being specially appointed to a position of authority was quite foreign to Paul's thinking. Instead, all those who had received the Holy Spirit (and it was impossible to be a Christian without that) were 'office-bearers' in the church – though, if everyone was an office-bearer, then in effect no one was. Even the apostles themselves appear to have had no authority just because they were apostles, but only insofar as the Holy Spirit gave it to them. Ernst Käsemann, for example, described Paul himself as just 'one charismatic among many', while even a conservative theologian like Hendricus Berkhof has written that 'taking the charismatic structure of the church seriously would put an end to clericalism and a church ruled by ministers'.

There is a great deal of truth in all this, though it is important to realize that Paul's charismatic understanding of leadership did not lead to a free-for-all in the church. Paul made it quite clear that a Spirit-directed leadership would itself involve a certain limitation of the work of any given individual within a church, for not every Christian was equipped by the Spirit to perform the same tasks (1 Corinthians 12). But when Christians are prepared together to obey the Spirit, then the Spirit can be trusted to produce a situation in which 'everything must be done in a proper and orderly way' (1 Corinthians 14:40).

It is not inconsistent with this for Paul to refer elsewhere to specific leadership functions within various churches. The church at Philippi had its church leaders and helpers (Philippians 1:1), while

1 Thessalonians 5:12 also mentions 'those who work among you, who guide and instruct you in the Christian life'. But it is certain that such people owed their position not to some formal act of ordination (as later), but simply to their endowment with the Spirit.

When we turn to the church in Jerusalem, we get a slightly different picture. There, James seems to be very much a man in charge of the church, though no doubt he was guided and assisted by others ('the apostles and elders' mentioned in Acts 15:6, 22). Later Christian traditions credit him with having been the first 'bishop' of Jerusalem, and though that might well be an exaggerated description of him it seems likely that he owed his position to some sort of hierarchical arrangement.

Very little is known of the formal organization of other churches during the New Testament period. Even the church at Rome is something of a mystery. When Paul wrote to it, he mentioned no leaders at all, though his list of house churches tends to imply that its structure was much more like the earliest churches in Jerusalem than the later congregation led by James. Books like 2 Peter, 1 John and Jude mention no leaders at all, while others speak vaguely of 'leaders', 'elders' or 'shepherds' but without explaining their functions (see, for example, Acts 20:17; Hebrews 13:7, 17, 24; James 5:14; 1 Peter 5:1–5).

It seems likely that churches in different parts of the Roman empire developed in different ways and at different speeds, and no doubt this applied to their forms of organization just as much as to their theological development. Two conclusions can however be stated with confidence with regard to the churches of New Testament times: they all had a very loose and diverse form of organization, and the concept of official priests or ministers was completely unknown.

Heresy and orthodoxy

The single most important factor that led to the development of a well-organized and disciplined church in the second century was the emergence of arguments about Christian beliefs, which eventually led to the articulation of quite precise definitions of what could, and could not, be acceptable formulations of theology.

The charismatic view that we find in the early chapters of Acts and in Paul had always been open to abuse. That was clearly a large part of the trouble that Paul had to deal with in the church at Corinth. As long as Christians were truly led by the Spirit, then things could be expected to work smoothly, but the unscrupulous could easily manipulate such a situation for their own ends. It was all too easy for a person's own ideas and selfish motives to be put forward as the Spirit's guidance, and it was correspondingly difficult for others to prove that someone claiming the Spirit's guidance did not actually have it. Paul believed that the Holy Spirit would lead Christians to do only those things that were compatible with the way Jesus himself had lived, thereby producing the 'fruits of the Spirit', especially that supremely Christian virtue, love

(Galatians 5:22–26; Romans 13:8–10; 1 Corinthians 13). But even this was not enough to control the extremists in Corinth. Paul's own position as an apostle was itself called into question, for others were claiming that by the power of the Spirit they were 'super apostles', and their revelations were more spectacular – and therefore more valid and believable – than his (2 Corinthians 11:1–15).

Similar arguments are to be found in the background of the letters of John. Wandering teachers claiming the inspiration of the Holy Spirit were not only scandalizing other Christians by their behaviour, but were also putting forward theological ideas that the church and its leaders found unacceptable (1 John 4:1–21). How could Christians deal with such people? In the earlier period the apostles had been the final authority, but as they died, the problem became more difficult. Fringe groups such as the Gnostics were gaining ever more ground, and it soon became clear to those in the mainstream of the church that it was no longer sufficient just to assert that they had the Holy Spirit, for their opponents were making exactly the same claim. Faced with such problems, the church had no alternative but to begin a radical rethinking of its position. What did it believe? How could it be sure of knowing where to get authoritative guidance? And how could it ensure that the church in the second century would follow the guidelines laid down by Jesus and his apostles at the very beginning? To try to find the answers to these questions, the church began to reassess its life in three main areas:

BELIEFS
The Christians of whom we read in the early chapters of Acts had not been too concerned to set out their beliefs in any sort of systematic way. That is not to say they had no theology: Jesus himself had claimed the title 'Son of man', and in the early chapters of Acts we find him identified as the 'servant of God' (3:13, 26; 4:27, 30) as well as 'the Messiah' (2:31, 36; 3:18, 20; 5:42; 8:5). Because of their own experience of the coming of the Holy Spirit, they had no hesitation in associating Jesus with God, and giving him the title 'Lord', the personal name of God in the Hebrew scriptures (Acts 2:36; 7:59–60; 1 Corinthians 16:22). Of course, they also knew that Jesus had been a real person who lived in Galilee and died on a Roman cross. But they were not concerned with defining their beliefs about Jesus more precisely, and the kind of theological reflection that later led to dogmas about Jesus' 'divinity' or 'humanity' would at this time have seemed both irrelevant and unnecessary.

However, when other people came along with claims that Jesus had been only partly divine, or not really divine at all, the church was faced with a challenge. It was not a new challenge, for Paul had already met something of this sort in Corinth. Perhaps that is one reason why he wrote his letter to Rome not long after that as a kind of summary and exposition of his own Christian thinking. But, after Paul's death, the problem became more acute. 1 John was written to counteract views of this kind, and we shall examine the precise nature of these Gnostic or Docetic beliefs in chapter 24. The fact that there were people who called themselves followers of Jesus but had different views from the majority about his significance meant that everyone in the church had to do some hard thinking, to try to define more precisely what they really believed.

But where could they find their beliefs? The Gnostics and their associates had their own books, many of which are still known today (*The Gospel of Thomas, Gospel of Philip, Gospel of Truth* and various others allegedly containing secret teaching given by Jesus to some of his disciples). Up to this point, much of the church's teaching had been passed on by word of mouth. By the end of the first century, most of the New Testament books were already in existence, but virtually all of them had been written for specific situations in particular churches and, with the possible exception of the letters of Paul, they had not been gathered together in any sort of permanent collection. According to Eusebius (*Ecclesiastical History* III.39) some church leaders, like Papias, still preferred the spoken word to what they could read in books. But the majority felt that the time had come to try to decide exactly what they did and did not believe.

WORSHIP

At the very beginning, the Christians met together every day, and their worship was spontaneous. This seems to have been regarded as the ideal, for when Paul describes how a church meeting should proceed, he depicts a Spirit-led participation in worship by many, if not all members of the church (1 Corinthians 14:26–33). No doubt this was the natural way for things to happen at a time when the church generally met in someone's house. But as churches got bigger it was no longer possible for Christians to get together in this informal setting.

Then there was also the fact that anyone had the freedom to participate in such worship. In the ideal situation when everyone was truly inspired by the Holy Spirit, this was the perfect expression of Christian freedom. But it was accompanied by the danger that those who were out of harmony with the church's beliefs and outlook could also use this freedom to pervert the faith of the community. Because of this it became necessary to ensure that those who led the church's worship could be relied upon to be faithful to the Christian message as it had been delivered by Jesus and the apostles. By the end of the first century a fixed form of service was in existence for the celebration of the eucharist, and other forms of Christian worship were also becoming less open and spontaneous than they had been. Not everyone welcomed this, and even the *Didache* (itself a handbook of church order) asserts that the ministry of Spirit-inspired speakers should not be curtailed in the interests of a formal church order. But in the face of growing threats from fringe groups in the church it was inevitable that this should happen eventually, in order to preserve the integrity of the Christian faith.

AUTHORITY

If the conduct of worship was to be controlled so as to exclude undesirable elements, two groups had to be created within the church: those with the authority to conduct its worship, and those without such authority. It is important to realize that the movement towards a more authoritarian church hierarchy also originated in the fight against unacceptable beliefs. At a time when Gnostics were claiming a special authority because of their alleged endowment with the Spirit, it was important for the mainstream church to have its own clear source of power. Even if it might have been true, it was of little practical use for the church's leaders to claim that they, rather than their opponents, were truly inspired by the Spirit. They needed something more than that – and they found it in the apostles. In the earliest period, supreme authority had rested with them. So, they reasoned, anyone with recognized authority in the church must be succeeding to the position once held by the apostles. They were the apostles' successors, and as such could trace their office back in a clear line of descent from the very earliest times. They stood in an 'apostolic succession'.

Church growth and debates about heresy and orthodoxy were undoubtedly the major reasons for the changing pattern of church life at the end of the first century. But others have claimed to find different reasons for this change, and we must give some consideration to two further suggestions:

Social change

The sociologist Max Weber has argued that any group started by an inspiring leader will inevitably change after the leader is dead. As the second-generation followers try to adapt the original charismatic lifestyle to the normal concerns of everyday life, the structures they create will inevitably become more institutionalized. This happens for a number of reasons, according to Weber, but economic interests are the most significant. The original leader's close associates subsequently become his or her official representatives. They therefore have a vested interest in developing an organization, and setting themselves up as a privileged hierarchy with the main job of other members of the movement being to support them economically and in other ways.

In the course of this process, the dynamic inspiration of the original leader is lost, and the charisma is changed into a more tangible quality that can be handed on from one holder of an office to another.

Historically, there can be no doubt that this is what has happened in the church, and it is possible to find early traces of it in the New Testament itself. For example, in 1 Timothy 4:14 the reception of spiritual gifts is identified with the act of appointment to an office – something that has been widely held in the church ever since. The odd thing is that it should have taken so long for this new development to happen. The early church became fully institutionalized not in the first generation after Jesus, but in the second and third generations.

Up to that point, the experience of the church runs contrary to what we would expect using Weber's sociological theory. Though Jesus was undoubtedly what Weber would have called a 'charismatic leader', the institutionalization of the church was not a simple linear development. Paradoxically, the church seems to have had elements of institutionalism from the very start. For example, it observed the Lord's supper as an exclusive community meal, it practised baptism of its converts as a rite of initiation, and it was conscious of having traditions to hand on to future generations. Its leaders had great authority, and were, at least on some occasions, paid by other church members. But there was one conviction that prevented the church developing into an organization existing for the sole benefit of its leaders, and this was the universally held belief that Jesus was not in fact dead, but alive, and continuing to work among his followers through the power of the Holy Spirit.

For as long as the church saw itself as the community founded by the Holy Spirit, this state of affairs could continue. But once it became suspicious of the exercise of charismatic gifts (because of their misuse), the real presence of Jesus became more of a dogma than a living reality, and it was a short step from that to the institutionalized church. There is no doubt that sociological analysis is helpful in explaining the course of later church history, and also certain aspects of the life of the earliest churches. But when we look for an explanation of the change from a charismatic to an institutional church, the main reasons lie elsewhere.

Frustrated hope

It has also been argued that the loss of the hope in the future return of Jesus (*parousia*) led to this change in the church's structure. The weight given to this consideration will depend on the extent to which any particular interpreter believes that Jesus and his first disciples expected the arrival of God's future kingdom to be imminent. Jesus had declared that it would soon come with power (Mark 9:1), and after his resurrection the disciples seem to have lived in daily expectation of the return of Jesus himself in glory. When nothing happened, the argument goes, they had to come to terms with the fact that the world was going to continue as it had always been, and in order to cope with that a visible and tangible form of church organization was required.

Others, of course, have argued that when Jesus spoke of the coming kingdom he was referring to a spiritual experience that his disciples could enjoy in this present life. We have already examined this whole issue in considerable detail in chapter 6, where it was suggested that both these elements can be found in the teaching of Jesus: God's new society had already arrived in the person of Jesus himself, but its complete fulfilment was yet to come in the future.

Naturally, different groups in the early church found different parts of this message more attractive than others. The Christians in the Greek city of Thessalonica became so excited about the fact that Jesus was to return that they gave up work in order to concentrate on preparing for this great event. Paul rebuked them for this, for though he shared their sense of anticipation, he was quite sure that scaremongering and imaginative speculation were not the way Christians should behave (1 Thessalonians 4:13 – 5:11). He reminded them in the words of Jesus himself that 'the day of the Lord will come as a thief comes at night'. In the meantime, Christians should be good citizens – work for their living and encourage and help other people. That is the way they will be ready for the coming of Christ.

Despite Paul's reticence in making pronouncements on such matters, many people still find it possible to believe that he was obsessed with nothing but the supposedly imminent end of the world. In reality, however, Paul and other leaders of the early church reflect in their writings exactly the same tension between present and future as is found in the gospels. They believed that Jesus would return one day, but they were also quite sure that in an important sense, Jesus was already with them in the person of the Holy Spirit.

In even his earliest letters, Paul gave instructions for Christian behaviour in a settled period of church life. Had he supposed that it was all to come to an abrupt end, such instructions would have been quite unnecessary. He describes the *present* experience of Christians as 'eternal life' (Ephesians 2:1–5; Colossians 2:13), and John uses the same expression. 'Eternal life' was not just a life that might go on forever in the future, but just as significantly it was the life of God as it can be experienced by Christians here and now in the present (John 4:23; 17:3).

With this kind of outlook, the non-occurrence of the second coming of Jesus would hardly be a problem. But there is one New Testament writing where it seems to be taken more seriously. This is 2 Peter, where the writer explains the apparently unexpected delay in the coming of Jesus by the observation that 'there is no difference in the Lord's sight between one day and a thousand years' (3:8). But we ought to note that the problem had occurred here because unbelievers had raised it, mocking the church by saying, 'He promised to come, didn't he? Where is he?' (3:4). Perhaps the issue would never have arisen otherwise, though it certainly became more important to Christians at a later period. Eventually the prospect of a future return of Jesus was lost altogether, and theologians were content to think of the church itself as the new society which Jesus had promised. But this was long after the New Testament period, and the disappearance of a future hope was not the cause of the church's institutionalization, but was one of its results.

In the final analysis, the church became an institution not out of conviction but out of practical necessity. It is easy to look back with hindsight and to imagine that the problems created by rapid church growth and emerging theological diversity could have been tackled in some other way that would have been less inhibiting to further development. But there can be no doubt of the sincerity of the second-century church leaders, nor of their genuine regret that, because of excess and abuse, the charismatic ideal no longer seemed to be a practical way forward.

The 'communism' of the early Jerusalem church

Some scholars have questioned the accuracy of the picture of life among the first Christians as a community based on the mutual sharing of goods. It can be pointed out that in Acts 2:44 and 4:32, the believers are said to have shared all their possessions, and yet in a later episode both Barnabas and Ananias still have property to sell (4:36 – 5:11). But there is no real contradiction here, for the earlier passages themselves make it clear that the members of the Jerusalem church did not dispose of everything at once, but sold things as the need arose, and then shared the profits with the rest of the Christian community (2:45).

There are no good reasons for doubting the general accuracy of Luke's account at this point. The sharing of goods was nothing new, and was regarded as an ideal by Greek writers, while the Jews were well aware of the need to be charitable. The community at Qumran practised a similar sharing of resources, though in this case a convert's possessions were not handed over until a year after joining the sect.

The distinguishing mark of the Christian 'communism' was its spontaneity. At Qumran, such sharing was carefully regulated by rules, as was the distribution of charity among Jews in general. But Jesus had laid down no hard and fast economic policy for his disciples to follow. Admittedly, he himself lived in relative poverty, and his immediate followers left all they had to join him. When a rich man wanted to become a disciple, he was told, 'Go and sell all you have and give the money to the poor' (Mark 10:21), and it is difficult not to conclude that Jesus believed a rich person would find it harder to follow him than a poor one (Matthew 19:24). But even the poor could become obsessed with riches, and they too were expected to give away their last coin in the service of God (Mark 12:41–44).

So it is not difficult to understand why these early Christians wanted to share their resources with one another. Yet it does not seem to have been an altogether successful enterprise, for we hear nothing more of such wholehearted sharing, either in Jerusalem or elsewhere. It can be argued that after its humble proletariat beginnings, the church soon moved into the middle classes of society, where the ideals of communistic life were not so attractive. It is certainly true that as the church expanded into the wider Roman world, some of its converts came from the higher social classes, but that seems never to have been the case in Palestine, and everything we know of the church in Jerusalem suggests that it continued to be poor throughout its existence. The church at Antioch in Syria sent a gift to Jerusalem (Acts 11:27–30), as did Paul's Gentile churches (Romans 15:22–29). Paul twice refers to the Jerusalem church as 'poor' (Romans 15:26; Galatians 2:10), and later Jewish Christians in Palestine called themselves 'Ebionites', a term which seems to have meant simply 'the poor'.

It is more likely that this early experiment in community living broke down simply because the Christians ran out of money. In their enthusiasm, perhaps they had forgotten to balance a sharing of goods with a sharing of labour, with the result that they disposed of the resources they already had, but could find no way of replenishing them.

Putting the New Testament together

To establish their position, Christians had to decide which books contained an authoritative statement of the church's beliefs, and it was thinking on this subject that eventually led to the collection of the twenty-seven New Testament books as having supreme authority. This collection is often called the 'canon' of the New Testament. The word 'canon' here comes from a similar Greek word meaning 'a measuring stick': the New Testament was to be an accurate measure by which all theological and doctrinal viewpoints could be tested.

It is not too difficult to imagine that somebody in the early church actually sat down and decided which books would form a part of this special collection, but it did not happen like that. The books of the New Testament were not accorded a special authority overnight, and in fact it was well into the fourth century before an actual list of books was drawn up. Four stages may be traced in this process:

● Right from the earliest times, Christians gave special authority to certain collections of teaching. The Old Testament, for example, was regarded as sacred scripture by the New Testament writers, and the sayings of Jesus also had a special place in their thinking. But in the very earliest times there was no fixed and clearly defined body of such teaching. We can see this from the fact that the New Testament occasionally refers to sayings of Jesus that are not contained in the gospels (see Acts 20:35), as well as the existence of later

AD200	AD250	AD300	AD400
New Testament used in the church at Rome (the 'Muratorian Canon')	**New Testament used by Origen**	**New Testament used by Eusebius**	**New Testament fixed for the West by the Council of Carthage**
Four gospels	Four gospels	Four gospels	Four gospels
Acts	Acts	Acts	Acts
Paul's letters:	Paul's letters:	Paul's letters:	Paul's letters:
Romans	Romans	Romans	Romans
1 & 2 Corinthians	1 & 2 Corinthians	1 & 2 Corinthians	1 & 2 Corinthians
Galatians	Galatians	Galatians	Galatians
Ephesians	Ephesians	Ephesians	Ephesians
Philippians	Philippians	Philippians	Philippians
Colossians	Colossians	Colossians	Colossians
1 & 2 Thessalonians	1 & 2 Thessalonians	1 & 2 Thessalonians	1 & 2 Thessalonians
1 & 2 Timothy	1 & 2 Timothy	1 & 2 Timothy	1 & 2 Timothy
Titus	Titus	Titus	Titus
Philemon	Philemon	Philemon	Philemon
James	1 Peter	1 Peter	Hebrews
1 & 2 John	1 John	1 John	James
Jude			1 & 2 Peter
Revelation of John	Revelation of John	Revelation of John	1, 2 & 3 John
Revelation of Peter		(authorship in doubt)	Jude
Wisdom of Solomon			Revelation
To be used in private, but not public, worship:	**Disputed:**	**Disputed but well known:**	
The Shepherd of Hermas	Hebrews	James	
	James	2 Peter	
	2 Peter	2 & 3 John	
	2 & 3 John	Jude	
	Jude		
	The Shepherd of Hermas	**To be excluded:**	
	Letter of Barnabas	The Shepherd of Hermas	
	Teaching of Twelve Apostles	Letter of Barnabas	
	Gospel of the Hebrews	Gospel of the Hebrews	
		Revelation of Peter	
		Acts of Peter	
		Didache	

Stages in the formation of the New Testament canon.

collections of sayings of Jesus, some of which are almost certainly genuine. The fact that there are four gospels in the New Testament instead of just one also shows that there was no idea of a fixed and exclusive collection of Jesus' teaching, and John 21:25 mentions many other sayings and deeds of Jesus not included in his gospel, but no doubt known to some of his readers in one form or another.

The apostles themselves had considerable authority, and their writings were highly respected. Notwithstanding the fact that the epistles were all written to specific people for particular purposes, they do nevertheless contain indications that their authors felt a special authority attached to their words (see, for example, Galatians 1:7–9). By the time 2 Peter was written, Paul's letters at least were regarded very highly, and could be classed as 'scripture' (2 Peter 3:16).

● When we move beyond the first century, into the period of the so-called Apostolic Fathers (people like Ignatius, Clement of Rome and Polycarp), we find a similar situation. These writers clearly respected many of the New Testament books, though they did not generally regard them as 'scripture', and over and above these books they also valued many other Jewish and Christian writings.

● This state of affairs received a serious challenge from Marcion, who in about AD150 left the church at Rome and declared that he had unearthed a new message which had allegedly been given in secret by Jesus to the disciples. They, however, had not preserved it intact, and so its secret was later entrusted to Paul. To back up his claims, Marcion compiled a list of sacred books, which included only one gospel (identical with none of the New Testament gospels, but not too different from Luke), together with ten letters of Paul.

At about the same time there was an explosion of other fringe groups, all of which had their own sacred books. In response to this, the leaders of the church began to write their own lists, and towards the end of the second century, Irenaeus, bishop of Lyons in France, had a kind of 'canon' of New Testament books. He also laid down a rough test for deciding the relative value of different Christian books, suggesting that those of most value were connected with the apostles themselves (*Against Heresies* III.11.8). This principle, applied by Irenaeus to the gospels, was refined and extended in the years that followed, and in the third century the church historian Eusebius listed in his *Ecclesiastical History* III.25.1–7 three different categories of Christian writings: those that were certainly authoritative (the four gospels, Acts, the letters of Paul, 1 Peter, 1 John and Revelation); those that were certainly not (*Acts of Paul, Shepherd of Hermas, Apocalypse of Peter, Epistle of Barnabas, Didache, Gospel According to the Hebrews*); and those whose status was disputed (James, Jude, 2 Peter, 2 and 3 John).

● Eventually in the fourth century, we find an actual list of authoritative scriptural books, from Athanasius in the eastern section of the church (AD367), and from the Council of Carthage in the western part of the church (AD397), and the books they listed are the twenty-seven books of our New Testament. But, of course, these books did not gain their authority then, for they had already been widely used and highly regarded for centuries, and the decisions made in the fourth century were simply the formal acknowledgment of a state of affairs that had existed for practical purposes for many years before that.

23 The Church and its Jewish Origins

It is impossible to understand fully the story of the early church without appreciating that the Christian movement was deeply rooted in the Jewish faith. Jesus was a Jew, as were all his original disciples, and so were most if not all of the converts on the Day of Pentecost. But, even in the earliest days, people like Stephen were asking whether Christianity was just another sect within Judaism, or whether it needed to become something distinctive and new. These questions became more pressing once Paul and others had moved out into the wider world to take the message about Jesus to Gentile people with no previous Jewish connections. Paul clearly regarded himself as the 'apostle to the Gentiles' (Romans 11:13), yet wherever he travelled he always took his message first to the local Jewish synagogue (Acts 13:14; 14:1; 17:1–2). As a result, many of the issues dealt with in his letters have a distinctively Jewish flavour – questions about the Old Testament Law, and the nature of Christian belief and behaviour over against Jewish traditions.

These issues were to become increasingly important for every aspect of life in the early church, as Christians took over the Jewish scriptures and the Hebrew Bible (usually in its Greek version) became the Old Testament. They naturally needed to know what relationships there might be between the inherited faith of Israel and their own new experience of Jesus and the Holy Spirit. Paul's epistles deal repeatedly with this question. But there are other writings in the New Testament which show how other Christians were tackling these issues. These 'general epistles' are mostly shorter than Paul's letters, and they are also for the most part considerably less complex. But they are no less valuable for that, for they give us direct access to areas of the church's life and thinking that are mentioned nowhere else in the New Testament.

Four books in particular shed light on different aspects of the Jewish dimension in the life of the earliest churches: James, Hebrews, 1 Peter and Revelation. They all have a clear orientation towards Jewish interests, but their concerns are not identical. Indeed, their very diversity makes them all the more useful, for they provide an insight into at least four different aspects of Jewish spirituality that were adopted and further developed among the first Christians.

Christians and Jewish morality

Judaism had always been deeply concerned with behaviour. In the Roman world, Jewish people were often distinguished not so much by what they thought as by what they did. They circumcised their male children, kept the sabbath day apart and observed distinctive laws about the preparation and consumption of food. These were the things that announced to the Romans that the Jews were different. But they were not the only things. For the Jewish people also had a comprehensive code of moral behaviour. Many of the things that were taken for granted in a regular Hellenistic lifestyle were avoided by Jews – not just because they were un-Jewish, but because they seemed to be against the Law of God. As Jewish people in different parts of the Roman empire explained their ancestral faith to other people, they found that Gentiles were often attracted by their moral standards. After the self-indulgence of much Greek and Roman culture, many Gentiles found the Jewish way refreshingly simple and disciplined. Not a few Gentiles actually converted to the Jewish religion, becoming full proselytes, while many more were like Cornelius (Acts 10:1–2), adopting the beliefs and lifestyle of Judaism without necessarily taking upon themselves the requirement of full obedience to the Torah.

The foundation of Jewish morality had been laid many centuries before in the Old Testament. Besides its concern with matters of religious ritual, the Torah has a strong moral core, in the ten commandments (Exodus 20:1–17) and elsewhere (especially the book of Deuteronomy). It was concerned to ensure that worshippers in ancient Israel should carry their religious beliefs over into the affairs of everyday life. The notion that there could be a division between the sacred and the secular was quite foreign to Judaism, for all of life was lived in the presence of God. As Amos and other Old Testament prophets never tired of pointing out, it was a waste of time to make high-sounding religious affirmations in the temple if they made no difference to the way people behaved at home and in the market place.

James

Jesus' himself had made the same emphasis, and the letter of James continues this theme: it emphasizes that religious belief is worthless if it does not affect the way people live. Devotion to God does not end at the door of the church. It only begins there: 'What God considers to be pure and genuine religion is this: to take care of orphans and widows in their suffering and to keep oneself from being corrupted by the world' (1:27). The heart of real devotion to God is to love one's neighbour as oneself (2:1–13) – and without deeds that will put such sentiments into action, religious faith is worthless (2:14–26).

Like Jesus, James uses many illustrations to deliver his message. In one passage he draws a vivid verbal picture of the apparent splendour of a rich person. Like the flowers whose beauty they try to copy, such people will last for only a short time: 'The sun rises with its blazing heat and burns the plant; its flowers fall off, and its beauty is destroyed. In the same way the rich will be destroyed...' (1:10–11; 5:1–6; cf. Matthew 6:28–30). James also turns his attention to the dangers of thoughtless talk. Just as a small rudder can steer a ship many times larger than itself, so the tongue has an influence that is out of all proportion to its size – and if we are not careful it can make trouble for ourselves and for other people. Once a person loses control of their tongue, it can create conditions like a forest fire, which is started by just one small spark but is very difficult to put out (3:1–12).

James takes many illustrations from the familiar world of Palestinian agriculture. He condemns the selfishness of the employer who refuses to pay workers a proper wage for a day's work (5:1–6). Jesus had used a similar story to make a rather different point. He told of an employer who hired workers for the vineyard. They started work at different times of the day, so that when the time came for them to receive their wages some of them had only worked for an hour, while others had worked the whole day. But they all received the same pay! Jesus' hearers must have rubbed their eyes with amazement when they heard that, for in their experience employers were more likely to treat them in the way James describes. But, of course, Jesus was speaking of a different kind of employer – God – who can always be trusted to deal with people in a way that is overwhelmingly generous.

The book of James has no coherent 'argument' as such, any more than Jesus' Sermon on the Mount has a consistently argued theme (Matthew 5–7). But its message would not be lost on its readers. These people were suffering the kind of discrimination that James mentions, and they are urged to be patient and to trust in God for deliverance. What God has promised will come true, and God's people will be vindicated in the end (James 5:7–20).

A CHRISTIAN BOOK?

There are several unsolved questions about the letter of James. But two things are quite clear: it is an intensely Jewish writing, and it is concerned above everything else with correct behaviour. Some have thought it so Jewish that they have doubted whether it could really be Christian. Martin Luther had no time for it, and dismissed it as 'a right strawy epistle, for it has no evangelical manner about it' – though in assessing his opinion, Luther's narrow comprehension of Judaism and his tendency to equate it with the failings of his own medieval church need to be taken into account. Others, however, have pointed out that James mentions the name of Jesus in only two places (1:1; 2:1), and that when he gives examples for his readers to follow, he chooses Old Testament figures like Abraham (2:21–24), Job (5:11), Elijah (5:17) and even the prostitute Rahab rather than Jesus (2:25). Moreover, no

significant facts about Jesus are mentioned anywhere in the book –
not even his death and resurrection. Indeed, if we were to look for
other books of a similar kind, we would most easily find them in
writings such as Proverbs in the Old Testament and other so-called
'Wisdom' books that were popular with Jewish readers in the time of
Jesus.

Some have therefore suggested that James was not written by a
Christian at all, and that the two references to Jesus were inserted at
some later date when Christians became embarrassed by the existence
of this apparently Jewish book in their scriptures. But there is no
evidence to support this idea. A later Christian editor who set out to
change what was supposed to be a Jewish book into a Christian one
would surely have inserted far more references to specifically Christian
ideas than just two mentions of the name of Jesus.

Similarities between the teaching of Jesus and James

God is the source and giver of all good gifts	Matthew 7:7–11 James 1:17
Christians must pay attention to God's word but also be prepared to put it into practice	Matthew 7:24–27 James 1:22
Christians should share God's mercy with others	Matthew 5:7 James 2:13
Christians should endeavour to make peace in the world	Matthew 5:9 James 3:18
'Love your neighbour as you love yourself'	Matthew 22:39 James 2:8
If this teaching is followed, the true nature of the Christian will be impossible to hide	Matthew 7:16–18 James 3:12
Followers of Jesus can pray to God confident their prayers will be answered	Matthew 11:22–24 James 1:6
God is the only judge, and the one to whom Christians are responsible	Matthew 7:1–2 James 4:11–12
Christians should make promises that others can accept and trust, because they intend to keep them, instead of trying to emphasize their sincerity by using unnecessary oaths	Matthew 5:33–37 James 5:12

JAMES AND JESUS

Far from suggesting that there is something deficient about the book
of James, its similarities to Jewish ways of thinking ought to challenge
the perception of those contemporary readers who have seen a sharp
dichotomy between the early church and its Jewish origins. For the
message of James is actually very much in harmony with the teaching
of Jesus. This is more than just a superficial similarity, for there are

many detailed points at which James' advice corresponds closely to specific aspects of Jesus' teaching as we know it from the synoptic gospels.

The words of James and the words of Jesus are not *identical* in any of these passages. But the language used and the sentiments expressed are so similar that it seems obvious there must be some connection.

The letter of James

Who wrote the letter of James? And who were its first readers? Most New Testament books contain some clues that enable us to answer such questions. But in the case of James, there is virtually nothing at all that provides specific indications about either the author or the recipients of this epistle. Indeed, it is not even certain that it was really an epistle, in the sense of a letter sent from one person to a group of others.

Who was James?

Apart from the mention of a person called James in the opening sentence, the book makes no further specific reference to its writer, readers or any other event or person. There is no hint as to where James and his readers lived, nor are we told who James actually was. This was a very common name among Jewish people, and a James who is described as 'a servant of God and of the Lord Jesus Christ' could have been any Christian of that name. Similarly, the way the book describes people and their behaviour could apply to many different situations not only in the ancient world, but in most social contexts, for it deals with basic traits of human nature that are the same the world over. It is as pointless to look for the identity of the rich people of whom James complains (James 2:1–4) as it would be to try to find out who the Good Samaritan was (Luke 10:25–37).

Early church traditions give no more real help. There is no trace of this letter of James in other Christian literature until the end of the second century. Eusebius listed it as one of the New Testament books whose value was disputed (*Ecclesiastical History* III.25.3). But he also added that the same disputed books 'have been produced publicly with the rest in most churches', and then linked this one with James, the brother of Jesus and leader of the church in Jerusalem (*Ecclesiastical History* II.23.25). Though this statement in Eusebius is obviously from a much later date than any possible time when the epistle of James might have been written, many scholars are prepared to believe it, if only because it is the only hard evidence we have, and so they regard the book as the work of James of Jerusalem.

If it is necessary to link this epistle with a person by the name of James who is mentioned elsewhere in the New Testament, then undoubtedly there are only two possible candidates: James the disciple and brother of John, and James the brother of Jesus. Faced with a choice between these two, most scholars would choose the second, on the ground that James the apostle was martyred in AD44 (Acts 12:1–3), and it is assumed that this date would be too early for the writing of any of the New Testament books. In addition, that particular James does not figure prominently in any of the stories of the early church contained in the book of Acts, whereas James the brother of Jesus became well known: he features as a central figure in Acts, and is also mentioned in Paul's writings. He would certainly seem to be the kind of person who could write to other Christians with no more introduction than his name.

But a number of arguments have been put forward against this idea that James of Jerusalem wrote the letter of James:

The most likely explanation is that the writer of James knew these sayings of Jesus in a slightly different form than they now have in the New Testament gospels. The gospel materials circulated by word of mouth for some time before they were written down, and the fact that some of this teaching has a more primitive form in James than it does in Matthew might imply that James had access to it at an earlier stage than the writers of the gospels.

The letter of James
continued

● It is written in very good Greek, in an elegant style that seems to imply some acquaintance with Greek literary arts. But would this be likely if it was the work of someone from rural Galilee? This argument was often given considerable weight by scholars of previous generations, who drew a sharp distinction between the culture of Palestine (which they believed was largely insulated from Greek influence) and the culture of the wider Hellenistic world. But this is now known to have been an over-simplification of a complex set of cultural interactions between the various regions of the Roman empire. Certainly, in an area such as Galilee with a large non-Jewish population a person like James could easily have learned a good deal about the Greek language. Moreover, at a number of places in the book, the distinctive idiom and style of the Semitic languages Hebrew and Aramaic seem to have influenced its style of writing (2:7; 3:12; 4:13–15; 5:17), which in turn suggests that the writer also knew one or both of these languages.

● If this book had been written by James the brother of Jesus, would he not have made more specific mentions of his famous brother? Indeed, since James was not a disciple during Jesus' own lifetime, would it not have been natural for him to have included some account of his conversion (alluded to by Paul in 1 Corinthians 15:7)? As it is, the writer seems to go out of his way to avoid mentioning Jesus directly: surely, therefore, he cannot have been this particular James. There is some weight in this argument, but it is an argument from silence, which really depends on guesswork. If we are unsure of the identity

of an ancient author, then making judgments about what he or she might or might not have been expected to write is, at best, a very subjective business.

● In James 2:14–26 there is a passage which contrasts faith and actions as the basis of true commitment. Paul also draws the same contrast, especially in his letters to the Galatians and to the Romans, and what James writes has often been regarded as a deliberate reply to and correction of Paul's opinions. If that is the case, then James must have been written after Paul's time, probably after his views had become a source of controversy – and on any account, this must therefore have been long after any possible date for the death of James of Jerusalem. But there is no reason to suppose either that James knew Paul's writings, or, as some have suggested, that Paul knew of James. Certainly they use the same terminology, but their concerns are different – and in any case, the differences between them are nothing like as far-reaching as Protestant (especially Lutheran) interpreters have generally supposed.

● The strongest reason of all for doubting that James of Jerusalem could have written this book is its conviction that true belief should be described in purely ethical terms. James had faced this question over the admission of the Gentile converts to the church: were they to obey the whole of the Old Testament Law or not? While James did not go along with those extremists who insisted that Gentile Christians should become Jews by being circumcised, he did agree that they should observe not only the moral laws of the Old Testament, but also some of the ritual and food laws as well

ORIGINS

Two main conclusions seem justified. On the one hand, the evidence for associating this book with James of Jerusalem is not especially convincing; but on the other, there are strong reasons for placing it in a very early period of the church's life. So where did it come from, and what was its purpose?

We must recognize that we do not have enough information to give a

---

(Acts 15:13–21). Is it therefore likely that he would have written that the 'law of the kingdom' could be kept by loving one's neighbour (2:8)? There is here a significant difference between what we know of James from Acts and Galatians (and what we learn from Josephus and other historians) and what we read in the book that bears the same name. In the view of many, this difference is so crucial that it alone must cast doubt on the alleged connection between the two.

The date

Though this book might well have no connection with James of Jerusalem, a number of facts suggest very strongly that it belongs to an early period of the church's life rather than a later one.

● In its opening sentence, it addresses itself to 'the twelve tribes in the Dispersion' (1:1). Taken literally, of course, that could mean the whole of the Jewish people scattered throughout the world. But it is probably to be understood in the same way as the similar address in 1 Peter 1:1 or Paul's designation of his Galatian readers as 'the Israel of God' (Galatians 6:16). From an early time, Christians understood themselves as being part of the people of God whose story is encapsulated in the Old Testament, and for that reason they found it was natural to apply to themselves language that had previously been used of Israel. Of course, the only period in the church's history when anyone could write to the whole of God's people in this way (as contrasted with 1 Peter, which was addressed only to certain areas) was at the very beginning of its history, when the church was still visibly

Jewish and centred on Jerusalem. This implies a time after the death of Stephen, but before Paul's travels had begun.

● This is further supported by the fact that there is no sign anywhere in James of a break between Judaism and Christianity. The well-to-do oppressors of the poor (2:6–7) were almost certainly Jewish people, but they are not condemned because of that, as they might have been at a later period. They are condemned for their selfishness, not their religion or ethnicity. Moreover, the gathering so vividly described in James 2:1–4 is said to be in 'the synagogue' (2:2). This situation is very similar to that described in Acts 4–5, when Jewish aristocrats were oppressing a lower-class proletarian Christian movement.

● The background to much of the imagery of James is clearly Palestinian. The mention of 'autumn and spring rains' (5:7) would have meant nothing at all in other parts of the Roman empire, while the agricultural practices mentioned in the preceding verses are of a type that disappeared for good in Palestine after AD70, but which were widespread in the days of Jesus.

● There is no evidence anywhere in James of the later practices and problems of the church. Not only is the Jewish/Gentile controversy unknown, but there is no mention of heresy, and no reference to the organization of the church or to doctrinal arguments of any sort. In addition, the moral teaching of James makes no mention of later ethical concerns over the adoption of unacceptable Hellenistic standards in the church. Instead, it is almost exclusively directed to the kind of problems that would occur in a Jewish environment.

full answer to that question. But the kind of teaching found in James is so similar to that of Jesus himself, and uses so much of the same rural imagery, that it is not unreasonable to suppose it has a similar background. It is not inconceivable that it had its origins among those followers of Jesus who remained in Galilee after the main centre of the church moved to Jerusalem. It is impossible to prove this, of course, for we know next to

---

'Faith' and 'works' in Paul and James

When Martin Luther called James 'an epistle of straw', his main reason for doing so was that he believed James' theology was fundamentally different from Paul's – and, since Paul was his hero, he was forced to relegate James to a secondary position. A comparison of James 2:24 with Romans 3:28 will readily demonstrate what led him to this conclusion:

● James 2:24: 'You see that a person is justified by works and not by faith alone.'
● Romans 3:28: 'For we hold that a person is justified by faith apart from works of the law.'

These two statements have every appearance of being mutually contradictory. Not only do they seem to be saying opposite things to each other: they also use exactly the same Greek words to do so! But when we examine them more carefully, and especially when we place them in their proper contexts, this alleged contradiction becomes much less obvious.

● Though they both speak of 'faith', James and Paul seem to mean rather different things by this word. For Paul, it has almost a technical sense, referring specifically to that belief in and commitment to Jesus that characterize the Christian life. In James, however, 'faith' has a much broader meaning, almost being something like 'faith' as belief in God, as opposed to atheism. For James, the term 'faith' is more akin to the intellectual acceptance of theological propositions, whereas Paul's concern was more focused on faith as personal commitment.

● A similar distinction may be drawn in the way they each use the term 'works'.

When James mentions 'works', he refers to the kind of behaviour that naturally stems from commitment to Christ (1:25; 2:8). But the 'works' that Paul writes about are attitudes of self-sufficiency, the kind of acts that religious people might do in order to commend themselves to God, or to gain God's approval. James refers to the things a person will do because he or she already has a living relationship with God through Christ.

● Paul and James were addressing themselves to different practical problems, and this inevitably affected the way they expressed themselves. In Galatians and Romans, Paul appears to have been contending against the self-righteousness of people who thought that by external religious observance they could commend themselves to God. So he condemns such things – and in doing so, he echoes the teaching of Jesus (Luke 18:9–14). James, on the other hand, was fighting against the temptation to suppose that right belief of an abstract, propositional kind is all that matters – and he accordingly emphasizes that doctrines with no practical effect are worthless. Again, he also echoes the teaching of Jesus (Matthew 7:21–23).

● This entire debate depends on the mistaken understanding of Judaism as a religion of legalism, propounded by Luther and repeated by most generations of Protestant scholars until relatively recent times. But once Judaism is seen in its own terms as a faith combining both personal commitment and loving actions, the alleged dichotomy between Paul and James can be seen for what it is: the imposition of an alien modern, Western agenda on an ancient text.

nothing about such Galilean believers. But the message of James would certainly be especially appropriate to those who were worshipping in the Jewish synagogues of rural Palestine, and at the same time were trying to put into practice what Jesus had taught them. Such people might easily have been tempted to substitute religious formality for the spiritual realities of which Jesus had spoken – and, as a relative minority, they would also be open to the kind of persecution that James mentions.

If the book originated in such a context, this might also explain why its value was unrecognized in the wider church for so long. Its eventual association with an important person like James of Jerusalem would then have been a means of justifying its inclusion in the canon of the New Testament. It could also reflect the possibility that the church in Jerusalem was included in 'God's people in the Dispersion', to whom James was originally dispatched at an early stage in the history of the church.

Christians and Jewish ritual

For generations, the temple in Jerusalem had occupied a special place in the life and thinking of Jewish people. In the stories of the nation, the construction of the first temple was associated with the reign of King Solomon, who was highly esteemed as the one king (along with his father David) who had really put ancient Israel on the political map of the day (1 Kings 8:20–21). Though this empire collapsed almost overnight on Solomon's death, the temple stood as a monument to his achievements, and was to be the lasting symbol of the royal dynasty of David. It could on occasion be invested with an almost mystical significance, and even in the dark days just before its destruction by Nebuchadnezzar, king of Babylon, the people of Jerusalem managed to convince themselves that, against all the odds, the physical presence of the temple in their city would somehow save them from invasion. They were wrong, of course, as the prophet Jeremiah was quick to remind them, pointing out that they were pinning their hope on a purely outward form of religious activity instead of taking seriously the moral and spiritual demands placed upon them by their relationship with God (Jeremiah 21:1 – 23:32).

Almost 150 years after Nebuchadnezzar had plundered Solomon's temple, it was eventually patched up and brought back into regular use under the influence of Ezra and Nehemiah, whose period is documented in the Old Testament books named after them. But by the New Testament period it was in the process of being replaced with a structure even more splendid than the original had been. In 20BC, Herod the Great decided to build a new temple that would be as grand as any monument in the Roman world. But he did not live to see it finished. The work was so ambitious and costly that it went on for something like eighty years. By the time this new temple was completed, the Jews were in revolt against the Romans, and soon afterwards it was destroyed by the Roman general Titus in AD70, and was never rebuilt.

This was the temple that Jesus and the first Christians knew, and it was a centre of devotion for Jewish believers from all over the Roman empire. By New Testament times synagogues had been established in every town or city where there was a Jewish population of any size. But worship in the synagogue was not the same as worship in the temple. The synagogue had originated as a social convenience for Jews living in lands far removed from Palestine. But it was at the temple in Jerusalem that Israel's religious past could be seen in true focus. The worship of the synagogue could incorporate some of the ancient rituals such as circumcision and the old food laws, but most of the rites prescribed in the Old Testament could only be carried out in their entirety in the temple at Jerusalem. Here, the priests still offered sacrifices as their predecessors had done for generations past, and all the great religious festivals had special significance when celebrated at the temple. Pilgrims travelled from all over the empire to worship in its holy places, and it was an ambition for every pious Jew to visit the temple at least once in a lifetime. The crowds who gathered to hear Peter on the Day of Pentecost were not unusually large, and at the times of special festivals the population of Jerusalem regularly increased tenfold, or even more.

How did all this relate to Christian faith? For Gentile believers, with no previous connection with the Jewish faith, this question seemed trivial: the Jerusalem temple had never featured in their spirituality before, so why should it do so now? But for those with a Jewish heritage,

this was a matter of more fundamental importance. Moreover, it highlighted a real problem for the early Gentile mission. For the early church everywhere seems to have adopted Jewish moral standards, as laid out in the Torah. But in reality, the Torah was far more than a collection of ethical teachings. It also contained detailed regulations for the proper conduct of worship. So how should Christians relate to the ritual practices of the Jewish religion? And why adopt the morality of the Torah as normative, and not take seriously those passages that were more specifically related to formal worship?

Putting the question that way merely serves to highlight its complexity, for ultimately the role of the temple in Jerusalem could not be dealt with independently from matters like circumcision that proved to be such a problem in the churches associated with Paul. In the event, as the church became more and more Gentile, that question was ultimately solved in favour of those who, like Paul, believed that the Old Testament Law was not directly relevant to the Christian life. But in the first century there were many Jewish Christians who not only continued with practices like circumcision but also felt a special affection for the priesthood and ritual of the Old Testament. The first followers of Jesus in Jerusalem had participated freely in the services at the temple: it never occurred to them not to do so, and in any case that was where they would find others willing to listen to their new message about Jesus as Messiah (Acts 2:46; 3:1). But as time passed, things soon changed. Many

The temple in Jerusalem occupied a site with a long-established tradition of sacrifice. Temple worship came to an end in AD70 when the Romans sacked the city. The Dome of the Rock mosque was built in AD691–92 on the same site.

Hellenist Christians shared the opinion of Stephen, that the day of the temple and its rituals was finished altogether. The death of Jesus was often interpreted using the language of sacrifice familiar from the Hebrew Bible, which made it easy to conclude that Jesus' death on the cross had in some way superseded the repeated sacrifices of the Jerusalem temple. At the same time, the church in Jerusalem seems to have continued to worship in the temple, and was allowed to do so because of its relatively conservative stance on the issue of Gentile Christians. There were many others who wished to join them. After all, the first generation of Hellenist Christians had all been born Jews, and there was never any suggestion that they should deny their Jewishness in order to follow Jesus. In addition, their non-Christian compatriots were naturally eager to know where they stood. Did they support and approve of the Jewish way of doing things – or did they, like Stephen, believe that even the temple was now redundant?

Hebrews: author, readers and date

The author

According to Eusebius, the third-century church leader Origen wrote of this book, 'only God knows the truth as to who actually wrote this epistle' (*Ecclesiastical History* VI.25.14). Some translations and ancient versions of the Bible give it the title, 'The epistle of Paul to the Hebrews'. But these words are not original, and it is highly unlikely that this book has anything to do with Paul.

● For one thing, it is not really an epistle at all. When Paul wrote letters he always followed the normal practice of Greek letter-writers (see chapter 16). He also leaves us in no doubt as to who his readers were and what has caused him to write to them. But Hebrews is not addressed directly to anyone, and the only possible reason for supposing it to be a letter of some sort is the inclusion of what appears to be a personal greeting after the benediction with which the book closes (13:22–25). Some have suggested that this section was added later, to make Hebrews look more like one of Paul's letters. It has even been suggested that Paul himself added the news of Timothy given in 13:23 to a book that Timothy had originally written. But there is nothing to support either of these conjectures.

● The language and style of Hebrews is in any case totally different from that of Paul's writings. Hebrews has just about the best Greek style of any New Testament book, and reaches a far higher literary standard than Paul could ever aspire to. Origen noticed this: 'The character of the diction of the epistle entitled "To the Hebrews" has not the apostle's rudeness in speech... that is, in style. But that the epistle is better Greek in the framing of its diction, will be admitted by everyone who is able to discern differences of style' (quoted by Eusebius, *Ecclesiastical History* VI.25.11–12).

● The concerns of Hebrews are also quite different from Paul's interests. If, as many believe, it was written primarily for the benefit of Jewish Christians, then Paul is unlikely to have written it in any case as his ministry was almost entirely among Gentiles. But even if it was written for Gentiles, its interest in the Torah is quite different from Paul's. Though Paul's attitude to the Law raises many questions, there is no doubt that his approach to it was primarily concerned with its *moral* demands. The ritual of tabernacle, priests and sacrifices which is so important in

Hebrews

This is the kind of question that inspired the New Testament book of Hebrews. The sort of encouragement and advice its author gives seems to imply that its readers were being persecuted – perhaps because of their resistance to accepting Jewish practices. This might explain why the question of Jewish worship had become so important to them: if they were prepared to conform to the traditional practices, life could be a lot easier. The stories of Acts show how religious fanatics could make life really difficult for Christian believers (Acts 13:50; 14:5, 19), and some scholars believe a similar situation is envisaged here. On the other hand, Christians throughout the Roman empire must always have been tempted to try to link themselves to Judaism, especially in times of persecution – for Judaism was a permitted religion under Roman law, whereas at this stage Christianity was not.

The writer of Hebrews argued that it was both pointless and

Hebrews simply never features anywhere in the writings of Paul.

We can therefore be quite sure that Paul did not write Hebrews. But it is not easy to decide who did. There is so little specific reference to people and events that the most diverse characters have been suggested, all with more or less equal plausibility: Barnabas, Apollos, Timothy, Aquila and Priscilla, and Luke have all been put forward as possible candidates. In reality, we are no nearer to a solution than Origen was. But it is possible to deduce some key facts about the unknown author from a close reading of the text of the book.

● The author of Hebrews did not belong to the same group as the apostles. Explaining how the Christian message had reached him, the writer comments: 'The Lord himself first announced this salvation, and those who heard him proved to us that it is true' (2:3). Some scholars have drawn inferences from this about the possible date of the book. But this statement does not necessarily imply that the writer belonged to a different generation from the apostles – only that he was not among their number. A person like Stephen would fit this description just as easily as someone from a later period.

● The author was clearly well educated. He knew how to write Greek, and was also well versed in the literary and rhetorical conventions of the Hellenistic age. Hebrews also reveals a person with some acquaintance with ideas that were common among Greek thinkers. The way the heavenly world, where Christ dwells, is contrasted with the material world in which traditional ritual worship operates, is not all that different from Plato's notion about the world of forms, or ideas, that gives meaning to the world we know through our senses.

● At the same time, the author's real background seems to be in Judaism. It has been argued that his knowledge of Plato's system came not through direct acquaintance with Greek thinking, but through knowledge of the work of a Hellenistic Jewish philosopher like Philo, who flourished in the early years of the Christian era at Alexandria in Egypt. But he also seems to have been familiar with the way Jewish teachers in Palestine interpreted the Old Testament, and some of his most distinctive imagery was very popular in various groups on the fringes of Judaism. The people from Qumran, who wrote the Dead Sea Scrolls, were expecting a Messiah who, like Jesus in Hebrews, would also be a high priest. They too had

unnecessary for Christians to keep the ritual requirements of the Old Testament Law. For this author, the message of Jesus was God's final word (1:1–3). Previous prophets in ancient Israel had spoken in God's name to the people of their own time, but they were now all summed-up and replaced by Jesus. Jesus is compared not only to the angels whom Jewish tradition identified with the giving of the Torah (1:4 – 2:18), but also to Aaron, the archetype of every Jewish priest, and other Jewish heroes like Moses and Joshua (3:1 – 4:13). But none of them was able to match Jesus. They were mere mortals, but Jesus was 'Son of God' and therefore greater than them all. Yet because of his human experience, he understood how people felt when faced with the power of evil (2:17–18; 4:14–15). He was the fulfilment of all Judaism's aspirations, 'a great high priest' who both summed up and superseded all that had gone before (4:14 – 5:10).

Continuing to write of Jesus under the imagery of the Jewish

Hebrews: author, readers and date *continued*

considerable interest in the Old Testament figure of Melchizedek and, like the writer of Hebrews, had a particular fascination with the rituals of the Day of Atonement. This has led some scholars to suggest that Hebrews was written to Christians who had come under the influence of the community at Qumran. But some of these ideas are also to be found in other Jewish documents such as the *Testaments of the Twelve Patriarchs*, while purification ceremonies like those mentioned in Hebrews 6:2 were observed by many groups in the Jewish community.

The readers

Since it is impossible to make a clear identification of the author of Hebrews, it is unrealistic to imagine that we can be certain who its first readers might have been. But there are a number of indications in the book itself that can give some impression of the kind of people they probably were.

● In recent times, it has generally been supposed that they would be Jewish Christians. This seems to be implied in the title, 'To the Hebrews'. But the ancient author did not give the book this title: like all the titles appended to the New Testament books, it was added for convenience in later centuries. It could

therefore be misleading, and some prefer to think of Gentile Christians as its recipients. Against that, it is not easy to see why non-Jewish Christians should have had such a detailed interest in the sacrificial system of ancient Israel, whereas for Jewish Christians the Old Testament and its rituals had been given by God, so it is obvious that they would have some significant questions. What was its status now? Had God's mind somehow changed with the coming of Jesus? These questions would certainly have more point for Jewish Christians than for Gentiles. They would be of greatest interest for people living in Jerusalem itself, where the temple was a feature of everyday life, and some have suggested that this must be where Hebrews originated. But a number of facts speak against this.

The church at Jerusalem was always a poor church, whereas the readers of Hebrews seem to have been reasonably well off (6:10; 10:34).

Surprisingly, in view of its subject matter, the temple itself is not actually mentioned in Hebrews. Instead, the author describes in great detail the worship associated with the tent of worship (tabernacle) used by Moses and the Israelites in their desert journey from Egypt to Canaan. This might suggest that the

priesthood, Hebrews goes on to suggest that a more suitable Old Testament image to illustrate what Jesus had done may be found in the figure of Melchizedek (5:11 – 7:28). In the original stories of the Hebrew Bible, this Melchizedek is a shadowy figure of whom we know next to nothing. In one of the psalms, the king in Jerusalem is called 'a priest for ever in the line of succession to Melchizedek' (Psalm 110:4), and later generations of Christians have applied this description to Jesus. He also appears briefly in a story about Abraham (Genesis 14:17–20), where again very little is said about him. But the writer of Hebrews uses the obscurity of these Old Testament references to argue that since 'there is no record of Melchizedek's father or mother or of any of his ancestors; no record of his birth or of his death', he must be 'like the Son of God', who is similarly timeless (7:3). He also draws attention to the fact that Abraham had recognized the greatness of this priestly figure (treating him with reverence, and giving him gifts) long before Aaron was even

---

readers did not have first-hand experience of the temple, and their only direct access to rituals like sacrifice and priesthood was through what they could read for themselves in the books of Leviticus and Numbers. This would obviously suit the situation of Hellenist Jewish Christians living elsewhere in the Roman empire.

● The readers of Hebrews also seem to have been suffering some kind of persecution. Not long after they became Christians, they had 'suffered many things, yet were not defeated by the struggle… at times publicly insulted and ill-treated, and at other times… ready to join those who were being treated in this way. You shared the sufferings of prisoners, and when all your belongings were seized, you endured your loss gladly' (10:32–34). But the author then goes on to encourage them not to evade further persecution. At the time of writing, unlike some of the early Jerusalem Christians, they had 'not yet had to resist to the point of being killed' (12:4), but that seemed as if it might be a distinct possibility.

● The book of Hebrews gives the impression that it is not addressed to an entire church, but to a group within a church. In 5:12–14 the readers are criticized because they have not yet realized their God-given potential to be teachers – a function that not every Christian would expect to have. Then 10:25 could be taken to suggest that they were reluctant to meet with other Christians – while 13:24 asks them to convey 'greetings to all your leaders and to all God's people'. It has been suggested that Hebrews might have been addressed to some sectarian group mentioned elsewhere in the New Testament – perhaps the Colossian heretics, who were opposed in the letter to the church at Colossae. These people were certainly interested in the role of angels, and in some aspects of Jewish ritual practices. But their underlying world-view shows that they were not understanding them from the perspective of normative Judaism. For them, the Old Testament rules were a useful way to achieve quite different objectives, and that would seem to distinguish them from the concerns of Hebrews.

● The recipients of Hebrews lived in Italy, perhaps in Rome. This is made clear in 13:24: 'The believers from Italy send you their greetings'. The author was in the company of a group of Italian Christians who wished to be remembered by their friends at home. If this was in fact in Rome, then certainly the circumstances of the church there do have some interesting

born. If the great ancestor of the Jewish nation had himself paid homage to Melchizedek, then that in itself was enough to demonstrate the superiority of his position over the later priestly line descended from Aaron; more than that, for as one of a generation yet to come, Aaron was at least potentially present in Abraham's body when he met Melchizedek, and therefore in a sense he too had shared in Abraham's reverence for this person. If more proof of Jesus' supremacy was needed, then the writer of Hebrews reminded his readers of the further fact that the Old Testament priests died and were succeeded by others, while Jesus, like Melchizedek apparently, lived for ever.

Most of today's readers will struggle to comprehend exactly what Hebrews is claiming. The actual form of the author's argument depends on a way of reasoning that is simply alien to most of us. The idea that all future generations are somehow contained within the reproductive organs of their original parents might easily be dismissed as nonsensical.

Hebrews: author, readers and date *continued*

similarities to the situation envisaged in Hebrews. The last chapter of Romans shows that in the late fifties the Roman church was not one unified congregation, but a collection of separate, though not unrelated 'house churches' (Romans 16:3–15). Other evidence from the Jewish community in Rome suggests that as the Christian gospel was proclaimed in different synagogues, they made different responses to it and formed Christian congregations distinguished by their various viewpoints on questions connected with traditional Jewish observances. We also know that the Jews of Rome had a close interest in the kind of ideas that Hebrews shares with some fringe sects within Judaism.

The date

So when was Hebrews written? Various dates have been suggested, ranging from the early sixties to the end of the first century. On no account can it have been written later than about AD90, for it is referred to in *1 Clement* which was written in Rome no later than AD96. A number of arguments are involved in fixing a more precise date:

● Some have pointed to the statement in 2:3 that, 'The Lord himself first announced this salvation, and those who heard him proved to us that it is true.' They argue that this shows the author was a second- or third-generation Christian, in which case an appropriate date might be between AD80 and 90. But we have already seen that this is not a necessary inference from that verse.

● It has also been pointed out that the book seems to emphasize the human character of Jesus. It is natural to suppose that this might have been a subject of controversy at the time, which in turn would most obviously take us to the arguments about Jesus' humanity and divinity ('Docetism') that emerged towards the end of the first century. But when we examine such references closely, many of them are seen to be based on the outline of Jesus' life contained in the gospels, and they are used in Hebrews to provoke a specific recollection of Jesus' behaviour and actions as an example and encouragement (2:14; 4:15; 5:7–9; 13:12). If we compare this with the way 1 John opposes heresy (see chapter 24 below), there are undoubtedly significant differences.

● In fact there are few signs of the interests of the institutional church in Hebrews. The tension between present experience (1:2; 6:5) and future hope (9:28; 10:34–38) that was so characteristic

But this is the kind of logic that would make perfect sense in the context of the prevailing physiology of the first-century world. The more important thing to notice is the conclusion reached by the author on the basis of this discussion, which is remarkably simple considering the convoluted route taken to arrive at it: 'we have such a High Priest, who sits at the right side of the throne of the Divine Majesty in heaven. This one serves as High Priest in the Most Holy Place, that is, in the real tent which was put up by the Lord, not by humans' (8:1–2). Everything that had been achieved through the rituals of Old Testament worship – first in the 'tent' (or tabernacle), then in the temple – was only a temporary alleviation of the human condition, and those things to which the temple had looked forward had now been achieved permanently by Jesus. The sacrifices offered by the priesthood had to be repeated, because they could only account for past wrongdoing. But the sacrifice of Jesus (himself, on the cross) had more far-reaching consequences. Not

---

of the age of the apostles is still found – and there is no more church hierarchy in view than might be suggested by the vague title 'leaders' (13:24).

● The writer of Hebrews seems to suppose that the kind of worship described in the Old Testament was still in existence. 'The same sacrifices are offered for ever, year after year… the sacrifices serve year after year to remind people of their sins…' (10:1–3). These, and other similar statements, suggest that the temple in Jerusalem was still standing, and if that is the case then the book can be dated before AD70. It may be objected that Hebrews refers not to the temple, but to the tent of worship in the desert. But the Old Testament regulations were the same in each case, and might indeed have been of the same origin if the findings of much Old Testament scholarship are to be believed. In the present form of the Old Testament, there are no temple regulations as such. Solomon's temple is just assumed to have taken over the pattern of tabernacle worship laid down in the Torah. If the temple had ceased to function when Hebrews was written, it is impossible to believe that the author would not have mentioned the fact, for the literal destruction of the Old Testament ritual in AD70 would have been the final

confirmation of the whole argument of his book.

● If Hebrews was directed to readers in Rome, then the statement that they had not yet given their lives for the gospel would seem to point to a time before Nero's persecution reached its climax in AD64. The earlier persecution that they had suffered could then have been connected with the disturbances that led Claudius to expel the Jewish people from Rome for a time in AD48.

We may tentatively conclude that Hebrews was written by an unknown author in the period leading up to Nero's persecution. Its first readers were a group of Hellenist Jewish Christians in Rome who were trying to escape the political consequences of being known as Christians by observing the rituals of traditional Judaism. They wanted the protection that the empire gave to Jews, but they also wished to enjoy the privileges of being Christians. The author of Hebrews deplored this attitude: in his opinion, not only were they betraying their fellow-Christians, but their acquiescence in Jewish rituals was also in effect a denial of their faith in Christ. If they truly wished to serve him, they must be prepared to stand up and be counted as his followers, whatever the cost might be.

only was it the basis on which humanity could be accepted and put right by God, but the divine power released by it could also set them free from 'useless rituals, so that we may serve the living God' (9:14).

Now, 'God does away with all the old sacrifices and puts the sacrifice of Christ in their place' (10:9). Because of that, those who are tempted to turn back and perpetuate the old rituals of Judaism are actually denying the effectiveness of what God has done in Jesus. They are 'despising the

Hebrews and the Old Testament

The most distinctive feature of the book of Hebrews is the way that it uses the Old Testament to back up its arguments. Taking up Old Testament figures like Aaron or Melchizedek, and rituals like the Day of Atonement, the author suggests that these things were a kind of symbolic preview of the work of Jesus. Just as Aaron was a high priest, so was Jesus – though with significantly greater effect. His position was more directly comparable to that of Melchizedek, and the sacrifice that Jesus offered had more lasting benefits than the traditional ritual of the Day of Atonement.

If we ever think about the Old Testament at all today, this is not the way we generally approach it. We may ask questions about its morality or its picture of God, but we would not expect to find detailed descriptions of the person of Jesus (who was born at least two centuries after its latest events) hidden within its pages. Yet the underlying question that puzzled the author of Hebrews is still a relevant one: namely, in what sense is the Old Testament a 'Christian' book? Obviously, it was not written by Christians, but the author of Hebrews shared the conviction of the early church (and of later Christians) that the God of whom the ancient scriptures speak is the same God as Jesus revealed. Since God is unchangeable, it is therefore legitimate to look for some sort of unity between the Old Testament and the New Testament.

The author of Hebrews found this unity by supposing that, since the same God is involved in both parts of the Christian

Bible, God's activities in the earlier stages of its story can be taken as a pattern or visual aid for what God does in the later stages. It is in this light that we can understand the way the writer of Hebrews uses the Old Testament. He is not suggesting that the people of Old Testament times understood their history and priestly rituals as a psychic glimpse into the unknown future. To them, these things were the facts of everyday life and faith. But, Hebrews argues, when Christians looked back with the benefit of hindsight, they could see how the life, death and resurrection of Jesus might appropriately be described as the 'fulfilment' of all that had gone before. Peter, for example, described Jesus as 'the servant of God' (Acts 3:13, 26; 4:25–30), no doubt referring to those passages in the book of Isaiah that have come to be known as 'the Servant Songs' (Isaiah 42:1–4; 49:1–6; 50:4–9; 52:13 – 53:12). For Isaiah and his contemporaries, the Servant was a real person or persons – the whole nation of Israel, or perhaps the prophet himself. But as Peter looked back, he found that these passages provided the imagery with which he could most authentically sum up Jesus' ministry. Hebrews is doing the same thing with other Old Testament people (Moses, Joshua, Aaron, Melchizedek), events (the Day of Atonement) and artifacts (the tent of worship in the desert).

This way of interpreting the Hebrew Bible was not unknown in Judaism. Philo of Alexandria had elevated it to an art, arguing that the apparently 'historical' events of the Old Testament could be understood as symbols of the insights of

Son of God', and insulting the Holy Spirit (10:29). They have effectively joined with those who reject Jesus, and God has no time for such people. To turn back to the old ways is to be lost, but those who trust in God and accept what Jesus has accomplished will find true and lasting salvation (10:39).

All this is strong stuff, capable of being interpreted as a sternly anti-Semitic polemic. But our author insists that it was nothing new, but the

---

Greek philosophy, at least as he understood them from his own Jewish background. Many of the church fathers later read not only the Old Testament but also the New Testament in this way, ignoring the reality of its stories and regarding them instead as complex allegories of theological truths. The fourth-century writer Hilary of Poitiers described the reasoning behind this: 'Every work contained in the sacred volume announces by word, explains by facts, and corroborates by examples the coming of our Lord Jesus Christ... From the beginning of the world, Christ, by authentic and absolute prefigurations in the person of the Patriarchs, gives birth to the church, washes it clean, sanctifies it, chooses it, places it apart and redeems it: by the sleep of Adam, by the deluge in the days of Noah, by the blessing of Melchizedek, by Abraham's justification, by the birth of Isaac, by the captivity of Jacob... The purpose of this work, is to show that in each personage, in every age, and in every act, the image of his coming, of his teaching, of his resurrection, and of our church is reflected as in a mirror.'

For people with that mindset, it mattered very little whether any of these people or events had ever truly existed. The important thing was the underlying truth that they were held to symbolize. Hebrews, however, pays some attention to historical reality, and does not treat the Old Testament as a story with no meaning apart from what later generations might choose to read into it. On the contrary, it regards all that it reports as being the actions of God in real history, and when Hebrews compares Old and New Testaments, its view of God is central, emphasizing that God is the one who gives

continuity and coherence to the grand sweep of history, for what God has revealed through Jesus is the next and final stage of the revelation in the Old Testament.

This method of interpretation has often been labelled 'typology'. But to be useful this term needs to be applied quite precisely, to indicate a way of interpreting past events that treats them with integrity in their own context, while seeing within them a pattern running through history that reveals some greater underlying cause or purpose. Used in this way, 'typology' can be set over against the kind of 'allegory' found in the work of Philo and the Church Fathers, as well as books like John Bunyan's *Pilgrim's Progress*, in which their own message is the most important thing, and history is at best a subsidiary aid in the presentation of their own insights. The message of Hebrews draws attention to correspondences between Old and New Testaments, claiming to show how God's work in one period of time was fulfilled by God's work in Jesus.

This method of expounding the Christian message is not found in any comprehensive form anywhere else in the New Testament. Its main appeal would obviously be to Christians with Jewish connections. It is far removed from the questions that modern Christians ask about the Old Testament, but its essential message is not irrelevant, for it is a reminder of the faithfulness and consistency of God's dealings with people at all times and in all places (13:8).

Hilary of Poitiers (AD315–368).

natural outworking of the Jewish faith. Far from being redundant, Judaism was an essential prerequisite for the full articulation of Christian faith – and so Hebrews goes on to list a 'large crowd of witnesses' taken from the Old Testament and Jewish history, whose experience of God is part of the ongoing narrative that culminated with the coming of Jesus (11:1–38). These people will receive the same reward as faithful Christians (11:39–40), and their story should be a lasting encouragement to Christians to get their priorities right and to keep their eyes firmly fixed on Jesus alone as their example and inspiration (12:1–11). To do this, they must live at peace with others and show love for other Christians, as well as members of their own families (12:14; 13:1–21). By doing so, they will please God, who in turn will 'provide you with every good thing you need in order to do God's will' (13:21).

Christians and the covenant with Israel

The debates in the early church about Jewish morality and ritual were symptomatic of more fundamental underlying issues in the self-understanding of the earliest Christian communities. In Old Testament times, to be a member of the people of God had not been simply a matter of behaving in the same way as other like-minded people. It also involved inclusion in the covenant relationship that God had established with Israel's ancestor Abraham (Genesis 12:1–3; 15:1–21; 17:1–14; 22:16–18) and with Moses at Mount Sinai (Exodus 19:5–8; 20:1 – 24:18). The relationship had started with God's concern and care for this people. Abraham was called from Mesopotamia and found a new homeland not because of any moral or spiritual superiority that he might have possessed, but simply because God's affection was centred on him. His descendants later emerged from the shattering experience of the exodus not because of their own moral perfection but simply through the care of a loving God.

On the basis of these undeserved acts of kindness, God had made certain demands of the people. Abraham and his family were promised a great and prosperous future (Genesis 15:1–6). In response to God's goodness, Abraham had accepted that both he and his descendants should give tangible and lasting expression to this new covenant relationship that existed between them and God: 'You and your descendants must all agree to circumcise every male among you... Any male who has not been circumcised will no longer be considered one of my people, because he has not kept the covenant with me' (Genesis 17:9–14).

The same elements recur in the covenant relationship established between God and Israel through Moses at Mount Sinai. God had rescued the people from slavery in Egypt, and they were to respond with obedience to God's laws, which included moral precepts such as are found in the ten commandments (Exodus 19:4–8; 20:1–17), as well as the ritual regulations that are contained in the books of Leviticus and Numbers.

When Christians claimed that Jesus had come to fulfil what God had promised in the Old Testament, these were the promises the Jewish people would inevitably recall. Moreover, the Christians themselves believed that what they were experiencing through the presence of Jesus and the power of the Holy Spirit made them the heirs of Abraham himself. This is why questions about keeping the Law and carrying out rituals like circumcision became such important issues in the life of the church; for, on a plain reading of the Old Testament, this was the only way that any person (whether born as a Jew or a Gentile) could ever be a full member of God's covenant people. To begin with, this was not an issue, for all the first Christians were Jewish believers, and naturally followed the expectations of their faith community in such matters. But when Paul and others accepted into the church Gentiles who had not been circumcised and who saw no reason at all for keeping the Old Testament Law, what might previously have been an interesting theological discussion between Jews who were Christians and those who were not, suddenly became the focus of a burning practical issue. Traditional Jewish thinking suggested that people who would not obey the Torah could not expect God to work in their lives. But the activity of the Holy Spirit among these Gentile believers seemed to be no less remarkable than what was going on in the lives of those Christians who were also faithful Jews (Acts 10:44–48).

Paul was one of the first Christian preachers to be faced with this problem. On a pragmatic level, he was quite sure that circumcision and keeping the Law should not be required of Gentile Christians. At the same time, however, the Old Testament had made it perfectly clear that to share in the blessings promised by God a person must become a member of Abraham's family. Paul did not wish to deny that the

Mount Sinai, the traditional place where Moses received the ten commandments, and other laws for the Israelites.

429

scriptures were the word of God, and his opponents were not slow to remind him that being a member of Abraham's family meant circumcision and obedience to the Law.

When Paul tackled this problem in his letter to the Galatians, he argued that the blessings promised by God to Abraham did not come to fruition because he kept the Law (Galatians 3:17). That did not even exist in his day. Instead, Paul argued, the relationship that Abraham enjoyed with God was a matter of faith: 'Abraham believed and was blessed; so all who believe are blessed as he was' (Galatians 3:9). Circumcision was an external sign to indicate that a person was trying to keep the Old Testament Law. But if the Law was now redundant, then circumcision had

---

Who wrote 1 Peter?

1 Peter was well known and widely read in the church from quite early times. *1 Clement* refers to it (AD96), as also does Polycarp (AD70–155), while Irenaeus stated towards the end of the second century that it was written by the apostle Peter himself. There are good reasons for accepting this view of its authorship:

● Much of its teaching is exactly what might be expected from a disciple of Jesus. Many aspects echo the teaching of Jesus himself, sometimes following it quite closely.

The author contrasts the readers' knowledge of Jesus, which was second-hand, with his own first-hand knowledge, and he seems to have witnessed both the trials (2:21–24) and the crucifixion of Jesus (5:1). Some scholars also believe that certain passages contain allusions to gospel stories in which Peter was particularly involved. Others, however, have claimed that if this letter was the work of Peter, then we would expect to read much more about Jesus. But this argument depends on the mistaken assumption that authors will write everything they know in everything they write. We should also remember that Peter's reminiscences of the life and teaching of Jesus might well have been recorded in a comprehensive way already, in Mark's Gospel.

● There are also a number of connections between 1 Peter and the speeches of Peter in the book of Acts. Jesus' cross is called 'the tree' in Peter's speech to the Jewish rulers (Acts 5:30) and in his sermon to Cornelius (10:39), and the same unusual terminology occurs here in 1 Peter 2:24. In 1 Peter 2:22–24 Jesus is referred to in the language of the 'Servant Songs' of the book of Isaiah, and according to Acts, Peter consistently called Jesus 'the servant of God' in his earliest preaching (Acts 3:13, 26; 4:25–30). Jesus is also linked with the stone mentioned in Psalm 118:22 by Peter in his defence before the religious authorities, and again in 1 Peter 2:4, while the emphasis on the fulfilment of Old Testament promises in Acts 3:18–24 is very similar to 1 Peter 1:10–12.

● There is no sign in 1 Peter of the concerns and interests of the later institutional church. There is still a tension between the present experience of God working in the lives of Christian believers (1:8–9, 23) and what God will accomplish in the future with the return of Jesus himself (1:3–5, 7, 13; 4:13; 5:4). Nor is there any evidence of a developed hierarchy in church organization, with the consistent emphasis on all Christians being 'priests', and the leaders of the church simply referred to as 'elders' or 'shepherds' (5:1–4).

There are, therefore, several good reasons for accepting the ancient view that Peter was the author of this letter. There are, however, some other facts which might point in a different direction:

also lost its value (Galatians 5:2–12). What should matter to the Christian is 'faith that works through love' (Galatians 5:6). We have already dealt with Paul's argument, but the question is important in this context because the same issues also surface in Peter's first letter.

1 Peter

Though many of the same themes are found here, they appear in a distinctive form. Abraham is mentioned only in passing, and in a different context altogether (3:6), while there is no sign of the complex theological arguments that Paul puts forward in Galatians and Romans. The conclusion, however, is the same, for 1 Peter conveys the clear conviction

● Like Hebrews, 1 Peter is written in an exceptionally fine Greek literary style. Not surprisingly, it might reasonably be asked whether a Galilean fisherman would be capable of writing like this, especially one who is specifically described as 'uneducated and common' (Acts 4:13). We have already seen that the Galilean origins of Peter, far from disqualifying him from knowing Greek, would actually point in the opposite direction, while the statement about Peter's educational achievements in Acts can hardly be taken literally. It certainly does not indicate that Peter was illiterate. Quite the reverse, for the comment is made by religious leaders who

Similarities between the teaching of Jesus and Peter

Christians should have an alert and watchful attitude	Luke 12:35 1 Peter 1:13
Christians have the privilege of calling God 'Father'	Luke 11:2 1 Peter 1:17
Christian conduct should cause non-believers to praise God	Matthew 5:16 1 Peter 2:12
Christians should not pay back evil for evil	Luke 6:28 1 Peter 3:9
There is joy to be had when the Christian is being persecuted for doing what God wants	Matthew 5:10 1 Peter 3:14
We will all have to give an account of ourselves to God on judgment day	Matthew 12:36 1 Peter 4:5
If Christians are insulted because they are followers of Jesus, they should be glad	Matthew 5:11 1 Peter 4:14
Christians should be characterized by humility, and God will make them great	Luke 14:11 1 Peter 5:6
Because God is caring for them, Christians should not be worried or anxious	Matthew 6:25–27 1 Peter 5:7

A 4th-century sculpture depicting Jesus and Peter.

that Gentile Christians have been incorporated as full members into 'the people of God' whose history began with the covenants of the Old Testament (2:9–10). It also asserts that they have achieved this position as a result of their response in faith to what God has done for them. Like the ethnic family of Abraham, Gentile Christians owe their knowledge of God not to their own piety or insight, but to God's undeserved love shown towards them. In the case of Israel, this had been demonstrated particularly in the exodus. For Christians, 'it was the costly sacrifice of Christ, who was like a lamb without defect or flaw' (1:1–19).

1 Peter was not written in the same controversial context as Paul's letter to the Galatians. But that only makes more striking its insistence

---

Who wrote 1 Peter?
continued

were expressing their amazement at the *unexpected eloquence* of people who had come from the remote hillsides of Galilee, and who (like Jesus) had not been trained in formal styles of religious speech or teaching. In order to take account of the high literary quality of this epistle, though, some take the view that Peter is to be associated with the actual content of the letter, but not with its written form. On this view, the fine Greek style would not be Peter's own, but that of Silas who is specifically identified as Peter's secretary (5:12). That of course would be true of most, if not all, Greek letters, which were generally dictated to a scribe who would then write them up in their own style.

● Why would Peter have written a letter to Gentile Christians living in Asia Minor when according to Galatians 2:8 he was 'an apostle to the Jews'? This question is often raised, but it is scarcely relevant to the matter of authorship. For one thing, in the context of Galatians Paul's statement was not intended as a hard and fast rule. He never even kept it himself as an inflexible dictum, for he preached the gospel to many Jews even though he described himself as 'apostle to the Gentiles'. In addition, we know that Peter moved about in the Gentile world from a relatively early period. Paul mentions Peter's extensive travels (1 Corinthians 9:5), and there is no good reason to suppose he could not have visited some of the places to which this letter was sent. According to Acts 16:6–10, Paul was

'forbidden' to go to this very area, and some commentators suggest that was because Peter was already working there. On the other hand, 1 Peter 1:12 seems to draw a distinction between the writer of the epistle and 'the messengers who announced the Good News' to its readers, implying that he had not been the one who first took the Christian message to this area.

● It has also been argued that 1 Peter is too similar to Paul's letters to have been written by Peter. But this is hardly convincing evidence against Petrine authorship. It presupposes that Paul was unique in the early church, saying entirely different things from anyone else. We have already argued that this is an unrealistic way to look at Paul, and we also noted good reasons for believing that he and Peter saw eye to eye on most issues. So why should 1 Peter be entirely different from Paul's writings? In any case, the two are not identical. It is significant that though the conclusions emerging out of Peter's teaching on the church and the Old Testament covenants is very similar to Paul's, in arguing for it 1 Peter uses altogether different language and imagery. The closest parallels between them are all in the ethical instructions. But these can be found in a similar form not only in Paul's writings, but elsewhere in the New Testament, which suggests that a more plausible explanation is that both Paul and Peter were passing on moral advice that was widely accepted throughout many sections of the early church.

that Christians – even Gentiles – are now the true 'family of Abraham' without compulsory obedience to the Law, for it shows how this issue was soon settled in the church along the lines that Paul had argued.

THE CHRISTIAN'S STATUS (1:1–12)

These themes appear in the very first verse of the epistle, with the greeting 'To God's chosen people in the Dispersion throughout the provinces of Pontus, Galatia, Cappadocia, Asia, and Bithynia'. This opening is similar to that of the book of James. We noticed there that 'God's people in the Dispersion' could indicate only Jewish people, though in the context it was more likely to be referring to the church. In the case of

---

Date and origin

If Peter did indeed write this letter, then obviously we must date it before his death, which took place in the persecution of Christians begun by Nero in AD64. But dating it more precisely than that depends on our interpretation of the various references to persecution that occur throughout the letter. A number of observations may be made about this:

● In all the organized persecutions of Christians that took place towards the end of the first century, obedience to the emperor – even worship of him – was a crucial test of Christian allegiance. But this was clearly not the case in the persecutions envisaged in 1 Peter. Christians are encouraged to 'respect the Emperor', and to accept his authority – even though it must come second to the authority of God (2:13–17).

● The readers of 1 Peter seem to have been surprised to be persecuted (4:12); after the persecutions of Nero, we might have expected them to accept suffering as the norm.

● The descriptions of persecution in 5:8 ('Your enemy, the Devil, roams round like a roaring lion, looking for someone to devour') and 1:7 (testing by fire) could well refer to the events of Nero's persecution itself. According to the Roman historian Tacitus, the hated Christians 'were covered with wild beasts' skins and torn to death by dogs; or they were fastened on crosses, and, when daylight failed, were burned to serve as lamps by night' (*Annals* 15.44).

Putting all these indications together, it seems reasonable to conclude that perhaps 1 Peter was written as Nero's persecution was in its early stages. We have no certain evidence that it eventually spread to Asia Minor. But even if it did not, the official persecution in Rome would certainly have encouraged people elsewhere to despise the Christians in their own cities. We do know that Peter was in Rome at the time. The term 'Babylon', used by this letter, was a favourite code word for Rome among the early Christians. As Peter saw what was happening there, he felt it would only be a matter of time before such a great evil spread to other parts of the empire. He wanted Christians to know that when their time of trial came, they were not alone in their suffering. Others were suffering too. But most important of all, God would not fail to care for them, for they were the covenant people.

The Colosseum, Rome, built by Vespasian between AD69 and 79 as a place of entertainment. Many Christians died here, in contests with gladiators or wild animals.

1 Peter, there can be no doubt at all that Christians are being addressed, and that they are for the most part, if not exclusively, Gentile Christians.

This initial greeting is followed by a thanksgiving to God, after which the letter turns to exhortation. Peter's readers are encouraged to celebrate God's goodness to them, 'even though for a little while you may have to suffer various trials' (1:6). The writer tells them that such trials are insignificant when set against God's power. Christians already know something of this power in the new life that they enjoy through Jesus. They can also look forward to 'the Day when Jesus Christ is revealed', when they will meet him face to face (1:7). Simple Gentile believers might find this difficult to understand – even the angels cannot fully do so – but what is happening to them now, and the destiny that is waiting for them in the future, is all part of God's plan that was first revealed in the Old Testament.

CHRISTIAN DEVELOPMENT (1:13 – 2:10)
The writer then goes on to remind his readers that acceptance of the good news about Jesus imposes responsibilities as well as bestowing privileges. Faith in Christ is not merely a private experience, but

---

The theme of baptism in 1 Peter

On the surface, 1 Peter appears to be an ordinary letter, written to encourage Christians who were being persecuted. But it has been suggested that there is more to it than this, and that the central part of 1 Peter (1:3 – 4:11) is not a letter at all, but consists of material originating in the worship liturgies of the early church, specifically in the context of a service of baptism. A number of features are claimed to support such an understanding of 1 Peter:

● This passage seems to be a self-contained section of the letter. The words of 4:11 would certainly make a suitable conclusion, for they contain a fuller benediction than actually occurs at the end of chapter five. Peter also says in 5:12 that he is writing a 'brief letter', and since the whole of 1 Peter is hardly 'brief', the actual letter that he wrote might only run from 4:12 to 5:14, while the rest of the book is an account of the church's worship.

● Baptism is mentioned only in one obscure passage (3:18–22). This may be thought a good reason for doubting its importance, but in this passage Noah's deliverance from a great flood in the Old Testament is said to be 'a symbol pointing to baptism, which now saves you'. The emphasis on 'now' suggests to some that those addressed had only just been baptized. Others have claimed to be able to discern subtle changes in the language towards the end of the first chapter, and they argue that the act of baptism had actually taken place between 1:21 and 1:22. On this understanding, this part of 1 Peter is regarded as a litany for a service of baptism, complete with hymns, responses, prayers, a sermon and a benediction. Other evidence for this is drawn from the exhortation to 'Be like new-born babies, always thirsty for the pure spiritual milk' (2:2). Evidence from the *Apostolic Tradition* ascribed to Hippolytus describes how towards the end of the second century a cup of milk and honey was given to Christians who had just been baptized, to remind them of the land promised to Israel ('a land flowing with milk and honey', Exodus 3:8). But 1 Peter mentions neither the honey nor the land,

something to be shared with others, in deed as well as word. Christ's death and resurrection has 'set you free from the worthless manner of life handed down by your ancestors' (1:18), and the recollection of that should lead Christians to obey God, and share God's love with other people.

They should also grow and develop in their Christian experience, being as eager for spiritual nourishment as babies are for their mothers' milk. As they grow as Christians, so they can 'come as living stones, and let yourselves be used in building the spiritual temple, where you will serve as holy priests to offer spiritual and acceptable sacrifices to God through Jesus Christ' (2.5–9). As Christians mature in this way, they will demonstrate how they are 'the chosen race, the King's priests, the holy nation, God's own people'.

Orthodox Jews still worship at the Western Wall, the only remaining part of the platform on which the temple was built. Peter uses the term 'living stones' to describe how Christians are being built together into the fabric of a 'living temple' which rests on the foundation of the work of Jesus Christ.

---

and the milk is described as 'pure and spiritual' which also suggests it could just as easily be understood metaphorically rather than literally. Another link with the *Apostolic Tradition* has been found in 1 Peter 3:3. Here Christian women are reminded that a person's character has nothing to do with 'the way you do your hair, or the jewellery you put on, or the dresses you wear'. In later customs, women removed jewellery and clothing and rearranged their hair before being baptized. But the emphasis in 1 Peter is not so much on this, as on the positive moral virtues that should be found in the Christian.
● There are a number of places where Peter uses language and imagery taken from the Passover story in the Old Testament. He says, for example, that Christ is 'a lamb without defect or flaw' (1:19), just as the Passover lambs had been (Exodus 12:5). Christians are told to 'gird up your minds' (1:13), in the same way as the Israelites fastened up their clothing on Passover night (Exodus 12:11). And 2:1–10 has many connections with the Old Testament books of Exodus,

Leviticus and Numbers. The relevance of this Passover connection is found in the fact that Tertullian, writing at the beginning of the third century, commented that the ideal time for Christians to be baptized was at Easter (Passover).

This way of looking at the content of 1 Peter has drawn attention to some significant aspects of the theme of the epistle, but they are not convincing when used to suggest that the document itself originated as a baptismal litany. There is no compelling reason for accepting that:
● There is no way of recognizing a first-century baptismal service, for we have no real idea how baptism was carried out in the earliest churches. Where the New Testament mentions it, baptism seems to have taken place at the same time as a person's initial commitment to Christianity. There is certainly no indication that baptism was an important event in formally organized worship, as it was later. No doubt Christians soon developed their own preferred ways of worshipping, but it is highly unlikely that these were as stereotyped in the New Testament period

There is not another passage of comparable length in the whole New Testament where more Old Testament imagery that was originally applied to Abraham and his descendants is taken over and applied to the Christian church as in some way being the 'new Israel'. But there are also some interesting connections here with Paul's thinking. The picture of the church as a building constructed out of living stones (one of which, the 'cornerstone', is Jesus himself) is not dissimilar to Paul's description of the church as a living body made up of many parts, 'Christ's body' (1 Corinthians 12:12–31). Indeed, Paul might well have been familiar with the same imagery himself, for in Romans he writes of Christians offering 'a living sacrifice' that will bring glory to God (Romans 12:1–2). When Peter describes all Christians as 'priests', he is saying the same thing as Paul did when he declared that all Christians had a God-given ability that they must share with the church at large. The fact that they use entirely different language from each other only serves to emphasize how important this concept of shared ministry was to the first Christian communities.

The theme of baptism in 1 Peter continued

as they became in the days of Hippolytus and Tertullian.

● It is also difficult to reconcile this view with the plain evidence of 1 Peter. There is no indication at all that the section 1:3 – 4:11 has originated in a different context from the rest. It is written in exactly the same style, and the same arguments seem to carry over from one section to the other.
● This baptismal theory has no way of explaining how a baptismal liturgy for the church at Rome could have got mixed up with a letter to Christians in Asia Minor. On the face of it, 1 Peter is a letter to persecuted Christians, and we must make sense of it in that light.

The evidence that has been claimed in support of this theory could no doubt carry some weight if there were other reasons to connect 1 Peter with Christian baptism, but by themselves these considerations are hardly sufficient to establish such a connection. In addition, there are some important differences between the accounts of Hippolytus and what is contained in 1 Peter. Later, the service of baptism included exorcism, anointing and

the laying-on of hands, none of which are even hinted at in 1 Peter.

The occurrence of themes that seem relevant to newly baptized Christians is probably due to the fact that Peter, like Paul, wanted to remind his readers of what was involved in being a Christian. To do this, it would have been natural to recall the commitment they had made when they first came to faith in Christ. Quite possibly he would repeat the sort of things that he was in the habit of saying to new converts, but that does not lead to the conclusion that he was giving an eyewitness report of an actual church service. Someone who has worked out effective ways of expressing things will always tend to repeat the same ideas in different contexts, and a better assumption is to suppose that the author of this book had regularly used themes found in these pages to encourage Christians in their faith. Perhaps they had been carefully crafted in the course of communication, and they were not being expressed this way for the first time here, but it is a big leap from that to the conclusion that the whole book is some kind of worship manual for the services of the church.

Peter and the church in Rome

After the stories of the early chapters of Acts, the course of the rest of Peter's life is unknown to us. Apart from Paul's reference to his missionary activity (1 Corinthians 9:5), and what is perhaps a cryptic mention of his death in John 21:18–19, the New Testament tells us nothing more about him. 1 Peter, of course, is evidence that he was at one time in Rome, but it gives us no further personal details.

It was not long, however, before Christians began to enquire about Peter more specifically. Just as they wanted to know about Andrew, Matthew, Philip and other disciples of Jesus, so they wanted to know what had become of the disciple whom Jesus had once called 'the Rock', on whose foundation he said the church would be built (Matthew 16:17–19).

The second-century *Acts of Peter* purport to tell of how Peter came at an early stage to the city of Rome and there established a large and thriving Christian community. Like Jesus, he performed many miracles, though his progress was continuously hindered by a hostile magician called Simon who, among other things, had the power to fly. According to this document, Peter's mission to Rome was cut short by the events of Nero's persecution. His Christian friends advised him to leave the city and escape martyrdom, thereby freeing himself for yet greater exploits in proclaiming the Christian message. But as he was leaving the city in disguise, Peter saw Jesus himself entering Rome, and asked Jesus where he was going. 'And the Lord said to him, "I am coming to Rome to be crucified"... And Peter came to himself... he returned to Rome rejoicing and giving praise to the Lord.' As a result of his return, Peter himself was crucified, insisting that he should be hung upside down on the cross.

Like the stories about the other disciples, all this is mostly fiction. But, like them, it probably reflects some facts, for there is no reason to doubt either that

St Peter's, Rome, beneath which is the tomb of Peter, and probably also of Paul.

Peter visited Rome and played an important part in the work of the church there, or that he was put to death in the persecution started by Nero. *1 Clement* 5 connects the deaths of both Peter and Paul with this period, and before the end of the second century the graves of these apostles had become a place of pilgrimage (Eusebius, *Ecclesiastical History* II.25.5–7). At a later date, when the emperor Constantine became a Christian, he constructed a more elaborate shrine at the spot (probably in about AD333), and today the Basilica of St Peter stands on the same site. Archaeological investigation has confirmed this general account, for not only has Constantine's monument been discovered, but traces of the second-century edifice have also been found. Further remains of bones and early graves, some going back to the first century, have also been unearthed, though there is no agreement among archaeologists about their significance, with some claiming that the actual grave of Peter himself has been laid bare, while others argue that these graves are not even Christian.

Whatever the outcome of such ongoing investigations, we may be sure that Peter did die as a martyr in Rome during the persecution of Nero, and that his grave lies somewhere on the site of St Peter's Basilica. There is, however, no evidence to show that he was the founder of the Roman church, though (along with Paul) he had some connections with it from an early stage, and it is therefore not surprising that he soon became its patron saint.

CHRISTIAN BEHAVIOUR (2:11 – 4:19)

Peter goes on to remind his readers that, as God's people, they have different standards from non-Christians. They are as much at home in the prevailing cultural value-systems of the Hellenistic world as 'strangers and refugees' (2:11). Their only true allegiance is to God and so everything they do should be intended to glorify God alone. Even when they have to 'endure the pain of undeserved suffering' (2:19), they can look to the example of Jesus. For 'when he was insulted, he did not answer back with an insult; when he suffered, he did not threaten, but placed his hopes in God, the righteous Judge' (2:23).

Exactly the same principles should determine how Christians behave at home. Christian wives should be ready to share the love of Christ with their husbands – and men for their part must treat their wives with respect and affirmation. In a word, every believer should follow the advice of Jesus: 'Love one another... and be kind and humble with one another. Do not pay back evil with evil or cursing with cursing; instead, pay back with a blessing' (3:8–9).

Peter knew that it is never easy to behave like this, especially when suffering from unjust persecution. For the Christian, it involves putting God first so that lifestyles are not controlled by personal whims and fancies, but by God's standards and values (4:7). Putting God first will always be worthwhile in the end. Suffering is just a temporary thing, and Christians must look beyond it to the judgment of God, when all things will be put right. 1 Peter assures its readers that they can trust themselves to God's care, for God's promises never fail (4:19).

SERVING CHRIST (5:1–14)

Finally, Peter gives advice to those who are, like himself, 'elders' or 'shepherds' in the church. Instead of being domineering, they should be 'examples to the flock' (5:3), recognizing that the church will flourish only when all its members have 'put on the apron of humility' to serve one another (5:5). In doing so, they are following the example of Jesus, who himself had worn the apron of a slave to wash his disciples' feet (John 13:1–17). But above all, they must not lose their trust in God in the midst of persecution. Even this hardship can be transformed in the light of God's intentions for the people of the covenant: 'After you have suffered for a little while, the God of all grace, who calls you to share in eternal glory in union with Christ, will personally perfect you and give you firmness, strength, and a sure foundation' (5:10).

Hope for the future

Peter was not the first writer to face the problem of unjust suffering. It was a question that became increasingly important in the centuries just before the birth of Jesus, as is evidenced by the many apocalyptic writings produced between about 100BC and AD100. We have already explored the distinctive features of this kind of writing in looking at the religious background to the life of Jesus in chapter 1. They were generally pessimistic works, despairing of God ever being able to put things right in this world, and therefore laying more emphasis on the heavenly world instead, and containing reports of visions and dreams in which God's plans were revealed to those who needed to know. On the face of it, the kind of escapism typified by these writings seems quite foreign to the outlook of the New Testament. But there is one New Testament book that has clearly been profoundly influenced by the style, if not the thinking, of the Jewish apocalyptists.

Revelation

Probably no book in the entire New Testament is less read and less understood than this one. All the great interpreters of the past had difficulty with it. Among the Protestant Reformers, Martin Luther found it an offensive piece of work, with very little to say about Christ, and John Calvin also had considerable doubts about its value. Many modern readers feel the same way. It is not surprising that Revelation should seem a difficult and complicated book, for people today do not generally think in the same terms as Jewish apocalyptists, and find their secret language and visions to be both meaningless and bizarre. Christians in particular are uneasy with the apocalyptist's conviction that God has no relevance to the world in which we live, and they find it difficult to imagine that God's sole intention could be to destroy human society and set up some sort of other-worldly kingdom instead. At the same time, there are others for whom the book of Revelation assumes far greater importance than any other book of the New Testament. It has been claimed that it gives an insight into God's ultimate plans for humankind, even down to detailed predictions of how the world will come to an end. So what can we make of it? Does it have any lasting significance, or is it to be dismissed as an unfortunate mistake by the early church, which should never have been included in the New Testament canon?

A CHRISTIAN BOOK?

There can be no doubt that despair and pessimism about human history is fundamentally at odds with the outlook not only of the New Testament, but of the Old Testament as well. The biblical writers faced up to the tragic realities of human experience, but they had no doubt that God can and does meet men and women in the everyday events of normal life. This is at the very centre of the gospel, with the belief that through Jesus God personally shared in human existence, thereby affirming the value of life in this world as something to be embraced and celebrated.

When we look at the book of Revelation in detail, it is clear that its author shares this positive Christian emphasis on God's involvement in human affairs. Though the language and imagery in which the book is written is apocalyptic in form, its message has this distinctively Christian world-affirming emphasis.

■ Unlike every other apocalyptic book, Revelation names both its author and its first readers. It was written by a person called John, and was sent 'From John to the seven churches in the province of Asia', in the towns of Ephesus, Smyrna, Pergamum, Thyatira, Sardis, Philadelphia and Laodicea (Revelation 1:4). These churches are addressed in quite specific terms, and incidents and individuals are mentioned by name. This kind of self-confidence was never shared by other apocalyptic writers. On the contrary, they were generally so afraid of their persecutors that to have identified themselves in this way would have led to certain death. Of course, that was also the outcome for some members of these churches, but that was evidently not a good enough reason for disguising the true nature of their Christian faith.

■ Even in those parts of the book which are most similar to Jewish writings, John's visions are always closely linked to his experience of life in the church. His vision came to him 'on the Lord's day', perhaps in the course of Christian worship, and the contents of the visions have many references to the worship of the church, its confessions of faith, prayers and hymns. For examples, see Revelation 1:5–6; 4:8, 11; 5:9–10; 7:10, 12; 11:15, 17–18; 12:10–12; 15:3–4; 19:1–2, 5–8; 22:13.

The seven churches mentioned in the book of Revelation.

■ Revelation looks forward to a future intervention of God in the affairs of this world. But its understanding of this is different from that of other apocalyptists, who without exception regarded this world and all its affairs as irretrievably evil. To them, history was a meaningless enigma, and the sooner its course was stopped, the better. This had not been the view of the Old Testament writers. Though some of the prophets had looked forward to the coming of a 'Day of the Lord' when God would intervene in a final and decisive way in the affairs of the world, they believed that this would be the continuation of what God was already doing in the present order of things (Isaiah 2:6–22; Hosea 2:14–23; Joel 2:28 – 3:21). For them, the God who would inaugurate a new world order in the future was also the God who could be known here and now in the events of human life.

The apocalyptic writers rejected this view, because they could make no sense of their own present experience. But like the Old Testament, the book of Revelation makes a clear link between what God is doing in history now, and what God will do in the future. Indeed, the entire meaning of God's plan for the future of humanity is to be found in a historical event, the life, death and resurrection of Jesus himself, 'the Lamb of God' (Revelation 5). Far from the sufferings of Christians being a meaningless interlude, John declares it to be one of the most powerful responses against all forms of evil (Revelation 12:10–12).

Revelation therefore does not follow slavishly the pattern of the Jewish apocalyptic books. It presents a distinctive and positive Christian explanation of the presence of evil in the affairs of human life. Its message is expressed through conventional language and vivid Old Testament imagery, but its content goes beyond the literary form of apocalyptic writing.

THE BOOK AND ITS MESSAGE

The first three chapters of Revelation are similar to many other New Testament writings: they contain seven letters to seven churches in the Roman province of Asia. They are not real letters like those written by Paul, for they purport to come from the risen Jesus himself, and John says that their content was given to him in a vision, just like the rest of the book. But they deal with very down-to-earth matters, and show a detailed knowledge of these people and their environment. Their churches were involved in disputes over Christian beliefs, their commitment to Christ was wavering, and as a result they were in no position to face up to the challenge of sustained persecution. To do that, they needed to be wholeheartedly committed. This is a message that we find many times in the New Testament, and it is not significantly different from that of 1 Peter.

But the second part of the book (4 – 22) is quite different. Here we come face to face with the language and imagery of apocalyptic writings. No longer do the visions seem to relate to real events and people, but instead they introduce monsters and dragons in a quick succession of terrifying events. The whole section is introduced in chapters 4 and 5 by a vision of heaven which sets the scene for what follows. Here the author lays out the underlying assumptions of the way in which he understands God's workings in history. God is the one who is 'high and exalted' in absolute majesty and holiness (4:2), and men and women (represented by the twenty-four elders in the divine court) find their true significance as they worship and serve God. But they are quite incapable of reflecting every aspect of God's personality, and when a sealed scroll containing God's revelation to the world is produced, the elders are unable to open it to reveal its contents. After an angel has searched unsuccessfully in heaven, on earth and in the underworld, God's own heavenly deliverer appears on the scene in the person of the Lamb of God, Jesus Christ (5:1–8).

This is a powerful and impressive presentation of the central importance of the life, death and resurrection of Jesus in the Christian understanding of life and its meaning. It is significant that at the very beginning of his visions, John links the future destiny of the world and its inhabitants with God's self-revelation in the historical events of the life of Jesus.

The chapters that follow then present a series of visions describing how justice will be served on all those forces that are implacably opposed to God's will. Many of the descriptions here are quite horrific, and much of the language in which God's judgment is described comes from the story of the plagues in Egypt in the Old Testament book of Exodus (Exodus 6:28 – 12:36). This gives a clue to the point that John is making, for in the exodus story God's main purpose had not been the plagues: they were merely a prelude to the salvation that God had planned for the people of Israel, and through them for the whole world. So too in Revelation, the main point of the book is not to be found in God's judgment upon evil, but in the conviction that God is now in the process of making a new world from which evil will be completely banished. In this new world, people will enjoy a fresh and unfettered freedom to know God in a direct way: 'God will be with them in person... God will wipe away all tears from their eyes. There will be no more death, no more grief or crying or pain. The old things have disappeared...' (21:3–4).

There have been many attempts to arrange the visions of Revelation according to some sort of schematic pattern. One popular suggestion is that, with the exception of chapters 4 and 5, and the description of the new heavens and earth, the whole book is arranged in a pattern of seven sections of sevens:

Seven seals (6:1 – 8:1)

Seven trumpets (8:2 – 11:19)

Seven visions of the dragon and his kingdom (12:1 – 13:18)

Seven visions of the coming of the Lamb of God (14:1–20)

Seven bowls of God's anger against evil (15:1 – 16:21)

Seven visions of the fall of 'Babylon' (17:1 – 19:10)

Seven visions of the end (19:11 – 21:4).

However they might be arranged, these visions present a kaleidoscopic picture of how God will finally overcome the powers of evil. It is the work not of a self-conscious theologian but of a great artist, and like a good artist John depicts the same subject from a number of different perspectives in order to reinforce the overall impression that he wants to create.

MAKING SENSE OF THE MESSAGE

Because of the many allusions to specific events and people known to the writer and his readers, it is difficult today to appreciate fully every detail of these visions. But their impact on the original readers of the book of Revelation is not difficult to imagine. John assured his Christian readers that their present suffering was only temporary (2:10; 3:10), for their great enemy 'Babylon' (a term which John, like Peter, used to refer to Rome) would ultimately come under the judgment of God (Revelation 18). God alone is the Lord of history, with a personal interest in the destiny not only of nations but of ordinary people as well: injustice and evil would not be allowed to win the day.

This view of Revelation is consistent with the way we have tried to appreciate the other New Testament books, by setting it in its context and attempting to understand what it might have meant for those who first received it. This approach to understanding Revelation is sometimes called the 'preterist' view (from the Latin word *praeteritum*, meaning 'referring to the past'), and it seems the most obvious approach to take. Over the centuries, however, the seemingly mysterious character of Revelation's message has encouraged people to seek out other hidden meanings within its pages. During the early centuries of the Christian era, it was frequently regarded as a symbolic presentation of some of the great truths of the Christian faith. Origen and Augustine regarded its imagery as a picturesque account of the principles of God's working throughout history, and saw its weird descriptions of persons, battles and beasts not as real events, but as a dramatic presentation of the age-long opposition between God and the forces of evil. This way of reading the book can be helpful: not only does it make sense of many of the most difficult passages, but it also succeeds in relating it to the needs of its first readers, who needed to be assured of the successful outcome of the struggle in which they were engaged.

But during the late nineteenth and early twentieth centuries, a significant body of popular opinion came to look at Revelation in a different way. These so-called 'futurists' argued that its real meaning is connected with events that are still in the future even now, and its full significance will become plain only to that generation which finds itself living in 'the last days'. Some even suggested that the seven letters with

The apocalyptic writings were full of strange and intricate symbolism, mysterious creatures and messages from angels. The German artist Albrecht Dürer captured the mood of these prophetic visions in his woodcut *The Four Horsemen of the Apocalypse*.

which the book opens are not real letters at all, but part of a detailed clairvoyant insight given to John consisting of descriptions of seven successive ages of church history, reaching from the first century up to the end of time. This 'Dispensationalist' view was popularized in Christian circles particularly through the *Scofield Reference Bible* published in 1909, which argued that the present generation had reached the stage of the seventh and final letter (to Laodicea), and was therefore the one that was living at the very end of world history. Throughout the twentieth century this view exercised considerable influence, though it presents many difficulties:

■ There is of course the plain fact that several generations have believed themselves to be living in the last days, some even putting a date on the end of the world – but they have all been wrong.

■ More significant is the fact that Jesus himself explicitly warned his disciples not to indulge in this kind of speculation: 'No one knows... when that day and hour will come – neither the angels in heaven, nor the Son...' (Matthew 24:36). It is therefore hardly likely that God would have given the information only to a select band of modern readers of the book of Revelation!

■ Another serious objection is that according to this view, the book of Revelation must have been totally meaningless and irrelevant to the people for whom it was ostensibly written. If the letters to the churches of Asia were not real letters, related to the concerns of real people, that would make Revelation quite different from every other book in the whole of the Bible. It also shares the general pessimism about existence in this world that was common in apocalyptic literature, but was quite foreign to New Testament thinking.

There is no justification for regarding either Revelation or any other book of the Bible as a blueprint for the future course of world events. That is not to suggest that the Christian faith has no expectation of a better world at some future date, for the whole New Testament presents the clear conviction that there will be a point at which God must deal decisively with the forces of evil, at which time the kingdom of peace and justice announced by Jesus will become a lasting and tangible reality.

The book of Revelation confirms that conviction by assuring its readers that this world belongs to God and not to the forces of evil. Through the use of vivid and powerful imagery it emphasizes that God will act to put things right, no matter how long such action may seem to be delayed. At that time, people will not simply be able to make a new start, but will have a part in the new world, where sin, misery and evil have no further place. Those who reject the values of this new world will have no part in it (Revelation 21:27), though it is not God's intention that any should be excluded, but rather that all should respond to the offer of a new way of being: 'Come, whoever is thirsty: accept the water of life as a gift, whoever wants it' (Revelation 22:17).

The author and date of Revelation

Revelation is the only New Testament book that was explicitly dated by any writers in the early centuries. Irenaeus stated that John saw his vision 'not long ago, but almost in our own generation, towards the end of Domitian's reign' (*Against Heresies* V.30.3), and this opinion was quoted with approval by Eusebius (*Ecclesiastical History* III.18–20; V.8.6).

This corresponds quite closely with what can be discerned from the concerns of the book itself. Though there is some doubt regarding the extent to which Domitian (AD81–96) demanded that he be worshipped as divine, there is no doubt that emperor-worship in general was especially deeply entrenched in the area of Roman Asia to which Revelation was addressed. From the time of Augustus onwards, honouring the emperor was a convenient test of political allegiance. Christians did not want to be disloyal citizens, but neither were they prepared to offer worship to the emperor, and as a result many of them were persecuted and hounded to death as enemies of the state.

A significant minority opinion, however, argues that the book of Revelation was written earlier, in the days just after the persecution of Christians by Nero. Reasons for this include the fact that there is no explicit reference to the destruction of Jerusalem in AD70, and if Revelation 11:1–2 is understood literally it could imply that it was written as the final assault on the temple was underway. There is also the fact that 13:3 mentions one of the heads of the 'beast', or antichrist, having been fatally wounded but coming to life again to rule the empire – and there was a widespread expectation that Nero was likely to return in this way. In addition, depending on how the list of seven emperors in 17:9–11 is analysed, it is possible to place the seventh and final one either in the time of Nero or his successor Galba (AD68–69). Such speculations however assume that John had actual historical figures in mind at this point, whereas in the light of his predilection for the number seven, it is just as likely that these seven emperors were never intended to be real people, but were a way of referring to the sum total of all the evil that is opposed to God. On balance, there seems no compelling reason to reject the traditional date for Revelation of about AD95.

The author of Revelation was a person called John, whom Justin Martyr identified with 'one of the apostles of Christ' (*Dialogue with Trypho the Jew* 91). The idea that he was this particular John seems unlikely, for the writer of Revelation mentions 'the twelve apostles of the Lamb' with no suggestion that he might have been one of them (21:14), while the way he introduces himself as 'your brother... a follower of Jesus... your partner' (1:9) hardly suggests he was a person of great authority in the church. But he was clearly steeped in the imagery of traditional apocalyptic writings, and we may therefore suppose he was a Jew.

At the same time, there are a number of unusual connections between Revelation and John's Gospel, which we argued in an earlier chapter had some indeterminate connection with Jesus' disciple of that name. Both John and Revelation refer to Jesus as 'the word (*logos*) of God' (John 1:1–14; 1 John 1:1–4; Revelation 19:11–16). Both of them also call Jesus 'the Lamb of God', though they use different Greek words to do so (John 1:29; Revelation 5:6–14). Furthermore, both the gospel and the letters of John seem to have had some connection with the city of Ephesus, which was also one of the churches addressed in Revelation.

One of the more plausible explanations of all this is that there was at Ephesus a 'school' of Christian thinkers established and inspired by John the apostle, and perhaps different members of this group, including John himself, were responsible for the final form of the various books which now go under his name.

24 The Enemies Within

One of the most influential factors in the changing pattern of life in the early church was the development of arguments about the nature of Christian belief, and in particular the emergence of various groups of people who, at a later period, came to be regarded as 'heretics' by the majority of Christian believers. In one sense, of course, those who were labelled 'heretics' were those who eventually lost the arguments, while the mainstream were those who won. But it would be a mistake to depict these disputes as little more than power struggles for control of the growing church. There were significant moral and theological issues involved, the origins of which can be traced back to currents of thought we have already encountered in discussing the letters of Paul. As early as the writing of Galatians, Paul mentioned people whom he believed to be proclaiming 'another gospel' (Galatians 1:6), while in Corinth he was opposed by some who clearly had a fundamentally different understanding of the Christian message (2 Corinthians 11:1–4). Probably none of these people were 'heretics' in the later, technical sense, and Paul certainly never went as far as the second-century church leaders

by suggesting that they should be excluded from the church. Rather than being the local representatives of any sort of organized group within the church at large, most of them seem to have been personal opponents of Paul, who sprang up spontaneously in different places,

It is clear that Paul was not wholly successful in dealing with these matters, and some of the later New Testament books reveal how people with similar ideas to those opposed by Paul were beginning to organize themselves into distinctive movements within the church. By the middle of the second century, Montanists, Gnostics, and others had become clearly identifiable groups. But in the first century, the tensions that led to the eventual formation of separate sects were only just beginning to surface in church life, and the tendencies that can be traced towards the end of the first century were much more loosely defined.

The book of Revelation

We have already looked at the message of much of the book of Revelation. But in its first three chapters, this book reflects the conditions of the seven churches in Asia Minor to which it was addressed. The advice given by the risen Jesus to three of these churches (at Ephesus, Pergamum and Thyatira) is about their attitude to various false teachers (Revelation 2:1–7, 12–17, 18–29).

The church at Ephesus is commended because it has 'tested those who say they are apostles but are not, and have found out that they are liars' (2:2). In addition, its members are said to 'hate what the Nicolaitans do' (2:6). In Pergamum, some church members had actually followed the teaching of these 'Nicolaitans', while others are described as following

The ruins of ancient Pergamum rise high above the modern Turkish town of Bergama. Pergamum was, according to Revelation, 'where Satan has his throne', possibly referring to the Altar of Zeus which was situated between the two trees overlooking the town. Pergamum also became a centre of the official cult of emperor-worship.

'the teaching of Balaam' (2:14). The church at Thyatira had also come under the influence of false teaching, in this case from 'that woman Jezebel, who calls herself a messenger of God' (2:20).

Given the somewhat cryptic nature of these references, there is room for debate as to the precise identity of these various groups, though it is likely that they were all connected with each other, rather than being separate groups in the different cities. The Nicolaitans are certainly mentioned in both Ephesus and Pergamum, and in the message to Pergamum the followers of Balaam appear to be the same people. Though neither of these names is applied to the heretics in Thyatira, the activities of the Nicolaitans/Balaamites in Pergamum are the same as those practised by 'Jezebel' and her devotees there: they all eat food offered to idols and indulge in practices which were regarded as immoral.

Paul had dealt with both these issues at an earlier period, though he never suggested that those involved in such activities were 'heretics' in the strict sense. He had declared that eating food offered to idols was a matter of indifference to Christian believers (1 Corinthians 8) and, though he typically had less patience with instances of immorality, he generally dealt with them in a tactful and generous way, seeking to persuade rather than to dictate. Things must have changed in the interim. In Paul's time, these concerns were mainly practical issues, arising naturally as Gentile converts struggled to understand how their new faith might affect their lifestyle. But they had now become theological and doctrinal issues and, though the book of Revelation gives no real indication of the kind of beliefs that led to such activities, a number of considerations suggest that these sects were an early form of what was later known as Gnosticism:

Beliefs that later came to be associated with Gnosticism feature in several New Testament writings. Shown here is an amulet engraved with Gnostic symbols.

■ Members of one of the prominent Gnostic groups of the second century actually called themselves 'Nicolaitans'. They traced their origins back to a man called Nicolaus who, according to Acts 6:5, was one of Stephen's Hellenist colleagues in the early Jerusalem church. It is unlikely that they had any real connection with this person, but some of their practices were not dissimilar from what we read about in the book of Revelation.

■ Though the heretics opposed in Revelation were undoubtedly less sophisticated and less well organized than these later groups, there are some signs of Gnostic terminology and ideas here. For instance, Jezebel's teaching in Thyatira is referred to by John as 'the deep secrets of Satan' (Revelation 2:24), and this phrase is found among later Gnostic groups as a description of their own beliefs. The very fact that a woman should have been so prominent in this movement is also consistent with some kind of Gnostic connection, for in the Gnostic movements of the second-century, women often enjoyed a significant and conspicuous role. Indeed, this was one reason why the church after the New Testament period officially excluded women from any form of public service.

■ The evidence of other New Testament books points in the same direction. The letters of John, as well as the letters of Jude and 2 Peter, all seem to have originated in the same geographical area as that referred to in Revelation, and in all of them there are mentions of wandering teachers who operated in the same way as those who are dealt with in Revelation. 1 John explains their theology in considerable detail, and we can see from this how close these people were moving towards classical Gnosticism.

The letters of John

Like John's Gospel, 1 John spells out its author's intentions quite clearly: 'I am writing this to you so that you may know that you have eternal life – you that believe in the Son of God' (5:13). John's Gospel was written to demonstrate that Jesus was Messiah and Son of God, and to win people to faith in him (John 20:31). By contrast, 1 John was written to people who were already Christian believers, but who needed to be reassured of the truth of what they believed.

'False prophets'

It is not difficult to see why these people needed such reassurance for, like the churches mentioned in Revelation, the Christian community to which they belonged was suffering from the activities of 'false prophets' (1 John 4:1). These people had originally been members of the community, but they had left and were now trying to subvert it from the outside (2:19). Of course, that was not how the false teachers saw things. They believed they had received special revelations that were not entrusted to more ordinary Christians, and spoke of 'knowing' God in an intimate way through some secret spiritual empowerment that allegedly enabled them to live on a different plane from the others (2:4; 4:1; 4:8). They were already spiritually 'perfect' (1:6, 8, 10), living in full appreciation of the 'light' which was God (1:5; 2:9) – and so the normal, earthbound rules of Christian morality no longer applied to them (3:7–12; 4:20).

All this sounds remarkably similar to the claims of Paul's opponents in Corinth. They, too, were claiming that, because of their personal mystical experiences, they were no longer bound by the normal constraints of bodily existence (1 Corinthians 10:1–13), but that through these experiences they had already been raised to a new spiritual level, far above that enjoyed by ordinary mortals (1 Corinthians 4:7–8). It was, they said, just as if the resurrection had already come: they might seem to be living in this world, but really they had been totally liberated from it, and so they no longer shared its concerns (1 Corinthians 15:12–19).

People with similar views are also mentioned in 2 Timothy 2:17–18. 1 John does not actually say that these 'false prophets' also believed that the resurrection had already taken place through their own mystical experiences, but it is likely that they held this view too.

Docetism

There is, however, a new element in 1 John. For the 'false prophets' mentioned here had a distinctive understanding of the person and significance of Jesus himself, and it is clear from what is said about them that John's opponents were denying that Jesus was the Messiah and the Son of God (2:22–23; 4:2, 15; 5:1–5, 10–12). It was not that they denied that Jesus had revealed the power of God – but they found it difficult to comprehend how an ordinary human person could reveal the character of the eternal God. So they asserted that Jesus was not truly human at all (4:1–3).

In Greek thinking there had always been a strong conviction that this world in which we live is quite separate from the heavenly world. The Old Testament prophets had always believed that God's activity could be seen in the affairs of human experience, but Greek thinkers more typically regarded life in this world as a miserable existence, and understood the true destiny of men and women to be not here, but in the spiritual world inhabited by God. On this view of things, true salvation could only consist of the escape of a person from the 'prison' of this world into the life of the supernatural world. There were many explanations as to precisely how this might be accomplished, and it is obvious that the desire for such liberation was what motivated both Paul's opponents in Corinth, and those whose teaching the author of 1 John was opposing.

At the beginning, Christians were interested in such ideas mainly because they were attracted by the promise of exciting mystical experiences. But, as these mystics began to think through the theological implications of their experience, they inevitably found it hard to cope with the church's belief that Jesus himself – as Jesus of Nazareth – could have come from God. For if God was a part of this mystical, supernatural world, then there was no way in which God could also be thought of as a real human person. For the all-powerful, transcendent God to be imprisoned in the life of a human being would be a contradiction in terms.

One way out of the dilemma was to suggest that Jesus had only *seemed* to be the Messiah or Son of God. This view is called 'Docetism' (from the Greek word *dokeo*, meaning 'to seem'), and it is something of this sort that is opposed in 1 John. A story told by Irenaeus recounts how the apostle John once went to a public bathhouse in Ephesus, but when he got there and recognized Cerinthus – a prominent Docetist – he refused to share the same water (*Against Heresies* III.3.4). Because of this, some have suggested that 1 John was a direct reply to Cerinthus himself. He certainly argued that the 'divine essence', or 'cosmic Christ', entered the human Jesus of Nazareth at his baptism, and left him before the crucifixion, and 1 John 5:6 might be interpreted as a direct and specific reply to this: 'Jesus Christ is the one who came with the water of his baptism and the blood of his death. He came not only with the water, but with both the water and the blood.' Cerinthus, however, had many other ideas that feature nowhere at all in 1 John, and overall the problems dealt with in this letter seem to be less complex and sophisticated than the theology of Cerinthus and his followers. Indeed, with the exception of their speculation about the person of Christ, the heretics of 1 John have much more in common with Paul's opponents in Corinth, and it is probably more accurate to regard them as an intermediate stage between the Corinthian heretics and the fully developed Gnostic systems of the second century.

1 John

The author of 1 John clearly had no time for these people, for he denounced their beliefs and opposed their practices in every section

---

The books by John

We cannot consider 1 John independently from the other letters of John, and John's Gospel. 2 and 3 John are related very closely to 1 John, though they are quite a different type of literature. Unlike 1 John, they are short, personal letters, one addressed to a church and the other to an individual called Gaius. Their author calls himself 'the Elder', and in 2 John he warns his readers against wandering teachers 'who do not acknowledge that Jesus Christ came as a human being' (2 John 7–11). He was concerned that these people should not be welcomed into the Christian community, and because of this many scholars think that 2 John must have been written before 1 John, as 1 John envisages a situation in which the heretics had already been excluded from the church (1 John 2:19).

3 John advises Gaius about a man by the name of Diotrephes, who was engaged in a power struggle for control of the church, in relation to which 'the Elder' says that he intends to pay a short visit to correct 'the terrible things he says about us and the lies he tells' (3 John 9–10).

The situation envisaged in 3 John seems to reflect a stage when new patterns of church government were beginning to emerge. As the apostles and their representatives died, the corporate leadership of the earliest churches began to disappear, and new leaders were trying to assert themselves in a process which eventually led to the formal appointment of just one authoritative leader in each local church. Perhaps 'the Elder' represented the older form of church organization, and that might explain his concern about the emergence of just one person claiming to be the church's leader. In the second century, anyone with the title of 'Elder' would himself have been a part of the organized hierarchy of the church, though the writer of these letters clearly does not belong in that context. He was obviously highly respected by his readers, but he does not seem to have had absolute authority over them as he can only appeal to them to do what he believed to be right.

The majority of scholars believe that 'the Elder' who wrote 2 and 3 John also wrote 1 John, for there are many connections between the three letters in vocabulary and style, and certain statements in 2 and 3 John seem to presuppose some knowledge of the issues dealt with in the first letter. If it was possible to decide the identity of 'the Elder', we could presumably, therefore, identify the writer of all three letters.

But this is easier said than done. Guidance has often been sought in a statement attributed to Papias, who is quoted by Eusebius as having written in his *Interpretation of the Oracles of the Lord*, 'If ever anyone came who had followed the elders, I inquired into the

of his letter. He realized all too well the strong pressure that they were placing on the members of the community, and he went out of his way to assure them that they, and not the 'false prophets', were the ones who had the truth.

Beyond that, it is not at all easy to define exactly what 1 John is about. It certainly has no linear argument running through it, which has encouraged some to rearrange the letter so its various sections can fit together in what they regard as a more logical and sequential fashion, while others have explained what they believe to be inconsistencies by supposing that the letter went through more than one edition and is, therefore, the work of different writers. But neither of these suggestions

---

The books by John continued

words of the elders, what Andrew or Peter or Philip or Thomas or James or John or Matthew, or any other of the Lord's disciples, had said, and what Aristion and the elder John, the Lord's disciples, were saying.' Eusebius goes on to observe that 'It is here worth noting that he twice counts the name of John, and reckons the first John with… the other Apostles… but places the second with the others outside the number of the apostles… This confirms the truth of the story of those who have said that there were two of the same name in Asia, and that there are two tombs at Ephesus both still called John's' (Eusebius, *Ecclesiastical History* III.39.4–6).

If the 'elder John' to whom Eusebius refers was the same person as 'the Elder' who wrote 2 and 3 John, then presumably this second-generation Christian was also the author of 1 John (and perhaps had some connection with the writing of John's Gospel). But Papias' statement is itself too ambiguous to provide much guidance, for he also appears to call the disciples themselves 'elders', and Eusebius might therefore have been wrong to infer that Papias was actually referring to two different people called John. In addition, this whole argument assumes that Papias had access to reliable information. But we must treat these statements with caution, especially when we only have second-hand knowledge of what Papias actually wrote. As far as the writings of John are

concerned, it is more helpful to begin with the documents themselves.

There is a certain amount of debate about the precise relationship between 1, 2 and 3 John, and John's Gospel. There are considerable and close similarities between the gospel and 1 John. Both use the same language in the same way, and distinctive expressions such as the contrasts between light and darkness, life and death, truth and error, and the emphasis on love (not to mention the description of Jesus as the Word or *Logos*) are all found in both gospel and letter. Both of them also use the same techniques for conveying their message, initially stating an idea in a simple and easily remembered way, and then examining its implications from a number of different angles.

But there are also a number of differences. 1 John has a more restricted vocabulary than the gospel, and its emphasis is also slightly different at some points. For instance, while the gospel lays most emphasis on the present experience of the Christian (so-called 'realized eschatology'), the letter has much more emphasis on the future hope. The letter also has a stronger emphasis on the church and its sacraments, though of course these things are not entirely absent from the gospel.

It has been proposed that the gospel was edited by the writer of the letter, to bring it into line with his own thinking on

---

is particularly convincing. The book contains not just the author's response to those who were opposing him, but also his own theological reflections on the situation he faced. His thinking seems to be expressed in a cyclical way, with themes being identified and then visited and revisited from different angles in order to tease out their significance and meaning. From a compositional perspective, it is more a work of art than of philosophy, and can usefully be compared to a musical composition in which the main theme is first expounded, and then taken up, developed and elaborated, as the composer moves on to other themes and ideas, yet always returns to the first thought.

Whatever the form of the argument, the message of 1 John is crystal

---

these points. There is certainly some evidence that the gospel contains the work of more than one person, but it is unlikely that the original form of the gospel has been revised by someone who found it theologically unacceptable. An attractive explanation of the complex connections between the various books connected with the name of John is to be found in the suggestion that there was in Ephesus a 'school' of Christian thinking associated with and growing out of the work of John, the disciple of Jesus. He served as the theological mentor of a whole group of Christians, and was the source of the information contained in the fourth gospel (see John 21:24), but the literature as we know it now was the product of this 'school' rather than of just one individual.

In dealing with John's Gospel it was suggested that it could have been first written in what might be called a 'Palestinian edition' and, if so, then the gospel would possibly be the first of these books to have been edited and reissued from the school in Ephesus. Perhaps its message was subsequently misunderstood and misapplied by its new readers. In a Jewish context, the contrasts between darkness and light, truth and error, life and death were all ethical contrasts, whereas the same terms had always been used by Greek thinkers to describe the cosmological distinction between the divine world of spirit, in which God lives, and the evil world of matter, where we live. Some

Greek readers of the gospel could easily have been misled by these terms, and that misunderstanding ultimately led them to the position adopted by the Docetists. The way the gospel emphasizes the present reality of the resurrection in the life of Christian believers would also lend colour to such speculations.

In response to this growing threat, 'the Elder' (presumably a prominent member of the Johannine school, if not John himself) wrote 2 John to warn against such false teaching. But things went from bad to worse, the false teachers broke away from the church to form their own sect, and 1 John was written as a more theological response to the problem. Not only was the Docetic view of Jesus challenged, but it was now emphasized that the resurrection hope was very much something tangible and future, and not just a part of the present spiritual experience of Christians.

If anything like this reconstruction is correct, the date we give to these letters will depend on the date assigned to the gospel. The kind of teaching opposed in 1 John is certainly more advanced than that encountered by Paul in Corinth. There is a clear idea of 'heresy' in 1 John, but it is not as complex or as well developed as we find in the second century. Since the heretics opposed in 1 John seem to have a number of features in common with those mentioned in Revelation, a date sometime towards the end of the first century is perhaps the nearest guess we can make.

clear. Like every other New Testament writer, John was convinced that mystical experiences, however elevated, would only have meaning if they could be integrated into Christian belief on the one hand, and expressed in appropriate lifestyles and behaviour on the other. It would be of no value talking about being liberated into the world of light, unless God's light truly informed and inspired behaviour, and to say that mystical experiences actually release men and women from the power of evil is dismissed as unrealistic and untrue, for human experience more commonly demonstrates that it is not possible for a person to make themselves totally perfect and free from the influence of sin (1 John 1).

True Christians must 'live just as Jesus Christ did', but they must also face up to the reality of their moral poverty, and accept the forgiveness which only Jesus can give (2:1–6). Living like Jesus is a practical affair: it is a matter of loving other people, and this in turn means that anyone who despises others (as did the Docetists) can hardly claim to be doing God's will (2:7–14). In reality, they are just indulging their own selfishness (2:15–17).

The fact that such people could ever have been a part of the church should serve to emphasize that the day of judgment is not far off (2:18–19). The others must not be intimidated by them, for whatever the sectarians might claim, those left in the church are the true recipients of the Holy Spirit, and they are the ones who have been accepted by God (2:20–29). Not that they have done anything to deserve that love, but having now been adopted as God's children, they should ensure that they continue to do God's will (3:1–10). Taking their example from Christ's love for them, they must love one another (3:11–18), and then

Authors and dates

Neither Jude nor 2 Peter contains any information at all that might link them to specific events or people in the early church. The only way their background can be understood is by trying to fit them into what is known about the development of the early churches in general. Several indications seem to suggest that both these books belong to the end of the New Testament period, rather than the time of the apostles themselves:

● Unlike Paul (and 1 John), Jude does not set out to argue with his opponents. He simply denounces them, and asserts that the answer to their problems is a return to 'the faith which once and for all God has given' (Jude 3). We have seen, in a previous chapter, that the development of

a standard form of belief like this was one of the things that characterized the emerging institutional church at the end of the first century.

● Jude 17 also indicates a date later than the age of the apostles, when the writer refers to 'what you were told in the past by the apostles of our Lord Jesus Christ'. Of course, that might refer to some occasion on which the readers had actually met the apostles themselves, but the same cannot be said of the reference to Paul in 2 Peter 3:14–16, where Paul's letters are mentioned as a recognized and well-known collection of writings, and are also classified as 'scripture'. Paul's letters were probably not gathered together in a collection until after his death, and it is reasonably certain that it would have taken longer still for them to

they can be sure that they are truly living in harmony with the Holy Spirit, and in personal union with God (3:19–24).

The author keeps returning to the theme that telling the true from the false is not just a matter of human judgment, but is a test of belief that can distinguish false prophets from true believers: 'Anyone who acknowledges that Jesus Christ came as a human being has the Spirit who comes from God. But anyone who denies this about Jesus does not have the Spirit from God' (4:2–3). Having God's Spirit naturally leads to love, just as God's own being is love (4:7–21). It also leads to obedience to God's commands, and to final victory over all that is opposed to God's ways of doing things (5:1–5). With this assurance, true Christians can be certain that they will know and understand God in a way that the Docetists never could (5:6–21).

Jude and 2 Peter

The influence of false teachers is also the subject of two of the most obscure books of the New Testament: Jude and 2 Peter. These books clearly belong together, for almost the whole of Jude (in a slightly modified form) is contained in 2 Peter. But otherwise, neither book contains any information to help us identify their original readers.

The way in which Jude and 2 Peter oppose false teachers suggests that they originated in a situation quite similar to that dealt with in the opening chapters of the book of Revelation. The term *gnosis* ('knowledge') is not actually mentioned, but these teachers are described in Jude 19 as 'psychics' ('controlled by their natural desires'), and we know that this was

---

be regarded as 'scripture' in any authoritative sense.

These facts are often taken to indicate that both books must be dated sometime in the second century, even perhaps as late as AD150, though there are difficulties about quite such a late date:
● It seems likely that 2 Peter was used (along with other New Testament books) by the unknown author of a work called *The Apocalypse of Peter*. But this is commonly dated sometime in the period between AD100 and AD135, and so 2 Peter can hardly be later than that.
● There is also the fact that the description of the false teachers in Jude and 2 Peter is quite different from any known second-century heresy. There is no hint even of a Docetic view of Jesus, let

alone of the more complex theories of the classical Gnostic systems.
● There is also no trace of much of the apparatus of the second-century church. There is a consciousness of a fixed body of Christian doctrine, but no indication of an organized ministry in the church. Both Jude and 2 Peter appeal to their readers on a moral basis rather than on the basis of their authors holding any position of authority.

A minority of scholars, therefore, have tried to explain the origin of these books by understanding them in the context of a much earlier age. Certainly, they both seem to be claiming to be the work of people who flourished in the age of the apostles themselves. 'Jude, servant of Jesus Christ, and brother of James' (Jude 1) is a

a technical term used by later Gnostics. These people certainly laid a great emphasis on their own spiritual experience (Jude 8), and they argued that because they themselves had been 'raised' to a new level of spiritual life, they had also been released from the normal constraints of Christian morality (Jude 12–13, 16, 18, 23). But all this was unacceptable to those in the mainstream of the church. Jude reminds his readers that, even in Old Testament times, people had suffered divine punishment for the same kind of wrongdoing and, unless they were prepared to repent, they could expect to share the same fate (Jude 8–16).

2 Peter also suggests that these people were denying the reality of the future coming of Jesus (3:1–18). No doubt they argued that, since they themselves had already been spiritually 'raised' to heaven, there would be no further need for the kind of literal resurrection hope held by the majority of the early Christians. In any case, they said, nothing had happened, even though the church had fervently expected Jesus to return in glory. This argument had first been put forward by Paul's opponents in Corinth, but 2 Peter 3:8 introduces a new answer to it, by asserting that God's timescale is not the same as a human calendar: 'There is no difference in the Lord's sight between one day and a thousand years.' The fact that the end has not yet arrived does not mean that God's promises have failed to be fulfilled. On the contrary, the delay in the coming of Jesus is itself to be seen as an expression of God's patience in allowing people more time to change their ways.

Jude does not describe the beliefs of these heretics so precisely. He simply asserts that they 'reject Jesus Christ, our only Master and Lord' (Jude 4). It seems likely that these false teachers had not gone quite as

---

Authors and dates
continued

description that invites readers to imagine it must be that Jude, who is named in the gospels as a brother of Jesus and of James in Mark 6:3, while 'Simon Peter' is clearly intended to identify the author of 2 Peter as the apostle himself (2 Peter 1:1). But there are other matters to be taken into account:

● The early church had a number of doubts about both these books. Jude is mentioned occasionally by early Christian writers, but 2 Peter is mentioned nowhere before the works of Origen (AD185–254), and as late as the fourth century both of them were regarded either as spurious or of doubtful value. This at the very least must suggest that they were not generally supposed to be the writings of leaders of the first generation of Christians.

● Coupled with this, there is general agreement among scholars of all opinions that if 1 Peter is the work of Peter, the disciple of Jesus, then 2 Peter is not. Many writers in the early church were perplexed by the differences between the two, for in style of writing, theological emphasis and general outlook they are so different that it is impossible to think the same person wrote them both. If we are correct to connect 1 Peter with Peter himself, then we must look elsewhere for an explanation of 2 Peter.

One possible solution might be indicated by the statement of Jude 3, where the writer of Jude reports that he was in the process of writing a letter to his readers, when he suddenly realized a more urgent need to communicate with them

far as those in 1 John. They had not challenged the church's beliefs on a theological level, by declaring that Jesus was not the Son of God come as a human person, but instead (like the heretics mentioned in Revelation 2:14), they had 'given themselves over to the error that Balaam committed' (Jude 11; Numbers 22:1–35). As we have already seen, that was more of a moral and practical problem.

As the years passed, the church had to change and adapt itself to deal with new threats, and take advantage of new opportunities. But it never forgot that its thinking and behaviour must always be firmly anchored in the experiences and outlook of those first followers who had actually known Jesus. Had it not been for the continuing commitment of a small group of Palestinian peasants, the wider world would never have heard this life changing message. It was not easy for them, for their courage and boldness were regularly rewarded with persecution, and even death. But their own experience of Jesus was such that they had no thought of turning back. They knew that Jesus was not dead, but alive, and working in power in their own lives through the presence of the Spirit. Not only did this inspire them to great exploits, but it also strengthened them in the face of trials. Perhaps it is appropriate that one of the most striking ascriptions of praise to Christ in the entire New Testament should be found at the end of this most cryptic of New Testament writings: 'To the one who is able to keep you from falling, and to bring you faultless and joyful before God's glorious presence – to the only God our Saviour, through Jesus Christ our Lord, be glory, majesty, might and authority, from all ages past, and now, and for ever and ever!' (Jude 24–25).

---

immediately, in response to which he wrote the letter of Jude itself. What, then, was the original letter that he was busy writing? In view of the close connections between them, could it have been 2 Peter – and further, could it be that the earlier letter referred to in 2 Peter 3:1 was not 1 Peter, as has generally been supposed, but Jude? Jude could have been writing as Peter's representative, for Acts 15:14 mentions the habit of leaders of the Jewish church of referring to Peter as 'Simon', which might then also explain the unusual use of that name in the opening sentence of 2 Peter.

Part of the difficulty with such a precise account of the origins of 2 Peter and Jude is that virtually nothing at all is known about the activities of the Jude who was the brother of James and of Jesus. But it might be possible to imagine that Jude and 2 Peter both originate from a group of Peter's disciples, in much the same way as the Johannine letters appear to have originated from a 'school' of John's disciples. This could account for both the similarities and the differences between 1 and 2 Peter. It could also explain why certain sections of 2 Peter (like the description of the transfiguration of Jesus in 1:16–18) have struck many readers as authentic reminiscences of Peter himself. Perhaps what we have in both these short letters is a fresh application of the teaching of Peter to the concerns and interests of a Hellenistic Jewish Christian congregation somewhere in Asia Minor towards the end of the first century.

25 Reading and Understanding the New Testament

The New Testament can be a frustrating book as well as a source of enlightenment. As we have seen, it is not one book at all, but a collection of twenty-seven writings compiled by different people at diverse times and places during the course of the first Christian century. In addition, the books themselves all have their own distinctive characteristics. Some of them, such as the gospels and Acts, contain narrative, while others are letters – either real letters like those written by Paul, or literary epistles like Hebrews, with few or no allusions to actual people. Even within individual books, there can be various literary styles. The gospels, for example, contain parables and stories, as well as teaching and the personal reflections of the evangelists on the lasting significance of what they report. Moreover, the question of how the New Testament should be understood is not only concerned with matters related to the different genres or literary styles to be found in its pages, but also relates to important considerations of ideological perspective and cultural change.

Beginning where we are

This book has been written from a Christian perspective. Though the preceding chapters have considered historical and literary questions related to the compilation of the New Testament, this has been accompanied by an exploration of the message of these books, which is motivated by a conviction that this message still has relevance for life at the beginning of the twenty-first century. Within this frame of reference, three underlying assumptions have been important:

■ For Christians, the New Testament is not just a collection of writings documenting the rise of the Christian church, it is also 'scripture', that is, it is in some way authoritative for the ongoing life of the Christian community. To a greater or lesser extent, therefore, this assumption implies that, as the New Testament is read and understood, it will serve as some sort of paradigmatic guideline or model for Christian belief today. If this is one of the purposes for which we read these books, we cannot limit ourselves to exploring them only in their literary and historical contexts. We must also explore their sociological, cultural and relational contexts, as they pertain to the spiritual search of real people in the real world, whether ancient or modern.

■ This principle leads to another, namely that modern Christians need somehow to be continuous with their roots and their heritage. To treat the New Testament as scripture means that there should be some demonstrable connection between what the church is today, and the message of Jesus and the life of the early church, together with whatever other spiritual streams have fed into these over the centuries. It is this connection with its history that allows today's church to claim with integrity that it is still, in some meaningful sense, 'Christian'.

■ The New Testament cannot and should not be separated from its total spiritual context, as if its authority and meaning were somehow insulated from other aspects of Christian faith and practice. These books form an important part of the Christian world-view, but they do not stand alone. They are part of a bigger picture and, in the context of Christian belief, their message integrates with a recognition that, because this is God's world, God is at work in circumstances and situations that can be far removed from overtly Christian influences, as well as taking account of the spirituality of those who struggle still to follow Jesus. In other words, in arriving at a fully comprehensive expression of Christian faith, the New Testament stories have to be related to a creation-centred spirituality which recognizes God's universal presence, as well as interacting with the continuing experiences of Christian people. The diagram illustrates this.

Starting points

In approaching the New Testament from this standpoint, it is important to be honest about our own presuppositions. There are many ways to read and interpret the New Testament, and Christians have no monopoly on it. Though so-called presuppositionless exegesis has often been flaunted as the only way to understand the text, the whole notion of a totally detached interpreter has deep flaws. It is neither desirable nor possible to have no starting points, and to pretend that 'objectivity' in understanding means starting with no convictions or opinions is pointless and unconvincing. No one can divorce themselves from who they actually are, and who they are becoming. Understanding any text begins with understanding ourselves, and in this context being honest about our prior faith – or lack of it – is going to be central to the enterprise of interpretation. We all have filters built into our lives, which serve to divert and process information reaching us – things like our basic values and beliefs about life, our own experiences and learning, the store of all those things we

Personal stories

Creation-centred spirituality

New Testament stories

Reading the New Testament is not primarily an exercise in ancient history, but is intrinsically connected to God's activity in the world, and the perceptions of the reader.

believe to be 'true', together with our feelings about those beliefs. The combination of these is what makes each individual's personality unique. Knowing and recognizing our own particular filters – their weaknesses as well as their strengths – is basic to all good interpretation. When scholars deny that they have such presuppositions, they lack credibility, and generally end up reaching untenable conclusions.

Reading and understanding the New Testament is, therefore, a two-way process. We bring something to the task (ourselves), and we hope to receive something from it. We speak to these books, and we expect them to speak to us. On this view, interpretation is a dynamic process, not a static one, and it is a holistic process, because it connects with other aspects of the reader's life and experience. This is quite different from the model that has been inherited from the Enlightenment, with its self-confident assumption that 'objectivity', in the sense of total detachment from the text, was both possible and desirable. That approach led to a way of looking at the text, which (like much within the world-view of recent Western culture) was mechanical and distant from human experience, because it was based on a linear view of reality that allowed the interpreter to think he or she stood completely outside the interpretive process, as the diagram shows.

> The historical-critical method encouraged the mistaken idea that it is possible to interpret the text without personally engaging with its message.

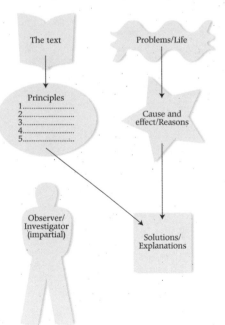

The text

Problems/Life

Principles
1...........................
2...........................
3...........................
4...........................
5...........................

Cause and effect/Reasons

Observer/ Investigator (impartial)

Solutions/ Explanations

This approach has its strengths, not least of which is its ability to highlight the concerns of the ancient world in which the New Testament books originated. But, by emphasizing interpretation as a window onto the ancient world, it can make it correspondingly more difficult to understand how the text can speak to the human condition in a time and place far removed from the first-century Roman empire. A more sustainable method of reading will take account of the contemporary setting right from the outset, and will view the text as a two-way mirror. It will certainly be possible to look through the text and back into its own world, but there will also be a conscious acceptance of the possibility that the reality of our own world can be reflected there, and the encounter of the two can then be used as a starting point for asking new questions of the text, which will go beyond only historical matters. This approach owes a good deal to the insights of non-Western Christians, wrestling with the reality of social deprivation and economic challenge, and seeking to use those experiences as hermeneutical tools with which to read the New Testament text. Robert McAffee Brown has described the process succinctly: 'We bring our experience *to* the Bible, we draw new insights *from* the Bible, we go back to our own situation *with* the Bible, and see it all in a new way.' A different kind of diagram can illustrate this.

Influences

What does 'objectivity' mean in this context? A great deal of postmodern philosophy now claims that there is no such thing as objectivity, and therefore there is no point in trying to achieve it. But most ordinary people still think it is important to try to understand things 'as they truly are', with as little interference as possible from our presuppositions (which can also be prejudices). Maybe the nearest we can come to that sense of standing back from the subject-matter of study, and being as detached as possible in order to see what the text is about, is to recognize our own starting points, and then make due allowance for them – perhaps asking tougher questions, being more provocative in the way we deal with the evidence, when we find ourselves arriving at conclusions that seem to match our preconceived notions too closely. If that is the case, then we need to have some idea what kind of personal factors might be operating to influence the way we read a text from the New Testament. There are several obvious ones:

Scripture

Events

Reflection on events/ Experience

Experience of life/God

Readers might begin their reading of the Bible at different places, but a holistic understanding will always integrate its message with the rest of life.

■ Our social context has more power than we often realize. As people throughout the non-Western world have turned to the Bible in ever increasing numbers, it has become clear how our own cultural context can influence our understanding. Rich, white Western people tend to see things differently from economically deprived people in other parts of the world – or, indeed, from poor people in Western society. The story of the good Samaritan (Luke 10:29–37) has a different meaning for Westerners – who generally read it and aspire to be like the Samaritan – than for others, who are more likely to identify with the person left for dead by the roadside. Western people take it for granted that, if they are anyone in that story, they must be in a position of power and control and so, even if they might be reluctant to claim identification with the Samaritan, they are more likely to debate whether they are like the priest or the Levite than to imagine they could be the person who is beaten up. The connection of that with the recent history of Western imperialism and colonialism is too obvious to require further explanation.

■ Who we are in terms of gender and age also makes a difference. A man will read the story of Jesus' encounter with a woman caught in the act of adultery (John 7:53 – 8:11) in a different way from a woman – though both of them might struggle with the way Jesus handled the situation, with many men still thinking that the woman got off too lightly, while women might wonder why, in the face of a female in danger of immediate execution, Jesus played games by drawing pictures and words in the sand. A child would perhaps see something different again – maybe not appreciating what the issue was, but recognizing that, by doing something inherently childlike, Jesus had got the woman out of a very sticky situation.

■ Our own state of mind can also affect how we read the New Testament. In previous chapters we have noted more than once how Martin Luther's chronic depression led him to imagine that Paul suffered from the same ailment, and so he portrayed him as a defeated, broken man, oppressed by a narrow-minded Judaism in much the same way as Luther believed himself to have been treated by the medieval church. Those who bring a sense of their own lack of value to the New Testament can easily exaggerate some of its teaching on sin, while those who are uncomfortable with their own feelings will be inclined to play down the sense of human interaction that was found in the early Christian communities, and others might be tempted to emphasize the futuristic aspect of eschatology over and against the realized aspect, because they find life in a material world burdensome and challenging.

■ The same thing can be said about mental attitudes. For generations, the more obviously supernatural dimensions of the New Testament have been marginalized by Western interpreters. Christians have looked at the prominence of charismatic endowments in the writings of Paul, felt this was not to their taste, and therefore sought for ways to justify their disappearance from the life of the church. Others regularly did the same with the miracles of Jesus, while no one ever quite knew what to make of Paul's claim to out-of-body experiences as part of his spirituality (2 Corinthians 12:1–10). In the light of the rise of the New Age, and increasing awareness of such things from cultures all over the world, few people would want to adopt either of those positions today. It is obvious that the scholars of a previous generation were too much influenced by the prevailing rationalism of the time – and, of course, it might turn out to be the case that some today are too willing to embrace such things more because of cultural pressures than anything else.

■ The influence of a rationalist-materialist world-view has been especially powerful during the last two or three centuries. Reality has been understood in such a way that the only things that really mattered were 'facts', defined in a particular way that could be scientifically verified. In the hands of sceptics, this often became a tool which could be used to place a historical or literary question mark against just about anything in the New Testament, as we saw in dealing with the question of the historical Jesus. But in the hands of Christians, this same world-view regularly led to the conclusion that 'truth' is something that can somehow be proved by logic and argument and, therefore, by definition any literary analysis of the New Testament, which might suggest some of it is in a different genre from narrative history, is to be rejected. There have even been those who have insisted that, since on this view

René Descartes (1596–1650), whose ideas encouraged the notion that autonomous, rational individuals should be able to escape their presuppositions and view things objectively.

fictional material could not be a vehicle for truth, all the heroes of Jesus' parables must have been real people who did what is recorded of them in the stories he told.

A major weakness of recent methods of interpretation has been their uncritical acceptance of a reductionist approach to knowledge, which has assumed that things can be understood best by taking them to pieces. This had its origins in the scientific methods of people like René Descartes (1596–1650) and Sir Francis Bacon (1561–1626), and the further assumption that the best place for such dismantling to take place is in a laboratory, a place from which all external influences have been excluded. That scientific paradigm has now been discarded, and it is widely recognized that, even in a laboratory, the presence of the investigator makes a difference to what can happen. But it lives on in much New Testament interpretation, and even those who are Christian believers frequently think it is important to lay aside all religious beliefs or presuppositions in order to unearth what is true. Study of literary texts more broadly (not only religious ones) has demonstrated that reading and understanding is a more holistic business. Since the texts arose out of human experience in the first place, the reader's own experience of life is going to be a key factor in understanding them. That in turn means that readers interact with the text, in much the same way as Bell's theorem describes how scientists interact with the materials with which they experiment. The way a person feels about a text is of fundamental importance, and their own emerging world-view (whether that be Christian or some other) will play a part in the act of interpretation. Faith (or doubt) is not something to be hidden, but to be acknowledged as a significant element in the process of reading and understanding. The idea that a Christian and an atheist could – if both were being totally objective – reach the same conclusions on the meaning of a New Testament passage is nonsense.

Sir Francis Bacon (1561–1626).

The key questions to be asked of any passage in the New Testament are, therefore:

■ What is the text saying? That is, what are the actual words, as contained in the most reliable ancient manuscripts?
■ What is the text's context? That is, what are the historical circumstances and literary style?
■ What is my context? That is, who am I as a person? What expectations, presuppositions and prejudices am I bringing to it?
■ What is our context? What is the wider social group within which I belong, and which is affecting my own perceptions?

The text's own context

The writers of all these books lived in a very different world from the one we know, and in order to have a full appreciation of the

New Testament, we need to take account of the specific cultural circumstances in which it originated. In reality, there are several different aspects of the text's own context, which should be considered.

The sociological context

This collection of writings as a whole was brought together as the literary heritage of a religious group, as a testimony to the faith of the early church. While it might be possible to extrapolate historical data from the various books, it is always important to remember that they were not primarily written to provide such information. Moreover, the church was certainly not in the mainstream of Roman culture and, in some situations, might even have had to operate in a clandestine way. Never fully accepted by the empire, these Christian communities were also struggling to define their identity over and against the social context of their origins in Judaism, and therefore the question of identity, and defining the boundaries of the church – both theological and cultural – was a major concern throughout the first century. In addition, the different churches consisted of people drawn from diverse socio-economic circumstances, though with a clear preponderance of middle and upper-class people, especially in the urban centres of Asia Minor and the western empire. Some leaders straddled these various spheres of influence. For example, Peter began in the culture of rural Galilee, then interacted with a different style of Jewish society in Jerusalem and Judea, before involvement with the multiracial church in Antioch, and then moving on to the great urban centres elsewhere in the Roman world. To understand how these people perceived and experienced God, we need to have some degree of familiarity with an extensive span of historical and cultural circumstances – while recognizing that we are ourselves bringing our own cultural baggage to the enterprise.

World-view

The first Christians lived long before the emergence of modern science and technology, and held the typical ancient understanding of human life as being at the centre of a three tier universe. The flat disc of the earth was sandwiched between the murky underworld beneath and the dome of the heavens above, beyond which was a dark and unknowable chaos. This was a magical world, inhabited by deities and demons of many different kinds. Petronius once wrote that, on the streets of Rome, it was easier to meet a god than a person! (*Satyricon* 17). In this context, religion and everyday life were intertwined, and everything had a spiritual aspect to it. In ancient farming, for example, the sowing of seeds was a religious act, requiring honour to be paid to the gods in an appropriate way in order to ensure the success of the crops. Building a house, going on a journey, forming a relationship – all these things had intrinsically religious dimensions built into them. Though at a

philosophical level the prevailing world-
view imagined a great separation between
the material and the spiritual, in everyday
life these two stood alongside each other, as
just different sides of the same coin.
It takes considerable effort for people
who live in a more fragmented culture
to understand how people in the ancient
world might have reflected on and reacted
to matters of life, death and meaning.

A missionary of
the Middle Ages
tells how he
found the place
where the Earth
touches Heaven.

Personal perceptions

The expectations of the average person
hardly changed from the start to the finish of the Bible story. In the
gospels, the concerns of a peasant economy predominate, and this
naturally affects the imagery used to illustrate the message of Jesus.
The imagery changed as Paul and others took their message into larger
centres of population, but there is still a strong influence of rural ways
of thinking running throughout the New Testament. For many
Christians, the city was a place of danger – a place where Jesus had
been crucified, and where persecution was often at its most violent.
The book of Revelation highlights this better than most, with its cryptic
references to Rome as 'Babylon' – something that had featured as a
symbol of destructive urban influences as far back as the story of the
Tower of Babel in Genesis 11. Eventually, Revelation 21:9 – 22:5 depicts
the life of the city being redeemed, but the idea that a rural life is to be
preferred over an urban one has been surprisingly persistent through
much of Christian history. All this was reinforced by the expectations
and horizons that were available to most people. Few people were
regular travellers – Jesus himself would have been typical, for he hardly
moved at all from his home area – and, in reflecting on the extensive
travels of Paul, it is hard to believe that he would not have been
familiar with so unsophisticated a mode of transportation as a bicycle.
Perhaps as part of this heritage, home and family life were always at
the centre of things, and the home was a major focus for spirituality
in both the Jewish and the Roman context. Indeed, in the cities of the
empire, many churches were, in effect, just one part of the typical
Roman household, and several New Testament passages describe the
heads of households deciding that their entire community would
convert to Christianity. As well as profoundly influencing the way
the Christian communities operated, this feature probably also had
an impact on the way that at least some parts of the New Testament
evolved. In the context of home based groups, the oral traditions of
storytelling would thrive very easily, and doubtless this was how many
New Testament narratives, especially the gospels, were shaped and
handed on in the early years.

Discovering the message

It might seem as if interpreting the New Testament is too daunting a business to be tackled at all by ordinary people. In some ways this is true, for there is a certain body of historical knowledge with which we need to be familiar in order to begin to understand these writings fully in their context. That is why this book has laid so much emphasis on the presentation and explanation of such information. But when we think of these books as part of Christian scripture, things start to look more hopeful. Three considerations can help to guide creative reflection on the message of the New Testament writings:

■ We need to read these books with some sense of empathy towards those who wrote them. It is impossible to divorce the New Testament from the processes of thought, experience, faith and interpretation that produced it in the first place. The writers and their own perceptions and expectations of life, along with their own personal stories, are all an intrinsic part of the mixture. When Christians read the New Testament, they do regard its books in a different way than others might, because they are themselves part of the same community of faith which created them. Many things have changed in the intervening centuries, of course, not least our world-view. But insofar as they are able to, today's readers

The historical-critical method

In dealing with the gospels, reference has been made to various interpretive tools that have commonly been used in analysing their message: source criticism, form criticism, and redaction criticism among them, together with the kind of historical criticism implied by the long story of the quest for the historical Jesus. All these methods are relatively recent developments in New Testament study, and owe their origin and rationale to the philosophical ideas of the European Enlightenment. Starting with the growing awareness among European people of the existence of other continents and cultures, and continuing through the next four or five centuries with the development of science and technology, Western people managed to convince themselves that their new ways of doing things would deliver the human race from, what they came to regard as, its previous captivity to mythology and superstition. Whereas previously, people had tended to look to religion to help explain the meaning of things, now it seemed as if the unaided power of human reason would be able not only to discover new things about the world, but also to enable people to live in a different way, reliant only on themselves. In this new world, for the first time in history, things would be understood as they actually were, rather than as they might be explained by religious teachers who in turn could only justify their opinions by reference to God as their source. As purely rational principles were applied to the study of the human condition, it was only a matter of time before even religion itself would be subjected to the same kind of rigorous scrutiny. This was the context in which the quest for the historical Jesus had its origins, and the historical-critical method of interpreting the Bible was to flourish.

By adopting the scientific optimism of the day, based on the assumption that everything can be traced back to some relationship of cause and effect, and therefore everything can be resolved by the

need to be open to hearing what the New Testament writers were saying within their own cultural context, while recognizing that all world-view perceptions (including our own) are tentative.

■ Theologically, the message of the New Testament needs to be set within a larger frame of reference. These writings themselves bear witness to the possibility of God being known in other places, most notably through what later generations have called 'natural theology' or 'creation centred spirituality'. The stories of Jesus' birth in Matthew 2:1–12 tell of eastern astrologers travelling in search of the Christ child, on the basis of their understanding of the star which led them. In his parables, Jesus uses imagery from the natural world in a way that makes it obvious he regarded the life of plants and animals as somehow reflecting aspects of the nature of God. In a previous chapter, we noted Paul's starting points for sharing his faith with others, and his policy of accepting other people's spirituality as pegs on which he might hang the gospel. The story told in Acts 17:16–31, of his mission to Athens, is a classic example in which he had no hesitation in identifying Jesus with the 'unknown god' on the assumption that, if this is God's world, presumably God could be expected to work in the most unlikely of places. In Romans 1:18 – 2:16 he explains the thinking behind this, and

---

application of human reason and logic, scholars of the New Testament devised their own procedures for reading texts which, it was imagined, would give unhindered access to the early church as it actually was, rather than as later generations of Christians might have imagined it to be. A key part of this process would involve setting the various New Testament books in their original historical and literary context, asking how they were written, why they were written, to whom and by whom, and for what purpose. Questions like this have featured prominently in our study of the New Testament here, and there can be no doubt that, by comparison with some of the methods of interpretation that went before, this led to significant advances in understanding. Previous generations had often ignored the historical setting of the New Testament altogether, which left the books open to subjective perceptions of their meaning being imposed on them by interpreters. Now, almost for the first time, there would be some sense of boundaries

within which it would be legitimate to operate, boundaries concerned firstly with the historical setting and secondly with critical (in the sense of detached and analytical) reflection on the meaning of these writings – hence the emerging description of this way of proceeding as the 'historical-critical method'.

Great advances have taken place as a result of a process which stressed objective detachment, and historical and literary context, and we have not only noted some of them, but we have also taken advantage of them throughout this book. But the historical-critical method was not quite what its exponents claimed it to be. In particular, it was not value-free, but was actually part of a struggle within European culture to break away from any sense of knowledge coming from anywhere other than the human spirit. E.B. Pusey (1800–82) described it at the time as 'a child of disbelief', and regarded it as an effort not to build up faith, but to destroy it. More recently, Helmut Koester has confirmed the ideological bias of this

places the knowledge of God gained through nature and conscience alongside the Old Testament Law as an equally valid revelation of the divine will. In reading the New Testament, it is a mistake to exclude this bigger picture of God's activity in the world. Ultimately, the New Testament needs to be set in a context of God's work that is much broader than itself.

■ The New Testament books cannot be divorced from their human origins. Many efforts to define the inspired and inspirational character of these writings have sought to reduce them to a collection of rational propositions, which can stand alongside other similar propositional notions of truth, emanating from the philosophical nostrums of the European Enlightenment. It is perfectly natural for Christians to want Bible interpretation to be as rational as possible but, in the understandable effort of doing so, it is easy to undermine two convictions that are central to Christian faith:

Paradoxical though it might seem, weakness and vulnerability are central aspects of the New Testament's message. At the heart of all it says is the incarnation, with its amazing claim that God was best known in this world not through a rich and powerful figure, but through one who came as a child and lived a life of relative obscurity. From the

The historical-critical method *continued*

method of interpretation, 'designed as a hermeneutical tool for the liberation from conservative prejudice and from the power of ecclesiastical and political institutions'.

This need not surprise anyone, for we all bring our own personal, philosophical baggage to every enterprise in which we engage. Stunningly obvious though that might be, it is only in relatively recent times that the implications of this for scholarly analysis have become clear. The optimistic atmosphere of the nineteenth and early twentieth centuries encouraged previous generations to imagine that they could indeed stand outside of themselves and see things 'as they really are'. That is why the procedures of the historical-critical method were so universally adopted, and why it was taken for granted that they could be used to question so many matters that previously had seemed settled. As the twentieth century progressed, it became increasingly obvious that human reason could not solve all mysteries, nor was it necessarily going to make the world a better place. Now, the rational approach

is itself being questioned, and the whole nature of New Testament study is far less stable than it once was – so much so that it is difficult to predict where it might go in the future. One thing is certain: that we should not now make a similar mistake to those who in the past have imagined that everything that went before them was to be rejected. No doubt the historical-critical method has many flaws – some of which have repeatedly been spelled out here – but it is important not to lose sight of its benefits. By anchoring study of the New Testament in the historical and social context in which it was compiled, great advances have taken place, and these should not be jettisoned just because we can now see that previous scholars were not as dispassionate as they thought they were. What is now required is a recognition of what they got right, an honesty about what they got wrong – and an openness which will not imagine that the exercise of rationality by itself is going to provide the answer to every human question.

A synagogue in Galilee.

perspective of Western images of power, control and rationality, this is a very weak message. But if the medium is indeed the message, then we need not be surprised if the Bible also seems to share this quality of strength within weakness.

This fluid, person-centred aspect of the New Testament is also one of its great strengths. The epistles in particular give a first-hand glimpse into the faith, doubt and struggles of those who wrote them, and those to whom they were addressed. They show real people working through a process of spiritual and personal development, discovering what it could mean for them to follow Jesus in many different situations. Readers of all generations have been able to make connections with them, for people of faith in all times and places wrestle with the same questions. If the New Testament had been couched in the propositional concepts of philosophical discourse, it would have ceased to engage with the human condition long ago, for there has always been a limited number of people who search for the meaning of life in strictly abstract, analytical terms. But, as a book of stories, the Christian canon speaks as powerfully to people today as it ever did. The stories of Jesus, together with the stories of his early followers, provide a bridge across the centuries to the human stories of today, rooted in the underlying conviction that, since this is God's world, God may be discovered in the most unexpected of places.

The text of the New Testament

None of the original documents of the New Testament books still exist. Modern translations are all based on copies of copies, which date back to the earliest centuries of the Christian era. To a generation accustomed to instant access to printed books and digital information, this can seem a distinct disadvantage, for how can we be sure that what the authors originally wrote has not been tampered with or somehow distorted in the process of transmission? Questions like this have to be put in perspective, and set in the context of other ancient literature. For example, Julius Caesar wrote in the first century BC, and less than a dozen manuscripts of his work now survive – the oldest of which was produced around AD800–900, almost 1,000 years after his time. Tacitus was a Latin author living towards the end of the first century AD, most of whose work is completely lost, and only two manuscripts survive – copies made in the ninth and eleventh centuries AD! The work of the Greek historian Thucydides (460–400BC) is contained in fewer than ten ancient manuscripts, the oldest of which dates from about AD900. Yet the accounts of these three authors are vital for our understanding of Graeco-Roman history and culture. By comparison, the New Testament is remarkably well served. There are many manuscripts dating from the period between AD200 and AD300, together with scraps of manuscripts which can be dated even earlier, one of them – the Rylands Papyrus of John's Gospel – originating in about AD130, which must have been less than fifty years after that gospel was written. In addition, there are many quotations from the New Testament included in the writings of early Christian authors.

The Rylands papyrus.

Ancient documents

Ancient books were commonly written on three different kinds of material:

Leather documents, made from the skins of animals, were used in Egypt from as early as 2800BC. According to the Talmud, all copies of the Jewish Law used in public worship were written on leather made from the skins of animals designated as 'clean', and stitched together into long rolls. There are no known leather New Testament documents.

Papyrus documents were made from the papyrus plant, which grew in the rivers and marshes of Egypt. The pith was cut into strips, which were laid in two layers, at right angles to one another, so that the fibres lay horizontally on one side and vertically on the other. The two layers were then fastened together by pressure and glue, so as to make sheets which could be attached side by side to form a long strip and rolled up. The height of the roll was limited to the usual length of the strips of pith, normally about ten inches, though a typical roll could be as long as thirty-five feet – large enough to contain the longest of the gospels. At a very early period (certainly by the second century), Christians had invented a new form of book, using papyrus sheets folded down the middle and stitched together like a modern book – the codex.

Vellum documents were written on animal skins, but were different from leather by not being tanned. Vellum was originally the skin of a calf, but skins of other young animals were also used. It proved to be a very durable medium, and by the fourth century it had replaced papyrus as the material most often used for significant books, including copies of the New Testament. The majority of early copies of the complete New Testament are on vellum, written in what is called uncial writing. This was a literary style of writing, which continued in use until the tenth century AD, when it was replaced by a cursive, or flowing script (technically known as minuscule writing), with smaller letters continuous with one another. This then continued to be used for copies of the Bible until the invention of printing in about 1450. The earliest New Testament manuscripts were all written without any punctuation, and often with no spaces at all between words, which creates its own problems of interpretation. Punctuation was added in due course and, though there were earlier divisions into sections, the present divisions into chapters dates only from the thirteenth century, while subdivision into verses was introduced in the sixteenth century.

New Testament texts

In textual studies of the New Testament, five types of source material are available.

Papyrus documents

Being a vegetable material, papyrus easily decomposed in damp climates, and most papyrus documents have, therefore, come from Egypt, where the dry, warm sand helped to preserve them. Almost seventy papyrus documents containing parts of the New Testament have been found there, varying from mere scraps like the Rylands Papyrus, which contains only five verses of John 16, to the Chester Beatty Papyrus II, which has eighty-six nearly perfect leaves of what was originally a codex of 104 pages, probably containing all the epistles of Paul. These papyrus documents were written between about the first half of the second century and the fourth century, or even later. The largest papyrus documents are:

● Chester Beatty Papyrus II, containing Paul's letters and dating from the beginning of the third century, more than a century earlier than the date of the great vellum codices.

● Chester Beatty Papyrus I, containing portions of the gospels and Acts, of similar date, and belonging to the collection of eleven codices of Christian writings dating from the second to the fourth centuries, acquired by Chester Beatty in about 1930 – hence the name.

● The Bodmer Papyrus has 108 pages which contain (with one missing section) the first fourteen chapters of John's Gospel,

and dates probably from the late second century.

Vellum codices

More than 250 of these are known, with the following being the most important of them:

● Codex Sinaiticus, which is always designated by the Hebrew letter *aleph* (א). This dates from the middle of the fourth century and contains the complete New Testament, as well as portions of the Old Testament, along with the *Epistle of Barnabas* and the *Shepherd of Hermas*. This is a large document, with pages 15 inches by 13 inches, and four columns of writing on each page. It came to light in 1844, when Constantin von Tischendorf was visiting the ancient monastery of St Catherine in the foothills of Mount Sinai and noticed some leaves of the Old Testament part of the codex in a basket about to be burned in the monastery furnace. After complex negotiations he managed to obtain the entire codex and, eventually, it was purchased by the British Museum in London, where it is still kept.

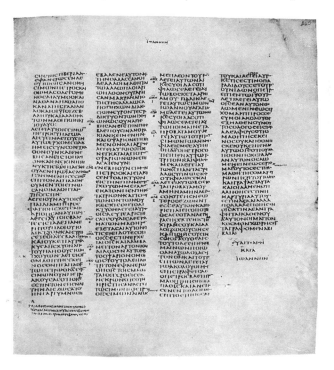

A page from Codex Sinaiticus, which contains the entire New Testament in Greek. It is written on vellum and dates from the 4th century.

Codex Alexandrinus (referred to as A) dates from the first half of the fourth century, and also originally contained the complete Bible, along with two epistles of Clement of Rome and the *Psalms of Solomon*. Most of the latter, along with small sections of the New Testament, are now lost. It might have been written in Alexandria, Egypt, but it was from Constantinople that it was presented to Charles I of England, and it has been in the British Museum since its foundation. The text is generally regarded as less useful than what is contained in Codices Sinaiticus and Vaticanus.

● Codex Vaticanus (known as B) dates from the fourth century, and was also originally a complete Bible, from which most of Genesis, some of the Psalms, part of Hebrews, the pastoral epistles and Revelation have disappeared. It has been in the Vatican Library at Rome since 1431, and along with Codex Sinaiticus, is highly prized as the most authoritative ancient source for the text of the New Testament.

● Codex Bezae (known as D) probably dates from the fifth century. Its pages are smaller than the others, only 10 inches by 8 inches, and it has Greek and Latin text on opposite pages, though it only contains the gospels and Acts, with a few verses from the general epistles. Its early history is unknown, but it was bought at Lyons in France in 1562 by Theodore Beza, who presented it to the University of Cambridge in England. It is of great interest to textual scholars as it contains, particularly in Acts, a very different type of text from what is found in the other great codices.

● Codex Ephraemi (known as C) dates from the fifth century. It originally contained the whole Bible, but of 238 New Testament leaves only 145 remain, though these represent all the New Testament books, with the exception of 2 Thessalonians and 2 John. This codex is a palimpsest; vellum writing material was very valuable in the ancient world, and it was a common practice to erase the original writing and use it again for a new book. In this case, what had originally been a Bible was used for the works of St Ephraim of Syria – hence its name.

Minuscule manuscripts
There are almost 3,000 of these, mostly of later date. Scripture passages are also contained in many ancient lectionaries (selections for reading in church worship). One group of these manuscripts has special interest for scholars because it contains a distinctive form of text which might have been connected with the traditions of the church in Caesarea, but many of them are of a later date and are obviously copies of inferior manuscripts.

Early versions
Versions were translations of the New Testament from the original Greek into other languages. The most important ones are in Syriac, Coptic and Latin. A particularly interesting text is the *Diatessaron* of Tatian, which is a harmony of the four gospels compiled in the second century. For a long time, this work was known only through references made to it by early Christian authors and an Armenian commentary of the fourth century, which included lengthy quotations from it. Arabic and Coptic versions of this work have been found, and there is also a fragment of the text in Greek, which might suggest it was originally written in Greek, though Tatian himself was a Syrian, and Syria is certainly where it first circulated.

Quotations in early Christian writings
Many early Christian writers are witnesses to the text of the New Testament, through the quotations from it that they included in their own writings. Unfortunately, accurate quotation was not as much appreciated in the ancient world as it is today, which makes most of these examples of limited usefulness. The most important of these writers in relation to understanding the development of the textual traditions is Origen, who seems to have used one kind of text while he was living in Alexandria

and then adopted a different one when he moved to Caesarea.

Scribes and copyists

Considering that all these documents were copied by hand, it is surprising how few and relatively unimportant are the differences between them. Substantial differences occur in well under 1 per cent of the entire text, and most of them are predictable errors that copyists might easily make. These include spelling mistakes, sometimes caused by a scribe writing down a word that was more familiar than the one that had actually been dictated. Sometimes a word, or even a whole line, was left out – an easy mistake to make when two consecutive lines began with the same word. The same word might be written twice over, or a sentence unconsciously altered to make it agree with the words of a similar sentence elsewhere.

This could happen very easily when the same story or saying occurred in slightly different words in one gospel than in the others. A note made by a reader in the margin could also be included in the main body of the text as if it were a part of it. This is probably what happened in the case of 1 John 5:7, which contains a clear statement of the later doctrine of the Trinity. This verse was included in the Latin Vulgate, and some other manuscripts used by the translators of the 1611 King James Version, but it does not appear in any of the oldest codices, which is why it is no longer included in more recent translations. Very occasionally, scholars suspect that a text has been changed a little to suit the copyist's theology. For instance, in some Latin versions of John 1:13 the plural 'were born' appears as the singular 'was born', in what looks like an effort to suggest a reference to Jesus' birth of a virgin.

Classifying texts

By comparing the actual words of different documents it has been possible to develop a system for classifying them into groups, on the assumption that if one particular ancient manuscript had an unusual reading, then all those that were copied from this one would be likely to have the same unusual reading. The definitive classification of texts was first set out in 1870 by Brooke Foss Westcott and F.J.A. Hort and, though some refinements have since been made, their description of four textual types remains the standard.

Syrian texts

These texts contain many readings not found in the oldest manuscripts or versions, but seem to have been used extensively from the fourth century onwards, particularly by writers living in the neighbourhood of Antioch. Westcott and Hort proposed that a revised text of the New Testament had been issued at Antioch towards the end of the third century, from which a great many of the minuscules now known were copied. These Syrian texts are of little value in helping to identify the original text of the various books, as their variant readings are presumably the work of the revisers at Antioch.

Western texts

These are best represented by the Codex Bezae and two others, and they are also found in the Old Latin and Syrian versions. These texts tend to include considerable additions not found in other texts. As this kind of textual tradition was the first to be translated into Latin, it is considered likely that it was used by churches in the western part of the Roman empire. Its additions typically take the form of circumstantial detail. So, for example, in Acts 12:10 it includes the information that when Peter escaped from prison he went down seven steps, while in Acts 19:9 it states that Paul taught in the lecture hall of Tyrannus from the fifth to the tenth hour, and in Acts 19:28 Demetrius is described as running out 'into the street' during the riot at Ephesus. These additions have generally not been taken seriously as part of the original text, though when this Western text omits something (for instance, the mention of a second cup at the last supper in Luke 22:20), its value is likely to be taken more seriously, for its general tendency is towards addition rather than omission.

Alexandrian texts

This type of text is found in the Codex Alexandrinus, and Codex Ephraemi, as well as in the writings of many Christian leaders who were resident in Egypt. Its distinctive characteristics are more related to style than subject matter, perhaps originating in the understandable concern of Christian scribes in the scholarly context of Alexandria to ensure that the text of their New Testament would be available in high quality Greek. If that was the reason for its production, then the Alexandrian texts obviously add little or nothing to our knowledge of the original text written by the New Testament authors.

Neutral texts

These are the ones which have most in common with other texts. Whenever a particular manuscript diverges from others in the same group, it generally reverts to this neutral text, which is the text represented by the two oldest and largest codices, Vaticanus and Sinaiticus. When these two agree (as they almost invariably do), they are likely to be as near to the original text of the New Testament as it is possible to be.

Textual study is ongoing, and two particular developments are worth commenting on:
● As well as the four classical text types listed above, it seems possible to identify another group, which shares some of the characteristics of both Neutral and Western texts. This is the so-called Caesarean text type. Some of the minuscule manuscripts have common peculiarities, such as the placing of the story of the woman taken in adultery, which in the received text (the basis for the King James Version) was at John 7:53 – 8:11, but which could also be placed after Luke 21:38, or even left out altogether. Luke 21:38 seems a more likely place for the story, as it is more in the style of Luke than of John. The Chester Beatty Papyrus I has a Caesarean text in Mark's Gospel, and one with some Caesarean characteristics in Luke

and John, although its text of Acts is Neutral. The precise characteristics of this textual style are still less clearly defined than the others, but when Origen left Alexandria and moved to Caesarea in AD231, his quotations from New Testament writings seem to show that he gave up using the Alexandrian text and used a different form of text similar to this – hence the reason why it has been called the Caesarean text, though it is not impossible that Origen might actually have taken it with him from Alexandria to Caesarea.
● The Western text has generally been accorded more value, the more it has been studied. Many early Christian writers seem to have used this Western text in quoting from the New Testament, and this suggests it must have been reasonably early in date. Moreover, much of the additional material found in it seems quite pointless unless it belonged to an original source; there is no obvious reason why anyone would wish to invent such details as the number of steps Peter took from prison, for example. Could it be that Luke wrote different drafts of Acts, and this textual tradition reflects one of them? The presence of a number of Aramaic turns of expression in the Western text also adds to the impression that it might be of early date.

For all that, the Neutral text is still regarded as the most authoritative, though textual experts are generally prepared to consider variations from it on good grounds. Textual criticism is a painstaking business and the value of each particular variant in the text must be decided on its own merits, by asking such questions as:
– Which reading gives the better sense?
– Which reading is least likely to have been made through a mistake in copying?
– Which reading is most likely to be due to later theological influences, such as Gnosticism?
– Which reading is supported by the oldest and most reliable manuscripts, even although it might not occur in the best examples of the Neutral text?

Other Books on the New Testament

General

Aune, D.E., *The New Testament in Its Literary Environment*, Philadelphia: Westminster, 1987.

Brown, Schuyler, *The Origins of Christianity*, New York: Oxford University Press, 1993.

Carson, D.A., Moo, D.J. and Morris, L., *An Introduction to the New Testament*, Grand Rapids: Zondervan, 1992.

Reumann, John, *Variety and Unity in New Testament Thought*, New York: Oxford University Press, 1991.

Schnelle, Udo, *The History and Theology of the New Testament Writings*, London: SCM, 1998.

Wright, N.T., *The New Testament and the People of God*, London: SPCK, 1992.

The World of the First Christians

GENERAL

Barrett, C.K., *The New Testament Background: Selected Documents*, London: SPCK, 1987.

Ferguson, Everett, *Backgrounds of Early Christianity*, Grand Rapids: Eerdmans, 1993.

Kee, Howard C., *Christian Origins in Sociological Perspective*, Philadelphia: Westminster Press; London: SCM Press, 1980.

Malina, Bruce J., *The New Testament World: Insights from Cultural Anthropology*, Louisville KY: Westminster John Knox Press, 1993.

Roetzel, C.J., *The World that Shaped the New Testament*, Atlanta: John Knox, 1985.

Stambaugh, J.E. and Balch, D., *The New Testament in Its Social Environment*, Philadelphia: Westminster, 1986.

JUDAISM

Chilton, Bruce and Neusner, Jacob, *Judaism in the New Testament*, New York: Routledge, 1995.

Dunn, J.D.G., *The Partings of the Ways: Between Christianity and Judaism and Their Significance for the Character of Christianity*, Philadelphia: Trinity Press International, 1991.

Hengel, Martin, *Judaism and Hellenism*, vols 1 and 2, Philadelphia: Fortress, 1974.

Maccoby, H., *Judaism in the First Century*, London: Sheldon, 1989.

Neusner, J., *Judaism in the Beginning of Christianity*, Philadelphia: Fortress, 1984.

GNOSTICISM AND HELLENISTIC SPIRITUALITY

Couliano, I.P., *The Tree of Gnosis*, San Francisco: Harper, 1992.

Filoramo, G., *A History of Gnosticism*, Cambridge MA: Blackwells, 1990.

Goehring, J.E., ed., *Gnosticism and the Early Christian World*, vols 1 and 2, Sonoma: Polebridge, 1990.

Hedrick, C.W. and Hodgson, Jr, R., eds, *Nag Hammadi, Gnosticism, and Early Christianity*, Peabody MA: Hendrickson, 1986.

Layton, B., *The Gnostic Scriptures*, Garden City: Doubleday, 1987.

Nash, Ronald H., *Christianity and the Hellenistic World*, Grand Rapids: Zondervan, 1984.

Perkins, P., *Gnosticism and the New Testament*, Minneapolis: Fortress, 1993.

Robinson, J.M., *The Nag Hammadi Library in English*, San Francisco: Harper and Row, 1977.

Walbank, F.W., *The Hellenistic World*, London: Fontana, 1981.

The Life and Teaching of Jesus

BIRTH AND EARLY YEARS

Brown, R.E., *The Birth of the Messiah*, New York: Macmillan, 1977.

Hendrickx, H., *Infancy Narratives*, Minneapolis: Winston Press, 1984.

Scobie, C.H.H., *John the Baptist*, London: SCM Press, 1964.

CHRISTOLOGY

Cullmann, O., *The Christology of the New Testament*, Philadelphia: Westminster Press, 1964.

Dunn, J.D.G., *Christology in the Making*, Philadelphia: Westminster Press, 1980.

Hengel, M., *The Son of God*, Philadelphia: Fortress Press, 1976.

Hooker, M.D., *Jesus and the Servant*, London: SPCK, 1959.

Marshall, I.H., *The Origins of New Testament Christology*, Nottingham: IVP, 1977.

Moule, C.F.D., *The Origin of Christology*, Cambridge: Cambridge University Press, 1977.

O'Collins, G., *Interpreting Jesus*, Mahwah NJ: Paulist, 1983.

Tuckett, C., *The Messianic Secret*, Philadelphia: Fortress Press, 1983.

THE KINGDOM OF GOD

Chilton, B.D., *The Kingdom of God*, Philadelphia: Fortress Press, 1984.

Dodd, C.H., *The Parables of the Kingdom*, London: Nisbet, 1935.

Kümmel, W.G., *Promise and Fulfilment*, New York: Oxford University Press, 1961.

Ladd, G.E., *The Presence of the Future*, Grand Rapids: Eerdmans, 1980.

Perrin, N., *The Kingdom of God in the Teaching of Jesus*, Philadelphia: Westminster Press, 1963.

Riches, J., *Jesus and the Transformation of Judaism*, London: Darton Longman and Todd, 1980.

PARABLES

Jeremias, J., *The Parables of Jesus*, London: SCM Press, 1972.

Kissinger, W.S., *The Parables of Jesus*, New York: Scarecrow, 1979.

Perkins, Pheme, *Jesus as Teacher*, Cambridge: Cambridge University Press, 1990.

Shillington, V.G., ed., *Jesus and his Parables*, Edinburgh: T and T Clark, 1997.

Stein, R.H., *The Method and Message of Jesus' Teachings*, Philadelphia: Westminster Press, 1978.

Wenham, David, *The Parables of Jesus*, London: Hodder and Stoughton, 1989.

MIRACLES

Fuller, R.H., *Interpreting the Miracles*, London: SCM Press, 1963.

Meier, J.P., *A Marginal Jew: Rethinking the Historical Jesus*, vol. 2, *Mentor, Message, and Miracles*, New York: Doubleday, 1994.

Remus, Harold, *Jesus as Healer*, Cambridge: Cambridge University Press, 1997.

ETHICS

Chilton, B.D. and McDonald, J.I.H., *Jesus and the Ethics of the Kingdom*, London: SPCK, 1987.

Hendrickx, H., *The Sermon on the Mount*, Minneapolis: Winston Press, 1984.

Lohse, E., *Theological Ethics of the New Testament*, Minneapolis: Fortress Press, 1991.

THE DEATH OF JESUS

Carroll, J.T. and Green, J.B., eds, *The Death of Jesus in Early Christianity*, Peabody MA: Hendrickson, 1995.

Crossan, J.D., *Who Killed Jesus?*, San Francisco: HarperSanFrancisco, 1995.

Hendrickx, H., *Passion Narratives*, Minneapolis: Winston Press, 1984.

Hengel, M., *The Atonement*, Philadelphia: Fortress Press, 1981.

Hengel, M., *Crucifixion*, Philadelphia: Fortress Press, 1977.

Jeremias, J., *The Eucharistic Words of Jesus*, London: SCM Press, 1955.

Marshall, I.H., *Last Supper and Lord's Supper*, Grand Rapids: Eerdmans, 1981.

Sherwin-White, A.N., *Roman Society and Roman Law in the New Testament*, Oxford: Oxford University Press, 1963.

RESURRECTION AND ASCENSION

Donne, Brian, *Christ Ascended*, Exeter: Paternoster, 1983.

Hendrickx, H., *Resurrection Narratives*, Minneapolis: Winston Press, 1984.

Lapide, P., *The Resurrection of Jesus: A Jewish Perspective*, London: SPCK, 1984.

Lüdemann, G., *The Resurrection of Jesus: History, Experience, Theology*, London: SCM Press, 1994.

O'Collins, G., *The Easter Jesus*, Valley Forge: Judson Press, 1973.

Perkins, Pheme, *Resurrection*, New York: Doubleday, 1984; London: Geoffrey Chapman, 1985.

Torrance, T.F., *Space, Time and Resurrection*, Grand Rapids: Eerdmans, 1976.

The Gospels

GENERAL, INCLUDING LITERARY-CRITICAL ISSUES

Barton, Stephen C., *The Spirituality of the Gospels*, London: SPCK, 1992.

Bauckham, Richard, ed., *The Gospels for All Christians*, Grand Rapids: Eerdmans, 1998.

Bellinzoni, Arthur J., *The Two Source Hypothesis: A Critical Appraisal*, Macon GA: Mercer University Press, 1985.

Blomberg, Craig L., *Jesus and the Gospels: An Introduction and Survey*, Leicester: Apollos, 1997.

Bultmann, Rudolf, *The History of the Synoptic Tradition*, Oxford: Blackwell, 1968.

Burridge, Richard A., *What Are the Gospels?*, Cambridge: Cambridge University Press, 1995.

Dibelius, Martin, *From Tradition to Gospel*, Cambridge: Cambridge University Press, 1971. Originally in German, 1919.

Dungan, David L., *The Interrelations of the Gospels: A Symposium*, Macon GA: Mercer University Press, 1990.

Evans, C.A. and Porter, S.E., *The Synoptic Gospels: A Sheffield Reader*, Sheffield: Sheffield Academic Press, 1995.

Farmer, W.R., *The Synoptic Problem*, Dillsboro: Western North Carolina Press, 1976.

Farmer, W.R., *Jesus and the Gospel*, Philadelphia: Fortress Press, 1982.

Gerhardsson, B., *The Origins of the Gospel Traditions*, London: SCM, 1979.

Green, J.B., McKnight, S. and Marshall, I.H., *Dictionary of Jesus and the Gospels*, Downers Grove IL: InterVarsity, 1992.

Hagner, Donald A., *The Jewish Reclamation of Jesus*, Grand Rapids: Academie, 1984.

Hilton, M., *The Gospels and Rabbinic Judaism*, London: SCM, 1988.

Hooker, Morna D., *Beginnings: Keys that Open the Gospels*, London: SCM, 1997.

Jacobsen, Arland D., *The First Gospel: An Introduction to Q*, Sonoma CA: Polebridge Press, 1992.

Perrin, Norman, *What is Redaction Criticism?*, London: SPCK, 1970.

Sanders, E.P. and Davies, Margaret, *Studying the Synoptic Gospels*, Philadelphia: Trinity Press International, 1989.

Stanton, G.N., *The Gospels and Jesus*, New York: Oxford University Press, 1989.

Stanton, G.N., *Gospel Truth? New Light on Jesus and the Gospels*, Valley Forge PA: Trinity Press International, 1995.

Stein, R.H., *The Synoptic Problem: An Introduction*, Grand Rapids: Baker, 1987.

Streeter, B.H., *The Four Gospels*, London: Macmillan, 1924.

Stuhlmacher, Peter, *The Gospel and the Gospels*, Grand Rapids: Eerdmans, 1991.

Talbert, C.H., *What is a Gospel?*, Philadelphia: Fortress, 1977.

Taylor, Vincent, *Formation of the Gospel Tradition*, London: Epworth, 1935.

MATTHEW

Balch, D.L., ed., *Social History of the Matthean Community: Cross-Disciplinary Approaches*, Minneapolis: Fortress, 1991.

Beare, F.W., *The Gospel According to Matthew: Translation, Introduction and Commentary*, Peabody MA: Hendrickson, 1987.

Hagner, D.A., *Matthew 1–13*, Dallas: Word, 1993.; *Matthew 14–28*, Dallas: Word, 1995.

Luz, U., *The Theology of the Gospel of Matthew*, Cambridge: Cambridge University Press, 1995.

Overman, J.A., *Matthew's Gospel and Formative Judaism: The Social World of the Matthean Community*, Minneapolis: Fortress, 1990.

Riches, John, *Matthew*, Sheffield: Sheffield Academic Press, 1996.

Schweizer, E., *The Good News According to Matthew*, Atlanta: John Knox Press, 1975.

Shuler, Philip L., *A Genre for the Gospels: The Biographical Character of Matthew*, Philadelphia: Fortress, 1982.

Stanton, G.N., ed., *The Interpretation of Matthew*, Philadelphia: Fortress, 1983.

Stanton, G.N., *A Gospel for a New People: Studies in Matthew*, Edinburgh: T and T Clark, 1992.

MARK

Gundry, R.H., *Mark: A Commentary on His Apology for the Cross*, Grand Rapids: Eerdmans, 1993.

Hooker, M.D., *The Gospel According to Saint Mark*, Peabody MA: Hendrickson, 1991.

Lane, W.L., *The Gospel According to Mark*, Grand Rapids: Eerdmans, 1974.

Schweizer, E., *The Good News According to Mark*, Richmond VA: John Knox Press, 1970.

Telford, W.R., *Mark*, Sheffield: Sheffield Academic Press, 1995.

LUKE

Bock, D.L., *Luke*, vol. 1, *1:1 – 9:50*, Grand Rapids: Baker, 1994.

Bock, D.L., *Luke*, vol. 2, *9:51 – 24:53*, Grand Rapids: Baker, 1996.

Danker, F.W., *Jesus and the New Age: A Commentary on St Luke's Gospel*, Philadelphia: Fortress, 1988.

Evans, C.F., *Saint Luke*, Philadelphia: Trinity Press International, 1990.

Green, Joel B., *The Theology of the Gospel of Luke*, Cambridge: Cambridge University Press, 1995.

Nolland, J., *Luke 1 – 9:20*, Dallas: Word, 1989.

Nolland, J., *Luke 9:21 – 18:34*, Dallas: Word, 1993.

Nolland, J., *Luke 18:35 – 24:53*, Dallas: Word, 1993.

Schweizer, E., *The Good News According to Luke*, Atlanta: John Knox Press, 1984.

Talbert, C.H., *Reading Luke: A Literary and Theological Commentary on the Third Gospel*, New York: Crossroad, 1982.

Talbert, C.H., *Reading Luke: A New Commentary for Preachers*, London: SPCK, 1990.

Tiede, D.L., *Luke*, Minneapolis: Augsburg, 1988.

Tuckett, C.M., *Luke*, Sheffield: Sheffield Academic Press, 1996.

JOHN

Beasley-Murray, G.R., *John*, Waco: Word, 1987.

Brown, R.E., *The Community of the Beloved Disciple*, New York: Paulist, 1979.

Cullmann, O., *The Johannine Circle*, Philadelphia: Westminster, 1975.

Ellis, E.E., *The World of St John*, Grand Rapids: Eerdmans, 1984.

Hengel, M., *The Johannine Question*, Philadelphia: Trinity Press International, 1989.

Lindars, B., *John*, Sheffield: Sheffield Academic Press, 1990.

Morris, L., *Commentary on the Gospel of John*, Grand Rapids: Eerdmans, 1971.

Porter, S.E. and Evans, C.A., *The Johannine Writings: A Sheffield Reader*, Sheffield: Sheffield Academic Press, 1995.

Smalley, S.S., *John: Evangelist and Interpreter*, Carlisle: Paternoster, 1997.

Smith, D.M., *The Theology of the Gospel of John*, Cambridge: Cambridge University Press, 1995.

Stibbe, M.W.G., *John as Storyteller: Narrative Criticism and the Fourth Gospel*, Cambridge: Cambridge University Press, 1992.

OTHER TRADITIONS ABOUT JESUS

General

Bruce, F.F., *Jesus and Christian Origins Outside the New Testament*, London: Hodder and Stoughton, 1974.

Ehrman, Bart D., *The New Testament and Other Early Christian Writings: A Reader*, New York: Oxford University Press, 1998.

Evans, C.A., *Noncanonical Writings and New Testament Interpretation*, Peabody MA: Hendrickson, 1992.

Jeremias, J., *Unknown Sayings of Jesus*, London: SCM, 1964.

Morrice, William, *Hidden Sayings of Jesus*, London SPCK, 1997.

Wenham, D., ed., *Gospel Perspectives 5: The Jesus Tradition Outside the Gospels*, Sheffield: JSOT Press, 1984.

Gnostic gospels

Crossan, J.D., *Four Other Gospels*, Sonoma CA: Polebridge, 1992.

Funk, R.W. and Hoover, R.W., eds, *The Five Gospels*, New York: Macmillan, 1993.

Koester, H., *Ancient Christian Gospels: Their History and Development*, Philadelphia: Trinity Press International, 1990.

Pagels, E.H., *The Gnostic Gospels*, New York: Random House, 1979.

Patterson, S.J., *The Gospel of Thomas and Jesus*, Sonoma CA: Polebridge, 1993.

THE QUEST FOR THE HISTORICAL JESUS

Chilton, B.D. and Evans, C.A., *Studying the Historical Jesus: Evaluations of the State of Current Research*, Leiden: Brill, 1994.

Evans, Craig A. and Porter, Stanley E., *The Historical Jesus*, Sheffield: Sheffield Academic Press, 1995.

Kee, Howard Clark, *What Can We Know About Jesus?*, Cambridge: Cambridge University Press, 1990.

Powell, Mark Allan, *Jesus as a Figure in History*, Louisville: Westminster John Knox Press, 1998.

Tatum, W. Barnes, *In Quest of Jesus: A Guidebook*, Atlanta: John Knox Press, 1982.

Theissen, Gerd and Merz, Annette *The Historical Jesus: A Comprehensive Guide*, London: SCM, 1998.

Wright, N.T., *Jesus and the Victory of God*, London: SPCK, 1996.

The Early Church

THE BOOK OF ACTS

Dibelius, M., *Studies in the Acts of the Apostles*, London: SCM Press, 1956.

Gasque, W.W., *A History of the Criticism of the Acts of the Apostles*, Grand Rapids: Eerdmans, 1975.

Hengel, M., *Acts and the History of Earliest Christianity*, Philadelphia: Fortress, 1979.

Marshall, I.H., *The Acts of the Apostles*, Sheffield: JSOT Press, 1992.

CHURCH ORDER

Bauer, W., *Orthodoxy and Heresy in Earliest Christianity*, Philadelphia: Fortress, 1971.

Dunn, James D.G., *Unity and Diversity in the New Testament*, Philadelphia: Westminster, 1977.

Judge, E.A., *The Social Pattern of Christian Groups in the First Century*, London: Tyndale Press, 1960.

Malherbe, A.J., *Social Aspects of Early Christianity*, Philadelphia: Fortress, 1983.

Meeks, W., *The First Urban Christians*, New Haven: Yale University Press, 1983.

Robinson, Thomas A., *The Bauer Thesis Examined*, Lewiston: Edwin Mellen Press, 1988.

Schweizer, E., *Church Order in the New Testament*, London: SCM, 1961.

Theissen, G., *The Social Setting of Pauline Christianity*, Edinburgh: T and T Clark, 1982.

Tidball, D.J., *An Introduction to the Sociology of the New Testament*, Exeter: Paternoster, 1983.

WORSHIP AND MISSION

Bartlett, David L., *Ministry in the New Testament*, Minneapolis: Fortress, 1993.

Cullman, O., *Early Christian Worship*, London: SCM, 1953.

Dunn, J.D.G., *Unity and Diversity in the New Testament*, Philadelphia: Westminster, 1977.

Hahn, F., *The Worship of the Early Church*, Philadelphia: Fortress, 1973.

Larkin Jr, William J. and Williams, Joel F., eds, *Mission in the New Testament*, Maryknoll NY: Orbis, 1998.

Martin, R.P., *The Worship of God*, Grand Rapids: Eerdmans, 1982.

Paul

GENERAL

Cousar, C.B., *The Letters of Paul*, Nashville: Abingdon Press, 1996.

Dunn, J.D.G., *The Theology of Paul the Apostle*, Grand Rapids: Eerdmans, 1998.

Elliott, Neil, *Liberating Paul: The Justice of God and the Politics of the Apostle*, Maryknoll NY: Orbis, 1994.

Fitzmyer, J.A., *Paul and his Theology*, Englewood Cliffs: Prentice Hall, 1989.

Jewett, R., *A Chronology of Paul's Life*, Philadelphia: Fortress, 1979.

Knox, J., *Chapters in a Life of Paul*, Macon: Mercer University Press, 1987.

Marrow, S.B., *Paul – His Letters and His Theology*, New York: Paulist, 1986.

Murphy-O'Connor, J., *Paul the Letter-Writer: His World, His Options, His Skills*, Collegeville: Liturgical Press, 1995.

Roetzel, Calvin J., *The Letters of Paul: Conversations in Context*, Louisville: Westminster John Knox Press, 1998.

Sumney, J.L., *Identifying Paul's Opponents*, Sheffield: JSOT Press, 1990.

Witherington III, Ben, *The Paul Quest*, Downers Grove IL: InterVarsity, 1998.

PAUL THE PHARISEE

Sanders, E.P., *Paul and Palestinian Judaism*, Philadelphia: Fortress, 1977.

Stendahl, K., *Paul Among Jews and Gentiles*, Philadelphia: Fortress, 1976.

Thielman, Frank, *Paul and the Law*, Downers Grove: InterVarsity, 1994.

Watson, F., *Paul, Judaism and the Gentiles*, Cambridge: Cambridge University Press, 1986.

Westerholm, S., *Israel's Law and the Church's Faith*, Grand Rapids: Eerdmans, 1988.

Ziesler, J.A., *Pauline Christianity*, New York: Oxford University Press, 1990.

CONVERSION

Kim, S., *The Origin of Paul's Gospel*, Grand Rapids: Eerdmans, 1981.

Longenecker, R.N., ed., *The Road from Damascus*, Grand Rapids: Eerdmans, 1997.

PAUL AND JESUS

Bruce, F.F., *Paul and Jesus*, Grand Rapids: Baker, 1974.

Wedderburn, A.J.M., ed., *Paul and Jesus: Collected Essays*, Sheffield: JSOT, 1989.

PAUL THE EVANGELIST

Allan, R., *Missionary Methods: St Paul's or Ours*, Grand Rapids: Eerdmans, 1989, orig., 1912.

Hock, R.F., *The Social Context of Paul's Ministry*, Philadelphia: Fortress, 1980.

O'Brien, P.T., *Gospel and Mission in the Writings of Paul*, Carlisle: Paternoster Press, 1995.

ETHICS

Furnish, Victor Paul, *Theology and Ethics in Paul*, Nashville: Abingdon, 1968.

Furnish, Victor Paul, *The Moral Teaching of Paul*, Nashville: Abingdon, 1985.

Meeks, W., *The Moral World of the First Christians*, Philadelphia: Westminster, 1986.

PAUL AS PASTOR

Best, E., *Paul and His Converts*, Edinburgh: T and T Clark, 1988.

Zuck, Roy B., *Teaching as Paul Taught*, Grand Rapids: Baker, 1998.

Colossians, Ephesians and Philemon

Barclay, J.M.G., *Colossians and Philemon*, Sheffield: Sheffield Academic Press, 1997.

Best, E., *Ephesians*, Sheffield: JSOT Press, 1993.

Bruce, F.F., *The Epistles to the Colossians, to Philemon, and to the Ephesians*, Grand Rapids: Eerdmans, 1984.

Donfried, K.P. and Marshall, I.H., *The Theology of the Shorter Pauline Letters*, Cambridge: Cambridge University Press, 1993.

Knox, J., *Philemon Among the Letters of Paul*, London: Collins, 1960.

Lincoln, A.T. and Wedderburn, A.J.M., *The Theology of the Later Pauline Letters*, Cambridge: Cambridge University Press, 1993.

Corinthians

Dunn, J.D.G., *1 Corinthians*, Sheffield: Sheffield Academic Press, 1995.

Fee, G.D., *1 Corinthians*, Eerdmans: Grand Rapids, 1987.

Hay, David M., ed., *Pauline Theology*, vol. 2, *1 and 2 Corinthians*, Minneapolis: Fortress Press, 1993.

Kreitzer, Larry J., *2 Corinthians*, Sheffield: Sheffield Academic Press, 1996.

Murphy-O'Connor, J., *St Paul's Corinth*, Wilmington: Glazier, 1983.

Galatians

Donfried, K.P. and Marshall, I.H., *The Theology of the Shorter Pauline Letters*, Cambridge: Cambridge University Press, 1993.

Dunn, J.D.G., *The Theology of Paul's Letter to the Galatians*, Cambridge: Cambridge University Press, 1993.

Romans

Donfried, Karl P., ed., *The Romans Debate*, Peabody MA: Hendrickson, 1991.

Donfried, Karl P. and Richardson, Peter, *Judaism and Christianity in First-Century Rome*, Eerdmans, 1998.

Hay, D.M. and Johnson, E.E., *Pauline Theology*, Vol. III, *Romans*, Minneapolis: Fortress, 1995.

Hultgren, A.J., *Paul's Gospel and Mission: The Outlook from His Letter to the Romans*, Philadelphia: Fortress Press, 1985.

Morgan, Robert, *Romans*, Sheffield: Sheffield Academic Press, 1995.

Sanders, E.P., *Paul, the Law and the Jewish People*, Philadelphia: Fortress Press, 1983; London: SCM Press, 1985.

Ziesler, J.A., *Paul's Letter to the Romans*, Philadelphia: TPI, 1989.

Pastoral epistles

Davies, M., *The Pastoral Epistles*, Sheffield: Sheffield Academic Press, 1996.

Houlden, J.L., *The Pastoral Epistles*, Philadelphia: TPI, 1989.

Young, F., *The Theology of the Pastoral Letters*, Cambridge: Cambridge University Press, 1994.

Philippians

Bruce, F.F., *Philippians*, San Francisco: Harper and Row, 1983.

Fee, G.D., *Paul's Letter to the Philippians*, Grand Rapids: Eerdmans, 1995.

Thessalonians

Marshall, I.H., *1 and 2 Thessalonians*, Grand Rapids: Eerdmans, 1983.

Williams, D.J., *1 and 2 Thessalonians*, Peabody MA: Hendrickson, 1992.

PAUL THE THEOLOGIAN

General

Barrett, C.K., *Paul: An Introduction to His Thought*, London: Geoffrey Chapman, 1994.

Brauch, M., *Hard Sayings of Paul*, Downers Grove: InterVarsity, 1989.

Fitzmyer, J.A., *Paul and His Theology*, Englewood Cliffs: Prentice Hall, 1989.

Ridderbos, H., *Paul: An Outline of His Theology*, Grand Rapids: Eerdmans, 1975.

Ziesler, J.A., *Pauline Christianity*, New York: Oxford University Press, 1990.

The church

Banks, R., *Going to Church in the First Century*, Beaumont: Christian Books, 1990.

Banks, R., *Paul's Idea of Community*, Eerdmans: Grand Rapids, 1980.

Ellis, E.E., *Pauline Theology: Ministry and Society*, Grand Rapids: Eerdmans, 1989.

Käsemann, E., *Essays on New Testament Themes*, London: SCM, 1964.

Käsemann, E., *Perspectives on Paul*, London: SCM, 1971.

Schatzmann, S., *A Pauline Theology of Charismata*, Peabody: Hendrickson, 1989.

The Church and Its Jewish Roots

Dunn, J.D.G., *The Partings of the Ways*, Philadelphia: TPI, 1991.

HEBREWS AND HELLENISTS

Bruce, F.F., *Peter, Stephen, James and John*, Grand Rapids: Eerdmans, 1980.

Hengel, M., *Between Jesus and Paul*, Philadelphia: Fortress, 1983.

PETER

Brown, R.E., Donfried, K.P. and Reumann, J., *Peter in the New Testament*, Minneapolis: Augsburg, 1973.

Brown, R.E. and Maier, J.P., *Antioch and Rome*, New York: Paulist, 1983.

Cullmann, O., *Peter: Disciple, Apostle, Martyr*, Philadelphia: Westminster, 1962.

1 PETER

Cross, F.L., *1 Peter, a Paschal Liturgy*, London: Mowbrays, 1954.

NABPR Special Studies, *Perspectives on First Peter*, Macon: Mercer University Press, 1986.

JAMES

Davids, P., *The Epistle of James*, Grand Rapids: Eerdmans, 1982.

Dunn, J.D.G., *Unity and Diversity in the New Testament*, Philadelphia: Westminster, 1977.

Hartin, P.J., *James and the Q Sayings of Jesus*, Sheffield: Sheffield Academic Press, 1991.

Mitton, C.L., *The Epistle of James*, Grand Rapids: Eerdmans, 1966.

THE EPISTLE TO THE HEBREWS

Casey, Juliana, *Hebrews*, Wilmington: Glazier, 1980.

Thompson, J.W., *The Beginnings of Christian Philosophy*, Washington DC: Catholic Biblical Association, 1981.

1, 2 AND 3 JOHN

Brown, R.E., *The Community of the Beloved Disciple*, New York: Paulist, 1979.

Edwards, R.B., *The Johannine Epistles*, Sheffield: Sheffield Academic Press, 1996.

Ellis, E.E., *The World of St John*, Grand Rapids: Eerdmans, 1984.

Hengel, M., *The Johannine Question*, Philadelphia: TPI, 1989.

Marshall, I.H., *The Epistles of John*, Grand Rapids: Eerdmans, 1978.

REVELATION

Bauckham, R., *The Theology of the Book of Revelation*, Cambridge: Cambridge University Press, 1993.

Collins, Adela Yarbro, *The Apocalypse*, Wilmington: Glazier, 1979.

Mounce, R.H., *The Book of Revelation*, Grand Rapids: Eerdmans, 1998.

Interpretation

Beasley-Murray, G.R., *Preaching the Gospel from the Gospels*, Peabody MA: Hendrickson, 1997.

Boers, H., *What is New Testament Theology?*, Philadelphia: Fortress, 1979.

Charpentier, E., *How to Read the New Testament*, London: SCM, 1982.

Coggins, R.J. and Houlden, J.L., *A Dictionary of Biblical Interpretation*, London: SCM, 1990.

Court, John M., *Reading the New Testament*, New York: Routledge, 1997.

Farmer, William R., *The Gospel of Jesus: The Pastoral Relevance of the Synoptic Problem*, Louisville KY: Westminster John Knox Press, 1994.

Fish, S.E., *Is There a Text in This Class? The Authority of Interpretive Communities*, Cambridge MA: Harvard University Press, 1980.

Green, J.B., ed., *Hearing the New Testament: Strategies for Interpretation*, Grand Rapids: Eerdmans, 1995.

Klein, W.W., Blomberg, C.L. and Hubbard, R.L., *Introduction to Biblical Interpretation*, Dallas: Word, 1993.

Krentz, E., *The Historical-Critical Method*, Philadelphia: Fortress, 1975.

Lührmann, D., *An Itinerary for New Testament Study*, Philadelphia: Trinity Press International, 1989.

McKnight, E.V., *Post-Modern Use of the Bible*, Nashville: Abingdon Press, 1988.

McKnight, Scott, ed., *Introducing New Testament Interpretation*, Grand Rapids: Baker, 1989.

Neill, Stephen and Wright, Tom, *The Interpretation of the New Testament 1861–1986*, New York: Oxford University Press, 1988.

Osborne, G.R., *The Hermeneutical Spiral: A Comprehensive Introduction to Biblical Hermeneutics*, Downers Grove IL: InterVarsity, 1991.

Index of Subjects

Index of Maps, Charts and Diagrams

Index of Quotations from Ancient Authors

Index of Secondary Sources